C000213099

PRIME MINISTERS' PAPERS SERIES

PALMERSTON I

GEORGE VILLIERS, 4TH EARL OF CLARENDON
by Francis Grant, 1843
Reproduced by permission of the Earl of Clarendon
Photographed by A C Cooper Ltd

ROYAL COMMISSION ON
HISTORICAL MANUSCRIPTS

Prime Ministers' Papers Series

PALMERSTON

I: Private Correspondence with Sir George
Villiers (afterwards fourth Earl of Clarendon) as
Minister to Spain 1833–1837

EDITED BY ROGER BULLEN
AND FELICITY STRONG

LONDON
HER MAJESTY'S STATIONERY OFFICE

© *Crown copyright 1985*
First published 1985

ISBN 0 11 440185 3

CONTENTS

PREFACE

The Commissioners wish to express their thanks to the Trustees of the Broadlands Archives Trust and to the Rt. Hon. the Earl of Clarendon for permission to publish these letters.

They also wish to thank Dr. R. J. Bullen and Mrs. Felicity Strong for offering to edit the correspondence, and for devoting so much of their time to the preparation of the volume. It has been seen through the press by Dr. R. J. Olney, as general editor of the Prime Ministers' Papers series, and Dr. J. G. Parker.

B. S. SMITH
Secretary

INTRODUCTION

George Villiers's correspondence will some day or other make one of the most valuable and entertaining publications that ever appeared, though I shall not live to see it.

Charles Greville, 1836.

The text of this edition of correspondence between the third Viscount Palmerston, Foreign Secretary in the three Whig Administrations of Lord Grey and Lord Melbourne between 1830 and 1841, and George Villiers (who succeeded as fourth Earl of Clarendon in December 1838), British minister at Madrid from 1833 to 1839, is taken from the in-letters and copies of out-letters preserved in Lord Palmerston's private papers (the Broadlands Papers), supplemented and corrected by reference to Villiers's copies of his private letters to Palmerston in the Clarendon Deposit in the Bodleian Library, Oxford.

The correspondence merits publication for a number of reasons. It illustrates Palmerston's conduct of foreign policy during his first two periods at the Foreign Office and the nature of his response to the problems of political change and modernization in continental Europe. For Villiers, his period as British minister at Madrid constituted his political and diplomatic education. He was the only nineteenth-century Foreign Secretary to have spent so long a time in a British mission abroad, and the experience accounts for the wealth of his political and diplomatic contacts and in part for his later reputation as a European statesman. The correspondence also demonstrates the endeavour and the failure of Great Britain and France to find a mutually acceptable basis for co-operation on an issue where they hoped and claimed that their new identity of outlook and their common principles would transcend their former rivalry. It was in London and Paris that the 'liberal alliance' of the 1830s was made; it was in Spain that it faltered and ultimately collapsed. The correspondence also shows how and why the Whig Governments of Grey and Melbourne gradually committed themselves to far-reaching political objectives in Spain, and the very limited means at their disposal for achieving them. As Villiers frequently pointed out, the logic of British policy was extensive military, naval and financial assistance, but Palmerston was never able to offer anything more than grand gestures such as the Legion, and piecemeal help of other kinds. Lastly, Villiers's letters reveal the ever-increasing dependence of the Spanish Government on British advice, and the limited aid which Palmerston was able to offer. When she signed the Quadruple Alliance of 1834 Spain acknowledged her dependence on Great Britain and France; after the collapse of Thiers's Government in 1836 Palmerston and Villiers seized the opportunity to attempt to transform Spain into a British client State. Anglo-French differences in the Peninsula in the late 1830s and 1840s were largely the consequence of this development.

The editors' original intention was to publish the complete correspondence from 1833 to 1839, with no omissions. Rising costs have made a modification essential. The period covered has been restricted to 1833 to 1837 inclusive, ending just after the disbandment of the British Legion. By this time the Quadruple Treaty of 1834 had ceased to be effective, and the strains between Britain and France were increasingly apparent. The Carlists, hitherto in the ascendant, had begun to lose the initiative in the war: although 1838 saw many setbacks to the Queen's cause through weak Ministers, bankruptcy, lack of leadership and military blunders and incapacity, the eventual victory of the Queen began to seem likely. Villiers's letters to Palmerston continue full of essential detail and interest until his return to England on leave in July 1838. Thereafter, until his final relinquishment of his post in 1839, they lose the involvement and immediacy that characterize the earlier letters.

The practice of supplementing official despatches with private letters was not new to British diplomacy in 1830. Lord Grenville had appointed a secretary on the Foreign Office establishment to deal with his private correspondence as far back as 1795. But from the start of his Foreign Secretaryship Palmerston laid great emphasis on the use of the private letter as a regular supplement to the despatch, and not merely as an exceptional method of conveying a particularly delicate or confidential matter. He expected his subordinates to write frequently, in some detail and with perfect frankness, although he was not always able to reciprocate. His reasons for attaching so much importance to the private letter are bound up with the parliamentary and Cabinet system of British government. Views and information contained in private letters could not cause embarrassment in Parliament to the Foreign Secretary or the Cabinet. Despatches were public property; there was always the possibility that they might be subjected to public scrutiny and discussion or published in a Blue Book. A motion in either House for the Government to produce papers was often opposed on the grounds that publication would prejudice negotiations still in progress or would be injudicious. If the motion was passed, however, the Government was bound to comply. The despatches were often skilfully selected and edited to conceal matters that the Government thought it premature to discuss or difficult to defend, but in principle the views, information and action reported in despatches might at any time be made public. Private letters by contrast were guarantees of confidentiality and retreat into necessary secrecy.

As a result of the potentially public nature of despatches, both the Foreign Secretary and his diplomats wished in them to be seen doing what they knew would secure parliamentary approval. Sometimes despatches were deliberately written for publication. For instance, Villiers wrote a great many on the atrocities committed in Spain during the civil war, for use as Government propaganda. Both sides were responsible for acts which violated the Eliot Convention (negotiated in 1835 during Wellington's brief tenure of the Foreign Office), but Villiers echoed the Queen's generals in the North and the liberal newspapers in Madrid in stressing the frequency and barbarous nature of the Carlist atrocities. In publishing these despatches, Palmerston's purpose was to show that the British Government was doing its utmost to secure strict adherence to the Eliot Convention, and to discredit the Carlist cause in England and those high Tories who championed it.

Potential publicity did not end when the Government fell. Incoming despatches and copies of outgoing ones were numbered and placed on record in the Foreign Office where they were available to any Ministry and for publication at any time. In the examination of these records by new Administrations, party spirit was by no means always absent. A new Government might decide to publish the despatches of a predecessor as a means of retrospective indictment or to disarm critics by suggesting that its policies were a continuation of those of its forerunner. Because Blue Books thus developed into a weapon of party warfare, despatches became unsuitable for the transmission of confidential information and interim judgements on men and events.

The decision to publish despatches might also cause a Government embarrassment in its relations with other countries. The absolutist monarchies of Europe did not always understand the limitations of English parliamentary monarchy or the rules of party warfare. Their own obsession with secrecy and their immunity from public scrutiny

3

made them exceptionally sensitive to criticism and the disclosure of information given in confidence. In Spain, the Queen Regent and her Ministers were hardly less sensitive to publicity than absolutist monarchs. They tended to assume that discussions on Spanish affairs in the British Parliament were opportunities for the British Government to reaffirm its loyalty to the cause of constitutionalism in Spain. Criticism of their activities and failings was resented. Villiers was therefore cautious in his comments in despatches on policies and their protagonists. He normally limited himself to describing what had happened, reserving comments on individuals and speculations on the reasons for and consequences of events for his private letters.

Palmerston later became notorious for the cavalier way in which he discharged his constitutional responsibility to consult both the Crown and the Cabinet about the conduct of foreign policy. Established constitutional practice demanded that outgoing despatches should be read and approved by the Sovereign, and that incoming despatches should be submitted to him immediately after they had been seen by the Foreign Secretary. Despatches conveying major policy decisions were supposed to reflect the considered view of the whole Cabinet. Partly to relieve the Foreign Office clerks of the immense labour of copying a large number of despatches for members of the Cabinet, Palmerston initiated a bulletin which summarized for the Cabinet the contents of the more important despatches received over a period of a few days. In the early 1830s Palmerston submitted to royal and Cabinet control more willingly than later in the decade. In his Spanish policy he had to contend with William IV's disapproval of Villiers because 'his first opinion rather abounded in liberalism', and because of his hostility to the British Legion. In the Cabinet he was forced to realize that his colleagues were anxious not to commit themselves too wholeheartedly to either side in a civil war. He undoubtedly took some of them further than they wished to go in their commitment to constitutionalism in Spain, although not nearly as far as Villiers would have liked. He sometimes showed private letters from diplomats abroad to selected Cabinet colleagues, but was adamant that he was under no obligation to do so. Privacy was thus the essential quality of the private letters exchanged by Palmerston and his diplomats, providing protection equally against parliamentary, public, royal and even Cabinet scrutiny. Secure in the knowledge that their letters would remain private, both the Foreign Secretary and British envoys abroad were free to develop their ideas and convey confidential information. This is why the private letters of Palmerston and his most trusted diplomats are so important. The despatches may reveal what British policy actually was, but the private letters show why a particular policy was pursued and what it was expected to achieve. From private letters it is possible to begin to reconstruct the underlying motives of Palmerston's foreign policy, his fears, aspirations and order of priorities.

The correspondence printed in this book was not exchanged between political equals. Palmerston was the political master to whom Villiers as a subordinate had to defer on all important issues of foreign policy. This statement of the constitutional position does not, however, explain the complex relationships which in fact developed between early nineteenth-century Foreign Secretaries and their envoys. A considerable degree of discretion was allowed to the diplomat abroad, partly because he was assumed to have local knowledge and influence, partly because of the additional delays which would necessarily occur if every decision had to be referred to London. Later in the century the extensive use of the telegraph diminished, but did not destroy, ambassadorial discretion. It was accepted that a diplomat would not always be able to fulfil instructions from London to the letter; he was expected to discern their spirit and apply them as best he might in the light of local circumstances. It was his responsibility to determine timing—exactly when to approach a foreign Government on a particular issue, and tone—whether to couch a request in menacing or conciliatory terms. In his letters to Palmerston, Villiers frequently described in great detail the way in which he had carried out his instructions.

The duty of the envoy to inform the Foreign Secretary about the issues and problems that confronted the Government in its conduct of foreign policy was not merely a matter of conveying information, although some diplomats acted as if it were. It was as much a matter of political, diplomatic, military and economic analysis as it was of stating facts. By selecting and arranging information in a particular way British envoys abroad were advising as well as informing the Government, who were therefore concerned to select representatives who shared their political outlook, assumptions and aspirations. Villiers undoubtedly owed his appointment to Madrid to the fact that he was a known Whig supporter. The replacement of Tory diplomats by friends and associates of the Reform Ministry could not be accom-

5

plished at once on all levels of the diplomatic service. Palmerston was content to allow some of Canning's appointees to remain at their posts. A complete change of diplomatic personnel would have added considerably to the cost of pensions at a time when Palmerston was attempting, in line with Government policy, to reduce expenditure in the Foreign Office and the Foreign Service. Grey was moreover opposed in principle to the dismissal of experienced and capable diplomats who were willing to serve the new Government. In any case, before recalling Tory diplomats, the Government needed to find able and willing successors, no easy task. The Whigs had been too long out of office to have a substitute diplomatic service waiting in the wings. As far as the lower ranks of the service were concerned, Palmerston was prepared to wait until new talent appeared. One such new man was George Villiers who in 1830, when the Grey Ministry took office, had been by no means an obvious candidate to fill an important post in the diplomatic service.

George Villiers, grandson of the first Earl of Clarendon of the second creation, was born in 1800 into a family which was Tory in outlook and affiliations. His uncle was a supporter of Pitt, his father a friend of Canning. He owed his first official appointment in 1820 as unpaid attaché to Sir Charles Bagot's embassy to St. Petersburg to his uncle, Lord Morley, who was a friend of Castlereagh. Villiers was attracted to diplomacy for a number of reasons. He had a flair for languages and had stayed on at Cambridge for one or two terms after taking his degree in 1819 to study modern languages. He did not know Spanish when he arrived at Madrid in 1833 but soon picked it up, and spoke and wrote it fluently by the time he relinquished his post. He was also interested in the social and political development of societies other than his own. By the time he left Cambridge he was Whiggish in outlook; living abroad would afford an opportunity to test his political and social assumptions, as well as widening his horizons. Finally, he believed that diplomacy offered him the prospect of a career, which he needed because his family was comparatively poor. In fact, lack of financial backing proved as inhibiting in diplomacy as it might have done in politics. Paid employment became essential. Villiers relinquished his unpaid attachéship at St. Petersburg and returned to London to seek a remunerative post. In November 1823 he was appointed Auditor of the Customs at £800 a year. Another opportunity to live abroad came in December 1831 when he was appointed a member of an Excise Commission to revise the customs duties between England and France. The Commission did most of its work in Paris, and his work and contacts there may have helped Villiers to enter diplomacy a second time.

Villiers claimed that it was Lord Granville, the British ambassador at Paris, who secured for him the post of British minister at Madrid. He certainly knew Granville and Holland far better than he knew Palmerston. Palmerston would have read the commercial reports written by Villiers and Sir John Bowring, the other British Excise Commissioner in Paris, but there is no evidence to suggest that he was anxious to employ Villiers in his Department. It was the refusal of Stratford Canning to succeed the Tory, Addington, as British minister at Madrid that forced Palmerston to look elsewhere, and gave Granville the opportunity to recommend Villiers.

The Madrid legation was a mission of the second rank in the early 1830s. The fact that it was no longer an embassy—the last ambassador had been recalled in 1822—was as much a recognition of the fact that Spain had ceased to be a great Power as it was of the British Government's wish to reduce the expenses of the diplomatic service. Nevertheless, when Villiers was offered and accepted the post as minister, it was an important one and likely to become more so. Canning's unsuccessful extraordinary mission in 1832 to secure Spanish recognition of Dona Maria as Queen of Portugal had made Palmerston aware that Spain too was on the brink of great political changes. Within a few months of his arrival in Madrid in September 1833 Villiers himself came to see the struggle between liberalism and Carlism in Spain as part of a wider European struggle between the forces of progress and those of reaction. He believed that as the representative of the leading liberal Power, he was at the centre of the contest. As a result, his letters are imbued with a sense of the importance of events in Spain and his part in them which others, including Palmerston, did not always share. Villiers's position in the diplomatic service was therefore not an easy one: he was not like the heir to a Whig peerage who could afford to be indifferent to his Government's attitude; he was in no sense a protégé of Palmerston, and was acutely aware that there was no reason why Palmerston should show him special favour, support him against critics or offer him preferment. His future in the diplomatic service depended on his abilities: with very little training in diplomacy, he had to prove himself.

Spain & Portugal
Showing principal places
mentioned in the text

0   40   80   120   160
English miles

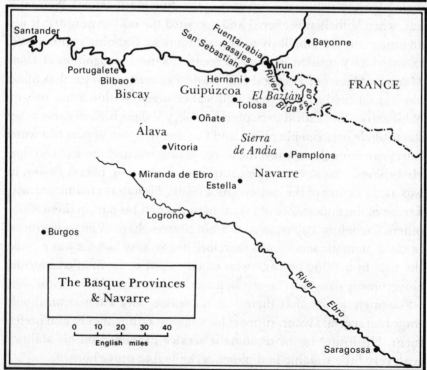

**The Basque Provinces
& Navarre**

0   10   20   30   40
English miles

When Villiers arrived in Madrid the legation staff consisted of Lord William Hervey as secretary of legation and MacPherson Grant as paid attaché (soon replaced by Newton Savile Scott). Villiers brought with him Henry Southern as his private secretary. In 1834 at Villiers's request Southern was attached to the legation as unpaid attaché, and in August 1835 he was made paid attaché when Scott moved to The Hague. In addition, Villiers employed a Spanish secretary to translate despatches to and from the Spanish Foreign Ministry which lacked translators who could work quickly and accurately. Villiers trusted his subordinates, and worked well with them. If he had a favourite, it was Southern, whom he described as his 'right hand man on a courier day'. Southern's contacts with Spanish politicians, particularly with the advanced liberals, seem to have been closer than Hervey's, and he was entrusted in 1836 with the handling of the Cadiz junta. The fact that all the subordinate members of the legation openly espoused the Queen's cause and mixed freely in the political society of Madrid was an asset which Villiers did not underestimate. His letters repeatedly refer to the contrast in attitude and conduct between the British diplomats at Madrid and the French, a difference which he did not fail to exploit.

One of the great difficulties with which Villiers had to contend was the maintenance of regular communications with the Government at home. The packet-boat from Falmouth was subject to the vicissitudes of wind and weather; the messengers on the overland journey to Madrid had to elude the Carlists. Carlist activity was often the cause of delayed despatches, and occasionally resulted in their seizure. The reciprocal arrangement whereby British and French messengers left Madrid and Paris on different days, carrying the bags of both legations, did not always work satisfactorily, and Villiers did not always have adequate notice of the departure of a courier. In addition, he often complained of the absence of instructions from Palmerston, especially in his letters to Lord Granville and his brother, Edward Villiers. He clearly did not understand the difficulties under which Palmerston worked. The business of the Foreign Office was steadily increasing throughout the 1830s. Palmerston corresponded with many diplomats besides Villiers, and had frequent interviews with foreign diplomats in London, as well as attending the Court, the Cabinet and the House of Commons. He did not neglect Spanish problems: his correspondence with Granville was often dominated by Spanish issues, which he frequently discussed as well with French and Spanish diplomats in London. He also received reports direct from Colonel Wylde, a British officer attached as an observer to the Queen of Spain's army in the North. On Anglo-French co-operation in Spain, Granville was the obvious diplomat through whom Palmerston worked. Thus, while his letters to Villiers contain an accurate account of his attitude to Spain and the line of conduct he was endeavouring to follow, they do not reflect fully the actual making of policy, particularly in so far as Anglo-French co-operation was concerned. This was especially true in 1834 and 1835, less so thereafter. As the entente declined, British policy towards Spain was made more often in the exchanges between London and Madrid than in those between London and Paris. At the beginning of his mission to Madrid, Villiers was helping to execute an Anglo-French policy; by the time he left, he was helping Palmerston to formulate an anti-French policy.

Throughout the period when Villiers was British minister at Madrid, Spain was in crisis. From the outset the British Government was committed to a particular outcome, and had to take account of every aspect of the Spanish problem. The correspondence printed in this book has therefore a number of distinct but related themes. Six major issues dominate it: first, the nature and extent of British assistance to the constitutional cause in its war against provincial separatism and Carlism; secondly, the problems raised by Anglo-French co-operation to end the war in Northern Spain; thirdly, the problems encountered by the Spanish Government in its conduct of the war; fourthly, the evolution and the vicissitudes of the new political order at Madrid; fifthly, the formation and the role of the British Auxiliary Legion; and lastly, the financial problems of the Spanish Government and the attempts of Villiers and the British Government to put Anglo-Spanish commercial relations on a new basis.

It was as a result of its attempt to settle the Portuguese question that the British Government became involved in the Spanish crisis in the 1830s. In 1826 Dom Pedro, Emperor of Brazil, had abdicated the Portuguese throne in favour of his infant daughter Dona Maria, with his brother Dom Miguel as Regent. In 1828, however, Miguel had assumed the title of King of Portugal, with clerical and absolutist support. Three years later Dom Pedro invaded Portugal on his daughter's behalf, and by the early autumn of 1833 was in control of Lisbon and Oporto.

Miguel claimed that Maria was excluded from the succession under Salic law. In Great Britain, however, the Whig Government that came into office in November 1830 upheld Maria's cause as one of constitutional monarchy versus absolutism. Both Palmerston and Grey were anxious to co-operate with Spain, and in the autumn of 1832 Stratford Canning was sent on a special mission to Madrid, empowered to make what the British Government regarded as significant concessions to the Spanish dread of constitutional government in Portugal in return for Anglo-Spanish mediation to expel Dom Miguel. Canning failed. The King of Spain, Ferdinand VII, was himself the greatest obstacle to an agreement. He continued to believe to the moment of his death that changing the order of succession in favour of his two daughters was compatible with the maintenance of absolutism throughout the Peninsula. The fact that his brother Don Carlos, who refused to accept his relegation to third place in the order of succession, left Spain and joined Dom Miguel in Portugal in no way convinced him of the need to change his Portuguese policy. Ferdinand resolutely opposed the Spanish recognition of the new order of succession in Portugal because it was associated with constitutional reform. He had never forgotten his humiliation at the hands of the Cortes Government in Spain, and he remained thereafter the implacable enemy of liberal ideas and institutions.

Ferdinand died in September 1833, and the events of the next few months revealed the hopelessness of his endeavours. The structure of government which he and his Ministers had so laboriously built immediately began to collapse, and his wife, María Cristina, who became Regent during the minority of her daughter Isabella II, prepared to abandon his Portuguese policy. It was clear to the Queen Regent and her advisers that if the new order in Spain was to survive, a re-alignment of forces was necessary throughout the Peninsula. Don Carlos, with the support of Dom Miguel, was gathering together an army in Portugal with which to make good his claim to the Spanish throne. If the challenge of Carlism was to be defeated, then it must be accompanied by the destruction of Miguelism in Portugal, which could only be achieved with the consent and co-operation of Great Britain. Out of the fear and confusion following the King's death emerged the liberal order in Spain; and out of the Spanish offer to co-operate with

Great Britain emerged the Quadruple Alliance of April 1834 between Great Britain, France, Spain and Portugal, the so-called 'liberal alliance' of the West. What Palmerston paraded as a grand design was in fact a makeshift measure.

Palmerston was quick to seize the opportunities presented by the Spanish volte-face on Portugal. He had for some time been convinced of the necessity for British intervention in Portugal. He and Grey had tried and failed to secure Cabinet support for such a measure. Spanish willingness to participate in the intervention enabled him to persuade his Cabinet colleagues that the action of the two Powers would be decisive, quick and cheap, an assurance he had been unable to give when he had proposed unilateral British action. The alliance was made in London. Palmerston presided over the negotiations, and Miraflores, the Spanish minister to the court of St. James's, acted on behalf of his Government. Villiers played virtually no part in the negotiations; the only contribution expected of him was to expedite the return to London of the Spanish ratification of the treaty. The negotiation of the alliance established the pattern which was to last until 1836, whereby British policy towards Spain was hammered out in discussions between London and Paris rather than between London and Madrid. At the outset, therefore, Villiers did not participate in the making of policy, merely in its execution. The treaty was undoubtedly an important landmark in the political development of the two Peninsular monarchies. It re-established close relations between England and Portugal, and for the rest of the 1830s it associated Great Britain and France with the attempt to create a new political order in Spain. It was the fixed point around which the relations between the Peninsular States and their Great Power patrons revolved for more than a decade. The treaty became both a symbol of unity amongst the four Powers and supposed evidence of their common faith in liberal ideas and institutions. It was also a source of constant conflict between them.

The key issue of conflict in the interpretation of the treaty was the question: what was it designed to achieve? The treaty itself stated that its purpose was to expel Carlos and Miguel from Portugal. This was quickly achieved. By late May 1834 both Pretenders had conceded that they were unable to resist the combined Anglo-Spanish forces, and both agreed to leave Portugal. Miguel went into exile in Italy and Carlos was brought to England in a British warship. By July Don Carlos, who was not a prisoner of the British Government, had returned to

Spain and associated himself with the revolt in the Basque Provinces. By so doing he transformed a provincial revolt into a war of succession and of opposing principles.

The Spanish Government claimed, not unnaturally, that the purpose of the treaty was to expel the Pretenders from the Peninsula and bring tranquillity to the two reforming monarcines, and that it was merely accidental that Carlos had been on Portuguese territory when the treaty was drawn up. It was a firm belief at Madrid that the treaty remained unfulfilled while Don Carlos was on Spanish soil, and that the three other signatories were bound to assist Spain to end the war in the North and expel the Pretender. In response to these claims Palmerston made the distinction between the letter and the spirit of the treaty. He asserted that although the letter of the treaty had been fulfilled by the expulsion of the two Pretenders from Portugal, the spirit was to pacify the Peninsula and to enable both the Peninsular monarchies to develop free from the fear of revolution and civil war. The return of Carlos to Spain was an affront to the spirit of the treaty, and consequently the other three Powers were morally obliged to assist Spain to end the war. It was from this distinction that the Additional Articles of August 1834 emerged. By them, Great Britain undertook to sell arms and supplies to Spain, and France agreed to prevent supplies reaching the Carlists across the Pyrenees. From the summer of 1834 onwards British policy was based on two premises: first, that there was a commitment to assist the Spanish Government; secondly, that there was no commitment as to specific measures of support except as stated in the Additional Articles. The British Government was therefore free to decide what form its support should take.

A great deal of the correspondence between Palmerston and Villiers from August 1834 onwards was concerned with this question. The difference between them was fundamentally one of perspective. The enthusiasm of Villiers for the new order at Madrid, his belief that liberal ideas and institutions had the capacity to transform Spanish government and society, were shared by Palmerston. What distinguished Villiers from his chief was his constant fear that the new order was in imminent danger of collapse. This danger, in his view, arose out of the failure of the Madrid Governments to end the war in the North. While the war continued the new order could not consolidate itself, first, because it faced the possibility of defeat by Carlism; secondly, because it might be overturned by its own armed forces since some of the leading generals were more anxious to control the Government than to be controlled by it; thirdly, because the moderate liberals, preoccupied with and divided by the war, were unable to combine and concentrate on resisting the challenge of the radicals; and lastly, because the financial demands of the war strained the resources of the regime beyond endurance. Spanish Governments were forced to find means to pay for a war which they could not afford, and the political uncertainty engendered by the war destroyed the confidence of potential creditors. Villiers was convinced that this Gordian knot had to be cut and that there was only one way to do so: Anglo-French intervention to secure a swift and decisive end to the war. In his opinion the collapse of the new order in Spain, as a result of either a Carlist or a radical triumph, was the greatest danger faced by British policy in the Peninsula, far greater in its consequences than the temporary presence of a French army in northern Spain.

Palmerston, as is obvious from the correspondence, did not share Villiers's assumption that the constitutional monarchy in Spain was likely to collapse unless the war was brought to a swift conclusion. He was convinced that the Spaniards themselves were capable of making greater efforts to end the war, and that Great Britain and France should not be expected to provide what, with more effort and organization, the Spaniards could provide themselves. In his view a more vigorous and sustained war effort in Spain would destroy Carlism, and the very fact that the Spaniards had achieved it themselves would immeasurably strengthen the new order at Madrid. Palmerston was therefore prepared only to supplement the Spanish war effort. He attached almost as much signficance to what he called the 'moral' effect of aid as to its practical effect. He believed that Anglo-French aid to the Constitutionalists would demoralize the Carlists. It would also convince the reactionary Powers that their supplies of money and arms to the insurgents were of no avail, since the two Western Powers would not permit a Carlist victory.

Palmerston knew, moreover, that he was not in a position to offer extensive aid even if he had wished to do so. Some of his Cabinet colleagues had had misgivings about the extent of British assistance offered under the Additional Articles. There was every indication that they would oppose further and more far reaching measures. In Parliament the Tories were bitter critics of the Whigs' Spanish policy, and in particular of the Quadruple Alliance. They advocated a policy of neutrality, ostensibly because this was the only way to avoid involvement in a war in which, they argued, Great Britain had no interest. In fact they hoped that if the British and French Governments pursued a neutral course, the position of the Spanish Constitutionalists would rapidly deteriorate and the Carlists would win. Palmerston realized that any attempt to augment the aid which the British Government was affording to Spain would meet with powerful opposition in the Cabinet and strident attacks in Parliament. At no stage in the years between 1834 and 1837 did he initiate a parliamentary discussion on Spanish affairs. In 1835 the Foreign Enlistment Act was suspended by Order in Council to enable the British Auxiliary Legion to be formed. This use of the royal prerogative meant that Palmerston did not have to seek the consent of Parliament for the measure itself: he merely had to ensure that Parliament did not censure the Government for its *fait accompli.*

The same consideration affected Palmerston's attitude to the question of French intervention in Spain. The Tories argued at the time of British intervention in Portugal that the Whigs had established a precedent in the Peninsula which the French would be eager to follow in Spain. Palmerston denied this vigorously; he argued that he had placed Anglo-French relations in the Peninsula on a new footing: that whereas in Portugal England should act alone but in consultation with France, in Spain the two Powers should act jointly and on a basis of equality. Full-scale French intervention in Spain would destroy this equality, and Spain would again become the client State of France. All these considerations separated Palmerston from Villiers on the question of aid to Spain. In 1836 Palmerston was prepared to accept and support Thiers's proposals for French assistance to Spain, partly because they fell short of full-scale intervention and partly because Villiers argued that they were the only means to avoid disaster. On that occasion only did Villiers lead and Palmerston follow on a major issue.

It was Palmerston who was the architect of the Anglo-French entente in the form in which it existed after the signature of the Quadruple Treaty in April 1834. The French Government had for some time sought a more general and wide-ranging alliance with the British, and during the negotiation of the treaty it had displayed a marked reluctance to undertake specific obligations in the Peninsula. The King of the French and Talleyrand, the French ambassador in London, eventually accepted the terms proposed by Palmerston, first because they thought that any agreement with Great Britain was better than none, and secondly because they feared that the exclusion of French influence from the Peninsula, particularly from Spain, would certainly follow if Britain alone was seen to be responsible for the expulsion of the two Pretenders from Portugal. From the outset the French regarded the entente as an imperfect shadow of a more general alliance. Palmerston, by contrast, believed it to be an ideal agreement: it recognized British pre-eminence in Portugal, placed the two Powers on an equal footing in Spain and presented a united front of liberal Powers to the absolutist Powers of the East. He assumed that by committing themselves to work with Great Britain in the Peninsula, the French had in fact conceded that they would neither take the initiative nor act in Spain itself without the prior consent of Great Britain. Thus from the outset there was little unity of purpose in the entente.

The development of the entente in the years after 1834 was also greatly affected by the instability of French politics. While Villiers was British minister at Madrid, eight Governments were formed and seven collapsed in France. Only one lasted for more than a few months. It was inevitable that French Foreign Ministers should differ in their attitude towards the entente. The Duc de Broglie was the only one in whom the British Government had any real confidence. Towards the end of the decade Palmerston became convinced that it mattered very little who was at the head of the French Foreign Ministry as in his opinion it was Louis Philippe, and to a lesser extent the officials of the Quai d'Orsay, who really directed foreign policy. He had also decided that the King of the French was an enemy of England and of the constitutional régime in Spain. It was certainly over Spanish issues that cracks first began to show in the entente.

The principal charge levelled by Palmerston and Villiers against French policy towards Spain was that it lacked consistency. By 1836 both were convinced that there was a wide gulf between what French Governments professed to be their policy in Spain and what that policy actually was. They assumed that what the French lacked was honesty of purpose, and in the late 1830s both devoted a good deal of their correspondence to speculation about the real motives of French policy. In reality the entente declined because the French would not act as the British wished. The civil war in Spain raised problems for France which were different from those faced by Britain; fragile Governments with slender majorities were in no position to act decisively in foreign affairs. A régime that feared its own radical opponents was likely to view with alarm the progress of radicalism in Spain, and a country attempting to restore its international prestige was suspicious of what it regarded as British encroachments on the French position at Madrid. Moreover, the French were conscious that they could not compete on equal terms with British exports, and they assumed that the British knew this. They consequently believed that any British attempt to renegotiate tariff agreements with Spain would result in the exclusion of French goods from Spanish markets. At no stage in the late 1830s did Palmerston and Villiers concede that they were giving the French any grounds for suspicion. By the time Latour-Maubourg was appointed ambassador at Madrid Villiers was content to allow the old pattern of rivalry between the British and French representatives to reassert itself. Naturally, he was determined to present his own conduct in the best possible light; this required that he should catalogue and explain the insults, vanities and bad faith of his French counterpart. Latour-Maubourg retaliated. The result was a vicious circle of intrigue and accusation, in which Palmerston loyally supported Villiers. In a sense, therefore, Villiers was as much responsible as Palmerston for the decline of the entente, and his attempt to salvage it after his return to England and his entry into the Cabinet as a means of settling the Near Eastern crisis is all the more strange. The only other explanation of his conduct is that while in Spain he did what he thought Palmerston expected. This, however, seems unlikely as in many matters, for example commercial affairs, Villiers often took the initiative and complained when he was not supported by the Government at home. It is difficult to escape the conclusion that he sought to establish a combative relationship with his French colleagues, and that in his dealings with the Spanish Governments in the late 1830s he lost no opportunity to inflame their increasing distrust of France.

When Villiers arrived in Madrid in the autumn of 1833 there was no reason to suppose that his relations with the Spanish Government would be any different from those of his predecessor, Addington. In 1837 a group of Spaniards gave a public dinner at which they heaped extravagant praise upon him as one of the most important and influential friends of the new order in Spain. There was some truth in this encomium. By 1837 Villiers was playing an important and occasionally crucial role in Spanish politics. The transformation of the position of the British minister at Madrid was the result of two facts: first, the

British commitment to the Constitutional cause; and secondly, the failure of the Spanish Government to end the war in the North. One of the unspoken assumptions of British policy was that what Spain could not do by herself, the British must assist her to do. This applied not only to military and naval aid and grants of essential supplies, but also to the conduct of the war itself. After the Quadruple Treaty was concluded, the British were benevolently paternal to their new ally, confining themselves to giving good general advice about the military operations in the North, above all encouraging the Spaniards to redouble their efforts to bring the conflict to a speedy conclusion. Palmerston displayed his usual breezy optimism; he did not doubt that the Constitutionalists would win and that they would win quickly. Villiers, who unlike Palmerston had no previous experience of the conduct of war, soon began to have doubts about the ability of the Spanish Government to control its generals, impose an overall strategy on the various military operations in the North and marshal and use the slender resources at its disposal. Within months of his arrival he had accurately diagnosed the ills which plagued the war effort of the Constitutionalists: incompetent and ambitious generals who would rather work against than with each other; insufficient funds; and insufficient authority to ensure that the funds which were available actually reached the army and were used for the purposes for which they were intended. For all these ills Villiers proposed remedies, most of which were impossible to adopt in the political situation at Madrid. The fact that he was fertile in suggestions for improving the Spanish war effort, combined with his eagerness to offer his advice to the Spanish Government, had important consequences. It meant that he soon acquired a special position in Spanish politics. The ease and speed with which he acquired it reflected not only his and Palmerston's belief that it was natural and proper that the British envoy at an allied Court should offer advice on internal matters, but also the Spanish belief that the advice could be helpful, and that to accept British advice in some way shared the burden of responsibility for the measures taken. Thus it was that Villiers became involved in the Spanish conduct of the war. At times he was exasperated by the failure of the Spaniards to do what he thought was both obvious and necessary, at other times he wrote as if he was responsible for the direction of the war.

Although Villiers soon identified the major deficiencies of the Spanish war effort, he found it impossible to place them in order of priority or to decide which would be most easily and effectively remedied. At times he placed his emphasis on the lack of direction at Madrid, at others he believed that the total want of adequate resources was the main problem, and sometimes he argued that the incompetence of the generals was the major obstacle to a successful conclusion to the war. His constantly shifting analysis reflected the fact that at certain stages in the war particular problems seemed to overshadow others, but it also reflected the assumptions and preoccupations of the politicians at Madrid. Villiers tended to accept the version of events given by the Spanish Government, or at least to offer one which differed only in details. His letters to Palmerston give an accurate picture of how the war was seen at Madrid and how it was conducted by successive Spanish Governments.

Villiers was not Palmerston's only source of information. From 1835 on he received regular reports from Colonel Wylde who was attached to the military headquarters of the Constitutional army. Wylde's position was officially that of observer, but he was in fact an unofficial adviser to and mediator between the Spanish generals. Moreover, when the British Legion began to take part in the military operations against the Carlists, Wylde became the liaison officer between the British and Spanish forces. This was a difficult and delicate position. Wylde reported directly to Palmerston. He also corresponded with Villiers, although far less frequently. That he and Villiers did not agree in their estimate of the characters and capabilities of Spanish generals is evident from the correspondence printed here. Palmerston's low opinion of Córdoba was derived from Wylde, whereas Villiers spiritedly defended him for some time against his British critics. Wylde drew his conclusions from what he observed at military headquarters, and Villiers from the despatches sent to the Government at Madrid.

An aspect of the war with which the British Government was especially, almost obsessively, concerned was the brutality with which it was conducted. This was as much a matter of propaganda as an expression of concern for the maintenance of humane and civilized values. It was essentially a party question in England although it did have European repercussions. What Palmerston was attempting to do was to apply lessons he had learnt during the Portuguese civil war to the conflict in Spain. In their struggle to destroy Dom Miguel in Portugal, the Whigs had succeeded in branding him as a cruel tyrant whose followers committed atrocities against soldiers and civilians alike. They were then able to taunt the Tory Opposition who supported the Miguelites with condoning crimes against humanity. The Tories were gravely embarrassed by these accusations, both because they were true and because, while Dom Pedro lacked a base from which to conduct military operations in mainland Portugal, the same charges could not be levelled against him and his followers. It was on this issue that Palmerston believed that he had rallied radical supporters behind the Government's intervention in Portugal and divided liberal Tories from their diehard colleagues. He hoped to do the same with respect to Spain. As far as Palmerston was concerned, Carlist atrocities condemned Carlism and those in Spain and the rest of Europe who supported it. It soon, however, became uncomfortably clear that the Constitutionalist forces also committed atrocities against both civilians and prisoners of war. This made it increasingly difficult for Palmerston to make the clear distinction between Carlism and barbarism on the one hand and the civilized and enlightened values of the new liberal régime at Madrid on the other. He was therefore forced to change his argument, and to allege that the Carlists committed more and worse atrocities than the Constitutionalists.

In Melbourne's second Administration the question of atrocities in Spain became if anything a more important issue in English party politics than it had been before the Whigs left office in November 1834. During the brief Peel Ministry of 1834-35 the main emphasis of Wellington's Spanish policy had been to persuade both sides to agree to a convention regulating the conduct of war. His aim was simple. He sought to introduce into civil war the rules of war which governed conflicts between States: that prisoners on either side should have prisoner of war status instead of being shot as traitors, and that civilians should be tried for alleged war crimes by civilian courts. Both sides agreed to abide by these rules largely because both were anxious to secure the goodwill of the new British Government. Wellington sent Lord Eliot to Spain to supervise negotiations, and the agreement became known as the Eliot Convention. After the return to power of the Whigs, Palmerston was particularly anxious to ensure that the Constitutionalists adhered scrupulously to the Eliot Convention, and equally anxious that Villiers should report in detail all those occasions when the Carlists violated it. These reports were collected and published at fairly regular intervals in Blue Books. When the Constitutionalists infringed the Eliot Convention or acted in a brutal or inhumane way, Palmerston protested to the Government at Madrid. These protests, like the Blue Books, were really intended for English rather than Spanish eyes.

Soon after his arrival at Madrid, Villiers began to play an active part in Spanish politics, and he quickly came to regard himself as a benevolent patron of the new order in Spain. He was drawn into Spanish politics at the invitation of the politicians themselves, as the envoy of a powerful ally and the natural patron of the anti-French groups in Spanish politics. Villiers was easily drawn into the labyrinth of Spanish politics; intrigue came naturally to him and he sincerely believed, as did Palmerston and most British diplomats, that Great Britain was the natural model and protector for States attempting to establish liberal institutions. He certainly thought it his duty to give the Spaniards the benefit of British wisdom and experience in constitutional government. Moreover, because he believed that the outcome of the war in the North depended on decisions taken at Madrid, he was not unnaturally anxious that these decisions should be the right ones taken by the right men. His involvement in the evolution of the new order at Madrid was on two levels: he advised Spanish Governments on basic constitutional problems, and he participated in the day-to-day operation of the new system. Particularly at times of crisis it was not always possible to separate the two aspects completely.

The fundamental problem of Spanish liberalism was its divisions. Many had been apparent before the liberal order was established, and in the five years after 1834 they hardened. The two main factions, the conservatives (later known as the *Moderados*) and the radical elements (later fused into the *Progresista* party), were separated by real differences of opinion on basic issues. It was therefore impossible to construct a political system to which both were prepared to give wholehearted support. Their differences were exacerbated by fear and jealousy; each party sought the permanent exclusion of the other from office. Within the parties, too, faction and intrigue predominated. The centre groups in both parties were neither willing nor able to co-operate with one another. Unable to resolve their differences amongst themselves, the politicians looked elsewhere either for support or for mediation. The Crown ought to have acted as a force for reconciliation both within the parties and between them. This was not possible because the Queen Regent was a partisan of the conservative groups in the *Moderado* party. In any case, her first priority was not the creation of a strong Government but the preservation of the royal prerogative. The Crown was therefore an active force in the struggle, but with interests of its own to safeguard. This was also true of the army. As a result of the war it had acquired a special place in Spanish society. It had interests and privileges which it was determined to protect, but it never acted as a single force: the generals were political as well as military rivals. The leading commanders had political allies at Madrid whom they supported, and enemies with whom they were not prepared to co-operate. In many important aspects the new liberal order in Spain was unique, if not in the principles underlying it, at least in its operation. Even Villiers, who understood it better than most, found it difficult to describe. 'Words', he wrote to Granville on 22 October 1836, 'which it is necessary to apply to things here, because there are no others, do not represent the same ideas as when applied elsewhere and they become therefore the medium of erroneous impressions. A new vocabulary is almost necessary in order to enable one to write upon or discuss the affairs of Spain with precision.'

Amidst the confusion Villiers attempted as far as possible to act consistently. His basic concern was to ensure that there was a strong Government, capable of creating and sustaining a majority in the Cortes and of prosecuting the war with as much vigour as finances would allow. In most instances he supported the Governments against their critics. Only rarely did he intrigue against a Government in office or advise the Queen Regent to change her Ministers. To Ministers, he suggested how best they could manage the Cortes, maintain good relations with the Queen Regent and control the generals in the field, as well as adopt measures for the good of Spain. His advice was for the most part tactical; he seemed to regard himself as the self-appointed manager of inexperienced politicians.

As far as Government policy was concerned, Villiers on the whole confined his advice to foreign and financial problems. In foreign policy no Spanish Government after April 1834 looked beyond the Quadruple Alliance. It was the cornerstone of domestic as well as foreign policy because the course of the war in the North, the outstanding domestic problem, was vitally affected by the attitudes and policies of the two Great Power allies of Spain. Within the context of the alliance it was possible for Spanish Governments to place more emphasis on co-operation with one Power than with the other. The exercise of this option was as much an aspect of domestic as of foreign policy, reflecting the wish of different factions to identify themselves with either England or France. Villiers certainly encouraged and supported anti-French groups, particularly after the autumn of 1836 when Anglo-French co-operation in Spain was purely nominal.

Villiers was deeply involved, as this correspondence shows, in the many schemes to attract foreign capital to Spain. There were several reasons for his involvement in these enterprises. He was genuinely convinced that the lack of resources was seriously impeding the successful prosecution of the war in the North. He also believed that if he, and more particularly the British Government, were involved, the loan negotiations would have a better chance of success. Moreover, he certainly thought that the Spanish Government would be more likely to agree to reform its tariff if it had previously secured a large supply of credit from the foreign money markets. Villiers acted on the assumption that successful loan negotiations would be a prelude to commercial negotiations. Lastly, Villiers was directly involved in the financial problems of the Spanish Government between 1835 and 1838 because he was an almost weekly suppliant for funds for the British Auxiliary Legion which was entirely dependent on the Spaniards for food, clothing, arms and pay.

In his correspondence with Palmerston on the affairs of the Legion Villiers made no attempt to conceal his exasperation. There is no doubt that the presence of the Legion in Spain added enormously to the burden of work imposed on the Madrid legation at a time of almost constant political crisis. Its problems strained and complicated the relations between Villiers and the Spanish Government. In addition to his regular dealings with the Prime Minister and the Foreign Minister (offices which were frequently combined), he had also to maintain close contact with the Finance and War Ministers. He found the officials as well as the Ministers wanting in almost every respect. They were slow to transact business, irregular in their methods and profligate with promises. In order to secure supplies of arms and money for the Legion he had to charm, cajole and threaten. He was blamed by the Spanish Government for asking too much and blamed by the Legion for securing too little.

Relations between the Legion and the Spanish army were almost continuously bad. In theory the Legion was a Spanish force composed of British volunteers and officers paid and equipped by the Spanish Government and under the orders of the Spanish Commander-in-Chief. In practice the Legion was organized as a British regiment, acting in accordance with British Army regulations, and Evans, its commander, was reluctant even to co-operate with, let alone obey, his Spanish superiors. The goodwill, high hopes and political idealism which accompanied the formation of the Legion in England soon evaporated when it reached Spain, and Villiers found himself at the centre of the constant bickering and mutual recriminations which characterized relations between the Legion on the one hand and the Spanish Government and army on the other. Once again he was forced to assume the role of mediator, and occasionally that of judge, in the many conflicts that occurred.

Villiers himself had little faith in the Legion. He thought that it would inevitably attract disreputable and inefficient elements in British and particularly in Irish society, and that it would be extremely difficult for Evans to transform such a motley crew into an effective fighting force. To him the sending of the Legion was first and foremost a gesture of goodwill; there were other gestures which might have been of more use to the Spaniards, for example a loan. He also believed that the Legion was intended as a substitute for the full-scale intervention of the French army in Northern Spain; in his view it was an inadequate substitute. In June 1835 when the Legion was formed he wrote bluntly to Granville that 'Foreign troops could do nothing in the insurgent provinces militarily speaking and nothing to restore confidence in the rest of Spain'. The military activities of the Legion from 1835 to 1838 did little to make him change this judgement, and he was greatly relieved when it was disbanded.

The fact was that the Legion was a small force, operating in unknown territory, fighting a type of war of which most British soldiers had no experience. Almost from the start desertion and indiscipline began to undermine its effectiveness. In England its importance was deliberately exaggerated; the English press tended to assume that it would win the war for the Queen of Spain. This attitude had been encouraged by Evans before he left London and in the first few months in Spain. He regarded himself as a crusader of liberalism and an accomplished soldier whose experience and tactical skill, once at the disposal of the Spaniards, would bring about a rapid reversal of fortunes in the war. It is difficult to escape the conclusion that the Legion was nothing more than a gesture, albeit a much publicized one. For Villiers it was principally a source of anxiety and frustration, and the difficulties with which it presented him undoubtedly added to his growing disenchantment with his post. He admitted as much to his brother in 1838.

Villiers's repeated failure to place Anglo-Spanish commercial relations on a new basis was also a great disappointment to him. His interest in commercial diplomacy was aroused in the early 1830s when he had been one of the two British Commissioners appointed to revise the Anglo-French customs duties. He was unusual amongst British diplomats in having a keen appreciation of the benefits to Great Britain of increased overseas trade. He saw that Britain's power was based on her wealth, and that her wealth was to a large extent based on the successful penetration of overseas markets. In the commercial negotiations he conducted with the Spanish Government, his aim was simple: to open up Spanish markets to British goods and remove the numerous restrictions and duties which prevented the free flow of commerce. Such a measure would, he believed, not only benefit British exports; tariff changes would lead Great Britain to import more goods from Spain, thus stimulating trade and industry in Spain itself. He also believed that a revision of the tariff would reduce the vast amount of smuggling which was encouraged by the existing prohibitive tariffs. The Spanish Government would in consequence receive more revenue from increased legitimate trade paying a lower duty than it did under the high duty arrangements. Like Palmerston, who enthusiastically supported his endeavours, Villiers was convinced that liberal States had a duty to pursue liberal policies, and this included lifting archaic restrictions on trade. Both men argued that the indifference of commercial opinion in England to the fate of Spain could be transformed into support for Spanish constitutionalism by tariff reform.

Although Villiers's attitude to the commercial question was straightforward, the actual negotiations were tortuous and ultimately unavailing. Despite his insistence on raising commercial questions with every successive Spanish Government, despite the many different schemes he proposed, and despite his efforts to surmount or circumvent the obstacles in the way of reform, Villiers failed to secure an agreement acceptable to both Governments. He was fully aware of the reasons for failure; his letters to Palmerston list them all and occasionally place them in order of importance. None of the Spanish Governments was prepared to give commercial matters a high place on its list of priorities. They were all shrewd enough to realize that the British Government would continue to support the Queen's cause even if the

Government at Madrid failed to reform the tariff. All were reluctant to face the opposition which reform would undoubtedly arouse in the Cortes, and particularly amongst the Catalan Deputies who were convinced that the commercial and industrial interests of their region required protection against competition from British manufactured goods. Villiers knew too that the French Government was determined to oppose any reform of the Spanish tariff even though the same terms of trade would be offered to France as to Britain. In 1838 Soult informed Latour-Maubourg that, as France could not yet compete on equal terms with English manufactures, the French Government would prefer English goods to face a highly disadvantageous tariff barrier in Spain. Villiers also believed, with what justice it is difficult to tell, that Poulett Thomson, the President of the Board of Trade, was placing obstacles in the way of the schemes which originated from the British legation at Madrid. He was convinced that vanity and jealousy of any success he might achieve rather than sound commercial arguments lay behind Thomson's objections.

The printed correspondence ends in December 1837, six months before Villiers left Madrid on leave of absence. After his return from England in October 1838 he was unable to recover his previous enthusiasm for the many struggles in which he had formerly taken part in Spain. By the beginning of 1839 the course of the war in the North had lost the drama of its early years. There was little prospect of another Carlist push southwards. The real question now was how long it would be before the Queen's army would restrict Carlist military operations to so small an area that they would be starved of supplies and their will to continue sapped beyond endurance. In Madrid politics there was an uneasy truce between the factions, earlier dramas having been transformed into the usual routine of small crises. Villiers was anxious to be recalled. He wrote to his brother Edward on 29 October 1838:

> The interest which I felt in this country and cause and which had grown by degrees to the height it had during five years of anxious watching has dwindled down very low. The thread was broken by my visit to England and I should not easily be able to splice it even if I had the wish to do so.

His personal circumstances also changed. When he accepted the post at Madrid he had been urgently in need of paid employment. In

December 1838 he succeeded to the earldom of Clarendon, and although the financial arrangements made by the previous Earl were far from satisfactory, he now had an independent income and a seat in the House of Lords. His political prospects were transformed. He was, moreover, engaged to marry Lady Katharine Barham. 'The progress made in the great Cathy affair', he wrote to his brother, 'since my departure has been beyond my most sanguine expectations, and as you may suppose occupies my thoughts rather more than the Queen's cause.' Villiers had served his political apprenticeship. As Earl of Clarendon his career entered a new phase. Palmerston had no wish to stand in his way. The worst was over in Spain, and in his opinion the total collapse of Carlism was imminent. In the new situation which was developing at Madrid Villiers was no longer indispensable. His talents were needed at home where Melbourne was looking for new men and new measures to revive his Ministry.

In Spain the war in the North ended a few months after Villiers's departure. Carlism was by no means a spent force, but by 1839 it was an exhausted one. The civil war was over, but Carlism was not destroyed and liberalism did not triumph. It was, as Villiers acknowledged, a Spanish compromise.

EDITORIAL NOTE

Palmerston's letters to Villiers survive only in office copies, now preserved among the Palmerston (Broadlands) Papers. The majority of Villiers's letters to Palmerston survive both as originals, now among the Palmerston Papers, and as copies in the Clarendon Deposit in the Bodleian Library. The copies are usually faithful, with only occasional slips or variations. Where differences are minor, the printed text follows the original in the Palmerston Papers without annotation or comment; where there is a substantial difference, the copyist's variant is supplied in a footnote. Palmerston's pencilled comments on and his amendments of Villiers's letters are also noted.

For reasons explained elsewhere, the text has been shortened by the omission of passages of peripheral interest. Comments on personal affairs and British domestic politics have been consistently omitted, and detailed and repetitious passages relating to the Latin American republics, the slave trade, loans and commercial questions have been pruned. The subject matter of excised passages is indicated by an introductory phrase or sentence followed by omission marks.

For ease of reading abbreviations in the text have been extended, capitalization has been reduced and punctuation has been modified. The original spelling has been retained, however, even though Villiers in particular was idiosyncratic and erratic in his orthography. Where the sense is obscured correct spellings have been supplied within square brackets. The transliteration of Spanish names is complicated, and Palmerston, Villiers and their copyists were inconsistent in their choice of alternatives. We have not attempted to impose consistency except in the footnotes and the index. Both Palmerston and Villiers used Don and Donna as Portuguese honorifics: we have retained these incorrect usages in the text. Neither regularly used accents, diaereses or tildes: we have not added them where they are lacking. Nor was their Spanish always accurate: some corrections have been supplied within square brackets, but where the original version is intelligible it has not been altered.

Where Villiers or Palmerston failed to designate a postscript by the abbreviation 'P.S.', this has been supplied editorially in italics. Otherwise italics appear in the printed version of the text only where they represent underlining in the original manuscript.

The statements of how Villiers's letters were sent (e.g. 'by French courier') are taken from the copies in the Clarendon Deposit. The dates of receipt of Villiers's original letters were recorded on them either as an endorsement in Palmerston's hand or as part of the official docket. We have given this information in a standard form ('*Received 5 April*'), preferring the earlier date when there are two.

MANUSCRIPT SOURCES

The following are the principal manuscript sources quoted or referred to in this edition.

PALMERSTON (BROADLANDS) PAPERS. The property of the Trustees of the Broadlands Archives Trust.

GC/CL/99-372	Villiers to Palmerston 1833-37
GC/CL/1216-1327	Palmerston to Villiers 1833-37

CLARENDON DEPOSIT (Clar. Dep.). Bodleian Library, Oxford.

C.451/2	Copies, Villiers to Palmerston 30 September 1833 – 4 July 1834 (letter book)
C.451/1	Copies, Villiers to Palmerston 8 July 1834 – 8 December 1834 (unbound)
C.452	Similar copies 2 May 1835 – 30 December 1836[1]
C.453	Similar copies 4 Jan. 1837 – 30 June 1838
C.460-461	Correspondence with General Sir George de Lacy Evans 1835-37, 1840
C.467	Letters to Edward Villiers 1835-39
C.470	Miscellaneous Spanish papers, including Villiers's queries on his instructions September 1833

FOREIGN OFFICE PAPERS. Public Record Office.

FO 72/406,412-413	Despatches to and from Villiers September – December 1833
FO 72/419-428	Despatches 1834
FO 72/439-445	Despatches 1835
FO 72/456-463	Despatches 1836
FO 72/475-485	Despatches 1837

GRANVILLE PAPERS. Public Record Office.

PRO 30/29/413,421-423 Private correspondence of the 1st Earl Granville (British ambassador to France) with Villiers 1832-41

ASTON PAPERS. Public Record Office.

FO 355/6   Correspondence of Sir Arthur Aston (secretary of embassy to France and minister plenipotentiary in Granville's absence) with Villiers 1835-37

HOLLAND HOUSE PAPERS. British Library Department of Manuscripts.

ADD MS 51617   Villiers to the 3rd Baron Holland 1833-40, nd

ARCHIVES DU MINISTERE DES AFFAIRES ETRANGERES (AMAE). Archives Nationales, Paris.

C[orrespondance] P[olitique] Angleterre 645-648 Correspondence with ambassadors to Great Britain 1835-37

C[orrespondance] P[olitique] Espagne 765-779 Correspondence with ministers to Spain 1835-37

THIERS PAPERS. Bibliothèque Nationale, Paris.

N[ouvelle] A[cquisition] F[rançaise] 20603-20604 Correspondence 1836

---

[1] C.452 consists of two folders, separately foliated, and covering the periods 2 May – 26 Dec. 1835 and 2 Jan. – 30 Dec. 1836 respectively. They are referred to in this edition as C.452/1 and C.452/2.

CORRESPONDENCE

CORRESPONDENCE

1 'Paper of Queries drawn up previously to my final conference in London with Palmerston, and his answers, September 1833'[1]

[V.] To ask for copy of Stratford Canning's instructions[2] and whether all the motives upon which they were founded are not now strengthened.

[P.] The motives to prevent bloodshed and restore peace are of course the same but the manner of bringing about those ends proposed by Stratford Canning is completely altered by circumstances.[3]

[V.] The rejection of his proposals renders many things difficult now which might then easily have been done in furtherance of Spanish views—

[P.] certainly

[V.] —for however much we may dislike Don Pedro we cannot deny that without his perseverence his daughter would have had no chance—and it would be hard now to eject him from the field of his conquest.

[P.] Certainly.

[V.] What truth is there in the Spanish assertion that Pedro intends to make himself master of the Peninsula?

[P.] Entirely false—some few rash or idle men may have held such language but Pedro never did, and the hatred which the Spaniards and Portuguese [? feel for each other] would, if nothing else did, always render such a project hopeless and chimerical.

[V.] If he thinks that Spain means war to the knife with him and that under no circumstances he is to expect anything but her enmity, it is not unnatural that he should endeavour to act offensively as well as on the defensive, and endeavour by the spread of constitutional principles to create for himself a party in Spain which should not only uphold him in Portugal but give Spain sufficient occupation at home.

[P.] Quite natural—it would in fact be a measure of defence.

[V.] In this case would England interfere, could she, ought she?

[P.] It might be difficult for England to interfere but she could by no means encourage or lend any countenance whatever to attempts against the internal tranquillity of Spain.

[V.] For should Bourmont[4] fail before Lisbon and should the King die it is manifest that Miguel[5] would with his army and Vendean officers[6] march into Spain to seat Don Carlos[7] on the throne in the expectation that there would afterwards be a reciprocity of good offices in Portugal.

[P.] It is more than probable that Carlos, Miguel and Bourmont, each for his own object, meditate such a course.

[V.] On the other hand, supposing that Spain is willing to be really neutral and to give reason for believing that she does not intrigue to prevent the establishment of Don Pedro's authority, and that when established she will honestly recognize it, how far will England interfere to prevent what Spain may consider revolutionary institutions being given to Portugal, and such as are likely to set bad spirits to work in Spain against public tranquillity? If she will interfere at all, what are to be considered revolutionary institutions, for it is clear that the Spanish acceptance of them will constantly have to be denied?

[P.] England cannot interfere to prevent Portugal adopting any institutions she may think fit. It is a mistake to think that England ever held out any hopes to Spain that she would dictate in such a manner to Portugal[8]—besides it is a dangerous principle to admit that the institutions of one country are to be modelled to suit the taste of another. England as a common friend to both countries might suggest to Portugal that though such and such measures might suit the Portuguese, yet such and such disadvantages externally might attend their adoption and that it would be desireable well to balance the two previously to final decision—but even this should be resorted to with reluctance. It is true that had Sir Stratford Canning's proposals been adopted we might then have made to Pedro, whose fortunes then appeared desperate, any conditions we pleased before we took measures to secure the throne to his daughter—but that time is gone by, and the opportunity has been allowed by Spain to slip through our fingers.

[V.] In the 3d case if Spain continues to profess the same kind of neutrality she has hitherto done, openly proclaiming one set of principles and secretly devising others[9]—if the consequence of that should be a continuance of bloodshed and tumult in Portugal and that kind of guerilla warfare on the frontiers which will inevitably lead to reprisals

and perhaps to some just ground of accusation upon its effects against Portugal by Spain, though its causes are created by herself, how far will England interpose to stop such a state of things and force the contending parties into a more correct view of their own interests?

[P.] A most important consideration, and Spain must be made to feel that upon her will rest the responsibility of the continuance of such a state of things. It is to be hoped however that it will not be of long duration, for Bourmont and his army cannot for any length of time keep the open field subject to desertions, without materiels of war, without a place d'armes, no supplies by sea and Spain unable to assist him openly. England cannot at present pledge herself to the moment or the circumstances when interference shall be imperative upon her, but Spain may be threatened with it and given to understand that it is not improbable.

[V.] If Spain will listen to no terms with Pedro, and that Napier[10] was to take his fleet to Cadiz, beat or turn the Spanish fleet there and proclaim a constitution, what language would England hold at Madrid? What answer would she make to a call upon her to prevent such a course by the exercise of force?

[P.] Napier would not be allowed to do this. Such a step might lead to a general war and certainly to the Spaniards entering Portugal, therefore it would be against our interests, therefore we should not allow it and Parker[11] would not let him leave the Tagus and our alliance and protection with Portugal would be forfeited. Spain however might be made to feel that this is one of the many dangers she incurs by not concurring to restore order in Portugal.

[V.] In the event of Bourmont's succeeding and getting possession of Lisbon, will England still persevere in her system of neutrality, and will she confine her interference to the protection of British life and property?

[P.] An event possible but daily becoming less possible. England would only interfere for the protection of the lives and property of British subjects.

[V.] The reconquest of Lisbon however will only complicate, not settle, the question, for Pedro will still have possession of Oporto, a portion of the Algarves, the means of blockading the Tagus unresisted together with the moral aid of those towns and that portion of the population who have declared in his favor—retaliation, vengeance and a state of things worse than before would then ensue.

[P.] It would be a tremendous complication and no effort should be wanting to avert it—the best way would be for Pedro to take into his service immediately plenty of foreign soldiers who would garrison Oporto and Lisbon and set free his Portuguese troops with which he might scour the country and drive away Miguel and Bourmont.

[V.] Would England then press the ejection of the two brothers and the establishment of the Queen and a regency; or would it not then be high time to determine upon interference and, as in the affairs of Belgium and of Greece, at once to declare that Europe can no longer remain a passive spectator of such ruin and needless misery?

[P.] It is very possible such a course might be desireable but it can only be determined upon according to circumstances as they arise—and no instructions can now be given without the sanction of the Cabinet, by whom the contingency has not yet been contemplated.

[V.] If the first, in what way should Spanish cooperation be invited, for it is manifest that the totally altered circumstances of Pedro and the increased apprehensions of Spain for herself enable us to hold a very different language to that which Sir Stratford Canning was able to do? In the event of Spain declining to cooperate, will England act singly as she thinks best? In the 2d case would other Powers be consulted, and if so upon what basis should their assistance be invited?

[P.] Ditto to last paragraph.

[V.] What are Don Pedro's views for himself? Does he intend to be Regent? If so, till his daughter arrives at what age? If the Queen marries, what course does he mean to pursue?

[P.] Don Pedro has certainly no intention or desire to set aside his daughter and reign in her stead. He does not intend to *make himself* Regent, and one of his avowed objects in calling the Cortes is to settle that question. By his Charter the Queen will not attain her majority till 18—, but these questions are all to be settled by the Cortes. He means to retire to Italy unless called upon [by] the Brazilian *nation* to return there.

[V.] In what manner is the Cortes to be convened? Will England not endeavour to give some shape to their deliberations upon the institutions in order to guard against their assuming a character offensive to Spain?

[P.] Not exactly known—if according to Pedro's Charter, the mode of electing is to be found in the State Papers 1825-26. It could only be done unofficially but it would certainly be desireable.

38

[V.] Are we prepared to declare ourselves in favor of the Duc de Leuchtenberg's[12] marriage with the Queen, and our unqualified veto upon her marrying Don Miguel (Vial[13] is evidently instructed to keep this latter in view)?

[P.] We need not *declare* ourselves at all. Either Leuchtenberg or Prince Charles of Naples[14] would suit us very well—the former preferable—positively not Nemours,[15] and under no circumstances would we be parties to or sanction a marriage with Miguel, though if Donna Maria and Pedro were by any (impossible) chance to desire it we could not interfere to prevent it.

[V.] Can any means be adopted for removing Don Carlos from Portugal?

[P.] The only means are getting rid of Don Miguel.

[V.] It is clear that his absence would diminish Miguel's and Bourmont's pretence for converting the Peninsula into another La Vendée and the arena of Carlist and Holy Alliance principles. Those principles would have a firmer hold in Spain than in any other spot of Europe if Don Carlos succeeds to the throne upon which he would be placed by the Apostolicals,[16] for to them he must be bound during his life or till he is overthrown by internal convulsion.

[P.] Quite true.

[V.] What then should be the policy of England upon the King of Spain's death? It is manifest that all depends upon the course pursued at the moment. It is contrary to the principles and practice of England to interfere upon a question so purely national as the succession to the Crown, but her interests clearly point to the exclusion of Don Carlos, and the interests of Spain, rightly understood, are identical with those of England. Carlos King, darkness and despotism will prevail. If the Princess succeeds she must look for support from the people by extending education, diminishing exactions and causing justice to be administered. Carlos has on his side the whole of the Church, much of the army, the Royalist Volunteers and many friends to his claim as well as his principles—a firm united party, acting resolutely together for a common purpose. For the Infanta there will be the moderate liberals forming perhaps the majority in Spain but they are inert, dispersed and suspicious of each other—to these add the Constitutionalists and ultra liberals, more from hatred to Carlism than any other motive, for the Queen contrived mortally to offend them before the expiration of her regency and to teach them how little favor they could really hope

for at her hands.[17] Much, if not all, must depend upon the leaders of the respective parties. The long established superiority of the Apostolicals will enable them to start with all the advantage of a dominant party—a leader among them will be more easily selected and more willingly obeyed than among their opponents who have contracted the ill habits which years of proscription and despotism engender, and whose passions when once let loose are wild and impatient in proportion to their previous subjection. During the regency of the Queen a host of advisers sprung forth, but not one seems to have been designated by opinion for a leader or now to live in the recollection of his party.

[P.] Quite true.

[V.] Under these circumstances should the Queen be advised to be prepared to act instantly and with vigor upon the King's death—to declare herself Regent and call together the Cortes? For if the Infanta's claim is to be set upon a basis of despotism or that there is to be a mixed regency or that she is to marry Don Carlos's son,[18] the rivalry of opinions now represented by the contending parties will still continue and the contest will still have to seek an issue.

[P.] It would be very difficult, very delicate and hardly expedient—for the Queen is a weak woman with nobody to guide or assist [her], and however well we may wish to the Infanta's cause (which circumstances doubtless make that of better government) it seems scarcely possible to avert a civil war—except by all parties consenting to acknowledge her claim, for it is evident that immediately on the King's death she must be proclaimed. Her case however is by no means a clear one or one easy to uphold—and Palmerston thinks that Carlos will eventually succeed. The marriage of the Infanta with Carlos's son would upon the whole perhaps be the best way of avoiding the greatest number of evils. We might regret it but Palmerston said if he were a Spaniard he should desire it.

[V.] In the event of Don Carlos marching into Spain with Miguel and Bourmont, what part would England take supposing her to have been neuter and silent upon the question of succession at the King's death—what part supposing her to have expressed herself favorably to the Infanta and to any form of regency established by the Queen?

[P.] Complete neutrality and non expression of opinion must be the course of England upon the King's death. I should be accredited to the Infanta when she is proclaimed Queen (doing business of course with the Regent) and so remain till she was dispossessed by Don Carlos when, if he is considered to be elected by the nation, I must in course of time be accredited to him.

[V.] Is the King really sincere in his daughter's cause? I incline to think that being in love with his wife he has yielded to her solicitations in behalf of her daughter, and provided he obtains tranquillity while he lives he cares for little after his death. This would account for his upholding Zea[19] to whose indisposition to his daughter's cause (in so many respects resembling that of Donna Maria's) he cannot be blind.

[P.] Very likely—and there is every reason to believe that Zea has been keeping Carlos in Portugal to use or not according to circumstances, and the severe language he has used to him during his stay there has all been affected, and upon previous understanding both with him and Don Miguel.

Clar. Dep. C.470

[1] This document, in Villiers's hand, is set out in two columns, the answer being written next to the question. It would have been difficult to follow this layout in the printed version. Villiers's questions have therefore been prefixed V. and Palmerston's answers P.

[2] Canning had been sent by P on a special mission to Spain in December 1832 to propose that Spain should join with Great Britain in mediating to end the Portuguese civil war. The mission failed and he returned to London in May 1833. See R.J. Bullen, 'England, Spain and the Portuguese Question in 1833', European Studies Review 4, no.1 (1974), 1-22.

[3] When Stratford Canning went to Madrid a military stalemate existed between the belligerents in Portugal. This was broken in August 1833 when Dom Pedro and his partisans captured Lisbon.

[4] An ultra-royalist French army officer sent by the absolutist Powers to assist Dom Miguel.

[5] Second son of John VI of Portugal and brother of Dom Pedro. In 1828 he left Vienna and returned to Portugal to assume the regency on behalf of his niece, Dona Maria, to whom he was betrothed. Soon after his return, Miguel suspended the Constitutional Charter granted by Pedro and declared himself King. His main support came from the clerical and absolutist factions.

[6] After the 1830 revolution in France a group of legitimist French army officers from the province of La Vendée served in Miguel's army.

[7] Brother of Ferdinand VII of Spain. He refused to acknowledge Ferdinand's right to alter the Spanish law of succession in order to place his two daughters by María Cristina of Naples above the male representatives of the Spanish Bourbons in the line of succession. He 'retired' to Portugal where he resided at Miguel's headquarters. In June 1833 he refused to return to Spain to take an oath of allegiance to his niece, the Infanta Isabella, elder daughter

of Ferdinand VII, who thereupon ordered him to live in exile in the Papal States. Don Carlos refused.

[8] Stratford Canning had been instructed to inform the Spanish Government that if they would participate in the proposed mediation, the British Government would attempt to 'persuade' Pedro to abandon the Constitutional Charter of 1826. They did not promise to force him to abandon it.

[9] In 1829 the Spanish Government recognized Miguel as King of Portugal. As a result of pressure from the British Government, Spain was then persuaded to adopt a policy of non-intervention in Portuguese affairs. The British Government claimed, however, that most of the arms and warlike supplies that reached Miguel came across the Spanish border with the knowledge and connivance of the Spanish Government.

[10] Admiral Sir Charles Napier, a British naval officer serving as Pedro's naval commander.

[11] Admiral William Parker, commander of the British fleet in Portuguese waters.

[12] A German prince, and son of Napoleon's stepson. His sister Amélie was Dom Pedro's second wife.

[13] Spanish minister to Great Britain.

[14] Prince of Capua, son of Francis I, King of the Two Sicilies, and brother of Queen Cristina of Spain.

[15] One of the sons of Louis Philippe, King of the French.

[16] The ultra-conservative party in Spain which opposed Ferdinand VII's change in the law of succession, and which was strongly supported by the higher clergy.

[17] Cristina was Regent for a few months in 1832-33 during the illness of Ferdinand VII. During the regency the Spanish liberals had expected her to ask them to form a Government.

[18] Some argued that a disputed succession and civil war in Spain could be averted by a marriage between the Infanta Isabella and the Conde de Montemolín, eldest son of Don Carlos, who would reign as joint sovereigns. This solution was rejected by both Don Carlos and Queen Cristina.

[19] President of the Council of Ministers. He was disliked by the Apostolicals because he supported the succession rights of Isabella, and by the liberals because he favoured the maintenance of an absolute monarchy.

2 Viscount Palmerston to George Villiers, 9 September 1833

Draft despatch no. 2. Foreign Office. The King having made choice of you to fill the appointment of Minister Plenipotentiary from His Majesty at the Court of Madrid, and it being desirable that you should repair immediately to your post, i have received His Majesty's commands to give you some special instructions for your guidance. You will, on your arrival at Madrid, assure the Spanish Cabinet that His Majesty's Government is animated by the sincerest desire to maintain and to improve to the utmost those friendly relations which so happily subsist between the two countries. The mighty efforts which Spain and England made conjointly during the last war,[1] and of which Spanish ground was the theatre, and Spanish independence the immediate object, have necessarily created between the two nations that community of feeling which is natural to those who have shared in the same dangers, and partaken of the same success. Nor are the interests of the two countries less identified in peace than they have been in war. The alliance of Spain with England must always have a powerful effect in preserving the tranquillity of Europe; and there are perhaps no two countries that could derive greater mutual advantages from the liberal encouragement of reciprocal commercial intercourse. His Majesty's Government are persuaded that these sentiments and opinions are fully shared by the Cabinet of Madrid, by which and by its representatives in this country they have been repeatedly and in the strongest terms expressed.

The lamentable state of things in Portugal, and the different views which the two Governments have taken of those affairs, have unfortunately tended for some time past, not indeed to diminish the cordiality of feeling between the two Cabinets, but to present perpetually for their consideration matters of the deepest interest and of the most urgent importance upon which divergent opinions prevented them from concurring in the same course. His Majesty's Government long flattered themselves with the hope that some middle term might have been devised, by which the two Cabinets might have been enabled to act in concert with respect to the affairs of Portugal. They had persuaded themselves that the Spanish Government looked to things and not to persons, to the interests of Spain and not to those of a Portuguese faction, and that security against aggression from Portugal in consequence of civil commotions there, was the real object which that

Government sought to attain. It was in this belief that the mission of Sir Stratford Canning was resolved upon, and that his instructions were framed, and it was hoped that the propositions of which he was the bearer might have led to a concert between the two Powers, from whence might have sprung a speedy settlement of the questions which have divided Portugal, and an early restoration of internal peace in that distracted country. The hopes of His Majesty's Government were disappointed. The contest was allowed to run its course and events have since occurred by which the proposals made through Sir Stratford Canning have become inapplicable to the present posture of affairs.

But though the existing state of things in Portugal precludes His Majesty's Government from instructing you to renew the propositions which were made to Spain last winter, yet His Majesty's Government are no less desirous now than they were then to act in concert with the Spanish Cabinet with regard to the civil war in Portugal, if the views and determinations of that Cabinet should render such concert possible; and therefore although the British Government have no fresh proposals to make, yet they are ready to secure and to consider any which the Spanish Cabinet may wish to submit. You are accordingly instructed to encourage any disposition which you may perceive on the part of that Government, to propose any practicable scheme by which the united influence of Great Britain and of Spain could be successfully exerted for the purpose of putting an end to the barbarous system of predatory warfare which still continues to desolate some of the provinces of Portugal, and which cannot long continue without affecting more or less the contiguous districts of Spain. There is another point of view in which the termination of the Portuguese contest becomes of great importance for the internal tranquillity of Spain. It is obvious that as long as Don Miguel has an army and a head quarter, that head quarter will be the residence of Don Carlos. The interests of Spain require the immediate removal of Don Carlos from the Peninsula and the Spanish Ministers have professed the utmost anxiety to accomplish that removal without delay. The sincerity of some members of the Spanish Government on this point has indeed been question[ed]; it has been imagined that Don Carlos does not linger in Portugal without the connivance of those who ostensibly urge his departure; and that a plan is in contemplation to appoint him to be the leading member of the Regency in the event of the death of King Ferdinand.

But be this as it may, His Majesty's Government are entitled to assume that the Cabinet of Madrid is in earnest in its declared desire to prevail upon Don Carlos to quit the Peninsula, and you are therefore instructed to dwell upon the consideration, that if the civil war was put an end to, it would no longer be possible for Don Carlos to continue in the territory of Portugal and that consequently Spain has a direct interest in the speedy termination of the contest.

In the meanwhile, and should the Spanish Government make no proposal which could be accepted, you will assure them nevertheless that the influence, whatever it may be, which Great Britain may be able to exert over the councils of Portugal, shall be jealously exercised to prevent aggression of any kind against Spain.

There are some matters of the greatest importance upon which His Majesty's Government forbear at present from giving you any particular instructions, from the conviction that it would be useless to enter into any discussion upon them until the Portuguese question shall be settled. Of this nature is the extensive subject of our commercial relations with Spain. Relations which require to be attentively reconsidered, and which might be materially improved to the mutual benefit of the two countries. But you will not fail to direct your attention to this subject, and you will omit no opportunity of acquiring information, which may be useful to His Majesty's Government, when the proper time shall come for taking this matter in hand. . . .[2]

FO 72/406

[1] The war against Napoleon.
*[2] The rest of the despatch is concerned with the recognition by Spain of South American States and the more rigorous enforcement of the slave trade treaty.

3 Palmerston to Villiers, 9 September 1833

Draft despatch no. 3. Foreign Office. With reference to my general instructions of this day's date, I think it right to add some particular remarks with regard to the affairs of Portugal. I have stated in the instructions above mentioned, that the present condition of things does not admit of a renewal of the propositions which were made to Spain through Sir Stratford Canning; but on the other hand, the change of circumstances which has arisen since the period when those propositions were made has not diminished the expediency of a concert between Great Britain and Spain for the purpose of restoring internal tranquillity to Portugal and the events which are passing in that country seem to shew how much the real interests both of Spain and Great Britain coincide as to the manner in which that object can best be effected.

The interests of Great Britain require that peace should be restored to Portugal; the interests of Spain equally demand that a civil war waged close to her frontier should cease. The character which that war is assuming will render its continuance every day more injurious to the interests of all parties concerned. British subjects and property will be exposed to increasing danger, and the chances will progressively be multiplied that the frontier of Spain may be violated by one or other of the contracting parties. The Spanish Government alleges that its principal reason for being adverse to the success of Donna Maria is that the triumph of that cause would place power in the hands of Don Pedro, that resistance to that power would spring up in various parts of Portugal and that the consequence would be a prolongation of the civil war. But it seems demonstrable on the contrary that the establishment of Donna Maria is the only thing which could now restore tranquillity to Portugal, and thus afford on that score security to Spain. The Government established in the name of Donna Maria, if it were acknowledged by Spain, would for its own sake necessarily abstain from anything which could give just cause of offence to that Power; and means would thus be created which would be certain and effectual for preventing Portugal from becoming the seat of intrigues directed against the internal tranquillity of Spain. But if the civil war continues, and if Spain becomes mixed up, as it may not improbably be, with the cause of Don Miguel, must it not be the natural tendency of things that while on the one hand, an alliance will be formed between the supporters of Don Miguel and the Spanish adherents of Don Carlos, so on the other a sympathy of feeling will arise between the Constitutionalists of Spain and the Portuguese partisans of Donna Maria, and thus the contest between Donna Maria and Don Miguel may cease to be a Portuguese, and may become a Peninsular dispute?

It must be needless to point out to the Cabinet of Madrid all the dangers to Spain which would result from such a state of things. The Government of Donna Maria has the command of the sea, and her fleet is under the orders of an officer of the greatest enterprize and intrepidity,[1] and if Don Pedro were driven by Spanish aggression to have recourse to measures of retaliation, the means at his disposal would be of the most formidable kind. His Majesty's Government would consider such a state of things as a great European calamity, and would do all which they properly could do to avert it, but they see no method so certain of preventing the possibility of such evils as a cordial and immediate union of Spain with Great Britain for the purpose of putting an end to the civil war.

That civil war can now end only by the full establishment of Donna Maria, and it is unnecessary to add that to a marriage between her and Don Miguel,[2] His Majesty's Government never can become parties, nor can such a union form part of any arrangement which Great Britain can look to, as a mode of settling the affairs of Portugal.

But there is still another point of view in which the continuance of the civil war may be looked upon as dangerous to Spain. Can it be supposed that Marshal Bourmont and La Rochejaquelin, and other Vendean Chiefs who are now in Portugal, have gone thither with no other object than to fight for the cause of Don Miguel? The cockade which they wear answers that question. They command the troops of Miguel but they fight for Henry 5th[3] and the union of the Miguelites and the Spanish and French Carlists at Coimbra is a sufficient proof that the adherents of the three Princes consider the cause of the three to be one and the same. If then, Don Miguel were to succeed in Portugal, Don Carlos would establish in the Peninsula a most dangerous point of support from which to act against the succession of the Infanta, and in the event of the death of King Ferdinand, Portugal would supply the elements of civil war to Spain.

You are instructed then in your conversations with M. de Zea, to press the foregoing consideration upon him, urgently, but in the most friendly manner, and you will omit no opportunity of assuring him that if His Majesty's Government feel the greatest anxiety for the termination of the civil war in Portugal, that anxiety is founded quite as much upon a regard for the interests of Spain as upon considerations peculiar to Great Britain.

FO 72/406

[1] Admiral Sir Charles Napier.
[2] A solution favoured by the Spanish Government.
[3] The Bourbon pretender to the French throne. In July 1830 Charles X had abdicated in favour of his grandson who was styled Henri V by French legitimists.

4 Villiers to Palmerston, 16 September 1833

Paris. Private. According to your desire I have shewn the Duc de Broglie[1] my instructions—he had both time and inclination to read them through. Having done so, he said he had only to express his satisfaction and entire concurrence. Your position with respect to Spain he thinks a perfectly proper one; the Spanish Government having declined to avail themselves of the offer made by Stratford Canning, that England can originate no fresh proposition, but should be willing to receive any that Spain might be desirous to suggest. The contest in Portugal ought not in his opinion to be tolerated much longer. If either of the brothers succeeds in finally ejecting the other, the course to be pursued by England and France will be simple, but in the far more probable event of neither being able to assert his superiority, De Broglie considers that an intervention of other Powers will be inevitable, and as in the cases of Belgium and of Greece a cessation of hostilities must in the first place be insisted upon—to such an intervention *the 3 Powers*[2] must never be admitted, that England, France and Spain were the Powers naturally entitled to mediate, and his earnest wish was that England should take the lead. After what has passed, he thought Spain was more likely to make a communication to France than to England, and though he could not invite this he would do his best to encourage it.

I asked him what confidence he had in Rayneval.[3] He said he was a great Tory, but a correct observer and faithful reporter of what passed around him, and that he had no reason to complain of him or to expect that he would not zealously pursue any course prescribed to him provided he was sure beforehand of the appui of his Government. At my request De Broglie will write to him to desire his cordial cooperation with me, and to say he considers the arrival of a new British minister at Madrid to be an opportunity for fresh exertions to induce a wiser policy towards Portugal on the part of Spain. He will moreover give me a private letter to Rayneval saying that I am one of his intimate friends in whom he places great confidence, and requesting him (R) to do the same—this will give me a good chance of acquiring an influence with the aimable routinier.

With respect to the succession in Spain, I told him it was impossible to believe that France would support Don Carlos and prefer some infinitely remote advantage to the immediate benefit of having a liberal

Government established next door to her. He admitted all the mischief likely to arise to France if Don Carlos succeeds to the throne, but said that it was an important question upon which it was not necessary to pronounce an opinion, that France had neither protested or interfered, and that she would be perfectly content to wait the course of events. I said nothing more upon the matter for I have no doubt that he wishes well to the cause of the Infanta without being forced to abandon the right of Don Carlos.

He spoke with considerable asperity of Don Pedro who he said was acting like a madman, and that no final settlement of Portuguese affairs could be hoped for till he was got out of the country, which he wanted to make the foyer of revolutionary principles. I said that there would not only be difficulty but some hardship in ejecting him now that the Queen's cause had been brought to a triumphant issue by his energy and perseverence, and that I had reason to believe that neither Pedro or the Constitution were by any means as unpopular in Portugal as was supposed.

I dined yesterday at St. Cloud and the King[4] was extremely desirous to give me for your information a detail of the ill usage he had experienced from Don Pedro. He has never received any account of Napier's victory or notification that Donna Maria's authority was established, or did he get even a civil answer from the Empress[5] when he in person offered her a frigate to accompany her to Lisbon, or did she reconduct him, as she was wont when he visited her, or did she say a word of acknowledgement to himself or the Queen[6] for the manner in which she and Donna Maria had been treated here—all this the King said was anterior to the Leuchtenberg story, and he was utterly at a loss to account for Don Pedro's hostility and grossiereté. I asked him if Don Pedro had ever made any application to him for money (as Louis Philippe's stinginess is I hear a favourite topic of Don Pedro's). He said there certainly had been an application for money made and not complied with, although 60,000 francs had been given to Madame de Loulé[7] out of the secret funds. I told him that the English public, who of course would not be aware of the causes of complaint he had against the Emperor and Empress, had been surprised at the treatment which the Queen[8] had met with at Havre. He said he did not wonder at it, and that if he had known how to make a distinction between her and the Empress he should certainly have done it (his original intention having been to send a frigate and Flahault on a special mission with her), although up to the hour of her sailing he had had no *official* notification of *where* or *why* she was going. He said he was uncommonly desirous to 'justify himself' to the people of England, and above all he wished you to know that this foolish squabble in no way diminished his good wishes for the Queen's cause or his determination to act with England for the settlement of Portuguese affairs.

I told him you were anxious that there should be no misunderstanding in his mind about the treatment which the Queen has received in England—that the King[9] had no cause of complaint against her, and that as she had been acknowledged by us and already treated as a queen in England it was impossible not to give her now the same reception as before. He said, I beg you will tell Lord Palmerston how very sensible I am to this attention on his part. I have had no feeling whatever of dissatisfaction upon the subject. The King of England could not have received her otherwise, and I only regret that it was not in my power to treat her in the same way.

Both the King and De Broglie have said most kind and satisfactory things about my appointment to Madrid, which I report to you not out of what is called in Benthamese *jactancy*, but in a sort of justification to you for stepping out of the *right line of succession* in diplomacy.

I have staid here to dine with the King and De Broglie and mean to start on Thursday night after the arrival of the courier.

Received 19 September.

GC/CL/99

[1] French Foreign Minister.
[2] Austria, Prussia and Russia.
[3] French ambassador at Madrid.
[4] Louis Philippe.
[5] Empress of Brazil, wife of Dom Pedro.
[6] Marie-Amélie, Queen of the French.
[7] Marquise de Loulé, wife of the Portuguese politician and diplomat, and aunt and supporter of Dona Maria, who was reported to receive large sums of money from Louis Philippe through the French ambassador at Lisbon.
[8] Dona Maria, Queen of Portugal. She arrived at Lisbon on 23 September, having visited England after leaving Havre.
[9] William IV.

5   Villiers to Palmerston, 30 September 1833

Madrid. Private. I have not much to add to my despatches[1] but there are a few topics which may be treated privately better than publicly. I found Zea precisely what you described—an indifferent pupil of a 2d rate actor at the Theatre François. It is needless to repeat to you all his eternal professions of regard for England and desire to do all that England wishes, for you know them probably by heart. I gave him the King's message and told him how kindly you had mentioned him when I last saw you, whereat he was touché jusqu'aux larmes or jusqu'à putting his pockethandkerchief to his eyes. He told me he had heard a great deal of good of me and should have infinite satisfaction in doing business with me. He was loud in his grief at Addington's recall,[2] and he told Wm. Hervey that he regretted much the shortness of his chargé d'affaires-ship.[3] He lauds the Queen to the skies and told me today that her energy and prudence were wonderful, that she transacts business with great facility and is not likely to fall into the error of the late King of listening to a multitude of councillors—which I conclude means that as yet she has allowed him to do everything. Under the circumstances she could have done nothing else than retain Zea at first—for her former friends (among whom however there was scarcely a man of ability) are absent, many of them exiled, and Zea would have been a very formidable enemy if she had ejected him—though I believe that he has no friends whatever. He has attempted to form a juste milieu where there were no elements for it; he has disgusted most parties without conciliating any; and his fall, which will not be distant if the peace of the country is preserved, will be unattended with a single regret.

Although I have not yet fully entered upon the subject of Portuguese affairs with him, I have of course not left them quite intact, and upon my asking him this morning how long he meant to permit Don Carlos to remain in Portugal, he told me of the strong and menacing tone which the King had lately assumed towards him, and that the Queen and her Government were determined to pursue the same course. He said that M. Cordova[4] had orders to procure from Lord William Russell[5] a sauveconduite for Don Carlos with which he was to go to him and ask for a categorical answer whether he would avail himself of it or not—if the latter, that Don Miguel was to be peremptorily ordered to send him away, and in the event of his refusing that Spain sçauroit agir as became her dignity. I enquired which way that was, and after some hesitation he said that if we should not object or suppose that they had ulterior purposes they would cross the frontier and *enlever l'Infant!* He declared that when we discussed the subject, which he would be prepared to do in 3 or 4 days, that he would put the whole before me as a friend and appeal to me in what way the difficulties which beset Spain could honorably be got rid of. I told him that promptitude and good will seemed the only requisites, and with both he said he was prepared.

Upon my asking him what news he had received from Lisbon by the courier that I learned had arrived on the 28th, he at first affected not to remember there had been one—then told me he had only brought news to the 14th, and upon my asking him to think again he said to the 24th, but that upon his honor he had merely looked at them to ascertain that they contained absolutely nothing. Shortly after my return home however this evening there arrived from him a bag to me from William Russell containing the dispatch of which I send you the copy with the important news of the defection of Bourmont and Co.,[6] and which has of course been kept back by Zea for two days. I intend tomorrow not to disguise my opinion from him upon the proceeding.

Many people here have considered that the title assumed by the Queen of Reyna *Gobernadora* was irregular and that she ought to have been *Regent[e]*, but having taken some pains to ascertain I find it is perfectly correct. The King's will could not be found yesterday but it was discovered by the Queen this morning. It is I understand the will made in 1830—the codicil prepared by Zea was to have been signed the day the King died—and appoints a Council of Regency of moderate men with the Queen at their head.[7] The most perfect tranquillity or rather perfect indifference prevails at Madrid, and an existing Government has such great advantages here that I think the Queen's chances are more favorable than otherwise. The Captains of the Guard went to Zea last night and announced that they had no intention whatever of obeying him unless they received orders from the Queen to do so, and she was obliged to send for them and direct that any orders she issued through her Ministers for the maintenance of public order should be obeyed.

I hope you will have the goodness with as little delay as you can to send me new letters of credit to the Queen Isabella 2d for till they arrive I cannot see the Queen Regent, the consequences of which might be inconvenient. Pray let me know how much of compliment and satisfaction upon the accession you chuse me to express upon presenting the credentials, for I have reason to know that the Queen Regent is most eager for the *moral support* of England.

The Duc de Broglie's letter to M. Rayneval has done great good and we already go on with great cordiality together.

PS. I have no English messenger[8] and as events may come thickly there ought to be somebody at hand to take them home.

GC/CL/100; Clar. Dep. C.451/2 (1-3)

[1] Announcing the death of Ferdinand VII on 29 September 1833.

[2] V's predecessor as minister at Madrid.

[3] Lord William Hervey, secretary of legation at Madrid, briefly acted as chargé d'affaires between the departure of Addington and the arrival of V.

[4] General Córdoba, Spanish ambassador at Lisbon.

[5] Sent by P on a special mission to the headquarters of Dom Pedro (unaccredited until August 1833).

[6] General Bourmont and the Miguelite army besieged the Queen's forces in Lisbon in September, but failed to defeat them. He therefore threw up his command, complaining of the conduct of the troops.

[7] The Council of Regency 'is a Council of Government to whom the Queen Regent may refer matters either of general or extraordinary importance, but by whose advice she is not bound to abide'. (V to P, 3 Oct. 1833, no. 4, FO 72/412.)

[8] V wrote to Granville on 30 September 1833: 'I have just written this week to Palmerston by M. de Zea's courier. I do not know whether I shall be able to dispatch one myself as the exit of all couriers from Madrid is prohibited by law upon the event of a King's death. M. de Zea was not able yesterday to grant urgent requests I made to him to be allowed to send one.' (Granville Papers, PRO 30/29/413.)

6 Villiers to Palmerston, 7 October 1833

Madrid. Private. I have adopted a line somewhat new with Zea and have as yet no reason to be dissatisfied with so doing. I hope you will not either. Zea is probably an insincere man, and I wish we had to deal with any other, but as he is Foreign Secretary here we have only to make the best of him. He is an actor because he is desirous to appear honest. To exhibit distrust, therefore, is to prove to him that he has failed in his purpose, and much of the irritation complained of in him both by Stratford Canning and Addington appeared to me, on reading their despatches, attributable to that. I have assumed a tone of great cordiality, and the consequence has been that in the several interviews I have had with him there has never been an angry word between us, and I have said everything I wished, even to praising Don Pedro's absence of personal ambition, and threatening him with Napier's taking Cadiz (though I gave the latter as my own idea and not Lord Cape St. Vincent's).

I told him that he would find my Government as anxious for the interests and honor of Spain as for our own, and that for my part I would never propose to him any thing which upon my honor as a gentleman I did not think he ought to do and which mutatis mutandis I would not do in his place—at which he not only expressed himself delighted to me, but has told Rayneval of it all, and said that he for the first time thought that England had no unfriendly intentions towards Spain, and that he would now meet us more than $\frac{1}{2}$ way. Nous verrons. He certainly was pleased at my suggestion for Cordova's recall,[1] thinking it a first step out of their difficulties; and we must allow that it *is* a great gulp to their pride at once to abandon a cause in which they have embarked so much personal feeling and despotic sympathy, but if we can make a bridge from Don Miguel to Donna Maria over which their honor can pass pretty safe, I do believe that they ask no better than to cross.

Zea asked me if I would have any objection to give him a little précis of our conversation in order that he might shew it to the Queen and his colleagues (whom he said he would assemble to submit to them my Cordovian proposition) in support of what he should urge of the necessity now d'aller au devant de l'Angleterre. I told him I would, but that our conversation had been so entirely unofficial, as I had not been instructed to make him any proposition, that I must beg of him to consider any précis as a mere private memorandum.

I have accordingly not adverted to it in my despatch but I enclose it to you in case you should have leisure to read it as well as my letter to William Russell, and I hope you will let me know if I am too bountiful in detail to you.

In my interview with Zea today, after discussing the internal state of the country, I reminded him how much he might want the army now idling on the frontiers of Portugal, and it would be entirely at his disposal if he would but settle la maudite question, as he calls it. That I had not rélévéd what he had said of intervention 3 days ago, because he thought it impossible to recognize Donna Maria, but if he had a mind to propose any thing likely to *give satisfaction* I would with pleasure make it known to you. He said he was getting every day more anxious for the settlement of the question by England and Spain—that they were the only two Powers really concerned,[2] that the influence of England in Portugal was most advantageous to Spain, and that the interests of England were more identical with those of Spain than any other country. Under these circumstances and in the interest of humanity (for that even if Don Miguel was beaten and driven away, great elements of civil war still remained in the priests and the adherents of Don Miguel who held property belonging to Don Pedro's supporters) he would be prepared instantly to unite with England and put a stop to the war. I asked again upon what basis—he said pour l'amour de Dieu find me one that I can accept. I suggested that, though the proposition would be a very strong one and one which Don Pedro would have every right to reject, yet that we might try if he would quit Portugal in order that his brother might go at the same time. He *might,* I said, make the sacrifice in order to secure the throne to his daughter and tranquillity to the country. Zea said, that is at once throwing over Don Miguel and we must not do that. After an hour's discussion, in which I saw how much he was hunting for a loophole, he promised to think over well what might offer a decent chance of being accepted by all parties and begged of me to do the same. I wish I knew your present views upon the subject as well as the real state of Portugal now. Upon the latter I am entirely in the dark.

The condition and prospects of Spain are far from satisfactory and the course which Zea has chalked out for the Queen in her manifesto, by making her cry peccavi for her former errors of liberalism,[3] goes far to secure the success of Don Carlos. The liberals are indignant and their exertions in the cause of course slacken.

When I was with Zea today I could not help giving him my opinion upon his ill-advised profession de foi, and telling him that however grateful it might be to the Holy Alliance ministers here[4] and however much it might tend to secure their recognition of the Queen, yet that he had overlooked what should have been his first consideration, the welfare of the country, and seemed to me to have thrown away his only chance of forming a middle party between the Carlists and the Constitutionalists, and for which I was sure the whole of the intelligent portion of the community was desirous. I of course said this, and he received it, in a friendly way. He declared that his whole object in the manifesto was to throw himself upon the masses, that they were essentially religious and monarchical, and that I should see he had hit the right nail on the head in making the appeal he had to the people. He was equally bitter against Don Carlos and les revolutionnaires and seemed perfectly aware of the danger he was in and the detestation which was felt for him. Indeed it is so strong at Madrid that I believe people would sooner forego having a better Government than receive it at his hands. There is something in his position not unlike Polignac's.[5]

I send a courier with this to Bayonne. Rayneval and I propose to take it by turns to send one about once a week as long as things remain troublous in Spain. Rayneval is very cordial with me and whenever he is not too idle, of much use.

I send you a list of the Council of Regency which you will see is not very likely to work well.

The funds have fallen 6 per cent since the manifesto.

First enclosure: Copy, memorandum by Villiers for Zea, summarizing their conversation, 3 October 1833.

Second enclosure: Copy, Villiers (Madrid) to Lord William Russell, 3 October 1833, private, describing the situation in Spain and his conversation with Zea.

Third enclosure: List of members of the Council of Regency, with comments. In Villiers's hand.

Received 16 October.

GC/CL/101; Clar. Dep. C.451/2 (4-7)

[1] V suggested that Córdoba should be instructed to break off diplomatic relations between Spain and Dom Miguel and return to Spain if Don Carlos had himself declared King of Spain in Portugal, or if Carlos crossed the frontier into Spain with intentions hostile to Queen Isabella, or if Miguel allowed Carlos to remain in Portugal to encourage his partisans in Spain. A letter on these lines was sent. V sent a copy to P with his despatch of 7 October 1833, no. 5, FO 72/412.

[2] 'I said that if we agreed upon a basis there would be no objection to include France in the intervention. He replied that France had behaved extremely well on the question throughout but that it was an English and a Peninsular question requiring therefore no other Powers. I told him that no Peninsular question could be indifferent to France and that I thought she would have

some cause of dissatisfaction if she were not consulted.' (V to Granville, 7 Oct. 1833, PRO 30/29/413.)

[3] The declaration stated: '. . . I shall religiously maintain the form and fundamental laws of the Monarchy without admitting innovations, dangerous although flattering at first, and which have, for our misfortune, been already sufficiently tried. The best form of government for our country is that to which it is accustomed.' (Translated from the *Gaceta de Madrid* of 5 Oct. 1833, enclosed with V to P, 7 Oct.1833, no. 5, FO 72/412.)

[4] The representatives of Austria, Prussia and Russia, who had not yet received letters of credence to the Court of Isabella II. Within a few weeks they, as well as the representatives of many smaller Powers, were recalled.

[5] Chief Minister of Charles X of France at the time of the 1830 revolution.

7 Palmerston to Villiers, 8 October 1833

Copy. Foreign Office. Private. I received yesterday your letter of the morning of the 30th by Zea's courier, and I avail myself of a messenger whom Vial sends off tonight to write two lines to you, chiefly to tell you that according to our etiquette fresh credentials cannot be sent you, until we receive here a letter from the Queen Regent announcing to the King the accession of the young Queen. No time therefore should be lost in sending us such a letter, if it has not been despatched before you receive this. We hope and trust that the apprehensions of civil war upon this occasion may prove unfounded and that the authority of the young Queen will be peaceably and universally acknowledged throughout Spain. It is highly desirable for the interests of all Europe that this should be.

Docketed: No.2. By Spanish courier.

GC/CL/1216

8 Villiers to Palmerston, 12 October 1833

Madrid. Private. I shall write very briefly because it is more than probable that this will not reach you. Communications with Madrid from the North are nearly cut off but as far as we can learn the provinces of Navarre, Alava and Biscay are in open revolt. Santos Ladron, a guerilla chief well known in 1823, has constituted himself Captain General of Navarre and issues passports or impedes at his pleasure communication with the north and north-east of the country. From a courier who arrived here this morning, having managed to pass through from Bayonne, I learn that he every where met great numbers of the peasantry armed and equipped in the roads, and as he likewise met troops moving northwards, people seemed to think in the towns through which he passed that there would shortly be a trial of strength. This town continues in the same state of apparent apathy.

Backhouse having desired that Grant should proceed immediately to Lisbon, he will set out on Monday, unless the post, if it arrives, brings any orders from you to the contrary.

Bourmont and Co. are performing quarantine at Badajoz—they are to embark at one of the southern ports.

GC/CL/102; Clar. Dep. C.451/2 (8-9)

9   Villiers to Palmerston, [12 October 1833][1]

You will observe in the Madrid Gazette today some strong expressions made use of by Rayneval in offering French support.[2] It is a great mistake to have published them—they have given offence here and the Queen will be taxed with seeking foreign aid.

Rayneval told me that he had suggested this to Zea before the article, which was at first much stronger, appeared. Zea disagreed and said it would be of great use, which shews him to be in alarm; though he professes to feel none, and is perfectly calm and composed. Rayneval, in the message he gave from me to the Queen, confined himself to friendly assurances, saying nothing respecting offers of assistance.

Our information here is so vague and scanty that I can give you no opinion as yet upon the probable turn of the struggle. There has been hardly any defection from the Captains General or the army, *but no party seems coming forward for the Queen, whereas the Armed Royalist Volunteers are declaring in great numbers for Don Carlos, and if insurrection bursts out in many places at once the Government, which is unaided by opinion, will not have power to put it down.* It is said that Don Carlos has receded[3] from Alcantara and that the Deputies from Biscay have been to invite him to go there by the north of Portugal. This is not improbable but is only a report.

I have pressed Zea much upon the Portuguese question. He is eager for intervention as the best way, he told me today, of saving the honor of Spain. Grant shall if possible be the bearer of an olive branch to Don Pedro.

Clar. Dep. C.451/2

[1] Enclosed, in cipher, with no. 8 above. The version printed here is that in the Clarendon letter book (C.451/2). The Foreign Office decipher differs in many minor respects and is clearly a less reliable text.

[2] Rayneval was alleged to have said that he had orders to offer the Queen Regent 'all the support which under any circumstances she might be pleased to claim from France'.(*Gaceta de Madrid,* 11 Oct. 1833, enclosed in V to P, 12 Oct. 1833, no. 8, FO 72/412.) According to V no such offer of assistance was given and the contents of Louis Philippe's letter to Queen Cristina were deliberately exaggerated in the hope of strengthening the Spanish Government both at Madrid and in the north of Spain. (V to Granville, 12 Oct. 1833, PRO 30/29/413.) Granville replied that 'the Duke de Broglie is not pleased with the article inserted in the Madrid Gazette with regard to the French offers of support—those offers are represented to be stronger than the instructions addressed to M. Rayneval authorized.' (Granville to V, ? Oct. 1833, PRO 30/29/15/14.)

[3] GC/CL/102 has 'a deputation' written above the line by P, presumably in an attempt to make sense of the Foreign Office decipher which has 'received' for 'receded'.

10   Villiers to Palmerston, 15 October 1833

Madrid. Private. The news I send you tonight is satisfactory and I hope there is now every reasonable expectation that things will go well here. For the last two days there was every reasonable expectation that they would go ill—the spirit of rebellion was rapidly spreading and the art of civil war is so well understood in Spain that there seemed no reason why it should not be waged as destructively and as protractedly as it has so often been before. The Captains General were well affectioned and the troops appeared steady but as the Government was unaided by opinion and that there was no party for the Queen, the cause of the Inquisition looked horridly in the ascendant.

The favorable turn which her little Majesty's affairs have taken[1] is really, I believe, attributable to the energy of Zea and to the spirit with which he declared that he would suffocate l'incendie at once, though it broke out in 100 places at the same time. I have not heard of and certainly not met any other Spaniard who would have been capable of doing as much, and the Queen was certainly wise in suffocating her detestation of him and resisting the urgent appeals made to her directly the King died to kick him out. If Don Carlos is suffocated too and tranquillity is restored, we must use our best endeavours to make Zea turn it to good account by some liberal and conciliatory measures, and I don't despair.

I was with him for 3 hours tonight and though he was prodigiously flushed with victory he listened to my advice against vengeance by wholesale, and upon the sympathy which he would produce in favor of des masses fusilées.

The Fabian system upon the Portuguese question has not been without effect. I have constantly, both in conversation and familiar epistles, set before him the dangers to Spain of the present state of things in Portugal, and as I did not appear over eager for intervention he has become extremely so. We have this evening discussed a long paper which I wrote upon the subject in the spirit of my instructions. He was much pleased with it and asked me to make an official note of it,[2] and pointing out for omission one or two expressions which might blesser l'orgeuil national and make it more difficult for him to carry his point. I am to take it to him tomorrow and he will shew me his answer before he sends it that I may make any alterations I please, and in 2 or 3 days I hope to be able to send for your approval some proposition likely to do good in Portugal. In the mean time I have communicated the whole of Zea's change of policy to Grant who set out on Monday morning for Lisbon, and charged him with every friendly assurance to Don Pedro and Palmella[3] on the part of Spain— quoting Zea's own words upon the desire he had to establish relations of good neighbourhood and reciprocal benefit. I hope this will prepare the way for whoever you may charge with the mediation. Without some such measure, even though we could sacrifice one brother to get rid of the other, I don't believe there would be any chance of settling the question of principle upon which the contest would continue to hang.

Bourmont is in quarantine and Zea said he was infinitely disgusted that he should be in Spain at all. Cordova had orders to permit refugees to enter Spain if the army of Miguel was beaten and had to fly, but that he never contemplated the solitary retreat of the Marshal, and that Cordova ought not to have given him a passport without asking permission. Bourmont applied to come to Madrid and embark at Barcelona for Italy, which was peremptorily refused, and he was allowed the option of Cadiz or Malaga for embarkation. Zea said there should be the strictest watch kept over him till he was on shipboard.

He is very grateful to France for the promptitude with which the Queen was recognized and takes no umbrage at the movement of French troops towards the South. There is now no chance I trust of their assistance being needed. The Holy Allies here are ridiculously uneasy at Zea, as they think, slipping through their fingers and hampering Spain with an Anglo-French alliance. I have had many opportunities of indirectly letting Zea see the glories which would await him if he put the commercial relations of Spain and England upon the footing of which they are capable—he promises great things.

I wait for a more favorable moment to try the Equipment Article.[4]

PS. Don Miguel has sent no answer to the notification which was made to him of the King's death and the accession of the Queen.

Received 26 October.

GC/CL/103; Clar.Dep. C.451/2(10-12)

[1] V wrote to P on 15 October 1833 that 'the Queen's forces captured Santos Ladrón and 800 Carlist volunteers. M. de Zea seemed to entertain no doubt, and I think there is every reason to believe him correct, that although partial disturbances may for a while continue, yet that the contest is virtually at an end.' (No. 10, FO 72/412.)
[2] V to Zea, 17 Oct. 1833, enclosed in V to P, 19 Oct. 1833, no. 12, FO 72/412.
[3] Portuguese politician, a supporter of Dona Maria and the Charter of 1826.
[4] Part of a proposed treaty to suppress the slave trade.

11   Villiers to Palmerston, 19 October 1833

Madrid. Private. I shall be very anxious to know if you approve of the course I am pursuing upon Portuguese matters. The satisfaction which William Russell assures me is felt at Lisbon upon the altered tone here is very encouraging, and it is quite unnecessary to say any thing upon the favorable chance which the present moment affords of bringing matters to a conclusion. Zea of course yields upon Portugal from the altered circumstances there and the troublous times here, but says it is owing to being now convinced that England n'en veut pas to the institutions of Spain *viâ* Portugal and that she does not mean to encourage revolution in that country in order to bring about a constitution in Spain. As far as I am concerned I have only to speak with commendation of him—it is impossible to have discussed the Portuguese question with more temper and apparent desire to make it the means of rapprochement with England. He is very angry with Don Miguel, and only desires not to make the recognition of Donna Maria follow too closely upon the final rupture with him. He looks to the mediation for help there, as it will be sure to put Don Miguel dans son tort. I hope I have made him feel that Spain must not attempt to dictate, or interfere at all, either in the institutions of Portugal or the selection of functionaries. I told him I had no doubt that the influence, whatever it might be, of England would be exerted to prevent just cause of uneasiness being given to Spain, but that he must be aware that it could only be upon our being convinced that such measures or such men would be mischievous to Portugal herself that we could be justified in offering our advice, and beyond that I thought our interference could not go. He said he was convinced that with the profound ignorance and superstition of the Portuguese nation, that Donna Maria would not be 2 years upon the throne if Pedro's Charter were brought into play, and that he was sure in the interest both of the Queen and the nation that we should wish to see it modified.

I read him an extract from a private letter to me from William Russell which had an extremely good effect. I enclose a copy of it. With respect to the mission of M. Castro here, he wished that it should be postponed, because the Spanish Government could not yet receive him publicly, and that as a private agent he could do nothing more than what William Russell was doing through me—assuring the Government here of the desire which Don Pedro has to cultivate friendly relations with Spain. In short, he said, it was beginning by where he hoped we should end. I told him that as Don Pedro could not know that we proposed a mediation or that the feelings of Spain were so neighbourly now, that this offer to send M. Castro should be considered as one of peace. Zea said that he did so consider it and only wished it to be deferred because he did not see in what way either the rapidity or success of our measures would be promoted by Castro's presence.

I am going to send a messenger to William Russell tomorrow with many courtesies to Don Pedro, and I hope to pave the way for this mediation if you approve of it. Any expression from you of good will or satisfaction with Zea either in a public or private letter to me would do great good.

Zea encourages me to talk (and I see him 4 or 5 times a week) upon

Spanish matters, and his tone is marvellously improved towards the liberals since the Carlists have declared a war to the knife with him. I by no means despair, however little probable you may think it, of seeing amelioration gradually (and by gradually I don't mean slowly) adopted here, for the Queen desires to be popular and Zea desires to keep his place—thus from their respective desires will spring measures of usefulness, even a little Church reform is possible. Zea's brother and the Duc de San Fernando are both detained by the insurgents at Vitoria and the Carlists here affect to consider their lives in danger as the Government has slain Santos Ladron. The priests of course have been very active and have stirred up rebellion in many places where it would not have been thought of without them. Verily they will have their reward if Zea can catch them.

PS. The Minister of Police at Madrid, a known Carlist, has been turned out and his successor Latre is a man who had a considerable post under the Cortes.

Enclosure: 'Extract of a letter from Lord William Russell dated Lisbon, October 12th 1833', stressing Dom Pedro's friendliness towards Spain and announcing the proposed mission of M. de Castro to Madrid.

Received 27 October.

GC/CL/104; Clar. Dep. C.451/2 (13-15)

12   Villiers to Palmerston, 21 October 1833

Madrid. Private. I have received your letter of the 8th and upon reading it to a person here it was considered so friendly and satisfactory that my permission was asked to shew it to the individual whom it most concerned.

Lord Granville will have better means than I possess at this moment of sending you information from hence. I entirely concur in all that he will say.

I sent a courier to Lord William [Russell] last night, paving the way for better things I trust.

Received 31 October.

GC/CL/105; Clar. Dep. C.451/2 (16)

13   Villiers to Palmerston, 24 October 1833

Madrid. Private. I send you an extract of a private letter I have written
to William Russell and which will put you in possession of Zee's [*sic*]
sentiments upon Portugal. He is not only desirous to be out of the
scrape but to be out of it quickly and to get if possible a good neighbour
in Portugal as well as to throw over Miguel with whom he is naturally
in a towering passion. I have endeavoured to sustain these various feelings, and circumstances are so favorable that I have been anxious to
avail myself of them though it has not been without fear that I may
have gone beyond your instructions. Don Pedro however seems to me
to have so little hold on the country beyond the range of his guns (and
they do not reach very far) that if we can get Spain's assistance to conquer for him, Zea's own words, peaceably all the provinces which do
not own his daughter's authority, and if in the mean time we can procure for this harassed country a suspension of bloodshed, decided good
will be done. Were Miguel hung or shipped off tomorrow, I believe
that the intervention of Spain would still be useful with the Apostolical
party who from what I can learn must always have at their command
a large amount of tumult and civil war. I am not sufficiently
acquainted with the pledges of the Emperor or the wants of the nation
to judge of the desirableness of the constitution, but I believe Palmella
considers that to have a chance of permanent tranquillity conciliation
must be employed and concession, quite as much to be wished for by
the liberals as their opponents, should be made.

Upon all this you must have far better means of judging than I have
and I hope that you will send instructions to Lisbon and here as soon
as may be. Zea can be driven to nothing, but led to a great extent,
and I feel no doubt of being able to carry whatever you may direct
concerning Portugal.

I think you will be pleased with the Madrid Gazette of today—the
omen which it contains is as satisfactory as the present good which it
effects.[1] It is an *amende* for the manifesto which appeared upon the
King's death and made the nation believe that it was not to reap any
advantage from the event, and which the Holy Allies here say was only
a recognition-trap for their Courts, and that time having been given
to dispatch their letters of credit, Zea now will not care for them, but
only make the *gentil* to England and France. They certainly all speak
of him with great bitterness. Rayneval and I see him every day, and

he seems very willing to receive any suggestions we like to offer.

I have had much conversation with him upon commercial subjects, and if he can overcome a few private interests and the rascality of every department we shall effect something, and ere long. At all events he has promised me that one of the first acts of the Government on the restoration of tranquillity shall be to mettre à la raison the whole Guarda Costa service.[2] I have tried him upon Cortes Bonds,[3] but find him rather wanting—not intractable though—but he says, what I can believe without any stretch of imagination, that they have not a shilling just now. I have tried him upon South America[4] and found him more Spanish than upon any other subject, and he won't see that he is inflicting a great injury upon Spain in order to inflict a little one on Mexico. He has however told me that we will discuss it again. Do you think the recognition of Spain is of sufficient importance to those States to make them willing to pay for it, or acknowledge themselves indebted to Spain for some of the confiscated Spanish Crown property; that I think would alter the view taken here of their past delinquencies and present forms of government.

It is so extremely difficult to procure information from the revolted provinces that it is hard to speculate upon the issue of the contest now going on there and which is very formidable. If Sarsfield[5] has sufficient troops, and is able at once to gain an advantage, the guerillas will be off to the mountains and the peasants to the villages, but if he fails or is obliged to be inactive, the revolt will spread over the whole north of Spain. In that case a little neighbourly assistance will be indispensable and right well bestowed.

The Queen was delighted with your letter to me and considers it the counterpart forerunner of recognition to that sent by Louis Philippe. The greatest eagerness prevails in the town for the arrival of my letters of credit and, with an 'ignorant impatience' of dates, the Madrid folks think they should have been here with Rayneval's. I should write to Alava[6] that he is amnestied and will you have the goodness for I have not the time to offer my congratulations to Lord Holland on his friend Bauza[7] being now able to return. Except for one or two very black sheep, I think there will be no difficulty about the return of those who are not included in the amnesty of today and above all those who *do* return will now, so Zea swears, not be bullied or vexed.

Copy.

Enclosure: Extract, Villiers (Madrid) to Russell, 20 October 1833, describing Zea's willingness for Anglo-Spanish mediation in Portugal, on the basis of terms proposed by Palmella to Dom Miguel.

GC/CL/106; Clar. Dep. C.451/2 (17-19)

[1] *Gaceta de Madrid*, 24 Oct. 1833, enclosed with V to P, 24 Oct. 1833, no. 14, FO 72/412. The Queen Regent issued a general decree of amnesty, releasing all political prisoners except Carlists. V had urged the measure on Zea in order to rally the moderate Constitutionalists behind the Government. He also urged it on the grounds that 'such a decree would give universal satisfaction in England; for there, the persecution of political opinions in Spain has long been viewed with the deepest regret.' (V to P, 19 Oct. 1833, no. 12, FO 72/412.)

[2] The British Government had for some time complained that the Spanish Coast Guard service was inefficient, corrupt, and in some areas involved in contraband trade.

[3] Bonds raised by the so-called Cortes Government between 1820 and 1823. Their repudiation by Ferdinand VII and his Ministers after the French invasion was a source of great resentment on the London Stock Exchange and the Paris Bourse, and led to a successful boycott of Spanish stock on these money markets. Ferdinand was thus forced to raise money by a private loan which also became a source of embarrassment to the Spanish Government in the mid 1830s. In London there was a Bondholders' Committee which sought the support of the British Government.

[4] The British Government was anxious that the Spanish Government should recognize the independence of the former Spanish colonies in South America and enter into diplomatic relations with them.

[5] Commander of the Queen's forces in the north of Spain. In late October 1833 he was preparing for an attack on Burgos. (V to P, 24 Oct. 1833, no. 15, FO 72/412.)

[6] Spanish general who had fought alongside Wellington in the Peninsular War, and who had been exiled after the collapse of the Cortes Government in 1823.

[7] Spanish liberal exiled in 1823.

14 Palmerston to Villiers, 27 October 1833

Copy. Foreign Office. Private. I send you your credentials and hope they will reach you in safety. Vial was delighted at presenting his, and is become a staunch Christino. We heard 3 days ago by the Bayonne telegraph that the Spanish Government had acknowledged Dona Maria, but your despatch and private letter of the 15th which I received last night make me doubt the truth of the report. I hope it may turn out to be correct; if it is so, it is a most important event in its necessary consequences, not only as affecting the Peninsula, but as bearing upon the rest of Europe. But whether the step has actually been taken or not, taken very soon it must be. The Ministers of the Queen Regent of Spain cannot support Miguel; and when they turn against Miguel they must acknowledge Maria. Indeed Miguel will soon save them the pain of a decision if Saidanha follows up with vigor the successes gained on the 10th, 11th and 12th.[1] The moment it was decided in Spain to oust Carlos and uphold Isabella, it was necessarily decided to pursue a more liberal system of policy than that of Ferdinand. An estrangement from the Holy Alliance and an approximation to England and France must follow such a change of system; and we shall ultimately have England, France, Spain and Portugal united in a liberal alliance in the West, and by their moral power keeping in check the Unholy Allies in the East, and preserving the peace of the world. It is not necessary for this that Zea should throw himself into the hands of the foolish theoretical enthusiasts who invented that precious monument of absurdity, the Constitution of 1812 and 1820; but it is necessary for his own continuance in power, and for the maintenance of the Queen, that he should conciliate the moderate liberals, that is to say, the men who want practical improvements and the correction of daily felt abuses, without being wedded to any particular fancies as to forms of government.

Since writing the above, I have received your despatches and private letter of the 19th. They are, like every thing we have received from you, perfectly satisfactory; your note to Zea is excellent and cannot fail to lead to good. The advice you give him is very wise, and if he will adopt it, will be worth many thousand men to him. I have some doubts whether at present any mediation except that of the bayonet will be effectual in Portugal, but it will be important to get Spain to agree to the principle and to consent to make the offer. We could not well begin by proposing armistice unless Miguel was quite on the ground; to leave him with anything like an army secure from attack would not do. But I hope Saldanha will have followed up his success.

Pray tell M. de Zea how much I rejoice to think that the only subject of difference which ever existed between us is likely to be got rid of by the force of events, without the necessity of any relinquishment of principle on either side. The unfortunate Portuguese question was the only point upon which England and Spain could differ, and if that is got rid of, as it now seems likely to be, I trust that no two Powers in Europe will be more closely connected, or communicate together with more full and unreserved confidence than England and Spain.

I am excessively glad to find that you and M. de Zea agree so well, and are upon so pleasant a footing, and indeed I must do him the justice to say, that excepting the Portuguese question, on which I had the misfortune so widely to differ with him, our conversations upon other matters convinced me that if Miguel had only broke his head in some hunting party, we should have agreed on almost every topick.

I am delighted to hear the good news which you send me as to the state of the Spanish provinces. The Queen's cause seems to have virtually triumphed, and there is only wanted now a little mercy to temper justice. I hope the Government will think of Arguelles and Valdes[2] and some others, who by their good conduct and personal respectability are most deserving of being allowed to return, and of being protected when in Spain. Even Vial volunteered yesterday the expression of an opinion that such men ought to go back, though he was very savage against Mina.[3] You are quite right not to press other matters till the Portuguese question is settled. There is no denying now that Zea is in earnest against Carlos and his adherents, whatever might have been thought before. I must end, it is late, the messenger will barely be in time for the morning's tide at Dover, and I do not like to keep back your credentials another day.

Docketed: No. 3. By Messenger Draffen.

GC/CL/1217

[1] After the failure of Marshal Bourmont and the Miguelite army to capture Lisbon, the garrison and the Queen's army under Saldanha attacked the Miguelites on 10 and 11 October and drove them back to Santarém.

[2] Spanish liberals living in exile in London. Argüelles later became tutor to Queen Isabella II.

[3] Navarrese liberal and general, exiled after the collapse of the Cortes Government in 1823. He did not accept the Pragmatic Sanction of 1830 which excluded Don Carlos from the succession, and hoped to lead a successful invasion of Spain, with French support. The liberal invasion of 1831 was a total failure, and Mina escaped back into France.

15   Villiers to Palmerston, 27 October 1833

Madrid. Private. We have had a little émeute here today which has been put down, but as Rayneval and I think that by the time the news of it journeys to Paris and London it will assume a traveller's privilege of magnifying itself, we send off a courier with the facts. The Royalist Volunteers are disarmed—better late than never. They did not like it and shewed some fight, but 5 or 6,000 regulars who have been patroling and galloping about the town all day soon restored order, though not calm, for the enthusiasm which was displayed for the Queen seems not to be so easy to keep within bounds. Her party is very vociferous for arms and every person suspected or *supposed to be suspected* of Carlism has been maltreated today. It is impossible to tell yet what results these events may have and we shall therefore send another courier in a day or two.

The liberals are delighted that the Royalists are disarmed and when the Queen appeared at the balcony of the palace this morning some gentleman delivered an *eloquent address* offering 10,000 men to march against Her Majesty's enemies which is not looked upon in Madrid as a very orthodox proceeding. Zea has been too busy to attend to Portuguese affairs since I last wrote to you, but I have been very urgent with him to send away Gomez, Miguel's chargé d'affaires, from here. He assures me that he expects Cordova to cross the frontier in a day or two and that passports shall then be immediately sent to Gomez.

PS. We have nothing later than the 12th from Lisbon. Don Miguel is supposed (according to news from the frontier) to be at Abrantes.

Received 6 November.

GC/CL/107; Clar. Dep. C.451/2 (20)

16   Villiers to Palmerston, 31 October 1833

Madrid. Private. A courier by whom I wrote largely to you left Madrid this day week. He arrived at Burgos dispatchless, pennyless, and cruelly thumped. Another left this on Sunday last and I expect that he will fare likewise. I have accordingly sent you duplicates of the dispatches which they have borne to the Curé Merino, and for form's sake I add those of my private letters to you though it is improbable that you should have time for so many brochures.

The town is upon the whole quiet although patrols of soldiers and decrees against coffee housing or crying vivas or muertas for any body are every now and then considered necessary. The disarming the

Royalist Volunteers everywhere and the extensive measures of reform already in operation[1] are worth 20,000 men to the cause of the Queen. Sarsfield writes in good spirits and news has arrived this evening that the rebels in Navarre have been routed foot and horse.

It is now nearly 5 weeks since the King died and Don Carlos has only sneaked up and down a space of 20 leagues upon the frontier without attempting to cross it, or ever giving a signe de vie to his partisans in the country—they are accordingly much disgusted and one hears little about him personally. Hatred to the Queen, obedience to the priests and a sort of innate love for civil war keep up the strife, and provided it ends well, and *one way or another* I am sure it must, there will not be much harm done; it will make the Queen's course more simple and more difficult to swerve from.

I sometime ago told Zea that I had suggested Cordova's final recall being made contingent upon Don Carlos's crossing the frontier merely because it was the most probable hostile act that he would perform, but as he had not done so but had committed other acts of hostility equally overt, I hoped he would order Cordova home forthwith. He said it would probably be necessary to do so, but that he would write to him to come back immediately that he had notified to the Infant that he was a rebel. Zea has a letter tonight from Cordova to say that he has done so and that he was to set out next day from Elvas with his legation.

I shall tomorrow hope to hear that M. Gomez has been furnished with passports to leave Madrid.

Bourmont has written to Zea to complain about not being allowed to come through Spain (to go to Italy by Barcelona) and asking leave to return to Portugal, saying that he had no letters of credit upon the places at which he was permitted to embark—Malaga, Cadiz or Gibraltar. His request has been refused and Zea has written him word that the Spanish Government will advance to him at one of those ports the funds necessary for his passage.

The non arrival, for some reason or other, of that[2] which your private letter of the 12th gave reason to expect has produced the greatest uneasiness here.

PS. We have nothing later than the 12th from Lisbon.

Received 12 November.

GC/CL/108; Clar. Dep. C.451/2 (21-22)

¹ Extensive measures for the relief of famine, for reform of the administration and for the removal of some forms of censorship were published by the Government in decrees of 23, 26 and 29 October in the *Gaceta de Madrid*. (V to P, 31 Oct. 1833, no. 20, FO 72/412.)

² 'his new credentials' added in pencil by P.

17   Villiers to Palmerston, 8 November 1833

Madrid. Private. I don't believe the post goes at all now, as we have had nothing by it for more than a fortnight, and I therefore have determined to report progress by a courier whom I shall send to Barcelona that he may not run the gauntlet of all the Supreme Juntas on the Bayonne road and risk the loss of his dispatches, which always seems to depend upon the caprice or the sobriety of the particular brigand on duty.

My credentials arrived safely but the messenger Draffen had great difficulty in preserving them, *the deputation,* as he says, at Villafranca having opened the bag and torn off all the covers from the letters and parcels under pretence of seeking any that were for the Spanish Government. The presentation of them caused a great sensation and joy here.

I yesterday sent a courier to Lisbon with a proposition which may lead to better things and which will, I trust, be viewed by Don Pedro as an indication of good will and sincerity on the part of Spain.¹ Matters stand as follows and I think you will allow something has been gained. Spain desires to cooperate with England in the pacification of Portugal. She is willing to accept the proposals made by Palmella to Don Miguel as the basis of the joint mediation, preparing the way therefore for the recognition of Donna Maria. She admits that she must not interfere with the institutions of Portugal. She breaks off all relations with Don Miguel and sends a messenger to inform him that she is henceforth going to act with England upon the affairs of Portugal, and Zea told me yesterday that if Miguel is refractory he hopes that England will assist Don Pedro to force him to submission, and that if Spain had not her hands full at this moment she would aider à le chasser.

The recognition of Donna Maria will not be long delayed if Pedro behaves himself decently, but he does his best to disgust every body and by way of helping matters here he has taken to sneer at Zea in his newspaper for being a convert to liberal opinions, and by way of propitiating the Queen he attacks Ferdinand. I read the trimming you gave him with the greatest satisfaction. It was high time to put a stop to his insane proceedings—they naturally produce distrust here, and surrounded as he is by the worst counsellors, keeping Palmella and men of moderate views in disgrace, and issuing decrees of vengeance and confiscation, totally regardless of the prejudices and wants of the country, it is impossible to blame Zea for not being eager to gain the alliance of such a madman.

I have written to Palmella for his opinion how to turn the present dispositions of Spain to the best advantage and Zea is so extremely desirous to do whatever he thinks may be agreable to England that I trust we shall in one way or the other arrive at a result. If the Portuguese nation, i.e. Don Pedro and his present Ministers, chuse to have their Constitution, I suppose we cannot prevent it, but if we were to hear of the King of the Esquimaux giving his people a charter we should think it very absurd.

I read to Zea all your kind expressions towards himself and he was perfectly delighted. They have been of great use—and he has told me several times since qu'il tenoit à coeur de meriter les éloges de Lord Palmerston. In my long, almost daily, conversations with him I endeavour to make public opinion in England the guide of his actions here and he has lived long enough there to understand the value of such support if he can contrive to gain it.

Grant left Madrid 3 weeks ago. . . .

Don Pedro will probably be indignant with me for not having his letter presented to the Queen Regent,[2] but it would only have been productive of mischief. You never saw such a composition—6 sides of foolscap upon liberal institutions and march of intellect, enclosing a copy of the letter which Ferdinand would not receive and of the proclamation which he issued when he was at Belleisle.

The Queen's cause is perfectly safe, I think, and there would be no fear of the insurrection spreading, if the impunity which has hitherto attended it, owing to the ineffective state of the army, did not offer a temptation to the ill disposed in other provinces.

Received 20 November.

GC/CL/109; Clar. Dep. C.451/2 (23-25)

[1] The proposition was one of joint Anglo-Spanish mediation between Dom

Pedro and Dom Miguel, with a threat of British and Spanish assistance for Dona Maria if Miguel declined the mediation. (Enclosure with V to P, 7 Nov. 1833, no. 21, FO 72/413.)

[2] The Duque de Bragança (Dom Pedro) to the Queen Regent of Spain, enclosed with Lord William Russell to V, 1 Nov. 1833, and with V to P, 8 Nov. 1833, no. 23, FO 72/413. Russell described the letter as an attempt by Pedro 'to unite the two nations in amity and by a mutual understanding to enable the respective Governments to proceed *pari passu* towards interior improvements'.

18   Villiers to Palmerston, 12 November 1833

Madrid. Private. My despatches today tell you nearly all I have to say. I hope you will like the tone of Zea's note to me[1] and his letter to Santarem, and his announcement in the Gazette.[2] In each I think you will see evidence of desire to be upon good terms with England.

I have every reason to believe that the mediation will be agreable and necessary to Don Pedro—whether it is accepted or not by Don Miguel will I conclude depend upon how near his last shifts that amiable prince may find himself. In the former case Zea proposes (that which we understand Palmella did) to secure a general amnesty, oblivion of the past, and the full protection of the law for Miguel's followers as well as a *retiring allowance* for himself. This Ramfort[3] is instructed to communicate to Don Miguel in the event of his inquiring the terms which are to be made for him, and in the event of his rejecting the offer Zea says he can only hope that England or France may help Don Pedro to *écraser* him: he should see it with pleasure and help it if he could.

The mediation need not I apprehend lead to much trouble or many protocols in order to secure the above conditions, which the moderate liberals desire, and the Miguelite party should be contented with. We have a great interest, as well as Spain, in bringing about the pacification and good government of Portugal, but we shall never see either, I am convinced, without giving ourselves some trouble for it, and taking it out of the hands of Don Pedro, for the war is not merely between the two brothers but one of opinion which cannot be settled by the sword.

Unless my views are very erroneous or any great change of circumstances has taken place in Portugal since I last heard from William

Russell, I believe that the proposed mediation offers a better chance of bringing together opposing factions, and of establishing a state of things which there will be a general interest to maintain, than if Spain were to confine herself to recognizing Donna Maria and to leave to the foreign troops and admirable discretion of Don Pedro the conquest and reconciliation of the many provinces who shew no symptom of acknowledging the rights of his daughter. Such a course would not I believe detach a single follower of Don Miguel's from his cause while it would encourage Don Pedro in the career of mischief which you have so severely and deservedly reprobated. If we interfere to give peaceable possession of Portugal to Donna Maria we may surely impose the terms without which it can never be obtained, and as all fear of and squabble with Spain upon this subject is at an end, any course may be pursued by England which she may consider for the advantage of Portugal. You will I daresay let me know the instructions you give Howard de Walden.[4]

I hope by the next opportunity to give you an account of active operations against los rebeldes here—it is more than time.[5]

We have nothing from England since the arrival of the messenger Draffen on the 5th. Rayneval has received an account that a Cabinet courier who was coming to him was robbed, stripped, beaten and made to walk about 10 leagues back to the frontier of France.

Received 22 November.

GC/CL/110; Clar. Dep. C.451/2 (26-27)

[1] Zea to V, 11 Nov. 1833, officially announcing that the Spanish Government had broken off diplomatic relations with Dom Miguel, that it proposed to recognize Dona Maria as Queen of Portugal, and that Spain was prepared to act with England to end the Portuguese civil war by Anglo-Spanish mediation. (Enclosed with V to P, 12 Nov. 1833, no. 24, FO 72/413.)

[2] *Gaceta de Madrid,* 12 Nov. 1833, announcing that as the Government of Dom Miguel had encouraged 'the intrigues of Don Carlos against the legitimate succession to the throne and against the tranquillity of Spain' the Spanish Government had broken off diplomatic relations with Miguel's Government. (Enclosed with V to P, ibid.)

[3] A brigadier in the Spanish army sent on a mission to Miguel's headquarters to inform him of the Anglo-Spanish mediation proposals. (V to P, ibid.)

[4] Charles Ellis, 6th Baron Howard de Walden, had been appointed British minister at Lisbon in succession to Lord William Russell. He arrived at Lisbon on 14 February 1834.

5 'The insurrection is certainly alarming in the North. The time which has elapsed since it broke out has been sufficient for organization and renders its spreading and the seduction of the troops more likely. The priests are everywhere active, the Government to all appearances the reverse. The army has not been considered strong enough to quell the revolt.' (V to P, 12 Nov. 1833, no. 25, FO 72/413.)

19   Palmerston to Villiers, 15 November 1833

Copy. Foreign Office. You seem to be making good way in Spain, and on the whole the aspect of affairs there appears to be improving. The progress of Sarsfield has been slow, or rather, as far as our present accounts go, none at all; but I suppose he is waiting till he is strong enough to be quite sure of success; and if so, this is wise; for a defeat in the outset would produce the worst consequences, even though accidental and owing to numerical superiority on the other side. But we do not hear of any measures for augmenting the Spanish army; would it not be wiser to increase the Queen's military strength that way, rather than call in foreign auxiliaries? Every body knows the great jealousy the Spanish nation have always felt of foreign troops; and if the Government *can* put down the insurrection by an exertion of Spanish means, it would be incomparably better for them to do so.

We are delighted with the decrees which you have sent us; they prove that Zea, though adverse to a change of institutions, is a friend to improvement, and heaven knows that he has an ample field of reform to labor in without the form of the Spanish Government. This is certainly the wise course; for if Spain is, at some future time, to have more popular institutions, it is only by such preliminary reforms and improvements that the nation can be prepared for taking its part in a different system of government.

In Portugal the case is somewhat different, and I fear that the basis of mediation proposed by Zea in his note to you is no longer practicable. If he had accepted the proposals we made in January last through Canning, I think that *at that time* some understanding might have been come to for indefinitely suspending the Portuguese Charter. Pedro was then cooped up in Oporto; and if Spain and England had united to place Maria on the throne, we should have had a right to prescribe conditions. But as soon as Pedro got to Lisbon by his own means, the Constitution became inevitable, and moreover, it was from that moment excessively difficult, if not impossible to find any means of establishing a regency in any hands but those of Don Pedro. Unfortunately for all parties, the Spanish Government allowed itself to be swayed by the Holy Alliance, and miscalculated the relative chances of success on the sides of Pedro and Miguel.

We are doing all we can to check the impetuosity of Pedro's Ministers; but till the war is over, and Miguel driven out, it is hardly possible to effect a change. I think that when that shall have been accomplished, and Portugal is at peace, the Portuguese themselves will insist upon having an Administration under Palmella[1] and men of that stamp. The more therefore the Spanish Government can assist in stifling Miguel, the more they will contribute to a moderate system in Portugal. They should immediately acknowledge Maria, and send a minister to Lisbon; such a decision would be quite as effectual as the march of an army, and is indeed almost the only way in which in the present state of things, Spain can usefully cooperate with us. It is too late now for us to send troops to Portugal; and it would not look well for a Spanish army to enter the country alone; besides the Spanish Government wants all its army for its own purposes; and people would say, why do they not put down the civil war in their own country before they go meddling with that in their neighbour's.

It seems by our accounts from Petersburg, Vienna and Berlin, that those 3 Courts refuse to acknowledge Isabella, at least for the present. In such a state of things, will not Zea think it for the honor and dignity of the Spanish Crown, to request the defunct representatives of those 3 Powers to quit Madrid till they can return with proper credentials? Their continued presence at Madrid while their Governments refuse to acknowledge the Queen will be a direct encouragement to the Carlists; it will be as it were raising the Carlist banner under the throne itself, and proclaiming to the rebels that the 3 ministers are only waiting for the arrival of Carlos at Madrid to resume with him those functions which they refuse to perform towards the Queen. It will certainly be a great humiliation to the Queen and a great injury to her cause if those 3 gentlemen are allowed to remain to carry on intrigues at Madrid, or to be suspected of doing so.

Howard has arrived at Copenhagen and will be here in ten days. The time of his departure for Lisbon will probably depend on Lady Howard's health.

Docketed: No. 4.   GC/CL/1218

¹ Regarded by the British Government as a moderate liberal.

20 Villiers to Palmerston, 18 November 1833

Madrid. Private. We have been having a sharp struggle, which is not over yet, between the Council of Ministers and the Council of Regency, who are about to commit¹ their rights to wager by battle between Zea and Las Amarillas,² and a contest is beginning in which, as usual, only the public will suffer. The Regency won't hear of being treated as cyphers, or the Ministers as Chefs de Bureaux—the former will not have the responsibility of the latter and as they will generally be opposed to them, and as the people in this country (more even than in ours) love opposition to their Ministers, the Regency will always be the popular body, and between the two a prospect of uninterrupted worry seems open to the Queen. Las Amarillas is a man of fair abilities, as despotic in his character as Zea, more aristocratic though professing liberalism, and not so good a man of business. They will never draw well together and are now openly at war. The command of the army was offered to Las Amarillas, with guarantees that he should return here whenever he pleased—he refused it. The Ministry of War was offered to him, *ad interim* only if he chose it—he accepted, but upon certain conditions which the Queen would not agree to, and as she, like every other woman, likes to be served par devouement, she resents the selfishness he has exhibited.

The liberals look to him now not so much on account of his principles as because he is opposed to Zea, and if he were to take Zea's place they would in a fortnight probably hate him worse and eject him more easily.

I have been pressed to take an active part against Zea, and I have little doubt that if Rayneval and I had chosen it we might have compassed his downfall, but I have declined, not only because his conduct towards England now is satisfactory, but because upon the shewing even of his enemies there is nobody to replace him who would offer the same prospect of keeping things together. With the ignorance which exists here and the passions and intrigues that are in activity, a dictator is necessary at this moment to prevent a state of anarchy which would be frightful in its consequences, and Zea is the only man whom I see with firmness sufficient for the purpose, but his very fitness makes him obnoxious to the would-be governing multitude. He has committed some faults since the King's death and he shews a most ill grounded fear of the liberal party, confounding them all together as if there was not among them every shade of opinion from himself almost, down to Mina. By so doing he binds them together and by giving them a common cause against the Government makes them dangerous. Upon this matter I should not fear that he would be stubborn if tranquillity were once restored, for though he would sooner lose his head than *unsay* any doctrine to which he has committed himself, I see that he may be led to *undo* any, and he will yield the substance if he be allowed to retain the form.

The Holy Alliance ministers are becoming bitter against him and consider that he is already embarked in a course which puts the influence of their remote monarchs at nothing—about its real value—and from all Zea says himself and the messages I receive through him from the Queen, I believe that he perceives the *blessings* which may be in store for this country by coming to a cordially good understanding with England and France. His apprehensions of French propagandism seem extinct, and I never miss an opportunity to make him feel that England can have no sinister objects in this country—that we naturally think a constitutional is the best form of government and cannot therefore be without a hope of one day or other seeing it established here, but we have no object in pressing it, and only desire to see Spain prosperous and happy after her own way—that in her present condition reforms had better be given by the Government than taken by the people, and that if he will call around him men who are most distinguished for their talents and whose characters may be guarantees of the sincerity of the Government, and will honestly labor to effect administrative improvements, and above all adopt such a system as shall call to the aid of this country the commercial capital of England, that there could be no reason why Spain should not only be lifted up from her degradation but placed in that rank among nations to which nature has given her a just title.[3]

I see Zea constantly and he always invites this kind of conversation and enters into it in a very encouraging manner for he is a good Spaniard, and by constantly keeping in his view the honor and advancement of his country I think he will go hand in hand with us to promote them. Till he fails in the expectations I have of him, or that I see some man better qualified for his place and more likely to advance the interests of England, I shall view his downfall with regret but he will have infinite difficulty in maintaining himself against the unreasoning clamor which is raised against him.

I have more than once preached forbearance and mercy to him when he has told me of some successes gained over the rebels, and he assures me that they shall be the rule of the Government when the contest is once over, but I am inclined to think him right when he says that such a course would now be looked upon as an indication of weakness, for the horror and disgust with which a fusillade of 8 or 10 men at a time without a shadow of trial would be regarded in England are quite unfelt here, and one might as well lecture a Cherokee against scalping as a Spaniard upon mercy to an enemy who has fallen into his power.

There is of course a good deal of fear felt by each of the contending parties lest the other should succeed, but I have never heard from anybody a single expression of regret upon the existence of a civil war, or does any body bestow a thought upon the misery it inflicts or the consequences it will entail.

In short this country is a passing strange one, and nobody can have an idea of the state of things here without having seen it—it is only a marvel how they go on at all. The Government orders, but nobody obeys—every one thinks he knows best, and does just what he likes. This last week two generals (Sarsfield and Quesada)[4] both in the highest command, have sent up to Madrid, for the information of their friends, copies of ill written dispatches from the Minister of War and of their own insolent answers, and they have been discussed on Change and in the streets,[5] so that in times of excitement or dangers, subordination is so little to be depended upon, and disorder is so universal, that society seems always on the eve of being resolved into its original elements.

These matters are full of interest to a spectator, at a distance they may possess but little; however as Rayneval's courier goes by Perpignan and that I am not therefore likely to figure in Carlist print, I take my chance of your liking these details.

Aguado sent an offer to lend this Government £300,000 for present purposes, to be repaid at their convenience and without interest. I need not tell you that it was accepted. Aguado is *nominally* influenced by gratitude, attachment to Spain and I don't know what other unbankerlike feelings, but *really* by a wish not to be torn in pieces by

Spanish stockholders in Paris if their dividends were not forthcoming next Quarter Day and very little if any of this loan will come here.

Not a single individual of intelligence, station or note has joined the cause of Don Carlos. It is entirely supported by the priests and such of the rabble rout as they can seduce, for which purpose Mammon has become quite as necessary as God.

The ministers of the 3 Powers have as yet got no letters of credit, respecting which there is among the people of Madrid a profound and affronting indifference. The recognition by England and France was considered an object of necessity, by the others a mere *luxury*.

GC/CL/111; Clar. Dep. C.451/2 (28-32)

¹ C.451/2 has 'submit'.
² A member of the Council of Regency who, V thought, 'will be the leading man of the Council'. (No. 6 above, third enclosure.)
³ 'why. . . title' altered by P to: 'why Spain should not be lifted up from her degradation and placed in that rank among nations to which nature has given her a just title'.
⁴ Inspector of the Infantry and Captain-General of Old Castile.
⁵ 'What more could newspapers do' added in pencil by P.

21 Villiers to Palmerston, 23 November 1833

Madrid. Private. I enclose you a copy of a letter which I wrote a short time since to Palmella, and of the answer which I have received from him. Don Pedro's military triumph appears far from secure, and Palmella earnestly desires that suspension of hostilities which we thought it would be unfair to propose to his all but victorious master. If Don Miguel accepts the mediation the armistice follows as a first consequence, if he rejects it I see no chance of a cessation of the war unless we are prepared to take a decisive part.

The real state of the question appears to me this. England has throughout the contest been neuter and has declared her intention not to interfere for Donna Maria unless Spain took any active part in favor of Don Miguel—the casus foederis would then have arisen, and England would have immediately resisted the aggression. The circumstances of England remain unaltered—those of Spain are completely changed. Her interests are becoming identified with those of Donna Maria; she has grounds for making war upon Don Miguel, and would desire to do so but she is not sufficiently powerful. England is so, but has no more grounds than before for going to war. This is of course a difficulty, but the question is beset with difficulties, and if ever interference can be justified this is surely the case, and the present moment is more favorable than any that has yet occurred.

The contest has arrived at that pitch when neither of the Belligerent Brothers can assert his authority—the more it is prolonged the more irretrievable the disasters of the country must become, and the more probable must be the chances of embroiling the whole Peninsula in the struggle. Can England then refuse to interpose by force if necessary and put a stop to this horrible contest, to insist upon a cessation of bloodshed, to procure amnesty and protection for all parties, and thus acquire the right to assist in establishing a Government in accordance with the wishes and likely to promote the happiness of the nation?

To such interposition she is loudly called by humanity—it is eagerly invited by one of the contending parties and desired by Spain, the only Power whose right to have a voice upon the question we have admitted. It would be upheld by public opinion at home and approved by France, while in the Peninsula it would be received with gratitude by the exhausted Portuguese nation, and by every friend to the Queen of Spain it would be viewed as a removal of the chief source from which danger to her cause can spring. I can only perceive the personal interests of Don Miguel and those of his followers who have no property to be saved from confiscation to be set in the balance against these great advantages to be gained and great calamities to be avoided. If, as Palmella affirms, it be only necessary for England and Spain to adopt a decisive tone to secure a suspension of hostilities, and the triumph of the Queen's cause, no measure of coercion need be resorted to; if they were necessary it could only be against Don Miguel himself and a handful of adventurers who could soon be brought to reason by Parker's Marines, and Spain might at the same time march the troops which are now in Galicia and Estremadura into Portugal against Don Miguel with whom (under the circumstances of being assisted by England) she might declare war, and in pursuit of Don Carlos whom he protects. A joint notification however on the part of England and Spain simultaneously made to both brothers that the non-acceptance of the mediation would be treated as a declaration of war would I think render the application of force quite unnecessary.[1]

In the event of this mediation being entered upon I apprehend it should be so on neutral ground. The individuals appointed to conduct it must be supposed to be unbiassed and they would not be thought at Lisbon any more than at Santarem[2] to be beyond the reach of party spirit or the intrigues of faction. Madrid would seem the fitting seat of the negociation, Spain having many minor interests to be considered in establishing a solid foundation for good neighbourhood which it would be difficult to confide to any one in London in a manner which should not render reference to Madrid and consequent delay often necessary, whereas England has only to consider the cause of humanity, her own commercial interests, the security of the Portuguese throne and that the political institutions looked for by the nation are not withheld. The whole might soon be settled if Palmella were sent here with sufficient powers. Upon these matters your instructions would be plain and I think I can engage that Zea will comply with whatever you desire upon any part of this question. It excites great interest here and many persons have expressed to me their satisfaction at seeing that England has placed Spain upon a perfect equality with herself in contributing to the pacification of Portugal when she might have taken advantage of Spain's now helpless condition to settle the question as she pleased.

With respect to that part of Palmella's letter in which he declares he never made any propositions to Don Miguel, Zea says that he did not mean that Palmella had made any to Miguel independently, but had been a party to those which were sent to Bourmont, who had advised their adoption, and had quitted Don Miguel upon their rejection. It is of little consequence though whether we adopted for a basis of the mediation that which Palmella *did* say or *would have* said—the object being to guard against any future misunderstanding upon the main points of England's not receding from her engagements and Spain's ultimate recognition of Donna Maria.

I have nothing particular to add to this long letter, upon Spanish affairs. The news from the provinces during the last two days has not been so good—small bands of insurgents here and there create disturbances and agitate the public mind. In Valencia and Arragon, both most important provinces, this appears to be the case, and the disgraceful inactivity of Sarsfield has served, as it could not fail to do, for encouragement. It is difficult to form a correct opinion of Sarsfield. Every body who knows him says he is a brave soldier and an honorable man, but if he had been the contrary of both he would, as it appears to me, have acted just as he has done. If he, or rather his successor in the command Valdez, does not obtain some signal success within the next 8 days the whole aspect of affairs in Spain may be completely changed.

I will send the courier Vigo about the middle of next week. I must keep Draffen till the road is clear—at present no couriers but those on horseback have a chance of passing safely.

First enclosure: Copy, Villiers (Madrid) to Palmella, 7 November 1833, private and confidential, with a proposition for Anglo-Spanish mediation.

Second enclosure: Copy, Palmella (Lisbon) to Villiers, 16 November 1833, confidential, in reply. (In French.)

Received 5 December.

GC/CL/112; Clar. Dep. C.451/2 (33-36)

¹ 'If you agree in all I have written upon Portuguese matters will you urge Palmerston to take a decided tone, the moment was never more favorable and I see no other way of settling the question or acquiring any kind of influence over Don Pedro.' (V to Granville, 24 Nov. 1833, PRO 30/29/413.)
² Dom Miguel's headquarters.

22   Villiers to Palmerston, 30 November 1833

Madrid. Private. I have received your letter of November 15th. Zea was highly pleased with the passage which I read to him from it upon his good disposition towards reforms and preparing the nation for more popular institutions. He said that the tone now adopted by England and France was so generous, and the not attempting, in the moment of her weakness, to impose a change of institutions upon Spain shewed such knowledge of the real condition of the country, that if the lights of the Holy Alliance countenances were to be withdrawn from Spain the loss would be more than compensated for by the improved understanding with us and with France. Vial constantly writes from London upon the kindness he receives from you and the interest you always display upon whatever regards his country.

Upon the subject of Portugal there are one or two passages in your letter which give me reason to fear that I have not made myself understood, and as the Portuguese question derives a new and an immense importance from the present state of Spain, I will, though at the risk of being tedious, trouble you with a recapitulation of what has passed since my arrival at Madrid.

First—I was instructed to encourage the Spanish Government to make proposals by which the united influence of Great Britain and Spain might be exerted to restore peace in Portugal. That as long as the civil war there lasted, British interests and British property would be exposed to danger, and the Spanish frontier would be constantly threatened by the residence of Don Carlos in Portugal. That a sympathy of feeling would arise between the Pedroites and the Constitutionalists of Spain on the one side and the Miguelites and the Carlists on the other. That both would be equally dangerous to Spain and that a cordial union with England could alone prevent the Portuguese from becoming a Peninsular question.

I did accordingly so encourage the Spanish Cabinet and propositions were made in the spirit and with the objects of your instructions, which though wise and politic during the life of Ferdinand, have become so in a tenfold degree since his death, it being now impossible to attempt to separate or to *unpeninsularize* the Spanish and Portuguese questions, for so long as troubles exist in Portugal, as long will they be taken advantage of in this country. If Don Miguel should triumph —and this should not be lost sight of for his condition is not one jot more desperate than Pedro's when he was pent up in Oporto and he (Pedro) may any day by quarreling with the foreigners lose Lisbon by their defection as he gained it by their support—should, I say, Miguel triumph, the sympathy which you contemplated between the Miguelites and the Carlists would instantly be exhibited, and a most dangerous point of support established from which Don Carlos might act against Spain, and Portugal would be constantly supplying the elements of civil war against her neighbour. But can the triumph of Don Carlos be looked upon in any other light than as a European calamity, and is it not a European interest to avoid every thing which could contribute to his success? Will not the interests of England in Spain be better promoted under the necessarily liberal government of the Queen than under that of Don Carlos, who could only be the helpless tool of the worst of despotisms, and is not France interested in seeing good government peaceably established on her frontier and the agitation of Carlist claims and Apostolical principles put down?

On the other hand, if Pedro succeeds singlehanded, not only will England and Spain have lost the right to interfere, but I really don't see upon what ground they could pretend to offer advice or to check the system of revenge and confiscation which he will infallibly pursue, and which, however much the people may insist upon more moderate government, will be a system grateful to his followers, and effectually prevent tranquillity. Should he chuse to revenge himself upon Spain, the elements of civil war will still be found in Portugal, by a junction of the Pedroites with the Spanish Constitutionalists, whom the oncoming events of this country tend to render more dangerous even than the Carlists.

In either of these views then the Portuguese is now a Peninsular question.

There is one point more to be considered, the immediate recognition of Donna Maria by Spain—and this in my humble opinion would not advance the pacification of Portugal. If the struggle were between the two brothers only it would do so, but the war is one of opinion, of bitter inveterate factions independent of either Pedro or Miguel, and whose relative positions would be in no wise altered by the presence of a Spanish minister at Lisbon. It would only increase the fanatical desperation of Miguel's adherents and bind them more closely to his personal cause, while the state of affairs in Portugal, with its attendant evils and alarming consequences, would remain nearly where it now is.

All moderate men acquainted with Portugal concur in thinking that conciliation is the only way of meeting these difficulties—that concessions must be made—that oblivion of the past must be guaranteed—and that security of property must be maintained.

These are the objects sought by the mediation, with no intention on the part of Spain of asking a change or suspension of the Constitution, with no intention of removing Don Pedro from the regency or of not recognizing Donna Maria as soon as time has been given for effecting that which will afford her a chance of possessing her kingdom in tranquillity. The question in all its main features appears to be the same as in the time of Sir S. Canning's mission but the motives are increased and the facilities are greater for bringing it to a successful issue.

The condition of one of the belligerents is to all appearance desperate. Party spirit is perhaps more bitter and the country more exhausted, but the cause to which we wish success is in the ascendant, and Spain instead of being hostile cordially adopts and desires to cooperate in our views—while Don Pedro by soliciting our joint intervention admits his incapacity to finish the contest himself and gives us the right to interfere and check his misgovernment which we should have been able to exercise if Sir S. Canning's proposals had been accepted, and which we certainly do not now possess. All then that appears wanted is the adoption of the tone which must have been used had Sir Stratford Canning been successful and had, as he certainly would, Don Miguel been refractory—less would now suffice in proportion to his increased weakness.

When the real objects of the mediation became known to both parties there would, as I expressed a hope in my last letter, be no necessity for following up the decided tone with which the intentions of England and Spain to put a stop to the war ought to be announced, but some measure of coercion may be necessary and should be prepared for. If the struggle however is now nicely balanced, a very small addition of force would turn the scale. Spain too might take a hostile position. She would from the perfectly tranquil provinces of Galicia, Andalusia and Estremadura have troops to spare, and nothing could be more popular at this moment with the Queen's party than an attack upon Don Miguel and a hunt after Don Carlos, whose poltroonery might, upon the near approach of such danger, very likely induce him to take boat for Italy.

I think I have now redeemed my pledges of recapitulation and tediousness.

By a stupid mistake of Baron Ramforts who did not consider his instructions complete, a whole week was lost in making the communication to Don Miguel, but the answer is now hourly expected.[1]

I some days ago told Zea that several of the moderate liberals resented his making no attempt to call them into activity and that I thought if they were not separated from those who desired suddenly to change the institutions of the country that they would end by adopting their opinions. After some discussion he said he would put himself into my hands and he begged of me to be the medium of communication for him with the persons alluded to. I have spoken to them—it has been well received—and I hope I have laid the ground for some useful men being brought forward, amongst others Martinez de la Rosa[2] who I am anxious to see placed at the head of public instruction for his name carries great weight in Spain. He desires ardently to see more liberal institutions here, but as he feels that his countrymen are not yet enlightened enough to turn them to advantage, he would devote himself to their political education. I much doubt however that any thing will now sustain Zea—the intrigues and the clamor against him are too strong, and the Queen's popularity will be, indeed is, damaged by retaining him. Those who are the loudest against him have little else to urge than that his present policy is too much opposed to that which he pursued during the King's life to be honest—for the advantages they derive from such change of policy they care nothing, and as I remember writing to you some time ago, they would sooner continue under misgovernment than be indebted to Zea for reforms.

There is of course now no more fear of foreign intervention and I must do Zea the justice to say that he never looked upon it but as a last and most desperate resource.

GC/CL/113; Clar. Dep. C.451/2 (38-43)[3]

[1] The answer reached Madrid by 8 December 1833. Miguel rejected the proposed mediation. (V to P, 8 Dec. 1833, no. 34, FO 72/413.)

[2] Spanish writer and politician. A moderate liberal, he had formed a Government (February-July 1822) under the Cortes.

[3] C.451/2 (37) is a cancelled letter of 28 November.

23 Villiers to Palmerston, 8 December 1833

Madrid. Private. I shall merely trouble you with a few lines having written at such length in my despatches. I have told you in one of them a long story about Portugal though I have not said half of what I feel upon the imminent danger to the Peninsula and consequently to the peace of Europe of leaving things in Portugal to settle or rather *not* to settle themselves.[1] I really don't know if I conform to diplomatic etiquette in giving my opinion upon these matters in a despatch,[2] but it seems to me that the principal use of my being on the spot is to tell you all I think of what passes around me. You were desirous that Spain should be brought to cooperate cordially with England for the pacification of Portugal. She is so, and I need not say with what anxiety I await your instructions for my future proceedings. Should you intervene in Portugal and insist upon a cessation of hostilities I hope that such a great service will not be performed for Don Pedro unconditionally—for unless he is in some way bound beforehand either to give his Constitution or his absence, which would be far better, he has already shewn us what manner of dependence is to be placed upon his gratitude or his good faith. It is most desireable too that he should explain what the rôle is which he has selected for himself. He has no right to be King for he resigned the throne—he has no right to be Regent for the Cortes alone can appoint one—he has no right to issue decrees the preambles of which are usually a précis of the law he is about to violate. In short unless there is some check upon him he will be not one bit less of a European nuisance than Miguel. I treat it all very lightly to Zea but we can't wonder at this Government resenting the revolutionary projects against Spain which are openly discussed and avowed if not by Don Pedro himself, certainly by his most immediate belongings; and William Russell writes me word that Mendizabel[3] had declared that Portugal was only a secondary object in bringing foreign troops to Lisbon—it was against Spain that their operations were to be directed.

Zea is quite ready to put in the Gazette that Spain casts off Don Miguel and never will forgive the injuries he has committed against her, etc., etc. immediately if it is insisted upon, and would do so as a matter of course if we were inclined to use force on our side, but without that he thinks no good would come of it for Miguel in a fit of desperate revenge might throw up his Portuguese chances and march his whole army with Don Carlos into Spain. Zea says they are collecting troops on the frontier as fast as they can be spared from the provinces and that when they are in sufficient number he is ready for whatever we please.

The cry still continues against him though not so loudly, but he will have infinite difficulty in maintaining himself, for his unconciliating personal character prevents his having any friends. I have promised him to say a good word to you for the new consul general he is going to send to London of whom he speaks highly. He has turned out the one who was there for Carlism—ditto those of Bayonne and Gibraltar. Ditto several in his own office.

GC/CL/114; Clar. Dep. C. 451/2 (44-45)

[1] 'I have probably bored His Majesty's confidential advisers to death about Portugal but the more I learn of Spain the more dangerous and Peninsular do I think the question. Why even at this moment, although the Queen's cause is to all appearances safe, it is impossible to calculate to what perils it might not be exposed if Don Miguel were at once to bring 5,000 men with Don Carlos over the frontier. . . . If the struggle in Portugal were settled and a regular Government established it would not only do more to settle the Queen on her throne than anything else, but it would be a mortal blow to Apostolical principles in this their last and strongest hold.' (V to Granville, 8 Dec. 1833, PRO 30/29/413.)

[2] In his despatch V urged Anglo-Spanish mediation to put an end to the civil war in Portugal for three reasons: (1) it was in British commercial interests

to put an end to the devastation of Portugal; (2) it would prevent a fusion of Miguelism and Carlism, and thus a war of principle in Spain as well as in Portugal; (3) mediation was the only means to restrain Dom Pedro who would otherwise attempt to create a 'revolutionary party in the Peninsula'. (V to P, 8 Dec. 1833, no. 34, FO 72/413.)

[3] Jewish banker and liberal politician.

24   Villiers to Palmerston, 14 December 1833

Madrid. Private. If the newspapers[1] are a fair criterion, the interest and the ignorance concerning Spain remain undiminished, and as I see they are getting up a call for the Cortes I will give you my opinion upon the question in case you should think it worth having.

In the 1st place there exists no power in the State which *could* call together the Cortes after the manner of the years 1812 and 1820, and I believe that few of those who did, and still fewer of those who did not, belong to them at those periods, desire to see them so assembled again, for the same scenes with the same deplorable results would be repeated during the time which would then in all likelihood precede the ultimate triumph of the Apostolicals. But to call the Cortes together after some old fashion is I believe the desiderandum, and this is rather indefinite, for the Cortes have never been assembled according to any fixed rule; in whatever way elected, however, they must be a constituent assembly of nobles, clergy and people. From the first of these it would be impossible to select men of capacity or any not below the average, and that average a Spanish one; from the clergy there would come bishops and other dignitaries—Carlists to a man, and not very fit agents to promote extensive reforms or give stability to a liberal Government; the Deputies of the people would be chosen by the corporations of the towns compared with whose corruption that of Dublin or Leicester is of angel-like purity. These then would be the representatives of the nation and fitter machinery for the cultivation of abuses cannot be conceived. Whether they deliberated together or in separate Chambers they would not operate as a check upon each other for they would all have an interest in upholding the present system, and where responsibility would be so much divided public opinion, even if it existed, would be inoperative. From such a body acts as mischievous might be expected in an absolutist sense as from the Cortes of 1820 in a democratical. This country will only be well governed when it has a proper representative system, not the old Cortes which are totally unfit for Spain in a regenerating state or the modern Cortes which are not fit for her in any state, but a Cortes, neither imported or imposed, but adapted to the national character and understood and desired by the country.

For this there do not now exist the elements and if instead of waiting till they are matured, crude and unfit materials are employed, misgovernment will be indefinitely prolonged. If tranquillity is maintained, I think the political education of the people is in fair train. Already opinion and the press are acquiring a power which would astonish any one who had been absent 3 months from Spain, while the excellent appointments and the practical improvements which are making, and the determination to move onwards which seems to animate the Government, will induce the people, so often deceived, to believe that their advantage has at last become matter for consideration with their rulers. Zea will notwithstanding have great difficulty in maintaining himself, and his great unpopularity in the provinces certainly damages the cause of reform. The acts that have been performed by his Government should have rendered him popular, but party hatred is here so much stronger than public principle that the clamor against him is louder and more unreasoning than before the King's death. His anxiety for the approbation and alliance of England increases every day—indeed this is the general feeling—and if we can act together upon the Portuguese question, the public will be so delighted, so lifted up in their own estimation that I should hope to turn the political influence to great commercial advantage.

It would of course be desireable that the 3 Powers should recognize the Queen, because their not doing so is an element of strength and hope to her opponents, but their influence is no more to be apprehended here than that of the Hottentots. Their ministers sneer at Zea for the liberal tendencies of the Government, and he is not very measured in his expressions concerning them now that he does not feel the want of their assistance. I don't believe either of them has seen him $\frac{1}{2}$ a dozen times since the King's death.

The hunt after Don Carlos[2] will probably not be resumed and it has perhaps ended in the best way it could—for he has been scared away from the frontier, and the Government have shewn themselves to be in earnest and are spared the embarrassment of having him a prisoner in the country.

I have begun upon the slave trade with Zea. . . .

Received 27 December.

GC/CL/115; Clar. Dep. C.451/2 (46-50)

[1] English newspapers.

[2] News reached Madrid at the beginning of December that Don Carlos was at Bragança. General Rodil was instructed to cross the Portuguese frontier in pursuit, but when he entered Bragança Don Carlos had left. (V to P, 14 Dec. 1833, no. 37, FO 72/413.)

25   Villiers to Palmerston, 23 December 1833

Madrid. Private. I enclose a copy of the letter which I wrote to you by M. Perier last week—he has been taken up to the mountains near Bergara and if he ever comes down again he will probably be minus the innumerable letters and dispatches he has with him. I accordingly send duplicates of all mine which you will see has been no light labor.

I have not a very flourishing account to give this time. The state of things upon the Portuguese frontier has become alarming since I last wrote—the hostile attitude of the Miguelites attracts refugees from this country and a border warfare of pillage and politics has begun which may any day extend itself and become very formidable. Should it do so and should any of the frontier provinces become demoralized, we shall see Portugal, the lesser and the weaker country, dragging Spain down into the abyss of desolation in which she is herself plunged. I am not given to croaking but I can't disguise from myself that the tranquillity of Spain is in jeopardy, greater at this moment than it has been during the last 6 weeks. The Portuguese is becoming every hour more a Peninsular question and there is neither honesty, patriotism, union, activity, or money here to meet such a smash as that may turn out to be.

The Council of Regency and the Council of Ministers have had a conference and have settled not to quarrel. I think I was of use in bringing together the respective champions, Las Amarillas and Zea, but they hate each other at heart and they will probably squabble again. Zea bends and yields and abandons his system whenever he is sufficiently pressed but nothing can abate the deadly hatred there is against him. His enemies, i.e. every body except the Queen, don't profess a wish for any other system or even to have a fit successor to him but insist upon his being turned out, and as this feeling is even stronger in the provinces than at Madrid it can't be denied that his continuing in the Government damages the cause both of the Queen and of general improvement.

In Navarre and parts of Biscay the insurrection is not yet put down and we learn that all the people who were unwillingly pressed into the service of the rebel leaders have now got a taste for the plundering guerilla life they have been lately leading, and few in those provinces have availed themselves of the pardon which has been offered. They never wait for the arrival of the troops who are harassed by useless marches in the mountains at this time of year and who of course are not in sufficient numbers to make a clearing of such extensive districts. Valdes however is a very clever general and will make the most of the means at his disposal.

I intend to make the most of the means at my disposal this week upon the subject of the slave trade, and I shall be much obliged to you to tell Vial how much importance you attach to an immediate compliance with our demands, for I find that the Queen makes a great point of always seeing Vial's dispatches and she appears to have at heart to do any thing that can be agreable to England as much as Zea has to do any thing that can be agreable to her. The Duchess of Kent desired me, through Backhouse, to obtain for Princess Victoria an autograph of the Queen's. . . .

GC/CL/116; Clar. Dep. C.451/2 (51-54)

26   Villiers to Palmerston, 31 December 1833

Madrid. Private. I have not much to add to my long despatches today. The feeling against Zea gets stronger and it is evident nothing will alter or even abate it—it is even more violent in the provinces, and the Queen's popularity is suffering. The great necessity for Zea is certainly passed—a man of his firm purpose and decided character was useful in the moment of crisis but he is rather in the way now although he wanders from his system as much as one can desire. As long as he appears to understand the real interest which Spain has in *earning* for herself the goodwill of England, I shall take no active part against him, but I think if it were adviseable to do so Rayneval and I could upset him in a week. We have had one or two squabbles about Portugal in which I do not think I have come off worst, and we may now dictate what we please upon the course to be pursued by Spain.

You probably think me a great bore about Portugal, but my feelings upon that subject are so strong and I do so earnestly desire your foreign policy successful and great that I should think myself wanting in what I owe to you both as a minister and a friend if I did not on this as on all other occasions frankly declare to you my opinions and the grounds upon which they are formed. If I thought the alternative was armed intervention or doing nothing, I should press the subject no further, but I solemnly believe that the choice lays between intervention now under every favorable circumstance, and intervention hereafter when difficulties will be indefinitely complicated and the prospects of success miserably diminished. The Portuguese contest is at the very point which is ripe for interference. The two brothers are equal in force and the unassisted triumph of either would be the only remaining calamity which could be inflicted upon the nation; every respectable individual of either party desires foreign aid without which they feel their misfortunes must be interminable, and with this state of opinion the very *shew* of such intention on the part of England would nearly suffice for the work. The prolongation however of the Portuguese struggle will, I may say *must*, be the beginning of a similar state of things in this country, and if ever such a time comes I believe that the horrors of the French Revolution will be light as compared with the scenes which must take place in a society completely disorganized as this would be where brutal passions were contending in a war of opinion. It must be remembered that the priests think that their great stand must be made now, that they are (and so they are too) in their last ditch, all those moreover who live or intend to live upon the abuses which have so long crippled the country, all these begin to snuff reform in the distance and would upon slender cause throw off a liberating Government, preferring the Inquisition and things as they are to the progressive improvements in which the Queen must lead the way.

As another justification of myself for having written so much upon this cursed question, I must beg of you to remember that I have not even a clue to your opinions at the present moment upon the subject,[1] as I am unwilling to consider them now represented by the despatch to Lord Granville of November 12,[2] considering the alterations which have since taken place in the main features of the question, and judging from that despatch I think I must have made myself ill understood for there never has been any proposition to get rid of the Constitution on the part of Spain. British interests too cannot be said to be out of danger when Oporto is hourly exposed to being recaptured and when the commerce of Great Britain with Portugal, fast sinking into a desert waste, will be absolutely worthless. My last date from England is November 30th of either letter or newspaper. You may therefore have written to me but I am at a loss to guess by what possible arrangement it can be that all communications are stopped. I mention this, because in the event of your wishing any letter to arrive without delay some method different to the present one must be adopted.

Burgos[3] will I feel sure do great things for the country if the opposition to him and to reform in any shape is not too powerful. To him I look eventually for recognition in rebus South American provinces and Cortes Bonds.

Received 9 January 1834.

GC/CL/117; Clar. Dep. C.451/2 (55-58)

[1] V complained to his family that he lacked instructions from P. These complaints reached the ears of Charles Greville, who noted them in his diary. (*The Greville Memoirs,* ed. Henry Reeve, new edition, 1910, vol. 3, 10.) In fact V received no instructions from P between November 1833 and February 1834.

[2] In his letter to Granville of 12 November 1833 P set out three objections to intervention in Portugal: (1) tension with Russia was such that it would be difficult to spare ships from the Mediterranean fleet; (2) British intervention in Portugal would be regarded by the French Government as a precedent for France to intervene in Spain; (3) the Spanish Government only wanted to intervene in Portugal in order to prevent the introduction of a liberal Constitution. P believed that this was no longer possible. (P to Granville, 12 Nov. 1833, PRO 30/29/406.)

[3] Appointed Minister of the Interior, 28 December 1833. (V to P, 31 Dec. 1833, no. 43, FO 72/413.)

27 Villiers to Palmerston, 7 January 1834

Madrid. Private. My communications today are not rose colored—the measure of Zea's unpopularity, upon which I have said so much to you, is filling to the brim, and if the hate which the country seems to bear him is not speedily gratified by his dismissal bad things will be in store both for the Queen and for Spain. This measure has already perhaps been delayed too long, for the want of confidence that his daily departures from his absolute system has inspired furnished a pretext to the many restless spirits which abound here and combine for his overthrow and to bring about changes to which the more thinking part of the community were at first averse. Public opinion goes on simmering here for a long while, then bubbles and boils over almost at the same moment. Thus till within the last 10 days a change of institutions was generally reprobated; guarantees and charters are now freely discussed.

I have rather understated this in my dispatch to you[1] because as yet people scarcely know what to think they desire and are inclined to wait to receive their impulse from Catalonia, but when next I write I expect that much which is now crude and undefined will have assumed a specific character and the Queen will have, as many a Sovereign has had before, to decide upon going with or against the revolution—the first stone of which, strange to say, has been the improvements which have so long been demanded. Burgos is a clever man, but he has been in too much haste to exchange his tarnished character for a new one, and instead of the magical results which all hoped he might achieve I fear that he has only called into activity a spirit which will retard the ameliorations he meant to promote. His excellent measure of a territorial division[2] has perhaps been undertaken with too much haste, before tranquillity was restored, and when the funds necessary for carrying it into execution were not forthcoming, but to this as to every other attempt at reform the most deadly opposition will be offered by that omnipotent class in this country, the livers by abuse and corruption. The Captains General have determined among themselves to resist the measure and Llauder's[3] coup d'état is the first of a series which is in readiness. A combination among them will render the Queen's authority absolutely null, and whether she yields or resists they will equally be able to dictate. Zea has at this moment complete possession of her mind as he entertains in her a dread of revolution and the idea that he alone can effectually hold it in check. He himself never seemed to be aware that the ameliorations which the King systematically rejected during his life, and which were systematically adopted after his death, were in themselves a revolution, or that the appointment to places of power and trust of all the men who most detested him secured the downfall of his system. The longer he is retained in office the greater must be the changes which will follow his dismissal for the public clamor will only be raised to the pitch necessary for that by the pledges and offers of his opponents. Las Amarillas is upon the whole the man most designated by opinion for his successor—he is a man of some merit though not of great capacity; he would fret his hour usefully upon the stage and introduce some measures which would make his coming into office well worth while, but he would have no permanent hold upon public opinion, and must be swept away like Zea whenever he attempted necessary unpalatable improvements.

This is all gloomy and discouraging, and if I could have found any man who took, within the last week, a cheerful view of things to come I would give you the benefit of his opinion, but no one I think would honestly pretend to foresee what the course of events will bring in a fortnight hence.

Zea's conduct with me today was that of a madman—sitting in his office to deny that which was notorious to the whole town and which a hundred letters from Catalonia had this morning confirmed.

The quibble with which I believe he will try to save his conscience is that Llauder's letter was not *given* to the Queen—it was stopped by the Minister of War and it is to be sent back to him, in order not *to ruin a valuable public servant*, that he may reconsider it. I endeavour to steer a prudent course, keeping clear of the many intrigues I am invited to assist, without being on bad terms with the mouvement where I may ere long desire to have influence.

Received 15 January.

GC/CL/118; Clar. Dep. C.451/2 (59-63)

[1] V to P, 7 Jan. 1834, no. 2, FO 72/420.

[2] Burgos had issued decrees dividing the provinces into new administrative units and appointing Sub-delegates to govern the new units. The Captains-General of the provinces realized that, if effectively instituted, these new measures would curtail their powers. 'They have agreed amongst themselves not to submit and as you may easily imagine . . . the Government has no means of resisting them.' (V to Granville, 5 Jan. 1834, PRO 30/29/413.)

[3] General Llauder, Captain-General of Catalonia. In an open letter to the Queen he declared that 'the province under his command had viewed with disapprobation the course pursued by the Government and in the event of the present Ministry not being dismissed General Llauder was reported to have declared to Her Majesty that he would not answer for the allegiance of Catalonia.' (V to P, 7 Jan. 1834, no. 4, FO 72/420.)

28   Villiers to Palmerston, 11 January 1834

Madrid. Private. I have very little time for writing and not much to add to my dispatches. Dangers are gathering thickly, but they are greater in the west than in the east of Spain, for if the Catalonians insist, the Queen must yield and things may go on, but on the side of Portugal destruction may come any day, and if an invading Carlist army, though only of 3 or 4,000 men, enters Spain there will not be a district from one end of the country to the other which will not be fighting its own cause in its own way, and French intervention (of which you must know much better than me the European consequences) will then only avert the ultimate triumph of Carlism, and the Inquisition in more than all its pristine atrocity. If, as I see by the newspapers, you are going to send ships to the Mediterranean why should they not call at Lisbon, save Portugal, save Spain, kick out Miguel, bind Pedro hand and foot, establish a regency, marry Donna Maria, and procure the recognition of her and the Constitution by Spain at any hour you please? Upon the request of this Government to be furnished with a little money for present purposes (and till they can manage to raise some at home and abroad) and some arms, not above 1 or 2,000 muskets, neither to be given unless to be employed *for Donna Maria* as well as *against Don Miguel,* I trust that you will be able to give them some hope or they will surely perish—before they do so however they will, and who can blame them, throw themselves heart and soul into the arms of France however unpopular it might be, for the great desiderandum of every liberal here from the most moderate to the most democratical, is to establish a bona fide cordial alliance with England, to look to England for advice and support, and to raise their country by uniting her material interests with those of England.[1]

There is a slight reaction in public feeling here since I last wrote and some alarm that the Catalonians are going too far and too fast, but every body would now be glad to see what they demand accomplished, though they think that institutions acquired by dictation may not work well, and that the bayonets of a hot-headed militia are not precisely the guarantees which the nation desires.

Zea has lashed himself to the mast and means to go down with the ship—it never seems to cross his mind that he might relieve the Queen from a world of woe by insisting upon going out. It is difficult for her to turn him out at General Llauder's word of command—and not very

easy to retain him against the united voice of the whole nation—I fear
that Plebs may step in some morning and settle the question.

Received 23 January.   GC/CL/119; Clar. Dep. C.451/2 (64-66)

[1] 'M. de Zea said we would place ourselves in the hands of England to secure
Portugal being on terms of good neighbourhood with us for the future; and
for the present we should look on the arrival of British troops in Portugal as
the salvation of the Peninsula from an endless train of disasters.' (V to P, 11
Jan. 1834, no. 5, FO 72/420.)

29   Villiers to Palmerston, 16 January 1834

Madrid. Private. The event which I have for some time past contemplated has taken place—Zea was dismissed yesterday—and although
I should have regretted it 6 weeks ago I have lately been anxious for
it. His unpopularity was so unbounded both here and in the provinces
that it damaged every measure however beneficial proceeding from a
Government of which he formed a part, and what was of more importance it served as a pretext for all those who would have produced disorder by resistance to necessary reforms or by agitating questions for
which the public mind was not prepared. I have had great suspicions
of Zea upon the Portuguese question ever since he proposed to me that
Spain should *protect* Portugal, and although I have not doubted that
we could force him into complying with whatever we desired, yet it
was better to deal with a willing negotiator, and one who would not
be in the false position of Zea in adopting those decided measures in
Portugal which become every day more vitally important to Spain. I
have accordingly used some indirect means for letting the Queen know
that the continuance of Zea in power was far from indispensable to the
good relations between England and Spain, and that it appeared to
me he was pursuing a policy which, while it did not acquire the good
will of the *Barbarous Powers*, failed to inspire confidence in England and
France—the allies upon whom alone Spain can reckon in the various
ways in which she will need support. I don't pretend to say that this
intimation had any influence in turning out Zea,[1] but the Queen
received my congratulation upon the event with marvellous
complacency this morning.

I cannot yet predicate the effect which the new Government[2] will
produce in the country after the first exultation at Zea's fall has passed

away for Madrid is not Spain, scarcely more of it than the ground it stands upon—and the accounts from the provinces must determine the fate of Martinez de la Rosa. He is a liberal and an enlightened man but I doubt his practical capacity. I remember telling you once I thought him fit to be at the head of Public Instruction, which is very different from being at that of Public Affairs. From my previous knowledge of him I expect to find him amenable to all we wish respecting Portugal and South America.

Upon this latter question, if we succeed it may be as well that the English Government should have some credit for it, and I hope therefore you will let me know what are the objects sought by the representatives of the States in England. If we could obtain any pecuniary advantages for Spain it would be a friendly act—but at all events you might undertake their cause with the new Spanish Government. Nothing appears definitely settled about assembling the Cortes—no objection will be made to it either by the Queen or the Government if the necessity of the measure is at all demonstrated, but they seem determined not to proceed in that or any other fundamental change in a crude hasty manner.

I shall be able in my next to give you some clearer ideas upon our futurity.

PS. Llauder appears somewhat alarmed at the storm he has assisted in raising, and writes less like a rebellious Pacha—he has moreover admitted the new Subdelegados of the Interior to their functions which is a very beneficial act of submission.

Are you satisfied with Vial?

I find by a letter from Sir John Conroy that the Duchess of Kent is likely to feel embarrassed at receiving the Order which the Queen Regent sent to Princess Victoria . . . .

GC/CL/120; Clar. Dep. C.451/2 (67-70)

[1] To Granville V reported differently: 'I think I have had my part in his ejection.' (V to Granville, 16 Jan. 1834, PRO 30/29/413.)

[2] Martínez de la Rosa formed a Government on 15 January 1834.

30 Villiers to Palmerston, 28 January 1834

Madrid. Private. I continue writing but I have no idea whether my letters are of any interest to you.

Martinez de la Rosa lacks the energy and knowledge of business which distinguished Zea and in that respect is not so satisfactory to deal with, but on the other hand he is less obstinate and more liberal and his whole political career has been consistent and honest. I am upon the most friendly and satisfactory footing with him and he, as well as the Queen and the Council of Regency, are all eager to prove how little store they set upon Russian or Austrian alliance and how entirely they wish to identify the interests of Spain with those of England. No moment in the history of the two countries was ever more favorable for establishing our influence here—it is desired by the nation and any friendly demonstration on the part of England would give an immense moral strength to this Government. It is a kind of support they will stand in need of for they are upon slippery ground and if they fall I see none but adventurers and ignoramuses to take their places.

The convocation of the Cortes has become indispensable but I adhere to the opinion which I expressed to you some time ago that more evil than good is likely to result from the measure. If the basis upon which they are elected be too confined we shall see all improvement checked—if it be too liberal we shall have over again the mischievous absurdities of 1822 leading perhaps to such a denouement as in 1823. If a middle course is attempted I doubt its producing the satisfaction which is to be desired and I still more doubt any such middle course being à la portée of the men who have undertaken to discover it; for they none of them, Martinez de la Rosa as little as any, seem to me proceeding upon any fixed principles or to have any idea of the effect of men acting together in bodies—they are like children playing with chemical apparatus charged with they know not what destructive elements.

I have strongly advised Martinez to complete his loan or any other financial arrangements before the Cortes meet—to take warning from the example of Louis 16th and not to put the Queen in a position to submit to any conditions which may be imposed upon her from having to supplicate of the Cortes to untie the national purse strings. He is quite of the same opinion and was delighted when I told him that I did not doubt my Government would in any way that did not commit themselves to a guarantee (in any shape whatever) assist any financial operations of Spain in London by giving official information of her condition and prospects as well as of the means to be adopted for developing her many dormant resources and placing her credit upon a sound and permanent footing. He said he felt the immense advantages which Spain would derive from such an act of friendship and begged of me to write to you upon the subject, but I told him that there was one condition absolutely indispensable without which the London Stock Exchange would be as a deaf adder, charm the Government never so wisely—the recognition of the Cortes Bonds—and I exerted myself, not altogether without success I think, to prove how much this measure is in the interest of Spain.

The complete nullity of Holy Alliance influence here has been effectually proved during the last 4 months. There was a general gladness when the recognition of France arrived and a most feverish anxiety till that of England came but I believe that an Extraordinary Gazette containing some 2d. $\frac{1}{2}$y. [twopenny-halfpenny] victory over the rebels would produce more sensation in Madrid now than the recognition of the Three Powers, and their representatives look truly wretched and sheepfaced at being found out. I think Martinez will make considerable changes among his diplomatic agents in which he will probably act wisely—he is dissatisfied particularly with the man at Petersburg.

I say nothing more about Portugal because I can add nothing to what I have already said but every day I feel more confirmed in the opinions I have given.

We have weather here which we should say Te Deums for in England if we could have such in August—it is worth a few revolutions to have such a sun and I yesterday saw a bull fight for the first time which more than fulfilled my expectations, but as you will be bullfighting yourself in the House of Commons by the time you get this letter I won't give you any account of it.

Received 6 February.

GC/CL/121; Clar. Dep. C.451/2 (71-74)

31   Villiers to Palmerston, 9 February 1834

Madrid. Private. You will see by my dispatch No. 13 that my position here cannot be overpleasant with respect to the Portuguese question, and as I have never heard from you upon the subject and do not know how much or little of the newspaper reports may be true, I am somewhat embarrassed as to the tone I should take with the clamorous frightened friends of the present Government. The means for invading

Portugal do not exist, but if they did I do not apprehend we could object with any shew of reason or at least without giving some confirmation to the idea which now generally obtains here that England has some interest in not promoting tranquillity in the Peninsula.[1] It is a question however upon which I am anxious to know your opinion, for it may arise any day if the Government get money or the Cortes chuse to begin their reign by a popular act—which entering Portugal would be. The advantages which Don Pedro has lately gained ought to have important consequences, but without some lucky accident upon which one has no right to speculate he can't drive out Dons Miguel and Carlos, and till that is achieved no permanent quiet can be reckoned upon here.

Martinez de la Rosa tells me that he knows from authority which he considers good that Don Miguel, having failed to give sufficient security for payment to the persons of whom he was going to buy some vessels in London, sent to Holland where he has bought some and that the purchase was *much favored* by the King of that Ilk, by and with the advice of some Holy Allies. Martinez seems to have got the account both from England and Portugal.

You will be satisfied with the new minister to London, Count Florida Blanca—he is an honest little man—ever since I have been here he has been *memorializing* the Queen against Zea and putting strong (for Spain) articles in the newspaper against the Government—he is a liberal and has taken pains with himself. As a grandee he has done what is almost without precedent in accepting a mission, and some of the other grandees consider he has lowered his order by not being an ambassador.

You will see by my dispatch how likely the Government are to bedevil their two most important subjects—the Cortes and Finance. Upon the former I have done my utmost to warn them against the errors into which they are about to fall but they appear so pleased with their project and so blind to its consequences that I have faint hope of their amending it.[2] It is here however so little uncommon to see a general law made for or against a particular individual or a whole set of principles twisted to serve some crochet that it is not surprising that the invariable answer of 'Oh you don't know our country' should be given to every foreigner who offers advice or an opinion. One may say that one knows what human nature or common sense are, but you are again met with 'Oh but that is not Spain.'

With respect to the new Minister of Finance,[3] however mischievous such repeated changes may be, I shall do my best to have him dismissed. He is the very incarnation of prohibitive tariffs and as long as he is at the head of the Finances the commercial relations of Spain with England will only become narrower than unfortunately they are at present. Florida Blanca I find sets out this day week.

PS. I have some reason to suspect that the timid termination of Martinez de la Rosa's note to the 3 Powers arises from a doubt of our being prepared to take the Peninsula under our own special care and protection.[4]

Received 21 February.

GC/CL/122; Clar. Dep. C.451/2 (75-78)

[1] 'Much uneasiness and agitation have been manifested here during the last week in consequence of information which has been received through the medium of foreign newspapers, as well as private letters, that His Majesty's Government had come to the resolution of not taking any active part in the affairs of Portugal.' (V to P, 9 Feb. 1834, no. 13, FO 72/420.)

[2] The main point of difference between V and Martínez de la Rosa was that V thought that the grandees, of whom there were ninety, should be hereditary members of the Upper Chamber. V argued that 'It will be extremely difficult for a monarchy such as that of Spain must now become, to exist without an aristocracy, or for that aristocracy to maintain itself unless it be hereditary.' (V to P, 9 Feb. 1834, no. 14, FO 72/420.)

[3] 'M. Martinez de la Rosa confessed that he had never heard of M. Imaz until he was proposed to the Council by the only one of his colleagues who was acquainted with him, and that he had been appointed because no other person better qualified had been suggested.' (V to P, ibid.)

[4] Martínez de la Rosa to the Spanish ambassador at Vienna, 11 Feb. 1834 (copy enclosed with V to P, 12 Feb. 1834, no. 16, FO 72/420). The passage to which V referred stated that the Spanish Government did not insist on the prompt recognition of Queen Isabella II by the Austrian Emperor.

32 Palmerston to Villiers, 11 February 1834

Copy. Foreign Office. Private. Well may you say that you do not know whether your letters interest me, at least as far as you can be enabled to judge of that matter by my letters, but I have been overwhelmed of late with business of every possible kind including long attendances at Cabinets, Councils, Courts, etc.; moreover silence gives consent, and you may have justly inferred from not hearing from me, that which is true, that we are greatly pleased with your manner of going on, and highly approve all your doings and sayings.

I have not time today to write you any despatches, and indeed I should not know precisely what to say to you. You, and Martinez, and William Russell, and the Government of Pedro make out a very strong case to shew the expediency of an immediate interference on our part, to put an end to the civil war in Portugal. I cannot deny that it would be the wisest thing we could do, for our own sake, for that of Portugal, for Spain, and for Europe; and a slight effort would I have no doubt accomplish our purpose. I have always held this opinion individually from the moment when Pedro left this country to go to Terceira, to place himself at the head of his expedition. But in this world, the best things are not always the most feasible, and in the present case there are difficulties in the way of the execution of such a measure, which upon a balance of motives and results have induced us for the present at least to renounce it.[1] This decision undoubtedly leaves us somewhat in embarrassment with respect to Spain; we have been urging Spain for a twelvemonth to concur with us in a particular mode of settling Portuguese affairs, and when at last Spain says she is ready to join us and begs we will *go it,* we stop short and say we are much obliged to her, and delighted to find her of the same opinion with us, but are very sorry that just at present we do not think it convenient to carry our own proposals into effect. However so it is, and you must make the best of it you can; lay it on the ground of our general dislike to interfere by force of arms in the internal affairs of other countries, and in our hope that Maria's cause is in a fair way to triumph without foreign aid. But we shall have no objection to an attack upon Miguel by Spain provided it is made with the consent of Maria's Government, but on the contrary shall wish it every success. I really however expect, from the accounts we have last received which were from Lisbon of the 2nd instant, that Miguel will very soon be put out.

Howard is halfway to Lisbon by this time, and will be fairly installed long before this letter reaches you. The change will be useful; William Russell had got mixed up with the former state of things, and a new man was wanted, to say no more.

Pray say to Zea whenever you see him every thing from me that is personally kind; he is a good natured man, and I am glad he has got out of office with a whole skin, which at one time seemed hardly probable.

Your accounts of the present Ministers are satisfactory as shewing that they are not inclined to hurry on changes faster than the force of circumstances may render necessary, and you will of course encourage them in that prudent resolve. All changes in national institutions, to be useful and permanent, should be made to grow out of what is; and should be in harmony with the antient institutions and habits of the people. Total and sweeping alterations never can answer. It is very doubtful therefore whether it would be expedient, even if it were possible, to establish at once in Spain two Houses upon the English model, which however is better, as to the Peers, than the French. I take it the provincial feeling in Spain will be found a strong obstacle to a comprehensive Constitution; some of the provinces and especially Biscay are in fact almost pure republicks, though nominally parts of a despotic monarchy, and to them a Constitution would be a curtailment and not an enlargement of freedom.

Nothing could be more prudent and discreet than the course which you have steered as to ministerial changes, abstaining from interference but at last letting be known your opinion as to the real state of affairs. I can only recommend you to pursue the same line and to keep as much as possible aloof from such matters; for it is not easy always to foresee the ultimate bearing of changes of men.

With respect to the acknowledgement of the young Queen by the 3 Powers I think that matter cannot stand better than it does, and you may let it rest as it is. I would almost rather, now, that the Three Powers should *not* renew their diplomatic relations for some little time to come. They are losing their hold upon Spain, and riveting the connection of that country with England and France. The great object of our policy ought now to be, to form a western confederacy of free States, as a counterpoise to the eastern league of the arbitrary Governments. England, France, Spain and Portugal united as they now must be, will form a political and moral power in Europe which must hold Metternich and Nicholas in check. We shall be on the advance, they on the decline; and all the smaller planets of Europe will have a natural tendency to gravitate towards our system. Our objects will be the independence of individual States and peace among all; theirs, vexations and perpetual interference of the strong in the internal affairs of the weak, and a peace which may be called war without ball cartridge. Sweden and Denmark have formally declared that in the event of a rupture between us and Russia, they would be *neutral*; this is all we want. However there will be no war *this year* between us and Russia. She has found that we and France are in real earnest about Turkey, and not only determined but *prepared* to resist her further encroachments in that quarter, and she will take good care not to put us to the test at least till her famine is over, and her fleet and batteries in the Baltic and Black Sea put into better condition. Pozzo, when over here last year, had written the report which he was ordered to come and make and painted the constitution of England in the darkest colours; according to him, we were water logged as to finance, and 'sûr de perdition' as to internal organization. Soon after this report, came the unanimous vote of 20 millions for the West Indians, a staggerer for Nesselrode; then came accounts from all quarters of our manufacturing prosperity; then the decided tone of the Government upon Turkish affairs, our quiet naval preparations, and the universal expression of public indignation against Russian policy. The result has been that we have been smothered with fine words from Petersburgh, and that we believe them so far as to be satisfied that Russia is not this year ready for war.

You ask me what I think of Vial; I believe him to be a very honest good sort of man; I have had a good opinion of him on account of the very bad grace with which he told me a lie about Bourmont last year, and since Ferdinand's death he has been quite an altered man; he has become what he was, what an apprenticed negro will be to a field slave. If they chuse to leave him I shall not complain, if they send another I shall not repine; he and I are very good friends and go on very well together. Alava has been talked of here as a person likely to be sent as minister to us. I own I have my doubts whether that would be a good selection. There is not a better fellow breathing, and personally I should find him far pleasanter to deal with than probably any other Spaniard would be. But first, he is under the deepest obligations to the Duke of Wellington, and he is too honourable not to be devoted to him. Could I expect that Alava would have any secrets for[2] the Duke, and must he not be more in the intimate society of the Duke and the Duke's adherents than might be convenient? Next, Alava hates the French like a Spaniard and a Waterloo man; he is too frank and talkative to conceal his opinions, and would it be desirable that the Spanish minister in London should be running down Louis Philippe and the Barricades, and might not his opinions be represented in some degree as reflections of what he found entertained secretly in other quarters? Lastly Alava has not been in Spain since 1823 or 24 and are his impressions and connections those of 1833–34?

I merely throw out these doubts that you may make such use of them as occasion may seem to require.

Is there at Madrid a man by name Carneiro who is supposed to be a secret agent of Louis Philippe? If so, try to learn what he is about, and what is supposed to be the object of his mission—information or influence? And if the latter, for what purpose.

Mendizabel, the man who has been employed by Pedro, has been trying very hard to persuade me to listen to his opinions about Spanish affairs, with the intention obviously of quoting me, as if his opinions were mine; I have civilly declined his overtures, and therefore if you hear from any quarter that he has written to any of his friends representing me to have expressed to him any wishes or opinions with respect to Spain, I beg you will say that I have told you that Mendizabel has no authority to make any such use of my name. I say this because I heard that when he was at Lisbon in the autumn, he quoted me in a way which he was by no means authorized to do.

I send you a letter from the Duchess of Kent about the Order . . . .

We have reason to believe that the Spanish minister at Rome, Labrader, is not quite as zealous in the cause of the Queen as he would be if Don Carlos was in the Piazza di Spagna, instead of being on the frontiers of Spain.

Poulett Thomson wanted the other day to persuade me to send Bowring[3] to Madrid to help you to talk about commerce. I told him that was really too impudent a proposal . . . .

If anything can be done about the acknowledgement of the American States, it would be a great thing, but I can conceive it to be difficult.

I shall soon send you another messenger.

Vial spoke to me two days ago about some law proceedings in which the Spanish Crown is concerned . . . .

If the Spanish Government want any quantity of muskets, we can supply them at a cheap rate. We cannot *give* them because we must account to Parliament for the disposal of the Public Stores; but we have some 200,000 more than we want in our Stores.

Every thing is going on well here . . . .

PS. I hear from Vienna that Metternich has no intention at present to acknowledge Isabella; and from Petersburgh that Nicholas *dresses* by Austria.

Docketed: No. 1. By messenger.

GC/CL/1219

[1] The Cabinet would not agree to intervention in Portugal even though both Grey and P favoured this course.

[2] *Recte* from?

[3] Dr. John Bowring and V had together conducted the abortive commercial negotiations with France in 1831-32.

33   Palmerston to Villiers, 12 February 1834

Copy. Foreign Office. Private. *Asks Villiers to show Martínez de la Rosa the enclosed letter and papers from Count Irving, relating to a financial project.*

No enclosure.

Docketed: No. 2. By messenger.

GC/CL/1220

34   Villiers to Palmerston, 20 February 1834

Madrid. Private. I have but a few moments allowed me by the Yankee courier for writing and I cannot employ them more to my satisfaction than in thanking you for your letter of the 11th which I received this morning by the courier St. Martin.

The kindness with which you express your approbation of my proceedings gratifies me extremely and the clear and full manner in which you discuss every topic of interest here will be most useful to me.

In the absence of clear ideas upon your intentions my position has of late been embarrassing and it has vexed me to find England looked upon with distrust by the Government and the public here—but you have now wound me up and I shall be able to go on for some time. Since the arrival of the courier I have seen Martinez and *Burked* the few faint hopes he still entertained of English intervention in Portugal. He is of course very unhappy about it for Spain can do nothing there without an immense increase of her army and she cannot even make a small one without money. In the mean while the danger is daily increasing, the number of Don Carlos's refugees augment, and they keep up, without its being possible to prevent it, upon such a line of frontier, an active communication with his agents in Gallicia and

Estremadura. I fear your wish is father to the thought that Don Miguel is likely to be expelled by Don Pedro. I believe it to be *impossible*—Don Pedro's generals are not skilful, if they obtain any success they don't know how to take advantage of it. They are jealous of each other and the Emperor inspires them with no confidence. Don Miguel's army is faithful to him and the country is decidedly with him—where then is the expelling force to come from? Should he however be driven from Portugal I have no doubt that he and his followers would come into Spain and he would be a cunning man who foretold the termination of the state of things which would then begin.

Martinez has pressed me again to ask you if it would be impossible for England to lend or give some money towards bringing some Spanish troops to the Portuguese frontier. I have told him it was of no use and that in fact we could more easily send troops, for then we should know what we were paying for, but if we advanced money we could have no security for the manner in which it was spent. He said we might surveiller that ourselves and only give so much per man upon his being brought into the field and that we should then have the right to interfere upon all Spanish military operations in Portugal.[1] When M. Sarmento arrives, if he is able to enter into an offensive and defensive alliance with Spain, would you consider it impossible to lend the assistance of the British fleet and the Marines now actually in the Tagus for the purpose of any combined movements with Napier or for the defence of Lisbon and the setting the garrison free to join the army? The force might do much and the moral influence of English support would do more.

This Government is weak and I feel every day more confirmed in my original opinion of Martinez that he lacks all the qualities of a commander for a crisis and that he will be overwhelmed by the revolution which he does not know how to lead. Since he has been in office I have always preached to him the intimate connexion of Spain with France and England as a counterpoise to the despotic league in the east of Europe. He seems entirely of our opinion and told me today that Florida Blanca's instructions were altogether framed in that sense. Florida Blanca sets out for London viâ Barcelona tomorrow.

I have no more time.

Received 3 March.

GC/CL/123; Clar. Dep. C.451/2 (79-82)

35 Villiers to Palmerston, 20 February 1834

Madrid. Private. *Recommends the Conde de Floridablanca.*
Received 8 April.

GC/CL/124

36 Palmerston to Villiers, 21 February 1834

Copy. Foreign Office. I have got your despatches of the 8th today. I
have only time to write two lines. Could you not get the Spanish
Government to acknowledge Leopold King of the Belgians? They
ought to do so; the 2 countries have much commercial intercourse and
they now belong to the same political brotherhood. The acknowledg-
ment of Belgium by Spain would of course be agreeable also to France;
and it would shew that Spain is no longer in the trammels of the Holy
Alliance.

Your view of the peerage question is perfectly sound and just. The
Spanish Government will make a fatal mistake if they do not put the
grandees as a class, and as a hereditary class, into the House of Peers.
If the House of Peers is not founded upon a substantial and hereditary
aristocracy it never can afford a real and useful support to the throne,
of which however it is the natural ally. Compare the House of Peers
in England with the Chamber of Peers in France and see which has
most influence and power in the country, and which is the best element
of stability. By trying to have the peers too much under the¹ controul,
the Spanish Government will destroy their influence in the country,
and though they may have two assemblies sitting, they will have in fact
and as far as the country is concerned but *one* Chamber. Pray press this
as far as you can, without appearing to interfere improperly in matters
which do not concern us.

Here we are going on well, and the session looks as if it would be
neither difficult nor long.

Docketed: No. 3. Sent to Lord Granville to go by a safe opportunity.

GC/CL/1221

¹ *Recte* their?

37   Villiers to Palmerston, 1 March 1834

Madrid. Private. My accounts today are not over cheering. The content and hope which Martinez de la Rosa's appointment produced are vanishing fast, and look to which side one will stormy elements seem to gather and blacken.

In the revolted provinces matters go on very ill. The spirit of disaffection and the numbers of the rebels increase. The Queen's troops have hitherto behaved to admiration, and if their success had been in proportion to their efforts they would have continued so to behave, but one knows by oneself that one should be monstrously tempted to give up shooting if every day for 5 months whenever one came in at the corner of a field one saw all the birds get up at the opposite end. These rebels are just like wild birds and the troops never get a shot. If they get demoralized and take to deserting (some few already have) French intervention will be the next thing asked for by this Government, and from some information which I have lately received I don't think it would be disliked in those provinces, particularly in Biscay and Arragon, though upon very different grounds from those upon which it would be solicited by the Government. The cause of Don Carlos has at this moment very little to do with the insurrection—it was at first a banner and is now not wanted, though the *fond* of the population is essentially Apostolical. It is for their exclusive privileges[1] that they wage war—they know they are not defensible and from experience reckon upon being deprived of them by a liberal or reforming Government. In all these provinces and particularly in Catalonia there exists the greatest hatred of *Spain*. They deny ever having been legally or willingly incorporated with Spain and there is a burning desire for independence—this feeling has become stronger of late and there are projects in circulation for shaking off the yoke of Spain, making the provinces into a confederation and inviting the protectorship of France. The latter notion exists more particularly in Biscay where it is thought the offer would be so tempting to France that I have been informed (though I don't feel certain of it) that Deputies are gone to Paris for the purpose of sounding the ground. All this is at present very crude but in this country things remain long in that state and then start all at once into maturity. I shall keep a watchful eye upon the proceedings of those provinces.

With respect to Portugal I have little to say—you will see Martinez de la Rosa's fresh appeal for assistance.[2] I have given him no hopes of any result from it, but he likes better to stand and scream for help than to put his own shoulder to the wheel and try to get his cart out of the mud. I try my best to infuse a little vigor into him, and I have written privately to Howard to have M. Sarmento's instructions framed with reference to the difficulties of this country and the fears of the Government.[3] If he is the bearer of any proposition for a combined movement of Don Pedro's forces with those under the Captains General on the frontier, it will I hope be favorably received here, and if the British ships and Marines now in the Tagus might be charged with the defence of Lisbon in case of attack during the absence of the army to cooperate with Spain, Rosa might perhaps be brought to the scratch. Of this however I am more and more convinced every day—that unassisted, neither Spain or Portugal will be able to extricate themselves from their present difficulties. If the former falls into the confusion which now prevails in the latter, I defy the wit of man to foresee to what part of the world the flame which will then be lighted may not extend. It is for the wisdom of enlightened Governments to calculate the chances for and against waiting for the conflagration or extinguishing it in the *first intention*. Come it will however if it is not speedily checked.

This Government is weak and irresolute though well intentioned. They will run their round of blunders and then make way for others not more capable than themselves, but there are no eminent men here, patriotism and knowledge are at the lowest ebb and one cannot gather figs from thistles.

In reply to your enquiries respecting Carnerero (not Carneiro), he is a very clever well informed man and was chargé d'affaires at Vienna during the time of the Constitution—he was selected when only 20 years old to go and invite the Duke of Orleans to put himself at the head of the revolution here and was with him afterwards at Cadiz. There has been since an intimacy between them but I find no trace of *agency* whatever, or does he seem suspected of it. I know him pretty well and was in hopes that Martinez de la Rosa who is a friend of his would have made him his Under-Secretary as there would then have been a chance of some current business being got through. I see none now.

Oddly enough I had an opportunity of making use of your information respecting Mendizabel the day after I received your letter. I

found that he had been writing to Toreno de omnibus rebus et quibus-
dam aliis connected with Spain, and though he did not actually quote
you Toreno said he knew by *another letter* from Mendizabel that he had
long conversations with you respecting this country and that he was
therefore sure that Mendizabel was speaking from authority. Toreno[4]
as I need not tell you now thinks no such thing.

I hope you won't disapprove of my having shewn a little fight about
the Guarda Costas.[5] Their outrages have become intolerable and are
only equalled by those of the tribunals before whom their victims are
dragged, and a painful experience has proved that nothing but lofty
praise of both is to be expected when their iniquities are represented
to the Government.

The step being taken by me in order to profit by the accidental
presence of the ships[6] is much less hostile than if they were sent by you,
and I have made a favor of the whole to Martinez, as a check to piracy
and a promotion of good understanding.

Will you tell Lord Holland how much Martinez de la Rosa was
delighted with his letter? He says few Spaniards can write in such correct and graceful Castellano—if it had been [*sic*] contained troops for
Portugal the letter would have been perfection.

Your accounts of the state of things at home and in Parliament
rejoice me most heartily.

PS. I have received your letter of the 21st this evening. Ever since I
have been here I have been *saying a word* for Leopold.[7] Zea was like
a deaf adder upon the subject and Rosa strange to say cares more for
being recognized by Holland than recognizing Belgium, however I will
be at him with your letter tomorrow.

As you mentioned in your letter of the 12th ultimo that you should
shortly send another messenger I shall direct the courier St. Martin to
wait at Bayonne—he knows the road and will come much more safely
than one of those worthy English gentlemen in an undersprung
britchka and without a word of Spanish.

Received 9 March.

GC/CL/125; Clar. Dep. C.451/2 (83-88)

[1] The regional laws, *fueros,* gave the provinces where they were still in force
a quasi-independent political status and valuable economic advantages.

[2] Martínez de la Rosa asked V whether the British Government would
'adopt any means which might appear expedient to the British Cabinet for
the removal of Don Carlos from Portuguese territory'. (Martínez de la Rosa

to V, 25 Feb. 1834, enclosed with V to P, 1 Mar. 1834, no. 21, FO 72/421.)

[3] V to Howard de Walden, 26 Feb. 1834, copy enclosed with V to P, ibid.

[4] Toreno, an Asturian nobleman and historian, was one of the leading spokesmen of the liberal movement.

[5] V complained to Martínez de la Rosa that their 'acts were nothing short of piracy'. (V to P, 1 Mar. 1834, no. 22, FO 72/421.)

[6] Three ships, HMS *Barham*, HMS *Raleigh* and HMS *Favourite*, were in Spanish waters.

[7] V had tried to persuade the Spanish Government to recognize the kingdom of Belgium.

38   Villiers to Palmerston, 8 March 1834

Madrid. Private. My report today will be but a continuation of my last. The state of things here reminds me singularly of the last days of the Goderich Administration, except that the head of this Government is in a palmy state of satisfaction at what should fill him with alarm— his poetical imagination enables him to think whatever he wishes and prevents his seeing that he is reeling from weakness and soon must fall. It is a pity for he is an honest man and had a great reputation—commodities too scarce here to be wasted. He might yet be saved if he was sensible of his danger but of that I see no chance.

We have however another and greater cause for alarm springing up—Her Majesty the Regent having unfortunately got le diable au corps has ceased to demean herself as the angel she was at first represented. She selected for her private use some time ago a very large Garde du Corps[1] and although this choice from its extreme publicity produced no small scandal, yet as it appeared to have no political results, I did not think it necessary, or prudent in the state of the communications, to make mention of it to you. Such however is not the case now and her proceedings bid fair to produce 'everlasting smash' as the Yankees say. She goes out shooting from morning till night with her lover, the Ministers can scarcely see her and public business is mischievously impeded. She has become offended with the brothers Carrasco (who rendered her service when Ferdinand was supposed to be dead at La Granja and who till lately had great influence with her) and with Count Parsent and desired that they should forthwith be exiled. To this the Government objected and declared that things could not be done after that fashion any longer, upon which she sent for some of the Ministers and said that there was no use being Queen of Spain if she could not do what she pleased and that if her will was thwarted she gave fair notice that she would go with her hardes et bagages back to Naples. She has quarrelled with her family, and as her sister[2] is to a certain degree connected with the movement, she seems disposed to head the resistance, and there are some fears that she will not permit the Cortes to be convoked. The decree has been ready for her approbation and to send to the Council of Regency during the last 4 days but as yet she has not found a moment to consider it.

All this I have from an authentic source but in *the greatest confidence.*

It is said, but of this I am not sure, that Zea, through the means of her lover, is in constant communication with her. Martinez, whom I asked about it, declared he did not believe it. It is said, and of this I *am* nearly sure, that Oubril is in constant communication with the Queen's favorite.

Sarmento is an honest intelligent man and I hope that his mission here will turn out usefully, but you could scarcely believe, if I were to tell you, all the difficulty I have had respecting him with Martinez de la Rosa—he wanted at first to see him incognito at my house but I positively insisted that he should be received at the Foreign Office. Upon every thing however which has been proposed he has exhibited timidity and irresolution. I have at last screwed up his courage to *declaring* he will take active measures, but it has been like persuading a little girl to have a tooth out. Upon the immediate recognition of Donna Maria I have as yet failed and he still harps, whenever I bring forward the topic, *entirely upon Spanish grounds,* upon some 'appui', be it ever so small, from England or France. Men or money we can't give, and I know of no other appui—if there were any it would be unto him as a dram and we should see a little burst of energy. If England could together with Spain in any manner guarantee the measures of mercy and justice which Don Pedro now seems willing to pursue, their moral influence in Portugal might be powerful and perhaps destroy Don Miguel by defection as effectually as if an army were brought against him. Miguel's followers seem only to want confidence in Don Pedro in order to range themselves on his side.

Things remain in nearly the same state in the Biscayan Provinces but I have good reason to know that many French Carlists have lately come there and are very active in exciting and organizing the rebels.

Will you take an opportunity of telling Florida Blanca that I have complained to you of the impossibility of getting any attention paid to current business since Martinez de la Rosa came into office? No notice whatever is taken of representations however urgent, and unsatisfactory as it always has been to do business with the Spanish Government, it is now worse than ever. I have remonstrated seriously upon it and Martinez always pleads his own press of business and the inefficiency of his office—but still nothing is done to lighten the one or reform the other. I can't even get him to give me $\frac{1}{2}$ an hour, which is all it would require, to the consideration of my note on the slave trade.

PS. I have just learned that the Queen has been brought to permit the decree for the Cortes to be sent to the Council of Regency. It may therefore be expected to appear in a few days—notwithstanding all the promises I have received that it shall be framed *with reference to common sense* I expect that the Ministry will hardly survive its publication.

Received 17 March.

GC/CL/126; Clar. Dep. C.451/2 (89-93)

[1] Muñoz, the Queen Mother's lover, later created Duque de Riánzares.
[2] The Infanta Luisa, wife of Francisco de Paula, youngest brother of Ferdinand VII.

39   Palmerston to Villiers, 11 March 1834

Copy. Foreign Office. Private. I have received your letter of the 1st but have not time today to write more than a few lines. You know that we can give no money without a vote of Parliament and that we should not have the slightest chance of obtaining. We should be met by an unanswerable objection, that the Spanish Government has only to recognize the Cortes Bonds and it might then get what money it wanted in the market. With respect to arms we are tied up in the same way though not to the same extent. We have plenty in store and could send 20 or 30,000 stand in a week, but the Government cannot give away the public stores without the consent of Parliament. We could however sell them; and if the Spanish Government chose to buy some thousands we would let them go cheap to a friend and sell them on credit.

Tell this to Martinez de la Rosa and let me know what he says.

Docketed: No. 4. Sent to Lord Granville to go by a safe opportunity.

GC/CL/1222

40   Villiers to Palmerston, 16 March 1834

Madrid. Private. You will see by my long report[1] of that which is not one half of what has passed upon the subject since Sarmento's arrival, the labor there has been to make Martinez À la Rosa renounce the errors of Zea upon the everlasting Portuguese question. We have not got all we wanted but we have a good instalment of it. An accredited agent of Don Pedro's is received by the Queen, an apology founded upon the present critical state of Spain is made by the Government for not publicly recognizing Donna Maria, and Don Pedro's consent is asked for the entry of (about 7,000) Spanish troops into Portugal which, though their principal object is the expulsion of Don Carlos, cannot fail to be most useful to Don Pedro if he cooperates properly with them.

In the course of several conversations with Martinez I have expressed my surprise and disappointment at finding that a liberal policy towards Portugal had retrograded since he came into office, and he frankly, though hesitatingly, declared that having found that Spain in her extreme need could reckon upon no assistance from England and upon honied words only from France—the two Powers now the most natural friends of Spain—that he must be cautious how he increased the number of her enemies. It was in vain to tell him that a liberal policy was indispensable to the existence of the Queen's authority, and that as such policy never will be looked upon with favor by the Holy Alliance it was unwise to weaken the confidence and moral support of England and France by a course which must throw doubts upon his sincerity. It was of no use, and his friends all say that when he once has an idea fixed it cannot be driven out, though one rose from the dead to do it.

The state of opinion here is far from satisfactory and an idea is spreading even among the liberals that the present order of things cannot last. They do not contemplate the ultimate triumph of Carlist and Inquisition principles, to which the country will *never* again submit, but they expect a fearful struggle and that Isabel the 2d will never be seated upon the throne. It must be admitted that Her Majesty's illustrious Parent does all in her power to favor the notion. She has quite thrown over appearances and there is no more effectual mode here of securing unpopularity. None of the Court Ladies are appointed to attend her at Aranjuez where she is going a month earlier than usual, and by dividing the Cabinet, which is in the habit of meeting every day, [she] seriously impedes the public business. All this is much disapproved, and there was no concourse as is usual to see the departure of the Court yesterday, or any Vivas upon the appearance of the Queen. Rayneval and I mean to go to Aranjuez in the course of this week because some great row or some great act of folly may happen any day, and, though we could probably not prevent either, the blame would be laid upon us if we were not at our posts.

Torreno is becoming the rallying point of the opposition. He would join the Government and bring with him much support if Burgos was to be turned out, but Martinez has not courage to make the change and Torreno will probably end by taking his place.

Las Amarillas sees with no dissatisfaction all that is now going on for he contemplates the Queen's being set aside and the Council of Regency, in which he is supreme, taking the place of King—a short-sighted speculation for the country would not tolerate the authority of such a body for a fortnight.

I have reported to you at various times conversations with Zea, Burgos and Martinez upon the Cortes Bonds. They were all of opinion that they should be recognized, not so much upon motives of honesty as in the hope of getting more money upon better terms; but some of the hungry speculators who are now tempting the Government propose to lend without reference to the Bonds, and I see that Rosa is frail and means to be seduced. He now discovers that the Minister ought to lose his head who should venture to saddle the country with this NEW incumbrance on the eve of the Cortes assembling, and that the representatives of the people can alone decide so great a question. Nothing is yet settled because all the financial proposals received by the Government are to be referred to the Council of Regency, in which there is not I believe a man who knows the first rules of arithmetic, but Martinez says it will remove all responsibility from the Ministers.

The Sardinian minister who has just received an unasked for leave to quit Madrid[2] is a gentleman of very agreable absence. He is a rank Carlist and his doings here have long been of a suspicious character.

I am very much obliged to you for your prompt compliance with my request respecting Southern.[3] He begs me likewise to offer you his best acknowledgements.

Received 26 March.

GC/CL/127; Clar. Dep. C.451/2 (94-98)

[1] V to P, 15 Mar. 1834, no. 30, FO 72/421.
[2] Solaro della Margarita.
[3] To make Southern, a friend of V who had been acting as his private secretary, an unpaid attaché. (V to P, 18 Feb. 1834, private, FO 72/420.)

41 Villiers to Palmerston, 27 March 1834

Madrid. Private. I send you a gloomy account of things here and I see little hope of their not becoming worse. The public exasperation is greater than in Zea's time, for disappointment is to be added to other grievances. Weakness and vanity have marred a fine conjuncture of circumstances, and I fear that the time which must yet elapse before Martinez de la Rosa gets his first idea of his mistaken course from his abrupt fall will produce dangers and difficulties perhaps insurmountable for his successor. At present the more his friends warn him of his errors, the more like Dr. Panglos he keeps thinking que tout est pour le mieux dans le meilleur des mondes possibles, and he is much more occupied about a storybook which he has just published and a comedy which he is about to have acted than the danger of his country and the triumph of the principles which he has always opposed. Every thing is at a standstill for want of money but he fears to take upon himself the responsibility of a loan—yet keeps a Minister of Finance who is not fit to be a clerk in his own office. Burgos, who is a most able man but who feels that his unpopularity renders him useless at this moment, is willing to resign, but Martinez won't permit him because Torreno must be his successor. His constitutional ardor has entirely cooled because the Council of Regency have amended the blunders of his 'travail' upon the Cortes, which he had the vanity to desire should be his own without assistance or advice. But of all his freaks the most unaccountable is the Portuguese; it is true that Sarmento has delivered his credentials and a Spanish army is ready to cross the frontier, but it would be difficult to give you an idea of the outlay in threats and coaxings I have made to bring him to these points—for he is notoriously obstinate, and it is not a month ago that he composed his notes for assistance to France and England, and declared that singlehanded Spain could attempt nothing; and when Sarmento arrived his only idea was to see him privately, at night, and in my house. Even now he makes a secret of Sarmento's audience; and as Don Carlos has retreated into the interior[1] and will probably take refuge with Don

Miguel, I shall not be surprised if the entry of the Spanish troops is delayed or perhaps prevented because he cannot bring himself openly to take part with Don Pedro, although he admits that the two Queens have an identical cause, and he would rather risk the success of his expedition for want of proper cooperation and lose the moral effect which the *fraternization* of Spain could produce in Portugal than take a step which would be displeasing to the Holy Alliance.

I have heard that before his departure from Madrid Brunetti held out distant hopes to Martinez, if his conduct was Apostolical and good, of recognition from His Highness Metternich and His Holiness The Pope, and this may account for a world of vacillation.

If the expedition takes place to Portugal it will be commanded by two most excellent men, Murillo[2] and Rodil.[3] They understand the Portuguese question perfectly with reference to Spain, and as nobody here ever misses an opportunity of disobeying orders which they do not approve I have great hopes that they will do all that the Government ought but won't direct. I have had some means of getting a few facts conveyed to Rodil for his guidance, I need scarcely add without any danger of compromising myself.

I have received your letter of the 11th instant and have communicated its contents to Martinez de la Rosa who at last sees the impossibility of our giving any money. He was much pleased with your offer of letting him have some arms cheap and said he would consult the Minister of War upon it and let me have an answer immediately—which he has not done.

Till the Cortes meet the Cortes Bonds will not be taken into consideration. The Government shrink from the responsibility of recognizing them; they can get money without—and honesty is no stimulus.

I have been for a few days to Aranjuez but as nobody was there but Her Majesty and a *very minimized* society I found it impossible to be au courant of passing events, so I have returned here for a while, and as Martinez is occasionally obliged to come up my business with him is not impeded.

I hope you may not think it inexpedient to move the Colonial Office to reimburse to Sir William Houstoun the expenses he incurred for the embarkation of the French officers.[4] He will never get them from this Government who ought of course to pay them, and he says that the Gibraltar treasury is as pennyless as the Spanish.

I received 4 days ago your letter dated *February 12th* with some inclosures from Count Irving[5] ....

As I am of course desirous to maintain my present friendly relations with Martinez while he remains in office I shall be obliged to you not to let Florida Blanca, who writes to him the minutest details, know my opinion of *men, women* and *things* here.

Received 5 April.

GC/CL/128; Clar. Dep. C.451/2 (99-103)

[1] Don Carlos had left Vila Real and moved to Coimbra.
[2] Morillo had made his reputation during the war against Napoleon; he had risen from the ranks.
[3] Rodil, 'who alone had emerged with credit from the American wars' (E. Christiansen, *The Origins of Military Power in Spain 1800-1854*, Oxford, 1967, 32), was Inspector-General of Carabineros, a force created to prevent revenue evasion.
[4] Bourmont and the other French legitimists who had resigned from Miguel's army.
[5] No. 33 above.

42 Villiers to Palmerston, 4 April 1834

Madrid. Private. Rayneval's courier is going so much sooner than I expected that I am somewhat hurried today in my communications. I can report a shade of improvement in the present and a little better hope for the future than I have lately been able to do. The conscription is making with a facility—an alacrity almost—which is unprecedented; the Milicia Urbana now that it is left to itself is popular and progressing; and money enough has been scraped together, by fair means or foul, for carrying on the public service till the middle or end of May. Still however the inefficiency of Martinez de la Rosa and the unpopularity of Burgos are so great that unless the latter is removed and the former strengthened or neutralized every thing will tumble to pieces. This has become so manifest that contrary to your precepts and my own practice I have taken some part towards bringing about a reconstruction of the Ministry. Torreno appears to me, and Burgos himself is of the same opinion, the only man possessing the requisite knowledge and energy for the moment. He is a man of large views and much experience—a tried good orator—liberal without exaggeration in his opinions—and above all he is convinced that in close political and commercial alliance with England lies the only hope of regeneration for Spain. Burgos is willing to retire in his favor and Torreno does not object, though he does not much like, to take office under Martinez. I wish if possible to bring about this fusion of parties (Torreno is piqued at Martinez's neglect of him and Martinez is afraid of Torreno's abilities, but they are old and intimate friends) because Martinez has many good qualities as well as a high character in the country, and if he were to go out it would look both here and abroad as if the Queen had broken with the moderate liberal party, and that that of the movement was making undue strides. Rayneval is entirely of the same opinion with myself and he yesterday took an opportunity in a long interview which he had with the Queen Regent of expressing his opinion upon a reconstruction of the Ministry, and the Queen entirely agreed with him. He was much pleased with her—she shewed a great deal of intelligence and knowledge of her real situation (except upon one *ticklish* point which Rayneval of course did *not touch*), with a desire to do whatever was thought most advisable for her daughter and the country. Las Amarillas, with whom I have latterly put myself more in relation, is likewise of opinion that a general bouleversement will be the consequence of the present Government, constituted as it now is, remaining much longer in power. The difficulty will be with Martinez himself for he is more than ever convinced of his own vigor and capacity for governing, but I hope in a few days we shall effect some change which will be satisfactory to the public who are justly indignant at two months having been wasted at such a crisis.

I have labored incessantly in the cause of Spain and common sense with respect to Portugal, and Martinez is beginning to admit that the cause of the two Queens is the same and that the military operations of Spain in Portugal are likely to fail without the previously combined support of Don Pedro—but though he won't publicly announce the recognition of Donna Maria he told me yesterday that he meant to recognize the Brazils directly.[1] I hope I made him see that the doing so apropos de bottes at this moment, not in conjunction with Portugal or as a part of a general measure, would only be affronting to Don Pedro, and we shall probably hasten the recognition of Donna Maria in order that Martinez may gratify his Brazilian whim—which he told me *had occurred to him* the day before. Sarmento shewed him the project of amnesty, etc. which was about to be proposed to the Miguelites and we both of us begged him to remember that if it was accepted and

Miguel driven from Portugal, that he would have no right to count upon the good will of Don Pedro either to deliver up or expel Don Carlos, and this produced some effect upon his mind.

The whole Cabinet appear much pleased with the offer I made to them of muskets by your directions—not only because they will be of great use but as an evidence of good will on the part of the English Government which will produce a great effect in the country. If you will order 12,000 to be delivered in the quickest way possible at Coruña they will arrive at the time when they are most needed.[2] I said you would let them go cheap to a friend.

The advertisement for a loan which they have put into the paper is a very foolish proceeding—it will gather round them an abundance of adventurers and scare away the men of substance and capital who will neither submit to such competition or to the publication of their proposals.[3]

The news from the Northern Provinces is very bad. The little army which is there is perfectly impotent for such a war against such numbers in such a country—but if we can tide over the next 6 weeks there will be force enough under arms to give hope of better things.

I write in much haste.

PS. I have just received your letter of the 21st ultimo in re the muskets. You will see that your previous offer has been accepted. As there appears to be a large stock in hand it is possible that many of them may not be good, and I hope therefore you will give orders that those which are not likely to *go off* may not be sent.

Received 15 April.

GC/CL/129; Clar. Dep. C.451/2 (104-109)

[1] The recognition of Brazil as a sovereign State and of Dom Pedro's son as its Emperor. Ferdinand VII had insisted that Brazil should be treated as a colony of Portugal.

[2] The official Spanish request for twelve thousand muskets was forwarded with V's despatch to P, 4 Apr. 1834, no. 35, FO 72/422.

[3] The Spanish Government sought tenders for a loan of two hundred million reales. The tenders were to be judged by a committee of financial experts and their recommendations were to be published. (*Gaceta de Madrid*, 3 Mar. 1834, enclosed with V to P, 4 Apr. 1834, no. 36, FO 72/422.)

43 Palmerston to Villiers, 10 April 1834

Copy. Foreign Office. Private. For the first time I think I see daylight in Peninsular affairs, and I hasten to give you benefit of the gleam. The day before yesterday I saw Florida Blanca (I returned to town from Broadlands the night before). We had a very satisfactory conversation and I was extremely pleased with his frank and direct manner of meeting the subjects we discussed. He began by repeating the wish of his Court that we should send troops to Portugal. I told him that I individually entirely concurred with him in thinking that such a measure would be the best and speediest means of restoring peace to the Peninsula, in the manner the most satisfactory to all parties concerned, but that there were difficulties in the way which were at present insurmountable; that these difficulties had no reference to external considerations, nor to the good or ill will of the Holy Alliance about which we care not at all, but were founded entirely upon domestic circumstances, parliamentary considerations etc. That consequently there was no use in discussing the advantage of doing what could not be done and that we had better turn our thoughts to something else which might be practicable.

I then asked him, how stood by his last accounts the projected arrangement with Portugal for the entrance of Spanish troops into that country. He said he had not heard very recently from Madrid, owing to accidental circumstances. I told him that as far as I was informed the matter rested thus. That his Government was willing to send troops into Portugal, but wanted to limit the operations of those troops to the expulsion of Don Carlos, and did not see the necessity of any previous convention with the Portuguese Government before those troops should enter. That the Portuguese Government, however anxious for the advance of those troops, wished that there should be a previous convention between the two Governments upon the subject, and that the object of the operation should be, not only the expulsion of Carlos, but an attack upon Miguel.

I said that it seemed to us that the Portuguese Government were perfectly right on both points; that in the first place it is usual, but at all events certainly proper, that when in time of peace, the troops of one State enter the territory of another, there should be a previous convention between the two Governments, to define the object of the entrance; to regulate the proceedings of the entering troops, while within the territory of their neighbour; and to fix the time when they should withdraw; that such a convention was made between France and Belgium when the French went to besiege Antwerp and would be found to have been concluded in many other like cases; that in fact it was necessary for maintaining the rights of an independent States [*sic*]. I said that with regard to the second point, it seemed but reasonable that when the Portuguese Government was giving leave to a Spanish force to enter Portugal for a Spanish purpose, they should require that force at the same time to accomplish also some Portuguese purpose; that this must be allowed to be only just; but moreover that if the Spanish troops entering Portugal confined their operations to the expulsion of Carlos, they would not merely be doing no good to Maria but would actually be doing her harm; because, as happened at Bragança the other day, her partisans, not able to draw beforehand these nice distinctions, and looking upon the Spaniards as friends, would be led to declare themselves at the approach of the Spanish troops, and would then be left by the retirement of those troops or by their sanction to the vengeance of the Miguelites, who would only be emboldened when they found that the Spaniards did not dare to face them.

Florida Blanca said that this might be true, but that there would be great inconvenience in the other course, and he chiefly dwelt upon the consideration, that if by cooperating with Doña Maria's troops, the Spaniards placed an unconditional triumph in the hands of Pedro, they feared that such was the character of Pedro, and so little the dependence to be placed on him, that he might use in a way injurious to Spain as well as to Portugal, the unlimited ascendancy which he and his party would then acquire. This inconvenience he said would not arise if England was to interfere, because from our different position with respect to Portugal, the success of *our* interference would give us proportional means afterwards to controul Don Pedro. I also collected from what he said another objection, which however he did not distinctly express, and I inferred that the Spanish Government was averse to incur singly the displeasure of the northern Trinity by an apparently officious interference against Miguel, whereas if they were backed up in such a course by the cooperation of England, they would snap their fingers at Metternich and Nesselrode.

I admitted that his first objection was not without force; I said that in the present state of things in Portugal, Pedro with all his faults seemed to be the only man who could be Regent, at least till the Cortes shall have met and shall have otherwise provided; that his being a Prince of the Blood places him above competition and gives stability to his regency, and that his personal qualities of activity, courage and easiness of access have given him popularity with the army and with large classes of the people. But assuming his regency to be a necessity, it certainly would be desireable to tie him up to prevent him and his party from endeavoring to make use of their victory, to exterminate their defeated adversaries. I said that his observations and suggestions seemed to point at a treaty between Spain and England. That to such a treaty, Portugal would naturally be a party, and that it appeared to me by no means impossible to turn that idea to account and to combine, in such an arrangement, the means of accomplishing the fair objects of all three of the parties. I begged him to turn the matter well over in his mind, and said that I would think of it myself and consult my colleagues.

This morning I received from him the note of which I enclose a translation,[1] and after a previous communication with Lord Grey, I read the note to the Cabinet today and proposed to them the arrangement to which it points. The plan which Lord Grey and I suggested is that there should be a convention between the three Powers, the object of which should be the restoration of peace in the Peninsula by the expulsion of Miguel and Carlos. That for the attainment of this object, Spain and Portugal should cooperate with their troops, England by her ships, blockading ports, and cutting off all supplies by sea. The Governments of Spain and Portugal have each a manifest and direct and immediate interest in the transaction, and England becomes naturally and almost necessarily a third party, in consequence not merely of her general interest in putting an end to the civil war in an important part of Europe, but because of her peculiar treaties with Portugal, by which she is as it were a trustee for the Portuguese estate, and bound to be a party to a transaction which brings within its limits a Spanish army. Connected with such a convention and naturally growing out of it would be some stipulations on the part of Don Pedro as to what he would do when Miguel shall be expelled; what retired allowance he would give his brother upon reduction; what amnesty he would grant to the Miguelite party, and how he would confirm promotions and appointments made by the usurper.

The Cabinet have so far approved of this plan as to authorize me to prepare a draft of such a convention for their consideration the day after tomorrow, and I think this so important that I forthwith despatch a messenger to inform you of it. Further consideration may alter their views, and this plan may be essentially modified or entirely rejected; therefore breathe not a word upon the subject to any human being; but prevent, till you hear from me again, the adoption of any measures which would clash with such an arrangement. It is not likely that the Spanish troops should be ready to march when this reaches you, but if by any marvellous accident, the Spaniards should have been guilty of unforeseen activity in their preparations for entering Portugal, contrive to stop them till you get another messenger, and if you can find no other reason, you may at once say that Florida Blanca having again proposed to the British Government that it should unite itself in some way or other with that of Spain in this matter, you think it highly important that the Spanish Government should wait ten days to know what our answer has been.

I believe that the publication of such a treaty would give a death blow to the two Pretenders, and that Miguel's army would dwindle down to nothing, and that he and Carlos would quit the Peninsula. But even if this were not to come to pass, I am quite sure that the united action of the 3 contracting parties would very soon squeeze the two gentlemen as flat as a pancake. It is certainly most desireable that England should bear a part in the proceeding, it is befitting her dignity, and almost necessary for her security, under her standing engagements to Portugal. For if the Spanish troops were to enter, and Pedro to quarrel with them, and require us to come and turn them out, we should be bound by treaty to do so. We had better therefore take security beforehand than have to exact[2] forfeit afterwards.

Pray say how very much pleased I am with Florida Blanca, and how convinced I feel that our personal intercourse must tend to cement the good understanding between our two countries. There was but one unlucky subject discussed by us, and that was the Golden Fleece. . . .

I shall send this open to Granville, that he may read it on its way to you.

Docketed: No. 5. By messenger. Sent under flying seal to Lord Granville.
GC/CL/1223

[1] No enclosure survives in the Palmerston Papers.
[2] 'exert' deleted and 'exact' inserted in pencil.

44   Villiers to Palmerston, 15 April 1834

Madrid. Private. I have been very unwell the last 2 or 3 days or I should have sent my courier sooner. The delay however has enabled me to forward to you the long looked for, Cortes convoking decree.[1] Martinez has just sent it to me and I have barely had time to look through it. It contains some provisions which are wise and good but others, and particularly the high qualification, which will give great dissatisfaction.[2] You would however think it a chef d'oeuvre if you could compare it with what it was when it left the hands of Martinez and had not been revised by the Council of Regency.

The plan for reconstructing the Ministry has failed for the present.[3] The Queen told Rayneval that she felt it was impossible to continue her present Ministry, inefficient and unpopular as it was. Burgos said the same thing—admitted that he himself did harm to the Queen's cause by the unreasoning clamor that existed against him and he offered to give in his resignation to the Queen in favor of Toreno—the only man in his opinion capable of satisfying public opinion and of giving to the Government a vigor and unity of purpose which it had always wanted since Rosa's nomination.

He at the same time made one or two trifling conditions for himself to which I got Toreno to accede without hesitation. This really all seemed the beau idéal of a means for arriving at a most desireable end —but when the time arrived either the love of power overcame him or a new loan scheme which I know was submitted to him the evening before, but in short he offered his resignation so feebly and without any of the potent reasons by which it was to have been supported that the Queen refused to accept it and Burgos came away apparently over-joyed at the failure of his own project. I am sorry for it, for the Queen might have done a popular act and sponte sua taken an able man to her Councils. He will end by being imposed upon her by popular clamor and in the time which intervenes he will become much more of a party man than he is now, and he will then be forced by circumstances and in order to maintain himself to do things which he will not approve and for which there would now be no occasion.

We have made some progress in Portuguese affairs both by leaving the entry of Spanish troops to the discretion of Murillo and Rodil and by the appointment of Perez de Castro on a special mission to Lisbon. Upon the latter I may take a little credit to myself, for I attribute it in some measure to a severe dressing which I had occasion to give Martinez. He called upon me about 10 days ago and when I asked him why he didn't announce in the Gazette that M. Sarmento had delivered his credentials he asserted that he (Sarmento) had done no such thing, that they had merely been letters of condolence and congratulation. I reminded him that he had had copies of the credentials some days before he appointed the interview with the Queen—but it was to no purpose. He said that would amount to a recognition of which he had no intention whatever. I then told him that I had been miserably deceived, that I had misinformed you and misinformed Don Pedro, but that I should instantly send off couriers to London and Lisbon stating the circumstances and I assured him I didn't think there was a man in Europe who, when they became public, would not believe the whole was a trick—that Sarmento had been allowed to present his credentials, but that upon Don Carlos having withdrawn from the frontier a few days afterwards and the assistance of Don Pedro not being of the same necessity, the Spanish Government had bethought themselves of getting up a wrangle about forms with the minister whom they had received in order a little while to curry favor with the Holy Alliance. As Rosa is particularly cheery [chary] of his reputation he did not like this and begged me not to be so hasty for that all would go well, and so it has for a better appointment than that of Perez de Castro could not have been made. He was named ambassador at Rome upon Martinez's first coming into office and will return from Lisbon to go there whenever His Holiness turneth away from the wickedness which he is committing and doeth that which is lawful and just.[4]

I have proposed to Martinez that I should write to Howard to send an English ship or Government steam boat to fetch M. Perez de Castro either at Vigo or Cadiz. I did so for two reasons, 1st that he has no other means of getting to Lisbon—and 2d that it would exhibit an identity of purpose and interests between England and Spain which would probably produce a good effect in Portugal, but here it would work wonders. It would put an end to a hundred idle rumors which have their believers and their ill consequences.

My circular to the captains of King's ships on this coast respecting the Guarda Costas[5] has produced the greatest alarm throughout the whole 'Empresa'—they don't know what to make of it or what to do, and therefore do nothing which is just what we want. I feel sure it is the only way of dealing with this people, and if after a little longer delay you adopt the same course respecting the slave trade you will put a stop to it, and you will never hear a remonstrance worth listening to.

Since I have been here I have not sent you the commercial cases and questions upon which I have been engaged with the Government, thinking that they were of no particular interest and that you would have confidence in my not neglecting them—but I have perhaps not done rightly in thus deviating from what appears to have been the practice of my predecessors, as enquiries may often be made at the Foreign Office to which it would be desireable to have answers ready. I shall therefore by degrees work off these arrears. I don't think I have been more unsuccessful than others upon these matters.

Received 24 April.

GC/CL/130; Clar. Dep. C.451/2 (110-115)

[1] A copy of the *Estatuto Real* was sent as an enclosure to P by V, 15 Apr. 1834, no. 42, FO 72/422.

[2] Members of the Lower House were required to have an income of 12,000 reales (£120).

[3] 'I have some reason for supposing that the French Government is hostile to Toreno's coming into office, either with or without Martinez de la Rosa, from some erroneous notion that he is too liberal or perhaps too English.' (V to Granville, 24 Apr. 1834, PRO 30/29/413.)

[4] i.e. recognize Isabella II as Queen of Spain.

[5] Directing them not to submit to any attempt to stop and search them. (V to P, 15 Apr. 1834, no. 43, FO 72/422.)

45 Villiers to Palmerston, 19 April 1834

Madrid. Private. I avail myself of a commercial courier about to be despatched to Bayonne to acknowledge the receipt of your letter of the 10th.[1] It arrived last night. That it did not do so weeks ago you probably regret as much as I have done, and there is no use in discussing the altered value of the service now offered. The grand difficulty during the last 6 weeks has been to bring these people to the scratch. My object has been to rouse them to a sense of their danger and to make them do something themselves to avert it. The moment they got sufficient courage for this half the difficulties vanished. Don Carlos, upon the mere report of Spanish troops moving, fled from his quarters—his different chiefs quitted him and his little army dispersed.

Napier then came and reduced (aided slightly by the troops as well as moral influence of Spain) the whole north of Portugal, as well as all the seaports that had not yet acknowledged Donna Maria—so that the battle has been already won by mere demonstration. Today news has arrived of Rodil's advanced guard being in Portugal—of its having surprised Don Carlos and his family at Guarda: they went out of the town on foot, their baggage followed them and the whole of it has been seized, papers, money, etc. I send you the Extraordinary Gazette which has this moment been published and which has caused the greatest joy in the town—the funds have risen 7 per cent.

You see therefore that to stop the entry of Spanish troops is impossible, but no endeavour of mine shall be wanting to give effect to your wishes as far as circumstances will permit, and if the Convention arrives in a few days it will be in time for Perez de Castro to act upon when he arrives at Lisbon. Martinez is at Aranjuez where I have been to[o] unwell to return yet, but I have sent him a courier to say that the English Cabinet were taking into consideration the proposals of Florida Blanca.

Burgos is out and is succeeded by Moscoso—a weak and inefficient man. The public want Toreno and would resent this appointment as an affront if they were not in high good humour with the Portuguese news and the Cortes decree.

Enclosure: Supplement to the Gaceta de Madrid, *19 April 1834. (In Spanish.)*

Received 28 April.

GC/CL/131; Clar. Dep. C.451/2 (116-118)

¹ P has added at the top of the page: 'desiring him to prevent the entrance of Spanish troops into Portugal, if he could, till he should hear from me again. P.'

46   Palmerston to Villiers, 22 April 1834

Foreign Office. At last I send you our treaty. I have had a good deal of difficulty and bother about the details of it, in consequence of the French Government objecting to the form in which their accession was at first proposed;¹ but we have all been agreed as to the substance throughout. I trust the treaty will produce a good effect in the Peninsula; I am sure it will in the rest of Europe. The union of the four constitutional States of the West for any common purpose is an event, but much more so, for the purpose of expelling from Portugal the types of absolutism Carlos and Miguel. I cannot allow myself to believe that Pedro will refuse to ratify, but Sarmento has no instructions, and next to Metternich, Pedro and Carvalho will perhaps be the persons to whom the treaty will be the least acceptable. They want the continuance of the civil war, or victory without conditions. Still I think they will not venture to reject such a treaty signed by England, France and Spain.

I will suggest to Granville to ask the French Government to communicate without delay to Madrid their intention to ratify; and I will desire Howard to give you the earliest notice of the decision of the Portuguese Government; so that when the determination of those two Governments is known at Madrid, the Spanish Government might forthwith begin its arrangements without waiting for the return of the messenger who may bring the ratifications to London. At all events as soon as we exchange ratifications we will send off a messenger to Calais; from thence to Bayonne the intelligence will go by telegraph in a few hours, and from Bayonne to Madrid I presume a couple of days or three at most will be sufficient. The Spanish Government should I conceive issue the declaration to the Portuguese people when its troops enter Portugal.

The 12,000 muskets are packed up, and will be sent off the moment the ship is ready to convey them; which will be in a few days.

I am delighted with Miraflores; we go on together and understand each other perfectly. His manners are very agreeable; he is extremely quiet and intelligent and does not let nonsensical trifles stand in the way of business. I tell him he has accomplished in a week what I have laboured at in vain for a long time, namely to determine the English Government to take an active part in Portuguese affairs and throw over neutrality. It is true we do not send troops, but if the matter can be settled without them, which I am convinced it can, it is better for the whole Peninsula that *no* foreign troops should go thither, ours not excepted.

Expedite the ratifications, even if Rodil shall have entered Portugal before you receive the treaty.

You will see by the papers that our procession of yesterday was a failure as to its particular object . . . .

Copy. Docketed: No. 6.

GC/CL/1224

[1] For the text of the Quadruple Treaty see Michael Hurst, *Key Treaties for the Great Powers 1814-1914*, 1972, i. 232-35. P proposed that the French Government should accede to the treaty after it had been signed by the British, Portuguese and Spanish Governments. The French refused to accept this proposal on the grounds that it was an insult to the dignity of France, and insisted on becoming a full contracting party to the treaty. The change of form necessitated considerable alterations to P's original draft.

47 Palmerston to Villiers, 22 April 1834

Copy. Foreign Office. Mira Flores has just shewn me the decree for the convocation of the Cortes. I am glad it is out; and that it contains a hereditary peerage; but how in the world could they be such asses as to establish triennial parliaments, and then to make another mistake in the opposite direction by requiring a man to be *30* before he can be a Deputy?

In a country like Spain where they all have to learn their business and where a little steadiness will be much wanted in the outset of their career, it would have been most desirable to have taken five years at least for the natural life of their Parliament, with a power to the King of extinguishing at any time; and, as to the age, one should have thought that with the example of France before their eyes and all the inconvenience that still exists there even under the modified Law, from the creation of a Fourth Estate called the Jeunesse, who labour under exclusion from the Chambers, they might have opened their doors a little wider—however felix faustumque sit, and perhaps they may mend their flaws by and by.

PS. I am sorry to say that the King cannot be persuaded to change his decision about the Golden Fleece . . . .

Docketed: No. 7.   GC/CL/1225

48 Villiers to Palmerston, 24 April 1834

Madrid. Private. My letter of the 19th will have told you of the entry of the Spanish troops into Portugal but I think it so important to keep you informed upon their movements that I send off a courier with this day's intelligence as Rayneval has disappointed me about the one he promised to dispatch.

I have told Martinez de la Rosa that you had been much pleased with Florida Blanca's frank and satisfactory manner of treating the subject he had to discuss with you, and that you had submitted to the Cabinet his proposition for British assistance in the affairs of Portugal. He was very anxious to know what my expectations were upon the result. I told him that the desire of yourself and your colleagues to put an end to the struggle in Portugal would be greatly heightened by the hope of rendering essential service to Spain at the same time, and that I was very sure if the proposal of Florida Blanca was not complied with it would be exclusively upon domestic or parliamentary considerations. It being impossible to stop the entry of the troops, the next best thing was to gain time by inducing the Spanish Government to sign a convention with Don Pedro, and to sign it at Madrid instead of letting M. Perez de Castro do so at Lisbon, as Sarmento has to send for full powers—consequently if your convention arrives within the next seven days[1] it will find the Spanish and Portuguese plenipotentiaries (unknown to themselves) in readiness for it.

It has occurred to me however that the full powers asked for by Sarmento will only be to treat with Spain, and if England is a party to any engagement we should have again to send to Lisbon and fresh delay would be incurred which is if possible to be avoided, because events have been going at such a tremendous pace in Portugal during the last fortnight that I am afraid of the whole game being up and every object of the convention being fulfilled before it is signed save our obtaining a hold upon Don Pedro. I have accordingly written this day to Howard upon the subject of an extension of powers to Sarmento and I hope I have guarded against your being in the most distant manner committed. I enclose you a copy of my letter. Martinez de la Rosa tells me that the proposed convention will be on a broad base of *offensiveness* and *defensiveness* and in terms of great cordiality—the two nations assisting each other in every manner and giving the reciprocal right of entering their respective territories.[2]

No orders have been sent for the withdrawal of the troops. That is to be determined by circumstances and left to the discretion of Rodil, upon whose activity as well as zeal for Donna Maria you will have perceived I did not misinform you. The declaration of Almeida for the Queen was much assisted if not brought about by Spanish means— Rodil caused fair words and hard dollars[3] to be scattered abroad and promised arms and supplies to the inhabitants which he has since sent and 1,200 prisoners of Don Miguel's were released.

I am afraid that they will catch Don Carlos—the Government is very desirous of it but I see no advantage to be derived from having such a prisoner. They cannot expect the good luck which the French Government had with the Duchesse de Berri that he would turn out to be with child, and if he were shut up his partisans would invest him with all manner of glorious attributes but of which power he takes good care to deprive them while he is a free agent. I have spoken very seriously to Martinez about his not being treated with violence if he is taken prisoner and I think there is no fear of that.

Things have taken a favorable turn here—Rodil in Portugal and Amarillas upon the Cortes decree are principally to be thanked for it. The reaction will be speedy I hope in the revolted provinces and the Carlist spirit may be expected to cool there.

The *tendency* in some members of the Government to accept French intervention is I consider at an end—it was much stronger than I liked about 3 weeks ago.[4]

PS. The consul at Bayonne[5] has taken upon himself to send on my last dispatches by the messenger Clewes and I am therefore obliged to send my courier to Paris as I cannot in Rayneval's absence at Aranjuez get an order for an estaffette from Bayonne.

2 o'clock A.M. Martinez de la Rosa has just sent me word that a dispatch is arrived from General Rodil dated the 20 instant saying that the Governor of Almeyda had announced to him that he had received a letter from the Duke of Terceira written from Freixa de Nemao (half way between Lamego and Almeyda) on the morning of the 19th stating that he was about to enter with his troops into the interior of Beyra having reduced the provinces of Entre Duero y Miño and Tras os Montes.

Enclosure: Copy, Villiers (Madrid) to Lord Howard de Walden, 24 April 1834, private, asking him to ensure that Sarmento receives the necessary powers for signing the convention.

Received 2 May.

GC/CL/132; Clar. Dep. C.451/2 (119-123)

[1] 'seven days' underlined by P, who has added above 'which it will have done'.

[2] 'giving' to 'territories' underlined, probably by P.

[3] 'hard dollars' underlined, probably by P.

[4] 'I never miss an opportunity of telling Martinez de la Rosa what lasting

disgrace would, in my opinion, await the Spanish Minister who countenanced such a measure.' (V to P, 24 Apr. 1834, no. 45, FO 72/422.)

[5] J.H. Harvey.

49   Villiers to Palmerston, 29 April 1834

Aranjuez. Private. Little has occurred since I wrote to you on the 24th. That little however, as you will see by my dispatches today, is good. Affairs have taken a favourable turn—*why* it would be difficult to say, except that the general system of disobedience which the nation appears to have adopted as the correcting power of the misrule they have been exposed to is occasionally very successful. When things get as bad as they were a month ago the press does not mind the censor, the militia does not care for the Corregidor, the Captains General care for nobody and nobody cares for the Government. All this has latterly been in operation with good result, but as for arriving at any result by regular modes or with any regard to established forms or usages, it is idle to expect it. Two months ago I used every argument I could devise to induce Martinez de la Rosa to enter into a defensive and offensive alliance with Don Pedro and to sign a convention (as secret as he pleased) to that effect. He had no good reason to give against it but was as obstinate as a mule in refusing it. He is now doing, and doing very well, more than would have been stipulated for by the convention, and he is now ready to sign one and bind Spain to do that which has already been almost completed. Much is due (as I always thought it would whenever they were permitted to act) to Generals Rodil and Murillo who were ordered to confine themselves to driving away Don Carlos from the frontier, but who immediately took upon themselves the responsibility of assisting the cause of Donna Maria by money, arms and men as well as by cooperation with her troops and the population who were hostile to Don Miguel.

As I have not received another messenger from you and that it would be inexpedient, even if it were possible, to stop the operations of the Spanish troops, I have not again adverted to the possibility of Florida Blanca's proposals being favorably entertained except in general terms. If the Spanish troops are as successful in the next fortnight as they have been during the last (and as they will now have to cooperate with the armies of Terceira and Saldanha, I see no reason to expect a reverse) both Pretenders must be driven from Portugal.

The Queen held her first Court since the King's death on the 27th—her own birthday. A great concourse of people came down here upon the occasion. It would of course be better if she hadn't a lover and didn't display him in the way she does, but if she must have one it is most fortunate that her choice has fallen upon a very ignorant stupid man who is only desirous of living with those of his own calibre and making as much money as he can without caring for politics or meddling with them.

The Spanish ministers are to be withdrawn from the Northern Courts in a sensible decent manner which will embarrass the Autocrats as much as it vexes their representatives at Madrid.[1] The folly of that Trinity with respect to Spain must now be pretty apparent even to themselves. Don Carlos by his own vis inertiae and baseness is effete— his party sinking daily—the Government carefully avoiding all that tends to revolution and the people as carefully avoiding to hurry the Government into changes which are not legal or well matured—during all which time the absence of Holy Alliance ministers except for purposes of mischief has destroyed every remains of prestige upon their influence and made every one remember with shame that they ever submitted to what was so unnatural and unnecessary.

Martinez de la Rosa was much obliged to you for the communication of Seymour's dispatch.[2] The General Toledo[3] of whom Mr. Aubyn speaks is one of the most infamous men in Spain—a spy, deserter, and what not.

Received 8 May.   GC/CL/133; Clar. Dep. C.451/2 (124-127)

[1] The reason was the continued refusal of the Northern Courts to recognize Queen Isabella.
[2] A copy was enclosed with Backhouse to V, 11 Apr. 1834, no. 12, FO 72/419. It concerned Carlist activities in Portugal.
[3] According to Martínez de la Rosa Toledo was a Carlist agent: 'Copies of his instructions have been found among the papers belonging to the Infant [Carlos] which were seized by General Rodil in Portugal.' (V to P, 23 May 1834, no. 63, FO 72/423.)

50   Palmerston to Villiers, 2 May 1834

Copy. Introduces J. B. Renny, who is 'connected with some considerable houses in Glasgow', and who is going to Madrid with the object of improving Anglo-Spanish commercial intercourse.

Docketed: No. 8. Original sent to J. B. Renny Esq., 26 Mortimer Street, Cavendish Square.   GC/CL/1226

51 Villiers to Palmerston, 5 May 1834

Aranjuez. Private. Florida Blanca sent the original treaty by his footman—it has accordingly been delayed upon the road and if it had not arrived last night Rayneval and I had induced Martinez to prepare a ratification of the copy, *sauf* to send another afterwards in proper form.[1] My letter to Lord Granville on the 2d[2] will have informed you that no difficulties existed about ratifying either with the Queen, the Council or the Cabinet—all were equally pleased and all seem to understand the future and general effects of the treaty as well as its immediate advantages.

There is a feeling of laudable pride too at seeing Spain lifted up to the level of England and France in a measure which may have such important results upon the policy of Europe. I have spoken to Martinez about issuing a declaration, which you suggested I apprehend in the idea that the troops had not entered Portugal, and I am disposed to agree with him that there would be no good now, after the troops have been there for more than 3 weeks, in accounting for the objects with which they have been sent.

A long article appeared in the Gazette about 6 weeks ago stating the grounds of complaint which Spain had against Dons Carlos and Miguel and that if Spanish troops went into Portugal it would be solely to drive away their own Pretender and not to meddle with the internal affairs of the country. Martinez tells me that some thousand copies of this article as well as of Rodil's General Orders were struck off and distributed in the Portuguese villages by Rodil and Murillo—and he thinks that a declaration similar to that issued to the Greeks by the three Powers would now have a most beneficial effect both here and in Portugal. He has promised me however as soon as Don Pedro's ratification is known that Rodil shall proclaim the treaty and its objects. I sent a courier on the 2d instant to Howard to inform him that the treaty was as good as ratified. I have not yet heard from him—as soon as I do M. Perez de Castro is to set off for Lisbon.

I think you will be satisfied with the language of Martinez respecting Belgian and South American recognitions . . . .

With respect to the triennial parliaments Martinez says that if they had been made of longer duration people would have been frightened at having to live so long away from their provinces and many might have refused to serve in the Cortes. As the elections moreover won't be particularly *popular,* many of the objections to short parliaments cannot exist.

It was originally intended that the Cortes should only meet once in two years, and you will allow that triennial parliaments are better than that.

With respect to the age of the Deputies, it is a most unaccountable bit of nonsense to require them to be 30 years old while the peers are ripe for legislation at 25. Martinez could give no reason for this, though he told me it was his own particular clause—there is no Jeunesse however here to make a troublesome class of as in France.

I am sorry that the Admiralty are in a huff at my having ventured to address any of the captains of His Majesty's ships. I think that they have not read or misread my letter, the greater part of which was taken verbatim from the instructions I received on leaving London. I gave no orders. I stated that His Majesty's Government would never protect a smuggler, but that the Guarda Costas constantly violated the laws of Spain and captured British vessels engaged in lawful traffic or in places where they could not be legally interfered with—to *such cases I begged to call the attention* of Captain— —*so long as the ship under his command continued on the Spanish coast.* It would of course be dangerous for captains of ships to receive orders from any persons but their superior officers, and it never would have occurred to me to send a recommendation, even, to do anything to a captain which was likely to clash with his orders, though I think that *some* discretionary power might often be of advantage to the public service. For instance suppose Don Carlos who seems likely to go to the Alemtejo or Algarves was to write to me for a passage to Italy in one of the King's ships lying off Cadiz, I think we should better serve our ally here and fulfil the objects of the treaty more effectually by my being able to answer Yes, instead of that I must ask Sir Josias Rowley. With respect to the measure itself it has most completely answered—it produced no remonstrance or appeal from any Department of the Government but much alarm to the 'Empresa', a total cessation of their piratical acts and of the complaints which were weekly transmitted to this mission and afterwards disregarded by the Government.

You would very much oblige me by reading the letter I addressed to the captains and pray excuse this long story which I have thought necessary for my own justification in your eyes.

PS. I have heard upon what I believe to be good authority that Lieberman is immediately going to leave Madrid—he keeps it a profound secret.

I made as good a case as I could for the non-acceptance of the Golden Fleece . . . .

Received 15 May.

GC/CL/134; Clar. Dep. C.451/2 (128-133)

[1] The Spanish ratification was despatched from Aranjuez on 5 May 1834. (V to P, 5 May 1834, no. 54, FO 72/423.)
[2] V to Granville, 2 May 1834, enclosed in Granville to P, 9 May, Palmerston Papers GC/GR/573 (copy in PRO 30/29/413).

52   Villiers to Palmerston, 13 May 1834

Aranjuez. Private. The effect of the treaty continues to be exceedingly good—it is a death blow to the Carlist party—and the public seem to understand and appreciate the advantages it offers to Spain. The Holy Alliance people here were totally unprepared for it and when the report was first circulated in Madrid Oubril wrote off to his Court that it had been concocted by Rayneval and myself at Aranjuez. I had a long talk with the Queen upon the subject today. She said she was most grateful for the treaty to which she should consider she was indebted for the pacification of the Peninsula. I told her what anxious interest the English Government took in the prosperity of Spain and that she was looked upon in England as the most constitutional Sovereign in Europe, for she was averting revolution by gradual reforms and I felt sure her daughter's throne would be more firmly established than any of her predecessors for years past. She said that that was comme elle entendoit sa position and that she should never scruple to make any sacrifice which might be thought necessary. I told her too how much you were satisfied with Florida Blanca.

There is a strong feeling here that the said worthy little gentleman has been making a tripotage with Rothschild and that that is the reason why no regular loan is to be made at present, Rothschild having engaged to lend money now till the meeting of the Cortes upon conditions not very advantageous to Spain.

Perez de Castro is to go in a few days to Lisbon. I have explained to him very fully the difficulties in which Howard finds himself with the Government of Don Pedro and he will I am convinced cooperate heartily with Howard. A Mr. Comyn whom you probably know, as he was one of the commissioners for Spanish claims in London, has been appointed by Martinez de la Rosa consul general at Lisbon. Perez de Castro was very anxious to go in an English vessel but I backed out of the offer I made some time ago as civilly as I could.

Nothing particular has occurred in the revolted provinces, but I am afraid that in Navarre the insurgents have been very successful in their recruiting. The Minister of War tells me that he is assembling all the troops he can muster from different parts of Spain and he intends shortly to make a general and combined attack upon the insurgents in all the provinces. I have shewn him a statement which I have received from the consul at Bilbao of the rebel force in Biscay which he says is perfectly correct—it amounts to 7,500 men.

A step has been gained in re the slave trade, and I have some hopes of bringing that matter at length to a successful issue. I shall not despair either of mending the treaties and creating some trade between the two countries if I can get a good commission appointed.[1] Such important advantages can scarcely be expected *gratis* and I may perhaps have to draw upon the Secret Service if you think it adviseable.

In the event of my being able to make a clear statement of the extra expence to which I have been put in transporting my effects here owing to the state of the country, will you entertain it? It will not be very large in amount but it will be of great consequence to me for the *mise en scène* here is ruinous. I should be sorry however to ask for any thing which you might consider it your duty to refuse.

PS. The conduct of the Milicia Urbana in the row yesterday was not of good omen—they armed themselves and displayed a tumultuous and uncitizenlike spirit.[2]

Received 24 May.

GC/CL/135; Clar. Dep. C.451/2 (134-137)

[1] V proposed to Martínez the appointment of a commission to review the whole system of Anglo-Spanish treaties and commercial relations. (V to P, 13 May 1834, no. 58, FO 72/423.)

[2] See V to P, 13 May 1834, no. 57, FO 72/423.

53   Villiers to Palmerston, 23 May 1834

Aranjuez. Private. I have been somewhat longer than usual without writing to you as Rayneval delayed his courier's departure, but there has been nothing particular to communicate and I am now able to send you word of the evacuation of Santarem and the good effect the news produces here. Nothing certain is known of the movements of Dons Miguel and Carlos, but the Minister of War tells me that his opinion as well as Rodil's is that they are at Ebora which is a position from whence military operations may be made in the Alemtejo if they have a mind to fight or take their chance of escaping from a sea port— whereas if they go to Elvas it would only be to stand a siege which the scarcity of provisions, the absence of heavy artillery, and the demoralized state of the troops would make of very short duration and all retreat afterwards would be cut off. Rodil however does not intend to leave them a day for preparation—he will march upon them without waiting for Carandolet (vide dispatch)[1] and his rear guard, and he will be reinforced by the troops who entered Portugal at Mertola. It is difficult to contemplate any thing which could now prevent a speedy and favorable dénouement. Great credit is due to Rodil for the spirit, discretion and judgement he has displayed, as well as the admirable discipline which he has maintained and which seems to have prevented all jealousy or hostile feeling on the part of the Portuguese.

The whole of Don Carlos's papers which fell into the hands of Rodil have been examined by the Cabinet, and Martinez de la Rosa tells me that such a mass of folly, cruel intention and contemptible nonsense never was got together. The Bishop of Leon was Prime Minister and 3 or 4 French Carlists, one of them a redacteur of the Quotidienne, the principal agents. I have urged Martinez very much to publish the whole in order to give the Holy Alliance the full benefit of their protégé and let the world see in behalf of whom their efforts have not been wanting to throw the whole Peninsula into confusion, and they have hesitated to recognize the Sovereign who was supported by all the rank and wealth and intelligence of the community—he has promised me he will do so.

I have piqued his vanity a good deal upon recognizing the South American republics before the meeting of the Cortes for I have no great reliance upon the large or liberal views of those legislators, and he is now very desirous to enter upon negociation with any agents who may have come to Europe for the purpose. He says he has written to this effect to Florida Blanca and the Duke de Frias—the latter is in communication with M. Le Hon at Paris respecting Belgian recognition. In short I think we may consider that the Holy Alliance yoke is fairly thrown off here and that the real interests of Spain in cordially adopting the course pursued by England and France are at last becoming understood.

The Loan business is bad and I fear that Rothschild has been *doing* our Miraflores.[2] An intimate friend of Martinez de la Rosa's, a certain M. Allende who is Secretary of the Bank, though wholely guiltless of any knowledge of finance, or of any language save Spanish, has just been sent to Paris and London to superintend the affairs of the Loan which the Government at the same time profess they do not mean to contract till the Cortes meet[3] and the propositions of capitalists and the deficits of the country can be discussed by 4 or 500 representatives.

Florida Blanca's[4] letters are full of gratitude for the reception he meets with and of eulogiums on your franchise as well as interest for Spain.

Will you have the goodness to write me an ostensible dispatch expressing satisfaction that the questions of treaties and commercial relations are to be referred to a commission, and enlarging upon the political advantage of creating a trade between the two countries (for really when compared with what it might be it can hardly be said to exist) that it would establish the Alliance on the only firm basis—that nothing would ever be asked of Spain but that which was demonstrable to be in her own interest etc., etc? It would be of great use to me by stimulating Martinez who is far too much of a poet to be an economist, and will you have some conversation upon the subject with Florida Blanca as the Queen and the Cabinet see all his dispatches, for I am anxious to turn the present moment to commercial account when they are abounding in gratitude and cordiality towards us?

PS. I have a courier waiting at Bayonne—if you wish to write to me by messenger.

Received 3 June.

GC/CL/136; Clar. Dep. C.451/2 (138-142)

---

[1] Rodil had originally intended to wait until Carondelet joined him from Andalusia with 20,000 fresh troops before he continued the pursuit of Don Carlos. (V to P, 23 May 1834, no. 64, FO 72/423.)

[2] See also V to P, ibid.
[3] V believed that the Government was anxious that the Cortes should assume responsibility for any loans contracted because the bankers would exact very hard terms. Thus the Cortes, and not the Government, would incur the public disapproval which they believed would inevitably follow. (ibid.)
[4] i.e. Miraflores's.

54 Villiers to Palmerston, 27 May 1834

Aranjuez. Private. The Cura Merino is upon the road again with a few Cavaliers whose principal object seems the plunder of travellers and the interruption of couriers—two arrived last night from the Duke de Frias and Rothschild completely de-valised and Martinez sends off one this morning to Paris to fetch duplicates of the dispatches.

I have just had a long conversation with him upon the manner in which Don Carlos should be dealt with in the event of his surrendering himself or being taken prisoner, either of which may happen any day in his present desperate condition. I took care to express my conviction that he would not be treated with violence or in any way unbecoming his rank or fallen fortunes. There was however no necessity for my doing so. The views of Martinez de la Rosa, which he said were those of the Queen likewise, upon this point are most proper and generous. His object is to provide that the two Pretenders (for the arguments which are applicable to Don Carlos are equally so to Don Miguel) shall not take up their abode at a Court which has not recognized the Queen of Spain and given, as it were, thereby a pledge not to countenance those who dispute her rights. He considers that if they went to Vienna or Petersburg they would be kept in the leash of the Holy Alliance ready to be slipped at Spain whenever the peace of Europe may become troubled or internal commotion, of which much must be looked for during the early struggles against constitutional government, manifests itself in the Peninsula. He would therefore make the future provision for these Princes dependent upon their residence, as well as their abstaining from all attempts upon the thrones of Spain and Portugal. He was not prepared to say where he should wish these gentlemen to be transported to but he was desirous that I should submit these views to you. What he wished and what I positively objected to was that we should take charge of them, but I made him understand that the English Government with every friendly disposition to the Queen was absolutely without power to control the proceedings or order the comings and goings of the Pretenders if they came to England—that the Tory party would not fail to honor and exalt them—perhaps even in time of need to equip them for a hostile expedition as effectually as Russia or Austria—and that as the Carlist party here would not fail to represent the favorable reception of the Princes in England, either as the underhand work of the Government or the general sense of the country, I thought that the moral effect of the Quadruple Treaty from which so much support to the present order of things was expected would be destroyed. Martinez de la Rosa completely agreed with me, and I believe he would now as soon have the Dons in Madrid as in London.

There is another matter which he wished me to represent to you, and which I ought perhaps to have made a dispatch upon but the short notice I have had of the courier's departure leaves me no time. As soon as matters are concluded in Portugal Rodil and his army are to proceed to the Northern Provinces and the Government are going to direct all their energies to that quarter. They are desirous therefore that some English vessels of war should for a time cruize on the northern coast of Spain, partly in order to prevent supplies arriving to the insurgents, but principally to make them feel that le traité est une vérité and that we not only intended to eject the Pretenders but to prevent their return—and to assist by all proper means in the re-establishment of tranquillity.[1] The Government think that this would have more effect upon the rebellious *masses* in the provinces, if properly explained to them, than the addition of Rodil's army, as well as be a practical denial of the versions given by their chiefs of the treaty, and of the audacious lies propagated by the Carlists here respecting our sincerity. I told Martinez I thought you would not see any inconvenience in this and that he might be assured, whenever it was in their power, he would find the present Government cordially ready to come to the assistance of Spain.

PS. I have advice today from Coruña of the arrival of the muskets.

Received 6[2] June.

GC/CL/137; Clar. Dep. C.451/2 (143-146)

[1] The British Government later acceded to this request. (P to V, 26 Aug. 1834, no. 48, FO 72/419.)
[2] Apparently corrected from '5'.

55 Villiers to Palmerston, 30 May 1834

Madrid. Private. Having ascertained that my slave trade notes were to be discussed at the Council of Regency today, I came up this morning from Aranjuez in order to speak to Amarillas and others upon the subject and intending to return tonight, but I have this moment received a courier from Martinez de la Rosa with a copy of the dispatch he received this afternoon from Rodil—and to tell me that a courier will pass through Madrid on his way to Paris in ½ an hour. I have only had time therefore to make a hasty translation of the dispatch. Rayneval, who came up with me this morning, will send a dispatch for the telegraph. Nothing is known about Don Miguel.

I sent a courier to Howard two days ago requesting on the part of the Spanish Government that Don Carlos might be well treated and closely guarded, in the event of his surrendering himself, till the Four Powers had conferred upon his future destination—promising on their part, le cas échéant, to do the same by Don Miguel.[1] William Harvey has just arrived from Aranjuez, having heard that a courier was to be sent off, and has brought me a copy of the above dispatch which I accordingly send.

Enclosure: Memorandum by Villiers, summarizing a despatch from General Rodil to Martínez de la Rosa, 27 May 1834. (The despatch announced that Don Carlos had agreed to leave the Peninsula, and had accepted everything that Grant, the British secretary of legation in Lisbon, had proposed. The Miguelite General-in-Chief was also prepared to negotiate a surrender.)

Received 9 June.

GC/CL/138; Clar. Dep. C.451/2 (147-148)

[1] V to Howard de Walden, 28 May 1834, cypher no. 6, enclosed with V to P, 30 May 1834, no. 70, FO 72/423.

56 Palmerston to Villiers, 31 May 1834

Copy. Foreign Office. I have no time to write and yet I should wish to do so to vent my wrath upon the stupidity of Pedro's clerks or the bad faith of Pedro's Government. We have taken however the only course which was feasible and we shall lose only a couple of days by it, but I cannot lay the treaty before Parliament nor communicate it to other Courts till we get back the corrected copy of the Portuguese ratification. The progress of events in Portugal seems however now to be so rapid that I expect the whole thing to be over before the mail of tonight reaches Lisbon. How provoking that the northerly storms should just have chosen to blow while the blundering ratification was on its way here. Miraflores has a little mistaken the nature of Caradoc's duties,[1] and in his communication to the Spanish Government represents them as somewhat more extensive than they really are; you had better set that right by shewing Martinez and Zarco del Valle the copy of Caradoc's instructions.

Varium et mutabile semper Anglica administratio; here is a change but it is only of men[2] and not of principles or policy . . . .

Docketed: No. 9.

GC/CL/1227

[1] Caradoc was sent by the British Government to observe and report on the operation of Rodil's army in Portugal.

[2] The Earl of Ripon, Sir James Graham, the Duke of Richmond and Lord Stanley had resigned from the Cabinet.

57   Villiers to Palmerston, 2 June 1834

Aranjuez. Private. Events have followed each other with such unexpected rapidity that the objects of the treaty have been accomplished before the ratification of it has been received. A blunder, not an irreparable one I hope, has been committed in not communicating with Rodil previously to the arrangements being made for Don Carlos's departure.[1] My dispatch of the 28th to Howard will probably have arrived in time to prevent his sailing. Should it not have done so this Government will stand in the predicament of having borne the brunt of the war and brought every thing to a successful issue except the object for which they entered the Portuguese territory, for although the unconditional departure of Don Carlos would have satisfied the country 2 months ago it would certainly not do so now, when Rodil might have made him prisoner if he had not desired to leave the triumph of terminating the contest to the Portuguese, when Don Carlos shewed himself prepared to accede to any terms which were offered to him, and when proper conditions have been imposed upon his brother Pretender. I hope Howard will be able to repair this blunder[2] though His Highness may perhaps not be so amenable on board a

British man of war as at Ebora.

Martinez is very desirous now that the objects of the treaty have been fulfilled that some fresh agreement should be entered into by the Four Powers in order to prevent the revival of all that has been destroyed, and that the tranquillity which may now be expected should not be disturbed or threatened. He desires to leave this matter to the conference in London but he considers that the ultimate purposes of the treaty will be but half accomplished if England and France do not hold out to the intriguers of Europe that they intend to keep the peace of the Peninsula. Such a declaration would I think keep the absolutists every where in order and the Pretenders will be little inclined to risk the loss of their pensions if they are given quamdiu se bene gesserint. This course would produce an admirable effect here. It would strengthen the Government and give confidence to the liberal party—it would render this Western Confederation more compact and give us fresh power and new rights in the Peninsula—founded upon real gratitude—the expectation of future advantage.

Rodil and his army are going to the North and I have good reason to hope he will carry an olive branch with him—every day makes it more evident that those provinces are not to be conquered by the sword.

PS. Caradoc arrived here yesterday morning.

Received 13 June.

GC/CL/139; Clar. Dep. C.451/2 (149-151)

[1] 'General Rodil is much dissatisfied at the want of courtesy exhibited towards him by the Portuguese marshals who . . . have contracted an engagement with Don Carlos without any previous communication with the Spanish headquarters and without even stipulating, as in the case of Don Miguel, that Don Carlos should not return to Spain, nor again disturb the tranquillity of the Peninsula.' (V to P, 2 June 1834, no. 72, FO 72/423.)

[2] 'At the earnest request of His Excellency [Martínez de la Rosa] I am about to send a courier to Lord Howard de Walden to request that the Infant Don Carlos shall, at least, be required to enter into engagements similar to those subscribed to by Don Miguel.' (ibid.)

58 Villiers to Palmerston, 8 June 1834

Aranjuez. Private. As Martinez has given me short notice of the departure of his courier and that I am in the fifth day of a sharp fit of the gout I will only add a few lines in supplement of my dispatch to say how seriously this Government have at heart that Don Carlos should *take the pledges*. No set of repealers were ever more anxious to bind a doubtful candidate than are the Queen and her Ministers to impose upon Don Carlos the obligation, which to him would be a sacred one, not again to disturb the tranquillity of the Peninsula.[1] Had Don Miguel been suffered to depart unpledged neither the Government or the public would have been so anxious upon this subject, but now they think that Spanish interests have been neglected by the very people whom Spanish aid had rendered victorious, and at a moment when the generous forbearance of Rodil, who was only 5 leagues distant, prevented his making Don Carlos and his family prisoners and imposing upon them any conditions he pleased. If therefore it is possible to get a promise from Don Carlos before he goes to Holland (if to Holland he is going—for nothing is known here upon that except its being incidentally mentioned in Howard's dispatch)[2] this Government would be infinitely indebted to you and we should be considered to have done a great act of friendship. I don't think Don Carlos, if he intends to keep quiet, should hesitate in saying so, but if he will not, I much doubt whether in the present state of public opinion the Government could allow him a pension, or if they did whether the Cortes would not withdraw it afterwards. There is every wish on the part of Martinez and as he tells me on the part of the Queen to give him a princely provision. If His Highness is made to give any promise it would be well worth while to let this Government know of it by the telegraph.

We have heard, but without any authentic particulars, of the changes in the Government. I need scarcely say what my anxiety is for further intelligence.

Received 19 June.

GC/CL/140; Clar. Dep. C.451/2 (152-153)

[1] V, however, told Martínez that he thought it was now too late to impose conditions upon Don Carlos, for which there was no provision in the April treaty. (V to P, 8 June 1834, no. 75, FO 72/423.)

[2] Howard de Walden to V, 1 June 1834, enclosed with V to P, 8 June 1834, no. 75, FO 72/423.

59 Villiers to Palmerston, 14 June 1834

Madrid. Private. We have all returned from Aranjuez by reason of the cholera being supposed to be about 160 miles off, and I don't believe that any number of people, not being gypsies, ever decamped with such speed before. Her Majesty however upon the matter of cholera is a monomaniac and if it come Madridways I foresee we shall have to undergo every form of prevention which panic or ignorance have yet devised.

Martinez has just been here, I not being able to go to him owing to a severe fit of gout, and I have requested him to write to Perez de Castro to cooperate with Howard in whatever measures you think fit to direct for keeping Pedro in order, and some will I am sure be necessary to prevent our new ally being a clog and a shame to us. He seems not to understand that the prosperity of Portugal and not the indulgence of his caprice was the object of the treaty and from all I can gather he will not learn it unless he is threatened by the other 3 Powers with opposition to his regency when the Cortes meet. Nothing but an appeal to his personal interests or personal fears will make him select moderate Ministers and put away the adventurers who feed his vanity and fill his purse. The question of very bad government in Portugal is of great importance to Spain—measures of confiscation or vengeance there will not lack imitators here, and we are not so steady upon our legs here as to make it impossible for the lesser Power to drag us down to its level. I am quite sure that in order to make the influence of the treaty of wide spreading utility, in order to realize the fears of Metternich, and the hopes of the German States, that Portugal should for some time to come have the benefit of Your Lordship's active consideration.

Martinez de la Rosa has an odd way of doing business—he pops a decree into the Gazette this morning giving a Grand Cross of Charles III to Talleyrand . . . .

Things in general look well here—save the Milicia Urbana which for its age is an unruly bantling, and when it waxes stronger will I fear give us much trouble—it has been mismanaged throughout and it is saucy, overbearing, and hyper-constitutional.

I heard today viâ Paris that there was a chance of the secretaryship of embassy at Constantinople being vacant and of your appointing William Hervey to it. Both reports may be untrue and although I should be sorry to say any thing which might interfere with advancement of his, I cannot let the opportunity pass of saying how great a loss I should consider his removal, or of telling you what a zealous intelligent perfect man of business I consider him.

I have just received from Lord Granville the account of your triumphant majority on the 2d . . . .

Don Pedro means to keep up his army on a war footing, i.e. 30,000 men he says.

Received 26 June.

GC/CL/141; Clar. Dep. C.451/2 (154-157)

60 Palmerston to Villiers, 17 June 1834

Copy. Foreign Office. Private. I send you copies of my instructions to Backhouse and of his report to me,[1] you will see from these what has passed about Don Carlos. It was on Friday last the 13th that we heard of the arrival of the Donegal at Portsmouth. Miraflores came to me much disturbed at Carlos having been allowed to leave Portugal without entering into engagements as to Spain similar to those taken by Miguel as to Portugal. Upon talking the matter over together, we agreed that the only thing to be done was that he should go down to propose an arrangement to Carlos, and that I should send down somebody to sound the way for him, and at the same time to afford him all the assistance which an authorized representative of the English Government could give. I pointed out that the 4th article of the Treaty furnished him an obvious ground for a negotiation. No provisions could be asked from Carlos till a provision could at the same time be offered to him. There was nobody at Lisbon authorized to offer the latter, and therefore nobody who could be justified in prescribing the former. He might do both. To this he objected that he had no instructions as to the amount of income which his Government would assign to Carlos though he was sure the Queen would do whatever was right and handsome on this matter. After some consideration, Lord Grey and I pressed him to fix it at £30,000 a year, that being about the amount of his former income in Spain and that appearing to bear such a proportion to the allowance made to Miguel as becomes the superior dignity and power of Spain, compared with Portugal; and as might fairly follow from the circumstance that Carlos is married and has children; while Miguel has neither chick nor child; and that Carlos has lost all his property in Spain while Miguel is to be allowed to dispose of his private property in Portugal.

Miraflores immediately took the gentlemanlike view of this matter, and feeling all the importance of doing the thing handsomely as well as promptly, drew up a set of articles upon this basis, and two remarkably well written letters for Carlos, and off he went to Portsmouth on Saturday morning. Backhouse could not go quite so soon as I had to send his instructions down to Windsor for the approval of the King, but he got to Portsmouth on Saturday evening. The King not only approved entirely the instructions which I proposed to give, but by a private letter from Sir Herbert Taylor, authorized Backhouse to say in case of need that if Carlos refused the offers and conditions of Miraflores and should take up his residence in this country, he would not be noticed in any way whatever by the King, who would refuse to have with him any communication of any kind, direct or indirect.

The King is accordingly very much disgusted with Carlos's refusal and particularly indignant that a man who has not had the courage to expose his own person, and who has fled from the scene of danger, should still persist in endeavouring to involve his country in the misery and bloodshed of civil war, himself keeping aloof from the contest. He says this conduct is neither Spanish nor English.

It appears that Sampayo, Miguel's consul general here, and Saraiva the ex secretary of the Portuguese mission, went on board the Donegal on Sunday, and are to be employed by Carlos to manage his arrangements. Two more active marplots he could not have to do with. But Saraiva has I suppose told him of the million of francs sent by Charles 10th and while that lasts Carlos will not think of submission. It was quite right to make the attempt and it would have been a very good thing if it had succeeded, because a promise by Carlos not to return to Spain would have thrown a damp over the spirits of his partisans, but I do not think that in reality the failure is of much consequence. In the first place it was to be expected. It was very unlikely that Carlos advised by his Princesses and by the Bishop of Leon would ever give such a promise. I do not believe he would have given it in Portugal, unless in Rodil's hands, and with a shooting party drawn up in front of him and the handkerchief ready to bind his eyes; and if he *had* made such a promise in Portugal under duress, he would have been supported by public opinion in afterwards refusing to be bound by it. It is perhaps lucky that he was not asked to give the promise before he sailed from Portugal; for it would have been awkward to have detained him as prisoner for refusing to give it, and equally so to let him go, after he had so refused.

But after so prompt and complete an accomplishment of the first object of the Treaty and with the moral effect which this will produce all over Europe, the Spanish Government need give themselves very little uneasiness about Carlos; besides his personal character is a security against much danger from him. He will not land like Murat with half a dozen followers, nor march like Bonaparte in triumph from a sea port to the capital. I believe that on the whole it is desireable that he should remain in England; he can do less harm and be less troublesome to Spain here than in many other parts of Europe, and I do not think the Tories will find their account in making any fuss with him.

I took care that Miraflores should be received at Portsmouth with all the attentions due to his rank and position and he was saluted on his arrival and departure and had a guard of honor during his stay. Pray express in the strongest manner to Martinez de la Rosa my thanks to him for sending me such a colleague as Miraflores. He is so intelligent and handy and at the same time so perfectly single minded and straightforward and so free from all the humbug of diplomacy that it is a real pleasure to do business with him. While I am on this subject, pray tell our minister plenipotentiary at Madrid how very much satisfied all the Government are with his ability and zeal.

Domestic matters are settling down . . . .

Docketed: No. 10.

GC/CL/1228

[1] See P to John Backhouse, Permanent Under-Secretary at the Foreign Office, 13 June 1834, and Backhouse to P, 15 June 1834, nos. 1 and 2, FO 72/432. Backhouse reported 'I regret to have to acquaint you that Don Carlos refuses in the most positive manner to enter into any negotiations with the Marquis de Miraflores or to give any promise that he will abstain from encouraging his partisans in their hostilities against the Government of Queen Isabella II. On the contrary, he declares that he will never cease to assert his title to the Crown of Spain and he repudiates all pecuniary provision to be furnished on the condition of his making such a declaration as that which has been made by Dom Miguel.'

61 Villiers to Palmerston, 21 June 1834

Madrid. Private. We have received intelligence from Lisbon that the Portuguese erratum has been corrected and amended copies of the ratification furnished to the three ministers—this is of importance as far as it regards the good faith of Don Pedro, though of none, as you will have learned long ago, in the fulfillment of the objects of the Treaty.

Howard is very angry with the Spanish Government and calls them illiberal, ungrateful, cruel, selfish and what not. It is hardly worth while entering into long details upon this matter, for with a little good will and good temper all this may be settled, but Howard is wrong—the Spanish Government had a right to complain of no communication being made to General Rodil who was only at a distance of four leagues when Don Carlos surrendered—and as others acted on behalf of Spain, that the same conditions were not imposed upon our Pretender as upon the other—the same right, or no right, existing under the treaty; they had a right to complain of the enormous list (upwards of 250 Martinez de la Rosa assures me) given by Don Carlos of persons composing his suite and who may now be helping intrigues abroad before this country is finally pacified; they had a right to complain that the greater part of these persons were to be shipped off in two merchant brigs (one of them I believe a Russian vessel) unconvoyed by a ship of war and without security against their being landed in the North. The Spanish Government were wrong in having allowed Perez de Castro to delay his departure so long but if in the absence of any agent Don Carlos had been permitted to remain on board the Donegal till a courier had arrived from Madrid, and 8 and 40 hours longer would have been sufficient if one had been dispatched either from Ebora or by Rodil, suitable provision might have been made for Don Carlos and his family, their effects would have been restored, the amount of allowance fixed and the terms of the amnesty settled. This Government accordingly feels that they have played a somewhat sorry part in the denouement of a drama in which they were the principal actors, and are sore about it—but I daresay their equanimity will be restored when they receive tidings from England of the disposal of the Carlist Cargos.

Quesada has been removed from his command in the provinces, which has been marked by a series of disasters such as might be expected to befall a passionate ignorant sabreur. Rodil has been appointed Commander in Chief—he is a brave officer and his justice and good discipline have always made him popular with the army, but I doubt his tact and *politique* to carry on this war in a manner to give a chance of permanent peace. I have therefore made some exertions successfully to put about him the cleverest fellow I have met with in Spain—and he is Cordoba—who was minister in Portugal. When I left England my impressions of that man were very erroneous. I thought him the purest Miguelite that ever lived and the incarnation of Holy Alliance principles—he certainly acted up to his instructions with zeal while he was at Lisbon—but I found by his correspondence that he was always warning the Government against their mistaken course. His activity prevented Don Carlos from entering Spain when the King died, and when he returned here and held strong language to Zea upon his madness in upholding Miguel Zea quarrelled with him and became his bitterest enemy. I have seen a great deal of him and think most highly of his abilities. Rodil is delighted at having him and if I am not greatly mistaken you will see that he will be the real pacificator of those provinces. I shall be in constant correspondence with him and be able to communicate my views (which I have the vanity to think are sound) upon this, to Spain, most important question.

Caradoc finding his occupation gone in Portugal is very desirous to accompany the chef to whom he was to have been attached to the North. I gave a hint of this, at Caradoc's request, to Martinez de la Rosa quite unofficially and in confidence telling him you knew nothing about it, and begging him not to give it a second thought if he considered there would be an objection on the part of any body, but that as the campaign was likely to redound to the credit of Rodil and his troops, he might perhaps like to invite Caradoc to be a spectator, and I didn't doubt he would be a faithful reporter, of their deeds, and that he would accept with gratitude such an act of civility. He seemed much pleased and flattered and said he would speak to the Minister of War about it. I hope you will have no objection.

The appointment of Toreno[1] is a good deed and I hope there will now be a chance of establishing some commercial relations with Spain—his predecessor[2] was the creator of the present system which is destructive of all trade except the smuggler's. Toreno will infuse a little vigor and fixity of purpose into the Cabinet of which it stands greatly in need.

Martinez de la Rosa has set his soul upon a Quadruple Declaration with respect to the future[3]—pray therefore send me some mollia verba for him if you don't comply with his proposal—he is certainly prepared to cut the Holy Alliance dead and put Spain entirely under the protection of England and France but more particularly of England.

Received 1 July.

GC/CL/142; Clar. Dep. C.451/2 (158-162)

[1] As Minister of Finance.

[2] Imaz.

[3] Martínez was anxious that the Powers that signed the Quadruple Treaty should declare 'that in the event of Don Carlos, or Don Miguel, seeking to assert their pretensions to the throne of Spain or Portugal, the Treaty should be considered again to come into operation and that the same means which have been used to expel the Pretenders would then be resorted to to prevent the tranquillity of the Peninsula from being endangered'. (V to P, 21 June 1834, no. 78, FO 72/423.)

62   Palmerston to Villiers, 21 June 1834

Copy. Foreign Office. I have little to add to what I wrote to you some days ago. I have had no communication from Carlos since he landed, and know nothing directly of his proceedings. Indirectly I hear that the[1] means to come to the neighbourhood of London as soon as Sampayo can find him a house. Perhaps he is as well here as any where else, for though he has a great freedom and opportunities of private communication, yet on the other hand all he does may be known, and if he was resident in the dominions of any Power hostile to the Queen, the Government of the country might by its connivance give him even more facilities and certainly greater secrecy than he will find here.

I shall try if it is not possible in answering Miraflores' note to say something that may satisfy the Spanish Government as to our future intentions of supporting them, but we do not like to engage blindfold in prospective engagement, nor to guarantee crowns on particular heads.

We are still *hoping* upon the slave trade question. I should be very glad if we could get something to communicate to Parliament on this matter before the session is over.

Docketed: No. 11. By messenger.

GC/CL/1229

[1] *Recte* he?

63   Villiers to Palmerston, 28 June 1834

Madrid. Private. My dispatch of this evening will give you but a slight notion of the confusion which exists and is likely to continue in this place. Martinez assured Rayneval and me yesterday that he should return from St. Ildefonso immediately though at the time he had ordered his family and his office to remove there. He sent us passports this morning without telling us a word that when we got half way we should not be allowed to proceed, and he separates himself by a long quarantine from the Corps Diplomatique without announcing the fact or appointing a deputy. To be sure he has just named an Under Secretary—one Villalba—the most notorious booby in Spain, who has hitherto filled to the utter confusion of the Corps Diplomatique on Court days the important post of Introducer of Ambassadors—but even this appointment he has not announced to us and all foreign business is for a time suspended which places it upon a perfect equality with the domestic. Nothing can be less decent or less wise than the Queen's betaking herself to an exceeding high place on the first approach of danger, with just as much of her Court as is *necessary* for her personal service, and then establishing instantly two cordons and a quarantine between herself and the town where her Ministers are publishing twice a day that the cholera does *not* exist. The Cortes are still to be called together on the 24th July but the Cortes probably won't come, call they never so loudly, if the cholera is bad, for the alarm is excessive. Every body's first impulse was to run away and while they were debating where they should go, as the whole south of Spain has got the cholera and the whole north has got the rebels, the Government steps in with parental kindness and solves their difficulties by preventing any one quitting Madrid except themselves. The whole must be seen to be believed.

I am very glad that you seem to have given your opinion to Miraflores upon the manner in which the war is waged in the provinces for it has produced a great effect upon Martinez who has no objection to cruel things provided they don't injure his reputation for humanity. He told me how much your erroneous notions upon the subject had vexed him for the Government were acting with all mildness, only shooting the rebel officers[1] whom they took prisoners, while the soldiers were sent to the gallies for life. I took the liberty of reminding him of the glee with which he had only 5 minutes before informed me that the

Queen's troops had obtained a victory and left 800 men dead upon the field—Spaniards killed by Spaniards—and that he must expect that such facts and the dreadful system of retaliation which was adopted by both parties could not but produce a most unfavorable impression in England—he assured me such things were inevitable and that in our civil wars we had been quite as cruel. I assured him he was indebted to his imagination for his facts, and begged him at all events to look at Portugal where during 3 years of civil war there were no instances of such barbarities in cold blood—however Miraflores's dispatch did good for Martinez told me that he was in the act of composing a full amnesty for Rodil to publish before he took the field.

M. de Rigny has written to M. de Rayneval that Don Carlos refuses all pension unless given unconditionally. The Government are a good deal annoyed at this as it will be a triumph and an encouragement to the Carlist party and it shews they were right in regretting that the same conditions were not imposed upon Don Carlos at Ebora as upon Don Miguel where with the fear of Rodil before his eyes he would have consented to any thing.

PS. I believe you have learned from Howard that certain papers containing an account of Holy Alliance proceedings with respect to Don Carlos were stopped moyennant a large sum of money on their way to Lisbon—Howard's agent in the business brought the papers here and I am endeavouring to get him reimbursed. Previously to delivering them to Martinez I took a copy of the only one which is now of any importance—the history of the money which Don Carlos has found at his disposal in England. I herewith enclose it and I am sorry that there is not time to have it translated.[2]

June 29th. Rayneval has delayed his courier till this morning but I have nothing new to add except the publication of a Royal Order that the Queen, considering it a most sacred duty that no employé should be absent from his post at this moment of crisis or fail to give examples of courage and unselfishness, forbids all such to stir from their posts which will be declared vacant if they do. There is a general disposition however to prefer Her Majesty's example to her precepts.

The Minister of War called here last night—he was very obliging about Caradoc and seemed to think that his accompanying the army was a flattering compliment to Rodil—he wrote last night for the Queen's final permission and when it arrives Caradoc will set out.

The Deputies for Madrid are designated, though not yet elected, they are good men—having a knowledge of business—but not over-friendly to the Government.

First enclosure: Memorandum of 'Supplies of officers, men, ships, arms, money, etc., which have at different times been procured in England for Dom Miguel and Don Carlos. Mr. Villiers, no. 33, March 27 1834.'

Second enclosure: Copy, M. Saraiva (formerly Portuguese secretary of legation in London) to Dona Maria Francisca de Asis (wife of Don Carlos and sister of Dom Miguel), London, 22 April 1834, offering his services as an accredited representative of Don Carlos. (In Spanish.)

Third enclosure: English translation of the above, endorsed 'Received from Lord Howard de Walden'.

Received 8 July.

GC/CL/143; Clar. Dep. C.451/2 (163-167)

¹ 'officers' underlined in pencil, possibly by P.
² Possibly the second enclosure.

64 Villiers to Palmerston, 3 July 1834

Madrid. Private. Martinez de la Rosa's foolish new Under Secretary has given me such a minimized notice of the courier's departure that I have no time for writing.

I received your dispatch of the 21st and letters of the 13th and 17th nearly at the same moment the day before yesterday.[1] I sent a copy of the dispatch no. 31 to Martinez de la Rosa and I enclose you his answer to my letter. I likewise communicated it to M. de las Amarillas and Toreno. I likewise sent an extract to Martinez from your private letter as to the King's opinion of Don Carlos and your own upon Miraflores—the result of all which is that the Cabinet and the Council of Regency are delighted and grateful for all the interest which the English Government take in the concerns of Spain and the cordial *and graceful* manner in which you render service to this country.

I took care yesterday at the tail of my letter containing all these good things to Martinez to make a contrast between our activity and good faith and the manner in which they had dealt with the slave question, upon which they ought to be influenced by 100 motives of honour, honesty and humanity which did not apply to us. . . .

I hope you will approve of my not quitting Madrid—Rayneval is principally induced to do so by the fears of his family, but the quarantine will prevent his reaching St. Ildefonso before the 14th and Martinez de la Rosa must be here on the 22nd—besides the real seat of government is here and the excessive unpopularity which the Queen has earned for herself within the last week is alarming. The people openly declare that she has left Madrid in order to accoucher quietly at St. Ildefonso (I don't believe that there happens to be the least truth in the reports which for some time have been circulated about her condition) and if Don Francisco[2] had any intelligence wherewith to assist his wishes, in the ungarrisoned state of the town and the disaffected spirit of the National Guard, he might be King in 4 and 20 hours. Amarillas, who *is* the Council of Regency, and Toreno, who *might* at any moment be the Council of Ministers, are very much pleased at my staying and I think in the event of any catastrophe I might be of some utility here—these considerations have alone influenced me as it is personally quite indifferent to me going to St. Ildefonso or staying here.

The Government were pleased and flattered at Caradoc's wish to accompany Rodil. He set out yesterday muni with all proper recommendations to the General and I have taken care that there should be no misunderstanding about the character in which he goes—that of an invited spectator.

Many thanks for your approbation of my proceedings which it was most agreable to me to receive.

I think it will be desireable not to tell Miraflores what I say upon the state of public opinion here and the Queen's danger, for Martinez de la Rosa who never comes down from the uppermost regions of poetical optimism is blind to all that is passing around him.

Rayneval will do his best to induce the Queen to open the Cortes in person but I do not think there is much chance of his succeeding.

Enclosure: Martínez de la Rosa (San Ildefonso) to Villiers, 2 July 1834, thanking him for the copy of Palmerston's despatch. (In French.)

Received 14 July.

GC/CL/144; Clar. Dep. C.451/2 (167-170)

[1] P's despatches related to the British Government's attempt to persuade Don Carlos to renounce his pretensions to the Spanish throne in return for a life pension.

[2] Youngest brother of Ferdinand VII.

65   Villiers to Palmerston, 4 July 1834

Madrid. Private. I avail myself of the departure of a commercial courier to tell you that accounts have been received this morning from most of the provinces of the elections of the Deputies. Toreno assures me he is well satisfied with them and that although among the number there are some of the hotheaded heroes of 1820 he thinks they will upon the whole turn out a reasonable manageable body with a fair portion of intelligence and knowledge of the wants of their country.

I enclose you a letter I received this morning from Martinez in reply to mine communicating your instructions to Backhouse and his report of the interview with Don Carlos. He pledges himself as you will see to a speedy answer upon the slave question.

I have been taking some pains to make him understand the rationale of our parliamentary forms and proceedings, as he is quite unequal to the task, which he is determined to execute singlehanded, of drawing up a set of regulations for the internal government of the Cortes.

I have endeavoured to make him feel the immense importance it is to the liberty of the Assembly and the maintenance of order that a power should exist in it delegated by the Assembly and respected by it. I have pointed out the means by which we arrive at this and the evils, far beyond what at first might be calculated, which spring from disorder—evils which, however much they may be dreaded by us, should be guarded against in a tenfold degree here, where ardent passions and ignorance of the tactics of deliberative assemblies render them still more probable.

There is a great deal of cholerine and serious illness here though no decided case of cholera. The Queen however appears not to think herself sufficiently out of the reach of danger at St. Ildefonso and is preparing to go to Galicia upon the first announcement of cholera in Madrid. She is surrounded by contagionist physicians who encourage her fears and if she is so rash as to remove still further from Madrid she will put her daughter's throne in imminent peril.

I feel satisfied that I have done rightly in remaining here.

Enclosure: Martínez de la Rosa (San Ildefonso) to Villiers, 3 July 1834, on the slave trade negotiations, etc.

Received 16 July.

GC/CL/145; Clar. Dep. C.451/2 (170-171)

66   Villiers to Palmerston, 8¹ July 1834

Madrid. Private. Things are not very flourishing and unless some adviser not so troubled with optimism as Martinez de la Rosa makes the Queen sensible of the dangers of her position, they will get worse. The people don't believe in the cholera and are indignant at the sanitary regulations, while all ranks and parties agree that the Queen has retreated in the way she has done, cutting off all communication between herself and the capital, for the purpose of laying² in away from vulgar observation. I have no reason for believing this opinion to be correct, but if it is false it makes her return to Madrid more imperatively necessary.

Rayneval is performing his nine days' quarantine and has been treated with so much indignity that he would have returned at once if he had not resolved to tell the Queen some truths which may be worth her daughter's throne to her. A recital of the almost incredible absurdities which have been committed since the first report of the approach of the cholera would only weary you, and I should not have insisted upon them as much as I have, if it were not for the universal unpopularity which they have procured for the Queen and the political consequences which may ensue from that. All parties avail themselves of it and many steps have been gained during the past fortnight towards familiarizing men's minds with the impossibility of the present state of things lasting. The factious insolence of the National Guard increases every day—the infantry have made a formal demand to be furnished with ball cartridges, and the cavalry, which were assembled two days ago to hear their regulations read, declared they would not submit to them. It is now more than a month ago that Rayneval and I formally communicated to Martinez various facts respecting the National Guard which had come to our knowledge, and warned him while it was yet time to repress the spirit by which it was animated, but he assured us that the whole corps was devoted to the Queen and that he had the utmost confidence in its loyalty.

In all this there is perhaps nothing really formidable now except the impotence of the Government to prevent its becoming so; and at a moment when the Government should be utilizing such energy and abilities as they possess, one half of it places itself in incommunication with the other, and the Prime Minister occupies himself in concocting measures of precaution against a non-existing epidemic, while all the great questions which have to be submitted in a fortnight's time to the Cortes are as crude and unprepared as they were 3 months ago.

I of course know very few of the new Deputies by name or reputation, and have therefore to take my opinion of them from others. Toreno declares himself to be well satisfied, but the movement party is so much elated that I expect the liberalism of the Chamber will go beyond that of the Government.

There is a certain M. Ardouin here; a French banker—with whose name you must probably be acquainted. . . .

The news from the provinces is not good. In Navarre, although the departure of Don Carlos and the approach of Rodil were generally known, the insurgents are far from being disheartened. They are making fresh levies and seem disposed to act more upon the offensive than hitherto, while Merino and one or two other leaders are preparing to harrass Rodil's rear, though their banditti will probably not do much more than intercept his communications with the Government.

Toreno has just sent me word that he is in hopes the Queen will now be induced to open the Cortes in person. If she does this she will avert many a disaster.

Received 18 July.

GC/CL/146; Clar. Dep. C.451/1 (1-4)

[1] C.451/1 is dated 7 July.
[2] C.451/1 has 'lying'.

67 Palmerston to Villiers, 10 July 1834

Foreign Office. Private and confidential. You will learn by this messenger that the Government is virtually dissolved. . . .

Copy. Docketed: By M.de Miraflores' messenger.

GC/CL/1230

68 Villiers to Palmerston, 14 July 1834

Madrid. Private. I received your private letter of the 27th the day before yesterday. . . .[1]

I have again told him [Martínez] that the pressure of business of which he complains was no excuse in re the Equipment Act. . . .

It is impossible to pronounce with any certainty upon the composition of the Cortes—many of the Procuradores are unknown, and others who have figured in former times may now be very altered men. My impressions from what I have been able to collect are that there will be little intelligence and much crude liberalism, the tendency of which will be to exhibit itself in faction. I look to the tact and vigor of Toreno for guiding this assembly, and to his knowledge of the necessary reforms and firmness of purpose in effecting them, for carrying public opinion with him, at least during the first session. If he had been in opposition I would not have given a week's purchase for Martinez's Government.

I have had a letter from Caradoc—he has been very well received by Rodil who expressed himself flattered at Caradoc's being appointed to accompany him. He finds, as I was afraid he would, a most unconciliatory feeling towards the provinces among the military—their only idea is complete conquest and then complete assimilation to the rest of Spain. This will never do I am sure—for even if Rodil were to succeed in conquering them he would not pacify them. The Government might easily if they undertook it with judgement and good will retrench such of the privileges as exempt the provinces from contributions, recruits, etc. the same as the rest of Spain—these they would be quite willing to treat about and these are what principally signify to the Government, but the provinces insist upon maintaining their local administrations and taxing themselves as cheaply (i.e. in the collection) and as equally as they have hitherto done. Their mountainous country is too poor to support a system which has reduced the fairest provinces of Spain to poverty and waste.

Leopold is at last recognized.[2] I have known the M. Argaiz who is appointed chargé d'affaires in Belgium for many years—he is a sensible good sort of man and a near relation of Alava's.

The Holy Allies are beside themselves with disgust at the favorable aspect of things in this country. I hear that Lieberman has been pledging himself to M. Ancillon that the whole fabric here is one of straw and that its days are numbered. The Sardinian chargé d'affaires here who seems an unprejudiced man has been writing the simple truth to his Court upon Spanish affairs—nothing extenuating, but not setting down all in malice as his chef did. This has given such offence at Turin that a private friend has written to warn him that if he wished not to be ruined in his profession his dispatches must be in a completely contrary sense. This of course was communicated to me confidentially.

Received 24 July.

GC/CL/147; Clar. Dep. C.451/1 (5-10)

[1] No copy of this letter survives in the Palmerston Papers. It related to a proposed gift to P from the Queen.
[2] As King of the Belgians.

69 Palmerston to Villiers, 15 July 1834

Copy. Foreign Office. $\frac{1}{2}$ past 1 a.m. Private. I send you a messenger because I think it may be of importance that you should have the earliest information that the new ministerial arrangements are virtually settled; that is to say subject to the King's approbation to be taken by Melbourne tomorrow at Windsor. . . .

I am very glad you remained at Madrid; it was quite the right thing to do; and it is there that you can be of most use; I will send you an official sanction, but I have no means of sending you anything but this letter tonight. I hope you will be able to make good the expectation you hold out to me about the slave trade convention. There is nothing the Spanish Government could do that would be so acceptable to us.

Carlos has set off incognito to go as it is supposed to the Spanish frontier; I shall believe him in Spain when I know the fact, but till then shall doubt his intention of going thither. It seems more probable that he may intend to have some meeting with Calomarde[1] and some people from the Spanish Carlists, and that when this meeting is over he will return to England. The French Government could not allow him to linger on the frontier, and his own timidity will prevent him from entering Spain. It is however just possible that he may be encouraged by a notion that he could always in case of defeat make good his retreat into France.

The Spanish Government ought not to be so much disturbed at the sending away from Portugal of so many of Carlos's officers. Rodil would infallibly have shot them if they had fallen into his hands, and that would have cast disgrace upon the whole alliance. I heard the other day an anecdote of him at Callao which shows what a quick shot he is. He was told during the siege that some of his garrison were sick of the confinement and wished to get away. He mustered all hands, said he wanted to keep no man against his will, let those who were tired fall out and they should be sent off immediately: a few foolish fellows, officers, did fall out, and they were shot by his order on the spot and immediately.

I hope there will be no attempt to get rid of the Queen Regent, for it might be feared that this could not be done without disturbance. But it would be no affair of ours, and you would of course not interfere, unless you were to see some very strong motive and clear case for doing so.

PS. Pray explain to Martinez that not having foreseen till late this evening that I should have occasion to send you this messenger I have not been able to let Miraflores know of his going, so as to give him an opportunity of writing by him.

Docketed: By Messenger Kaye.

GC/CL/1231

[1] Former Minister of Ferdinand VII who went over to Don Carlos in September 1833.

70   Villiers to Palmerston, 19 July 1834

Madrid. Private. I have only two hours notice of Rayneval's courier in his passage through Madrid from St. Ildefonso and I have only time to give you a correct though not a full report of the many events which have crowded into the last 5 days[1]—all of black omen I am sorry to say. My predictions, when I determined upon not quitting Madrid, that this would become the scene of action have not been falsified, any more than those upon the spirit of the Urban Militia and the mischief they would cause whenever an opportunity arose.

The authorities are solely responsible for all the blood spilt on Thursday, for the example of disorder which has been given, and the state of excitement which still prevails in the town. Their conduct has been worthy of execration and it creates melancholy forebodings of what may be expected under the probable recurrence of similar disasters. The Government is cut in half—nothing can be done without the Queen's signature and under 4 and 20 hours an answer cannot be had from St. Ildefonso. In short it seems as if some demon drew a line beyond which this country was not to stir from affliction and degradation.

Martinez de la Rosa is down at St. Ildefonso surrounded by women and old doctors disbelieving, because he wishes to disbelieve, the imminence of the danger and quite incapable of taking any resolution except upon the establishment of quarantines, for the service of which the whole garrison of Madrid, save a few hundred men, has been withdrawn. The cholera which is really very formidable (nearly 400 died yesterday) of course adds to the general dislocation of society, and the active exertions which were some time ago used by the Carlists to make the people believe it was a Government *ruse* to prevent the meeting of the Cortes have increased the public ferment. With all this there are *only* two men, Las Amarillas and Toreno, who are likely not to sink under the difficulties that surround them. They will rise superior to them if they are not neutralized by the Queen and her Premier. If the news of Don Carlos's arrival in Navarre is confirmed, it will be even betting upon the throne for both the provinces of Castille will rise.

I must now conclude, having no more time and having endeavoured to give you as *clear an idea* as I can of the *complete confusion* which exists here.

I have had a bad relapse of gout which has grieved me to the heart for if I had been able to see the slaughter of Thursday and had gone to the authorities I feel convinced I could have been the means of checking the disgraceful outrages.

PS. I have sent you full details of a Mr. Hunter's case. . . .

Received 28 July.

GC/CL/148; Clar. Dep. C.451/1 (11-13)

[1] During the panic resulting from the spread of cholera in Madrid, the monks were accused of having employed agents to distribute poison. Several monasteries were attacked and many monks were killed. The Urban Militia assisted the mob. (V to P, 19 July 1834, no. 89, FO 72/424; V to Granville, 22 July, PRO 30/29/413.) See also V to Granville, 19 July, forwarded by Granville to P on 26 July, GC/GR/609 enc.

71 Villiers to Palmerston, 21 July 1834

Madrid. Private. An hour after I had closed my dispatches to you the day before yesterday I received from Lord Granville the tidings of Lord Grey's and Althorp's resignations and the consequent dissolution of the Government. . . .

In the mean while, though I have not much hope that you are Secretary of State or I minister in Spain, I may as well proceed with my account of men and things in Madrid. It is somewhat less gloomy than my last. The fear of forfeiting her daughter's crown being greater than that of the cholera, the Queen Regent has resolved upon opening the Cortes in person—but it required all the weight of last week's tumult, the reported presence of Don Carlos in Spain and the conviction of what the consequences of a prorogation of the Cortes would be, to induce her to take this resolution. It is a courageous one I must confess, for the cholera is very formidable and increasing with such velocity as the hottest weather, constant storms, ignorant doctors and the necessary medicines being already used, can impart to it.

The dismissal of all the authorities who permitted the massacre of the friars on Thursday last is a most un-Spanishlike act of vigor, and I hope it will shew to the country and above all to Europe the real character of the outrage—for the Northern Trinity and their English friends will of course proclaim that it was the natural and predicted consequence of an extension of liberty, whereas it was only the popular excitement which has been seen in every town in Europe upon the first breaking out of a great epidemic, seeking to attribute it to tangible causes, which carries the ignorant and the ill disposed into excess, if permitted by those whose duty it is to restrain their fury. À quelque chose malheur est bon too, and I hope the opportunity will not be lost of remoulding this villainous National Guard which would assuredly have upset the new order of things and been the means of *passing* the country through those various phases towards anarchy and then despotism with which it is unhappily so familiar.

Nothing further is known respecting Don Carlos in Navarre. I incline to disbelieve the report notwithstanding the credit which it has obtained in the provinces where it is said there have been public rejoicings, levées, distribution of rewards, etc., etc. by His Majesty in person. When one remembers the state of stupefaction from terror to which he was reduced in Portugal by the mere vicinage of Rodil's army it is difficult to suppose that a man should so far lay aside his natural character as to run all the risks of detection in crossing the sea or passing through France in order to run greater risks of every kind than he did in Portugal, for he would now have to make himself a guerilla and to incur all the chances of the war with the meanest peasant, and of some ugly consequences to himself in the event of being made prisoner. Still however Frias's dispatch by the telegraph leaves no doubt that he has left England in disguise, and that must be almost as much out of his natural character as coming to Navarre.

Poor Martinez is nearly overwhelmed with this complication of difficulties—he is a bad subject for the cholera moreover and as he is greatly afraid of it, his forced return to Madrid adds nothing to his composure.

PS. I open my letter to say that I have this moment received yours of the 10th which I have only time to thank you for as Rayneval's courier is setting off. Your letter confirms all my apprehensions for our futurity.

July 22nd. Rayneval's courier being put off till this morning on account of his being unwell and very uneasy respecting his daughter, I am able to congratulate you and myself upon continuing to serve the King our master. A courier from Bayonne has just arrived with the telegraphic dispatch of the 18th from Paris announcing the recomposition of the Government. May you all live and prosper and God send you a speedy prorogation of Parliament.

We still keep not believing that Don Carlos is in Navarre although we receive proclamations signed by him.

I have had an agreable visitor in the house—the cholera—one of my English stable people died of it yesterday. William Hervey has been pretty bad but is now better. Scott is hors de combat though only choler*ish* as yet.

Received 30 July.

GC/CL/149; Clar. Dep. C.451/1 (14-17)

72 Villiers to Palmerston, 24 July 1834

Madrid. Private. The messenger with your letter of the 15th arrived last night in time for me to communicate its contents to Martinez de la Rosa, and I made him understand that you had dispatched your messenger *on purpose* that he might be here before the opening of the Cortes in order to allay the anxiety which might be felt by the Spanish Government or public upon the change of Government in England. He was extremely grateful and begged me to express how much he was indebted to you for the proofs of active good will which he was constantly receiving at your hands.

He inclines to believe the report of Don Carlos's arrival in Navarre although Rodil and other officers write word that it is an idle rumour. The very doubt however is mischievous, it will embolden the Queen's enemies and increase the number of those lukewarm in her cause.

I have not time to write more as Martinez's courier is going instantly but I will write more at length tomorrow. It is impossible at this moment to tell, neither does the Government know yet, to what extent the conspiracy of last night has gone[1]—if it is not very serious it may be turned to good account and many dangerous disorderly men put hors de combat.

The Speech is too long but it is a sensible and well written document.[2]

I had already been very civil to Mr. Maberly and to Mr. Irving[3] upon hearing from Lord Granville that the latter was the agent of a paper friendly to you. I will be of all the use I can to him.

I need not tell you that Easthope will be eternally grateful if you can send him a copy of the Speech before other papers get it—as far as in me lays I have taken precautions that they shall not get their copies of it so soon as they expect. I send you one or two spare copies.

GC/CL/150; Clar. Dep. C.451/1 (18-19)

[1] 'I was informed by M. de las Amarillas that a conspiracy had been discovered in the night to proclaim the Constitution of 1812 in the Chamber at the moment of taking the oath of allegiance to the Queen, and that the confusion which would thereby be created was to have been the signal of a tumult without among the people. M. de las Amarillas appeared to think the conspiracy very serious.' (V to P, 24 July 1834, no. 95, FO 72/424.)

[2] *Discurso pronunciado par la Reina Gobernadora en la solemne apertura de las Cortes Generales,* enclosed with V to P, ibid.

[3] Both newspaper correspondents. Irving was the Madrid correspondent of the *Morning Chronicle.*

73   Villiers to Palmerston, 25 July 1834

Madrid. Mr. Irving is about to dispatch a courier to his Court and I avail myself of the opportunity to send you [a] duplicate of the dispatch which went by the Spanish courier yesterday and who will probably linger on the road.

There is but little more known respecting the conspiracy; that which it is important to discover is the assistance which the conspirators expected to receive from the troops or the people, as it can hardly be supposed that without some well founded expectation of this kind, two or three men would have raised a cry of revolution in the Chamber where they certainly would have found no sympathy. General Palafox,[1] who appears to have been at the head of the plot, is known by the English for his defence of Saragossa (of which place he was created Duke only 3 days ago by the Queen) during the Peninsular War, though Spaniards say he should have been shot for his conduct there. He has always appeared to me a mere nullity and I believe him now to have been an instrument in the hands of Romero Alpuente[2] who is an atrocious compound of all the worst men of the French Revolution. All this however and the events of the 19th from which the anarchists and the returned emigrants,[3] reckoning upon the *favorable neutrality* of the Captain General, had hoped a complete *bouleversement*, give a sickly aspect to the Queen's cause. Some of the troops are not entirely to be relied upon on account of their Jacobinism not Carlism and the Urban Militia is always ready for mischief. I remember saying a great deal about the composition of that corps, more perhaps than you may have thought *tanti* at the time, but I foresaw that arming the dregs of society must be productive of evil. The Government are aware of their perilous position and the majority of the Cortes is I think disposed to stand by them. The initiative is not with the Chambers on any subject, but all are open to them in the Address in answer to the Speech. I have spoken to several members of [the] Cortes respecting the Address and strongly advised that they should exhibit firmness and a readiness to support the Government in maintaining order.

About 50 Proceres and 70 Procuradores were present at the opening of the Cortes yesterday. The ceremony was very cold, but it must be owned that the news of the conspiracy, which began to circulate in the Chamber, and a distant aperçu of the gallows, for the mere fact of being there should Don Carlos arrive from the provinces at Madrid, were not altogether enlivening reflections.

The state in which ladies wish to be, etc. was supposed by the candid spectators to be that of the principal person there.

There is nothing new today respecting Don Carlos and the same doubt prevails as to whether he is or is not in Spain. Proclamations, amnesties and anathemas are published by cartloads in his name, still Rodil and his army disbelieve the *real presence*. If he is there he will be an encumbrance to Zumalacarregui[4] which will not be balanced by the good his presence will do his cause (for the people want no rousing, their spirit is already the worst possible), as he must be furnished with large escorts and the insurgents must change the whole nature of their warfare which has been so advantageous to them and must now take to outposts and avant gardes and all the other harassing duties of a regular army from which guerillas are free.

Copy.

Clar. Dep. C.451/1 (20-22)

[1] Arrested as a leading member of the conspiracy. (V to P, 24 July 1834, no. 95, FO 72/424.)

[2] Also arrested, a member of an advanced liberal group. (ibid.)

[3] Those liberals of 1812 and 1820 who returned from exile after the general amnesty proclaimed by the Queen Regent.

[4] A colonel in the army of Ferdinand VII who was deprived of his regiment in Zea's purge of 1832. In July 1834 he was promoted Lieutenant-General by Don Carlos after he had successfully raised an army of partisans in Biscay and Navarre. He was the most successful military commander of the civil war.

74 Villiers to Palmerston, 27 July 1834

Madrid. Private. You cannot complain that there is, or is likely to be, any lack of events in this country—they have come showering down upon us too quickly within the last 10 days, and the arrival of Don Miguel, whether in Catalonia or Portugal, is a most unnecessary addition to them.[1] Still however I see no reason to despond. Miguel can do nothing here and Carlos will embarrass rather than serve his cause—he will have priests and a Court round him with their intrigues and the war on his side will no longer be carried on with the irregularity which rendered it so formidable to the Queen's troops. The contest has now changed its outward character, but I see no reason to alter the opinions which I expressed some time ago to you respecting the Northern Provinces. The privileges have all along been the main point. The insurgents took up Don Carlos at first because despotism had always respected those privileges and liberalism had made war upon them—when Don Carlos was demonstrating his baseness in Portugal they first cursed and then forgot him—they now readopt him partly from the original cause and partly because he is the symbol of all that is obnoxious and dangerous to the Queen.

The position of Spain as respects the Treaty is one of considerable embarrassment. She has borne the brunt and the expence of driving out the two Pretenders from Portugal in order to bring them under the most favorable circumstances upon her own territory, and the Government will be exposed in the Cortes to the various reproaches which ignorance or malice can suggest.

I need scarcely tell you that neither in the Cabinet or the Council of Regency does there seem to exist an idea that the English and French Governments do not regret these 'untoward events' and would have prevented them if they could, but the generous public, who nowhere look beneath the surface, are not quite of this way of thinking, and you can easily conceive the unfavorable results at which they arrive when they put together the circumstances of Don Carlos's hasty embarkation and that of his 300 followers—his landing in England—his escape to France—unnoticed for several days—his stay in Paris without any attempt at disguise—his journey to Bourdeaux and Bayonne and his being escorted over the French frontier by a commandant of gens d'armes who it appears has been *reprimanded* for his conduct. The public therefore conceive that England and France are lukewarm allies and their opinion would be of no consequence if it were not a source of weakness to the Government, and of great encouragement to their enemies, Jacobins as well as Carlists. It would vanish however into thin air upon any public demonstration of the contrary on the part of England. A few ships sent to the northern and eastern coasts, where I hope they need not be detained long, would calm much anxiety, but if you could in your place in Parliament announce the views of the Government upon the Treaty again coming into operation I think it would set this Government upon its legs once more. Some months ago several ships of war appeared upon the eastern coast and their captains announced to the governors of the different towns that they were ready to be useful to the Queen's cause. The good effect produced by this was more even than could have been expected—it would be much greater now, and if Don Miguel should have any intention of going to Portugal instead of to Catalonia the measure appears to me to be one of imperative necessity.

Martinez has received accounts of the arrival of the 250 officers at Hambro' [?Hamburg] and that they are actively engaged in organizing schemes against the Spanish Government and for returning to join Don Carlos.[2] Upon this subject Martinez seems no longer to be sore but he regrets our generosity in placing any reliance in men whose inveterate enmity to the Queen was sure to lead them into plots against her cause. I cannot agree in the opinion that they would have been shot if they had fallen into Rodil's hands or that he would have dealt with them as he did at Callão where you must remember that he was in imminent peril, that Lima was in the hands of the insurgents and that a spirit of disaffection was spreading in his garrison. If a mutiny broke out on board a ship and that the captain hung up $\frac{1}{2}$ a dozen of the ringleaders in terrorem to the rest, it would be most unfair ever after to reckon upon such a man's cruelty and injustice—but these officers need no more have fallen into Rodil's hands than the 600 soldiers who were safely placed in the dépôt where they certainly ought to have been sent likewise as Don Carlos originally stipulated only for his suite.

A courier was sent by Martinez to Lisbon today and I wrote a short report to Howard of the conversation which I have given you an account of in my dispatch.[3] I likewise saw Sarmento and engaged him to write to his Government respecting an active police upon the frontier, and Rayneval will I conclude write in the same sense to M. de Rigny. In short Martinez seems confident that if the allies will but make a ring for him and keep it that he shall be able to double up Don Carlos in no time.

The conspiracy is an awkward business though it might have been much more so if it had only been discovered in the Chamber. I fear it has more extensive roots than the Government believe or at all events allow—there is a bad spirit afloat which sooner or later will produce mischief. The emigrants have returned hungry and clamorous, and there is besides a large and turbulent portion of society always ready for a scramble, whom the Tories, here as elsewhere, are ready to assist for their mischievous but short-sighted purposes.

A regency was to have been declared in the name of the Queen after the fashion of Cadiz in 1812—a 13 years minority being considered no more hurtful to the Constitution than an absent King, and the country is not yet ripe for a republic.

Some days ago I wrote you a dispatch upon the subject of the succession[4]—Las Amarillas pressed me so much to do so that I could not refuse. You will probably not send me an official answer to it, but I shall be particularly obliged if you will write me a private letter which I can read to him with some friendly expressions towards himself. He will be much flattered by it and he is, with the exception perhaps of

Toreno, the most reasonable and statesmanlike man I have yet met in Spain.

Received 7 August.

GC/CL/151; Clar. Dep. C.451/1 (23-28)

[1] 'M. Martinez de la Rosa informed me yesterday that he had received intelligence from the Duke de Frias that Don Miguel was about to leave Genoa to make a hostile descent upon the coast of Catalonia.' (V to P, 27 July 1834, no. 98, FO 72/424.) This report proved to be unfounded.

[2] These officers were with Don Carlos in Portugal and had been transported from Lisbon to London in British ships. The Spanish Government had hoped that the British Government would either intern them or prevent them from leaving England. (ibid.)

[3] Martínez de la Rosa asked whether the British Government thought that, in view of the return of Don Carlos to Spain, the Spanish Government had the right to demand 'effective aid under the terms of the Treaty of April'. (ibid.)

[4] Amarillas had asked V for the views of the British Government on the determination of the Spanish Government to change the order of succession, removing Don Carlos and his heirs and placing Don Francisco de Paula after the Queen and the Infanta Luisa Fernanda. (V to P, 19 July 1834, no. 88, FO 72/424.)

75 Palmerston to Villiers, 28 July 1834

Copy. Foreign Office. Private. I have this morning received your letters and despatches to the 19th. I am truly sorry for all the distressing events which they announce. I hope that the cholera will have run the same course at Madrid as elsewhere, and that after spending its fury in a violent outbreak, it will in a few days diminish its ravages. I shall be very anxious however for further accounts from you. I send you copy of my answer to Miraflores which contains all we can at present say.[1] The best measure that could be taken in the first instance by the Spanish Government if they want troops would be to have round by sea some of Pedro's regiments. This would relieve Portugal from some trouble and afford an efficient aid to Spain. But the Spanish Government must make an effort to put the insurrection down soon, or it may grow more serious.

Talleyrand has been pressing us to acquiesce in a contingent interference of France in this war. We are all strongly against it. We think that if the war does not spread, French assistance cannot be necessary;

and that if the war should spread, such assistance, to be effectual, must be upon a very great scale; that even then it may fail, and that if France should fail in a great effort in Spain, it would be fatal to Louis Philippe as well as to Isabella. The other Powers of Europe moreover would not remain tranquil spectators of the entrance of a large French army into Spain; and if that army did not succeed, and succeed promptly, those Powers would prove very troublesome to France. If the Spanish nation are really divided in any great degree, it is difficult to see the right of any foreign Power to interfere; at all events that right is as good for one as for another; and the 3 Powers would be perfectly justified in affording openly and effectually aid of all kinds to Carlos, the moment France marched a regiment into Spain. The Portuguese case was quite different in all its circumstances. Pray then endeavour all you can to persuade Martinez from asking French assistance. The Portuguese are ready to march, but they object to pay their own expences, and it is fair perhaps that Spain should defray the additional charge of the operation and she might take all the foreigners at once into her own service.

The question about the exclusion of the sons of Carlos is certainly one with regard to which we should be shy of giving opinion or advice. But nevertheless I think it may fairly be considered upon grounds somewhat different from those on which you placed it in your conversation with Amarillas. If Carlos had remained quiet and continued a peaceable and loyal subject of the Queen, it would have been the height of injustice to have meddled with the contingent rights of his children to the throne. But he has become a rebel against his Sovereign and against the law of his country; and the example of many other States might be quoted to justify an act of attainder and exclusion against himself and his descendants. If the justice of the measure might be defended both by precedent and by abstract reasoning, I confess I should not be inclined to dispute its expediency in the present state of affairs in Spain. Such an act of vigour would tend to give strength to the liberal party, and matters are now gone much too far to admit of any chance of peaceful compromise by a coalition of opposite extremes. I should vote for the Exclusion Bill if I was a Procere [Procer] or a Procurador. I hope the Queen has opened the Cortes in person instead of postponing their meeting.

Carlos and Miguel have destroyed their cause by want of personal energy and enterprize, let the Queen take warning by their example.

Those who in times of crisis will not expose their persons to danger cannot hope to direct the storm.

Docketed: By Spanish messenger.

GC/CL/1232

[1] A letter in reply to Miraflores's request to know what assistance Spain could expect from the other signatories of the Quadruple Treaty in suppressing the revolt in the Northern Provinces now that Don Carlos had placed himself at its head. P replied that the request was as yet premature, that the Spanish Government could take more energetic steps to suppress the revolt and that the Treaty of April 1834 as drafted had been fulfilled. Nevertheless he promised that the British and French Governments would give the problems of Spain their fullest attention and sympathy. (P to V, 28 July 1834, no. 38, FO 72/419.)

76 Villiers to Palmerston, 30 July 1834

Madrid. Private. You will see that I do my best to keep Martinez up to the non-intervention mark but I must say that hitherto his language upon the subject is all that we can desire.[1] To intervention, however, it must come unless something decisive takes place shortly.[2] I don't expect the insurgents will be such fools as to give regular battle to Rodil for they would infallibly be beaten. Nothing but defection could enable them to beat him and I see no reason to expect that—but I think there *is* reason to expect that the two armies will hold each other in check and then will begin after a time the wavering of people of influence, the appearance of fresh factions, and all those elements of disorganization which are so well known in this country. The Government must then make an appeal to the 'exalted' (as it is called) part of the nation which will be more dangerous in its[3] consequences and be as certain to lead to mischief as the Apostolicals. France will not look calmly on at a Carlist or a revolutionary party gaining ascendancy, and she will be placed in the dilemma of opposing the former in order to assist the latter which she will view with quite as evil an eye, although it has been called into activity by the moderate party.

The embarrassment of such a state of things both to England and France and the advantage that would be derived from it by the Holy Trinity need no expatiating upon. It may still be avoided I think by vigorous naval and frontier demonstrations of friendship—and they become more necessary at this moment for the acharnement of the public against the English and French Governments is very serious; nothing will induce even the more enlightened classes to believe that the return of Don Carlos might not have been prevented, and the Carlists, knowing well that lukewarmness on the part of the two Governments is a deadly blow to the Queen's cause, foment the opinion to the utmost.[4]

The information respecting the expedition from England to be commanded by Captain Eliot[5] was received this morning from Alava who is at St. Sebastian on his way here and says he can rely upon its correctness.

Most of the insurgent leaders are *buyable* and if this Government had any money I think the war might be put a stop to in that way and Don Carlos placed in *security*. Would the English and French Governments do any secret service of this kind? I don't know what are Martinez's views upon the matter or have I said any thing to him upon it in order not to raise false hopes.

The arrival of Don Carlos has induced the Government to prepare immediately a law for altering the succession and it will be introduced into the Chamber in a few days. In this I think they are right,[6] for it will nail the waverers. Nobody would dare vote against such a law now and in a month's time the *Mighty* only knows what will happen, but as all those who vote for it would be the very first for hanging if Don Carlos gets here their support of the Queen may be more securely depended upon.

Toreno's plan of finance is to acknowledge and to create one fund of the whole foreign debt—a portion of it ($\frac{2}{5}$ths he thinks, though that must to a certain degree depend on the Cortes) is to be what is called Active Debt i.e. bearing interest and in process of redemption. As soon as that is accomplished, another portion of the Passive Debt (which bears no interest) is to be made active and so on till the whole is paid off. . . .

PS. The law for altering the succession passes over Don Carlos and his children and gives the crown to Don Francisco and his children upon the death of the Queen and her sister without issue.

The cholera is subsiding.

Received 9 August.

GC/CL/152; Clar. Dep. C.451/1 (29-32)

[1] In an interview with Martínez de la Rosa 'His Excellency declared his con-

viction that the means at the disposal of the Spanish Government would be sufficient to quell the insurrection, provided that England, France and Portugal would cordially assist in preventing any aid from without being afforded to the insurgents. To England and France M. Martinez de la Rosa said he appealed not merely as parties to the Treaty of London but as powers deeply interested, on European grounds, in the success of a moderate constitutional government in Spain, for it was every day becoming more evident that the enemies of all progress hoped to fight a battle in the Peninsula which should be decisive as to the success of their policy.' (V to P, 30 July 1834, no. 100, FO 72/424.)

² 'to intervention' to 'shortly' sidelined in the margin in GC/CL/152, possibly by P.

³ 'begin' to 'dangerous in its' sidelined in the margin in GC/CL/152, as n.2 above.

⁴ 'by vigorous naval' to 'utmost' sidelined in the margin in GC/CL/152, as n.2 above.

⁵ In support of the Carlists. See V to P, 30 July 1834, no. 100, FO 72/424.

⁶ 'immediately' to 'right' sidelined in the margin in GC/CL/152, as n.2 above.

77 Villiers to Palmerston, 2 August 1834

Madrid. Private. I have been all the morning at the Chamber of Proceres and you will be glad to hear how satisfactory their first discussion has been. There was some opposition of which Martinez availed himself to explain the past and future course of the Government, and with respect to Don Carlos, his embarkation in Portugal and escape from England, il s'est tiré d'affaire with a tact and dexterity which were perfectly admirable and afterwards, without acknowledging that the Pretender was in Spain, he laid down the conduct of every good Spaniard with a courageous frankness which cannot but have a useful effect and which will I hope check the *composition with felony* which is probably revolving in many a good Spaniard's mind. The whole assembly was orderly and dignified and looked as if it had done nothing but debate for the last 50 years.

The Procuradores are to debate their Address tomorrow which is a very foolish document—such a one as conceited semi-educated schoolboys would produce, chattering about trial by jury, agriculture, individual liberty, arts, commerce, and no check upon the press. This *may* be in order to avail themselves of the best opportunity which will offer to glorify themselves in the eyes of their constituents and that having done so they will be all the more tractable—but I confess, without any positive data to go upon yet, that I have only a slender reliance upon their sagacity or discretion.

We are waiting anxiously for the next news from Rodil—it may be decisive if he has had troops enough to surround the insurgents before he attacks them—if not, they will all escape like fish out of a net with a hole in it.

The presence of Don Carlos (if it is really him) continues to produce no effect upon the army or much in the provinces—in the former the spirit is as good and in the latter as bad as possible.

I sent you by the last messenger an account of the expences which I incurred in bringing my effects here over and above what they would have been in quiet times, and I begged Backhouse to move Your Lordship to sanction the payment.

This place is very expensive which I regret because by feasting the members of both Chambers perpetually I think I could exercise a useful influence over them. I am prepared to spend my whole official income in this, but I *happen to have a particularly good reason* for not exceeding it.[1]

Received 11 August.

GC/CL/153; Clar. Dep. C.451/1 (33-34)

[1] 'not having any other income' added by P.

78 Villiers to Palmerston, 5 August 1834

Madrid. Private. Affairs in this country go through such various and rapid phases that four and twenty hours will sometimes completely change their complexion and prospect. If I had written to you yesterday my account would have been very unfavorable, today it is materially improved. There was a pleasing expectation that the Government of the country would be that portion of the Chamber who composed and supported the Address of which I gave you an account in my last letter. There is now fair ground for hoping that the Ministers will have the support of those who don't wish to hurry the country into revolution. I hope too that the Ministers are at last convinced of what it is so hard to make them understand, that difficult matters are better not left to chance—but to chance the elections were left, to chance the Deputies have hitherto been left, and the Government are then surprized at finding that others more active than themselves have filched the votes which they should have secured. However they have now had a pretty intelligible hint to be careful. It must be said though that these Deputies are most difficult to deal with—scarcely any of them will go to a Minister's office for fear of compromising their independence, and there is no society here or house where they can be met on neutral ground. The ease and fluency with which they speak in the Chamber is very striking, and if the press is not suffered to drive them into excesses, and if no sympathy is established between the Chamber and the gallery into which rush daily 300 at least of the canaille, and if the Carlists don't make a progress which will on the other side give an impulse to Jacobinism—*if* none of these take place, the Cortes may become what they ought to be—securities for improvement and better government.

The last two days have given me ample cause to rejoice at having taken an active part in the nomination of Toreno to the Ministry.[1] He is the only Minister to whom the Deputies are favorably inclined, and if he had been in opposition he would have swept away Martinez in the first debate, but he would have come into the Government pledged to a dangerous party over which he would have soon ceased to exercise any retarding influence.

Martinez announced today that some English vessels had arrived on the northern coast of Spain and that the French Government were taking active measures to prevent supplies being furnished to the insurgents—he carried in consequence a good amendment to the Address upon foreign politics.

The escape of Don Carlos has created doubts upon the sincerity of the English and French Governments even among the reasonable orders of society, and it is not to be wondered at that Martinez should be anxious for some authentic means of extinguishing the idle and mischievous rumours which are in circulation.

Maberly is perfectly convinced that so far from his having any thing to learn here, he is in a condition to instruct Spaniards about their own country. . . .

I have transmitted to you today an application from Scott, the paid attaché here, for leave which I hope you will grant. . . .

William Hervey is still very unwell and as there is a great deal to do here you may perhaps not think it inexpedient to send me some one from the Foreign Office during the 2 or 3 months which Scott ought to be absent.

Received 15 August.

GC/CL/154; Clar. Dep. C.451/1 (35-38)

[1] As Minister of Finance.

79   Palmerston to Villiers, 8 August 1834

Copy. Foreign Office. We have bothered the parties engaged in fitting out the United Kingdom steamer at Helvoet by setting the Firebrand to watch their proceedings. They must have been in a hurry because they hired the County of Pembroke steamer to tow the Samuel Cunard over to Helvoet instead of letting her sail, by which they could not at this season gain 24 hours in time; but nevertheless the Cunard had[1] been 4 days in Helvoet roads without transhipping her cargo of guns and arms. The master of the Firebrand has been ordered to try to engage for the King's service sailors serving on board the United Kingdom, and this also may tend to delay her. But when the United Kingdom does sail, we cannot stop or molest her consistently with our own law and the law of nations.

But the Spanish Government may surely take measures on their own coast. Cannot they lay on a sort of embargo upon the whole of their northern coast, forbidding all vessels for a limited time from sailing or arriving? Can they not prohibit the importation of all arms and warlike stores on any part of their coast, and seize any ship within their own jurisdiction of the maritime league, which should endeavour to violate this order? Could they not do something upon the principle of our Hovering Act against which nobody could protest or make any complaint? If they station some Guarda Costas along their northern coast they could surely prevent the landing of arms. The ports are all in the hands of the Government and therefore the arms could not be landed in a port; but to land 5,000 stand of arms on the open beach, and to carry the cases containing them up the country, requires time, concert, previous arrangement between the ship and the people ashore, and considerable means of transport. To be sure 4 or 5,000 unarmed peasants might be moved rapidly down to a given spot, and each man might carry off to the mountains a couple of muskets; but a small force properly posted and employed on the coast would be sufficient to prevent this. I believe the Lulworth cutter has sailed for the coast of

Spain as she does not seem to be in the Dutch ports.

I hope soon to hear of the cessation of cholera at Madrid and of the end of the civil war in Navarre. Pedro would transfer 3,500 foreign troops to the Spanish Government; what could they do better than send for them and land them at once at Fuentarabia in the rear of the insurgents?

Docketed: To be forwarded from Paris.

GC/CL/1233

[1] *Recte* has?

80   Villiers to Palmerston, 9 August 1834

Madrid. Private. I received last night your letter and dispatches of the 28th ultimo. I am quite at a loss to account for Talleyrand's anxiety for French interference, if such interference is to be founded upon Spanish solicitation. The Cabinet and the Council of Regency as well as the national feelings are all opposed to it, and in the face of these I do not apprehend that it can be contemplated to send a French army into Spain.

Martinez has told me again today that Frias and Miraflores have both been instructed to say that the Queen is quite able to fight her own battle provided her enemies are not assisted from without. She hopes her allies will do her some preventive service[1] and she asks for nothing more.

The return of Don Carlos is a Holy Alliance and not a Spanish plot. Not a village out of the insurgent provinces has risen for him, not a soldier or an authority has deserted to him and to this day the Carlists doubt the reality of his presence in Spain.[2] On the other hand there is abundant evidence of the advice and assistance which he received in England and France. His leaving London without a Spaniard,[3] the arrangements made for his transit through France, the armaments fitting out in England and Holland for his service are no *Spanish* Carlist contrivances, and it seems to me that the parties to the Quadruple Treaty have every right to resist these external attempts at defeating the object of the Treaty. If they are not resisted, stoutly and successfully too, they must lead either to the success of Don Carlos and the signal discomfiture of the Quadruple Alliance, or to that very intervention which England is so anxious to avoid. A declaration then, or publication, be the form what it may, on the part of England that no foreign Power would intervene in the national quarrel in Spain, the Queen's party being quite strong enough to assert her rights, but that in pursuance of the Treaty for establishing tranquillity and putting an end to the effusion of blood in the Peninsula, the parties to that Treaty intended to prevent hostile Powers or persons from fomenting the war—such a declaration would gratify the national vanity and strengthen the Queen's cause by weakening that of her enemies, while it could not give just ground of complaint, or excuse for interference, to other Powers.

Martinez has no taste whatever for the foreign legions of Don Pedro—they would be just as offensive as any other foreigners to the Spanish pride and would destroy what the Government are so desirous to maintain, the strict nationality of the quarrel;[4] besides I believe they are all the scum of the earth though they used to fight like devils when they chose or were not drunk. There is another consideration however which is conclusive against their employment—what is to prevent all these mercenaries qui n'ont ni foi ni loi going over to Don Carlos with their arms and baggage after they have been duly landed in his neighbourhood at the Queen's expence, if they happen to be discontented or to see a prospect of better pay or greater plunder on the other side?

With respect to my conversation with Amarillas upon the succession to the Crown, you must remember that it took place when we thought that Don Carlos was in England and quietly submitting to his destiny. My remarks were not offered as objections to the course which the Government were desirous of pursuing, but only as considerations of what might be said out of Spain under the circumstances of Don Carlos taking no active part against the Queen. Those circumstances are now changed and the Law of Exclusion has become a measure not only of expedience but of necessity.[5]

I received your dispatch about the Cortes Bond holders the day before yesterday,[6] and although I had settled with Toreno the manner in which they should be dealt with in the many conversations I have had with him upon their claims, I lost no time in firing off a note to Martinez in order that there should exist a written record of your interference for them, coming as it did so opportunely the day before the Budget.[7] Considering the state of the country I think they ought to be satisfied with the arrangement, and I hope you will take credit for the Government that their interests have not been neglected.

You will be satisfied with the passage in Toreno's statement respecting commerce and moderate duties *vice* prohibitions.[8]

PS. Rodil has had an advantage over the insurgents but I doubt its being of much importance.

Received 18 August.   GC/CL/155; Clar. Dep. C.451/1 (39-43)

[1] 'do her some preventive service' underlined, probably by P.
[2] 'Carlists' to 'Spain' underlined, as n.1 above.
[3] 'leaving' to 'Spaniard' underlined, as n.1 above.
[4] 'the strict' to 'quarrel' underlined, as n.1 above.
[5] 'Law of Exclusion' to 'necessity' underlined, as n.1 above.
[6] P to V, 26 July 1834, no. 36, FO 72/419.
[7] V to Martínez de la Rosa, 6 Aug. 1834, enclosed with V to P, 7 Aug. 1834, no.111, FO 72/425.
[8] See ibid.

81 Villiers to Palmerston, 13 August 1834

Madrid. Private. The news respecting Don Carlos is somewhat more favorable today and the predictions of the mischief his presence would do his cause seem in a course of gradual fulfillment—he has run his head into the very same noose from which he was so anxious to extricate it in Portugal, and he is now flying before Rodil as he was three months ago. Rodil is a bad correspondent and a giver of few details but Martinez gathers from his dispatches that Don Carlos is in a miserable plight, without good advisers and his troops shewing the best inclination to vanish upon the approach of danger. He himself seems to have no hesitation about running away but a great deal as to where to run *to*. At one time he went within two leagues of the French frontier and then something seems to have turned him like a hunted fox and Rodil does not say what direction he was taking—but the scent seemed very fine and the hounds were running breast high, so that they will perhaps run in upon him and kill him in the open.

Martinez has kept his promise of inserting a passage about foreign intervention in his exposé to the Cortes,[1] and that matter is now set at rest—particularly as the French Government are taking most active measures in every direction to prevent assistance being afforded to the insurgents. If they would have done a tithe of what they are now doing 6 months ago the war would long since have died a natural death.

Martinez was somewhat mystified that the two English brigs on the

Northern Coast had received no instructions recently to give assistance to the Queen's cause[2]—the more so perhaps as the French ships are numerous and active. I had little to say in reply as I know nothing of whether it is your intention to send more ships or if so what the nature of their orders will be. Martinez however wisely said that he did not wish the French Government to go one jot beyond what the English Government was disposed to do, for that it was far more important to Spain that a perfect unanimity should subsist between those two Governments upon all Spanish matters than that any extra services should be rendered by France and disapproved by England, and that nothing would hold the Carlists here and elsewhere in such check as a unity of opinion and action between our Government and that of the French.

I have found it very useful occasionally to shew a dispatch of yours or read a passage from a letter to Amarillas—he is flattered by the confidence and I secure the good will of the Council of Regency which he entirely leads, and their advice to the Government may often be of importance to us. I shewed him your note in reply to Miraflores's request for additional articles to the Treaty and I enclose you a letter upon it which I have received from him.

I suggested to Toreno to write an official answer in reply to the note to Martinez upon the Cortes bondholders in order that you might send it to the chairman of the meeting as the result of your intervention, and it would at the same time afford Toreno an opportunity of making known to the monied men of London any thing he pleased respecting his future plans either of meeting existing engagements or developing the resources of Spain by way of security for the new engagements which he may contract. He is however afraid of doing this, thinking he shall be accused of preference for the English creditors and that it will increase the storm which is raised against him at Paris. The great fault which is found with his plan by the Cortes is that it goes too far and recognizes too much—there is a growing disposition to throw over the Aguado loans[3] and to scrutinize very severely every transaction since 1823. Toreno is determined to resist any gross violation of the public faith though I don't think he would consider it necessary to resign if his plan was a little *pared down*—the disposition to do this which has already manifested itself in the Cortes is a proof that he would have failed if he had attempted more and should be taken into consideration by the grogneurs.

I forgot to mention some days ago that the Queen Regent means to write to you herself. . . .

The law for excluding Don Carlos from the throne is a bald and meagre document,[4] but Martinez tells me that when it comes to be discussed he shall put it upon higher grounds of State necessity.

I hope you will have the goodness to send me a good workman from the Foreign Office if you can spare one, for to my sincere regret I think that I must not even wait for your permission to send away William Hervey. I am under much alarm for his intellect and that alarm is increased by the disposition to madness which exists in his family. . . .

Enclosure: Las Amarillas to Villiers, n.d., thanking Villiers for showing him a despatch.

Received 22 August.

GC/CL/156; Clar. Dep. C.451/1 (44, 45, 49, 50, 62)

[1] 'It states that Her Majesty is rejoiced to have this opportunity of acknowledging the kind disposition of her august allies, whilst at the same time she places her confidence in the fidelity of the Army, in the support of the Urban Militia, and on the firm will of the nation which will alone be sufficient to prove to the imprudent Prince that he has made a fresh mistake and has before him a fresh warning.' (V to P, 13 Aug. 1834, no. 112, FO 72/425.)
[2] The captains of the *Leveret* and the *Saracen* were asked by the Spanish authorities at Biscay to prevent ships carrying munitions to the Carlists from landing on the Spanish coast. They refused on the grounds that they 'had no instructions to detain or search vessels supposed to have warlike stores on board'. (V to P, 13 Aug. 1834, no. 113, FO 72/425.)
[3] Loans privately contracted by Ferdinand VII through the banker Aguado at exorbitant rates of interest. To repudiate them would in effect have placed them on the same basis as the Cortes Bonds.
[4] The document drawn up by the Minister of Grace and Justice merely stated that as Don Carlos was in treasonable revolt against the authority of the Crown, he and his line must be excluded from the line of succession. (V to P, 13 Aug. 1834, no. 114, FO 72/425.)

82   Villiers to Palmerston, 16 August 1834

Madrid. Private. Martinez seems much pleased with the news from the provinces this morning, but I confess I see little to rejoice at. Rodil has been foiled in his intentions of hemming in Zumalacarregui, of forcing a battle, of catching Don Carlos, and of preventing his junction with the main body of the insurgents. He seems in short to be pursuing just the same sort of hare-hunting on foot system as his predecessors, and with the same results. The Minister of War thinks it very advantageous that Zumala and Co. should be in Biscay now instead of Navarre, but it cannot be said that they have been driven there. They have left their fastnesses of their own accord and for their own purposes as it seems to me although I don't pretend to say, with the slender details which come from the army, what those purposes are. All accounts agree upon the efficient activity of the French army upon the frontier.

There has been a gloom and panic the last 3 days upon the prospect of affairs which have served to shew how little dependence will be to be placed upon people here in the event of a real crisis arriving. Martinez told me today that I should not believe, if he were to tell me, the class or numbers of those who within the last few days have come to supplicate that the Government would ask for French intervention as the only means of salvation. To all he says he has given the same indignant refusal. The Government are however committing many acts of injustice and despotism strangely at variance with their professed liberality, and I fear that what with the discontents of the returned and unemployed emigrants, the total absence of foresight on the part of the Government or of police to supply its place against the activity of the movement scramble party that an awful storm is brewing.

I am not a croaker, still less do I affect in this land of chance to be a prophet, but I have a presentiment of coming ills which is far from pleasant.

I have such short notice of the departure of Rothschild's courier that I cannot write any more.

PS. Martinez is more than ever anxious for moral support as the best means of avoiding that which is material—*any* declaration on the part of the English Government he says he can trade with here to the greatest advantage.

PS. the 2d. I have this moment received your letter of the 7th instant.

Received 26 August.[1]

GC/CL/157; Clar. Dep. C.451/1 (58-59)

[1] C.451/1 docketed 'By commercial courier Rothschild'.

83 Villiers to Palmerston, 23 August 1834

Madrid. Private. I have received and shewn to Martinez your letters of the 6th and 8th instant. He admits the difficulty we should have in stopping our own or neutral flags (the French have no difficulty of the kind) but says that your proposition for English cruizers to keep company with the Spanish and come to their aid if they were in a wrangle without enquiring the cause of it, would answer every purpose they have in view, and he is very much obliged to you. The worst of it is though that no English cruizers arrive, and the commanders of the two little things which have been at Bilbao for many weeks past, finding nothing about ammunition for Don Carlos in the instructions which they got from Admiral Parker 3 months ago, remain quietly in port and add to the number of doubters of our sincerity.

I have explained to Martinez our Hovering Act and recommended to him to publish a prohibition to import arms and military stores. He promised to do so immediately and to make the prohibition and its penalties known in England, France and Holland.

Matters in the provinces go on ill and I see no ground for hoping that the war will soon terminate. It is evident that the insurgents go where they please and do what they like. Don Carlos has made a complete tour with impunity and, I believe, in security. The Queen's troops were never more but never less than three leagues from him—the whole peasantry is so favorable to him and those who conduct him are so dexterous that I doubt not he might make the same expedition $\frac{1}{2}$ a dozen times more with the same results. His supposed object in going to Lequeitio was to meet the armament from England and the bonhomie of his people in taking the 'Perla' frigate for the 'Samuel Cunard' schooner must have been disappointing to His Highness.[1] As usual with Spaniards they came with all their secrets written down, their signals, countersigns, etc., which were Charles X, Charles V, La Vendée, Duchesse de Berri and others shewing their connexion with the Carlists of France.

Rayneval shewed me a letter which he had received yesterday from Harispe who seems very successful in preventing the rebels drawing their supplies as they have hitherto done from France. He has a poor idea of Rodil's strategy or even activity. I enclose you an extract of a letter which I have received from Caradoc today—his account is entirely confirmed by what I learn from other quarters. In Rodil's report of the action of the 31st which has been published in the Gazette he says 'that the English Colonel Caradoc who is at my head quarters as a volunteer exhibited on the 31st ultimo *good disposition,* knowledge, and the *serenity* characteristic of the nation to which he belongs, as well as the captain of the Navy who accompanies him'. The latter is a Captain Dalling who Caractacus brought with him from Paris.

Aston has sent me the proposed Additional Articles to the Treaty which are quite satisfactory to the Government.[2]

Alava told me the other day that Miraflores was likely to leave England on the plea of the expence of his mission being greater than he could support, but in reality because he wanted to come into the Government here, in which case Alava said he should apply for the mission. I told him that I did not doubt the pleasure it would give you but I suggested for his consideration whether after the violent and I would add wrongheaded part which the Duke of Wellington had taken upon Peninsular affairs he might not find himself in a false position with respect to the Government, for he was not likely to give up his intimacy with the Duke, and though you never would, yet others might suspect him of playing a double part—all which might damage Spanish affairs. Alava thanked me quite cordially for this and said that he had not been aware of the part which the Duke had taken lately about the Treaty, etc.[3] which would embarrass him greatly and he should therefore not think again of going to London.

The French Government are furious with Toreno's scheme, but I believe they speak more as the representatives of *their own* breeches pockets than of the French rentiers.[4] De Rigny told Rayneval to make a formal protest against the measure but to consult first with me as I should probably have received instructions to the same effect. I strongly advised him not to do so, first because it is no longer in the power of the Government to alter a project which is before the Cortes, and 2dly that if the French were to take any strong measure of the kind it would so exasperate the Cortes that they would be sure without regarding the consequences to throw over the whole French debt. I told him too that with respect to the Cortes Bond holders, which was a far grosser case of injustice than that of the French rentiers, the English Government never claimed a *right* to interfere as if the question had been a national one and they had been prepared to push that right to extremities—they had done every thing short of that. Rayneval agreed with me and he has merely communicated to Martinez and

Toreno how strongly his Government felt upon the subject, which may perhaps be useful in preventing their *adhesion* to a measure for throwing over the loans since 1823 to which neither of them in their hearts were disinclined.

You have probably heard of the imprisonment at Pamplona of a Mr. Mitchell, the correspondent of the Morning Herald. . . .

PS. Martinez has this moment sent me the decree prohibiting the importation of arms, etc.[5]

Enclosure: 'Extract from Colonel Caradoc's letter to Mr. Villiers dated Ochandiano 17th Aug. 1834', complaining of Rodil's inactivity.

Received 2 September.[6]

GC/CL/158; Clar. Dep. C.451/1 (60-61, 51-52)

[1] A despatch published in the *Madrid Gazette* of 21 August stated that between 80 and 90 Carlists had mistaken the frigate *Perla* for a vessel which they were expecting from England with arms and stores. The Carlists were encouraged to board the ship and were all taken prisoner. (V to P, 23 Aug. 1834, no. 119, FO 72/426.)

[2] By the Additional Articles the British Government agreed to sell arms and supplies to Spain, and the French Government undertook to prevent arms reaching the Carlists across the Pyrenees. See Michael Hurst, *Key Treaties for the Great Powers 1814-1914*, i. 235-37.

[3] For Wellington's critical view of the Quadruple Treaty see, for instance, Wellington to Aberdeen, 20 May 1834, printed in *Wellington I : Political Correspondence 1833-November 1834*, ed. by John Brooke and Julia Gandy, 1976, 537.

[4] Toreno's scheme was to recognize the old Cortes Bonds but not the loans contracted after 1823.

[5] 'A decree was to be published on 24 August prohibiting the import of arms and warlike stores, and announcing that the most vigorous measures will be taken to that effect along the whole line of coast from Cape Finisterre to the mouth of the Bidassoa.' (V to P, 23 Aug. 1834, no. 120, FO 72/426.)

[6] C.451/1 docketed 'By French courier'.

84   Palmerston to Villiers, 26 August 1834

Copy. Foreign Office. Private. I send you a very unsatisfactory despatch[1] but we have no choice; the learned in the law lay down these doctrines and there is no denying the soundness of them. If we were to issue a declaration of war against Carlos our situation would be changed and we should then become entitled to all the rights of a belligerent, but this would not be tanti and the Spanish Government itself can hardly wish that we should to such an extent mix ourselves up in the civil war in Spain. The fact is that there is very little to be done in order to prevent the landing of arms and stores for the insurgents, and that little the Spanish Government will be able to do for itself. We will give them every assistance and facility for fitting out ships here; we will give officers and men leave to serve; and we will give according to our recent engagements, arms and stores. One or two good steamers could easily be bought and equipped and they would effectually prevent any supplies from being landed, if assisted by other small vessels to keep a look out and let them know of the approach of any vessel. Besides, as the season advances, landing arms on the open beach in the Bay of Biscay will become not so easy a matter. The United Kingdom still lies at Helvoet watched by one of our steamers and though another cargo of arms has arrived for her in another merchantman, the transhipment has not yet taken place. I believe that the owners of the arms and vessel have not yet been paid for them by Carlos and his bankers, and that they do not like to part with their property till payment is made or secured.

The war in Navarre and Biscay does not seem likely to come to an end because the two parties never meet. If the Spanish Government want more muskets to arm additional troops with, we can supply them; but is it impossible to disarm the minds of the population of their angry passions by some arrangement upon the points in dispute? We, removed as we are from the scene of action and necessarily ignorant of details, can be but bad judges, but it seems to us that compromise would be the shortest way of putting an end to the insurrection. It is uncommonly hard to reduce to submission by force the population of a mountainous district when the whole of that population is determined to resist, and after all, suppose obedience re-established for a time by the complete occupation of the country by twice the present number of troops, those troops cannot stay there always, and who will answer for the continuance of submission when the troops shall have been withdrawn?

The request of the bondholders seems really very fair and reasonable; it would be unjust that they should be permanent sufferers from the want of punctuality on the part of the Spanish Government in fulfilling its obligations in former years; and nothing can be more moderate and reasonable than the request that the interest, which ought to have been paid but which is still due, should be now considered as so much additional capital and that interest should be paid upon it.

We are daily hoping for some good news about the slave trade articles.

I am amused with your account of Maberley. . . .

PS. If the Spanish Government would send to the northern coast some of those Guarda Costas which amuse themselves by capturing our merchantmen in the Mediterranean, they would do two good things at once.

Docketed: By messenger.

GC/CL/1234

[1] Announcing the British Government's reluctant decision not to instruct its cruisers to take an active part in patrolling the northern coast of Spain. See P to V, 26 Aug. 1834, no. 48, FO 72/419.

85   Villiers to Palmerston, 29 August 1834

Madrid. Private. I have received your letter of the 19th in which you say that you send the Additional Articles—but they did not arrive. I received them however from Aston. The Government are delighted and Martinez expects a great moral effect will be produced throughout Spain, for the Carlists were beginning to shew their heads every where and to proclaim that England and France did not intend to renew the Treaty.

Where moral effect however is most wanted the Treaty will never penetrate—in the Northern Provinces where the possession even of a Madrid newspaper is punished by death and the people are stuffed with lies about Russian armies and English fleets coming to their assistance. We have no news from Rodil this week and it is evident that he makes and probably will make no more progress than the French when they were in that country with 48,000 men commanded by able generals and never possessed more of it than what they actually stood upon. Every movement of the army is instantly made known to the insurgents whereas no amount of bribing or punishing can procure an iota of information respecting the plans of the latter. General Carandolet last week offered to several peasants (at different times) 1,500 francs to carry a letter three leagues and they all refused—not only from attachment to the cause they serve, but from fear of Zumalacarregui's police and his vengeance. He last week shot two Alcaldes for having delayed one $\frac{1}{4}$ of an hour forwarding a report to him. The manner in which he blockades a town *morally* is singular but as effective as if it were done by an army—he declares that such a place shall receive no provisions and he leaves a handful of spies who are acquainted with all the inhabitants of the surrounding villages to watch that his orders are obeyed. The man who introduces even a sack of flour finds himself infallibly shot next day, and all attempts at such smuggling never last beyond a few days. Vitoria has in this way been reduced lately to most of the privations of a siege and the inhabitants have been putting themselves upon short allowance although there was not an armed man within sight of the town.

The blockade has now been raised because, no traffic being allowed, Zumala received nothing from his different lines of Custom Houses, and provisions are again carried to the town after paying the rebel tariffs. Mina adopted the same system with the same success against the French and all persons who know those provinces well speak despondingly upon the prompt termination if not the eventual issue of the war.

On the other hand, Her Majesty the Regent seems playing the game of Don Carlos as if he paid her for it. In my last dispatch, notwithstanding Martinez's assurance that he expected her here, I ventured to disbelieve, and sure enough three days ago the Cabinet learned *by accident* that she had prepared every thing to decamp from St. Ildefonso and pitch her tents near Cuenca at an out of the way village about 25 leagues from Madrid and in a very factious country. The Ministers informed her that the cholera was raging there and moreover indicted a savage round robin to say that by the King's will the Council of Regency was entrusted with the safe keeping of the young Queen and they would no longer tolerate being separated from her. Toreno too added a letter of his own upon certain financial exactions which exceeded all decent bounds. These together with a severe pelting which the Chevalier grimpant got yesterday from the St. Ildefonsians seem to have moved the Court i.e. the two Queens and the Muñoz family to come to the Pardo, a royal shooting place about two leagues from the town, which will be a great facility to public business as her signature is necessary for every act—even for a royal order issued yesterday by the Minister of the Interior for the discontinuance of the indecent practice observed at some schools of whipping little boys.

Mina has been restored to his rank, but he declines taking it unless it is a part of a general measure; he has however written word that as there is now a national representation he shall be ready and desirous to serve the Queen in any capacity.

Rayneval has addressed a confidential note to Martinez urging him to recognize and pay the whole of the French debt. . . .

Upon seeing that Melbourne in answer to Lord Londonderry had stated that Caradoc was sent to Rodil's army in order to transmit correct information, I wrote to him immediately to recommend that he should not quit his post till he heard from you, and I have written to him again tonight to say that you desire him to stay.

The reports of Maberly and Irving must be received with great caution. . . .

As I have no belief here in any but accomplished facts, I am afraid of again promising any thing upon a matter where I have been so constantly disappointed, but I think that in a few days I shall bring the undecided Martinez to swallow the Equipment Articles in return for the Additional ones. Alava has been of use to me in this. He begs to be most especially brought to your Lordship's recollection.

Miraflores has asked for and obtained two months leave of absence—he has been thereunto moved by those mighty passions, ambition and love—he can't bear that the Proceres should separate without hearing him speak and he is afraid that an enormous old dowager whom he has loved not wisely but too well for fifteen years should pass into the arms of another swain.

PS. William Hervey is somewhat better and he will not leave Madrid unless absolutely forced by his state of health. I think then if you please I will postpone having Mr. Otway of whose working capabilities it strikes me I have not heard a very high report.[1] I hope you will be amused by my extract from the Royal Order respecting the cholera—we are great hands at legislation here.[2]

PPS. I open this to say that I have this moment received a letter dated the 20th from Caradoc—things appear much in the same state except that the insurgents are more in want of shoes and powder. Don Carlos is terribly frightened, bored and disgusted and Zumalacarregui is supposed to be desirous of getting rid of him.

Received 8 September.

GC/CL/159; Clar. Dep. C.451/1 (53-57)

[1] The copy in C.451/1 ends here.

[2] 'The local authorities were directed whenever the cholera appears to adopt means for promoting mirth and composure in the minds of the inhabitants, avoiding all that may affect them with melancholy.' (V to P, 29 Aug. 1834, no. 123, FO 72/426.)

86   Villiers to Palmerston, 3 September 1834

Madrid. Private. I must be very brief this evening as I am already keeping Maberly's courier waiting. I have given you the debates of the Cortes more in detail perhaps than you may think called for, but it is the best means of exhibiting the manner in which they are composed, a matter of no small importance as the futurity of Spain depends upon their proceedings. There is not a single man of talent in the Opposition, but the Government possesses little or no influence. Their supporters give their votes as victims and their opponents with a kind of insolence which has created a friendly sympathy with the gallery, where 3 or 400 of the Madrid prolétaires are packed and who I foresee will soon acquire the same influence in the debates as the galleries did at the time of the Convention.

The *Bill of Rights*[1] and crude declarations of principles which the opposition seems bent on introducing discredit the Government by placing them upon the slippery ground of shrinking from or opposing the opinions they have always been advocating and upon which they came into power. They don't either manage these questions with dexterity but Martinez is as obstinate as a mule when he meets with opposition. Upon the whole I don't like the parliamentary better than any of the other prospects of Spain. I read to Martinez and Toreno the passage in your letter eulogistic of their speeches and proceedings—they have of course taken care to make it known and I really believe it has done them infinite good here.

No news has been received from Rodil since I last wrote. Martinez told me today that the Government had desired him to be more active and to adopt a rather less regular strategy even if he were to run some risk by it, and above all not to pursue Don Carlos and his 2,000 $\frac{1}{2}$ armed ragamuffins with a corps d'armée which of course encumbers his march. The general commanding at Vitoria has written word that Don Carlos was again making his way to the Bastan, pursued closely enough never to have a day's rest, contused as to his head,[2] very angry at the false promises by which he was induced to enter Spain, and at some insults he had received from Zumalacarregui who now discovers him to be the incumbrance which every one predicted he would. Rodil is inactive certainly but he appears to have taken up good positions, to have routed the insurgents from their fastnesses and to have reduced them to greater straits than they have yet been for clothing, provisions and ammunition.

If you take the same view as I do of Lieutenant Trail's conduct I hope he will receive a reprimand.[3] The Carlists in Biscay are of course perfectly well informed of every thing that passes. They will know that the commander of the only British ship on the station refused to leave the port and cruize at the request of the Governor of Bilbao (in this perhaps he may have been justified),[4] and if he and his officers have been holding angry language at the conduct of the captain of the 'Perla' decoying out 90 rebels from the shore and afterwards at the request of a rebel junta has directed the English vice consul to interfere with the Spanish authorities in their behalf, it will be immediately magnified into English good will for the Carlist cause and more mis-chief will be produced than the Additional Articles will be able to undo. I don't know if the hoisting the colors of another country is a mortal offence against naval law but I know it is a very general prac-tice, and in the present instance it would seem to be perfectly in accord-ance with the kind of assistance we have pledged ourselves to give to Spain and it was completely successful in catching a parcel of fellows upon whose objects there does not appear to be a shadow of doubt.

Received 12 September.[5]

GC/CL/160; Clar. Dep. C.451/1 (69-71)

[1] Discussed in the Chamber of Procuradores on 1 September. (V to P, 3 Sept. 1834, no. 126, FO 72/426.)

[2] 'Don Carlos appears to have fallen from his horse and to have received a severe injury on his head.' (V to P, 30 Aug. 1834, no. 124, FO 72/426.)

[3] Captain of the *Leveret* stationed at Bilbao. He had ordered the release of the insurgents who had boarded the *Perla,* and had also asked the British consul at Bilbao to plead for leniency with the civil authorities. V instructed the vice-consul on no account to intercede on behalf of the rebels. (V to P, 3 Sept. 1834, no. 127, FO 72/426.)

[4] C.451/1 contains the additional words 'by his want of instructions'.

[5] C.451/1 docketed 'By Mr. Maberly's courier'.

87   Palmerston to Villiers, 5 September 1834

Copy. Foreign Office. Private. The French Government have asked me to instruct you to support Rayneval in the remonstrances which he is ordered to make upon the subject of the Royal Bonds as distinguished from the Cortes Bonds; the French Government appearing to think that there is an intention at Madrid of drawing a distinction between these two parts of the public debt of Spain and of acknowledging the latter and refusing to pay the former. I have said in reply that I could not give you any official instructions on that subject. That the rule which we have laid down for ourselves with respect to all these foreign loans in Europe and America, advanced to various Governments by British individuals without any previous understanding between the lenders and the British Government was that such loans and the claims founded upon them cannot be made the subject of formal discussion between the English and other Governments; but that English ministers abroad may be instructed to present memorials sent by parties in this country interested in such transactions and may be authorized to support the prayer of such memorials unofficially by arguments and reasoning, and by an expression of the interest which the British Government must necessarily take in such claims. But I observed that even in the case of such debts due to British subjects, the Government does not take the matter up on its own account, nor originate remonstrances, and solely confines itself to support remonstrances coming from private parties. That what the French now ask us to do would be going a great deal further, since it would be not only to change our character from that of supporters and backers of the representations of others, to that of originators of representations of our own, but moreover we should be taking up this new position not in favor of our own subjects but in favor of the subjects of France (if MM. Mauguin & Co. will allow me to use that expression). Now I observed, if we felt a delicacy as to speaking as from ourselves about debts due to British subjects, still more must we hesitate to do so about debts due to the subjects of another country. In reply to this, the French request that I would authorize you to point out in private and unofficial conversation, if you have an opportunity of doing so, all the motives of honor and good policy which ought to induce the Spanish Government to make no distinction between the different proportions of its foreign debt. This I said I could have no objection to do; that my own opinion was decidedly the same as theirs on this subject; that loans contracted under the authority of the existing Government of a country ought to be held sacred by all who come after; whether of the same or of totally opposite political opinions. That no country which did not act upon this principle could ever hope to enjoy any public credit in Europe; and that every motive of sound policy seem to me to combine in forming the strongest inducement to Spain to keep faith with all her foreign creditors. I said that I would certainly write to you to this effect and authorize you to draw the attention of the Spanish Ministers to these considerations, privately and unofficially, and not as British minister but as a well wisher to Spain.

There is also another consideration which the Spanish Government ought not to overlook. In the present state of their affairs, they stand in need of the good will and moral support of France; they require more; they want a certain degree of indirect assistance. Is it wise then, or, on a balance of considerations, advantageous to do that which may excite against them the interested passions of a vast number of persons in France, and which, by creating an impression that justice has not been done by Spain to Frenchmen, must not only disincline the French Government towards the Spanish cause, but create obstacles to the execution of their good intentions by exciting an adverse public opinion? I leave you to deal with this matter with your usual tact and discretion; but talk to Rayneval about it and tell him what I have written to you.

Carlos's wife is dead. . . .

No progress seems making in the equipment of the United Kingdom at Helvoet; she and the Cunard still lie looking at each other and watched by the Phoenix Government steamer. I fancy money is wanting to pay for the steamer and the arms. If the Spanish Government can get a few more ships and especially a good steamer or two upon the little bit of coast upon which alone any landing could be effected, this Helvoet plan must fail.

Docketed: Sent under flying seal to Mr. Aston, to be forwarded.

GC/CL/1235

88 Villiers to Palmerston, 9 September 1834

Madrid. Private. You will not be surprised at my agreeing with your private letter of the 26th ultimo and thinking your dispatch of the same date very unsatisfactory upon the doctrines of intervention. With all reverence for the learned in the law it appears to me that a declaration of war against Don Carlos is as unnecessary for us as it would be complimentary to him, for if the Treaty does not mean hostility to those who are disturbing the tranquillity of Spain it means nothing. England is not at war, it is true, but she is solemnly bound to keep the peace in this country, and towards those who break it she cannot be even in a position of neutrality. The warlike stores which we are supplying, the naval force which we are engaged to furnish are surely facts hostile enough and of a nature to render the stopping supplies to the enemies of our ally a matter of course and of secondary consideration in our own policy though not in its importance to Spain. Could you if called upon tomorrow refuse to send a naval force to Spain, and if you did, against whom would that force act? Against the supporters of the rebels and conveyers of supplies, come by what means they might, or the fleet would be a mockery of the Treaty, and it seems to me therefore most practicable that under our new engagements with Spain we should help her to enforce her own laws. She has declared that arms and ammunition shall be liable to seizure within two leagues of the coast—why should not our cruizers stop any vessel within that distance and carry them into a Spanish port or deliver them over to Spanish ships to make lawful prizes of? And there is a wide difference between stopping ships on the high seas and in a corner of the Bay of Biscay when they can only be coming to Spain and at a distance from the shore when their cargoes have become an illegal importation. Why should not an Order in Council be published as many a time it has before, prohibiting for a limited period the exportation of arms? This would be an immense check, for arms can be procured nowhere so cheaply or so easily as in England, and if it was once publicly known that under the Treaty we intended to assist Spain in enforcing her new decree within two leagues of the coast I'll warrant that our cruizers will have a complete sinecure. There is precedent, if I mistake not, for more than this when two vessels with men and arms were prevented from leaving England at the request of Zea (I believe, though I don't remember the circumstances clearly) because they were going to levy war against our ally Ferdinand.

If the French Government was to pursue a system of non-interference with the trade in warlike stores and permitted that men and arms should cross the frontier I declare to God I believe that before Christmas Don Carlos would be upon the throne and the Holy Alliance would have a triumph which it makes one sick to think of. To avert this, some, and not much, aid is necessary for Spain—the Treaty has gone far to rescue her from the jaws of the Inquisition and to render her an important ally to us; the Additional Articles will complete the work if they are acted up to, but we have no right to expect that our good wishes alone will suffice or that a series of lucky and unlooked for events should occur here as in Portugal. Hitherto we have only had a brig at Bilbao commanded by a lieutenant who seems to me to be a regular Carlist, and should more ships arrive and permit without interference the landing of stores for the insurgents, the moral influence of their presence will quickly pass over to the other side, and afford all the encouragement to the Carlists which we intend it should give to the Queen's party, while the public at Madrid, thinking we are insincere and either indifferent to or wishing for the success of Don Carlos, will be dispirited or vent their fury against the Government. This will be very ignorant and very stupid but it is not the less certain.

I am sorry not to be of the same opinion with you and I have no expectation that my views will alter any determination of the Government, but I am here upon the spot, I know the spirit of the people and the manner in which affairs are managed, the want of foresight in the Government and the tardiness and disobedience of their agents. I foresee the almost impossibility of Rodil's finishing the war in the provinces, and the almost certainty that if it continues much longer we shall have Carlist parties rising in every part of the country, which the Government will have no means of repressing. Feeling all this I am sure you will consider that I am only doing my duty in frankly telling you my opinion upon the necessity of boldly finishing what has been gloriously begun. Little is wanted to complete the federation of the constitutional nations of the West as a check upon the despotic federation of the North and as the greatest achievement of modern times, but that little, if withheld, may eventually be the means of plunging Europe into a general war and of retarding, at least for our days, the progress of better government.

Martinez has been much bullied by ci-devant Governors of Cuba and others not to accede to the Equipment Articles and you may suppose it has been no easy work to obtain his consent. I scarcely think I should have succeeded if I had not enlisted Alava in the cause. Pray send me powers to sign the Articles quickly lest he should change his mind and it would save time and chance of error if you would at the same time send me the form in which they should be drawn up. The Articles signed at Paris in 1833 would I suppose do but I have not been supplied with them and they are not in the State Papers, or the slave trade correspondence.

I hope I shall succeed in obtaining the request made in the memorials of the Cortes Bond holders. . . . [1]

The French Government ordered Rayneval to make a formal protest against Toreno's project and they have been loud and bitter in their denunciations of it. This has had a very bad effect not only with some portion of the Chamber and the public but with Martinez and Toreno (particularly the former). I have availed myself of this and stated that the English Government had no intention to interfere with a ministerial measure and they are both much pleased with the line I have taken.

Pray let me know if you like to have the kind of précis I have hitherto sent of the debates in the Cortes or whether they are not of sufficient interest in England to make it worth while. The Government are a good deal discredited by the debate on the Bill of Rights. They have shewn a great want of parliamentary tact and have permitted themselves unnecessarily to be put in a false position. I have endeavoured to make Martinez see this but he is like a deaf adder or one of his own mules when there is any question of concession. He is a wonderful man in the Tribune. It would be difficult in England to find a more able dexterous and powerful debater.

I don't know what Mr. Mitchell was put in gaol for but his case seems one of shameful persecution and I have done my best, I believe with success, to procure his liberation. . . .

Caradoc has left the army and returned to France as he will of course have informed you himself—he appears never to have received my letters desiring him to remain which is very unfortunate as his departure may give rise to misrepresentations of various kinds.

Received 20 September.[2]

GC/CL/161; Clar. Dep. C.451/1 (72-76)

[1] See V to P, 9 Sept. 1834, no. 128, FO 72/426.
[2] C.451/1 docketed 'By French courier'.

89 Villiers to Palmerston, 10 September 1834

Madrid. Private. I avail myself of Rayneval's usual impunctuality[1] in sending off his couriers to let you know that my dispatches dated yesterday do not go till today.

There has been a debate in the Procurers this morning[2] in which Martinez has distinguished himself and shewn that he no longer thought it wise to put himself in apparent hostility to the principles he has been advocating all his life. The effect I hear has been excellent and he has carried the whole Chamber with him—this will give the Government stability and improve their chance of carrying their finance measures which are more important than any other.

There is no news from the army except a report that Baron Carondolet, the general who has twice been surprised and had his regiment cut to pieces by the insurgents, has shot himself.[3] I did not believe any Spaniard capable of such an act and if true it is rather creditable to the Baron.

Received 20 September.[4]

GC/CL/162; Clar. Dep. C.451/1 (77)

[1] C.451/1 has 'unpunctuality'.
[2] On the Declaration of Rights, article 8, that 'All Spaniards are obliged to pay in proportion to their properties the taxes freely voted by the Cortes'. Martínez de la Rosa spoke in favour of this, and it was unanimously adopted. The Government had been defeated on articles 3, 5 and 7. (V to P, 10 Sept. 1834, no. 133, FO 72/426.)
[3] This rumour was false.
[4] C.451/1 docketed 'By French courier [?] delayed'.

90 Villiers to Palmerston, 11 September 1834

Madrid. Private. Happening to call just now upon Maberly I found him in the act of expediting a courier with an account [of] the report of the Finance Committee which has this morning been presented to the Chamber, and as he has offered me a copy of it I enclose you one. Its principal interest is that it affords a sort of justification for Toreno's scheme and proves that if he had brought forward a larger measure of justice for the French creditors he would have had no chance of carrying it. I still think his original project will pass and I hope that the chances of the Cortes Bond holders improve. I have endeavoured to impress upon him that without something more being done to conciliate the London market he will never get his loan. He is uncommonly pleased with my not having protested and stormed as Rayneval was obliged to do.

This will probably arrive before the French courier who left Madrid yesterday with numerous but not very important dispatches from me, except one in which I announce Martinez's readiness at last to consent to the Equipment Articles and asking full powers for me to sign them.

Nothing good or very new from the provinces—Carlos seems running in a ring like a frightened hare followed by a remarkably slow and ill hunted pack of hounds.

I am writing in Maberly's room and as his courier is on his horse waiting you must excuse this hasty scrawl.

PS. Martinez yesterday took the line which I have pressed him all along to do and put an end to these schoolboy discussions upon abstract principles. It produced a good effect—the Chamber is in better humour and the stability and prospects of the Government are improved—at least jusqu'à nouvel ordre.

Enclosure: Summary of proceedings in the Chamber of Procuradores on the presentation of reports by the Finance Committee. (All its members reported in favour of allowing the Government to raise only two hundred million reales, instead of the four hundred million for which Toreno had asked. A majority reported against acknowledging loans contracted between 1823 and 1834.)

Received 19 September.

GC/CL/163

91 Villiers to Palmerston, 15 September 1834

Madrid. Private. I have but little time given me for writing by Martinez's courier—there is however not much to report since I last wrote.

The death of Don Carlos's wife is an important event as it deprives him of the only source from which he ever drew any thing resembling courage. It may possibly complete the disgust he has for his present vagabond dangerous mode of life and oblige him to take refuge in France. Even then, though, the war would not be put an end to—his presence has exercised little influence upon it, and additional enthusiasm in some places has been more than counterbalanced by the inconvenience which he has entailed upon his partisans, and if he were to be killed or to run away the struggle would remain as deadly and unchanged for a republic or the independence of the provinces as it now is for absolute monarchy. The time for compromise has been permitted to pass—the spirit of the people is now too bitter and their anxiety for victory is too great to permit them to remember the original cause of the war or the means which once offered for its termination. The character of the people is the same now as in the most remote periods, and a war in those provinces has from all times been the grave of the reputation of the general sent to conduct it. In 11 months four generals have failed in every thing except increasing the numbers of the insurgents and improving their mode of warfare. The Government are now as much dissatisfied with Rodil as with his predecessors. They have had some difficulty in persuading the Council of Regency to appoint Mina to the chief command of the army, but when it was proposed to the Queen she refused to give her consent *at present* i.e. till it is too late to be of use. I do not myself think he would have done much good—it is true his name has a great *prestige* in the provinces but the population are too deeply committed in the war to feel deference for the prestige of a man fighting against themselves and whom they would therefore consider an apostate to his former opinions. Mina is moreover jealous and ambitious, he will take council of no man, his broken health would prevent his former activity and it must be remembered that his fame was gained in the command of guerillas and making war after their fashion—he has never commanded regular troops; still his appointment would have been a kind of homage to public opinion and would have made the Government popular.

The present intention and the Queen's wish is to send Llauder to replace Rodil—he is very desirous of it himself, and certainly the manner in which he has kept down the whole province of Catalonia ever since the King's death shews him to be no ordinary man. His activity and determination in whatever he undertakes know no bounds, but his absence may be fatal to the tranquillity of Catalonia, which is pretty equally divided between Carlists and republicans, and a more terrible set of devils than both are don't exist on this side of Pandemonium. In short there is no question whether of men or of things here that is not bristling with difficulties and my constant wonder is that we scramble on towards improvement as much and as fast as we do.

Don Carlos's edict of death against the Government and all the members of both Chambers will greatly serve the Queen. Well may the Ministers in their acts against him style him ill advised Prince for instead of endeavouring to throw doubt and dissension in the Cortes he has now united Carlists, Christinos and Waverers by the common tie of self preservation against his cause.

I am doing my best for the Cortes Bond holders and I have little doubt that the prospect held out to them in Toreno's original scheme will be ameliorated. The reports of the Finance Commission and the uncertain temper of the Chamber upon the whole subject prevent Toreno from giving any decided answer at present, but he has promised me to make honorable mention of the memorials in his speech and I have asked him to send as favorable an official answer as he can to my note in order that you may have some proof of their interests not being neglected to shew the Bond holders.

I keep speaking and writing to Martinez about Mr. Mitchell. . . .

September 17th. I had written thus far the day before yesterday when I learned that Martinez meant to postpone his courier's departure for a few days. I accordingly send one myself, first because there is plenty of one kind or another to say, and next in order to have a courier stationed at Bayonne in the event of your sending me full powers to sign the Equipment Articles by a messenger—for a gentleman accustomed to travel in his undersprung britchka makes very bad work of galloping lame mules over a couple of hundred miles of goat paths.

Yesterday morning I received your admirable letter of the 5th instant. It came just at the right moment when the discussion upon the finance question was about to commence and it has produced the best effects. I read it to Rayneval who was delighted and said that if he had received similar instructions at first from his Government he should have been able to make a much more successful fight. I afterwards read it to Toreno and Martinez who were both equally pleased and said it was impossible not to adopt views so just or take advice given in such a friendly spirit. The report of the majority of the Finance Committee is so grateful to the roguery and antipathies of the people that there is of course some danger that it will be adopted by the Opposition, but Toreno assured me he should use every effort to modify his original project in the sense of the minority of the Committee. You will see in my report of today's debate that Toreno used the opinion of the English Government against the intention of throwing over the French creditor which will I hope be satisfactory to De Rigny.

By the courier who brought me your letter of the 5th I received one from Aston informing me that De Rigny had told him that the question of French intervention had been discussed in the Spanish Cabinet and that Martinez and Toreno had been the only Ministers who were unfavorable to it—that the French Government were no longer so much disinclined to the measure under certain restrictions, etc., etc. of which Aston has doubtless sent you a report. I disbelieved the report of the question having been discussed, but as I thought it highly important to know the truth I communicated to Toreno with caution and in confidence that the French Government were aware of the discussion, etc. which had taken place in the Cabinet. He interrupted me at once and exclaimed, It is false—no discussion whatever has taken place upon the subject. I don't mean to say that it *might* not have been matter for discussion but the fact is, it has never once been mooted by myself or any of my colleagues and nothing but the clearest demonstration that the throne or the life of the Queen depends upon it will ever induce Martinez or myself to consent to it. I afterwards went straight to Martinez and made to him the same communication in the same manner. He interrupted me in the same place and with the same words as Toreno—It is false, no discussion has ever taken place—and then repeated to me with great earnestness the opinions I have so often heard before from him upon the subject.

Now if we call to mind the dislike which the French Government has always expressed to intervene at the time when they were best disposed towards the existing order of things here and compare it with the readiness which they now profess to march into Spain when they are all thunder and protest against the measures of the Spanish Government, it looks much more as if the intervention would be in favor of the Perpetuelles than against Don Carlos, and as if they thought that Harispe and 40,000 men would send up Royal Bonds better than Rayneval and diplomatic notes. They have therefore improvised a discussion in the Spanish Cabinet which Rayneval never could have reported to them and which if they had derived it from any other source they might have verified through Frias, in order to justify their proposed change of policy and to tâter le terrain in England. I am accordingly very glad that I made the communication to Martinez and Toreno for they will be more loud than ever in deprecating the measure and will moreover I think be very active in taking means to prevent the necessity of it ever arising.

There are endless present and future European objections to it but the main objection, to my mind, would be found here—the entry of French troops would be so universally unpopular among the liberal party that it would raise a Jacobinical spirit which the Government would be wholly unequal to control, which would produce general confusion and eventually turn to the profit of Carlism.

Aston wrote me word that De Rigny would have preferred a blockade to the preventive regulations respecting the importation of arms—his reasons appeared to me to be good and I communicated them to Martinez. He asked me to write him a private letter upon the subject in order to shew his colleagues, which I did and they agreed upon the Royal Order for a blockade which I send tonight. I suppose you will have it officially announced in the Gazette and at Lloyds.

I hope Montilla will come here upon Martinez's invitation. . . .

You will of course have seen a furious fight between the Times and Chronicle about the respective veracities of Mr. Turnbull and Mr. Maberly. . . .

PS. Mitchell is at large. Mr. Otway is not yet arrived. I hope that if *above* one half of what I hear of his inutility turns out to be true, you will permit me not to consider him a fixture here upon Scott's return.

GC/CL/164; Clar. Dep. C.451/1 (78-85)

92   Villiers to Palmerston, 23 September 1834

Madrid. Private. In my last letter I told you that the command of the army in the North had been offered to Llauder—three days ago I learned from Toreno that he had declined it on account of the landing of Romagosa and the extensive Carlist conspiracy which was hatching. I asked Toreno then what the Government intended to do; he said that they had again proposed Mina to the Queen who had again refused and had named in his stead one Cantarac[1] who is the poorest of God's creatures, of doubtful loyalty and by birth a Frenchman which Toreno said put them to great embarrassment. I told him it was more shame for him if it did as the disgrace of such an appointment would not fall upon the Queen but upon his and Martinez's shoulders, for that they ought not to remain a moment in the Government if the Queen rejected measures which they and the Council of Regency considered necessary, at a time too when Her Majesty had surrounded herself with triple sanitary cordons (which are not against infection but against intruders and advice) and was shut up with her paramour and a venerable old lady yclept Minister of Grace and Justice, so that she had no means for forming a correct judgement and they ought not therefore to bear that she should trifle with the destinies of the nation as if they were matters for caprice or Court patronage. Toreno said this was very true and that the Cabinet were much too courtierlike for a crisis like the present one—but that they were thinking of a remonstrance against Cantarac's nomination.

Yesterday I learned that Mina had been appointed to the chief command in Navarre and Osma to that of Biscay—he having been the man who has all along asked for Mina as the only chief likely to put down the rebellion and he will therefore be the most active in his cooperation with him—but the division of the army is manifestly very unwise. I have no reason for supposing that my conversation with Toreno had any influence upon this decision, but I had for some time past resolved to take an opportunity of expressing an opinion upon the deference which the Ministers (principally Martinez) pay to the royal caprices when exercised upon points of vital importance—the more so because I feel sure that the Queen's tendencies are good and that she is never unwilling to relinquish her own opinions if it is proved to her that they are wrong or likely to be injurious.

I still retain my opinion that Mina will do little more than his predecessors in the provinces but if he is not a successful general he will become a much less dangerous citizen—which *is a hedge*. His appointment will not be popular with the officers but the soldiers will like it which is of more consequence—they are somewhat disgusted now not with their fatigues and dangers but their want of success. Mina was written to yesterday[2] but there is some fear that his bad state of health will prevent his accepting the command. The landing of Romagosa and the Carlist conspiracy in Catalonia prove how dangerous it would have been to remove Llauder.

September 24th. Rayneval delayed his courier till today thinking that the Chamber would come to some decision upon the most important article of Toreno's project that all the foreign debt of Spain should be recognized, but nothing has been settled and I avail myself of a commercial courier to send my letters. I don't like the proceedings of the Procurers at all—not above 120 out of 180 are come or appear to intend coming—of these between 50 and 60 are generally against the Government—45 always so—among the rest there are waverers and very few thick and thin men such as a Minister loves in a representative assembly. The President's weakness absolutely invites disorder and his partiality towards the Opposition is only exceeded by that of the Secretaries who are 4 rank radicals—2 of them editors of newspapers. The côté gauche has already fallen into the Opposition jargon with which you are not *altogether unacquainted in England* of not wishing to embarrass the Government and deprecating any desire to be in office—at the same time nothing is left untried to force the Ministers out and if they succeed I don't believe that le bon Dieu himself could prevent every thing going to the Devil.

If any instructions have been issued to the English cruizers on the north coast of Spain will you direct that I may be furnished with a copy of them? Martinez has more than once spoken to me upon the subject.

I yesterday received your official announcement of the death of Doña Francisca. The day the *melancholy intelligence* was known here the Infant Don Francisco, his wife and family, were all gaily dressed at the bull fight.

Mr. Otway is arrived. I never saw *his* like before.

Received [?] 3 October.[3]

GC/CL/165; Clar. Dep. C.451/1 (86-88)

[1] General José Canterac: this nomination was withdrawn.
[2] Mina was still in France.
[3] C.451/1 docketed 'By Ardouin's courier'.

93   Villiers to Palmerston, 24 September 1834

Madrid. Private. I have already written to you today by a commercial courier to Paris but as I have just had an offer of writing by one to London I send a line to say that Rodil is recalled and Mina is appointed to the chief command in Navarre—General Osma to that in Biscay—the army being divided into two.

Little or no progress has been made in the discussion upon the finance question. The Government obtained so far a triumph yesterday that they carried the question of discussing the project of law before the reports of the Committee. It is hoped, though it is still doubtful, that tomorrow the 1st article of Toreno's project—the recognition of

all the foreign debt—will be carried—except the Guebhard Loan[1]—
that seems likely to go overboard. Even then however the payment will
be another and an equally difficult question and it will be some days
before the Chamber arrives at discussing that part of the project which
has created such an uproar in all the foreign stock exchanges. Till
Toreno sees his way more clearly he can of course say nothing positive
about the Cortes Bond holders but I still hope to get improved terms
for them.

The Chamber has of late been so difficult to manage and Martinez
has once or twice appeared so heartily disgusted, that he may retire
any day. I hope therefore you will lose no time in giving me powers
to sign the additional slave articles for if Martinez goes out the whole
question would have to be begun again with his successor and with a
less favorable issue perhaps.

PS. Mina is still in France and it is by no means certain that he will
accept the command. The appointment is upon the whole popular
here though some are, as was to be expected, indignant at it.

We have just had news of the 20th from Lisbon announcing the
alarming state of Don Pedro's health—that the Queen has been declared of age by the Chamber and has sworn to the Constitution—and
that Palmella has been charged to form a new Government.

Received 2 October.[2]   GC/CL/166; Clar. Dep. C.451/1 (89-90)

[1] The Guebhard Loan or Spanish three per cents were loans contracted by
Ferdinand VII between 1823 and 1833. The French loans, made in 1828,
were distinct from the Guebhard Loans.
[2] C.451/1 docketed 'By Buschenthal's courier'.

94   Villiers to Palmerston, 25 September 1834

Madrid. Private. There has been a stormy debate today in the
Chamber upon the first article in Toreno's project acknowledging the
foreign debt and nothing that the bad faith of the President and the
factiousness of the Opposition could effect has been left undone—but
the Ministers carried the question by a majority of 63 over 47. It is an
important triumph for if the loans contracted since 1823 had been
thrown over the credit of Spain would have been ruined in the London
as much as in the Paris market. She then would get no money and Don
Carlos would have beau jeu.

I avail myself of a courier which Rayneval dispatches instantly to write you this. It is of great interest to the French Government, and Rayneval will telegraph it from Bayonne in order to dévancer the squadron of commercial couriers which is now sallying forth from Madrid.

There is nothing fresh from Rodil or from Portugal.

GC/CL/167

95 Villiers to Palmerston, 26 September 1834

Madrid. Private. Notwithstanding the vote of yesterday which recognized the whole of the foreign debt the Chamber has this day thrown over altogether the Guebhard Loan (Emprunt Royal it is generally called at Paris). Feeling that this will render some new modification of Toreno's plan necessary in order to secure good humor in London, I went to him directly the Chamber was up to urge some better terms for the Cortes Bond holders. The result of my interview has been that he has promised this night to propose to the Committee of Finance that the *whole* of the principal of the Cortes Debt shall be made active i.e. immediately bear interest, instead of the *half* according to his original project. He told me likewise that he had little doubt of being able to carry it.

I write in great haste by a commercial courier.

Received 4 October.

GC/CL/168; Clar. Dep. C.451/1 (91)

96 Villiers to Palmerston, 27 September 1834

Madrid. Private. Although these interminable finance discussions are not of great interest in England I avail myself of the couriers which go every day to give you a short account of our proceedings.

I wrote yesterday to you to say that Toreno intended to give the Cortes Bond holders better terms than those which he originally proposed, in order to put the London market in better humor and to repair the additional shock to public confidence abroad given yesterday by the rejection of the Guebhard Loan. He fulfilled his promise this morning, and carried his proposition of making the whole of the principal of the Cortes Debt active, instead of half of it as was at first intended. . . .

Public attention is entirely taken up with the finance subject and the proceedings and intriguings of the Procurers and nobody seems to care for the non-arrival of news from either the army or Portugal.

We have never heard what effect the death of his wife had upon Don Carlos.

Received 6 October.

GC/CL/169; Clar. Dep. C.451/1 (92-93)

97 Villiers to Palmerston, 29 September 1834

Madrid. Private. I avail myself of a courier which Maberly is about to send to let you know that financial matters look better here. The whole of the foreign debt is to be recognized and made active—1/40th part of the interest due upon the Cortes Debt is to be made active every year until the whole becomes so. This is not quite so favorable an arrangement as I had hoped to effect or as Toreno was disposed to carry but he found that the Commission was averse to doing more and he was afraid of disturbing the good humor and almost unanimity to which they have at last been brought. . . .

Received 7 October.[1]

GC/CL/170; Clar. Dep. C.451/1 (95-96)

[1] C.451/1 docketed 'By Mr. Maberly's courier'.

98 Villiers to Palmerston, 30 September 1834

Madrid. Private. I wrote to you yesterday by Maberly's courier to say what a change had come over the spirit of the Finance Committee's dream—that all the foreign debt was to be acknowledged and forthwith to bear interest—the loan of 4 million reales[1] (effective) was to be granted—in short every thing, except the Guebhard Loan and the arrears of interest upon the Cortes Bonds—the former of which was thrown over altogether and the latter to be made active debt only in 40th parts annually—was considered to be settled amicably and in the best way for Spanish credit. All was joy and gladness—jobbing was looked upon as over—and young Rothschild and Toreno had embraced each other—when lo! this morning, when every one thought the finishing stroke was about to be put to all this good work, the Chamber upon no other ground than caprice decided that $\frac{2}{3}$rds of the debt should be made active and $\frac{1}{3}$ passive. This will not only destroy the high hopes which will have been raised in London and Paris by the herd of couriers who have left this place during the last two days, but it will be the severest blow yet given to Spanish credit because it will demonstrate that no reliance is to be placed upon the reason, the good sense or the good faith of the Chamber which has acted throughout upon the whole question as if it were composed (as it is for the most part) of wayward ignorami.

Rayneval sends his courier immediately and I have not had time to see Toreno so that I can tell you nothing of what you will be most desirous to know, whether any thing further can be done for the Cortes Bond holders. By the vote of today they will stand in the same position as if their last memorial had been complied with, i.e. £75 of their debt (£150) is made to bear interest—yesterday they were to have got £100. I shall do my best in every quarter, both with Ministers and Deputies, to get something more for them—and as State matters in Spain seem always decided by tossing up I may perhaps succeed.

There is no news from the army and no answer is yet arrived from Mina to the offer of taking the command in Navarre. We received yesterday the intelligence of Don Pedro's death. I hope the Queen will marry Leuchtenberg—it would be exceedingly popular and useful here, for things will never go well in Portugal unless there is a good man upon the throne and when I left England you had a very high opinion of the Duke of Leuchtenberg. There is a great deal of intrigue however going on at Lisbon against him I understand and I should think that some indirect English influence would be of use.[2]

PS. The letter which you wrote to me upon Spanish finance had great influence in determining the course lately taken, though now unsuccessfully, by the Government—which I shall request Lord Granville to communicate to De Rigny.[3]

Received 11 October. GC/CL/171; Clar. Dep. C.451/1 (97-98)

[1] C.451/1 has 'sterling', which is presumably right.

[2] The French Government was strongly opposed to Leuchtenberg's marriage to the Portuguese Queen. The marriage took place, but he died soon after his arrival in Lisbon.

[3] V to Granville, 30 Sept. 1834, PRO 30/29/413. V was anxious to demonstrate to the French Government that the British Government had not sought better terms for the British bondholders at the expense of the French creditors. The postscript is omitted from C.451/1.

99   Villiers to Palmerston, 2 October 1834

Madrid. Private. Martinez has just sent me word that he is about to dispatch a courier and I avail myself of the opportunity to tell you that I have nothing to say except that permission was given to Toreno by the Chamber this morning to contract a loan of 4 millions. The question now will be if, after all the folly and recklessness displayed by the Cortes upon the finance question, so large a sum of money will be to be found at London or Paris except upon ruinous terms. I fear not. Toreno has one great pull in his favour—he has Rothschild completely in hand, and certainly the Jew never did any victim himself more completely than he has been done by this Government. In order to keep up the Spanish funds in Paris he paid the dividend of 15 millions of francs due in July upon the *full understanding* that he was to be immediately reimbursed but without a scrap of guarantee or even acknowledgement of the debt. He has of course become alarmed and has been roaring for his money, appealing to the fear and the honour and gratitude of the Government, but though he has charmed never so wisely Toreno has as yet been like a deaf adder declaring that although he means to pay he can only do so when he has got his loan—the *last* instalment of which will probably fall to the Jew's share whose inclination therefore to run a muck at it will be wonderfully softened.

I wrote to you in much haste the day before yesterday and I find I rather overstated the amount upon which the Cortes Bond holders will receive interest—it will not be £75, but $\frac{2}{3}$rds of £100. A proposition was yesterday made by an independent Procurer to make the interest due upon the Cortes Bonds active debt, but the Chamber would not hear of it, and Toreno told me yesterday he feared that nothing further could be effected at present but there may arise means of favouring the Bond holders in the settlement of the details of the project and he has promised me to avail himself of them to the utmost.

There is no news of any consequence from the army. An officer who left head quarters on the 29th said today that the appointment of Mina had been very well received by the troops and he considers that as soon as severe weather sets in the insurgents will be driven to submit.[1]

Received 12 October.[2]

GC/CL/172; Clar. Dep. C.451/1 (99-100)

---

[1] 'as soon' to 'submit' underlined, probably by P.
[2] C.451/1 docketed 'By Spanish courier 12 o'clock night'.

100   Villiers to Palmerston, 8 October 1834

Madrid. Private. I have very little to tell you. The army in the North since the recall of Rodil seems to be more than ever troubled with the slows, and the Chamber has been resting from its labors of contradicting and stultifying itself for a fortnight. Since I last wrote however a step has been made towards getting money and towards putting down the rebellion. The Rothschilds seem willing both to support and take a share in the loan. . . .

Towards putting down the insurrection, the knowledge that Mina has accepted the command will do much, perhaps quite as much as his assuming it, and the man who by a mere chance has become his locum tenens[1] is the very fittest one in the army and we shall now for the first time see the officers acting zealously in concert together. The insurgents appear to be put to great shifts and the more the season advances the more difficult will it be for them to keep their mountain fastnesses—they seem to be in no want of money but utterly unable to procure arms. If the insurrection could be mastered in Navarre it would die a natural death in Biscay directly—the country is there less mountainous and the rebels are very sick of the hardships they are suffering. Martinez de la Rosa will send the proper introductions for Colonel Wylde[2]—he was much pleased with your instructions particularly with the one forbidding Colonel Wylde to receive the body of Don Carlos even if the Infant offered it in person.

The Queen is still at the Pardo surrounded by sanitary cordons at two leagues from the healthy city of Madrid and nobody thinks about her which I believe is exactly what she wishes.

Received 17 October.[3]

GC/CL/173; Clar. Dep. C.451/1 (101-102)

[1] General Lorenzo. See V to P, 8 Oct. 1834, no. 152, FO 72/427.
[2] The British Government had appointed Colonel Wylde 'to proceed to the headquarters of the army in the North in order to transmit correct information of the operations of the army in the disturbed provinces'. (V to P, 14 Oct. 1834, no. 156, FO 72/427; Martínez de la Rosa to V, 10 Oct. 1834, enclosed with no. 156.)
[3] C.451/1 docketed 'By Ardouin's courier'.

101 Villiers to Palmerston, 14 October 1834

Madrid. Private. I have not much of importance to narrate. The army seems stricken with inactivity—it did nothing before by running about and it is now arriving at the same result by keeping still. We occasionally have pompous narratives of trifling skirmishes which all end in the greatest glory to the army and the most perfect impunity to the rebels. Mina, by a letter which I saw yesterday from General Harispe who is with him at Cambo, is much more likely to die in France than to take the command in Navarre and although his friends here have persuaded him not to resign it I understand that he himself has little expectation of being able to encounter the hardships of the campaign and the season.

We have news from Paris of the 8th and the state of the money market and of public opinion with regard to Spanish affairs generally have spread alarm here. . . .

Martinez tells me that as the Pope still persists in dressing by Austria and not recognizing the Queen, he has written to his Holiness to propose that he should at least not continue to gratify his political feeling at the expence of his ecclesiastical functions in this country, and that he should accordingly direct the Nuncio not to present his credentials as ambassador, but to perform all those duties connected with the Church which are incumbent upon the Pope's delegate in Spain, and for the want of which the Church and the clergy are put to serious inconvenience. As we have no representative at Rome I have not reported this conversation in a dispatch, but Martinez is very desirous that you should back his proposition by any means direct or indirect which you may have at your command. If the Pope would consent, it would not only do away with a vast many accumulating grievances here, but perhaps pave the way to political recognition which would be a deadly blow to the Carlist party.

I have spoken both to Martinez and Toreno upon the subject of Donna Maria's marriage and told them my reasons for thinking the Duke of Leuchtenberg the fittest husband for her. They would both in their hearts rejoice at his success, but they will have a difficulty in taking any steps to promote it, because the Queen Regent is desirous that a Prince of Naples[1] should be selected. I told them however that I had no instructions from you upon the subject. I cannot but think that there have been and are quite Bourbons enough upon the thrones of Europe, and that as it seems in their blood to restrict and never to promote the liberties of the people, no great advantage could be expected from setting up one of them to govern a constitutional country. Under the present circumstances the tendencies of a Neapolitan prince in Portugal would be towards France, to the detriment of English influence in that country. The tendencies of the Duke of Leuchtenberg, both on account of his own principles and the ill will he bears to Louis Philippe, would be towards England, and that would go far to strengthen the alliance between Portugal and this country where anti-French feelings are daily gaining ground.[2]

As it is now five weeks since I announced that Martinez was ready to adopt the Equipment Articles I was in hopes to have heard from you upon the subject and am somewhat alarmed at not doing so, for as it became known that Martinez was occupying himself upon the slave trade, there are endless intrigues at work to prevent his throwing any impediments in its way, and I am always afraid that his resolution, which it cost so much to bring to the sticking point, may at last yield to some new persuasion. He may moreover *any day* be turned out by the Cortes or what is more likely retire in disgust, and the same ground would then have to be gone over with his successor though perhaps not with the same result.

I am at a loss to conceive what General Montillo and the other South American deputies can be about. . . .

I hope you will excuse my taking this opportunity of saying a word in favor of my friend Sir Robert Ker Porter. . . .

You may suppose that I have not been unmindful of commercial affairs. I have made some progress in them with Toreno and although as much will not be done this year as I would wish (principally owing to the *political* circumstances of Catalonia) I hope to effect some alterations in the tariff favorable to England.

Arguelles is arrived rather sulky and undecided but leaning more to Toreno than to the Opposition who are greatly disappointed at his not putting himself at their head.

Received 27 October.[3]

GC/CL/174; Clar. Dep. C.451/1 (103-108)

[1] One of her brothers.
[2] 'this' to 'ground' underlined, probably by P.
[3] C.451/1 docketed 'By French courier'.

102   Villiers to Palmerston, 18 October 1834

Madrid. Private. Rayneval sent to me while I was at dinner to say that he should dispatch a courier at 8 o'clock. I have therefore hardly had time to send you a brace of hurried dispatches and have none for a letter. You will see that Toreno has kept his word with me respecting the Cortes Bond holders[1]—the amendment will be sent down directly to the Procuradores and by bestirring myself (if it is lawful for a gouty man to speak so) among them I hope to secure its adoption even though the Guebhard Loan, the pill which the Cortes Bond amendment is intended to gild, should not be swallowed. The Bond holders will then stand very well—at least far better than they could ever have hoped to do, but it should be remembered that if they make opposition and that the monied men in London raise such an outcry against the Spanish Government that the loan cannot be raised, all these new engagements cannot be fulfilled; and if Spain is obliged to declare herself insolvent and the Government to throw themselves upon the nation for support in order to put down the rebellion and establish the existing order of things, they will of course take all the advantage as well as the disgrace of bankruptcy and throw over at one fell swoop the whole of the foreign creditors.

The ejection of Burgos from the Chamber of Proceres today was a terrible exhibition and Alava's motion was unnecessarily cruel,[2] but Burgos happens to be one of the Afrancesado party (those who addicted themselves to Joseph Buonaparte) and that is the only crime for which there is no expiation in this country—rape, murder and robbery are mere child's play in comparison to it.

Received 27 October.[3]

GC/CL/175; Clar. Dep. C.451/1 (109-110)

[1] Toreno agreed to introduce into the Lower House a double motion, one part improving the terms to be offered to the Cortes Bond holders, the other recognizing the Guebhard Loan. V suggested this to Toreno as a measure which would restore the confidence of the London and Paris money markets in the Spanish Government. (V to P, 18 Oct. 1834, no. 162, FO 72/427.)

[2] Álava's motion was that Burgos (former Minister of the Interior) should leave the Chamber until he had cleared himself of the charge that he had appropriated part of the Guebhard Loan. The motion was carried by acclamation. (V to P, 18 Oct. 1834, no. 164, FO 72/427.)

[3] C.451/1 docketed 'By French courier'.

103   Villiers to Palmerston, 22 October 1834

Madrid. Private. We are still without news of any importance from the army, and although Mina writes word that he shall be able shortly to assume the command, the letters which have been received from Bayonne and Cambo give small hopes of his recovering sufficiently to do so. As I expected, and as I believe I wrote you word when there was first question of his appointment, the prestige of his name in the provinces rather does harm than good and the insurgents, forgetting that it is they and not he who have changed sides, are exasperated more than frightened at his taking part against them.

I remember the Duke of Wellington's telling me that Mina was excellent as a guerilla chief provided he had only specific orders to execute, but that if any thing was left either to his judgement or discretion he was one of the most incapable men he had ever had under his command. At the head of regular troops therefore, and not assisted as he has always been before by the whole population of the country, I look to his effecting nothing more than his predecessors.

I think exceedingly ill of matters here at Madrid—the Government is only maintained because Martinez and Toreno happen to be more dextrous, as yet, than their opponents, but there is a fixed determination per fas et nefas to get rid of them and enact over again the scenes of 1822, in utter recklessness or forgetfulness of 1823. These emigrants like all others seem to have forgotten nothing and learned nothing—they appear never to bestow a thought upon the enemy at their gates and are wholly engrossed in obtaining power for themselves at the same time that they are every day proving their entire unfitness for it. Among other worthy means to which they are resorting for their purpose, they have informed Muñoz (the Queen's swain) that they will vote the enormous Civil List upon which the Queen insists provided the whole Government is turned out, otherwise Her Majesty will not have above a tithe of what she asks. Arguelles on his first arrival was very reasonable, though sour, and admitted all the dangers of encouraging the revolutionary party but I suppose his head has been turned by the adulation he has met with since his arrival and he now seems inclined to play the game of the canaille. I am to see him by appointment tomorrow and shall do my best to turn him away from the wickedness which he has committed and make him do that which is lawful and right. The Carlists are overjoyed, and no wonder, at the progress of events, which is only much more rapid than they could have anticipated. In fact if the worthies who call themselves the Opposition here were paid by the Holy Alliance to further the interests of Don Carlos I don't see how they could earn their wages more honestly than by proceeding in their present course. Martinez is in bad heart and nothing but a strong sense of duty makes him remain in office.

I think there is little fear that the mixed Finance Commission will agree to the additional bonus to the Cortes Bond holders—it will probably be decided tomorrow.

You will I hope approve the note which I have sent to Martinez respecting the British crew imprisoned at Santa Cruz and the rights and privileges generally of British subjects in Spain.[1] It is Southern's composition.

Received 31 October.[2]

GC/CL/176; Clar. Dep. C.451/1 (111-112)

[1] V to Martínez de la Rosa, 19 Oct. 1834, enclosed with V to P, 22 Oct. 1834, no. 166, FO 72/427.
[2] C.451/1 docketed 'By Ardouin's courier'.

104 Villiers to Palmerston, 24 October 1834

Madrid. Private. Your dispatches of the 12th arrived here after a rapid journey yesterday. The courier brought me no letter from you.

I shall of course as in duty bound use all exertions to get the slave treaty accepted, but I will not disguise from you my regret at having to do so—the translations, the notes, the discussions to which it must lead will in my opinion occupy more time than Martinez will stay in the Government unless things take a different turn to what they now seem disposed to do, and by grasping at too much we may lose all. Some of the articles of the treaty it would be utterly impossible for any Spanish Minister to hear of, and there can be no greater mistake than supposing that Spain is sincere in wishing to put down the slave trade. . . .

If therefore I find, as I expect, Martinez very averse to the treaty, or that I think he is on the eve of resigning I will close with the Equipment Articles which he promised to accede to, not the least from admitting their necessity (on the contrary he thinks they will be detrimental to Spain) or desiring to check slave trading but simply as an '*obsequio*' as it is called here, a civility to England.

I had a conversation of nearly four hours yesterday with Arguelles and my opinion is that he is an honest, inflexible, most dangerous man, cherishing and caressing the Constitution of 1820 as a young mother does her first born, and uniting all the qualities most requisite at the present moment and with the Chamber constituted as it is, for securing the return of Don Carlos after a due period of anarchy. I never met with so unadulterated a doctrinaire—give him his theories then 'ruat coelum'.

Don Carlos went from Guernica on the 10th and with 4,000 insurgents made a sort of attack upon Bilbao—they skirmished for 3 or 4 hours and then retired with a loss of about 15 killed and wounded on each side.

Received 3 November.[1]

GC/CL/177; Clar. Dep. C.451/1 (113-114)

[1] C.451/1 docketed 'By courier of French embassy Mr. Katz'.

105   Palmerston to Villiers, 31 October 1834

Copy. Foreign Office. Private. I am sorry to get your letter of the 22nd, but still hope that matters may turn out better than at that time you seemed to expect. I send you another memorial from the Spanish bondholders which was brought to me an hour ago by Mr. Thornton, a most *warm* man of the City. . . .

I never see the King that he does not lament that the Spanish Government can find no way of making any amicable arrangement with the population of Navarre and Biscay and again the day before yesterday he reverted to the same subject. He says it is evident that the insurgents are fighting not for Carlos for whom they do not seem to care sixpence, but for their local privileges, and is it then impossible for the Spanish Government to make some compromise with these people so as to take from them any motive for further resistance? The King is well aware that this is a delicate matter for any foreign minister to speak about, because it relates entirely to the internal affairs of Spain, but he is so anxious to see this war brought to a prosperous end that he desired me to write to you on this subject, and to beg you to press this consideration upon the attention of the Spanish Ministers in confidential and unofficial conversation, whenever you may have an opportunity of doing so.

I hope you will be able to send us back the slave trade convention such as I sent it to you. It will redound greatly to the honor of the Spanish Government.

I highly approve of your note about the privileges of British subjects in Spain; it is very ably drawn up, and the matter is one which urgently requires that the two Governments should come to an understanding upon it.

We have sent muskets and sabres enough to exterminate the Carlists, if every weapon kills but one man.

The fire in the House of Lords is proved to a demonstration to have been mere accident. Mr. Cooper the ironmonger stands alone in his dream.

GC/CL/1236

106 Villiers to Palmerston, 3 November 1834

Madrid. Private. During the last week there has been a dearth of events and of couriers both diplomatic and commercial—little public business was transacted in the Cortes, no news arrived from the do-nothing army, and financial matters were before committees who wrangle and intrigue and do any thing but report, so that nobody sent a courier because every body was waiting for something to write. Part of this deficiency has just been supplied in the most disastrous manner by the destruction of two battalions of the Queen's troops near Vitoria as you will see in my dispatch. The consequences of this will be even more mischievous than the disaster itself for the insurgents have now been enabled to supply their main deficiency—want of arms, and the moral effect of their achievement will be as encouraging to the Carlists as it is disheartening to the Queenites. Here, the consternation it produced was extreme for the upper and middling classes are a most white feathered race—their first impulse on any approach of danger is fear, their second flight, and their moral state on the 'untoward event' becoming public was much the same as when the cholera broke out with its first violence. There are among both the Proceres and Procuradores some who have their mules harnessed and their trunks packed ready to be off—others cry out for French intervention or for a change of Ministry or its modification or the return of the Queen to the capital.

In short things were just in that state two days ago when panic hurries on revolution. The Carlists and the anarchists (for lack of a better word for the wanting-a-scramble part of the community) have both been working with the same object of upsetting the Government, and on Saturday there was some apprehension for the tranquillity of the town—but proper precautions were taken, some busy Carlists were arrested and now things look much calmer. Luckily there has been no important business to discuss and consequently no session of the Cortes, or the Opposition would not have missed such an occasion for availing themselves of public irritation to embarrass the Government.

The conduct of the Government has often of late been unwise and what is perhaps worse, at critical moments unfirm, but their position is one of singular difficulty. The generals who have been sent to conduct this unlucky war have all been the men designated in turn by public opinion which would have raised a cry of treason if they had not been appointed—not one of them has obeyed a single order sent from Madrid and not one has hit upon a successful expedient of his own. Then there is the Queen whose misconduct and dévergondage has altogether destroyed that prestige of royalty and royal authority which is, and has from all times been, the most powerful instrument in the Government of this country and which in the hands of a well intentioned Ministry might have been turned to vast account. She is shut up in the Pardo two leagues off surrounded with cordons as if the plague were at Madrid and 2,000 troops to do the service of those cordons (which every human being here is ready to swear are placed to keep off spectators of her being with child), and having no medium of communication with her Ministers but through an old woman of a Minister of Grace and Justice to whom his colleagues are obliged to write and explain every thing in order to get the Queen's consent and signature not only to the important measures of the Government but to all the current business of the country. Martinez went down to the Pardo two days ago to see this colleague, for the first time since July, and how do you think the interview was conducted? The Minister of Justice came to meet him at the first cordon and they conferred together at the distance of a couple of yards, guards standing by to watch that they didn't approach nearer.

Then although the necessity of having money is as clear as the sun in order to give the country a chance of salvation and that the Budget which displayed the most beggarly account of empty boxes has been for 3 months before the Cortes, nothing can yet be called finally settled and it must be at least another month or 6 weeks before one shilling of the new loan can reach the Treasury, the Chamber having in the mean while damaged itself and the credit of Spain by its senseless mode of proceeding. The Ministers have no sure majority and the Opposition only make ad captandum declamations and contend for shreds of abstract principles of which they generally exhibit their own misapprehension. The cholera by intercepting all communications and preventing both the collection and remittance of revenue did infinite mischief—and it is very expensive and difficult to keep down the numerous bands which at times like these never fail in Spain under political pretences to rise up every where for purposes of pillage. To all this must be added the Church, powerful, united, sensible of coming danger, and putting secretly, but actively, its vast means into operation against an order of things which it reasonably enough abhors. The Carlist party too which in every corner of the kingdom is more or less strong, and that army of employés appointed under another régime and dreading investigation or reform of the abuses by which they live, all are laboring to prevent change.

I might go on adding items of this kind till they would puzzle Joseph Hume to *tottle*, but I think I have said enough to prove that the position of the Government is not one of ease, and that that agreable concurrence of events, a long minority, a disputed succession, a civil war and a national bankruptcy does not present itself here in a form particularly mild or mitigated. I have great satisfaction in always finding Martinez and Toreno stout hearted and nothing appalled by the present or the future—they have their faults as Ministers, but they have great merits, and I shall consider their overthrow by the movement party as fatal to the chance which Providence seems now offering to Spain to creep out of the abyss of degradation into which she has been cast by a misgovernment which has scarcely a parallel in history.

What with the insurgents and the Chamber, the Government are now carrying on a mortal strife, and there is no use at the present moment expecting Martinez's attention to the slave treaty. . . .

I send you my Commercial note which I hope will have some effect.[1] Whenever, if ever, the country is at peace and Toreno remains in the Government, he will introduce great commercial reforms, but he is at the present moment checked by the political condition of Catalonia where there are 40,000 armed manufacturing militiamen quite as ready to fight for the prohibitive system as for the rights of the Queen—a good deal more so perhaps.

The Queen has insisted upon offering the Ministry of War to Llauder, the Captain General of Catalonia. If he accepts it I shall be in great alarm for the tranquillity of that most important province.[2] The appointment will be mightily distasteful to the movement party, for under the partial guise of a liberal Llauder is, next to the Grand Duke Constantine,[3] the most finished despot of modern times.

If Mina can begin by any success, public confidence will be greatly restored—if he appears like his predecessors to be on the high road to failure, the cry for French, or rather perhaps should I say for Anglo-French, intervention, will be strong and general, except with Martinez, Toreno and Alava who have it in horror.

PS. My dispatches are dated yesterday but Rayneval did not send his courier as he intended.

Received 12 November.[4]

GC/CL/178; Clar. Dep. C.451/1 (115-120)

[1] V to P, 2 Nov. 1834, no. 169, FO 72/427.
[2] He did accept this post, and was Minister of War from 2 November 1834 to 24 January 1835.
[3] Governor of Poland.
[4] C.451/1 docketed 'By French courier'.

107 Villiers to Palmerston, 8 November 1834

Madrid. Private. Nil desperandum, as I have often said, in this country. People are now almost as contented and full of hope as they were irritated and dejected when I last wrote to you. Nobody reasons here—all are impelled by passion and act according to their hopes or fears—the latter being generally the impulse which takes precedence of any other. Five days ago if Martinez had declared his conviction of the necessity of French intervention, it would have been joyfully and almost generally approved, but as he did no such thing, and as the public alarm wanted something to cling to, the Chamber wisely selected the Government for that purpose, and the ministerial ranks have been nearly doubled this week. When the Guebhard Loan was finally disposed of a month ago, the Government were in a minority of 28—today upon the same question *plus* the offence of its being sent back to the Chamber by the Proceres, they were in a majority of 80.

If Mina can but now make a good hit or two business will go on smoothly in the Cortes and then they may be dismissed quickly which I apprehend is the great desiderandum of all constitutional Ministers and one not altogether unknown to the Cabinet of His Britannic Majesty.

The more I live and learn here the more convinced I feel that it is Arguelles and men of his class who are ignorant of the real state of the country. The *nation* does not wish for liberal institutions—they are essential to its prosperity and for the correction of abuse—but they must be administered as medicine to a child in small doses and well disguised or they will all be *brought up*. Almost every Deputy has received letters from his constituents full of anger and disappointment at the conduct of the Opposition—they say they care nothing for the Bill of Rights and the abstract principles which the Cortes have been wasting their time in discussing, but they want to see the Government strong in order that it may crush the common enemy, instead of embarrassed as it has been by the Chamber, which by proclaiming its disunion has exhibited its weakness to the Carlist faction both in and out of Spain. Two days ago a man who was a general in the time of the Constitution and has ever since been in exile, came up to Madrid from Estremadura, where he has been residing for some months, purposely to warn his friends, Arguelles, Galiano and others, against the course they are pursuing, and he declares that the ejection of Martinez and Toreno, and the admission of the movement party into the Government, would be the signal for revolt in Estremadura—which is perhaps the most liberal province in Spain.

These are all favorable omens and may be turned to good account. Such matters are of importance here, but I sometimes fear that I give you more details than you can have time or inclination to read.

I hope the Cortes Bond holders will be tolerably well satisfied now. . . .

Poor Martinez in addition to his other labors has now the War Portefeuille[1] and he is moreover very ill, so that the Mighty only knows when we shall complete the slave business. You may rely upon my not letting it sleep one moment longer than can be helped.

Received 16 November.[2]

GC/CL/179; Clar. Dep. C.451/1 (121-123)

¹ Zarco del Valle had resigned as Minister of War. The Queen had offered the post to Llauder who had not yet accepted.

² C.451/1 docketed 'By French courier'.

108 Palmerston to Villiers, 14 November 1834

Copy. Foreign Office. Private. I am not the least surprized at your being disgusted with the mass of paper which I sent you about the slave trade; but it would be desirable to have such a treaty signed if it can be done, and the Spanish Government ought to make no difficulty, for there is nothing in the treaty to which in principle they have not already agreed. But if you find that there is likely to be any considerable delay, resulting from an attempt to get the whole, cut the matter short and get the Equipment Article signed out of hand. There are many reasons which would render such an article of great importance at the present moment, and if matters are in statu quo when this reaches you, get us our Equipment Article forthwith.

Thank you much for your very detailed and interesting letters. The prospect of affairs in Spain is not at present very brilliant, but it is to be hoped their condition may improve. Mina *must* understand mountain war better than those who have preceded him in command, and I confess I expect a good deal from him. It is all very well for a few frightened people at Madrid to cry out for French interference, but if it took place, there would be a fine outcry the other way.

GC/CL/1237

109 Villiers to Palmerston, 15 November 1834¹

Madrid. Private. No event of any particular importance has occurred since I last wrote to you except the repulse in a very gallant manner of Zumalacarregui and his whole force by a body of cavalry not above 1,400² strong. The spirit of the people in the provinces is somewhat improved, and savors more of division and a desire to go over to Mina. Llauder has accepted the Ministry of War. It is a very bad appointment as it endangers the tranquillity of Catalonia, and he and Mina are sworn foes and neither of them with natures very forgiving or forgetting.

The Chamber has been all the week discussing the laws for the

National Guard and, upon the occasion of some of the Opposition wanting to introduce the phrase Constitutional King and others of the same kind, Martinez defied them to tell the Chamber what was the opinion in their provinces upon this matter as well as upon the whole course of the ultra liberals in the Chamber. He asked them if throughout Spain the memory of the Constitutional régime was not painful and bitter, and if the use of the terms proposed was not likely to produce mischief by recalling odious associations. Not one of them had a word in reply. The Government seems now sure of a majority and the political quacks are at a discount, for every body feels that Spain cannot be liberalized by a coup de baguette.

In the first place the whole nation have a profound veneration for *The King*—they have had the same from all times, and it is as their adoration of saints, but The King is the patron saint common to all and all therefore like to glorify his power. They have as much pride in his omnipotence, as much fear of his wrath, as much gratitude for his bounty, and as much desire to be beholden to him, as any individual has for the saint whose name he bears and under whose protection he considers himself to be. The King is the fountain from which flows all worldly good and evil—the people know no other and seem not to wish to know any other. This will partly explain a cry which has not been uncommon here and which has always appeared inexplicable to us of Viva el rey absoluto—for the power of an absolute King is undivided, the people think, and his will to dispense favors uncontrolled. The King is accordingly the only really acknowledged authority. Among individuals, there reigns the most perfect equality, and the lowest peasant can perceive no difference, except in the gifts of fortune, between himself and the first grandee. There is no feature in the Spanish people more striking than the ease which reigns between different classes— there is no servility, no set of men trying to ape another and to get out of the sphere in which they are placed in order to get into the one immediately above them—it is an unaffected real equality. The authorities are powerful and absolute but it is because they are emanations from the King, and the people are always ready to attribute to them, and never to the King, the misfortunes which misgovernment entails upon them.

With these feelings then which are the growth of ages, it is easy to understand why liberal institutions and the residence of power in a set of men comparatively independent of the King find no sympathy with the people, for they are in discordance with their ideas of fitness by checking the will of the Sovereign, and by investing individuals with a sort of supreme powers they disturb the equality which the people look upon as a right. A malefactor upon a more gigantic scale than Ferdinand never existed. He was over and over again proved to be false, and treacherous, a robber, and an assassin, and yet that man, to the day of his death, was loved, respected and obeyed by the people, *because he was the King*. There was enthusiasm in 1820 because glorious things were promised and vague hopes were held out, but it must never be forgotten that the people considered that the Cortes were instituted and convoked by the King's free will. As soon as they perceived that he was not a free agent, the tide began to turn—not but what the conduct of the Cortes, their thoughtless legislation and their selfish intolerant despotism, helped that tide greatly—and it is idle to assert that the French were not looked upon as saviours in 1823 by the great majority of the nation. No people in the world are so irresistibly persevering or capable of such immense sacrifices when once roused by a national spirit in a national cause. If Ferdinand and his system had been so universally odious would they have submitted to it so long and so resignedly? Would the French, who are detested in Spain, have been allowed to march with scarcely a shot fired at them, and almost in triumph, from one end of the country to the other, and would the people, if they regretted the restoration of despotism, have persecuted with the savage zeal of fanaticism every one who was suspected of a tendency to a liberal opinion? Those men then who disregard experience and insist upon restoring the Constitutional régime with all its associations, unmindful or careless of what the consequences may be, are either doctrinaires who would let the country perish to save their theories or they are scramblemongers who wish disorder for their individual ends.

The state of things here however is very different to any which has as yet obtained, and is the only one which appears to offer a prospect that better government by being gradual should become permanent. The improvement begins from above and not from below—it is given and not taken. Abuses are acknowledged and reforms declared by the Government with the free consent of the Sovereign, and in the Administration are men whose early enthusiasm in the cause of liberty has been tempered by experience and misfortune, but whose principles remain the same, and who are deserving of praise rather than of the outcry raised against them by a handful of men for not yielding to clamour and for determining to carry the country with them in the march of improvement, and not to brusquer the prejudices and opinions which it is their hope to modify.

Toreno has stated that the public service is provided for till the 1st of the year—by mere administrative reforms and taking care that what comes out of the people's pockets should go into the Treasury the revenue has never been more productive though under every variety of adverse circumstances.

Ardoin, the French banker who is here, told me yesterday in confidence that he had just received a letter from Mendizabel saying that the English Government and particularly Lord Palmerston was highly displeased (sumamente disgustado) with the Spanish Government.[3] I am sure that Mendizabel's object in writing this to Ardoin was that it should be told to Toreno. I said that I heard nothing whatever of the kind from you and that I had no reason to believe any alteration had taken place in the friendly feelings of my Government towards that of Spain. I think it right to tell you this although you never put any confidence in *Mr. Mendizabel knowing his inexhaustible* powers of mendacity. Pray make no allusion to this that might come round to him.

Received 24 November.

GC/CL/180; Clar. Dep. C.451/1 (124-129)

[1] At the King's desire P sent a copy of this letter to Wellington, omitting, however, the final paragraph. (Southampton University Library, Wellington Papers, 17/45-49.)

[2] GC/CL/180 has '1,400', possibly written over '1,000'; C.451/1 has 'a thousand'.

[3] 'a deliberate untruth and totally unfounded. P.' added by P.

110 Palmerston to Villiers, 16 November 1834

Foreign Office. 11 p.m. I am glad to hear the good accounts I have just received from you. I am hard at work winding up, having this morning received notice to deliver up the seals tomorrow at two. I have therefore no time to write more than 2 lines. The Duke of Wellington is Prime Minister; I hear that Ellenborough is to succeed me; Peel is sent for but he is now in Italy; the Speaker will take the Home Office in the meanwhile and Murray will go back to the Colonies. All this cannot last, but I fear much mischief may be done by the storm it may raise in the country. I trust and hope that they may leave you where you are, and I hope you will not yourself furnish them with an excuse for sending anybody else. As long as you find their policy consistent with your opinions, you can be of more use in Spain in present circumstances than any body else could be.

Copy.

GC/CL/1238

111 Villiers to Palmerston, 20 November 1834

Madrid. Private. I received two days ago by that rapid conveyance the post, your letter of the 31st ultimo. I have forwarded to Martinez the memorial of the Cortes Bond holders which arrived at the same time and consequently about ten days too late to have any influence, if it ever would have had any, upon the determination of either the Government or the Chamber. The Bond holders in general ought to be satisfied with the present arrangement, but Mr. Thornton in particular should be overjoyed. . . .

It is now about a fortnight ago since I had a long conversation with Amarillas upon the war in the Northern Provinces and the possibility of coming to some arrangement with the insurgents. I said that both sides now appeared too much exasperated to render it probable that the initiative coming from either would not be liable to misconstruction or be attended with a successful result, but that I was sure, although I had received no instructions upon the subject, that my Government would gladly lend themselves to such a mediation as would stop the effusion of blood and restore the tranquillity which alone seemed necessary for the consolidation of the Queen's power. I told him that it was neither the principle or the practice of the British Government to interfere with the internal affairs of other countries, but that they had such a sincere desire to see this unfortunate struggle brought to a prosperous end, that, if invited to mediate by the Spanish Government, I had no doubt their best efforts would be used in the cause, and their interference would be a guarantee to the provinces far better, under existing circumstances, than any which the Spanish Government could offer. Amarillas liked this proposition exceedingly and said that he would submit it as his own idea to the Council of Regency who might then propose to the Government to invite the mediation of England.

Upon the receipt of your letter, I immediately went to Martinez and Toreno and read to them the passage containing the wishes and opinion of the King upon the subject of the war. They both expressed themselves most grateful for the interest taken by His Majesty in the affairs of Spain, and said they should at all times be happy to receive advice coming from such a quarter. Both seemed to admit that the war had begun for the maintenance of the privileges, but that the original object had been obliterated by the very nature of the struggle—it has been a war of savage retaliation and both sides are now too exasperated to seek or to be satisfied with any other end than victory. The Catalonians moreover, from whom the same privileges were taken by right of conquest, and the other provinces of Spain who never enjoyed them, have long looked with a jealous eye upon the exclusive advantages of the Biscayan Provinces, and all now expect that, in retribution for the loss and misery which the war has occasioned to the country, the present opportunity will not be neglected for bringing down these Provinces to the common level. The question has thus become national and consequently more complicated. Toreno however informed me that it is the intention of the Government whenever Mina has obtained success sufficient to prevent a misconstruction of the motive, to guarantee to the provinces some of the advantages, particularly those of local administration to which the people are justly the most attached, and then to make the measure general and confer the same advantages upon the remaining provinces of Spain.

I shall miss no opportunity in every quarter which I consider influential to endeavour to give effect to the benevolent wishes of the King.

Martinez has had a most satisfactory letter from Mina disapproving of much of the conduct of the Opposition and expressing his devotion to the Queen's cause and to the Government, both with regard to its constitution and its principles. He has conferred the principal command upon Cordoba telling him that he considered he was the best officer in the army—which I am particularly glad of as it was through my instrumentality that Cordoba was appointed to Rodil's staff.

Martinez a long time ago applied for some Congreve rockets but he was told there were none to spare. He is however very anxious to have some, were it only 100, to *rouse* the rebels when they get into the woods

233

or fire at them across the valleys when they stand laughing at the troops on the opposite mountain. Can you accommodate him?

The Government is now very strong in the Chamber and every body, except the agitators in the Cortes and the newspapers, seems mightily pleased thereat. The letters which come pouring in from the provinces all contain the same expressions of satisfaction.

As soon as Martinez is relieved from the Portefeuille of the War Department we shall have the Equipment Articles. . . .

My letters tonight go by a Spanish courier to Bayonne who will deliver them to the King's messenger there as you may perhaps be in want of him and he has already been waiting some time.

Received 1 December.[1]

GC/CL/181; Clar. Dep. C.451/1 (130-134)

[1] C.451/1 docketed 'By Spanish courier to Bayonne and thence by King's messenger'.

112   Villiers to Palmerston, 25 November 1834

Madrid. Private. It was extremely kind and friendly of you to write to me on the 14th when you must have had so many more important matters to think of. The news of the King's determination produced here, as you may well believe, equal surprise and dismay among all those attached to the cause of the Queen, who comprise within their ranks nearly the whole of the aristocracy, wealth and intelligence— those who have no pretensions to be classed under those heads are insultingly overjoyed at the appointment of the Duke of Wellington.

The regret of Martinez and Toreno for your loss is great and genuine for they considered you a sincere friend to the order of things which they have gone far to establish in this country, but in which without the auspices of England, they would have encountered insurmountable difficulties. My answers to their anxious enquiries as to the probable policy of the Duke of Wellington are not much calculated to diminish the terror with which they view his accession to power, for although I do not apprehend that he can make any violent change in the policy of England towards Spain, there is a wide difference between a non-violation of existing engagements and a liberal performance of services dictated by sympathy and good will.

As soon as it is known that the Duke of Wellington's Government is constituted I believe that Alava will be sent to England on a propitiatory mission with olive branches and presents and orders to cry Ogre, Ogre, don't eat us.

There is no particular news to write to you from hence and I suppose it will not be long before I have an opportunity of talking to you upon Spanish affairs.

GC/CL/182; Clar. Dep. C.451/1 (135-136)[1]

[1] C.451/1 docketed 'By commercial courier (Gaminde)'.

113 Villiers to Palmerston, 30 November 1834

Madrid. Private. I have received your letter of the 16th. I need scarcely say how much I feel the kindness of your again writing when in all the hurry of démenagement and doing so in order to advise me with respect to my future course.

I will follow your advice if I possibly can, for I believe that my remaining in this country at the present moment may be useful to the maintenance of the system which the influence and friendship of England have so powerfully contributed to establish. I may to a certain degree judge of this by the hopes and the apprehensions which the expectation of my departure creates among the Carlists and the liberals. If I were recalled, it would be looked upon as a disapproval of the policy of which I have for the last twelvemonth been the organ—if I resign, it would be said that I was unwilling to lend myself to the change of system which I saw was preparing, and in either case the Carlist party would have a triumph. Although perhaps no one in England would give me credit for it, yet Spanish feelings, as much as any other, influence my desire to retain this mission now that my intimate relations with you and the confidence you placed in me—its principal charm—will no longer exist; but I feel so deeply interested in the progress of improvement in this country, which is so wretched and might be so powerful, and I am so convinced of the important effects which the success or failure of moderate constitutional government in Spain must exercise upon the policy of Europe, that I shall not hesitate to make any sacrifice, short of that which is dishonorable, to contribute to the objects which I know you to have had, as much as myself, at heart. Some sacrifice it *will* be to me to remain, for without pretending to political importance in my present situation, I feel that there are circumstances connected with my appointment which may subject my conduct to misconstruction, and render my acting cordially, albeit in a subordinate situation, with those to whom you are opposed extremely difficult. You dismissed my predecessor because you felt no confidence in his desire to give effect to your policy. You selected me because you knew that my views would be in unison with your own and as an act of friendship which I shall always look back upon with gratitude. There can be no doubt then that the course most agreable to myself when you go out of office would be to resign this mission for to you I need not say that my private interests will form no element in my decision upon the course which I may honorably pursue.

I will act however upon your advice and I will not hastily give the Duke of Wellington an opportunity of sending any one in my place, but the moment I perceive that he is about to depart from your policy and by so doing lend a helping hand to the most terrible revolution which this country has yet endured, I shall instantly resign and you will I am sure approve of my doing so.

Forgive me for having so long occupied your time about my own concerns. You have to a certain degree brought it upon yourself, and you are of all men the one by whom I am most desirous that my conduct should be considered straitforward.

Alava goes to England in four or five days. The Government have done wisely in appointing him, for he is perhaps the only man who can make the Duke of Wellington believe that the cause of Don Carlos is the cause of revolution and of all those who would maintain this country in its present degradation. He assures me that if he finds His Grace ill disposed towards the Queen and the existing order of things in Spain, he shall not sleep two nights in London but immediately return here.

Matters in general are going on smoothly. Mina is acting with caution, and although he considers the state of the provinces more alarming than he expected, he seems to entertain no fears concerning his final success.

GC/CL/183; Clar. Dep. C.451/1 (137-140)[1]

[1] C.451/1 docketed 'By French courier'.

114   Villiers to Palmerston, 8 December 1834

Madrid. Private. We have news only to the 25th from London by which it appears that the état provisoire is still in force, but a storm seems gathering which may make His Majesty sorely repent his coup d'état and will gladden every radical heart in the kingdom.

I received 3 days ago your circular dispatch desiring me henceforth to address my correspondence upon public business to the Duke of Wellington and I have availed myself of the opportunity thus afforded me to write a private letter to His Grace in which I have given him as succinct a summary as I could of the reports and opinions which I have at different times made to you upon the state of this country. I have told him that the conduct of the people at the time of the King's death sufficiently disproved the assertions of the representatives of the Northern Powers that the country would, from one end to the other, be found Carlist—that the time and manner in which the English Government recognized the Queen, a step second only in importance to the recognition of Louis Philippe by His Grace, had saved Spain from a civil war—that the insurrection in the North which began on account of the privileges of those provinces had been wretchedly mismanaged both in a political and military point of view, but that the war had never extended itself out of the mountainous districts or beyond an area of 20 square leagues, and that Mina was pursuing a system of which the good effects were already visible in the improving spirit of the population.

I likewise informed him that the monastic orders and the livers by abuse were the principal enemies of the Queen, while on her side was ranged the whole of the rank, the wealth, and the intelligence of the country, who were as hostile to revolution as to Don Carlos, but who would *literally* be prepared to die sword in hand rather than repose confidence in Don Carlos or the party in whose hands he would be but a blind and devoted instrument. If they were rendered desperate however, that they would probably excite a spirit of revolution as the lesser evil of the moment, and a war of opinions would then commence which it would be vain to hope would not extend itself beyond the Peninsula.

I stated my grounds for considering the present revolution essentially different from any other, and that if improvement is possible it can only be effected through the instrumentality of those classes who are now

237

deeply compromised in favour of the Queen.

I then added a few words respecting myself of which I enclose the copy and which I hope you will not disapprove. It made me miserable not to place on record the *public* grounds upon which alone I hesitated to resign when you quitted office.

If the Duke of Wellington disapproves or alters the policy of the late Government and sends another minister here, who would have believed that my non-resignation and total silence had not been influenced by private motives and that to them, if I had had the option, I was ready to sacrifice my principles?

There has been but little news from the North lately and that little not very important, but the spirit of the population seems slowly improving and Mina's good spirits seem to increase.

Alava set out for London four days ago approving ab imo corde of English policy towards Spain during the last twelvemonth and determined to return here if it is to be altered.

Martinez has begged me once more to express to you his sincere regret for the 'untoward event' which has removed so warm a friend to Spain from the Foreign Office. Javat had written him word that almost your last official act had been to order the equipment of a Spanish steam vessel.

Little Miraflores in his unofficial capacity appears to have written a high flown volume of a letter to the Duke of Wellington upon the condition and prospects of Spain.[1]

Enclosure: Extract, Villiers (Madrid) to Wellington, 7 December 1834, stating that he has refrained from offering his resignation 'purely upon public grounds'.[2]

GC/CL/184; Clar. Dep. C.451/1 (141-143)[3]

[1] Miraflores to Wellington, 21 Nov. 1834 (Southampton University Library, Wellington Papers, 16/81-83).
[2] For a complete copy see GC/CL/192 enc. The original is in the Wellington Papers (19/72-73).
[3] C.451/1 docketed 'By French courier to Bayonne'.

115   Villiers to Palmerston, 2 May 1835

Madrid. Private. My dispatches are still addressed to the Duke of Wellington until I receive the official announcement of your resumption of office, but I cannot omit availing myself of the first opportunity which has presented itself of congratulating you, myself, and all parties concerned, not omitting Pozzo, Bulow, Werther, Nicholas and Metternich, upon your again being at the Foreign Office. To myself personally the satisfaction is most sincere of again entering upon those relations of confidence by which business is so much facilitated, and which have been altogether suspended during your absence from the Department.

Now that you are there, pray hold tight.

Received 12 May 1835.

GC/CL/185; Clar. Dep. C.452/1 (1-2)

116   Villiers to Palmerston, 12 May 1835

Madrid. Private. I wish that our correspondence was about to recommence under more favorable circumstances, but my dispatches of today shew an unpromising state of things in this country.[1]

Although I have hitherto received no official communication upon the subject, you must I think shortly be prepared to receive a demand for foreign assistance in order to put down the insurrection. Much as we have deprecated such a measure as fatal to the independence of Spain, I have now arrived at the painful conviction that by none other can the cause of the nation and the cause of all that is worth upholding in it be saved. There is no defence for the conduct of the Government during the last year and $\frac{1}{2}$ except saying that they are Spaniards, and as none ever yet looked a difficulty in the face, or adapted his means to his end, or took a decisive step till it was too late to be of use, it is not much to be wondered at that these people, raw in the art of governing and destitute of machinery and materials, should have floundered as they have done. This is however passed and cannot be recalled—we must look onwards and consider whether the salvation of Spain is of sufficient European interest to warrant its being taken out of Spanish hands, for in no other way can it be brought about. If the question were simply whether Charles 5th or Isabella 2d should reign it might be open to some doubts, but it is between the latter and an anarchy of which no man can foretell the consequences or the termination.[2] Don Carlos can never be allowed to ascend the throne in peace by the hundreds of thousands who are compromised in favor of the Queen, and who would be the victims of the exterminating vengeance of the party in whose hands he will be, as he is now, the merest instrument—a party consisting of all that is bigotted and most likely to perpetuate the barbarism of the country. It is to avert such a state of things and to give a fair trial to a moderate constitutional form of government that it may be worth while to help these people in their present need, for it must be confessed that circumstances have borne hard upon them, and that a civil war without an army, and an enormous expenditure with a bankrupt treasury were puzzles to a nascent legislature.

I foresee all the difficulties you will have in complying with the demand for assistance if it is made, the unpopularity in England, and the objections of the Holy Alliance. These difficulties would probably be insurmountable if French intervention alone were asked for, but if we at the same time sent some ships and one or two regiments—a company even with the British standard—the measure would then be in accomplishment of the Quadruple Treaty, and much of its bitterness and danger here and elsewhere would be removed.

Poor Martinez had a narrow escape yesterday for there is no doubt it was intended to assassinate him, *because* he was party to an agreement for saving Spanish blood and mitigating the horrors of a civil war![3] It was the work of the Emigrados, whose machinations ever since their return have been those of fiends. They are detested by all parties however—by none more than the army, and if tranquillity were once restored they would sink into the contempt they deserve.

Martinez will now probably remain some time longer at his post. The Queen had intended to dismiss him when the Cortes closed and to make Toreno rule in his stead—in which perhaps she would not have been wrong, for although a more virtuous and better intentioned man than Martinez never lived he is far too poetical for the present crisis in Spain—but his retirement at this moment would be a triumph to the mob and place the future choice of Ministers in the hands of a few select assassins. I hope therefore that he will continue long enough to sign the slave treaty, and I am looking with great anxiety for your answer to my dispatch of the 18 ultimo upon the subject.[4] Should it be favorable no further difficulty or delay will take place, and I shall be glad that it was not concluded during your absence from the Foreign Office.

Martinez was greatly pleased to learn that you were satisfied at having Alava in England.

Received 21 May.[5]   GC/CL/186; Clar. Dep. C.452/1 (3-6)

[1] 'I have the honour to inform your Lordship that General Cordoba arrived here on the 2nd instant from Navarre charged by General Valdez with the important mission of representing to his colleagues in the Government the demoralized state of the army, and the hopelessness of conducting the war to a successful termination without the aid of foreign troops.' (V to P, 12 May 1835, no. 79, FO 72/442.)

[2] A marginal line has been drawn, possibly by P, against the words 'If . . . termination.'

[3] Martínez de la Rosa was attacked by a group of Urban Militia with drawn swords. 'The cause of the dissatisfaction expressed against Mr. Martinez de la Rosa was the convention for the exchange of prisoners signed between General Valdez and Zumalacarregui, which is asserted to be derogatory to the national dignity by recognizing the rebel army.' (V to P, 12 May 1835, no. 80, FO 72/442.)

[4] V to Wellington, 18 Apr. 1835, no. 54, FO 72/441.

[5] C.452/1 docketed 'By French courier'.

117 Villiers to Palmerston, 20 May 1835

Madrid. Private. My dispatch of the 12th will have prepared you for the one of today.[1] I wish I could have greeted your return to office with any thing rather than this unpopular and intricate question of foreign intervention, and I cannot but regret for your sake that it did not arise before, in order that the Duke of Wellington should have had the task of deciding upon it, although I would not have *detained* him in power a day longer for the purpose.

I learned from you with great satisfaction that you were pleased with his conduct upon Peninsular affairs although I trust you viewed my remaining here as an outward and visible sign that there was no foul play with the policy of his predecessor. The Duke's transit through the Foreign Office will have had the good effect of proving to him that to those who take a just view of the interests of England with regard to Spain and in connexion with other countries, a different line of policy is impossible, and I understand that not only His Grace, but Lord Aberdeen, are loud in favor of the abolition of the Salic Law, and look to it as the basis of the regeneration of Spain and her ultimate emancipation from the thraldom of France. A somewhat tardy conviction for gentlemen who were not without data a year ago for forming a judgement upon the question, but which must muzzle their opposition in the event of your complying with the present demand of Spain, for injur-

ious as this demand is at the present moment to the national independence, it is the only chance left to Spain for shaking off her restless
grasping neighbour.

France does not desire to see Spain tranquil any more than she does
to see her prosperous or free. France is always, at this moment even,
laboring to maintain here a state of things which may call for or justify
her interference whenever the moment is ripe for her to turn it to
account. It is not so now for the territorial and matrimonial object
which she is keeping steadily in view, and the advantages of present
intervention will be confined to removing from her frontier the elements of discord daily becoming more inconvenient to her, *because* our
ships, or troops—the British flag in short—will confine her to the
objects of the Treaty. But should the joint intervention be refused I
have not the shadow of a doubt that it will eventually be undertaken
by France singlehanded under circumstances of far greater difficulty
and therefore justifying the imposition of her own conditions in return.
I will go farther and say she *must* so intervene and that no one can
object to her right when she declares that sua res agitur paries cum
proximus ardet. Burn it will, and with a vengeance if no hope of foreign
aid is once announced here—the army would immediately disband
itself—part of it would go home, part join the rebels, and part set up
for itself. Don Carlos would march upon Madrid and those who have
taken part for the Queen would in every direction fly before him as
the angel or demon of death—but they would neither submit or remain
passive—the moderates would join the anarchists, they would proclaim
the Constitution, commit every sort of extravagance, but they would
oppose an enormous force of resistance to the Carlist factions which
would spring up in the different provinces and to the Government if
Don Carlos were able to attempt one. In short the extent of confusion
proceeding from things in such a state is boundless, and its consequences in Europe not to be calculated. *We* must always remember too
that a common fate awaits both Spain and Portugal. Can any one
doubt that France would be justified in falling upon all this demented
fury at her frontier, or that the circumstances under which she would
then do so would not be immeasurably more embarrassing than the
present?

Her primary object would be her own tranquillity, but in *what sense*
or in whose behalf could she enter Spain? The Apostolicals? Public opinion and the safety of the French throne would render that impossible.

The Exaltados? France would give no such allies to her own republicans. The moderate party? It will have ceased to exist by the mere force of circumstances. Could France then attempt to build up a state of things of her own? Would Europe allow it? Would it have any chance of taking root in Spain? Look at the question of this country which way you will, it is starting with future difficulties, but the joint intervention now proposed seems to offer a decent chance (for nothing must ever be looked upon here in any other light) of overcoming them. The Queen is upon the throne—we are bound by treaty and by our own interests to maintain her there if possible—there exists a Government such as we should like to see strengthened and lasting—and we should come in aid of the great mass of the nation which is exhausted by political turmoil and desirous of the repose which they will never enjoy so long as extreme opinions are strong enough to wage war against each other and the Government is too weak to control them.

I am beginning to be very anxious for the answer upon the slave trade—allowing your Lordship 10 full days for deliberation a courier might easily have been [here] yesterday and I fear he may not arrive while Martinez is yet in office—he is already half out and would have been quite so if he had not been half assassinated last week. The Queen is sick to death of so little energetic a man and considers her daughter's cause damaged materially by him. I formed and gave you my opinion of him soon after he came into office—it has only been confirmed by subsequent intercourse—however he will sign the slave treaty if your answer comes in time and then Que vaya con Dios.

Received 28 May.

GC/CL/187; Clar. Dep. C.452/1 (7-12)

[1] V to P, 20 May 1835, no. 83, FO 72/442. V related to P the desire of the Spanish Government for military and naval assistance to help suppress the Carlist revolt.

118   Palmerston to Villiers, 22 May 1835

Foreign Office. I send you back the slave treaty.[1] It has taken me some time and given some trouble to go through it, because the Spanish Government had made several alterations and it was necessary to compare it minutely with our draft. . . .

I send you a despatch about foreign interference in Spain.[2] We hope that no application for such aid will come; but you may anticipate what our answer would be. I have just had a conversation with Sebastiani who assures me that his Government is determined not to meddle with the civil war. He says that 20 or 30,000 men might have done the thing last year, but that now a much larger force would be necessary, and that they must occupy Catalonia as well as Biscay, and that less than 80 or 90,000 would not be sufficient. This of course is on the supposition that the entrance of French troops would excite insurrections in parts now quiet.

Eliot and Gurwood are both for interference,[3] at least they both say that without it the war cannot be ended, but neither can precisely tell me what the French troops are to do when they go in, which could not be done by an equal number of Spaniards. They say that the Queen's troops are afraid of going into the great valleys of the Orquil and the Sierra de Andià, and that the Carlists are afraid of coming out into the opener country; that therefore it is a war without much fighting.

I cannot conceive how the Chronicle yesterday came to suggest a marriage between Don Carlos's son and Isabella, unless it be that Baron Haber[4] who is now here, and who proposes such a plan to all who will listen to him (of whom I am not one never having seen him) must have found certain means of inspiring that notion into the head of Black the editor. But after all *is* such a plan out of the question? The objections to it are, that with the son [come] the partisans and principles of the father; and that thus the seat of civil war would be only transferred from Biscay to Madrid: from the [?field or] the mountain to the Cabinet and the Court. But undoubtedly if it could be hoped that absolutism is the minor current, and that it would soon lose its character by mixing with those of the larger stream, such a match would by mingling the conflicting claims together, save Spain from many future difficulties. However one should fear that the objections to such a scheme would be too great, but let me know the result of your own observations and reflections on this matter.

Some compromise about privileges seems more feasible. Could not the Queen's Government make Men of Kent out of the Biscayans?

I have read, and so have my colleagues, with great delight your despatches to the Duke during his reign. They are highly creditable and honourable to you.

Copy.   GC/CL/1239

[1] P to V, 22 May 1835, no. 3, FO 72/439.
[2] In it P stated that interference by one State in the the affairs of another was objectionable in principle, and only to be resorted to in an emergency. Such an emergency did not exist in Spain, where the Queen's Government was surely able to find the men and money necessary for prosecuting the war. Great Britain would supply further arms if required. Intervention might not in any case answer the purpose. Was it not possible to reach a settlement with the Biscayan Provinces on the matter of their privileges? (P to V, 22 May 1835, no. 1, FO 72/439.)
[3] Lord Eliot and Colonel Gurwood, the former a political, the latter a military protégé of Wellington, had visited the north of Spain in early April to negotiate with both the royal and the insurgent armies a convention regulating the conduct of the war. For these negotiations see Roger Bullen, 'Party politics and foreign policy: Whigs, Tories and Iberian affairs, 1830-36', Bulletin of the Institute of Historical Research, LI, no. 123 (May 1978), 37-59.
[4] Financier, reputed to have lent money to Ferdinand VII in the decade between 1823 and 1833.

119   Villiers to Earl Granville, 23 May 1835

Copy. Aranjuez. Private. On my arrival here a quarter of an hour ago I found that Rayneval was in the act of dispatching a courier. I have delayed him a few minutes in order to write you a line although I have nothing to add to my dispatches of a few days since.

I yesterday received a long and most important letter from Aston[1] for which pray have the goodness to thank him as I cannot do so now, giving me de Broglie's opinion upon intervention which as far as it goes is prudent and not to be contradicted, but it does not go far enough, and Aston is perfectly correct in saying that the refusal of aid would drive the Government or their successors into revolutionary measures as a last though frail hope of salvation, which however would be worth trying rather than submit passing [sic] to the gibbet. It is to the consequences of their refusal, rather than to those of their compliance, that the French Government should look. They may be assured that it will entail a state of anarchy which will be insupportable to them, and which they will have eventually to combat, but under circumstances of far greater difficulty and danger than the present— under circumstances too [in] which they would be much less likely to have public opinion in France with them than now, for the state of things then would have a revolutionary or republican appearance and the intervention would then seem undertaken in a Carlist sense, for the

Queen's Government would hardly be one fit to be upholden. The French would then be enacting over again the *drame* of eighteen hundred and twenty three which neither they nor *we* should like.[2]

The actual Government here, not the men exactly, but the system they intend, if they knew how to carry it through, is the only one to control the two contending factions of the country. It can only do so effectually by being made strong (and be it observed not much is wanted for that, the people at large are so dead sick of commotion, and so desirous of repose that if the civil war were once put an end to, the Government would become strong by the force of circumstances and the will of the people). It can only become so now by foreign assistance and we are rapidly approaching the last moment at which that assistance can be usefully rendered. All I am anxious that the French Government should bear in mind is that before six months pass they must take an active part in the affairs of Spain, and that *we* should remember that in whatever fate awaits Spain, Portugal must share.

I am inclined to believe, for he would be a bold man who talked with certainty upon anything future in Spain, that if the intervention were well managed it would be attended with as prompt success as the Antwerp affair,[3] and would afford as satisfactory an answer to the bouderies of the Holy Alliance. If the three Powers parties to the Treaty enter Spain in fulfillment of their engagements they must do so with the olive branch as well as the sword; if they attempt merely a military occupation they will be exposed to the same difficulties and probably the same results as the Spanish troops. They must come in as friends and neighbours determined to restore peace, requiring both parties to cease hostilities, declaring that no disgrace will attach to either party (overtures of peace NEVER CAN come *from* a Spaniard *to* a Spaniard), that they are bound to maintain the Queen's authority, but at the same time they intend not to neglect the interests of those who had denied it—that there should be no vengeance, no proscriptions, that it was the interest of Europe to maintain peace, and that peace should be maintained. I *believe* from all I know of the Spanish character and the nature of this war that such a way of proceeding would be successful. It would moreover have the advantage of shewing to Europe England and France closely united, and that whatever *they* determined upon must take place. The Holy Alliance people too should learn that the cause of Don Carlos is *really* the cause of revolution here, and that order can alone be brought about, and sustained, by upholding the Queen, who has on her side *every class* of society that can contribute to the well being of a country, and who will not stand and cannot submit to the ignorant brutal masses to whom alone Don Carlos can look for support.

I have written this in the greatest hurry, and I fear that you will scarcely be able to make me out—if you can I think you will agree with me, and then you can easily put matters in an intelligible form as the Duc de Broglie did me the honour through Aston to ask my opinion.

Will you have the goodness too to communicate this letter to Palmerston—and tell him at the same time how much I regret not receiving an answer upon the slave trade? The Cortes will close in five or six days and then I would not give Martinez a week's purchase for his place.

GC/GL/188

[1] Copy, Aston to V, enclosed in a letter from Aston to P dated 19 May 1835 (copy in Aston Papers, FO 355/6). For Broglie's non-interventionist views at this juncture see also Aston to P, 15 and 29 May (GC/AS/59, 63) and Broglie to Rayneval, 23 May (AMAE CP Espagne 765).

[2] The French intervened in Spain in 1823 and their troops remained in occupation until September 1828.

[3] The Anglo-French intervention in Belgium in 1832 to force the evacuation of Dutch troops occupying Belgian territory.

120   Villiers to Palmerston, 29 May 1835

Madrid. I only heard late yesterday, at Aranjuez, that the Queen was going to close the Cortes this morning, and I accordingly came up, when Martinez informed me he was about to send a courier with the speech, but I shall address you very briefly, by him, for I have not much to say and I am very unwell.

The Government have done rightly in proroguing the Cortes, as at this critical moment the half dozen demagogues which they contain, who bona fide desire to bring about confusion, might inflame the public mind to acts such as those against Martinez on the 11th and which may, any day, and as if by accident, produce a revolution, or else by indiscreet speeches and questions embarrass the Government in the cause which their own not *savoir fair* has rendered necessary.

The more I reflect upon this course in all its present and future bearings, the more indispensable does it seem to me and the greater is my conviction that this people have now seen the full length of the tether with which they can be trusted alone, and that those who would suffer by a continued mismanagement of this country's affairs should not, when invited to do so, refuse to take them in hand. By your directions and by my own sense of what was desirable for the independence of Spain and the nationality of the Queen's cause, I have hitherto deprecated in the strongest manner a resort to foreign aid, and if the Government had fairly looked their difficulties in the face and at first adopted the measures which they have too late had recourse to, tranquillity would long since have been established, but the whole history of Spain is there to prove that it is not *in Spaniards* thus to act and were they alone concerned they might be left to the consequences of their improvident folly. Unfortunately, however, a total *bouleversement* of things here (one greater than any which has been yet seen, for the struggle will be between the whole of the enlightened classes and the ignorant mass) cannot be a matter of indifference to Europe.

The policy of the English Government was to form a Western Confederation against the Powers of the North—for this great object it will not do, Hispanice, only to desire, however intently, and we must not shrink from the means. Disorder would have been endless in Portugal if she had been left to herself—it will be so here if England and France don't come to her aid. It is the first and last moment for doing it with effect. Both the Government and the country would have objected to it before, and thwarted it, till their own incapacity was proved and the oncoming danger made them ask for succour; and it is the last moment because, if once a complete dissolution of the existing order of things takes place, there will be no party in the State whom it will be desirable to assist, whereas now there is the immense advantage of a Government whose moderate system (ill-managed it is true) is the only one which will suit our purpose, and which, if enabled to make head against the two contending factions, can consolidate the tranquillity which the nation at large is eager to secure.

I feel the excessive difficulty, without going to a tedious length, of explaining why one should not reason upon Spain by analogy with other countries, and I fear therefore that I shall not have succeeded in conveying to you my reasons for thus earnestly desiring this measure of intervention.

The Queen's intention 3 days ago was to dismiss Martinez upon the closing the Cortes. I know not if she still intends to put it in execution, but if she does our slave treaty will be in the greatest jeopardy. I have no doubt that your next door neighbour is the cause of the unlucky delay, and that you regret it as much as I do and strange to say, now as Martinez does. I have had some conversation with him today upon the subject. . . .

Copy. Docketed: By Spanish courier.

Clar. Dep. C. 452/1(13-16)

121 Villiers to Palmerston, 2 June 1835

Aranjuez. Private. I yesterday received your dispatch upon foreign intervention and the materials for an amended edition of the slave trade [treaty]. I have only been able to see Martinez for five minutes since—he has promised to fix an early day for conferring, signing and sealing (I suppose in compliment to the subject it should be with *black* wax) but I doubt his having the power though he certainly now has the will, for it was communicated to me today that Her Majesty means to eject him forthwith from office. As there is no particular reason for doing so immediately, I urged several weighty reasons for letting him remain till the final answers in re intervention were received from London and Paris, in order that he should bequeath the Equipment Articles as his last will and testament to the niggers, but I fear Her Majesty is in too *ladylike* a hurry for the execution of her project to listen to my reasons.

I communicated your dispatch No. 1 to Martinez who was utterly cast down by its contents, but as he was going to the Queen [he had no time][1] to pour forth his sorrows. I shall venture a few remarks to you upon that despatch by a courier who goes tomorrow, as there is not time to do so by one of Rayneval's who is just starting, and you will have as much of my lucubrations as you will care to read in a dispatch which I had written before I received yours.[2]

You gratify me very much by what you say of my dispatches to the Duke of Wellington.

Received 11 June.[3]

GC/CL/189; Clar. Dep. C.452/1(17-18)

[1] 'he had no time' supplied from C.452. GC/CL/189 lacks these words because the signature has been cut away.

[2] V to P, 2 June 1835, no. 88, FO 72/422, again urging intervention. V communicated to Rayneval the tenor of this despatch, and Rayneval was 'very

desirous' that Granville should show it to Broglie. (V to Granville, 2 June 1835, PRO 30/29/421.)
³ C.452/1 docketed 'By French courier'.

122 Villiers to Palmerston, 7 June 1835

Aranjuez. Private. I have this day in a dispatch which I fear you will think very long, but which upon such a subject it was difficult to make short, endeavoured to supply some of the information which you must naturally stand in need of upon the actual state of this country in order to decide upon complying with or declining the demand for assistance made by Spain.¹ I have found myself with great regret compelled to advocate a measure which will be so embarrassing to you, and is likely to be so unpopular in England, but I should have altogether failed in my duty if I had omitted to lay before you the powerful arguments which to my mind exist for not permitting the Spaniards, not to settle, for that they would never do, but not further to embroil their own affairs.

As far as those arguments relate to the Peninsula I don't know that I have any thing to add to my dispatches, but with respect to our general policy they appear to me equally strong. The close alliance of England and France has kept Europe in order for four years, but when the Northern Powers see the Peninsula plunged into hopeless confusion, and that France and England deeply interested in the struggle, the one by her geographical position, the other by her ancient relations, refuse to interfere, the prestige of that alliance will be destroyed, and our unwillingness to maintain the system we have tended to create will be placed upon the most unfavorable grounds.

The recognition of the Queen immediately upon Ferdinand's death by England and France turned the scale in her favor. The Quadruple Treaty has since kept her upon the throne, and if we now shrink from the complete fulfilment of that treaty—for although we may *get up a wrangle* about the letter of it, its spirit was the exclusion of the two Pretenders from the thrones of Spain and Portugal, and the object, unavowed, but well felt and well feared by the Holy Allies, was the establishment of moderate constitutional Governments in the place of two tyrants—if then we now shrink from our engagement it will be, and with a fair show of reason, supposed, either that we abandon our idea of such Governments as dangerous or impossible, or that we fear the resentment of the Northern Powers, and the chastisement they may inflict upon us hereafter— or it will be believed that the ancient rivalries between England and France with regard to Spain still exist, and that our alliance, however cordial in appearance, is but shallow, and will dissolve upon the first shock of national prejudices, or of interests supposed to be contending. How then shall we make ourselves respected in the East or elsewhere if through fear or jealousy or economy we cannot help a friend or keep a weak next door neighbour in order?

Supposing however that France becomes alive to the impending danger, and says that although she has all imaginable deference for us she cannot have her house set fire to pour notre bon plaisir, and that we still refuse to take part, we should not cut a very good figure either at home or abroad. The intervention of France single-handed would be still more unpopular in England than the application now made by Spain. It would produce a coolness in our alliance for it would be undertaken against our will, and we should have to watch her proceedings with the utmost jealousy, but we should have lost the right of objecting to any terms France might make for herself in payment of a debt of gratitude, and as she would throw upon England all the blame of non-fulfilment of the Treaty, Spain would again, and perhaps as much as ever, fall into the trammels of France.

Supposing too that Portugal, as she unquestionably will, falls into the same confusion as Spain, and that Don Miguel, rigged out by the Holy Alliance, lands either with a foreign force, or that a body of Carlists march from this country to his assistance, could we then help intervening, or if Donna Maria makes out the casus foederis could we refuse to come to her assistance? And should we not then do so at greater risk and expence than in the manner now proposed?

The state of things here at this moment is appalling—the hundreds of thousands of people whose lives and fortunes are involved in the Queen's cause are now waiting, like people expecting the arrival of the plague, for the confirmation of the report that intervention will be refused, and beginning to exhibit all the selfishness to be seen in moments of public calamity—the wildest schemes are entertained by some and the most atrocious projects by others. I believe this state of things would at once be calmed by the official contradiction of the rumors, and the first French soldier who crossed the Bidassoa would turn the tide in the Queen's favor. It is a moral effect that is wanted. Some act which should convince the Queen's party that they have nothing to fear and the Carlists that they have nothing to hope—which should render palpable the inutility of further resistance—as a great battle sometimes decides the fate of an empire, not because the means of resistance are less than the day before, but because the moral effect of defeat renders it useless to recur to them.

It would be an error to suppose that the stability of the Queen's throne would be injured by foreign intervention. There is no doubt that it would be far better if that throne were supported alone by the national will, but the Spanish pride would take no alarm at a repetition of what they have seen before here, and what they have abundant examples of in other countries. Philip 5th was placed on the throne by a foreign force and his line has descended very quietly since. Ferdinand might have reigned till Doomsday for any harm which the French did to his throne in 1823. Donna Maria owed her crown last year to the Spanish army—Leopold's was not shaken by the French expedition to Antwerp which saved him from the Dutch. If Charles 10th had governed wisely, the means by which Louis 18th was restored to France would not have been remembered against him—and so far from the Spaniards thinking the cause of Isabella weakened by foreign aid they would consider it placed upon a securer foundation, because the same means by which it had been propped up might be reapplied if it should again chance to totter.

Of all the modes, however, for settling the affairs of Spain the marriage of the Queen with the son of Don Carlos is the most impracticable and the worst. In the first place he and all his family are attainted and banished for ever by the Cortes, and that decree will never be reversed for such a purpose. Moreover Don Carlos with his pigheadedness,[2] and his conscience, and his views of his rights, would never consent to it, but it would be far better for the country that he should reign alone than to create a never failing source of intrigues by maintaining two parties in a war which must be interminable so long as they have respective chiefs to look to, who must be supported upon antagonist principles and who would always be waiting for events. If the Queen were to die for instance her sister is her successor. Is it to be supposed that Don Carlos's son, who would look upon himself as King, would allow himself to be set aside in order to make way for her? Or if he did would his party permit it? Such a marriage bed would be the hot bed of discord and civil war—and the idea of it would dissatisfy the Carlists and exasperate every body else. The Queen and the present system of government are the only means by which a fusion of parties can ever be brought about, by an absence of persecution and letting the country see a futurity of repose.

I have given you an unmerciful dose of Spanish today.

Martinez is out as I predicted to you in my last,[3] and Toreno reigneth in his stead.[4] Martinez is a worthy man and full of Hell's pavement—good intentions—but they don't suffice in revolutionary times particularly when accompanied with more vanity, obstinacy, and weakness of purpose than I have hitherto seen collected in any three men. His successor is much more able—a man of the world—and fitter to be at the head of a Government. I wish when he was at school that his writing master had kept him exclusively copying 'Honesty is the best policy'—there is no knowing but what by dint of that he might have quedado enterrado of[5] the useful axiom.

Martinez wrote to me that if he was allowed he would sign the slave treaty with me as he had the full powers for the purpose and I have this day obtained the permission from Toreno for him to do so. I hope therefore that this week will settle the business.

Received 18 June.[6]

GC/CL/190; Clar. Dep. C.452/1 (20-25)

[1] V to P, 7 June 1835, no. 90, FO 72/442.
[2] 'highmindedness' in C.452.
[3] V to P, 2 June 1835, no. 89, FO 72/442.
[4] Toreno was appointed President of the Council of Ministers. He retained the office of Minister of Finance until 15 June when he was replaced by Mendizábal. (V to P, 15 June 1835, no. 97, FO 72/442.)
[5] 'continued to be guided by'.
[6] C.452/1 docketed 'By Courier St.Martin'.

123 Villiers to Palmerston, 13 June 1835

Madrid. Private. I have come up from Aranjuez and am living here in order not to lose a moment in concluding the slave treaty with Martinez who has the full powers for signing it. There are still various little hitches and difficulties, but the matter is proceeding as rapidly as any thing *can* do in Spain, and I hope to send the treaty off by the middle of next week at furthest.

I have this evening received a letter without a date from Alava, referring me to one from you which I have not received at all, for the reasons why England declines to give the assistance sought by Spain.

You are fully in possession of my opinions upon this subject and I need not add the expression of my unavailing regrets at the decision which appears to have been taken. Alava says that the Foreign Enlistment Act is to be suspended in the Queen's favour but I think my late dispatches will prove to you how inoperative such a measure will be to save her throne.[1] It will produce no moral effect here, neither will it give the Spanish Government any assistance which they had not already at their command. Alava knows well that General Bacon has been offering for months past to raise any number of men in England and land them within a given time in Spain. The English Government could not have prevented this without committing an act of hostility against this country, for they never effectually prevented it in the case of Don Pedro with respect to whom England was bound to be neuter, whereas with respect to the Queen of Spain she is bound to give assistance.

The courier which brought me Alava's letter arrived yesterday morning—the report was spread that French troops were about to enter, and it would be difficult to describe the satisfaction which the report produced or the manner in which it calmed the public excitement. People are here in an agony of fear, and they will commit the acts of desperation usual under such circumstances when they become convinced that they have no longer any ground for hope.

In the possible event of the Queen considering Cadiz more *pleasant* and *salubrious* than Madrid in a few weeks time and that she invites the friendly diplomates to accompany her I suppose you will not wish me to be ungallant and decline.

I have had such short notice of the transit of Toreno's courier through Madrid that I have no time to write more.

Received and answered 22 June.[2]

GC/CL/191; Clar. Dep. C.452/1 (27-30)

[1] V to P, 7 June 1835, no. 90, FO 72/442. V wrote to Granville that he thought Álava 'must have contributed to mislead Palmerston as to the nature of the assistance really needed by Spain'.(PRO 30/29/421, 13 June 1835.)
[2] C.452/1 docketed 'By Spanish courier'.

124 Villiers to Palmerston, 16 June 1835

Madrid. Private. I yesterday received by a French courier the copy of your note to Sebastiani[1] which should have been forwarded by Alava as it appears. Your letter to me to which he alludes has not arrived.

So long as the question of intervention appeared doubtful I thought it incumbent upon me to lay before you the arguments and the facts which bore upon it. The question is now settled and I shall say no more about it, or doubt that powerful and sufficient reasons have induced your decision.

The Government has with some dexterity given out that intervention has not been refused, and that French and English troops are about to arrive—not letting it be understood that they are merely mercenaries which, though they may prolong the war, would entirely fail in producing a moral effect. This together with the announcement of the new Ministry has produced a calm—of what duration it will be I cannot tell, but the Carlists are now quite confident, and there is no doubt that nothing but want of courage to avail himself of his present position hinders Zumalacarregui from pushing on to Madrid.

The appointment of Mendizabel who has always been looked upon here as the arch fiend of revolution has astounded every one. I am very glad of it, for I look upon him as a man of creative genius and the only Spaniard fit to undertake the cleaning of this great Augean stable of corruption. Alava's nomination will probably disgust him greatly.[2] I can neither tell you why it was determined upon or who is to be his successor, for Toreno is at Aranjuez where I cannot go, for immediately upon my arrival here to finish the slave treaty with Martinez I was laid up with the gout. . . .

As you were pleased to commend my dispatches to the Duke of Wellington I send you herewith a copy of the only letter which I wrote to him, and which although marked private certainly forms part of my official correspondence. Without having the presumption to suppose that I should influence his policy with respect to Spain I was desirous of giving him an exposé of the course his predecessor had pursued, and I considered a private letter the more convenient form for the purpose. I did not send you a copy of it at the time thinking that as you were no longer in office you would have considered such a communication improper.

PS. I have just received from Toreno an answer to a letter which I wrote to him last night informing me that Alava's successor is not yet appointed and will not be so until he has conferred with me.

Enclosure: Copy, Villiers (Madrid) to Wellington, 7 December 1834.[3]

GC/CL/192; Clar. Dep. C.452/1 (31-34)

[1] In reply to specific questions put to P by Sébastiani on Broglie's instructions, P stated that he did not think intervention the most effective measure to be taken at this stage in the conflict; that a proposal by the Government for naval intervention would be opposed in Parliament; but that Great Britain would support France if the Eastern Powers attacked her on the pretext of French intervention in Spain, although this would require parliamentary approval. (Broglie to Sébastiani, 28 May 1835, and Sébastiani to Broglie, 4 June, AMAE CP Angleterre 645.) Toreno considered that the French questions had been framed so as to throw the responsibility for non-intervention on Great Britain. (V to P, 22 June 1835, separate and secret, FO 72/442.)

[2] He was nominated Minister of Marine.

[3] See also above no. 114.

125 Palmerston to Villiers, 16 June 1835

Foreign Office. The French Government mean to offer, or rather have offered to that of Spain, the Foreign Legion now in the French service, which completed as it might be, would amount to near ten thousand men. Pray urge the Spanish Government strongly to accept this offer; it is of great consequence in a political as well as in a military point of view that it should be accepted. The worst possible effect would be produced in Europe if the application of Spain to France for military assistance were first declined, as it has been by France, after communication with us; and if then *we* were to send a corps of auxiliaries, and the offer of a similar corps by France were to be declined by Spain, it would look as if the Quadruple Alliance had already expired under the influence of petty national jealousies, and narrow minded feelings of mutual distrust. The Spanish Government may perhaps think some of the men, who may be found in the Foreign Legion, a little more enthusiastic in their political notions than might exactly suit the juste milieu; but these gentlemen will not fight the less well on that account, and they will vent their redundant energies in the mountains of Navarre.

The Tories here are furious at the selection of Evans[1] to command our volunteers;[2] but that is all nonsense. It is only men of ardent minds who are fit for difficult enterprizes, and if Alava had pitched upon such as Gurwood, either favourable to Carlos or lukewarm in the cause of the Queen, the whole thing must have failed. As it is I really think the measures now taking will bring it to a successful issue. Lord Holland has written a letter full of good advice and good Spanish to Martinez de la Rosa with whom he is personally acquainted.

Our Corporation Bill makes us safe for this year; and in times like these a year's lease of power is a good deal.

Copy.

GC/CL/1240

[1] Lieutenant-Colonel George de Lacy Evans. He had seen active service in India and in the Peninsular War, and took part in the battle of Waterloo. In 1830 he entered Parliament as a radical, sitting for Westminster from 1833.

[2] The Spanish minister, Álava, had asked the British Government for permission to recruit British volunteers for the Queen of Spain's army. The British Government agreed to the request. This was the origin of the British Volunteer Legion. (P to V, 11 June 1835, no. 4, and 12 June 1835, no. 5, FO 72/439.)

126   Villiers to Palmerston, 22 June 1835

Madrid. Private. I am writing in a great hurry to be ready for a courier of Rayneval's who is coming through this place from Aranjuez—the little I have to say you will find in my dispatches,[1] and if I had more to add I don't think I could do it for I am at this moment suffocating with fury. I came up from Aranjuez and have now stayed here for 12 days, at great inconvenience both public and private, because I felt sure that without hourly goading Martinez and the clerks of the Foreign Office I had no chance of ever getting the slave treaty finished. . . .

Alava has sent several couriers here lately but they brought me nothing either public or private from you. I saw in the Madrid Gazette the Order in Council for suspending the Foreign Enlistment Act and Toreno told me yesterday it had been done upon Alava's application to you. It produced a good effect here and in Madrid things are calmer—10 days ago we were on the very verge of revolution with all its concomitants in their worst form, as has since been discovered.

Soublette's negotiation still hangs fire. . . .

I must reserve till the next opportunity some details about Alava's recall and the appointment of his successor.

Received 8 July.[2]

GC/CL/193; Clar. Dep. C.452/1 (35-38)

[1] See especially V to P, 22 June 1835, no. 98, FO 72/442, in which V reported that he had urged Toreno to turn his attention to the subject of Anglo-Spanish commercial relations. He had reiterated that the political alliance which Toreno 'professed himself so desirous to promote . . . would have no solid foundation until it was based upon the reciprocal interests of the two countries'.

[2] C.452/1 docketed 'By French courier'.

127 Palmerston to Villiers, 22 June 1835

Foreign Office. I write you two lines by Mendizabal's messenger though I wrote to you on Friday[1] a letter which Granville was to forward you by the first opportunity. Alava has this morning received the approval of his Government of the levy of 10,000 men, which he proposes to make here. I am glad of this, and hope that this levy, and the transfer of the French Foreign Legion, will answer all purposes of more direct military [?aid]. The appointment of Mendizabal as Minister of Finance is a capital measure. He will put the Spanish finances in order if any man can, and what he has accomplished in Portugal, where he really has done wonders, is a pretty good pledge of his success in Spain. He is the best man in Europe for this appointment.

Alava declines the Department of Marine, and prefers remaining as minister here. I greatly exhort him to persevere in this determination, being quite convinced that he can render Spain more important services by being here as minister, than he could by going to be in the Marine Department at Madrid. Last year Alava would have been in a false position here; while the Duke of Wellington was hostile to the Queen, Alava would have been greatly embarrassed by being her representative at this Court. Now the case is altered and since the Duke has declared in her favor, Alava is far more useful than any other man could possibly be. Pray then impress upon Toreno the great importance of keeping Alava here as Spanish minister; he has the entire confidence of the present Government, and by enjoying also the confidence of the Duke of Wellington he is able to paralyze the Opposition, and

to render our task in assisting Spain far more easy than it would otherwise be.

I am glad to find by your letter of the 13th that you give me hopes
of a speedy signature of the slave trade treaty. It will come most opportunely and will render the Queen's cause popular. If you could also
announce to me some material improvement in the commercial system
of Spain you would do that which would be most highly advantageous
to the Queen's cause in this country. At present the liberal part of the
nation are all in her favour, as a mass; but there is hardly a single individual who has any commercial connection with Spain who has not
some complaint to make of hardship and injustice suffered by himself,
or of impediment to his commercial speculations arising from the
customs house regulations of Spain.

Copy.

GC/CL/1241

[1] P to V, 16 June (which was, however, a Tuesday), no. 125 above. See P
to Granville, 16 June, GC/GR/1548.

128   Villiers to Palmerston, 29 June 1835

Aranjuez. Private. Herewith at last the slave treaty, of which you have
probably begun to despair as much as I have done for the last twelvemonth. There is no use now recurring to the pains which it has cost,
or the annoyance attendant upon the transaction of any business with
such a man as Martinez; but if the good old custom still obtained of
giving a thousand pounds to the signer of a treaty my conscience would
not compel me to refuse it upon the score of not having worked for it.

I have received, and yesterday communicated to Toreno, your letter
of the 16th. He fully admits that it would be impolitic to decline the
offer of the French Foreign Legion, and begged I would assure you that
it had been accepted. He likewise told me in confidence that Frias, who
never loses an opportunity of shewing his dislike and his distrust of the
French Government, had been making some difficulties with the Duc
de Broglie respecting the formal acceptance of the Legion or the formal
demand for it—much as in the case of Eliot's mission—and had gone
so far as to write to Toreno that he should still hesitate to do so, *even*
though he received the express orders from hence to that effect, as he
considered that France had behaved shabbily upon a question which

was almost as much French as Spanish, and that the assistance now offered was only in consequence of the efforts making in England for the Queen's cause—which efforts he considered would be sufficient without exposing Spain to the humiliation of being beholden to France. Mighty magnificent for so small a man. However, I told Toreno that a perseverance in this line might produce a coolness between France and us, and although we were very fond of Spain we should not be disposed to pay that price for our friendship 'with her. I begged him therefore to give a better direction to Frias's zeal which he has promised to do, and he said he had already sent peremptory orders for him to accept the Foreign Legion.

I have done my best, and I think with some success, to explain to Toreno, Amarillas, and others, as well as to [the] Queen, through a confidential channel which I have, that the English Government could not in their present position intervene in the affairs of Spain otherwise than as they have done, and that the suspension of the Foreign Enlistment Act and the manner in which the Order in Council was drawn up, afforded ample evidence of the friendly feelings by which the English Government are now animated. Every body seems to agree in this, and to be grateful for the popularity of the Queen's cause in England.

Will you have the goodness to write me a few ostensible lines upon the subject of our commercial relations and the political advantages which their improvement and extension might at this moment procure for Spain—i.e. if you agree with me as to the fact. I feel convinced that if you were able to make some satisfactory statement upon this subject in the House of Commons, it would more than any thing else serve to popularize in England the existing order of things here.

I have expressed some discontent to Toreno upon his appointment of Alava to the Ministry of Marine, and told him that I thought it ni politique ni poli after you had declared your satisfaction at finding yourself in relation with Alava, and the reasons why you considered him the most useful representative Spain could have in London. Toreno said he should be exceedingly sorry if you were displeased, but he was convinced you would not view Alava's appointment as a recall to him or as an affront to yourself, when the only reasons for it were the Queen's service. He had felt that at a critical moment it was necessary to form an entirely new Cabinet pour frapper les imaginations here, and he had included Alava in it not only on account of his popularity and experience, but as a means de rassurer foreign Powers who might have taken alarm at Mendizabel's forming part of the Government.

Toreno is however in great embarrassment as to a successor for Alava, and has consulted me upon whom I think it would be agreable to you to have. He will not appoint one till he knows your wishes. I am going to offer you an opinion upon this matter with which you will perhaps be disinclined to agree, but I do so without hesitation because from the *local* advantages which I have I feel sure I am right.

I know *every body* who would pretend to be appointed minister at London, and I declare there is not one with whom you would have a satisfaction in doing business except Cordova. He is not only the most agreable man in every way here but the most acute and intelligent. When I came to Madrid I had a strong prejudice against him which was entirely destroyed by the evidence of facts. He was opposed to us in Portugal in compliance with his duty as a Minister of Ferdinand's, but always stoutly representing the impolicy of the course he was made to pursue, and affirming that the maintenance of Don Miguel upon the throne was treason to the system which must obtain here when the King died, and to which alone the young Queen could look for support. All this I have seen in his correspondence with Zea, who became his bitter enemy for having told me that Don Miguel ought to be expelled cost what it might and Donna Maria placed upon the throne in peace. It is true he was likewise for getting rid of Don Pedro at the same time and *we* should then not have been sorry for it either. Immediately upon the death of the King the measures which he took respecting Don Carlos prevented his entering Spain, and the Queen Regent has several times told me that she could never forget his conduct upon that occasion and that her daughter was infinitely indebted to him for her crown. His correspondence at that time has since been laid before the Cortes and received with universal approbation, and probably if Don Carlos had now the choice of the man who of all others he would best like to hang it would be Cordoba. He is the only general during the campaign who has obtained any success and suffered no reverse. He is now directed to take the Command in Chief of the army ad interim. Toreno told me that he should be most happy to appoint him if you liked it, and I agreed to ask you, but I have not mentioned it to Cordoba. He is an Anglomane enragé, 36 years old, clearheaded and unprejudiced. I am sure you would like him and am sure you would do what you pleased with him. *Them's my sentiments* as your Lordship's countrymen say, and the matter awaits your Lordship's decision.

PS. I have this moment heard from Toreno that Zumalacarregui is dead and *buried*.[1] It is really a miracle of good luck at this critical conjuncture of affairs.

Received 8 July.[2]

GC/CL/194; Clar. Dep. C.452/1 (39-45)

[1] He was wounded at the siege of Bilbao and died as a result of his wounds. (V to P, 29 June 1835, no. 103, FO 72/442.)

[2] C.452/1 docketed 'By Courier St.Martin'.

129 Villiers to Palmerston, 4 July 1835

Aranjuez. Private. I yesterday received and immediately communicated to Toreno your letter of the 22d ultimo. I had particular satisfaction in doing so, as I have all along told him that Alava would not accept the Marine Department and that you would not part with him, because he could be much more useful to Spain in London than at Madrid. He of course had nothing to object, but said that as Alava meant to accompany the expedition and in no case therefore could be at Madrid for some months, he would not appoint a new Minister of Marine—1st because Alava's name standing as part of the Cabinet was useful in and out of Spain, and 2dly because if matters turned out well and the civil war was terminated, it might happen that Alava's presence here when the Cortes next meet might be more desireable than at London. In the mean while however no new minister will be appointed to England.

The paragraph in your letter upon commercial matters came quite àpropos, and was just what I asked you for a few days ago. I have only confidence here in things accomplished, and I will therefore not promise you any improvement of the commercial system of Spain, but I have hope, and you may be assured that nothing which exertion on my part can effect shall be wanting.

I have been pushing Toreno hard lately upon the Honduras question but I have not made much way. . . .

Mr. Faxardo,[1] whose mission here I have mentioned in my dispatch of today, is a very intelligent officer, and both the Queen and Toreno are desirous that he should obtain permission from the English Government to accompany the expedition, for as a Biscayan by birth and a British officer by profession he would be peculiarly useful here in his own line, the Commisariat—he knows every inch of ground in Biscay and his family and connections live there. He is on leave at present, and I daresay there would be no difficulty in prolonging it if you approve. He goes home in the Castor and I hope you will see him when he presents himself at the Foreign Office as he can give you interesting information. He did so to the Queen and her Ministers con una franqueza that they are not accustomed to, but which will have a good effect. Among other things the Queen asked him what he thought of the strength, discipline, etc. of the faction. I think, Madam, he answered, that 2,000 of *our fellows* would walk through them all and Your Majesty's army into the bargain. If it had not been for the English squadron, and Captain Henry's[2] Englishmen who are in the service of Spain, Bilbao would have fallen long ago which is of good omen for those who are coming out. The zeal and activity of Lord John Hay and the officers under his command entitle them to great commendation.[3]

Toreno was much pleased with your approval of Mendizabel's nomination.

PS. So many strange things happen in this strange country that I shall not consider the slave treaty entirely safe until it is ratified. I hope therefore that you will enable me to do so with as little delay as may be.

Received 16 July.[4]

GC/CL/195; Clar. Dep. C.452/1 (47-50)

[1] He came to Madrid with despatches for the Government from Bilbao and Santander, and was anxious to be attached to the British Legion. He had joined the British army during the Peninsular War. (V to P, 4 July 1835, no. 104, FO 72/443.)
[2] Captain of the Marines who were on board the ships of the British squadron in Spanish waters.
[3] For the siege of Bilbao see Hay to V, 22 June 1835, Clar. Dep. C.459.
[4] C.452/1 docketed 'By Spanish courier'.

130 Palmerston to Villiers, 9 July 1835

Foreign Office. I have received your letter and despatches to the 29th

of June. I am delighted at having at last got your slave trade treaty
. . . . The effect will be excellent and I shall lose no time in sending
you the ratifications.

I was much obliged to you for sending me a copy of your letter of
the 7th December to the Duke of Wellington. It was a very handsome
letter on your part, and does you great credit, and it has been very
gratifying to me to read it.

I do not wonder that you find fault with us for not having determined at once upon the bolder course of direct interference. Perhaps
it might have been the most effectual, but still considering all the
inconveniences attending such a course I am satisfied that we have
taken the right decision. Evans's ten thousand will turn the fate of the
war. The Spaniards ought to give him the chief command, if he acquits
himself well when he gets to the ground. Their great want seems to
have been a good general; their commanders have been one worse than
another; and now they have got back again to Sarsfield, who bears a
high character, but who never happens to have done anything, anywhere.

I hope Torreno will have determined to leave Alava here; in spite
of your panegyric upon Cordova, I do not think that gentleman would
succeed well with us. He may be agreable and clever, but the great
requisite for a diplomatist at an allied Court is to inspire confidence;
and unfortunately Cordova's career has not been such as to lead one
to place very great personal confidence in him. However, if he comes
we shall make what we can of him; but I should strongly advise
Torreno to leave us Alava.

Mendizabal's appointment is a capital hit. If any man can put the
Spanish finances in order he will do so—I shall have some serious talk
with him, before he goes, about our commercial relations, and shall
endeavour to impress upon him how important it is for the political
alliance between the two countries that our commercial intercourse
should be extended. I have frequently touched upon this topic with
him, and he seems fully aware of the truth and importance of our opinions about it. In the meanwhile however pray omit no opportunity
of urging this upon Torreno. He is too enlightened a statesman to
require convincing, and I am sure you can say nothing to him about
this matter which has not already presented itself to his mind, but the
pressure of other matters may drive this from his thoughts, and it is
very important that you should recall it to his recollection, and endea-

vour to persuade him to take some decisive step, as an earnest of his future intentions—any measure of this kind would greatly facilitate Alava's operations.[1]

It would also be an amazing advantage if he would work up the long arrear of unredressed grievances and dispose of some of those thirty or forty cases of complaint of which you sent me a list the other day.

Copy.

GC/CL/1242

[1] In raising money on the London market.

131   Villiers to Palmerston, 10 July 1835

Madrid. Private. Toreno's courier is going early and it is only since dinner that I have had notice of his departure. I must therefore be very brief.

I hope the King our Master will be pleased with my conversation this afternoon with the Queen Regent—it was my doing. Her Majesty is in the habit of sending her private secretary to confer with me *independent* of her Ministers and he told me yesterday that *La Señora* did not know how to convey her gratitude to the King for the manner in which he had befriended her cause. I suggested that she should throw over Spanish etiquette and send for me, to say what she wished to have conveyed to the King. She gladly took the hint and I hope the conversation may be useful as a contrepoison to any Tory rabies, for I hear from all quarters of the fury with which Londonderry[1] and Co. are expressing themselves upon the enlistment which they fear, I trust with good reason too, will secure the Queen's throne. The feelings of gratitude not only of the Queen but the public towards England at this moment are very satisfactory. The French, or rather Louis Philippe, are at a great discount. The Queen today wanted to abuse her cousin of France, but as I thought it would not be civil to contradict her and I did not want to agree with her, I took the liberty of *talking across* her.[2]

Frias writes the most indignant dispatches—one of which Toreno shewed me the other day and which began El demonio es el padre de todos los Franceses. Toreno is rather inclined to agree with him and is so confident that the English auxiliaries will do all that is necessary here, that he is indifferent to French assistance and is glad of the delays which have arisen respecting the French Legion. I think I have been of use in making him see that this is very foolish as regards Spain, and very improper as regards England, when he knows the wishes of the English Government and the motives by which they are guided upon that subject.

Received 20 July.

GC/CL/196; Clar. Dep. C.452/1 (51-52)

[1] The Marquess of Londonderry frequently attacked the Government's Spanish policy in the House of Lords and openly espoused the Carlist cause.

[2] For an account of this conversation see V to P, 10 July 1835, no. 109, FO 72/443.

132   Villiers to Earl Granville, 13 July 1835[1]

Madrid. Private. Toreno is at last convinced that Frias should not be left to himself—for even if he had all the good will, which he has not, he would never know how to set about enlisting French officers and soldiers and giving them the information they must stand in need of. A brigadier of whom Amarillas speaks most highly is about to be sent immediately to manage every thing—and that does away with the necessity of sending any one from Paris here—indeed he never could have had any thing to do here.

I have had a letter this evening from Cordoba who has now the Command in Chief—he seems to think rather worse of things than I expected, although Valdez and Latten have done every thing which cowardice or treachery could effect to ruin the army and the cause. He tells me the following—that his parlementaire had just returned from the Carlist camp (where he had been respecting an exchange of prisoners) and that he had been prodigiously well treated by all the Carlist chiefs, who all said that if France intervenes they will immediately make an honorable capitulation and lay down their arms returning to their homes, but that they are quite indifferent to the arrival of the auxiliary corps and *are fully determined to give quarter to no foreigner.* They despise Moreno[2] who has the Command in Chief (he is the Malaga man who was hunted out of England last year); they neither esteem or like Don Carlos. The troops are attached to and have great confidence in some of their chiefs and although they were for a time inclined to despond at the death of Zumala they have now entirely recovered.

The not giving quarter to any foreigner is very important. In the 1st place Melbourne I saw in the papers in answer to Londonderry said that the English auxiliaries would be entitled to the benefits of the treaty.[3] It was quite reasonable that he should suppose so but in fact he had no authority to assert it and I fear that if English prisoners are shot much blame may be attached to the Government—and the families of the sufferers will of course endeavour to throw upon them the responsibility of having both encouraged the enlistment and guaranteed in a manner the lives of the prisoners. 2dly, should this hostile course be pursued with foreigners, England and France should be prepared with the course they will adopt—for having sanctioned the auxiliary force going to Spain they cannot consent to their being butchered. I am perfectly certain that Don Carlos will insist upon it—and I had heard from tolerable good authority some time since that he had publicly made the declaration but I never heard it so credibly stated as by Cordoba today—and in another part of his letter he says he has no doubt of it. Will you have the goodness to communicate this hurried scrawl to Palmerston as I have not another moment by a courier who is going to Oleron?

Your accounts of matters at home rejoice me very much. Still I cannot help having great misgivings about the Lords.

PS. I open my letter to say that I have just seen Toreno to ask him what were the terms of the treaty stipulating that prisoners were not to be shot— he says that Melbourne may consider himself perfectly justified in the assertion he made because there was not a word said in it about their being Spanish subjects. Don Carlos has plenty of foreigners in his service who would of course if taken prisoners by the Queen's army be entitled to all the benefits of the treaty which will be shamefully violated if any Englishman is shot after being made prisoner.

GC/CL/197

[1] Superscribed 'My dear Lord G.'

[2] He acted as Carlist Commander-in-Chief after the death of Zumalacárregui although he was never officially appointed to the post. Moreno was dismissed from the Royal Army by Ferdinand VII after he had sided with Don Carlos at La Granja in September 1832.

[3] See *Parliamentary Debates,* 3rd Series, XXVIII (House of Lords), 780, 15 June 1835.

133   Villiers to Palmerston, 20 July 1835

Madrid. Private. The spirits of the crestfallen army are reviving greatly, and the bad effects of Valdez's cowardice or treachery, or both, are diminishing.[1] Still, however, I don't believe that without *real* French intervention the insurrection will be put down, for the rebels look upon the auxiliaries as Spanish troops—and with the character of the Navarrese, their pride, their jealousy of every other part of Spain and their glory in the contest they have sustained it is not difficult to understand their repugnance to yield to the Queen's troops. For, with their inaccessible country, and their peculiar mode of warfare, they can never be *beaten*, unless they chuse to give in, or that the whole country is occupied militarily (which would require a well disciplined army of 150,000 men) or that the whole male population should first be caught and then deported—both of them impossibilities. But the country is exhausted, and the people and their chiefs want peace—or in other words I really believe a foreign army to surrender to.

I know that the English Government has done all it *can* do, and that that of France has done all it *will* do.[2] It would therefore be much more agreable to me to say that enough assistance had been given, but I think it the duty of an agent upon the spot to report what he believes to be true. My opinion is that the auxiliaries cannot put an end to the war in time enough to give a moderate form of government strength against Exaltados and Carlists—the former being now more to be feared than the latter—and if a moderate Government cannot sustain itself, the Peninsular Alliance, which the altered position of affairs in Europe owing to the giant progress of Russia has rendered so necessary, will only be an incumbrance, and may in moments of greater difficulty than the present embarrass us exceedingly. It is because I think I foresee that Spaniards left to themselves will fall into an inextricable confusion which will be injurious to us, that I have written, till you must be sick of my letters, upon the necessity of helping them—and it is likewise because the present moment appears so singularly favorable for setting Spain upon her legs, unless it is foredoomed that she is to lye for ever prostrate, when every notability and every class worthy of consideration are in favor of that state of things which actually exists (though they have not quite sufficient force to uphold it), and when France and England, instead of as heretofore having opposite and rival interests, have both now a common object in promoting by the same means the welfare of the Peninsula. But if they hang back from doing so, my fear is that such a course will be attributed to old jealousies revived, or to fear of the Holy Allies, and that the prestige of our Alliance, which under every circumstance most favorable to war has kept the peace of Europe for five years, will be materially injured.

When I wrote to you upon the subject of Cordoba I had not received your letter of the 19th ultimo (which came by the post and therefore in 16 days). There is now no thought of sending a successor to Alava, but I would gladly remove your prejudices against Cordoba, for I am certain they are founded upon an imperfect knowledge of his character and conduct, as my own were when I came to this country. If Alava lets it be supposed that Cordoba in whatever he does has only his own personal objects in view, he is a shabby fellow and the truth is not in him, for Cordoba when secretary of embassy at Paris, Ferdinand being in the best health and despotism at the time, risked every thing in order to shew marked and public attentions on every occasion to emigrants—particularly to those who were the objects of the King's vengeance—to none more than Alava himself. However, I rejoice that Alava stays in London and I fully admit that no one, be he who he may, could render his country as good service.

I omitted in my last letter to tell you what an admirable effect was produced here by your speech in answer to Mahon[3]—it sent up British alliance 50 per cent, and you are much more venerated at the Puerta del Sol than any Spanish Minister, though that is giving you but a mean idea of the public esteem for you.

On the other hand, that mild prig the ex Under Secretary did his late chef much harm, for there was rank Carlism in every line of his speech, and people here of course supposed he was uttering the real sentiments of the Duke of Wellington.

I fear the Zaragoza business is by no means over,[4] and that both in itself and by its example it is laying up a store of complication and trouble.

Received 28 July.   GC/CL/198; Clar. Dep. C.452/1 (53-57)

[1] Valdés had insisted that it was impossible for the army to enter the territory north of the Ebro. The result was that the army had retreated. Valdés also believed that Bilbao was lost to the Carlists and that there was no point in trying to relieve the besieged town. He was replaced as Commander-in-Chief of the army in the North by Córdoba. (V to P, 20 July 1835, no. 110, FO 72/443.)

[2] V was convinced that the French Government had given Spain all the assistance it was prepared to give, and that the real obstacle was the King. Louis Philippe had 'made it now quite a personal question and is like a bear with a sore head if anybody hints at intervention'. (V to Howard de Walden, 25 July 1835, Clar. Dep. C.541.)

[3] In a debate in the House of Commons on 24 June 1835, on the Government's policy towards Spain. P made a long speech in defence of Government policy and made no objection to the production of the copy of the Order in Council which was the object of Mahon's motion. (Parl. Deb., 3rd Series, XXVIII, 1133-56.) Lord Mahon had been Under-Secretary at the Foreign Office under Wellington.

[4] Four convents were burnt and the Urban Militia was about to proclaim the Constitution of 1812. The Captain-General of the garrison and his troops seized the ringleaders and immediately executed them. (V to P, 10 July 1835, no. 108, FO 72/443.) After these disturbances a deputation from the town council was sent to Madrid to demand complete freedom of the press. (V to P, 20 July 1835, no. 110, FO 72/443.)

134 Palmerston to Villiers, 28 July 1835

Foreign Office. As Mendizabal is sending off a messenger this evening I avail myself of his going to write you a few lines. I have this morning received your letter of the 20th. I see you still think a French army necessary to put an end to the war; I believe with you that it would be effectual for that purpose; but I trust and hope that the thing can be done without it, and if it can it will be far better for Spain, that a foreign army should not enter her territory under a foreign flag.

One cannot help thinking that the Spanish army is numerous enough to put down the insurrection, if the officers and men were fonder of fighting and had more confidence in their leaders; that spirit which they lack will be infused into them by the example of their English auxiliaries, and our ten thousand men will in this manner be worth forty thousand fighting men to the Queen.

Pray at the same time however take every opportunity of pressing upon Torreno the expediency of accompanying the increased exertions of strength which the Government are about to make with some attempts at conciliation. We quite admit the force of the remarks you made in one of your letters, that to grant all that the Basques ask might be almost tantamount to the establishment of a separate republic in those provinces, and that other provinces might be encouraged by their example to set up similar claims, which it would then be difficult to refuse. But perhaps some disposition might be shewn to grant indulgence, as far as it can be done consistently with the principles of that Constitution which *must* embrace within its scope the whole of Spain.

We have heard of the murder of three English Marines in the service of the Queen, in the neighbourhood of Bilbao; we have not yet got full particulars, but we shall suspend our decision as to the steps to be taken thereupon, till we learn the result of Colonel Wyld's mission to Carlos. It would certainly tend to simplify our position, if we were compelled to declare war against Carlos, and were thus enabled to give our cruisers on the Spanish coast instructions to act as belligerents.

I am glad Alava is to remain here; he has got into hot water with some of his Tory friends, and therefore it is still more important that he should be supported by his own Government and not be supposed to be thrown over.

I trust that Mendizabal when he gets to Madrid will be able with your assistance to do us all some good service about commercial arrangements. I have spoken to him much on these matters, and he has been talked to by Poulett Thompson; he is well imbued with orthodox doctrines about free trade, and professes to be full of good intentions—whether they will end in mere paving stones cannot be known, but we must trust to you to keep him up to the mark; and I think you will have no great difficulty in doing so. If any man can reestablish Spanish finances, and place the commercial system of Spain on a rational footing, he will do so. It is proposed by the Portuguese Government, he tells me, that he should take Lisbon in his way to Madrid; I tell him that whether he does so or not, he *must* go through Paris; that it is absolutely necessary for him to have personal communications with the French Ministers, before he goes to his post, and that if he appeared to avoid Paris he would give just cause for jealousy to the French Government. He means therefore to go to Paris, embark at Bordeaux, go from thence to Lisbon and then on to Madrid. This seems not a bad arrangement.

I think we are pretty safe here for the present and at all events till the end of the session. . . .

I am glad to hear that my speech on Mahon's motion was approved at Madrid. I have already had the satisfaction of hearing it was condemned at Berlin and Vienna. Poor Mahon himself made a wretched figure; but then as they say he knowed no better.

GC/CL/1243

Copy.

135 Villiers to Palmerston, 1 August 1835

San Ildefonso. Private. I have been disappointed at not having an opportunity of writing to you during the last 10 days, but Rayneval has the gout and would, like a wise man under such circumstances, as soon think of putting his foot as his hand to paper, and Toreno prefers junketing with a fat new wife he has taken so that the couriers have made nothing but false starts lately.

You will of course have heard long ago of Cordoba's victory on the 16th.[1] It is the only positive advantage which has been gained since the beginning of the war—the first time that prisoners have been made, and the first that a great moral effect has been produced upon the insurgents. All this too with the same troops which but a fortnight before had been reported by their General in Chief to the Government as so panic stricken, so completely *acobardados*,[2] that their loyalty must no more be depended upon than their valor. Their enthusiasm now, and their confidence in Cordoba are unbounded, and I don't believe, to compare small things with great, that Napoleon when he took the command of the army of the republic in Italy, produced a more extraordinary revolution in its morale than Cordoba has done in the Queen's army.

After the battle, Cordoba went with the army to Pamplona, in order to surrender the command to Sarsfield, and at the same time to give in his own resignation, because from what he had heard of Sarsfield, he considered that there was nothing but disasters in store upon his taking the command. Cordoba however having passed a day with him, found in him so much ability and knowledge, together with such enlightened views of policy for the pacification of the country, that he implored him not to refuse the command, and offered to remain with him as his aide-de-camp or his secretary. I mention this, because I think it a remarkable trait in an ambitious man, which Cordoba is, and because I think it shews him to be entitled to the confidence which you are disposed to deny him. Of one thing I am certain, that to renounce an intention of resigning which had already been made public, and to offer at the moment of victory to serve another in an inferior capacity, upon the conviction of the superior fitness of that other, is an act of unselfish patriotism which might in vain be looked for in any other Spaniard than Cordoba. Sarsfield declined the command for the present, and Cordoba retains it during the two months which Sarsfield asks for the reestablishment of his health (his complaints being occasional attacks of the brain and total deafness).

The progress of the insurrection, promoted, as if intentionally, by Valdez, has been checked—but that is all. The rebels are angry and disconcerted, and without confidence in their leaders, but it never occurs to them to change sides and join the Queen's army. They desert to their own homes, each man to continue his own rebellion as best he may—the women too, who are more immediately under the influence of the priests, are important obstacles to submission, and the whole population, upwards of 300,000, are at this moment in a state of *unmitigating* hostility. This population must not be judged by analogy with any other, for they are unlike any other—to a man they are ignorant heroes. No private interest, no prospect of advantage will make them abandon what they have taken up as a public principle, and the fear of shame would perhaps be found to operate more powerfully in Navarre, than in some neighbouring and more civilized countries. The restoration of the privileges would at this moment only be viewed as a proof of the Queen's weakness, and would encourage rather than quench the rebellion, and amnesties would only be laughed at by people wholly indifferent to life.

The Government is at length prepared to make any concessions which will procure peace, but their task of doing so with effect is not light, and requires the greatest caution. The first object must be to gain over the leaders, who are always more easily secured than the led. The Government for this have authorized the expenditure of any sum of money, amnesty and the conservation of grades. The people then must be gradually persuaded, and by their present leaders, that in laying down their arms they make no sacrifice of their principles respecting monarchy and religion—this done, they will gladly turn to any relief of their material wants, for their misery and exhaustion are extreme. The plan mentioned in my dispatch of opening public works in the provinces for the employment of the people will then come into useful operation, and the restoring some one or more privileges may complete the work.[3]

Cordoba is entirely of my way of thinking. I am in constant and unreserved communication with him, and am able to serve his views with the Government.

In the mean while the English troops have been received with enthusiasm at San Sebastian, and the most favorable reports are sent

273

up here of their appearance and *tenu*. The Duke of Ahumada considers that to send them upon active service before they are properly disciplined, and acquainted with each other and their officers, would be very *unfair*, and he proposes that they should for a time drill and do garrison duty at San Sebastian, Bilbao, and Santander, and thus set free for active service the troops now in those important towns. He wishes likewise to send an English division to Burgos, on account of the moral effect which red coats and the old associations connected with them will produce in Castille.

Alava will probably have left England before this letter arrives, but I suppose Mendizabal will still be superintending the final embarkations, and it would be well if he were to send a good cargo of salt provisions, for Cordoba writes me word that the supplies which the country affords are likely to run short. I have done my best to stimulate every body whom it concerned, against permitting any failures either in the Commissariat or pay departments for upon these, as I have told them, John Bull n'entend pas plaisanterie.

I beg of you to use your best powers of intervention with Santa Maria in order that he may come here *immediately*. The South American question has assumed an entirely different aspect since he last heard from Madrid. . . .[4]

Your letter of the 9th ultimo upon commercial matters was exactly what I wished and asked you for. I read it to Toreno who was flattered by its tone, and again admitted the expediency of putting the commerce between the two countries upon a better footing. My last note has certainly been taken into more serious consideration than ever yet befell a commercial representation from a foreign minister. I am pressing it with the departmental dii minores who have far more influence than the superi, and though I do not like to give you hopes upon this important subject, I am not without them myself.

I shall not feel entirely easy about the slave treaty until the ratifications are exchanged. I hope you will enable me to do so shortly.

I am delighted with this place. . . .

Received 10 August.[5]

GC/CL/199; Clar. Dep. C.452/1 (58-64)

[1] At Mendigorría over troops commanded by Don Carlos himself.
[2] 'terrified'.
[3] A plan of public works with 'liberal remuneration' was thought by the Spanish Cabinet to be a sensible move as most of the insurgent troops had

been for some time without pay. (V to P, 31 July 1835, no. 115, FO 72/443.)
⁴ Toreno admitted to V on 31 July 1835 that there were no longer any 'insuperable objections' to the Spanish recognition of Mexico. (V to P, 31 July 1835, no. 118, FO 72/443.)
⁵ C.452/1 docketed 'By Spanish courier'.

136 Palmerston to Villiers, 6 August 1835

Foreign Office. I send you the ratification of the slave treaty; send *me* back the Spanish one as soon as you can that I may if possible lay the treaty before Parliament this session.

We shall probably sit on to the end of the month and therefore there may be time. . . .

I have made Southern paid attaché instead of Scott, whom I have moved to the Hague; I thought that this would be agreable to you and be an evidence that I am aware of the merits of Southern. Mendizabal will start from hence on Sunday. He goes first to Paris, then by Bordeaux in one of our steamers to Lisbon, and thence to Madrid. His taking Paris and Lisbon in his way will be very useful. I strongly advised him to do so.

The Queen's cause seems to be looking better, and will thrive when our auxiliaries all arrive. Your friend Cordova is distinguishing himself, he seems to possess enterprize and capacity and the talent of inspiring his army with confidence. Pray write to him to communicate freely with Evans, whom I am sure he will like. I have written to Wyld to go and meet Evans, and to remain with him as long as they may both think it useful he should do so, but not to take any part in military proceedings.

The Government here will stand in spite of majorities in the House of Lords. . . .

Copy.

GC/CL/1244

137 Villiers to Palmerston, 9 August 1835

San Ildefonso. Private. I have received your letter of the 28th and thank you much for all the information it contains, the most valuable portion of which is that the Tories will not try their luck again just yet in your opinion. . . .

You will 'ere this have received Colonel Wylde's account of his mission to that most stupid barbarian Don Carlos, who prefers defying the power of England to not acting like an Ashantee. I fully agree with you that to declare war against him would much simplify your course, and I cannot but believe that such declaration, founded as it would be upon the announcement from his own lips of his resolution to butcher Englishmen, would meet with the approval of all parties and classes at home. England's declaring war upon him because he violates a treaty in order to commit murder[1] must *do* for him every where except with Lord Londonderry. I need scarcely tell you how delighted Toreno and Ahumada are with the hopes of it, and they reasonably expect most important results to the Queen's cause, if England in her own behalf decides upon entering the lists.

But if you declare war, how do you mean to wage it? The cruizers may act as belligerents, but the fight is a land fight, and the Englishmen to be slaughtered are soldiers not sailors, and our ships on the North Coast can do little more than what the zeal and activity of Lord John Hay and Co. have already done. Don Carlos may therefore pursue his system with impunity and laugh at our threats into the bargain, unless we have some means of getting at him inland. Sending troops however would I fear be next to impossible unless such a measure should chance to be demanded by the indignant public, but a landing of a corps of Marines and the unfurling of a British standard at Bilbao and Santander might be practicable, and that, together with the expectation of what might follow, would strike panic from one end to the other of the insurgent ranks.

His French Majesty must likewise take some decided part and avenge the murders of Frenchmen; but if exceptions should be made *in favor* of Frenchmen, it will go far to prove that which is believed by the whole Spanish army, that an understanding exists between Louis Philippe and Don Carlos. Toreno and Ahumada even, both told me yesterday they were convinced Don Carlos would not have dared give such an answer to Wylde if he had not counted upon French support. Upon this I don't pretend to give an opinion, but that the insurgents are receiving all kinds of direct support from the agents of the French Government I can no longer doubt. During the last week Ahumada has received reports from five different generals stating that 300 horses for the service of Don Carlos have been introduced from France, and

I never see Toreno but what he has some fresh proof to give me of the system which *during the last three months* has been permitted upon the frontier. I never allude to this subject in my dispatches because I think it matter for private rather than for public communication, but the more I reflect upon Louis Philippe's present course with respect to Spain, the more I feel confirmed in the opinion I gave you in a private letter some months ago upon his intentions.

Be his intentions however what they may, it appears to me that no interest of his can be served by his present policy. He cannot wish to have Don Carlos established in Spain or to extend over the whole surface of the Peninsula the intrigues and plots which are now chiefly confined to the south of France, but even this he could not contrive, for Don Carlos *cannot reign here.* His arrival at Madrid would be nothing more than the tocsin sounded by the most brutal part of the Spanish nation for a general civil war, which, rely upon it, would be full as acharné and (if left to Spaniards) perhaps nearly as long as the war with the Moors, and how would Louis Philippe like the contact of such an epidemic? The ultimate chances however would be in favor of the liberals, for the spiritual arms which in other times would have made their opponents strong are now broken and useless, and let the liberals arrive by their own means at mastery, inflamed by the very excesses of their own acts and opinions, and how will Louis Philippe like the changes that will then be rung upon every variety of federal and republican Governments by the madmen who will be tearing the country to pieces and preying upon its vitals? What he and the Holy Allies seem to be unable or unwilling to understand, is that the cause of the Queen is the cause of order, the cause of rank, property, and intelligence, the cause of *anti-revolution* in short, and that which they should all join to support, unless they desire to perpetuate tumult here by a determination to set up an impossible idol of despotism in Don Carlos.

This Government which has on its side the support which would be all-sufficient in quiet times is now tottering for want of strength between two parties each fiercely opposed to it, and wants a friendly hand to help it awhile. If it had only Carlism to contend with there would be no real danger—the army has been dispirited, but the example of Evans and his ten thousand will infuse new courage into it, and the insurrection will be *eventually* overcome. In the mean while however the Government may be knocked on the head by the Exaltados, and all that has been done go for nothing. Convents are burned and priests massacred by wholesale—seditions and conspiracies are forming every where, and the Government from its physical weakness being without moral power, is obliged to look on, a passive spectator of the steadily advancing dissolution of society. Yet if it had 20 or even 10,000 disposeable troops all would proceed quietly and not a Jacobin head would be reared. It was with these objects and in the well understood interests of order that I was in hopes France would have taken that decided line which would at once, and as if by magic, [have] restored strength where it would have been usefully employed.

I fully admit that the English Government in its present position could not have taken a more active part, and that it has done well and zealously all that it was in its power to do. But this is not the case with Louis Philippe—he might have settled the whole question by a pull of the telegraph, and there is no job I should have liked better than to have undertaken his *justification, upon their own principles,* at the Bar of the Holy Alliance. But it has neither been for the interests of Spain or for those of France that I have continued representing this matter till I fear my MSS. and their subject must be equally nauseous to you, but because I thought British interests were concerned, and I knew that in your mind they would longo intervallo stand before all other political considerations. I believed that if Spain were set free and started fair on the road of improvement, solving the great problem of the self-conversion of a despotic into a moderate constitutional form of government, that she might be to us a tower of strength, for the Western Federation of Constitutional Governments which was your object in the Quadruple Alliance would have made our general policy easy in comparison to what it will be if the Peninsula is thrown into inextricable confusion. This Government *may* pull through its difficulties, but it leans upon a broken reed, for it is dependent upon the more or less forbearance of the Exaltados, and I would not underwrite its safety for a week.

It is for this reason, to descend from generalities to particulars, and indeed because the whole history of Spain is but one long chapter of accidents, that I look with great anxiety for the arrival of the slave ratifications. Such a row as took place two nights ago in Madrid, such a one as is expected tomorrow, *any nothing* in short, is sufficient at this moment to produce a general outbreak, which would make the Government think much more of self emancipation than of that of the niggers.

Toreno was much satisfied with your arrangements for Mendizabal and your reasons for ordering him through Paris.

He promises me by all that is sacred (not that I know exactly by what *he binds himself* in that oath) that in the course of next week I shall have something satisfactory to send you upon commercial matters. I can safely say that I never leave him or any one else concerned in the matter unmolested for 4 and 20 hours together.

PS. I have put in my dispatch respecting General Iriarte and the Carlist prisoners what Toreno said jokingly about the French newspapers,[2] as I myself read in Galignani the paragraph in question, and I thought it might furnish a good answer to any attack in the House of Commons upon the Queen's Government. I am far from defending its humanity God knows, it is a word unknown to Spaniards, but I do not think this particular fusillade could have taken place without the knowledge of the Government or the retaliation of the Carlists.

GC/CL/200; Clar. Dep. C.452/1 (66-73)[3]

[1] In his interview with Colonel Wylde Don Carlos declared that the British Legion would not be treated in accordance with the Eliot Convention.
[2] It was alleged that General Yriarte had ordered Carlist prisoners to be shot, in defiance of the Eliot Convention. Toreno said that these and many other falsehoods appeared in the French press and that they were deliberately inspired by Carlists to create a bad press for the Queen's Government. (V to P, 9 Aug. 1835, no. 126, FO 72/443.)
[3] C.452/1 docketed 'By Spanish courier'.

138 Villiers to Palmerston, 18 August 1835

San Ildefonso. Private. Some *banking* couriers have I believe been sent from Madrid two days ago, and you will by their means have learned the news of our émeute. Nous l'avons échappé bel, *if* we are out of it yet. It has been the most alarming, because it would have been the most decisive, *turn up* which I have seen since I came to Spain.[1] As to precautions, the Government had of course taken none—it would not have been a Spanish Government if it had—firmness or presence of mind are always out of the question—and the only determination which was *really* taken was to wait here for events, and if they came off ill to go to Burgos with the Queen and talk big from the head quarters of the army of reserve—i.e. if one exists of which I have never been very clear.

I have done my best both before and during the row to induce Toreno to return to Madrid, and be at his post instead of down here, dividing the Government and the garrison, but he swears the Queen won't budge, Mr. Muñoz thinking he shall be arrastrado por las calles,[2] which is a delicate Spanish operation you may have occasionally heard of. Now however the Government are inclined to display some vigor, and instead of, as usual, hanging some wretched obscure culprit after a 9 months imprisonment and a 3 months trial, they have named a military commission before which various rebel members of the Lower House,[3] and Urban Officers are to take their very indifferent chance.

If their vigor is not froth, and that they make some examples and reform the militia, the Queen's cause may be incalculably strengthened by this event, or rather by the accident which determined its result, for had the people of Madrid taken part with the *émeutiers* during the last three days, the Queen's authority would have been destroyed at Madrid, and within a week shaken off in every other part of Spain by the extreme liberals. Every variety of excess would have been committed, and that would have called up Carlist risings, not in favor of the one tyrant, but in disgust at the many. This is chiefly the work of the Emigrants who, as I have mentioned before, have never been easy a single moment since they returned. They never would make any allowance for progress or change of political feeling in Spain during their absence, they fancied themselves gods at home because they had represented themselves so abroad, and being indignant that the entire Government of the country was not sacrificed for them like the fatted calf on their return, they have incessantly labored at confusion ever since they set their feet on their native soil. They have struck no roots, however, and have done little more than disturb the surface—certainly the incapacity of the Government and its utter ignorance of *how* to govern have powerfully aided its enemies, but this is only an additional proof that the country *will not have* that which is called liberty in the emigrant sense, for it knows by painful experience that it is only a change from one despotism to another and a worse.

To support the Queen's Government therefore which steers a middle course between the two, and *works well* with the majority of the country, *is a European interest,* quite as much that of Russia as of

England and France, for it is the interest of anti-exaggeration and anti-revolution on either side, et dans le tems qui court this is a great desideratum, be the country or the form of government what it may. I can only say that Louis Philippe ought to be eternally obliged to the barrios bajos[4] (the St. Giles's of Madrid) for they might have made a general revolution, and Spain would have proved a most infernal machine to him if once well set on fire crammed with such combustibles as she is.

Before I go further let me thank you sincerely for Southern's appointment. Nothing could have been more agreable to me not only on his account, but as a proof of regard to myself on your part. Let me add too that I have an additional pleasure in it from thinking the appointment honorable to yourself, for many others must have better claims than Southern on the score of seniority, and I am sure you would not have named him if you had not been satisfied of his worth and abilities—they are of a no ordinary kind, and I heartily wish that there were a few more such men in the diplomatic service.

I have received the slave ratification. I wish it had come before, for I cannot expect much attention to the matter at such a moment as this. . . .

Toreno has not kept his promise of enabling me to send you some satisfaction upon commercial matters, but in consideration of 'late panic', as Cobbett said, I excuse him for another day or two. Alava is arrived at Santander and he, as well as every one else who has seen them, sends brilliant accounts of the English troops. The English are in prodigious favor throughout Spain, and French influence and French prestige diminish every day. If we declare war against Don Carlos and the *ruction*, as the Irish say, at Madrid is turned to good account I shall once again think well of the Queen's cause.

You will have received an account from Bilbao that Lord John Hay's boat has been fired upon by the Carlists from the bank of the river although the British flag was flying in her—two of his men were severely wounded, so that we certainly now have got a sufficient case. Some Marines to land at the ports, a few of the King's soldiers in red coats to cooperate with the auxiliaries (which would then soon all pass for King's troops), the standard of England hoisted at different places, and above all a public declaration of hostilities and the reasons thereof, would act like magic, and need not, as it seems to me, cause offence to France, for she was no party to the Convention which has been violated. Not knowing what your intentions are upon this matter I have not ventured to broach the question to Toreno, but I really think we might in exchange for troops and material assistance, offer to stipulate for the concessions which the Government should make to the provinces—the course of general administration they should pursue—and a commercial treaty upon a grand scale. This you will perhaps think is a wild notion, but I don't believe it to be impracticable, though it may not be worth while to trouble you with the developement of the scheme at present. Pray let me know as soon as you can your determination upon the result of Wylde's mission. An estaffette goes from the French Foreign Office to Rayneval every Saturday and a letter from you would always be forwarded by that means.

Alava writes to me in terms of enthusiasm respecting Cordoba's deeds—my fear is that he is dying from the fatigues he is undergoing.

Received 27 August.

GC/CL/201; Clar. Dep. C.452/1 (75-83)

[1] There were disturbances in most of the large towns, and they were aided by the Urban Militia, which on 15 August set up barricades in Madrid and proclaimed a Constitution. The movement in Madrid subsided on 17 August. (V to P, 18 Aug. 1835, no. 136, FO 72/443.)
[2] 'dragged through the streets'.
[3] 'MM. Isturitz, Caballero, Galiani [*recte* Galiano], all members of the Cortes, were either members of the junta, or took an active part in its proceedings.' (ibid.)
[4] 'poor quarters'.

139   Villiers to Palmerston, 22 August 1835

San Ildefonso. Private. The accounts I send you today, though not so actively bad, are in fact progressively worse than those which went by the last courier. Many of the principal towns are now governed by juntas of Urbanos who appropriate the revenues of the State to *public purposes* as they say, and turn out the employés of the Government whom they consider *disaffected* in order to occupy their places—in short in the most loyal manner and always in the name of the Queen they are shaking off the authority of her Government. The Carlists may, and probably do, assist this, knowing that it must eventually turn to their advantage, but no Carlist cry is raised out of the Northern Provinces, and all this is the work of a handful of individuals in each town, who have no definite object but the places which others occupy, and who are as cowardly as they are noisy. I have no doubt that if an active Provost Marshal could make a tournée with 1,500 men to all these towns, and in each of them hang half a dozen ragamuffins, that the country would soon be quiet, and the Queen's authority generally respected. There are no troops however—half the army is in the hospital, or in garrison, or have deserted, or have been made prisoners, and Cordoba has not at this moment an effective force of 12,000 men. It must be still some weeks too before the English auxiliaries can be trained sufficiently to give them a fair chance of being useful. Anarchy in the mean while progresses with an accelerating velocity as the weakness of the Government becomes more apparent, and as there seems not only to exist no talent for governing but no personal courage in any one, every variety of disaster may of course be expected.

I have endeavoured to make Toreno and Ahumada feel that their proper place is Madrid in the hour of danger, but they are both of opinion that San Ildefonso being the safer is the *properer* post. They lay the blame upon the Queen, but I have ventured to suggest that in a constitutional Government that is no excuse for a Minister. It's *no go*, however. The consequence is that the orders they have telegraphed and couriered up from here have not been executed, and the people whom it would have been really desireable to catch and make examples of escaped at the moment, and most of them are now walking about the streets of Madrid—it being too late to do any thing with them! Some of them went away in the Diligence publicly and without disguise, the Intendant of Police telling Toreno that the idea of examining the public conveyances had not *struck him*. He was asked why he had not issued the order to arrest certain persons at the time that the state of siege was published, and he said he was dead asleep at the time and thought it would do just as well the next day. An agent of Police was sent to arrest Galiano—he found Isturiz, the most active and ferocious of the agitators, sitting with him. He asked, Are you come to arrest me as well? No Sir, replied the agent, the order for that was given to a comrade of mine who is now looking for you.

I give you these as specimens out of ten thousand similar ones, of the manner in which business is done in every department from one end of Spain to the other.

The plan which is fast gaining ground, and respecting the probability of which I wrote to you about 14 months ago, is the re-establishment of the kingdom of Arragon. I told you likewise that Deputies had gone privately to Paris in order to make this intention known to the King, or to offer in the event of the civil war continuing to place the Northern Provinces of Spain under the protectorate of France. Whether Louis Philippe is waiting for such an event, or whether he intends ultimately to intervene upon his own account, I of course know not, but the activity of French agents in Catalonia and the assistance afforded to the Carlists on the frontiers are now as notorious as the desire, long entertained by France, to possess some of the ports of Biscay. If any such schemes as these are entertained, they are wild and shortsighted ones, for I conclude France would not be permitted to settle down on this side of the Pyrennees, and as for the provinces setting up for themselves and forming separate republics—they would in a twelvemonth be in the same condition as the Kilkenny cats.

Having found Toreno and Ahumada together this afternoon I could not resist broaching to them the idea which I mentioned to you in my last, of making a treaty of reciprocal advantage between England and Spain. That is, if the former would declare war against Don Carlos, and send a few troops to this country in order to put down the two factions which are on the eve of swallowing up the Government, that Spain in return should admit all English manufactures, and allow us to settle the differences between the insurgents and the Government. I said that the moment appeared peculiarly favorable for this— Catalonia was in revolt and had stopped the payment of taxes, and France could have no right to complain, for the concessions to England would be in return for the aid which had been refused by France.

They both declared their readiness to enter into such a negociation, and said that if England would lend an effective aid at this moment she might impose her own terms—adding that they were sure they should have the public voice with them in any such arrangement with England for there was a general feeling in favor of a closer alliance with us.

I of course begged that this conversation should be considered entirely unofficial as I had no authority whatever for saying what I had, and I was afraid that, although my Government might be disposed to act in favor of the Queen, neither Parliament or public opinion would support them in an enterprize upon so large a scale. They both admitted that this was more than probable and there the matter ended. There will not be time before Toreno's courier goes to put this in a dispatch, but I will do so at a future opportunity.

I have this evening received a dispatch from you desiring me to report without delay upon the proceedings taken against the 'Isabel Anne'. . . .

Sir Arthur Chichester appears in common with at least four out of the 8 millions of his countrymen (*all* of whom have written to me upon the subject) to have been hoaxed with a will of Duke O'Neill, Governor of Mexico. . . .

Every day I make a point of annoying Toreno upon his commercial note, and I feel that by that means I have given him a personal interest in letting me have it, but it is still in the hands of a Finance Junta, who are probably in the pay of some manufacturers to delay it in hopes either to weary out my patience, or that every thing will be smashed here and then there will be no necessity for it.

I am likewise very troublesome about the ratification, which *is* upon the stocks and will I trust in a few days be launched.

Received 1 September.[1]

GC/CL/202; Clar. Dep. C.452/1 (85-92)

[1] C.452/1 docketed 'By Spanish courier'.

140   Villiers to Palmerston, 29 August 1835

Madrid. *Introduces M. Calderón de la Barca, whom he has known since they were both members of the* Corps Diplomatique *at Petersburg, and who while at the Spanish Foreign Office has been of assistance in connection with the slave trade treaty negotiations.*

Enclosure: Copy, Palmerston (Foreign Office) to Henry Fox (appointed British minister to the United States of America), 24 October 1835, introducing Calderón, the Spanish minister at Washington.

GC/CL/203

141   Villiers to Palmerston, 31 August 1835

Madrid. Private. I was in hopes to have sent off the messenger two days ago, but the delays of these people in exchanging the ratification have prevented me. Martinez wished to put the last hand to the work, and I could not object, but as I found the business would never terminate by letter I came up here to hasten it. There have been petty difficulties without end, and even the certificate of exchange had to be written three times over before the academical niceness of Martinez was satisfied. However all's well that ends well and the treaty is a good deed saved out of the fire, for a pretty *gintale* [? genteel] sort of a blaze there will be here presently.

You have for months past perhaps considered me a croaker, and that I could have no reasonable ground for my prophesies and fears, but events are unfortunately so turning out that I would, without fear of their contradicting me, refer to what I have written to you from hence for the correctness of my opinions. I admit that it required a large dose of faith in those not well acquainted with Spaniards to believe in the march that events would take, but I have always taken into account that there was no man in the country fit to govern it under difficult circumstances, and I felt the necessity of guarding against the passions of this people which when dormant are as if they did not exist, but which when roused proceed with the velocity of lightning. They are like the genii which the fisherman brought to shore and might have done as he pleased with when he had him pent up in the box, but which when let out, cannot be got back again and play the devil with those who free them from restraint. France, to whom the affairs of Spain are of far different importance than to us, will find, when perhaps too late, her error in looking upon them as a Spanish and not a French question, and by determining to believe that the miniature La Vendée in the North was the only ground for apprehension she neglected the opportunity for killing two birds (the very two which are bothering herself) with one stone, and giving strength to a Government which was endeavouring to pursue the system upon which she considers her own safety to depend.

Foreign interference was necessary in Greece, was necessary in Portugal, and so it will be some of these days in Spain, but under what accumulated disadvantages? For the revolutionary party will feel that a foreign army must be as much opposed to them as to the Carlists. Each party will therefore be hostile to the common enemy, and both will by that time have to be sought out and attacked in the remotest corners of the country.

In my black dispatch of today[1] I have confined myself to the simple statement of facts but you will easily imagine all the details of disorder which such a state of things must be engendering. Conceive that foolish Queen remaining with her Prime Minister and 1,500 troops to guard them 40 miles from the capital—and Toreno at such a moment as this appointing a Ministère pour rire.[2] Conceive that it was thought necessary to restrain the press here by a fresh Junta of Censors and yet that all the papers from Barcelona, Valencia and other places where these *gags upon knowledge* have been entirely removed are permitted to arrive and circulate at Madrid. Conceive the damnation which all these ejected monks are dealing through the land—however I will not proceed for you will be sick with the *puchero*[3] I am setting before you.

Soublette is very grateful for the energetick manner in which by his own account you spoke to Santa Maria. . . .

Mendizabal is not expected till the 4th of next month—he will find himself in the position of a man jumping naked into a nest of hornets. The Queen must make him Prime Minister and he must make the best terms he can with the Exaltados.

The Carlists are very proud of the answer given to Colonel Wylde by *His Majesty*, and all parties are waiting with anxiety to see how it will be received in England.

We have news from London to the 21st. . . .

PS. Since writing the above I have received from Toreno a note upon commercial matters. It, as well as its inclosure, is so long that I think I must defer sending it till the next opportunity, for the messenger is ready to go. . . .

Bad news has been pouring in all day. I wish you would let me know immediately what course I am to pursue in the event of the Queen being obliged to adopt the Constitution or take any violent revolutionary measure.

Received 10 September.

GC/CL/204; Clar. Dep. C.451/1 (63-68)

[1] V to P, 31 Aug. 1835, no. 142, FO 72/443.
[2] Several ministerial changes were made in the preceding week. V said that the new members were old and incapable of performing their duties properly, and that in Madrid the Government had become a laughing stock amongst the politically informed. (ibid.)
[3] 'mess' added in pencil, possibly by P.

142   Palmerston to Villiers, 4 September 1835

Foreign Office. I promised Mendizabal that I would write to you to beg you to communicate with him with entire confidence, but I know it is unnecessary for me to do so because you are already aware that I have long been in the habit of unreserved communication with him on the affairs both of Portugal and Spain, and I cannot doubt that you and he are already on the footing of old friends. I hope his energy and good sense will have enabled him to set things to rights, but certainly all the accounts we receive from Spain tend to shew that energy and vigour are greatly wanted. Addington told me that the people in the provinces used to say in the days of Ferdinand, no hay Gobierno, and I am sure that may be said with equal truth in most of the provinces at present. I hope the Spanish Government will take the 6,000 Portuguese, they are worth having at any price, and the Portuguese Government seem willing to lend them on very moderate terms.

The Emperor of Russia is full of plans for meddling with Spanish affairs[1] but I doubt much his two allies of Austria and Prussia joining in his schemes. But still this ought to be a reason with the Queen's Government for trying to put an end to a state of things which *invites* the interference of foreign Governments in the affairs of Spain. As to anything which the Three Gentlemen of Kalesch or Toplitz[2] can really do to help Don Carlos, that is not much worth thinking of. The only real assistance they could afford him would be money, and I imagine that he has never been allowed to want that.

Copy.

GC/CL/1245

[1] P's source of information on the Spanish policy of Nicholas of Russia was Granville's despatch of 31 August 1835, no. 147, which he sent to V on 4 September 1835 (no. 25, FO 72/439).

[2] The Emperor Nicholas, King Frederick William of Prussia and the Emperor Ferdinand of Austria had met at Toeplitz in Bohemia.

143   Villiers to Palmerston, 5 September 1835

Madrid. Private. I have only just learned that a courier for Paris is expected to pass through here from San Ildefonso in the course of an hour or two. I have had but time therefore to indict you a hasty dispatch[1] and send you some decrees which I had got translated beforehand.[2] Very imprudent ones in my opinion. Toreno thinks otherwise and that he knows the effect they will have upon the country. I cannot say his late attempts at vigor during the *siege of* Madrid give me much confidence in this new effort upon an enlarged scale. I believe it will make a vast number of people who have now their swords half drawn, throw away the scabbard.

These juntas and emeutes in Valencia and Andalusia would be no more than tempests in teapots if it were not for those in other places, but Catalonia and Aragon are very formidable—they are in open revolt, defy the Government and I see no means of bringing them to submission.

It is now 12 o'clock at night and I have just received a letter from Mendizabal at a town some leagues from hence saying that he shall proceed by a cross road to San Ildefonso without passing through Madrid and begging of me to come there immediately as my presence will be of great importance. I don't exactly know what he wants, and I shall be very cheery [chary] of advice in the present state of affairs, but I am going to set off directly.

Received 15 September.

GC/CL/205; Clar. Dep. C.452/1 (94-95)

[1] V to P, 5 Sept. 1835, no. 143, FO 72/444.
[2] Declaring the general juntas illegal and conferring unlimited powers on provincial governors to support the prerogative of the Crown. (ibid.)

144 Villiers to Palmerston, 15 September 1835

Madrid. Private. I am sorry that at this critical moment ten days should have passed without my writing to you, but Rayneval has kept his courier waiting for the ministerial dénouement, and I did not think myself justified in sending one while that important question remained undecided.

In my last letter I told you that I was going to San Ildefonso to meet Mendizabal—my doing so was of use, for he and Toreno were like two fighting cocks together, and I contributed to prevent an open rupture on the first day which would have been discreditable and injurious to Mendizabal, whereas now he has had the opportunity of gaining over many opinions to his side by his honorable conduct as well as discretion, and by insisting upon friendly discussions with Toreno upon the impossibility of his joining the Government as then constituted. You may perhaps think him wrong in not having done so, but I assure you he acted in that wisely both with respect to the public and himself.

You yourself might as soon have expected to retain your importance and power of being useful, if you had joined the Duke of Wellington in his three days attempt to form a Government during the progress of the Reform Bill, as Mendizabal if he had united himself with Toreno whose unpopularity is greater and more general than that of any man who has yet figured on the political stage of Spain. It is not worth while to analyze the causes of it—the fact is sufficient, though the deadly hate which exists against him may not be merited. He has thought of nothing for the last three months but taking his ease and *proclaiming* resistance without reflecting that though his countrymen do not require much force to control them, yet it must be of a different kind from that of decrees which long habit founded upon necessity has taught them to disregard.

It is impossible not to be struck with Mendizabal's energy and his unbounded self confidence which here more than any where is a certain element of success. I quite agree with you as to the utility he will be of to the finances of this bankrupt nation, for he seems a great bundle of ways and means, and it would be difficult not to like a man who appears English to his heart's core.

His views as a statesman I did not much fancy at first—he gave me the impression of a pilot who might weather the storm if he hadn't happened to be so terribly drunk, but the extreme danger of the ship has sobered him, for he has been quite a different man during the last few days, and I have been taking measures to secure his success which I should have hesitated to do 8 and 40 hours after his arrival. I fear he miscalculates entirely his power in the country, and that his name will not be to him the tower of strength he supposes when he turneth away from the revolutions he has committed and doeth that which is lawful and firm. I don't believe it is in the power of any man to subdue the elements of disorder which now rage here—however he is our derniere cartouche and if it does not take effect, why then sauve qui peut, for it will be all up.

Supposing that there were no insurmountable objections (I can divine none and have only heard one—le Roi ne le *veut pas*—soit fait comme il est desiré) against it, I shall always consider the refusal of Louis Philippe to intervene in the affairs of this country three months ago as the greatest error committed in the politics of modern times. 20,000 French troops would have produced precisely the same effect upon the equally balanced contest in the North as 8,000 Spanish troops did in Portugal by the moral conviction that further contest was hopeless, that there was no baseness therefore in submission, and that justice would be done between the victors and the vanquished—but the present state of Spain is that which suits Louis Philippe's policy, whether it be a despotic form of government here, or a slice of Biscay, or marrying some *chico* of his into Don Carlos's family. The system of France for the last 150 years has been to prefer having a weak disorderly beggar at her gate to being jostled by a thriving neighbour. His present Majesty in this as well as other matters is walking in the steps of Louis 14th, and he is not detained in so doing by his knowledge that if Spain were prosperous and at peace her interests and all her national tendencies would point towards England.

I have only just received your dispatch No. 21 of August 14th—enclosing your answer to the Duc de Broglie's note to Sebastiani—Rayneval had shewn it to me a month ago. It is scarcely necessary for me to say that I agree in every word of your note—a fine figure England and France would have cut going together hand in hand with all the pride of error to put out a burning fiery furnace with a drop of milk and water.[1]

I had written thus far when I went to see Mendizabal who is like a mad bull at the Queen having permitted Toreno to be present at their interview last night, and at his having spoiled all the projects he had cut and dried. The chief of which was to have published an address to the nation upon the new era about to dawn, and requiring all disobedient juntas and others to return within the pale of legality upon pain of his not being able to compose a Government which should meet the wishes of the country. Not a very regular mode of going to work but it would have been new and might have answered. He has however been forced in consequence of Toreno's expiring influence with the Queen to adopt another course, and Alava is named President of the Council. For the latter I am not sorry, and so much did I foresee what was about to happen that a week before Mendizabal's arrival I wrote to Alava that Toreno would be shoved out by Mendizabal and asking him if he would consent to occupy the very post to which he is now appointed. Like a wise man he did not answer and like a wise man too I conclude he will reject the proffered honor. The Queen has thrown over Mendizabal[2] for when I left her last night she distinctly said she should charge Mendizabal with the formation of a Government. I think I diverted her royal fancy from the scheme of retiring to Burgos upon which it has long been bent. She believes she could come Jeanne d'Arc over the Carlists which is all the more bold in her as her *present condition* appears to me very different from that of the renowned damsel.

We have reports here that Alava [*? recte* Córdoba] and Evans have sustained a severe defeat near San Sebastian but nearly all the communications are interrupted and the Government has no certain intelligence.

I have received your letter of the 4th. You were quite right in supposing that Mendizabal and I should be together as if we had not been apart for 10 years.

I have sent you a commercial note of Toreno's[3] which might have gone a fortnight ago if there had been an opportunity—these matters however do not much signify at this moment for every junta at the sea ports would decree just what it pleased respecting the admission of foreign merchandize, and it is as well that people in England should not be deceived by the decrees of a Government which is unable to carry them into execution.

Received 25 September.

GC/CL/206; Clar. Dep. C.452/1 (96-103)

[1] P had rejected Broglie's proposal for a joint Franco-British mediation between the Spanish Government and the insurgents on the basis of a recognition of the local privileges of the provinces. (Broglie to Sébastiani, 2 Aug. 1835, AMAE CP Angleterre 645; P to V, 14 Aug., no. 21, enclosing P to Sébastiani, 13 Aug., FO 72/439; Broglie to Rayneval, 24 Aug., AMAE CP Espagne 768.)

[2] C.452 has 'Toreno', which is correct.

[3] Enclosed (translated copy) in V to P, 8 Sept. 1835, no. 145, FO 72/444.

145 Villiers to Palmerston, 19 September 1835

Madrid. Private. The more I see of Mendizabal the more I regret not having known him before I came to this country, for had I had the confidence in him a year ago which I have now, he should have been in the Cabinet long before the necessity for placing him there had become pressing, and many disasters, present and to come, might then have been averted. He has now, as I said in my last, arrived too late—the torrent has broken its dykes and he himself begins to feel that to dam it up or even arrest its progress is beyond his power.

You will be pleased with his exposition to the Queen although he, like every other Spaniard, talks too much of himself in it. The passage announcing the reforms which he considers necessary is excellent, and the whole gave satisfaction here.[1] He thinks it will produce an equally good effect in the provinces but in this, as I have told him, he will be mistaken. The different juntas have just had time enough to learn how sweet, or rather how profitable is power, and they will no more leave it than a tyger the prey which for the first time teaches him the taste of blood. They make laws and execute them at their pleasure, give and take away employments, levy troops, etc., etc., but the attribute of government in which they display the greatest activity is in taxation, and atrocious robberies are now every where committing in the name of the Queen and for the sacred cause of liberty. The people still take no part and they, as well as the respectable majority of inhabitants in the junta-ridden towns, are no more than passive spectators of the farce which is enacting by a handful of worthless brawlers alike destitute of property, talent or respectability.

The Carlists in the mean while are increasing every hour, but the army not being reinforced is barely able to hold them in check, and yet the 'Exaltados' are sending agent upon agent to the head quarters to endeavour to seduce the troops from the Queen's service in order to join the *patriotic* standard. The moderate party, including the rich and the timid and those who have every thing to lose by the triumph of either Carlists or anarchists, might at least be expected to rally round Mendizabal whom they admit was the only man the Queen could select as her Minister, Toreno being no longer possible, and to support him in the anti-revolutionary path he has sworn to keep—so far from it however, they are all holding back and affect not to like his *antecedentes,* i.e. every minute act of a man's former life which is invariably treasured up against him here with appropriate additions, in case he should ever acquire power and *consequently* have to be dragged down. Was there ever a more extraordinary or diabolical state of things?

Rayneval in reply to his demand for instructions upon the points has been told by his Government that in the event of the Queen Regent's being deposed his functions are immediately to cease, and if she quits the capital and goes either to the army or the provinces he is to accompany her.[2] Upon the latter case I asked you a question about three months ago, but not having received an answer I thought you intended to let me act as I might think best under the circumstances. I do not therefore ask for instructions in a public dispatch, but I conclude you will think it expedient that in Rayneval's and my mode of proceeding there should be no divergency.

I shall be very curious to know whether the Emperor of Russia's projects concerning Spain find favor in the sight of his German allies. I don't look upon them as unimportant because I think that the restoration of tranquillity in this country lies between Mendizabal and His Imperial Majesty. It would be with bitterness of soul that I should see a Cossack or a rouble in operation here—still however the oncoming state of things is so horrible that one must have no bowels at all of philanthropy not to wish to see an end *quelconque* put to it.

I have received, wondering many things, your dispatch No. 23 upon which I beg to offer a remark or two. The said dispatch directs me to use my influence in behalf of the 27 Carlist officers now imprisoned at Coruña. Your instructions shall of course be obeyed, but it would be difficult for me to use the influence I possess in a manner more prejudicial to this Government. The persons in question are for the most part men of distinguished families—a chosen band of young and active officers whose emancipation would be of far more importance to the Carlist army than any prisoners of war for whom they would be exchanged could be to the Queen's. They are moreover not in the same category with other prisoners—they were taken long before Eliot's treaty and at a time when reciprocal massacre being in practice the Government not only was bitterly reproached for sparing their lives but they had difficulty in doing so—they were afterwards sent to Coruña instead of to the Colonies partly upon my intercession. I believe that their being let loose would produce great dissatisfaction in the army, and great triumph in the insurgent camp that the British Government had effected for them an object of so much importance. My conclusion therefore is that Mendizabal will be grossly wanting in his duty if he complies with the representations which I shall make in behalf of these gentlemen.

September 23rd. Mendizabal has kept delaying his courier till today when Rayneval has determined upon sending one. Las Navas and his rabble are not above 20 leagues from Madrid.[3] The Mighty only knows if any means will be found of stopping him—but if the whole does not, like most other Spanish enterprises, go off in smoke he may order as he pleases when he arrives for no resistance will be made, and as I suppose the Queen Regent will not agree to deposing herself she must go and wait for better days. In the mean while Don Carlos will *come* and then these revolutionists will all run away instantly—back again to England I conclude, but not to impose upon our credulity and our charity as before, I trust, for their conduct as well as that of most of the returned emigrants is the conduct of robbers and traitors.

Rayneval's courier goes early and I have no time to add more.

Received 1 October.

GC/CL/207; Clar. Dep. C.452/1 (104-109)

[1] The reform programme consisted of the following: 'a) to put a speedy and glorious end without other aid than that of the national force to the fratricidal war; b) to fix at once and with due respect the future condition of those religious corporations whose reform is required by themselves as well as by public utility; c) to embody in wise laws all those rights which issue from the representative system; d) to create and lay the foundations of public credit whose mighty force and magic power must be studied in free and wealthy England.' (*Gaceta de Madrid*, 18 Sept. 1835, translation enclosed with V to P, 19 Sept. 1835, no. 149, FO 72/444.)

[2] Broglie to Rayneval, 10 Sept. 1835, AMAE CP Espagne 768.

[3] For the demands of Las Navas, a junta leader at the head of five thousand men, see V to P, 27 Sept. 1835, no. 150, FO 72/444.

146 Villiers to Palmerston, 27 September 1835

Madrid. Private. I have but very short notice from Mendizabal of his courier's departure, and as I am laid up with the gout I shall add but a line or two to the dispatch which I have just written. Whereat you will probably rejoice, for I suppose the affairs of this country can excite nothing but nausea and disgust. Such a picture of selfishness, cowardice, rapine, and treachery as Spain now presents has been rarely seen in modern times, and in the midst of it all I declare to you that I see only Mendizabal and Cordoba who are actuated by a sense of duty, and who desire honestly to fulfill what they have undertaken. I have met with no others who are not moved by vile and sordid views. Nobody thinks of saving the country or the cause, nobody even thinks of his own eventual interest, but every thing is sacrificed in order that each man may avail himself of the present state of things which may possibly not again occur, to gratify his vanity or his vengeance, or to fill his pockets.

The returned emigrants still continue distancing all competitors in the contest of ruining the country. It is they who from the moment of their return have with unceasing labor been organizing confusion, and it is the chief men among them who now are bent on preventing Mendizabal from establishing order or attempting a Government but upon principles which they know are hateful to the country and which contain within them all that is necessary for failure.

I admit all the appalling difficulties of Mendizabal's position. I don't suppose one man was ever beset by so many—but I fear he is insensibly getting drawn into the stream of revolution—he is already going with much greater velocity than he intended, and is much less master of his craft than he was. If some lucky accident does not happen quickly he will be hurried down the rapids and never heard of more until the mangled remains of his reputation come up some of these days in the Portuguese Stock Market.

Alava accepted the portefeuille of Foreign Minister but refused the Presidency of the Council of Ministers. This was just as it should be—for his occupying the latter post would have been very distasteful to the gentlemen who are to be conciliated at this moment—but he has taken fright at what he has done and begs to retract. He writes to me to manage this for him, which I don't intend to do, for I think he may be useful and at all events it is his duty to try to be so. If he and Mendizabal quarrel (an infinitely probable circumstance for I don't believe they agree upon a single man or thing or principle) he can go back to London—and it is on that account that I have prevented Mendizabal from filling up the vacancy until Alava arrives.

The accounts which I receive from Bilbao are few and far between, and as I conclude the murders of British sailors (King's) and the insults to the British flag which are constantly committed there are reported to you, I do not allude to them, but I do not believe such outrages were ever before committed with impunity.

Don Carlos publicly announced that he had replied to the mission of the British Government that he should not respect the treaty[1] with regard to British subjects and that he didn't care for the consequences—this however applied to Englishmen in the service of the Queen of Spain, and though we may not think that a sufficient cause for quarrelling with that Potentate, yet surely the case is altered when he attacks and kills men in the service of the King of England.

I was very sorry to see by the King's Speech that the slave treaty ratification had not arrived in time. This is entirely the fault of the messenger Tylecote. I told him repeatedly how important it was for him not to lose a moment—he set out from hence on the night of the 31st and it appears he was not in London on the 10th. All commercial couriers go to Paris now in 5 days—the very longest time is 6—the news of the row in Madrid was conveyed to London by the same courier in 140 hours. Mr. Tylecote has therefore no excuse for he met with no accident, but so long as the pay of our messengers is not made in some way dependent upon their speed, they will continue to be as they are now, proverbially the slowest in Europe.

Received 8 October.

GC/CL/208; Clar. Dep. C.452/1 (110-114)

[1] The Eliot Convention.

147 Villiers to Palmerston, 2 October 1835

Madrid. Private. In these busy times notices of couriers are short, and as dispatches are necessarily long I must curtail my private lucubrations to you, in which there will be no great mischief for I sometimes fear that they are too lengthy upon matters which, though of high interest at Madrid, may assume a very different aspect in London.

Esto marcha as you will see by my dispatch, and Mendizabal begins to feel that which he would not believe when I told it him 3 weeks ago, the extreme difficulty of his position and the impossibility of managing this country à la Portugaise. He has been obliged to throw himself into the ways of revolution *much more* than he intended, and *a little* more than he likes. A fortnight ago he determined not to meddle with the Estatuto Real or to employ notorious Constitutionalists—every place of power and trust is now filled or filling with them and a Royal Decree has already appeared handing over the Estatuto to the Tormentors.[1] I do not the least blame him for this—it was no fault of his that, when he was called to the rescue, the Government was powerless and the country in confusion—he could only avail himself of the means at his disposal and these were revolutionary. Come what will however, the preservation of the throne and the postponement of complete anarchy during the last 15 days has been solely owing to him. 3 days more of Toreno's Government would have rendered the whole concern unsaveable—and I shall therefore never repent the part I took towards establishing Mendizabal in his present post. His only chance now is the being able to convert all the excitement which the juntas have stirred up into an anti-Carlist channel, and thus to put down the war in the North which will place the army then at the disposal of the Government—that is the only influence which will ever be respected here for many a year to come, and the only one under which salutary reforms can be effected. As for the moral power which this or any other Government could obtain over the nation, corrupted as it is to its heart's core, I would not give a brass button for it.

If Mendizabal is, or thinks himself, obliged to make many more concessions—if his new electoral law is bad—if he renders prolétaires eligible as in 1820—if the changes in the Estatuto are very radical, all is over with the throne of Isabella. What may come after, the Devil alone in his infinite cunning can tell, for to his charge this unfortunate country seems specially entrusted. A select committee of his imps surround Mendizabal and whisper diableries in his ear all day long. I see him constantly, and do my best to keep him straight, for, though I say it as shouldn't, I know both the country and the people much better than he does.

The juntas *cooperate,* like friendly Powers—they don't obey—and even if they were to dissolve themselves they would spring into life again whenever their old members were dissatisfied with the Government, i.e. with the distribution of places. Among other experiments which are likely each to fret its hour upon the revolutionary stage is that of a federal system—the language of the juntas *se ressent* of this, and the idea of independence would be popular in each province. I shall not be surprised to see it attempted, and a *very durable* and *satisfactory* state of things it will produce.

The proclamation of the Constitution[2] by the army of reserve is the most alarming circumstance which has yet occurred—Cordoba with his usual tact and promptness has stifled it all, but it is very probable that he will not master the evil if it inclines to spread. It is entirely the work of two returned emigrant colonels who wanted to be generals. Cordoba's worst enemies admit that during the last 3 months the Queen's throne has been preserved by him alone—he not only reinspirited the army, but has been able to effect with 12,000 men that which Valdez failed in with 40 thousand. Since these revolutionary proceedings commenced he has maintained the discipline of the army (the reserve was not under his orders) and kept it as a centre of order in the midst of surrounding confusion. Your sense of justice will I think admit that my partiality for him is well founded.

Alava is to arrive today—he has been rather twaddling about joining Mendizabal's Government. Some time before Mendizabal arrived I foresaw what must happen and wrote to Alava to know if he would take the Foreign Affairs in the event of Mendizabal's becoming First Minister. He answered me as if I had offered him an affront instead of a place in the Cabinet—quite horrified at the thought—and lest I should not believe him, he sent me afterwards two editions of his political creed each stronger than the other. Upon being *appointed,* however, President of the Council, he wrote to desire I would arrange for him only to have the Foreign Affairs and to leave the Presidency to Mendizabal. I did so—when two days afterwards I got a letter from him saying that the first moment of enthusiasm was passed, and that he wanted not to have any thing to do with the Government, because he hated all the men whom it would now be necessary to conciliate—he therefore looked to me to get him out of his *escrape* as he calls it. I have done that too—for he would be very miserable in such a Government as this, and as he was considered one of the stand-still party even in Martinez's time, his being *now* in the Government would only afford pretences for attacking its system. The fact is, friend Alava liked the thought of the Foreign Affairs and then took fright at indulging his fancy.

I did a good deed last night with Mendizabal in re South American question—he could not stand the idea of being less liberal or more afraid of responsibility than Toreno both of which I gave him to understand I considered him.

Received 12 October.

GC/CL/209; Clar. Dep. C.452/1 (116-121)

[1] The Royal Decrees of 3 September against the juntas were revoked by a new decree of 23 September. According to V this had the effect of improving relations between the juntas and the Government. Mendizábal also agreed to convoke the Cortes and set it the tasks of revising both the Estatuto Real and the electoral law. (V to P, 2 Oct. 1835, no. 158, FO 72/444.)

[2] Of 1812.

148 Villiers to Palmerston, 6 October 1835

Madrid. Private. We are improving, and Mendizabal is a great man—entirely. Like other great men he alarms little ones, and his mode of treating revolution upon the homoepathic [sic] system—simi-lia similibus—makes Martinez de la Rosa and Co. look upon him as a Grand Junction Consolidated Junta himself—but he has adopted the only means for stopping—at events for a time—everlasting smash.

I am perhaps wrong in calling the present state of things here a revo-lution for it is rather a dozen and a half of revolts, but as far as the Queen's throne was concerned one system would have *worked as well as the other*—the people having taken no part whatever has made the work of pacification easier. None of the dissolved or dissolving juntas would have reentered the pale of legality if they could have helped it, but the inhabitants of the towns they oppressed, sick of their rapacious and despotic proceedings, have in most places entirely withdrawn their support upon becoming acquainted with the policy of Mendizabal who, as a man said to me yesterday, has just tossed up and turned over public feeling like an omelette, except the moderate party, who like their namesake in the House of Commons are here of-use-to-nobody men. The Exaltados are however the class from which he must eventually expect the fiercest opposition—they are beginning to perceive he is not the man they hoped and therefore to run a muck at him, but if he can only obtain some anti-Carlist advantages before the Cortes meet he will be strong enough to prevent any revolutionary measures being carried, and upon that the futurity of the country depends.

'You Gentlemen of England who live at home at ease' may perhaps have thought that I was unnecessarily alarmed respecting the non exit of Toreno and then the advent of Las Navas, but I assure you that if the former had remained two days longer in office the Queen would at this moment have been somewhere in Navarre, nearly deserted, and in mortal trouble how to escape out of the country, and I have some right to be believed as I have not been a prophet après coup, but have foretold step by step three months beforehand all that would occur here.

With respect to Las Navas, if he had advanced with his troops and his rabble during the first week of Mendizabal's Administration, and before his measures had calmed the public excitement, he would have met with no opposition here, and in order to save the Queen from sub-mitting to his terms, Mendizabal had determined (and had got her consent) to *elope* with her to Galicia—begging Rayneval and me to follow *if the people let us*—leaving the town and *the country* first to the tender mercies of the scramble mongers, and then to those of the Carlists, who would shortly have arrived to put order dans tout cela. They were thus to be left for a few months to pillage and butcher each other, and then the Queen was to have appeared again upon the stage as a pacificatrix and granted all the same liberal measures which she is now doing. This would have been playing rather gros jeu, but it was all settled, and Mendizabal communicated it to nobody but me—under such strict promise of secrecy however, that I did not venture to write it to you, until it had become, as it has now, a mere marginal note in the history of the last month.

Alava is arrived and was in great trouble how to arrange his ministerial and diplomatic matters to the satisfaction of himself and others. Mendizabal put the whole into my hands, and it has all ended charmingly, Alava retaining his mission, and Mendizabal the Foreign Affairs ad interim, both *quedando en la mayor amistad*[1] possible.

I have likewise arranged Cordoba's matters—for many of Mendizabal's nominations displeased him—he looked upon them as betokening approval of revolution against which he had loudly and successfully pronounced himself with the army, and as he could not with honor continue his command under a Government with which he thought he must be in opposition, he insisted upon resigning. I have however satisfied his apprehensions, and he has assured me that so long as I think it right for him to do so he will retain his command. If he were to quit it the army would disband itself on the same day and on the next Don Carlos would be on the road to Madrid—however I will leave Alava to tell you his opinion of Cordoba—he passed a day with him on his road here and was *incantado,* as he said, never having met with so remarkable a young gentleman in his life.

By the bye Alava will be much obliged to you if you will cause to be published in some of the best public instructors the decree retaining him at London which goes with my dispatch of today.

About a month ago the junta of Barcelona addressed a circular to the consuls of that place explaining in modest terms their conduct and their reasons for opposing the Government. Mr. Montagu sent me a copy of this document and I wrote to him a private and confidential letter in answer (of which I enclose you a copy)[2] and directing him to make such use of it with the junta as he might consider discreet and safe—but on no account to give a copy of it. It appears he is well acquainted with every member of the junta, and he communicated the letter to each of them. It had the happiest effect, and they all assured him that they would be willing to submit to the Government and implicitly follow whatever course was thought most expedient for the good of the province.

Received 24 October.

GC/CL/210; Clar. Dep. C.452/1 (122-127)

[1] 'remaining on the best terms'.

[2] No enclosure found.

149 Villiers to Palmerston, 10 October 1835

Madrid. Private. The notice which Mendizabal has given me of his courier's departure is so short that I can add but little to the two hasty dispatches which I have just written. I have but little to add though. Our anti-revolutionary progress is great—so on the other hand however is that of the Carlist faction. The different juntas have each held out as long as they could, i.e. till they were left nearly alone in their glory, and their final dissolution proves what I have always said, that the movement party has no root and can expect no support from the country at large. The juntas were the work of the secret societies and were *all* composed of persons who neither possessed or deserved to possess influence, although by acts of violence and having on their side the armed prolétaires or Urban Militia they were able to *cow* the peaceful and respectable, who it must be admitted however felt great disgust at the apathy of the late Government—*not as* regards *liberalism* or *freedom,* but in putting down the Carlists. The circular just issued by the junta of Barcelona (the one longest established and therefore the first in bearing fruit) shews that the certain consequence of all these revolutionary movements is Carlism. The faction in Catalonia is I understand *trebled* and the patriots of course are all hiding themselves —this would have occurred in every other province (it was already beginning) within another month—which is precisely the state of things I had the honor to predict to your Lordship in the month of June last. But the only good thing in this land of strange chances is that there is always hope, and I *do* indulge a hope that for Mendizabal is reserved the glory of, singlehanded, saving his country.

We have again a chance, if it could be availed of, to make this country English. The people all incline us-wards and Mendizabal would *incorporate* Spain with England if he could. A declaration of war against Don Carlos and a few troops—a few Marines—but a British standard—landed in Biscay to avenge the murders of our sailors and the insults which have been offered to our flag, might still do wonders in the cause of humanity, for the rights of the Queen whom we are bound to support, and for English policy, which whether with reference to France, or to Russia and the East, or to having our own hands free for all unnecessary difficulty, should ever be to make Spain powerful and friendly. If we help her in the first we ensure the second. Vamos es preciso animarse,[1] for on my conscience I believe that it would be a right good speculation and that if we could eject Don Carlos we should within six months establish such commercial relations as would speedily exalt you (Lord Palmerston) above your fellows. The one might be made conditional upon the other—indeed there are a dozen ways from which we might derive advantage from the present state of Spain—but I don't feel myself at liberty to take any step, for before you take from the needy what they may have to give they have a right to know what you intend to offer, and I am in total ignorance of whether His Majesty's Government are generously disposed or whether they still consider that le jeu ne vaudra jamais la chandelle.

Received 20 October.

GC/CL/211; Clar. Dep. C.452/1 (128-131)

[1] 'We must bestir ourselves.'

150 Villiers to Palmerston, 15 October 1835

Madrid. Private. By the last courier we were rather up in the world, by this one we are rather down again—still however I believe we shall right after all. The state of this country is more like that of an old ship in a tempest than any thing else, but with every aggravation of difficulties, any of which would be sufficient to prevent her arriving safely at port. In the first place the vessel is so rotten and leaky that she is already sunk as low as is compatible with floating at all, and all her tackle has got into worse confusion than before during the great length of time that the gale has been freshening, so that it is now quite unfit for the hurricane which blows at this moment. There is an enemy too along side of her, who though of smaller calibre is active, well manned, and keeps up a brisk fire on her while she is unable to defend herself or bring half her guns to bear, because there is a mutiny among the crew. The man at the helm though a very able seaman is a little bothered by all he has to contend with, and having somewhat swerved from his course has met with shoals and rocks which he suspected nothing about, but he swears he knows whereabouts the land lays, and that he shall make it as soon as ever the storm subsides a little. I believe him, though I don't think the people at Lloyds would have anything to do with a vessel three parts foundered as this is.

However, to come ashore—Andalusia is the great difficulty and danger at present, but I have hopes it will be got over—if so you will not be sorry to hear that it is in great measure owing to His Majesty's mission at Madrid. I have done a thing which is perhaps a little out of the regular old diplomatic beat, but as it compromises nobody, and is likely to be attended with success I am sure you will not disapprove. The circumstances are these. About a year ago Southern and I had an opportunity of shewing kindness to and assisting a certain Don José Villalta, who was treated by Martinez and Toreno with a cruelty worthy of the Grand Duke Constantine. He is a very able man of great literary acquirements, and well known in England and Switzerland—he was profoundly grateful for what we did for him in his distress. We heard by accident that this man was the life, soul and mind of the junta at Cadiz—that it was he who was organizing the whole movement in Andalusia, and who would probably end by putting the Queen's throne in extreme jeopardy. I told this to Mendizabal offering that Southern, who had been in occasional correspondence with Villalta, should write to him upon the folly and mischief of his conduct. Mendizabal upon learning all the circumstances implored me to let Southern go to Cadiz himself, as he was convinced that more would be done by him in an hour than by a volume of correspondence. I at first refused, not chusing to have any relations, however indirect, with persons in revolt against the Government, and because, though Mendizabal might pursue whatever policy he thought best, nothing should induce me to countenance any compromise of principles, or to assist him in going further than he had already done. He solemnly assured me that come what might, he would make no compromise of principles, or go further than he had done, or yield to any demands from the juntas which still remained undissolved. After some further discussion I consented and I cannot give a better proof of my sense of the expediency and probable usefulness of the step than the voluntarily depriving myself of Southern's services at such a moment as this. It was almost like sending my right arm to Cadiz—however I gave him a bag of nominal dispatches to you, and he went as an attaché of the mission who was going to England by sea—his departure accordingly occasioned no sensation here, and at Cadiz he is supposed to be waiting for the Mediterranean steam boat. Things turned out as we expected, and if he had not been robbed on the road, one of his mules killed and he left to walk a stage on foot, he would have arrived at Cadiz in time to prevent the reestablishment of the junta.

I send you herewith the copy of a letter which I have received from him. It is, like the story I have now been telling you, rather long, and you may probably not have time or inclination to read it, but it serves to shew the real state of the country and is, I hope you will consider, a justification of Southern's mission. Mendizabal has not the least difficulty in consenting to the measures suggested by Southern and an approving courier is this day sent to Cadiz with the necessary orders to the authorities, as if the ideas had originated with the Government at Madrid.

The chief alarm under which Mendizabal at present labors is the semi-hostile disposition of France which is not confined to acts of assistance to the Carlists upon the frontier but to very decided indications of ultimately intending to recognize Don Carlos. I am sorry to say that of this there are not only proofs in Frias's dispatches, if[1] he reports at all correctly his conversations with De Broglie, but there are other signs which I do not venture to write to you upon the present occasion, which leave me no doubt that Louis Philippe is contemplating such a measure upon the ground that this country is plunged into irremediable anarchy, and that the course which the Queen's Government is pursuing will only make confusion worse confounded.

He is mistaken in this view as he has been upon the whole Spanish question. The country it is true is in confusion enough, but Mendizabal's present policy is the only way of getting out of the scrape, and of making the Government strong—or rather of making *any Government at all*—for the alternative is not Don Carlos or Isabella—it is Isabella or general, permanent civil war. Don Carlos *cannot* reign in peace here, or can he occupy the throne 6 weeks unless placed and maintained there by a French army. Now, though the French nation is most desirous of internal tranquillity and therefore submits to despotic laws, I don't apprehend that the feelings (principles I suppose there is not much question of) engendered by the revolution of July are so entirely laid aside as to render a crusade like that of 1823 very palateable —neither should we, I guess, view with any peculiar favor French intervention, which we could not stomach when in behalf of the Queen and desired by the Government, given to support Don Carlos against the wishes of every class of society which is worth consideration, and in the face of a treaty to which we are parties.

The present state of things then here is tending to interrupt our alliance with France, and every effort should be made to put a stop to it—nothing is so important as vigilance upon the frontiers, and a bonâ fide impediment to Carlist proceedings. A new experiment is being made in Spain at this moment, and all that is asked is a fair trial. If at the end of 3 or 4 months nothing has been achieved except an increase of confusion, why France must then adopt the line which she may think necessary for her own safety, but I feel now as convinced that the proper course for Louis Philippe to take at this crisis of Spanish affairs, with reference to his geographical position as well as to the policy which he is pursuing at home, is to support the Queen by every means in his power, as I was 4 months ago that a six weeks stationing of French troops on this side of the Pyrenees would have saved *all* the difficulties and dangers which now beset the Spanish throne and threaten to disturb the harmony which exists between other nations.[2]

Enclosure: Copy (extract), Henry Southern (Cadiz) to Villiers, 9 October 1835, on the Cadiz junta and the preparations by Villalta for its dissolution. At the end of the extract, a summary of the remainder of the letter in Villiers's hand.[3]

Received 30 October.

GC/CL/212; Clar. Dep. C.452/1 (132-139)

[1] 'if' underlined twice, probably by P.

[2] V was aware that the French Government regarded him as closely associated with the radical party at Madrid, and as committed to increasing British influence in Spain at the expense of French. V wrote to Granville on 15 October, asking him to set Louis Philippe right on both these points. (PRO 30/29/421.)

[3] For a copy of Southern's official report to V on his mission to Cadiz, dated 14 Nov. 1835, see GC/CL/222 (not printed). It was forwarded to P in V's despatch no. 180.

151 Villiers to Palmerston, 17 October 1835

Madrid. Private. Mendizabal, who cannot be said to keep late hours or early hours for he keeps none at all, has just sent me word that he has an opportunity of sending to England if I let him have my letter before 8 o'clock P.M.[1] I therefore write you one line to say that things are improving. A great defection of troops from the Central Junta has taken place—they are gone to help the people of Seville against the column of troops sent by the Central Junta under [? Osorio] to reestablish the dissolved junta of that place. These troops are afterwards going to Cordoba which they intend to reduce to order, and will then probably *volunteer* for the army in the North—after having been a month in mutiny against the Government. What a strange, almost incomprehensible people. I still adhere to my opinion that we shall pull through—but now is the time if possible to help us. If you could bring France to take a right view of the Spanish question and French interests, for they are identical at this moment, and then make a combined auxiliary demonstration—declaration—any thing—you would have ground to rejoice at doing so per saecula saeculorum— depend upon it. I shall now go to bed again.

PS. Mendizabal is flogging up public spirit and people are untying their purse strings sorely against their will but Mendizabal in his time has been so much dunned himself that he knows how to dun others.

GC/CL/213

[1] 'A' written in pencil above 'P', possibly by P.

152 Villiers to Palmerston, 21 October 1835

Madrid. Private. A few hasty lines which I wrote you on the 17th will have informed you of our improving condition. I am now able to confirm it and to add that in all things I don't see how we could be doing better. The revolutionary spirit is subsiding, and people are rapidly reentering the pale of such legality as ever exists in Spain, where the law appears to be only a set of regulations which need not be observed.

Southern in a quiet and unsuspected way has been doing excellent service at Cadiz. Mr. Villalta under his influence has been a powerful instrument of good—they together have stopped the supplies and the moral support which the Central Junta depended upon from Cadiz—they have prevented the public money from being disposed of, and have got the junta to pass the measures mentioned in my dispatch of today,[1] which if anyone had proposed but a week before he would have surely died. The junta is by this time dissolved, and Southern has not only brought about that fusion of parties which it was only in the power of an uncompromised and disinterested party to effect, but before he comes away he expects to make Cadiz the stronghold of Mendizabal in the South—his mission will therefore I hope be justified in your eyes.

Mendizabal is every day giving proofs that he is equal to the gigantic task he has undertaken, and as he is gaining strength every day, all parties are hastening à l'appui du plus fort, except the grandees (backed and helped by Toreno I fear) who are laboring in the only vocation they are fit for—petty intrigues—and endeavouring to prove to the Queen that the road taken by Mendizabal leads only to perdition, but she is behaving beautifully and he has her entire confidence. There is in that Señora, as I have always thought if she were but courageously and faithfully advised, the elements for making one of the greatest Sovereigns of modern times. She is capable of taking large views. She is ambitious of glory, and has at heart the prosperity of Spain. She is moreover acute, docile, and absolutely without fear—but is of course ignorant of the art of governing or how to turn her position to the account which she herself desires. She has always done whatever she has been advised to do, but her advisers have always been incompetent or false. Mendizabal was exactly the man she wanted to rescue her from her fallen state which she felt she did not deserve to be in, but from which she could not extricate herself, and she accordingly looks upon him as an angel from heaven. I have mentioned this because I know it is industriously put about—and there are proofs here of its having been told Louis Philippe—that she disapproves but has been forced to adopt the measures of her present Minister. There was an exhibition of popular feeling in her favor at the review two days ago very different from that which her presence would have called forth at any time during the last twelvemonth.

Cordoba is not yet sufficiently reinforced to take the offensive, but he has been employing himself in some operations which will straiten the enemy in the winter campaign, and he appears to have been very successful in promoting dissension in the Carlist camp. He has established a system of flags of truce upon every occasion, however trifling, and he has by that means communication with all the principal officers of Don Carlos's army. They are, nearly without exception, disgusted with his service, and nothing but a point of honor retains them in it—they admit that for some time past the juntas have been their only hope of ultimately succeeding. I believe the power of Don Carlos to have reached its maximum in Navarre—he can raise no more men there and the spirit of the country cannot be more favorable to him than it is. It is clear also that he cannot extend the field of his operations, for the Navarrese *will not* leave their own country or are they fit for any kind of warfare but their own. This is not the case however in Catalonia—*there* is a new field and new elements for insurrection of even a more formidable character than in Navarre. The prodigious increase of Carlists therefore during the reign of the *Patriots* was very alarming, and the victory which has lately been gained, near Figueras, is of the greatest importance, for it has checked the faction until reinforcements can arrive and has marvellously raised the spirits of the Catalans.

The English Legion is coming to Vitoria and Burgos which will be better winter quarters and bring them nearer to their work. The praise of their improvement, their good discipline and fine tenu is universal, and Evans and Cordoba are upon the best possible terms. In short the tide has turned in the Queen's favor, and now if ever is the moment for a friendly demonstration on the part of England—it would of course be better were it of England and France united. Any *published* measure of hostility by us against Don Carlos—or an order by the French Government to the authorities in the South respecting greater vigilance upon the frontiers would shorten the war by some months, and what is of almost equal consequence make Mendizabal strong in the Cortes. The Spaniards know so well that they can finish nothing by themselves, and are so accustomed to foreign influence, that the wishes and intentions of other countries, if they are but clearly indicated, have an extraordinary weight. I assure you that if you had an occasion to make a speech at a public dinner and pronounced yourself strongly in favor of the course now pursued by Mendizabal, etc., etc., it would be worth a Jew's eye to him.

Shortly after Mendizabal came into office he wanted to recall Frias, but I recommended him not at that moment, because as his object then was to conciliate Exaltado opinions, he would not have ventured to appoint any known moderate man, and any known revolutionist would have been distasteful to his French Majesty. The new ambassador therefore from the beginning would have been in an unfavorable position and the explanations he might have to give respecting the policy of his Government, coming through a suspected medium, would do Mendizabal more harm than good. I thought it better therefore to wait till the clouds which hung over the futurity of Spain had a little cleared away, and he might then with a better chance of success send a representative of the new order of things to Paris. He quite agreed in this—but Frias has since behaved in a manner which renders his continuance at Paris not only inexpedient but impossible,[2] and Mendizabal proposed to Alava to go there, but he positively declined it, saying that he would prefer being chargé d'affaires at London to ambassador at Paris—in which I think he is perfectly right, but at the same time he appears to me the fittest representative Spain could have in France at this particular moment, for the King knows him to be an honest man, who never meddles with intrigues, and who hates revolutions and the heroes of them as much as he does. He would therefore be inclined to believe what Alava told him of the real state of Spain, and of the necessity, upon conservative principles, under which his Government laid of pursuing its present policy.

Mendizabal and Alava having agreed to abide by any suggestion of mine upon the matter, I proposed that Alava should return to London but when at Paris that Frias should be recalled and that he should receive instructions to take charge of the embassy until the appointment of a new ambassador, receiving his credentials as ambassador extraordinary, and that after two or three months, when things went smoothly here, his successor might arrive and he return to his mission in London. Both of them were perfectly satisfied with this arrangement and so it stands at present. Mendizabal told me to communicate it to you and Lord Granville—but in confidence, as it is not yet finally arranged or has it received the Queen's sanction.

PS. Owing to the disturbed state of Catalonia several mails from England had become due and I did not receive till yesterday your dispatch No. 27. I need not add with what sincere satisfaction.

October 22d. Mendizabal yesterday put off sending his courier till this morning and he has just told me that unofficial news has arrived of the dissolution of the Central Junta and that nearly all the troops are now at the disposal of the Government.

I have this moment received a letter from Cordoba dated the 19th instant—he has had an action with the Carlists at Cirauqui and beaten them—he says that his late operations have succeeded beyond his best hopes, and that the half of Navarre is now his and all his strong places safe—he adds los recursos de subsistencias crecen mucho para nosotros y disminuyen para los enemigos. Esto no puede ir mejor.[3]

Mendizabal has begged me *earnestly to request* you not to refuse the 2 or 3 things he may now and hereafter have occasion to ask of you through Jabat. He says he knows perfectly your good will and the many difficulties you labor under for which reason he will never make you a request which is not of absolute necessity for him, but he says he is every hour more certain of his ultimate triumph. I have no more time.

Received 2 November.

GC/CL/214; Clar. Dep. C.452/1 (140-147)

[1] Measures which were intended to result in the dissolution of the junta. (V to P, 21 Oct. 1835, no. 166, FO 72/444.)

[2] It was believed at Madrid that Frías was a partisan of Toreno, and that he had misrepresented the acts of Mendizábal to the French Government and suggested that the Queen Mother was the 'prisoner' of Mendizábal and his policies. (V to Granville, 21 Oct. 1835, PRO 30/29/421.)

[3] 'Our supplies of provisions increase greatly while those of the enemy diminish. This could not go better.'

153 Palmerston to Villiers, 23 October 1835

Foreign Office. I am delighted at the turn which affairs have taken in Spain. I had always great hopes in Mendizabal, but the danger was that matters should have gone too far before his arrival—fortunately this has not been the case and I look upon Spain as saved.

I was sure that you and he would go on well together; he has a frankness and energy of character that was sure to suit you, and I was certain that he would look upon it as a Godsend finding such an English minister as yourself to help him at Madrid. Had he found Addington there, what would he have done—Addington who used to fall down on his knees and worship 'the noble minded Alcadia'? I hope Mendizabal will not be led too far and induced to make greater organic changes than may be really expedient and absolutely required.

He should remember that steps of that kind *never* can be retraced; and that mischief thus done is therefore irreparable. Mistakes in ordinances, laws of administration, or arrangements of departmental matters are easily set right; you may undo one year what you have ill done the year before, but you can never persuade those to whom you have given constitutional power to surrender it again; and the more they have abused it, the less willing they will be to give it up.

I say this with reference to the constitution of the Cortes which he ought to alter as little as possible till he has put other matters to rights and then he will not only be a better judge of what may be needful, but he will have created better elements to work with.

I am quite ready and glad to do justice to Cordova; he has behaved nobly in his command; has shewn great talent for managing men and things; and has rendered important services to his country. It is evident that had any of his predecessors been in command at particular moments instead of him, affairs would have gone very differently.

I am much obliged to you for your frequent and interesting private letters, pray continue to write. I am so hunted from morning till night by people I am obliged to see, and have such masses of papers daily to read through that my means of writing are very limited; you must not be surprized therefore, if tu pulsas, ego vapulo tantum.

I must say there is some force in the explanation given by the French Government as to the passage of supplies over the Pyrenees to the Carlists. They first deny the fact to the extent alleged. They say that Carlos has manufactories of arms and powder of his own: that muskets and horses to a considerable quantity have been taken by the Carlists from the Queen's troops, and we know that upon one occasion near 2,000 men surrendered to the Carlists; that the numerous seizures made on the frontier prove that vigilence is exerted by their guards, and lastly they say what is quite true, that in such a district, and with such an extent of mountain frontier it is out of human power to prevent things from passing clandestinely and, as Harispe says, if there were ranged on the frontier 20,000 men holding hand by hand the smugglers would contrive to make way through them. A good deal of irritation has grown up on this matter between the two Governments, try to soften it. Broglie is honest about the matter; Thiers very likely plays the rogue; what may be the case in higher quarters I cannot pretend to say, though I disbelieve the story brought by Cordova's aide de camp and founded on a report of a deserter from the Carlists.

I thought I had done good service to Evans and his Legion by getting him two Ordnance officers, Reid of Engineers and Colquhoun of Artillery, and as there is no half pay list of those Corps to which officers can exchange from full pay, and these two were on full pay, I got the Ordnance to place them on temporary half pay to enable them to serve. All seemed smooth, and Reid went, and Colquhoun was going when I was pressed by Javat and Colquhoun to try to get the King to allow some non-commissioned officers to be discharged in order to serve also. This the King refused, he having since the Order in Council been much worked upon by Tory advisers, and having inwardly repented of having signed the said order.

The discussion about the non-commissioned officers led to an enquiry about Reid and Colquhoun, and it turned out that the arrangement having been made while Vivian, the Master General, was out of town, there was a bother and a confusion about it, and the King's pleasure had never been taken. The King accordingly availed himself of this irregularity to refuse his sanction to the arrangement and he has required Vivian to tell the two officers that if they remain in the Spanish service, they will not be put back into their places on full pay, in their Corps as had been promised them, but that they must continue for ever on half pay. But if they chuse now to return to their Corps they may do so and resume their places. This is in fact recalling them from the Spanish service, at least in the case of Reid who is gone; Colquhoun being still here of course must remain here and cannot go. To him it is a prohibition and not a recall.

I have written and represented to the King in the strongest manner the impolicy of this order of his; and Vivian has done the same, but all to no purpose—I should think (as I have told the King) that Reid would determine to remain in spite of the communication and will take his chance of reinstatement hereafter. By reinstatement I mean coming back into his place, and not being put back at the bottom of the list of rank.

Pray explain all this as well as you can to Mendizabal and tell him not to look upon the communication which may be made to Reid as coming from the Government or as indicating any change of policy or feeling on the part of the Government, but as being a single piece of personal caprice and obstinacy on the part of the King, in the detail of a branch of the military service which he has always kept very much under his own immediate controul.

We were very unlucky about the slave treaty; however slow the messenger was he did contrive to arrive here the night before the prorogation, but slave trade despatches by an internal arrangement of the office go to a separate department and not at once to the Under Secretary. The clerk who had charge of that separate department in the absence of his principal is a muddle headed young gentleman, and he had not wit enough to see that it might be useful for me to have early notice of the arrival of a ratification of a treaty, accordingly instead of knowing the fact at nine in the morning as I ought to have done I did not learn it till one, and before I could get to Melbourne and tell him of it, the King was in his state coach with his speech in his hand and Melbourne waiting to receive him with the Sword of State, too big to mend a pen with, and so it was impossible to alter the paragraph, and to announce the actual arrival of the ratification.

I hope Mendizabal will soon give us a lift about commerce.

One of the people of the Chronicle came to me yesterday to ask me if I thought that a subscription in favour of the Spanish Government would take. I said I thought not; that subscriptions had generally been in aid of patriots fighting for liberty *against* a Government, or for people who like the Portuguese during the French invasion or after the earthquake had suffered by some great calamity out of all ordinary course of events. But to ask John Bull to subscribe in aid of the regular Government of a great country like Spain, in command of the resources of that country, and able to raise a loan in the money markets of Europe, if those resources should be insufficient, seemed to me a very hopeless undertaking.

Copy.   GC/CL/1246

154   Villiers to Palmerston, 26 October 1835

Madrid. Private. I have very little to add to what you will find in my dispatches of today. The decree of general armament[1] is a great measure, and will be a successful one, for Mendizabal is realizing every where his idea of turning against the Carlists the political excitement which he found raging his predecessor's Government.

The Carlists are panic-stricken. The juntas are now all dissolved, except in one or two places where their existence is ample punishment for the people of sense and property who continue to tolerate them, but their evil effects do not extend beyond their own narrow rayon. The troops have all returned to obedience poco a poco.

In any *regular* country to be sure the effect would be strange of hearing that after 6 weeks open rebellion Colonel or Captain such a one had addressed the Queen in the most extravagant style of laudation of his own patriotism, and the service he had done the legitimate cause (*by his mutiny*) and that he was *now* ready with his regiment or his company as it may be, to march against the Carlists at such and such a place as it may suit his fancy to designate—but chaque pays chaque mode. These things don't strike people here as extraordinary—they get what they want and are careless about the means—the same system pervades every rank and class in society, and the Government in this has always been in harmony with the people. In other countries a Government generally considers itself bound by its own acts, obliged to follow out the principles or system it lays down, and abide by the consequences. That's not the way here though, and it accounts for the inconsistencies and vagaries which out of Spain appear so inexplicable. Decrees right in the teeth of each other given by the same men create little surprise—consistency or good faith or wisdom would create much *more*—but then there is a *hedge*, for nobody obeys, and so the whole machine goes rattling and scrambling on. Mendizabal however will I really believe begin a new aera—he of course won't make bad men good, or fools wise, but I think he will force them to act according to what he knows to be for their interest.

Southern writes me word that the real elements of revolution in the South are contemptible, and that *one* regiment of incorruptible soldiers would secure tranquillity at Cadiz per saecula saeculorum.

I have nothing from England by the post later than the 2nd.

PS. William Hervey writes me word he is to return here—personally speaking I shall be very glad of it, but he so ardently hoped never to see Spain again that I am sorry for his disappointment. He is clever —and an excellent man of business. As a chef de chancellerie I should doubt his having an equal in the whole profession. I never met with such preciseness and love of order. . . .

Received 5 November.

GC/CL/215; Clar. Dep. C.452/1 (148-151)

[1] Calling to arms all Spaniards from 18 to 40 years of age, 100,000 of whom were immediately to be brought into active service. This would make four

million liable for military service; exemption could be purchased and Mendizábal expected the exemption payments to bring in two million sterling of revenue. (V to P, 26 Oct. 1835, no. 170, FO 72/444.)

155 Villiers to Palmerston, 31 October 1835

Madrid. Private. As I wrote to you only a few days ago and that things are now marching with a certain kind of regularity, I have but little to say by this courier—indeed I don't know why Mendizabal sends one unless it is to keep public attention abroad in a proper direction.

The Government are greatly pleased with Evans's movement from Bilbao in support of Cordoba. I am not sure that the latter will be as well satisfied, as his greatest desire is to get the Carlists to wait for him which he looks upon as synonymous with licking them. However the best spirit exists between him and Evans, and I have no doubt they will do good things together as soon as the Englishers are less raw—they have made great progress in their learning, but are still I fear very far from being what Evans wants.

I have had a letter from Ingestre representing to me his grief at the Admiralty having sent the Tribune upon the east coast of Spain whose captain is senior to him and therefore supersedes him in the duties of the station. When Ingestre first came upon the coast I thought it possible his Tory notions might interfere with his duty, and I accordingly wrote him a letter of *advice* (far be it from me to give *instructions* to any naval gentleman) upon the subject, which he took exceedingly well, and I must do him the justice to say that the interest which he has taken in the Queen's cause, and the tact and decision with which he has acted up to his instructions, have drawn forth the constant approbation and thanks (officially conveyed to the Spanish Government) of all the authorities upon the coast. If the Admiralty did not select the Tribune for the station in order to supersede Ingestre, and if it is indifferent to them by what ship our naval force there is increased, I think it is a pity not to leave him there in command after having established good relations with the Spanish authorities and the French fleet. Should you opine the same perhaps you will move My Lords to leave him.

According to your desire I have done my best to procure the exchange of the 27 Carlist officers still confined at Coruña. I have spoken to Mendizabal and written to Cordoba upon the subject, and

I hope to get it done—fear of the impression it will produce upon the public is now the only obstacle.

Talking of impressions you may perhaps like to know the kind of one you produce upon a foreign minister—Calderon de la Barca writes to a friend of his here that 'J'ai eu l'avantage d'etre presenté à Lord Palmerston dont je suis enchanté, car à une noble figure et à des manières tres distinguées il joint une attrayante affabilité. Je suis redevable à M. Villiers du plaisir que m'a procuré la connoissance de ce Seigneur'; and I accordingly am much obliged to you for the kind reception you gave him.

Southern discovered at Cadiz that another slave ship was fitting out and having made a proper representation to the owner upon the subject he has been enabled to stop it.

The calculation I sent you in my last dispatch of the harvest to be expected by the Treasury from those who would want to shirk the general enlistment will not prove correct. The Government found the tax would be too heavy if it was made general, and it is therefore confined to those who may be drawn for the service. This however is expected to suffice for the whole arming and equipment of the 100,000 men about to be raised.

The disturbed state of Catalonia prevents the arrival of the post as the French Post Office, notwithstanding many remonstrances, persists in sending letters to this country via Perpiñan instead of Oleron. The 6th is the latest date from England, and with the exception of the dispatch which I acknowledged by the last courier I have had nothing either public or private from you for nearly three months.

PS. Since writing the above I have seen Mendizabal who says you would do him a great service by communicating to Rothschild that the official reports you receive from Spain are very favorable, and that you are of opinion from them, that the Queen's cause will ultimately triumph and Mendizabal come out of the struggle not only with honor but with *credit* to the country. The fact is, as you may readily believe, that there is no money here and great need of it. Two months of stopped contributions from the provinces coming upon the exhausted loan and after the dilapidating Government of Toreno paralyse the great measures Mendizabal is taking in order to put down the civil war. The futurity of the country depends upon his prompt success in that; for then he will have means more than ample for meeting his obligations and carrying on the service of the State. In administrative reforms and reductions alone he will be able to save an amount nearly equal to half the present revenue of Spain, and he will double it by the measures which he projects for developing the national resources. He is determined to make no more loans, but he would be overjoyed if Rothschild would lend him $\frac{1}{2}$ a million—that, with the taxes returning to the treasury, would enable him to finish the war and to render the last loan quite secure. It would in short be a grand vivifier of all things here if this *rasgo de generosidad*[1] could be extracted from the Leviathan. I told Mendizabal that he knew well enough no one was more hearty in the cause of the Queen than you but that you could scarcely send for Rothschild and tell him this and I didn't believe you often saw him. He said that Melbourne constantly saw Rothschild and would perhaps, if you expressed your wish to that effect, undertake to *insense* him.

Received 10 November.

GC/CL/216; Clar. Dep. C.452/1 (152-156)

[1] 'stroke of generosity'.

156 Villiers to Palmerston, 2 November 1835

Madrid. Private. I avail myself of a traveller going to Paris to send you a decree which was published yesterday,[1] and upon which I have thought it worth while to say a few words in a despatch—it appears much ado about nothing, but Spanish nothings sometimes give a great deal to do, particularly if they get magnified and misrepresented out of Spain. Tories and Holy Allies know very little about the real state of things in this country, but the name of Riego will I am sure not be music in their ears, and they will consider that an act of grace to his name and fame emanating from Mendizabal stamps his Government as revolutionary—but I think you will agree with me that, vû the motion which would have been made in the Cortes,[2] this measure is well-timed and is unobjectionable in its object and its tone.

It must be remembered that the ostensible ground upon which Riego was executed was his having voted the civil death of Ferdinand. Galiano proposed and Arguelles seconded it. Alava and many others supported it. All these men were fully amnestied by the Queen, and it is therefore but an act of justice to place the name and family of

Riego—the only Deputy who was put to death—where they would have stood had he now been alive.

Mendizabal regrets extremely your objection to give Mr. Barreros, the Spanish consul at Gibraltar, an exequatur. He understands that it is on account of his being a military man. . . .

Alava will I believe set out for Paris—nominally for England—at the end of this week.

No fresh news from the army since I last wrote.

PS. Since writing the above the messenger Webster has arrived. I have only time to acknowledge him and to thank you for your thrice welcome letter. Mendizabal has just been here and I certainly never saw more unmixed delight than upon his reading your letter to him. This is a most revivifying courier and will do good in a variety of ways. Mendizabal tells me a courier from Cordoba arrived an hour ago with news to the 30th. Cordoba has taken the Queen's troops where they had not ventured to shew their noses these last 7 months. He has again beaten all the enemy he could get near—the rest, though collected for the purpose of giving him battle, having fled. He has established himself at Salvatierra, an important place disgracefully abandoned by Valdez, and had returned to Vitoria to meet Evans—the troops llenos de entusiasmo. *So am I today.*

Received 13 November.

GC/CL/217; Clar. Dep. C.452/1 (158-161)

[1] The decree of 1 November reversed the attainder of the late General Riego, executed for his support of the Cortes Government of 1820-23, and placed his family under the protection of the Queen Regent. (V to P, 2 Nov. 1835, no. 175, FO 72/445.)

[2] It had come to Mendizábal's knowledge that some radical Deputies intended to propose some mark of honour for Riego in the Cortes. Had it passed, the Government would have been forced to accept it with consequent loss of face. (ibid.)

157 Villiers to Palmerston, 3 November 1835

Madrid. Private. Having written to you twice within the last four days I have not much to say now, but I don't like to let Mendizabal's courier go without a line from me. I found him today as he was yesterday, rayonnant with pleasure at your letter, which seems to have delighted the Queen almost as much as himself. There never was praise more deserved or better bestowed than yours to him.

He jumped about his office like a Brobdignag schoolboy at play, with happiness at your reply to the Bishop of Leon[1] (I was very well inclined to make a pas de deux with him upon the occasion) and implored of me to let him publish it in the shape of intercepted correspondence or any other shape I liked, as it would be worth a Jew's eye to the cause. I would almost have given one of my own to have ventured. Should you see any objection? If not pray let me know by the next courier.

There never was a more useful arrangement than the one you have just made in re a regular messenger once a fortnight—at the moment I received the announcement of it from Strangways four mails were due here which, as well as the importance of the events which are passing here, will amply justify the additional expense. I have to thank you likewise for letting me know what has been done, or rather not done, at Toeplitz. It has served to correct a great deal of error here.

Alava will set out on the 9th and I really hope he will accomplish that which made me so desirous of his taking temporary charge of the embassy at Paris—doing away with that feeling of soreness which has grown up between the French and Spanish Governments. He fully enters into the necessity of this and feels that, however well we may wish to the Queen's cause, we cannot and ought not to brouiller ourselves with France upon the matter. I read him your correspondence with Lord Granville upon Mendizabal's complaints and De Broglie's replies—he admits that there must have been great exaggeration, and even if there had not that the surly remonstrances were impolitic. He promises however that as soon as he gets to Paris there shall not be another angry word upon the matter, let his instructions be what they may.

I have *compuesto* the affair of Reid and Colquhoun with Mendizabal who only sees in it a new proof of your friendly zeal in the cause. I have likewise explained it upon technical grounds to Evans, to prevent any misapprehension in that part of the world, and lest other officers should take fright at the Royal displeasure.

I am very glad to know the King's feelings about having signed the Order in Council, because I shall never miss an opportunity of lauding the Legion in my public dispatches. I have every expectation of often being able to do so, and that the conduct of that corps will grievously disappoint the hopes of the Tories and those who are advised by them. My only fear is from the jealousy of the Spanish army, and as they are now about to unite I have recommended to Cordoba a proclamation recalling the ancient glories of English and Spanish arms during the Peninsular War. Cordoba has not a particle of petty feelings and he will, I have no doubt, prevent them in others as he does whatever he pleases with the army. The enthusiasm for him is so great that the soldiers belonging to a regiment of Guards which left Madrid this morning to join the army, who were in the hospital, petitioned to be allowed to go likewise, as they should get well sooner with such a physician as Cordoba and in the field of battle.

Received 13 November.   GC/CL/218; Clar. Dep. C.452/1 (162-165)

¹ Not traced.

158   Palmerston to Villiers, 4 November 1835

Copy. Stanhope Street. I am just setting off for Tiverton to see my constituents, and have only time to write two lines; but I am glad to tell you that the King has at last consented to allow Major Reid to remain with Evans, and to let Captain Colquhoun go out to join him. So this is well. The good accounts you continue to send us are really delightful, but pray persuade Mendizabal not to overwork himself, for if he breaks down there is an end of the whole thing.

Jabat has asked for four cruisers on the coast of Catalonia. I have settled with Minto to send three in addition to those already there, and I have given you a list of those on the southern and eastern coast. But Mendizabal must remember that we are shy of neutrals, and he ought to send out a few cockboats with the Spanish flag on board to be the actual visitors and detainers. If he wants ships, let him order thither some of those Guarda Costas who now amuse themselves by plundering our commerce in the neighbourhood of Gibraltar.

I am glad to find that the French Government are coming back to the Alliance.¹ Austria is said to be sending money to Carlos, and to be still keener in his favour than Nicholas is. I can believe it, because Metternich dreads the effect on Italy of the example of rational government in Spain, whereas Nicholas cannot apprehend that what passes in this Peninsula can have any sensible influence on his Offs and Vitches.

PS. We highly approve of you having sent Southern to Cadiz, and are very much pleased with the ability and judgment with which he executed your commission.

GC/CL/1247

[1] The French Government had undertaken to conduct an enquiry into Spanish allegations that supplies were reaching the Carlists across the French frontier: if these allegations proved to be true, stricter measures of control to prevent the trade would be enforced.

159   Villiers to Palmerston, 7 November 1835

Madrid. Private. I write this morning not because I have much to say, but because I am going to send a courier to Oleron to meet the one from London under your new and most useful arrangement.[1]

Cordoba has been very angry and wrong about Evans, which I much regret just before they were about to meet for the first time. It is partly owing to disappointment at not fighting the factions, and partly to rheumatic fever which falling upon his nerves drives him nearly mad. He has moreover some ground of complaint against the Government, for his representations have not been properly attended to—he has not only all the responsibility and anxiety of his command, but all the details and manual labor of the Staff and Commissariat fall upon him for want of people to whom he can entrust them—he has repeatedly asked for assistance but has been told that the officers he wants are required here. Accordingly during the last two months he has every day passed 10 or 12 hours on horseback and 6 with a pen in his hand—the troops are without clothing too, upon very short rations, and much in arrear of pay. All this has disgusted and made him restive, and on the 4th he sent in his resignation.

As he always writes to me upon his grievances, I took Mendizabal seriously to task about it all last night, and told him that some change of system was indispensable now that the Englishers were united with the Queen's troops, for that *they* would never fight upon half rations and no pay, and that he could not make a difference in their treatment unless he wanted to lay a solid foundation for jealousy. All his *loose cash* should therefore be devoted to Cordoba, and it would be better to delay his embryo army coming into the field than to paralyze the full grown troops upon whose efficiency every thing now depends. Out of this conversation, preceded as it has been by several of the same kind, sprung the determination of sending the Minister of War[2] and Zarco del Valle in the course of a few days to the army, and £50,000 tomorrow. I have promised Mendizabal to write to Cordoba and it will all I hope be *compuesto*.

I have likewise at his request written to beg Howard will insist upon the Portuguese coming to Vitoria.[3] I don't know what the objection to it may be unless that it is too far from the frontier. There has been trouble enough to get them across it, and I suppose Palmella only likes their going with a string round their leg in order that he may pull them back at a moment's warning, but if their object is to fight the insurgents and that the insurgents won't come to them, a march to Vitoria does not seem an unreasonable request.

The only people except the Carlists who have not confidence in Mendizabal are the grandees and the extreme moderates. Both are intriguing against him as hard as their limited capacities will allow—the first because he is a man of no birth, *risen from mud*, and the second because he does not fall down before and worship the Royal Statute. Both admit that his predecessors have signally failed, and that he has accomplished almost incredible things, but so degraded are they, that I am convinced their necks feel *uncomfortable* when they are not chafed by the yoke of despotism, and they would at this moment rather put their faith in a treacherous amnesty of Don Carlos's than see their country liberated and their own chamberlainships perhaps endangered by an *adventurer*. All however I suspect are but catspaws of Toreno's whose unbounded vanity is wounded and whose Ministry receives a fresh condemnation at each success of Mendizabal's.

Martinez and Toreno are upon the worst terms, and though he (Martinez) is no more fit to be at the head of affairs than I am to teach Chinese, he is a very honest man, and I hope he will be got to support the Government. His only objection now to Mendizabal is the small favor which he thinks he will shew to that *hijo de sus entrañas*[4] the Estatuto.

As a little galanterie to Her Majesty I translated for her your letter to that pleasant Father in God the Bishop of Leon. She returned it delighted, but with regret at having 'respecté ma volonté' neither to take a copy or to have it published, which like her Minister she sorely desires.

Mendizabal trusts if you have an opportunity that you will say a word for him to Rothschild. Unless he thinks the *many pounds* of flesh which he could offer to be cut from off his person would be a temptation to the Jew I cannot conceive upon what his hope of monies is founded, but he has it, particularly since an old gentleman who he didn't know, walked into his room the other day and lent him £40,000 for a few months without interest—an instance of confidence from one Spaniard to another which is probably without a parallel.

PS. I have taken pains to soften the press and there will I hope be no more articles offensive to France and of odious comparison between the French and English Governments. The Morning Chronicle however has done infinite harm.[5] J'ai beau prêcher, few will believe that it is not the ministerial paper and, as it is the fiercest and most personal against every thing which now obtains in France, people suppose that that line must be more or less agreable to the Government.

My dispatches today are copied by Mr. Alonso because Southern is waiting at Seville for the departure of a caravan (I believe) with numerous guards in order to have a chance of passing through Andalusia alive—a very difficult matter now that there are so many loose Patriots upon the road. Otway is in bed with a fever.

Received 17 November.

GC/CL/219; Clar. Dep. C.452/1 (166-168)

[1] 'Palmerston's excellent (if it is regular) arrangement of a courier every fortnight seems to have failed at the outset. I sent a courier on the 7th to meet the English messenger at Oleron on the 10th according to the desire of the Foreign Office. He should have been back here early on the 13th but he has not appeared and my dispatches are probably waiting at Oleron to be taken on.' (V to Granville, 15 Nov. 1835, PRO 30/29/421.)

[2] The Conde de Almodóvar.

[3] V to Howard de Walden, 5 Nov. 1835, Clar. Dep. C.541.

[4] 'brainchild of his'.

[5] By a number of articles in which it claimed that the French Government was not fulfilling the engagements it had undertaken in the Additional Articles to police the frontier. These articles came from the Madrid, not the Paris, correspondent of the *Chronicle*. See for example the articles in the issues of 25 and 27 September.

160   Villiers to Earl Granville, 7 November [1835]

Encloses a letter from Mendizábal for forwarding to Palmerston.

Enclosure: Mendizábal to Villiers, 7 November 1835, private, asking Villiers to convey his 'most sincere *and* most grateful *thanks' to Palmerston.*

GC/CL/220

161 Villiers to Palmerston, 12 November 1835

Madrid. Private. No matter worth making a dispatch of has occurred since I last wrote to you except the preparatory meeting of the Cortes this morning. The aspect of the meeting was just *the least taste in life* radical, and the election as President and Secretary of the two men that Toreno did his best in August to catch and hang for their proceedings in the Plaza Major, did not belie the aspect.[1] They will both be confirmed in their temporary appointments when the Cortes meet for business on the 16th. They are both ragamuffins of the first water, yet I am glad of their nomination, for although they will probably be partial and dishonest, they will have more power than any other members of preserving order, and Isturitz has the inclination to do so. He was President during the time of the Constitution, and even Alava admits that he filled the Chair more decorously than any of those who came before or after him. The maintenance of order in the Chamber, and above all in the gallery, is a great point, for the moderate party are declaring that if there is not fair play they intend to take up their beds and walk—home to the provinces—which would be fatal to the Government, and drive the Exaltados into nonsensical excesses. Toreno and others who expect to have disagreable questions put to them, are announcing every where that there will be no liberty of speech for them and are endeavouring to get up a row. This being the case the odds are rather against one taking place.

No news of importance has arrived from the army. Cordoba is better and is gone I believe to Briviesca to meet Evans. They will probably get on well together hereafter, but the cordiality of their first meeting will be damped by the contretems of Evans not having been able to take the route to Vitoria which Cordoba had ordered him.

Mendizabal, in addition to his other brilliant and useful qualities, seems to add the tact of a *wise woman* (Gallicè) and he in consequence pitched upon the earliest day for the opening of the Cortes with singular nicety. Had it been fixed one week—I might say three days—earlier, a royal commission must have been charged with that which I trust the Queen Regent will now be able to do in person.

Alava was to have set out for Paris yesterday, but he has had a kind of nervous fever which still keeps him in bed and renders his departure very uncertain. I am sorry for it because I believe that a credible witness like Alava might do the royal mind much good, and that some improvement in that quarter with respect to Spanish affairs is wanting I have no manner of doubt.

I was talking with Rayneval yesterday about the *Junta* at Toeplitz, and he suggested as one of the possible causes of its having been formed that the Treaty of Chaumont[2] which was made for twenty years expired this year, and as that Treaty was not only against the aggression of France but against revolutionary movements likewise, the three Powers might perhaps have thought it well to come to some understanding upon the matter—if so, I daresay England came in for a share of their favors.

Southern is returned and in a whole skin, having effected all that he went to do and a great deal more—he has left Cadiz in perfectly good trim and the authorities in the way they should go. Mendizabal is, as he ought to be, very much obliged to him. Southern's journey is a proof, if others were wanting, of the miracles which a handful of honest and able men might work in this country.

PS. I reopen my letter to say that an express from Evans has just arrived with dispatches dated Briviesca the 9th instant. He and Cordoba have met and are upon the most cordial terms—the latter admitting that Evans was right in disobeying his orders. Barring that the Legion has spent its last farthing and is rather hungry, every thing looks well. The express is the Commissary General who comes as *Procurador* for 5,000 empty British maws and as you may suppose with very pressing instructions.

GC/CL/221; Clar. Dep. C.452/1 (170-175)

[1] Istúriz as President, Caballero as Secretary.

[2] The Treaty of Chaumont was signed by Great Britain, Austria, Prussia and Russia in March 1814. 'It had been designed, as its phraseology shews, to guarantee the settlement not only against France but against any disturber of the peace.' (Sir C. K. Webster, *The Foreign Policy of Castlereagh, 1812-1815*, 1931, 229.)

162 Palmerston to Villiers, 13 November 1835

Foreign Office. I have only time to write a few lines to say that I have no objection to my letter to the Bishop being *indiscreetly* published, and that Minto says that Ingestre is junior to all the other officers commanding ships in the Mediterranean, and could not have been left in command, unless he had been left alone. To send additional ships was to send senior officers.

Copy.   GC/CL/1248

163 Palmerston to Villiers, 15 November 1835

Copy. Stanhope Street. *The Colonial Office objects to the continuance of the practice whereby military men have been appointed Spanish consuls at Gibraltar.*

GC/CL/1249

164 Villiers to Palmerston, 16 November 1835

Madrid. Private. I yesterday received your letter of the 5th which put both Mendizabal and me in good spirits—we were rather in want of it for a *porcion de cosas* not very agreable had occurred within the preceding 4 and 20 hours. In the first place came Wylde with a melancholy picture of the no pay and summer trowser state of the army—then a courier from Lisbon with the news of the non entrance of the Portuguese troops and the breaking up of the Government[1]—and lastly the intrigues of the grandees and others which have not been without their effect upon the Queen Regent's mind.

Wylde's mission will be of great utility—almost as much as if Cordoba himself had come—for he is perfectly acquainted with every officer, and all the necessities of the army—the latter could be relieved by money but not a shilling has Mendizabal got, and Wylde says that the consequences of leaving the troops much longer in their present condition may be very dangerous. Evans is likewise pennyless, but Cordoba knowing the importance of not discouraging the English raised a loan of 50,000 dollars for him upon his own personal security at Logroño. Wylde and I are to have a meeting with Mendizabal tomorrow in order to consult upon what means can be taken to remedy this state of things. It is one of the most pressing importance—every

327

thing depends upon the war—two or three successes would enable Mendizabal to laugh at intrigues foreign and domestic, and to govern with as much or as little liberalism as he may think proper—whereas if nothing is done in the course of the next two months this easily disheartened people will be turning their wrath against him and swearing he has disappointed them.

I have had letters from Cordoba and Evans since they met, speaking of each other in terms of the warmest praise and satisfied that nothing will prevent their cordial cooperation.

The news from Lisbon is very disastrous and will produce a bad effect here but a worse probably in Portugal. Mendizabal has just sent a courier there and I have written to Howard a strong representation upon the consequences of this sudden resolution of the Queen's. Don Sebastian[2] is at the head quarters of Don Carlos—sent there probably by the Princess of Beira, but I suspect with objects which are more Portuguese than Spanish—he is the representative of the same principles as Don Miguel but without the personal objections attached to his cousin.[3] We have already had information that an incursion into the north of Portugal for the purpose of raising the country was meditated by the insurgents of Navarre, and it is probably with the object of favoring some attempt of Don Sebastian's in his own behalf. Yet with these dangers, and the fate of Portugal absolutely linked with that of Spain, a treaty is violated at a moment when circumstances are more favorable to its accomplishment than when it was concluded, and the Queen of Portugal is not made to see that her throne can be more easily defended at Burgos than at Elvas. It really almost makes one a republican to think of the mischief of power vested in irresponsible childhood.

The Queen Regent has within the last week been *coolish* to Mendizabal—the grandees who are learned in intrigues and in nothing else, have contrived to alarm her upon the revolutionary aspect of affairs. It is not more than that as yet, because in her heart she believes that Mendizabal is walking in the way he should go, but she like other Sovereigns is apt to repent of any cession of power and to lend a willing ear to proposals for getting it back cheaply. These have been made to her by the sapient Miraflores who declared that Louis Philippe told him he would never grant intervention till he (Miraflores) was at the head of the Government. This I believe to have tempted the Queen for a moment, but Mendizabal thinks the storm is blown over. Poor

Miraflores who between vanity and apoplexy acts a sad figure has deluded a few other spirits yet weaker than himself with the grand promises he has imported from France, and a set of these gentlemen are quite ready to undertake the Government of the country, to all appearance unaware that they would be run over by events as a steam waggon would crush as many pigs upon the rail road.

All this as you will allow does not make Mendizabal's a bed of roses—upon which moreover he has to lose his parliamentary virginity, but I see no very formidable danger except want of money.

A row was intended today by Grandees and Co. but none took place. On the contrary the Queen has rarely been so well received and the town never was more tranquil.

I think as a whole you will like the Speech[4]—it might have been better for it would have been easy to laisser entrevoir more schemes ad captandum even if they had never *come off*, but the announcement of *any* ameliorations or practical reforms is a novelty and will produce a good effect. I am very much annoyed after all that has passed that the South American question should be referred (most unconstitutionally) to the Cortes, but nothing could overcome Mendizabal's fear of responsibility about treating the subject in the only manner now practicable.

Wylde is delighted that you have obtained permission for Reid to stay and Colquhoun to come—he says the artillery would have been nothing worth without them.

An application will be made to you by Jabat for a pontoon bridge—it is of the utmost importance to Cordoba—pray therefore grant it. Wylde says that there are plenty in store at Woolwich and we may as well furnish this as any other implements of war. He writes to Sir Alexander Dixon by the messenger tonight to describe the kind of bridge wanted in the event of your giving the necessary permission.

Orders will be sent immediately to the east coast to have some Spanish vessels perform the searching and seizing duties under the command of our ships.

I cannot sufficiently thank you for the fortnightly courier.

Received 25 November.

GC/CL/223; Clar. Dep. C.452/1 (176-181)

[1] By a convention signed in September Portugal had bound herself to send an auxiliary army of six thousand men to the assistance of the Queen of Spain. On 11 November the Portuguese Ministers resigned because of opposition

within Portugal to the fulfilment of the convention, but they were reinstated on 13 November.

2 Son of the Princess of Beira, and grandson of John VI of Portugal. The Princess of Beira was the sister of Don Carlos's first wife, and herself became his second wife in 1837.

3 *Recte* nephew.

4 A copy of the Queen's Speech was enclosed with V to P, 16 Nov. 1835, no. 181, FO 72/445.

165 Palmerston to Villiers, 19 November 1835

Copy. Foreign Office. The Rodney, a large two-decker, is to carry the 15,000 muskets to Barcelona, and I send you a note which I have received about her motions from Minto.

Jabat was ordered to ask me for 50,000 muskets in addition to the 200,000 we have already sent or promised to send, and of which the last 50,000 are still in this country. I advised him to suspend making this demand for the present and to wait at least until all the arms we have agreed to give are safe in Spain. These accumulated requisitions will throw a ridicule upon the thing. We must see too, how many muskets we have now got left in store, and whether we can spare any more. If 200,000 are not enough for the Christinos, Carlos can have but little chance left.

We are delighted at the continued good accounts which we receive from Spain and consider it now only a question of time. Mendizabal has won the game, and has only to play it out. Pray thank him for his short note which you sent me through Granville, but tell him not to waste his time in writing to me unless he has something to ask us to do. We and I especially know all he can say, and every minute of his time must be too little for the demands made upon it by the business of his country.

As to [the] Chronicle, I did all I could to moderate its 'impetus animi', but it was ungovernable, and between you and I, it may be doubted whether its attacks on the French Government about Spanish affairs have done any harm.

There certainly was an intrigue on that matter at Paris, somewhere and among some people, Heaven knows whom or where; but that is I hope all over now, and the Tuileries like the gods will espouse the conquering side.

PS. I believe the report that Metternich is sending money to Carlos. Spain and Italy have too much sympathy not to make Metternich anxious to reestablish pure monarchy in the former.

GC/CL/1250

166 Villiers to Palmerston, 21 November 1835

Madrid. Private. We are going on well—the manner in which the general enlistment has been taken and is nearly effected is good. So is the general tone of the press and the prospects of Mendizabal in the Cortes—above all the unexcited state of public opinion and the reasonable spirit which prevails are good. The little cloud in which that conjuror Miraflores had for a moment wrapped the royal mind has now passed away and all is right again in that quarter. I thought it expedient however to throw out the hints which you will find in my dispatch of today.[1]

I would not underwrite affairs going well ultimately except at a considerable premium, but I don't see how they could be in a better way, all things past and present considered. Mendizabal, now that he has concluded the first chapter of his Acts, by putting down the revolution in which he swam a triton among minnows, is now beginning another in which he is certainly not so great. He is untried as a Parliament man, a statesman, and a Minister and I see that he is doomed to commit a few blunders—his mere ignorance of forms will get him into scrapes and make him many enemies, but he has tact and courage and untiring ardor—a quick and just apperçu of what is right when he gives himself time to think, and manners which *invest* him with an extraordinary power over his countrymen. These are just the qualities necessary for mastering all that he has yet to learn and I confess I share his own sanguine hopes of ultimately triumphing.

The happy termination of the Portuguese devildom is a grand thing for the two little Peninsular Queens. The fall of Saldanha's Government was not well known here before the news of its being set up again arrived, except to the Carlists who always know every thing immediately, and they had two days of quiet ecstasy, but now they are very chopfallen indeed.

We have no direct news from Cordoba. I suppose he is too actively employed somewhere to write, but private accounts are favorable—the Navarrese who had passed into Arragon were so hotly pursued by the division sent after them by Cordoba that they all came back—some other regiments of Navarrese have absolutely refused to go out of the province upon any terms[2] (which is a great point to have fixed and known), and two of them have been fighting together. These private accounts state that Cordoba has been to Estella—the sanctum sanctorum of the Carlists. Wylde is delighted with what Cordoba is said to be doing, and predicts most favorable results from it if no mischance befalls him in his way out of the awful country he is now promening himself in.

Alava has been very ill but is now better, and in a week will set off for Paris viâ Santander and Bayonne, where he will see with his own eyes and hear with his own ears what is going on there. I have this moment received a note from Mendizabal saying Al Lord Palmerston debe V decirle que por las Fronteras se deja pasar todo—todo—todo. Es preciso no hacerse ilusion[3]—but Alava has no *preocupaciones* upon the subject—he believes that the causes of complaint have been greatly exaggerated, and is determined, happen what may, never to have an angry word with the French Government. I have had a great deal of talk with him upon the subject and made him feel that we must not be driven into a quarrel or coolness with France respecting Spain.[4] I shall be disappointed if Lord Granville and De Broglie don't find him very amenable. To my mind there is little doubt that much of Louis Philippe's conduct respecting this country of late is attributable to Frias who has an understanding with the grandee intriguers here, and has spoken of Mendizabal as a mere revolutionist whose chances, even if he had the wish, of establishing a rational Government in Spain were infinitely small. Alava will always act honestly towards his Government and I should think will inspire Louis Philippe with confidence.

The manner in which the reinstated Portuguese Government have made that poor foolish little Donna Maria eat dirt reflects little credit upon them either as Ministers or gentlemen.[5]

PS. I open my letter to say that I have just received a letter from Evans dated the 19th confirming the reports of Cordoba's success at Estella and of the Carlists being driven back from Arragon. Evans is unwell —nothing of consequence.

Received 1 December.[6]

GC/CL/224; Clar. Dep. C.452/1 (182-187)

[1] In an interview with the Queen Regent V stated 'that public opinion was

strongly in support of the present Government and it would be a great disaster for the Queen to change her Government'. (V to P, 21 Nov. 1835, no. 184, FO 72/445.)

² 'absolutely' to 'terms' underlined, possibly by P.

³ 'You must tell Lord Palmerston that the frontier must be completely closed. Let there be no misapprehension about this.'

⁴ See also V to Granville, 7 Nov. 1835, PRO 30/29/421.

⁵ The Queen was made to write an apologetic note to the President of the Council, stating that she had received the resignation of the Ministry with regret, had tried in vain to form a Government without them, and reposed perfect confidence in them. The publication of this document by the Ministry aroused strong public feeling in her favour, contrary to their intention.

⁶ C.452/1 docketed 'By Courier S. Martin'.

167 Villiers to Palmerston, 28 November 1835

Madrid. The proposition of bringing up a child and, being admitted, its converse must be so likewise, and as I was not brought up in the ways of diplomacy so it is lawful for me to depart from them. Being then justified according to the Book of Proverbs, I hope I shall not be blamed by His Majesty's Government for the document which I send you today—it will perhaps cause you some surprize, but I am sure that in my place you would have proceeded as I have done. Mendizabal wants money, and the Spaniards want cottons. We can help them to both and as I think very much to our own advantage.¹ So the opportunity was not to be lost, which it probably might have been if I had hesitated to take upon myself the necessary responsibility—for Mendizabal has the means if he chooses to resort to them of raising money at home (by conversions of the interior debt). He at first proposed the treaty to me in joke—I thought it a devilish good one and we soon came to an understanding. It would of course have been far more agreable to me to have written to you upon the subject before I took any further step, but I could not deny first the importance of gaining time and next that if you did not approve of the treaty, and it was not ratified no harm would be done and nobody be the wiser. Under these circumstances I consented, and here I may as well mention that the Queen, Mendizabal, his English private secretary, Southern (who in this as in every thing else has been of the greatest use to me) and myself are the only individuals who have knowledge of the transaction.

Mendizabal having requested me to draw up the treaty, I endeavoured by every means to guard against *our taking any harm* and I confess the idea of admitting *bodily* into Spain and her colonies the whole
of the cotton manufactures of England at 30 per cent less duty than
that which the manufacturers have looked upon as their greatest desideratum does elate me exceedingly, not alone on account of the thing
itself, but because the achievement of that which has hitherto been
looked upon as improbable as it was desireable will be received with
such favor and give such an impetus to the manufacturing interests
that it will be a new element of strength and popularity to the Government. It will render the Queen's cause—every day becoming a
European question of greater importance—more popular in England
by embarking new interests in its favor, and you will have more powerful arguments to use and more votes to expect should circumstances
impose upon you the necessity of taking more vigorous measures than
you have yet been able to do to secure the prosperity and peace of your
new customers.

The principal objection which I anticipated to the project is that it
will be necessary for you to go to Parliament previously to taking any
measure which might ultimately impose a burthen upon the finances
of Great Britain—upon this you must of course be the competent judge
and I cannot pretend to give an opinion, but I will only remark that
Mendizabal's objections are to a certain degree valid. If this matter
were to be brought in a preliminary state before Parliament it would
be impossible for him without subjecting himself to justifiable attack
not to render like homage to the Cortes, and if the admission of foreign
manufactures had to be discussed there, the particular interests of a few
and the national vanity of all the Procuradores would cause the project
to be rejected or nullified and the Cortes might either by measures, or
the expression of opinions, render the future amelioration of our commercial relations more difficult than ever.

Did not the English Government guarantee a Greek loan and a Russian Dutch loan (some loan which I remember Baring used to bully
terribly), and was the previous sanction of Parliament asked in those
cases?

I cannot but think however that if the manufacturers of England
could be consulted they would have no difficulty in *advancing* (let alone
guaranteeing) such a loan vû the securities and the advantages under
which it is proposed. The introduction of a million and a half's worth

of cotton goods under the provisions of the treaty would pay off the loan in 12 years—in 9, if two millions sterling worth were introduced —and this is by no means an exaggerated expectation when it is considered we should have a complete monopoly in supplying Spain, Cuba, Puerto Rico and the Philippine Islands—and be it remembered that as the amount due for the arms and ammunition furnished by England must now amount to nearly £400,000, it is in fact little more than a million and a half that we are guaranteeing and it is no trifling advantage to get security for this debt, for with the present prospect of affairs here, political and financial, the Mighty only knows how or when we should have got paid.

The next objection which I feared was, the displeasure with which France might view the treaty and the difficulty you might in consequence have in adopting it.

This I think I have been able to obviate for France will have no right now to complain that we are acting ungenerously or with selfishness. We secure for her like advantages upon like terms with ourselves and if she does not chuse to avail herself of them she has no right to quarrel with our doing so. I took care so to shape my conversation upon this subject with Mendizabal that I should be able to make from it the dispatch I have this day written. In this dispatch I have taken up two or three objects which you will readily perceive, thinking that if the whole matter turns out well and *goes forward* you might like to communicate this dispatch to De Broglie, in proof that the question of the treaty had originated here, and as a testimony of the general feelings of the English Government as well as of the particular spirit of my instructions.

Now I believe I have said my say upon this matter and have only to hope that you will approve.

I have written so much today that I have left myself little time and you probably little inclination for a political bulletin: things are going on well—the intrigues of the moderate party against Mendizabal are dying away, the fears of his being out being rather stronger than the fears of his staying in, and he will have good majorities in the Chambers, but I am beginning to dread that which he seems perfectly at ease about—the Exaltado party—their exigeance and selfishness have no bounds and any attempt to satisfy them is incompatible with decent government. These people are all his Auld Lang Syne friends and he thinks therefore he can rely upon them—I know that any man that does will surely be betrayed.

The law of elections is a most detestable one and as I told Mendizabal I would have given £500 to have seen it before hand as I should have protested against issuing tickets of admission to the Cortes to all the worst canaille in Spain.[2] I ended by convincing him I believe of the badness of the law which is really as unwise as it is unnecessary. He assured me it should be 'neutralized' in its course through the Chambers—that is much easier said than done—but I hope it may be modified—or before 2 or 3 years elapse we shall have a second edition of the vagaries of 1820.

Mendizabal has a trick of referring every important question to a commission, the selection of which he makes in the most careless manner—he thinks by this to avoid trouble and responsibility, he increases both and this system as I have told him is not governing—it is merely administering.

If you have time to form an opinion upon the election law and that you think of it as I do, will you write me two or three ostensible lines upon the subject—as well as upon the recognition of the South American States and the disgrace which will attach to the present liberal Government of Spain if that business is not at once *handsomely* concluded? I cannot screw him up to the point and he is hawking the question about to royal commissions and commercial juntas till it will get into inextricable confusion.

Many thanks for your letter of the 19th and dispatches which arrived this morning. It is of infinite use to me knowing what passes at foreign Courts respecting Spain—it serves as a key to much that is going on here.

PS. Mendizabal begs that the treaty matter may be kept *most secret* till the ratifications are exchanged in order to prevent manufacturing remonstrances here and gambling in London.

Unless Lord Granville directs to the contrary I have ordered my courier to proceed to London and he can bring back your answer, if you please—there is not *upon any road* in Europe one more speedy or more trustworthy.

Copy. Docketed: Courier St. Jago with commercial treaty.

Clar. Dep. C.452/1 (188-197)

[1] The document enclosed with V's despatch of 28 Nov. 1835 (no. 189, most secret and confidential, FO 72/445) was a draft treaty under which Spain

agreed to admit certain British manufactures at a low duty, in return for a loan guarantee. The document was to be considered null and void unless ratified by the British Government.

2 What V saw as dangerous was the principle of direct election. He admitted, however, that if the property qualification was properly enforced there would be no more than thirty thousand electors. (V to P, 21 Nov. 1835, no. 184, FO 72/445.)

168   Villiers to Palmerston, 2 December 1835

Madrid. Private. At a most undue hour of the night I learn that Mendizabal is dispatching a courier and I avail myself of the opportunity to tell you that he is a little alarmed about the effect which the treaty (if you accept it) may produce here. We are as much interested as he is that it should be well received and not occasion him any undue loss of popularity and you may perhaps therefore not be indisposed to meet his present wishes upon the subject. He wants you to give me instructions to agree to an additional article agreeing that the treaty may be revised every 20 years if thought necessary by the contracting parties —likewise an article by which the Government of His Britannic Majesty, in order to draw closer the ties, etc., etc., and in order to promote the development of Spanish industry and resources, agrees to propose to Parliament a reduction of duties upon divers (the specification is not necessary) articles, the produce of this country. These additions to the treaty are not to be resorted to unless the state of public opinion should render them necessary in order to obtain the approbation of the Cortes. Upon this matter I should be just as good a judge as Mendizabal and I should consent to nothing that I did not consider indispensable.

If any other concession on the part of England should occur to you which may be of use to these people politically, commercially or financially, you will I hope give me leave to use it in the event of its being really wanted, for such a *cotton opportunity* as this may never occur again —it will be a bitter pill however to the prejudiced and smuggling part of the Spanish community and we ought to assist Mendizabal in gilding it.

There is likewise another consideration. If we shew ourselves generous and the thing *takes* here we shall be able forthwith to make another *general* treaty of commerce and settle permanently the trading relations between the two countries. Any sacrifice therefore that we made now would be capital very well invested and perhaps returning us profit before Parliament meets which is what I should much desire, for I am sure that opening wide the door to trade with Spain would be one of the most popular acts you could do and in every manufacturing district would strengthen the Government tenfold in the event of an election.

The discussions in the Procuradores upon the Address have been *most* satisfactory—far surpassing my best hopes—upon the 2d paragraph which contains an assurance of confidence in the Government, out of 116 members present 111 voted in favor—none voted against —and of the 5 who abstained from voting one was a Minister out of decency and another Martinez de la Rosa because the paragraph implied a censure upon his own Government. There was no division upon any other and the discussion ended today in the most triumphant manner for the Government.

In answer to the accusations of Las Navas against the French Government,[1] Mendizabal answered *very well indeed*—saying that he drew the widest distinctions between the conduct of the French Government and that of some of its subordinate agents, that satisfactory explanations had been given by the French Government, and that the Government of this country had never been treated with greater consideration by France than at present. I must take some credit to myself for this for I had the precaution to get up a *dressed rehearsal* the night before. Arguelles and Galiano both likewise defended the French Government and deprecated any discussion which might be offensive. I heard their speeches and was quite satisfied.

Isturitz promises to be one of the best presidents of any legislative assembly now existing, and if the present spirit of union and order continues the Government will be *very* strong.

I must not keep Mendizabal's courier any longer.

Received 14 December.

GC/CL/225; Clar. Dep. C.452/1 (198-202)

[1] In the Cortes he complained that the French Government was not fulfilling properly the Additional Articles, and therefore that it was not a trustworthy ally of Spanish Constitutionalism. (V to P, 1 Dec. 1835, no. 194, FO 72/445.)

169 Villiers to Palmerston, 5 December 1835

Madrid. Private. I think you will be satisfied with my report of things today. The Government has gained greatly during the last week by shaking off the doubt which hung over its future destiny till the turn which affairs were likely to take in the Cortes became known. In the late debates an almost unanimous desire for union and order has been exhibited together with a sense of the necessity of making the Government strong. Isturitz is an *admirable* President—his worst enemies admit that he displays a rare firmness and impartiality—and the results of his conduct upon the Cortes and through them upon the futurity of Spain may be incalculably great. I consider Mendizabal much stronger than when I wrote to you a week ago.

He has now become desperately frightened about our treaty, and is beginning to weigh its consequences to himself with the ignorant prejudiced public of Spain. He cannot say I took any unfair advantage of his *innocence,* for I begged him over and over again to reflect upon the difficulties it would give rise to, but he would not listen to me or admit it would give rise to any thing but renown. He now begs you *por Dios* to hold out some commercial concessions on the part of England. I have told him I was sure you would do all in your power but, not taking corn, you cannot offer much. In the event of your ratifying the treaty and my finding the opposition which it would meet with likely to upset Mendizabal's Government, I suppose you would prefer the ratification here being delayed awhile, or the provisions of the treaty being embodied in the comprehensive one of which I last night got him to say he should request me to present a project—that treaty will of course have nothing to do with a guarantee of a loan.

It will take some time to collect the information and materials for this, and as soon as I get them I shall send you an outline for approval and filling up as you think proper—not cut and dried as the last, which was done with an intention of commencing money operations in London immediately upon your approval being known, but in the 11th hour Mendizabal admitted this would be rather too hasty in the present state of affairs here, and when no one could tell whether ratification at Madrid would be possible when the treaty returned from London.

The Spanish Government could scarcely at this moment do gracious things towards France and this rather hampers me, for I feel all the importance to ourselves but more particularly to Spain, that France should not be irritated. This is another reason for wishing that France would go cordially along with us in our policy towards the Peninsula.

Were we to make a great treaty and really to sacar todo el partido[1] which, with a little management is now open to us in this country, we should want some popular support in the provinces, the press, and the Cortes—this can't be done without a little money. I have not enough to accomplish these needful extras, and I don't know whether you would think such an expense justifiable, but an experiment of the kind, though only for six months, might be worth while, for I believe the country is now ready, perhaps more than at any former period, to gather itself unto us.

The Portuguese are behaving like Portuguese. I can say nothing worse of them—there is a handful of men called an advanced guard at Zamora near the frontier where the rear seems to have no intention of joining them.

The Minister of War sets out on a visit to Cordoba the day after tomorrow. Alava goes with him and afterwards proceeds viâ Santander on his journey to Paris.

Poor Miraflores has spoken, and out of his own mouth has been judged—several joints of his sprouting little tail have dropped off since, and though he has probably no doubt about his being the fittest Prime Minister for Spain, he has some about the amount of support he should get. He disapproves of all that is doing, and still wants French intervention which he believes (or at least says so to me) will never be granted.

Received 14 December.

GC/CL/226; Clar. Dep. C.452/1 (204-209)

[1] 'take full advantage of the support'.

170   Villiers to Palmerston, 7 December 1835

Madrid. Private. As many hours have not elapsed since my last letter I have but little to say.

I was glad to find that Mendizabal answered Rayneval upon commercial matters almost verbatim as I reported to you his intentions a few days ago, and the instructions which Rayneval has received in consequence of an article or letter in the Chronicle shew that I was right in making terms for France whenever any commercial facilities were granted to ourselves.[1] I cannot however but look upon the threat of making the civil war perpetual as ungenerous—not to say indecent. At the same time it is an admission on the part of the French Government that upon their more or less fulfillment of the Quadruple Treaty depends the extinction of the civil war and putting an end to a state of things which consumes to the very dregs the resources of this country and prevents the reestablishment of order, without which not a single step can be taken in the road to permanent improvement. *Charity* should dictate a different course, and as France has the power so she ought to have the will to check all these dreadful evils, instead of coldly looking upon them with *her hands in her breeches pockets*. State policy would prescribe the same as charity, but perhaps interest may be more effectual than either, and now is the time when she might be engaged heartily in the cause of Spain by *taking some shares* in a commercial speculation.

This would be an excellent opportunity for turning the Quadruple Alliance to account by modifications of our respective tariffs, from which would naturally be excluded the non-recognizing countries, Potencias facciosas as they are called here. This would be popular in England and France, and the political varnish which would be given to such an arrangement would modify the prejudices we must always expect in this jealous country against any measure which appears to concede an advantage to foreigners.

I am very desirous that Mendizabal should reinforce his Government by some one who can speak. His three colleagues are perfectly useless in the Cortes—he himself has only the minimum of oratorical talent, and, as might naturally be expected, is as ignorant as a child of 5 years old how to manage a deliberative assembly. Of this latter I have great difficulty in persuading him and I fear he will only learn it by painful experience and getting into scrapes. The Chamber is luckily very friendly but he must expect attacks upon his harum scarum mode of legislating which circumstances may justify but which he will never be able to defend. He has got the South American question into such a mess, first by pledging himself in the Queen's speech to *consult* the Chamber upon it, and then by asking the opinion of every council and commercial body throughout the kingdom that I almost fear he will not clear himself of these gratuitous difficulties. I have offered and he has accepted my mediation between the Government and the South American representatives and I have arranged with Galiano how to satisfy the Cortes and not damage the question further, but I doubt if Mendizabal will take my advice, for his timidity upon this subject is quite incomprehensible vû his *calling* for coups d'état in other matters. A word from you upon the unconstitutional proceeding of making a treaty in a committee of the whole House might be very useful.

Received 18 December.[2]

GC/CL/227; Clar. Dep. C.452/1 (210-212)

[1] Rayneval told Mendizábal that if, as newspaper reports suggested, England and Spain were about to conclude a commercial agreement, the French Government would view it as an 'offensive measure' which, among other evil consequences, might entail the indefinite prolongation of the civil war. (V to P, 7 Dec. 1835, no. 201, FO 72/445.)

[2] C.452/1 docketed 'By Spanish courier'.

171 Villiers to Palmerston, 8 December 1835

Madrid. Private. I find from Mendizabal that his courier did not go last night and he has just begged of me (as far as I could understand him for with his mouth full of rice pudding he was roaring with the gripes) to recommend to your particular attention either the letter he writes to you tonight or the one he wrote 5 days ago to Poulett Thomson—both however would be upon the same subject, namely helping him here with some commercial *concessions* and friendly *professions* in the event of your ratifying the cotton convention. His fears increase every day and he is now taking the view of the consequences it may entail upon himself that I begged him to take, but which he wouldn't, at the time of our making it. He wants your instructions to me to be as ample, or rather as nearly approaching carte blanche, as you can. I have no desire whatever of the sort but I consider myself just as competent a judge of public opinion here and of what he can or ought to do as himself, and in the event of your giving me an ample marge you may be assured it shall be used with prudence. He likewise wants some power to be vested in me of making the money part of the transaction personal to the present Government lest when the money is received the intriguers here may oust him. I have told him that this would be utterly impossible—at least in that kind of crude *un-gaséd* manner—but that perhaps upon reflection a mode *might* be devised of shaking off our own guarantee in the event of certain contingencies, and I promised to mention this wish to you; but he was not clear himself what he wanted, for by the time he had got to this part of the conversation the gripes had increased and he was dancing round the room with contortions which were of the most horrible yet laughable description.

Received 21 December.

GC/CL/228

172 Villiers to Palmerston, 13 December 1835

The activities of Mr. Monck,[1] British consul at Malaga, in connection with the seizure of an English vessel by the Guarda Costa.
Copy.

Clar. Dep. C.452/1 (214-215)

[1] *Recte* Mark.

173 Villiers to Palmerston, 13 December 1835

Madrid. *The negligence of the courier Webster.*
Copy.

Clar. Dep. C.452/1 (216-217)

174 Villiers to Palmerston, 13 December 1835

Madrid. Private. I need hardly assure you of the satisfaction which I derive from your coinciding in Sarmento's flattering prophesy—Spain is on the *road* to salvation but it is by no means a macadamized one, and there are woods enough still to pass through and get out of which make it very imprudent to begin whistling.

Rayneval does not talk (at least to me) so gloomily as he appears to write, but I know he thinks that this country is doomed to pass through more phases of revolution before it becomes purified and enlightened enough for the establishment of social order upon a basis of liberalized institutions. The past history of Spain, and the present state of parties go far to justify these apprehensions, but he always declares that things might have been otherwise ordered, and throws the blame of their not being so partly upon us, but mainly upon his own Government. He considers that with such an extraordinary concurrence of events in favor of the Queen's cause and of a state of things which, with reference to their general European policy, it was the interest of France and England to *clench,* it shews an ill adaptation of means to ends that the Spanish question should gradually have been permitted to increase in complication, in defiance of two powerful nations pledged to its settlement, and that instead of a useful branch of the Western Federation being established in the Peninsula, the general peace of Europe is not only in greater danger from this quarter than it was two years ago, but France and England, upon whose good understanding that peace depends, are upon the verge of coolness respecting that which should have been a fresh bond of union. In short if France and England had for awhile towered over the Peninsula till they ascertained that the combatants were incapable of settling their own matters, and then pounced down upon the question like two hawks, or like the Austrians whenever there is a *'ruction* in Italy, every thing would have been concluded and *fixed* according to their wishes, and before other Powers could have said a word, or they might have said all the words they liked—they would have been like water upon a duck's back against the united will of England and France pronounced and acted upon.

I have stated these opinions of Rayneval's not only because I think him a wise and unprejudiced politician, and more alive than any Frenchman I ever talked with to the gigantic results of which the alliance of our respective countries is capable, but that they go some way to account for his view of things here at this moment—he thinks they ought to have been better, and that his Government therefore does not deserve a bed of roses upon the futurity of Spain.

In one of Lord Granville's dispatches of which you sent me a copy, I see with some alarm that Metternich has told the Neapolitan minister that Austria would neither approve nor disapprove the recognition of Don Carlos by Naples. This was probably not a volunteer of His Highness's, but in answer to (perhaps in previous concert with) the Neapolitan minister—and I think such a step would not be taken without an arrangement with Sardinia. The ships of both countries, or at all events the flags, will then be legitimately employed in the service of Don Carlos, and we should either have to suffer their landing arms and stores under the guns of our ships, or to stir up some ticklish questions for a maritime nation, if we meddle with them. As soon as I received this dispatch I went to Mendizabal and made him forward positive orders to the coast for some Guarda Costas and cruizers to put themselves immediately in cooperation with our ships in case any seizing work should be necessary. In the events of Naples and Sardinia recognizing Don Carlos and openly giving him assistance would not England and France be bound to prevent this mischief being done to their ally? These two Powers were first in the field, they recognized and have been aiding the Queen, and if others choose to lay aside the neutrality which for two years they have adopted, it will be an offensive, if not a hostile, act to us and France. A timely word in the ear of these little States which are probably the feelers of greater ones, might save a good deal of trouble and more than one knotty question.

I had yesterday a long conversation with a *canonigo,* a friend of mine, who was the confessor of Don Sebastian, and who I really believe was ignorant of that young gentleman's intention of joining his uncle. He *says* he does not think there are any Portuguese objects in the visit, because Don Sebastian is even more afraid of personal danger or putting himself at the head of a party than of his mother, which is saying a great deal. He believes however in the marriage of the Princess of Beira with Don Carlos and her intention of coming to Spain. If once she gets here she will of course take advantage of any disorders in Portugal, and would very likely go there herself with Don Sebastian if there was the slightest chance of success. In reply to some questions of mine upon this subject, Howard says that if Don Sebastian, to whom the personal objections against Don Miguel don't apply, were to promise the Constitution of 1820, recognition by the Pope, and the restoration of Church, not national, property, that he would probably unite in his favor the Miguelite and Exaltado parties—there is accordingly a good deal of work on hand before the Peninsula becomes *quite* tranquil, but I still maintain that if France were as *notoriously* determined as ourselves to make things go as they ought, most of these clouds would vanish into thin air.

I am glad you liked the election law[1] because I have no doubt your opinion will be that of others and that the effect abroad will therefore be good which is a great point. To know however what its real character is, it is necessary to understand how it will work, and I did and do oppose myself to it because it is calculated to deprive the *country* of representation and to throw all the elections into the *towns* where alone

345

there is a democratical spirit and where the *alborotadores*[2] and secret societies will be able to influence the electors—it is calculated to exclude property, and as it opens the door widely to what are *called* (grievously miscalled too) *capacidades*,[3] i.e. doctors, lawyers and id genus omne, the only turbulent class in Spain, the ensuing Cortes would be composed of exactly the same kind of men as those who in 1820 *did* for the very name of liberal government. I opposed it moreover because (among other reasons not necessary to trouble you with) I saw the profound disgust it produced among all those liberals, not absolutely Exaltados, by whom I the most wish to see Mendizabal supported—and I cannot offer a better proof of the justifiableness of my opposition than that Mendizabal after hearing my arguments said I was right, that the law would be mischievous in practice, and that he would therefore take care to neutralize it in its progress through the Cortes. It is still before the committee and the very framers of the law have had to make considerable alterations and concessions to *public opinion* upon it.

I can't quite persuade Mendizabal yet of that which I am very certain myself—that he has no idea how to *handle* a legislative body, or of what in form as well as substance is the duty of a Minister under a constitutional Government. His star and his system he thinks are sufficient, but neither of them will keep him out of great parliamentary blunders. The South American question is a specimen of this, and I took the liberty of *writir g him a hint* (of which I enclose you the copy) the other day upon the scrape he was getting into. It has done good or at *least I think* so because he is going to adopt it and has a meeting tomorrow of friendly members of both Chambers to inform them of the course he means to pursue and ask their support.

PS. December 14th. Rayneval has put off the departure of his courier till this morning but I have little to add to my letter. I last night saw Mendizabal from 12 to 2 (our usual hours of conference); he was in considerable alarm for the safety of San Sebastian which the Carlists appear to be attacking as vigorously and the Christinos defending as badly as they can. He sent off a courier to Santander with a letter from me to Lord John Hay informing him of the fact and begging him to give all the assistance which his instructions warranted.

The recent proceedings of Harispe upon the frontier have caused great delight here, and nothing would be more easy than to produce a reaction in favor of France if this line of conduct were persevered in by the French authorities.

I send you a Gazette of today in which you will see that Mendizabal has at length adopted a wise tone respecting the loyauté of the French Government.

Enclosure: Copy, Villiers (Madrid) to Mendizábal, 10 December 1835, on political tactics in relation to the question of the recognition of the South American States.

Received 24 December. Docketed by Palmerston: By French messenger to Paris.

GC/CL/229; Clar. Dep. C.452/1 (218-223)

¹ The proposed new electoral law fixed the qualifications of an elector as follows: (1) he must be twenty-five years of age, either born within the kingdom of Spanish parents or of a Spanish father if born out of the kingdom; (2) he must be one of the hundred inhabitants of a province paying the greatest amount of taxes, or one of those who paid taxes equal in amount to those paid by the lowest on the list of one hundred; (3) he must be in a profession or occupation such as that of advocate, doctor or professor.

² 'agitators'.

³ 'professionals'.

175 Villiers to Palmerston, 19 December 1835

Madrid. Private. I believe that my dispatch contains all I have to say worth communicating to you this evening.¹ Two days ago an angry and impatient state of feeling was springing up which alarmed me, not because it was justified, but because I knew it would be catching. It is now appeased, and has only added one more proof to the millions already existing of how little even the best earned popularity can be depended upon. I must do Mendizabal the justice to say that neither upon this or any other occasion have I seen him the least alarmed, and it *does* require a stout heart to look undauntedly at all the difficulties which stare him in the face. He now admits that which I told him at San Ildefonso but which he laughed at then, that he would find in all Spain but Cordoba and Cordoba alone who was really capable, and guided by pure and patriotic motives. Whatever may be the true political version of that old English dispute upon men and measures, there is no doubt that in Spain men and not measures are the first necessity. If they are good they will act well enough for the present circumstances of the country, if not, they will with their passions, their vanity, and incapacity neutralize every measure, though, like the Decalogue, it were to come strait from Heaven. This is the case at the present moment, and Mendizabal does not know which way to turn himself for intelligent and faithful agents.

The next want is money, and that I declare I can't comprehend how he is to find—there are one or two measures which he might, but he says he won't, have recourse to, and nobody has a guess what he means to do. He is perfectly calm however about it, and told me yesterday that he should pull through very well if the Cortes next week gave him carte blanche to act as he thought expedient under the circumstances of the country, *sauf* accounting for it all, and getting a Bill of Indemnity at the end of the session. But what should you think the army upon paper (i.e. upon the treasury, and for which money is actually drawn) amounts to? *178,000 men,* exclusive of the 100,000 now raising—the greater part of it robbery of course—but the same exists in every other department of the State—each is its own Augean stable—the mere cleaning out of them all would make this country one of the most *comfortable,* with reference to its necessities, in Europe. The strength which internal tranquillity alone can give to a Government is indispensable for this more than Herculean labor, and two millions sterling and 12 good men and true would put Mendizabal in a condition to attempt it at least. It seems hard to be struggling for life *in muck* for the want of *semejantes frioleras.*[2]

I daresay much more is thought in London of Portuguese misdoings than in Spain—here we absolutely haven't taken them into consideration, and I am far from thinking that the non arrival of a parcel of ill disciplined political troops is a mischief. Cordoba was at first inclined to regret it, but I believe he now agrees with me that they would probably have been more troublesome than useful to him.

I hope you will have the goodness to move His Majesty to give leave for Lord John Hay and Colonel Wylde to wear the Orders the Queen has bestowed upon them. . . .

I think you will be much pleased with the law of the press[3] which was yesterday presented to the Cortes.

Alava is ill at Burgos and expects to have to stay there a few days longer which is very unfortunate, as the Duc de Broglie writes word to Rayneval that he is impatiently waiting his arrival.

Received 28 December.

GC/CL/230; Clar. Dep. C.452/1 (224-227)

[1] The despatch recounted the intrigues of the Exaltados against Mendizá-bal's Ministry. (V to P, 19 Dec. 1835, no. 208, FO 72/445.)
[2] 'such trifles'.
[3] In the Queen's Speech of 16 November a law regarding the liberty of the press had been promised.

176   Palmerston to Villiers, 21 December 1835

Copy. Stanhope Street. Here is our commercial treaty at last. It takes so much time to do anything of this sort, on which so many people must be consulted, that I began almost to despair of ever sending it off. Tell Mendizabal, No treaty, no guarantee. We could not hope to get Parliament to agree to the latter unless it was accompanied by the former.[1]

I write in a great hurry as I am just starting for Brighton where we have a Council today at four.

GC/CL/1251

[1] P told V officially, in a secret despatch dated 21 December, of the British Government's refusal to ratify V's draft treaty, on the grounds that it excluded France, and that any pecuniary guarantee would have to be sanctioned by Parliament. However, he enclosed in a further despatch of the same date a draft of a purely commercial treaty. (P to V, 21 Dec. 1835, nos. 49 (secret) and 50, FO 72/439.)

177   Villiers to Palmerston, 26 December 1835

Madrid. Private. Rayneval sends a courier today according to the fortnightly arrangement, and I therefore write, but I have nothing worth your reading to say, for the last week has been singularly barren in events. So many have happened lately and in such rapid succession, that I feel, when I have none to report to you, as I used to do after a blank day out hunting. Taking an average of events however in Spain it is perhaps the best news I can send.

My courier who went last week to meet the London messenger and should have returned yesterday morning has not made his appearance whereat I am greatly annoyed, for (my treaty courier not having come back either) he must bring at all events your *opinion* upon my attempt at making England and Spain *cotton* to each other. To tell you how anxious I am for it would merely be to say a platitude for you will readily conceive what a *muy mal rato*[1] I am passing until I hear from you.

You will see by my dispatch of Cortes proceedings[2] that Mendizabal, contrary to the practice of other constitutional Ministers who only beg to be whitewashed for what they *have* done, has requested carte blanche for what he is *going* to do, and you will see that the commission to whom the proposed law was referred, have reported not only that he ought to have it, but that whoever doubts it is a particularly bad citizen. Now both the law and the report have produced considerable alarm here—the former appears to tie the hands of the Government tightly but the 3d article which is the real carte blanche gives them power over the whole property, national and private, of the country. Mendizabal admitted as much to me. The report is looked upon as a denunciation of the commission (which is composed of some monied men and some stock jobbers but none of them have any fixed property) against all those who may not like to place every thing they possess at the disposal of one man without at least asking a question concerning what he intends to do with it.

I have had a long conversation with Mendizabal upon the subject and represented to him the great and justifiable alarm which this measure will create if he does not in the debate on Monday declare that the report of the commission is too favorable to himself, and invite enquiry upon the future intentions of the Government. He must do this and *more* or he will be in a great scrape. We are upon such an intimate and friendly footing together that I venture to lecture him pretty often (I *may* say daily) which is not pleasant but is very necessary, for as he has never read at all and not reflected much he is ignorant but not the least aware of it, and the host of interested flatterers by whom he is surrounded only serve to increase his delusion.

You will think perhaps from this that like Alderman Wood I am laying claim to absolute wisdom, but il s'agit only of those rudiments of constitutional government which every Englishman in the habit of reading the debates in Parliament has at his fingers' ends. Mendizabal has a great deal of genius but he lacks the *ballast* necessary for a statesman and a Parliament man—however, though he may not be all we could wish him for the sake of his country and his own, there is certainly no other man who unites as many qualities necessary for the salvation of Spain at this moment.

The Portuguese troops sent with a bad grace and coming with ill will would never do any good here. I have written to Howard to suggest that the few which are already in Spain should, according as disturbances arise in Portugal (and por la gracia de Dios I daresay they will not be wanting) be gradually withdrawn; but that from the moment the Portuguese Government agree to this that the troops should no longer receive Spanish pay. I am certain this is the only way of maintaining friendly relations between the two countries for in the 1st place the delay asked in order to raise recruits in lieu of the absent troops is absurd—the new levies here will be ready by that time, and if more were wanted there are plenty of men in this country—then there would always be disputes respecting the collocation of the troops, and as they would cost more than an equal number of Spaniards the national jealousy would be excited, and the Government exposed to constant attacks in the Cortes and the press which would only produce bad blood between the two countries. If the troops had entered six weeks ago at the moment of crisis they would have done great good— that moment being now passed they had much better (for Spain, perhaps not for Portugal) stay at home.

Alava I am sorry to say still continues very unwell at Burgos and unable to move. This is a most untoward event.[3]

I have had a letter from my old friend and co-attaché in Russia, Bankhead. . . .

Now I believe I have said my say for this time.

PS. December 27th. Rayneval put off the departure of his courier till today in consequence of the non arrival of mine—he came this morning safely but had been detained by the almost impassable state of the mountains.

From the anxiety which I expressed in the beginning of this letter you may judge of my disappointment at not receiving one word either public or private from you. By a letter from Lord Holland of the 8th[4] and one from Thomson of the 13th,[5] both of which arrived today, I learn that the treaty has not found favor. Will you oblige me by telling them that I have received these letters? It is impossible for me to answer them today as Rayneval's courier having already waited 4 and 20 hours is to go early.

Received 7 January 1836.

GC/CL/231; Clar. Dep. C.452/1 (229-235)

351

[1] 'very bad time'.

[2] V to P, 28 Dec. 1835, no. 221, FO 72/445. A Bill presented by the Ministry to the Chamber of Deputies on 21 December 1835 authorized the Government to continue in receipt of the supplies voted in the law of 26 May, and to adopt the measures it deemed necessary for terminating the civil war. It was to render an account of the use made of these extraordinary powers in 1836.

[3] 'He has since moved on.' added in pencil, perhaps by P.

[4] V was extremely disappointed by Holland's letter. On 10 January 1836 he wrote to Holland, 'I humbly aimed at advancing the objects to which your own life has been triumphantly devoted—the glory and prosperity of England as connected with a liberal system of foreign policy.' (V to Holland, 10 Jan. 1836, Holland House Papers, British Library Add. MS. 51617.) The rest of the letter is a long defence of his reasons for negotiating the treaty with Mendizábal.

[5] For V's reaction to this letter, which he considered showed Thomson to have jealously preferred his own scheme, see V to Granville, 27 Dec. 1835, PRO 30/29/421. To his brother, Edward Villiers, he wrote that Thomson's treaty contained 'the same commercial stipulations, the same guarantee for the same sum, thereby practically refuting all his own arguments for the rejection of my treaty'. (V to Edward Villiers, 29 Dec. 1835, Clar. Dep. C.467.)

178 Villiers to Palmerston, 2 January 1836

Madrid. Private. As I want to have a bit of a *turn up* with you I will begin, after the fashion of boxers who shake hands before they *set to*, by wishing you a prosperous new year and that Your Excellency may live a thousand.

Having said thus much I will add that after having read your dispatches Nos. 49 and 50[1] I never to my recollection since I have been in Spain uttered a deeper or longer *Carajo*.[2] Had the treaty been rejected altogether I should have understood that some fixed determination had guided the decision of the Government, and concluded that some insuperable objection had presented itself. Neither of these however being the case, and finding that the terms of the treaty are accepted (though shorn of many of their advantages) but put in a form which renders their adoption impossible, I grievously took to heart that an opportunity should have been missed for doing a great political service to Spain and securing great commercial advantages for England, two objects which, with reference to the general state of Europe and the present position of the English Government, I look upon as inferior to none in importance, and which were the motives of my taking upon myself a responsibility which I fear has not been viewed with any very peculiar favor.

The two objections taken to the treaty are those which I myself suggested in the dispatch which accompanied it—the one I considered not to be fatal, and for the other I hoped I had provided a remedy. First as to the necessity of going to Parliament for the power of guaranteeing a loan, I was perfectly aware of the constitutional rule, and had provided for it accordingly in the draft of the treaty, but yielded to Mendizabal's reasons against it. I know however, or thought I knew, of exceptions to the rule, and you will I am sure admit that the instance which I quote in my dispatch today is not ill calculated to lead one into error[3]—but if I was *not* wrong, there surely never was a guarantee upon which a Government could have entered more securely or with better chance of public opinion in their favor, for, granted that Spain failed in the stipulated provisions for paying the interest, how would the loan have stood? One fourth of it was for a bad debt which would have been instantly paid off—the remainder would have been chargeable upon England—interest or principal—so long only as Spain continued to grant an *enormous* boon—perhaps at this moment the *greatest* desiderandum to British manufactures, and which as long as it lasted would have been considered dirt cheap at the money—a sinking fund moreover being established, and the exporters of British goods having a direct interest in contributing to the extinction of the loan. If all things went smoothly this would have taken place in 9 or 10 years —if not, the responsibility of England ceased. Now though I say it as shouldn't, I don't believe that in the annals of loans or treaties a similar arrangement of reciprocal advantages can be found, for I don't believe a similar concatenation of feasabilities ever before presented themselves for adoption.

Supposing however that the whole loan had fallen upon us, what fear need we have of not being reimbursed? The colonies of Spain, Cuba, Puerto Rico, the Philippines, all entered into the arrangement, and a few idle ships upon the East or West India stations would soon have put us in pocket, and no Government of Spain, be it the Queen's, Don Carlos's, or a republic, would dare reject our just reclamations.

Now as to the second objection to the treaty—the jealousy of France: most just would that jealousy have been—most desireable was it to guard against such feelings—and having as I had hoped taken the precautions which prudence and good faith dictated as between allies in reciprocal want of each other's good will, I confess I was hurt at finding this subject treated in your dispatch as a bran new idea, and as one therefore which had been unthought of and unprovided for by me—the fact being that even after the treaty was completed, I refused to transmit it to you unless Mendizabal altered his resolution of not admitting France to a participation. He then consented to all I proposed, and I wrote you a dispatch for the express purpose of being submitted to the French Government. That dispatch contained evidence of the knowledge I had of the generous unselfish feelings which animated the English Government towards that of France, and it at the same time contained evidence that the former was utterly unaware beforehand of the particular transaction in question. Upon me therefore—upon the agent—would have fallen the responsibility—the blame of haste, of unwarrantable zeal perhaps—to the Government the glory, and *the profit*, of a frank and friendly proceeding—which is a fitting state of things. If this course had been adopted, and if it had been declared that England would not proceed with the negotiation without the participation or be it consent of France, I believe that the object you have in view would have been better attained, and the sincerity of England less exposed to suspicion than by (after a lapse of three weeks) suggesting to the Spanish Government to make a joint proposition to England and France—the suggestion being accompanied however by a treaty all ready for signature—which treaty would still give us le pas of France, and have been beyond all comparison more offensive and injurious to her than one which was simply commercial—for it settles in favor of England alone all those disputed rights (rights be it observed which we claim under *French* treaties) which are the never ending causes of vexatious reclamations between the two Governments, and as French subjects in Spain are to British as 100 : 1 the offence and injury to France of being excluded from such a general arrangement and of not being consulted upon it would have been great in proportion.

So strong is my conviction of this that some time since when Mendizabal in answer to my note against his Consular Decree consented to a revision of the old treaties (which apply equally to all the most favored nations) I immediately communicated it to Rayneval, told him that I was collecting the necessary information which should be shewn to him as soon as I had made a digest of it, and offered to proceed de concert avec lui in the work.

I will not trouble you with any more remarks upon the old and now cancelled treaty—thus much I have said in my own defence for the tone of your dispatch and your own unusual silence upon a matter involving such important interests lead me to believe that I have not hitherto justified myself in your eyes.

Come we now however to the only matter worth consideration— that which is practicable—and I hope I need not assure you that no paternal feelings for my own treaty interfered with my wish to have your's accepted, but the objections stated in my dispatch of today are perfectly bona fide.[4] All that Mendizabal says is true to the letter, and I do claim to be some judge of the real state of public opinion here, and of what he should or can do upon commercial matters. Were he to follow the course proposed *I assure you* we should entirely ruin his position and he would never recover it. This would in no way answer to us, for we cannot hope for another *Englishman* at the head of affairs here, and if he lost ground or resigned, every thing would go to *Fidler's Green* in a month, and the Holy Alliance might then come forward with their guarantee. He has pledged himself so often and so publicly to make no loan that he cannot without a mask of some sort have recourse to one. *Advance of duties* is a fiction which will serve his purpose, and he cannot accept the guarantee unless coupled with a commercial treaty.[5] As the one would not go down without the other in the House of Commons, I trust you will not see any fatal objection to their being joined together in order to render the measure possible here as well as at home.[6]

It appears most irregular that I should undertake a counter project to the treaty which I myself had presented, but my position happens at this moment not to be an ordinary one. Mendizabal declares he has unbounded confidence in me, looking upon me as *a partner in the same house with himself*, and that I know how far he can go in meeting the wishes of the English Government—besides he has no time and is unpractised in treaty drawing, he says. I may perhaps therefore succeed in adapting forms now that principles are admitted. In the same way he has promised to adopt the general treaty if after we have collected the information necessary respecting the real state of all these old pending questions no change in it should appear desireable.

It is needless boring you with details upon this and the interests, British as well as Spanish, which it would affect, but I assure you that no Minister of this country be his power what it might—the Principe de la Paz himself—would not [sic] venture at a trait de plume to sign such a treaty without putting it through a certain ordeal of councils and juntas. If he did, a cry would instantly be got up that he had sold his country to foreigners, and that *does* at once and irrecoverably for a Minister here. With the good will and good faith of Mendizabal in these matters we may I believe get what we want, but in this country more than in any other it is necessary to proceed with tact, and cautiously to respect the ignorance and prejudices of the people.

It is now high time to release you and to apologize for having presumed to *set to* with my Chef. I do not think however my Chef will object to the expression of my opinions merely because on a point of practice they may not quite coincide with his own.

By the bye there is one thing which it is right you should know. Mendizabal learned from Rothschild's agent here, before he heard them from me, the terms in which the Spanish Government was to propose the loan to England and France and the readiness of the former to agree to it if a commercial treaty was simultaneously adopted.[7] These were the circumstances.

The courier arrived while the Cortes were sitting. Upon my return home I read your dispatches and immediately went to the Foreign Office. Mendizabal said Rothschild's man had just shewn him a letter from the Paris Rothschild saying that he had received information from his brother in London of the intentions of the English Government,[8] and desiring that, if Mendizabal agreed, a courier should be immediately dispatched to him in order that he might make extensive operations.

Mendizabal told him what was true, that he knew nothing about the matter. The agent came to me next morning to make enquiries and got walked out of my house for his pains. He gave me to understand he should buy largely here, and I suppose he has done so for an article indicating the principal points of the treaty and calculated to send up the funds appeared in one of the newspapers this morning.[9]

This week's discussion in the Cortes has been highly interesting. Mendizabal comes on very much as a speaker and will do very decently. He admits most *ansomely* that my advice respecting the explanations the Cortes had a right to demand before giving him the vote of confidence and which he ought therefore to give, was good, and he has followed it with success. I have several times been up till 3 in the morning with him concocting and *hearing* the speech he was to make the following day.

Received 11 January.

GC/CL/232; Clar. Dep. C.452/2 (1-11)

[1] Of 21 December.
[2] An oath.
[3] V quoted the additional article of the treaty of 13 August 1814 with the Netherlands for the payment of subsidies. 'The consent of Parliament was probably to be asked in some shape or other, but as the fact does not appear in the treaty, I conclude that my deduction of its not being necessary was erroneous.' (V to P, 2 Jan. 1836, no. 1, FO 72/457.)
[4] Mendizábal's objections were: (1) that the British draft treaty proposed more favourable terms for British manufacturers than the first draft; (2) that there was no formal guarantee of a loan; (3) that it would be impossible to secure the approval of the Cortes for the treaty; and (4) that it would be highly unpopular in Catalonia. (V to P, 2 Jan. 1836, no. 1, FO 72/457.)
[5] 'he cannot' to 'treaty' underlined in pencil, possibly by P.
[6] 'render' to 'home' underlined, as n.5.
[7] 'learned' to 'adopted' underlined, as n.5.
[8] 'saying' to 'Government' underlined, as n.5.
[9] 'an article' to 'morning' underlined, as n.5.

179 Villiers to Palmerston, 10 January 1836

Madrid. Private. Short will be my story today, 1st because I have little to say and 2d because I appear to have mistaken the hour at which Rayneval was to send his courier and I have just got a message from him to say he is waiting for my bag.

Nothing more has been done about the treaty for Mendizabal's difficulties are greatly increased. The article put in the newspapers here by Rothschild's man for stockjobbing purposes has alarmed the Catalans who have already asked some very disagreable questions in the Cortes and in private. Mendizabal had reckoned upon such queries being answered by public acclamation when the political advantages of the treaty became simultaneously known, as well as by means he should have taken to purchase silence. An article likewise which appeared in the Morning Chronicle upon the subject and has been copied into the French papers has got him into a scrape with his colleagues to whom he had said nothing about the matter feeling the vast importance of its being kept profoundly secret.

So that we don't at all stand where we did. I have however given him the draft of a note to write to Rayneval and myself proposing the guarantee upon the commercial conditions—he likes its form and he is in somewhat better heart but has not quite made up his mind in what way it will be best to proceed. I have told Rayneval that such a joint proposition to us was upon the tapis but said nothing whatever about the original treaty. All this stockjobbing and newspaper work must however cause suspicion in France and if the thing cannot now be done in a satisfactory way to all parties you will perhaps agree with me that it had better not be done at all.

By the next courier I hope to tell you something decisive, i.e. all that Mendizabal *can* do.

I have had some long talks with little Miraflores who promises me to support the voto de confianza and I have every reason to believe it will pass the Chamber of Proceres as successfully as it did that of the Procuradores.

Not so the election law[1]—upon that there will be great opposition. Mendizabal has got himself foolishly into a scrape about it and is not going the right way to get out of it. More of that however another time.

Pray excuse the great haste in which I write.

PS. Cordoba is pursuing the Fabian system in the provinces and it is answering perfectly. He never loses or fatigues a soldier and the insurgents being kept in inaction are entirely thrown upon the resources of the country and not having lies of victories to tell they are losing greatly in moral strength. Still however they get money.

Louis Philippe's speech has been uncommonly well received here. I hope in *yours* from the throne you will be able to insert something firm and encouraging about Spain. It is astonishing what importance will be attached to it and I should greatly regret our being less cordial than our neighbours. Just about that time too I hope we shall be in want of public opinion here to uphold us upon commercial matters. If you wish to see any more of my valuable MS. I'll beg to refer you to a long prose which I have just been inflicting upon Lord Holland in answer to a kind letter which I had from him last month about the treaty.

Received 21 January.

GC/CL/234; Clar. Dep. C.452/2 (13-16)

[1] 'The plan was to change the procedure for elections to the Cortes from indirect to direct elections based not on property but on the basis of tax paying 300 reals ($£3$-3-0) per annum.' (V to P, 9 Jan. 1836, no. 5, FO 72/457.)

180   Villiers to Palmerston, 16 January 1836

Madrid. Private. Four days ago I received by the common post your letter dated December 17th[1]—the day on which a fortnightly messenger left London. Why he was not the bearer of it I of course cannot tell, but I much regret it, for had it arrived in time some of Mendizabal's scruples and fears might have been overcome. Much of his lukewarmness was occasioned by the idea that you would only act with respect to the treaty as France did. Upon French intentions he knew nothing, he doubted the willingness to guarantee, and feared the exorbitance of the commercial price to be paid for it. In the absence of all information upon these subjects I could of course give no pledge, but had I known as I do now, that you would guarantee whether France did so or no, I think we might have struck while the iron was hot. It is very cool at this moment. Mendizabal is regularly frightened by the mobbing he has got here in consequence of the affair having become partly known, and he thinks in the present state of Catalonia that any measure which would be destructive of the manufactures, or rather smuggling, of that *detestable* province, would be immediately laid hold of there by the Jacobins and turned against the Government to the profit of the *Constitution*.

To a certain degree he is right in this, and rather than run the risk of adding that province to the number of those in open rebellion and perhaps of upsetting his own Government he may not be unwise in waiting awhile till calm is restored and he is somewhat stronger. His desire of concluding a good commercial treaty is as strong as ever, and well whetted as you may suppose by the hope of English guarantee. His apprehensions are in my opinion as exaggerated now as they were too slender at the time we concocted[2] the treaty, and I have accordingly urged him to proceed, but finding it of no use I left him alone as I have done on several occasions before, and shall be at him again when he is in better spirits, and in the mean while shall devote myself to proving according to the information I collect that the treaty you sent me is the one he should adopt.

Mendizabal's position is not quite what it was, even when I last wrote to you, and my predictions during the last 3 months of the scrape he would get into with his election law have unluckily been verified. It was to be the most important measure of the session—the one which the Cortes were assembled to pass and I therefore begged him to devote all the time and attention he could to it, to call to his aid the most able men of the country in order to make as good a law as circumstances would allow of, but to let it be understood that it was *his* law and one which the Government proposed upon their responsibility.

Instead of this he named a commission which inspired a general distrust and set people beforehand against the measure they might propose. They could not agree among themselves and made two reports—both these reports were introduced into the Chamber by the Government which gave no opinion upon either. A commission of the Chamber was then appointed upon them—*they* could not agree either and made 2 or 3 reports. Still the Government gave no opinion, but merely expressed a desire that the discussion should be *muy libre*. Then every body committed themselves according to their passions, or interests, or, what is more important here,[3] their vanity. This got to such a pitch and the whole question was getting into such confusion, that two days ago Mendizabal got up and without much tact or courtesy declared himself against the majority of the commission in which were his own particular friends and indispensable supporters, Galiano and Arguelles, etc., and the next day the commission being beaten by a majority of 2:1 they threw up the conduct of the measure angrily[4] and left it to the Government. The consequence has been that Mendizabal was forced to knock under, to adopt the report of the majority and to shew to the country, what it was not the least necessary should be known, that persons out of the Cabinet and not those in it really form the Government.

I need not add that this has damaged him. Then the want of money paralyses every thing—and Cordoba, even if the extreme severity of the weather permitted it, has neither the funds or supplies necessary for any operations upon a large scale.

In short *we stick*—which is one of the worst state of things that can happen for the people here get tired of a new Minister as a child does of a toy which ceases to amuse it however beautiful or gaudy it may at first have appeared. This fatal war which has already been the grave of three Ministers and three sets of principles may very likely swallow up Mendizabal—he is now at no immeasurable distance from the plight in which Martinez and Toreno found themselves when the Government had lost its moral power and had no physical force to put in its place. Mendizabal does not know this, or[5] would he believe it, or forgive me for telling it to you, but unless he can speedily find great pecuniary means for completing the half-ready resources which he has called into life but not into activity, in order to put an end to the war, the people unreasonable and ungrateful (but not more so here than elsewhere) will become first weary, then angry, and Mendizabal's prestige will be gone. Popular excesses incited by disappointed demagogues who have nothing to expect from the Government will take place in different towns, and the infection will spread as before, but that state of things will be incalculably worse than the former—against *that* there will be no remedy but leaving the Spaniards like the South Americans to cut each other's throats—unfortunately they are a good deal nearer to us than their trans Atlantic brethren, and we cannot, though we wished it, view the strife with indifference.

You will naturally say that my opinions have changed very quickly, but here events and their effects succeed each other with a very different kind of rapidity to other countries. The stagnation of warlike preparations and operations for want of money—the events of Barcelona[6]—Mendizabal's altered position in the Cortes and consequently the diminished power of his Government together with his inability to avail himself of the pecuniary aid of England have within the last fortnight produced a change in the aspect of affairs which, without some unforeseen event happens, may before much longer produce disastrous results. You will perhaps consider these as mere croakings or at all events that I prematurely inflict them upon you, but in the present state of European politics I am so afraid of Spain slipping through our fingers and I feel it would be such an important relief to England and France to have the Spanish question satisfactorily settled that I *make bold* to ask of you to consider whether in a *quiet way* some assistance might not be given to the Queen's cause.

Upon France it must depend more than upon us—the disposition there is now favorable and I think there are many opportunities for giving effect to it. The Carlists upon the coast fire upon the English and French flags whenever they can. This is now to a certain degree retaliated, but if it were followed up by taking possession of any places held by them—if assistance was rendered to the Queen's forces near the frontier—a prodigious moral effect would be produced upon the Carlists. The forces on the southern line of the provinces might then close in more upon the enemy if those to the north could count upon French assistance. The people upon the frontier are disposed now to rise in favor of the Queen. This might be encouraged by France—assistance in arms or supplies might be quietly given them—emigration to France might be encouraged by the French as it is now by the Spanish Government, and France might safely pledge herself that those who placed themselves under her protection should come to no harm at the conclusion of the war. Intervention cannot be asked for by Spain, but it would be gladly, gratefully, received if given in this way. In short should there be a disposition on the part of England and France to proceed in this way there are 100 measures which might be pointed out for *ensuring* (I will venture to affirm) the most complete success.

The war once terminated, the want of money would hardly signify here and all things might go on smoothly—without money (besides the consideration that Spaniard versus Spaniard never can settle *any thing*) I see no other *hostilité activée* against the Carlists on the part of England and France.

A long, false, and offensive article upon the subject of the slave trade signed AntiMetternich appeared in the Times of the 31st ultimo. Thinking that you will have to allude to the treaty in the King's Speech, and that public attention will therefore be drawn to the question, the letter seemed to me worth an answer. I accordingly send one which I think you will consider satisfactory this day to my brother Edward,[7] as you will probably have too many things to do just before the meeting of Parliament to attend to such matters—but should you like to see it or have any directions to give about it pray send a message to him at the Council Office. It is in a shape fit for publication as a leading article in the Chronicle. If he does not hear from you I shall desire him to have it published in any way he thinks best with reference to the effect which AntiMetternich may have produced or any replies which may have been made to his slander.

If any directions have been given for the free admission of Spanish newspapers in England in return for the like privilege which *is now in operation* here will you have the goodness to communicate them to me.

PS. I think you will agree with me respecting the entry of Portuguese troops. Mendizabal will have no reason to rejoice at having them here, i.e. if they feel sufficiently insured against having to smell powder to *come*.[8]

Received 24 January.

GC/CL/235; Clar. Dep. C.452/2 (17-28)

[1] Not traced.

[2] 'contracted' in C.452/2.

[3] 'and elsewhere' added in pencil, possibly by P.

[4] 'entirely' in C.452/2.

[5] 'or' turned into 'nor', possibly by P.

[6] The murder of eighty-five Carlist prisoners by the population of Barcelona in reprisal for the murder of some Cristinos from Barcelona by the Carlists. No attempt was made by the garrison at Barcelona to prevent this. (V to P, 16 Jan. 1836, no. 12, FO 72/457.)

[7] 'I quite agree with you that the Anti-Metternich required an answer and as that was not difficult Southern and I together have drawn up the enclosed. It is in fit shape for a leader in the Chronicle or any other paper except of course the Times. My first intention had been to send it to Palmerston partly out of compliment and partly because he is in communication with the Chronicle, but thinking he would probably be occupied and unmindful I have only written to tell him of it, saying I had sent it to you and that if he wished to see it or give any directions upon the matter he must send you a message accordingly.' (V to Edward Villiers, 16 Jan. 1836, Clar. Dep. C.467 (no enclosure).)

[8] V believed that the Portuguese troops offered to the Spanish Government were reluctant to go to the scene of the war in the North, and wished to remain close to the border. If that were so, they would be of little use to the Queen's cause. (V to P, 16 Jan. 1836, no. 11, FO 72/457.)

181 Villiers to Palmerston, 24 January 1836

Madrid. Private. Your messenger of the 14th is arrived but did not bring me any thing private from you. I have but little to communicate today and that little is not very agreable. You will find it in the dispatch which I have unwillingly written,[1] and had half a mind not to send when I had written it, for I should be sorry that there existed any premature or unnecessary record of mine upon Mendizabal's small knowledge of the art of governing, for he is an honest man with good intentions enough to lay down the whole of Hell with new pavement, but that is not sufficient at a moment like the present, and in a country like Spain, and he is rapidly being swamped by his frankness and his friends. I wrote you nothing public last week upon the general state of things hoping that they might take a better turn, but this not being the case I thought it my duty, naught setting down in malice as you may believe, to advise you of the smash which may now any day occur. Mendizabal's self confidence and occasional happy hits are successful at a moment of revolutionary crisis when it is necessary, in order to lead men, to strike their imaginations with something out of the common way, but the application of these *as a system* to regular government or even to the dispatch of ordinary business must in the long run fail.

There are two measures which I have besought him as his disinterested friend (and he admits I am the only one he has) to adopt—the one to make the electoral law a Government measure, and the other to strengthen his Ministry before his own want of parliamentary practice became apparent, and the business of every department was thrown into confusion. I besought in vain however—he fancied that he was cut out for a debater and *insisted* that *his star* would serve him in that as in every thing else—he believed too that giving a few general orders and dispatching a vast number of couriers would impart all the activity necessary to the five Ministries of which he had taken charge.[2] And with respect to the electoral law he thought it a frank and popular proceeding not to interfere in the discussion of the various reports made by the committees—the question being one upon which the passions and fears and interests of the Chamber were certain to be called into active play, and to want the control which the fear of turning out the Government would have imposed. Every thing I predicted to him two months ago has come to pass with fatal precision—he has latterly become a mere tool in the hands of Arguelles and Galiano[3] whose boundless vanity impelled them to reject every amendment of their own notions, and instead of helping their friend out of his scrape they have day after day been dragging him through the mud. This humiliating position of Mendizabal's together with other circumstances, such as the total wants of funds and to all appearance the means of getting any, the events in Catalonia and the dread of similar horrors in other parts, the torpor which now prevails in every department, and though last perhaps not least, the *highly liberal* friends whom (for *auld lang syne* I suppose, for they have no other discoverable merit) he suffers to swarm about him, all tend to produce the anxiety and distrust which will shortly assume a formidable shape.

Such is the present state of things—however bad it may be there is in Spain always the consolation that worse has been. I have heard nothing from Cordoba since his late actions[4] which in themselves are not much but in their moral effect they will be important and that is the great thing to look for in this cursed war.

Commercial matters, standing business, South American question, etc., etc., every thing is at a dead lock, for Mendizabal does nothing and his employés imitate his example.

January 27th. I little thought when I began this letter that my evil prognostics would so soon be fulfilled—neither had they any business to be so, for this dissolution of the Chamber is a wanton unnecessary act.[5] The smallest foresight upon framing or introducing the law, ever so little management in conducting it through the Chamber, or resolution in compromising the difference which arose in the debate might have prevented this gigantic stride which the revolution has made. Day after day for the last six weeks I have been telling Mendizabal what would happen, but he was completely satisfied with his own parliamentary powers and convinced that *because* he spoke, that he must therefore speak skilfully. I begged of him to strengthen his Ministry before his friends became his enemies and before he had to submit to them as masters instead of inviting them as allies—but he thought (and honestly thought too for there is neither guile or ambition in him—only blindness) that the business of the Cortes and of five Ministries could be better done by one man than by several.

However there is enough of causes—the deed is done, and unfortunate will be the results. You will see by my dispatch that I did my small possible to prevent it, but I was one against many and failed. Mendizabal admitting in his heart that I was right, and though feeling that he was sacrificed to the uncompromising vanity of his friends, yet he was unable to resist their false reasonings and their menaces. He will now take some of them into the Government where they will make use of him as long as they please and then kick him out. The new Cortes will be elected under revolutionary influence—moderate men and men of property will in the true Spanish fashion hide themselves in holes and corners, and a rabble rout will be returned with none of the good sense and desire of union which has distinguished this Cortes during the last two months, and as they will have no interest in order Mendizabal will find them much more unmanageable than those whom he has ejected for supposed factiousness. The only good to be hoped for from the present state of things is that the absence of Cortes during two months will enable the Government to devote itself to the necessities of the country. The first of these is money—whether Mendizabal, who is now all rayonnant with the step he has taken, will be able to get any from abroad remains to be seen. John Bull is *muy* gullable but I doubt his investing as much as a brass farthing here.

I have just returned from the Cortes. The business of the morning has passed off quickly though the announcement of the dissolution was received with tremendous applause by the galleries. Cries of Viva Mendizabal, mueran los Procuradores (of the majority)—the scene was of ugly omen. Rayneval sends off his courier immediately.

Received 5 February.

GC/CL/236; Clar. Dep. C.452/2 (29-34)

[1] 'The state of public opinion here is by no means so favourable as that which I have during the last three months almost invariably had the satisfaction of reporting to Your Lordship.' (V to P, 24 Jan. 1836, no. 16, FO 72/457.)

[2] Foreign Affairs, War, Marine, Finance and the Presidency of the Council of Ministers.

[3] His closest political associates: although not members of the Government, they acted on its behalf in the Cortes.

[4] A skirmish with the Carlists in which the Queen's troops took six hundred prisoners. (V to P, 24 Jan. 1836, no. 14, FO 72/457.)

[5] On 25 January Mendizábal informed the Queen that she must either accept his resignation or dissolve the Cortes. V had advised throughout against either course of action. (V to P, 25 Jan. 1836, no. 17, FO 72/457.)

182   Villiers to Earl Granville, 28 January 1836

Madrid. Private. Mendizabal has just sent me word that he is about to dispatch a courier but has given me but a moment for writing.

Hitherto we have had no row though a very serious one was intended last night. The National Guards known to be disaffected were to have been placed at some of the most important posts, and to have given them up to their companions and the revolutionary leaders who were then to proclaim the Constitution. Want of concert among the leaders however and my timely advice of it to Mendizabal (as I had learned the whole plan and the names of those concerned in the morning) frustrated the intention, and it went off in a charryvarry to Toreno and Martinez—which is a very different operation here from in France, for it is always with murderous objects—no other way being known or *desired* of proving to a man that he is unpopular than by assassinating him. Toreno and Martinez however had both left their houses.

You will observe that the new Cortes are to be called according to the Estatuto Real—the only existing law—the only one by which therefore they can be legally convoked. For this I am fallen into much disgrace with the Exaltados, who consider that it is my doing, and that if it had not been for me Mendizabal could have been got to set aside the Estatuto and convoke a *Constituent Assembly according to the election law of the Constitution.* His friends (or rather I ought to say his bitterest enemies) were working hard for this and I, certainly not wishing to see this last vestige of legality trampled upon and the country offering the shameful spectacle of being given up voluntarily to confusion by its Government, did work hard the other way.

Mendizabal poor man like Frankenstein is trembling before the monster he has created, and adding a new example to the many which are on record that weakness is often worse than wickedness in a public man.

Pray send this on to Palmerston as I have not time for another letter.

GC/CL/237

183   Palmerston to Villiers, 28 January 1836

Foreign Office. A multitude of papers, a long Cabinet and a dozen people to see afterwards prevent me from writing to you more than a few lines. Your answer to Anti-Metternich is excellent, and could not have been better, if you had known who your friend is. I had not seen his letter till yesterday, but I am clear from some passages in it that the writer is a Mr. Mackenzie, late Commissioner of Arbitration under slave trade Acts at the Havanna whom I was obliged to dismiss for discreditable and dishonest conduct towards a General Wavell. Some of your sentences hit him hard.

I have not had time to write you a dispatch about the Barcelona business, but pray urge Mendizabal to take effectual measures for preventing elsewhere a repetition of such atrocities and more especially with regard to the young gentlemen confined at Coruña. As the Spanish Government will not exchange them under the Eliot Convention they are bound to take care they are not murdered.

I wish we could find some money for Mendizabal, but we have no mines in this country, except the House of Commons, and that mine cannot be worked to advantage without the aid of some commercial arrangements.

PS. My unfortunate private letter which reached you by the post ought to have gone by messenger, its straying by post was owing to some accident which of course has now no acknowledged author.

Copy.   GC/CL/1252

184   Villiers to Palmerston, 30 January 1836

Madrid. Private. Owing to a blunder of Mendizabal's who forgot to advise the Corps Diplomatique of what was expected of them today (the Infanta's birthday) I have been obliged to go to the Pardo this evening, which has cost me four hours time and, as you will see, a dispatch. My epistle will therefore be laconic by which you will be the gainer for I have nothing agreable to communicate, except my own agreable surprise at there being no row here, nobody murdered, and no Constitution proclaimed—pleasant intentions which have been entertained, but not executed for want, as far as I can make out, of some spark to set fire to the train, and the whole has gone off in charivaris to Toreno and Martinez who were not 'at home' on the night of their concert. I hope the National Guard, taken as a body, has sufficient property likely to be pillaged in the event of a riot to induce them to keep the peace.

As for poor Mendizabal—da lastima[1]—he is so sorry for what he has done and so frightened for what may come of it, that instead of blaming him for the past I do my best to encourage him about the future, but the embarrassments of his position are really appalling. He told me yesterday that if he had taken my advice about the electoral law, and admitted some of his friends into the Cabinet while they stood well in public opinion, when responsibility would have made them moderate, and before their wounded vanity made them bent upon his downfall, that every thing which has happened might have been avoided. I only mention this as a proof of the state of mind in which he now is for you know what it must cost his self confidence to make such a confession. Some of his *friends* who told him they would not join him unless he dissolved the Cortes now hold back and pretend to fear the responsibility of the vote of confidence which has been given to him. He thinks however he shall be able to form a Government, but I am afraid he must take what he can get rather than what he would like. Galiano is his great embarrassment—he is as much puzzled about him as you have been about Brougham—whether he would do most mischief in or out of the Cabinet, and I believe he has decided the former.

What do you think of Miraflores coming to me the other day to say that there was but one mode of saving the country and that he was prepared to make the necessary sacrifice?

There is something in the *build* of Miraflores very unlike my idea of Quintus Curtius, but I was resolved not to be prejudiced and begged him to state in what way he proposed to devote himself, when to my astonishment he announced that it was by forming a Government with himself at the head and Isturiz at the tail—some $\frac{1}{2}$ a dozen individuals more incapable than himself being the intermediate vertebrae—the whole to be called a Coalition Ministry. I ventured to take one or two objections to the *plot* which he instantly overruled in a manner which appeared quite to satisfy himself, and ended by suggesting that I should propose this coup d'état to the Queen and *to Mendizabal* whose consent, founded upon his incapacity to carry on the Government, was to be first obtained, as the embryo little first Minister would not lend himself to any intrigues and wished to walk into office with his *head erect.* I applauded these latter intentions much, but told him I was not in the habit of Cabinet making—as however there could be no doubt in any man's mind of the patriotism or extent of the sacrifice he proposed to make, I suggested that he should himself go to Mendizabal and submit to him the whole project. He gave me to understand that I was totally incapable of comprehending a great State measure, and there our conversation ended—but the plan had I have every reason to believe, been submitted to and quasi approved by the Queen, *because* Miraflores had assured her that French intervention would only be granted to him [as] First Minister—hence my conversation with Her Majesty this evening[2]—hence too I thought it right to advise Her Majesty not to be intriguing against her Minister, for although I don't think it possible for him to get through his difficulties, yet no good object can be effected by augmenting them so long as there is not a prospect of forming another Government. The Queen could only now chuse between the moderate party who would at this moment be put down by a revolution, or the extreme liberals who are incapable of governing and have against them the antipathy of the country at large.

Received 9 February.   GC/CL/238; Clar. Dep. C.452/2 (35-40)

[1] 'have pity'.
[2] In which the Queen spoke of Mendizábal 'in a tone of some asperity'. (V to P, 30 Jan. 1836, no. 25, FO 72/457.

185   Villiers to Palmerston, 2 February 1836

Madrid. Private. I avail myself of a courier which Mendizabal sends, I don't believe he knows why, to write you a line—though I have nothing to say, which under existing circumstances is good news. Mina's success in Catalonia has come very a propos, but I believe the butchery part of it has caused a more agreable sensation here even than the prospect of its political advantages.[1] I doubt if this people ever *did* fairly emerge from barbarism, but it is certain they are now immeasurably distant from civilization. Mina's savage exploit—first the trick, then the slaughter—has really done Mendizabal good, and as for Mina he is the first of men. I don't think any thing could have put him higher unless he had had a *dead factious* cooked for dinner.

Mendizabal's friends who swore they would only join him in the event of his dissolving the Chamber now prefer to wait awhile, and see if he can sustain himself sufficiently to make it their interest to be his colleagues or his successors, and he is obliged therefore to remain as he was with his several portefeuilles.

I don't see much harm in this, except that no business is done in any department, because the Ministry must be in the same spirit as the Chamber, and until the result of the new elections is known, it is better that he should not select colleagues whom he might have afterwards to dismiss, which would be a sign of weakness—*ergo* a direct invitation to attack. Cordoba has written a very handsome letter to Mendizabal upon the dissolution, attributing the disagreement with the Chamber to the manner in which Mendizabal introduced and conducted the electoral law, but admitting that the preservation of order in Madrid had rendered the measure indispensable, and giving therefore the tone of approbation to the whole army. Mendizabal felt the importance of this and was greatly pleased.[2]

I have had two letters fired at me from opposite ends of Spain by a Mr. Renny and a Mr. Grant who each inform me that they are highly recommended by you and are come out to give me information respecting the treaty which I *am now concluding*—under which circumstances they desire instructions from me as to their moving on upon Madrid. . . .[3]

Received 12 February.

GC/CL/239; Clar. Dep. C.452/2 (41-44)

¹ A Carlist stronghold had been captured by Mina and his troops, and eight hundred Carlist prisoners put to death. (V to P, 2 Feb. 1836, no. 26, FO 72/457.)
² A copy of this letter was enclosed with V to P, 2 Feb. 1836, no. 27, FO 72/457.
³ See no. 188 below.

186 Villiers to Palmerston, 8 February 1836

Madrid. Private. I am very unwell today and not able to write. I shall therefore do nothing more than acknowledge your letter of the 28th.

I have for some time past taken all the charge I could of the 27 Carlist officers imprisoned at Coruña—they were not very safe there (from massacre) and have been removed to Cadiz where harm is less likely to befall them.

My constant theme to Mendizabal is upon measures to prevent the repetition of atrocities like those at Barcelona but his old revolutionary friends are his bane and will be his downfall. His system of purchasing tranquillity by rewarding outrage can only lead to bad consequences.

There are one or two matters upon which I should like to write to you but even if I were able to hold my pen which I am not, I would not do so today for the facciosos are upon the Zaragoza road and what I want to say is certainly not fit for Carlist eyes. My courier who brought the London bag of the 28th was chased and narrowly escaped—so no more at present from/ Yours sincerely,/ George Villiers.

Received 20 February.

GC/CL/240; Clar. Dep. C.452/2 (45-46)

187 Palmerston to Villiers, 11 February 1836

Copy. Foreign Office. Your last accounts are far from cheering, but we must hope that the vicissitudes of Fate may befriend us. I quite agree with you in the extreme impolicy of the dissolution of the Cortes. The point of quarrel with them was too small to require such a measure; and the uncertainty as to the results which the measure might produce was a strong reason against it, except in a case of absolute necessity.

I hope Mendizabal will not supply his want of colleagues by taking in Galiano and Arguelles, for it is to be feared that those men having a steadier aim at their object and knowing better by what means to attain it, will lead him out of the course which he intends to pursue. Nothing can be better than the conduct you have held and the advice you have given. The proposition made to you by Miraflores is admirable; just like my worthy little friend of the Quadruple Treaty. What does Mendizabal mean to do about money, can he get any? If he can, without asking for our guarantee, so much the better.

We are going on well here. . . .

I hope the French will get De Broglie back again and this seems likely.[1]

GC/CL/1253

[1] The Duc de Broglie had resigned. P was anxious for his return to office as he feared that a new Ministry would 'do mischief by shaking confidence in the alliance between us and France and by inspiring the intriguers with fresh hope!' (P to Granville, 9 Feb. 1836, GC/GR/1595.) Broglie was in fact succeeded by Thiers.

188 Palmerston to Villiers, 12 February 1836

Stanhope Street. *Confirms that he has given Renny and Grant letters of introduction, but does not wish Villiers to summon them to Madrid.*
Copy.

GC/CL/1254

189 Villiers to Palmerston, 13 February 1836

Madrid. Private. I am sorry that in return for the flattering Spanish passage in the King's Speech I can send you only a tale of gathering storms. During the last month however I have not left you unprepared for the present state of things. It is useless making to ourselves any illusion. Mendizabal is *no go*. It grieves me to think it, still more so to have to tell it to you, for I have a personal regard for him and know that he has many good—some great—qualities, but I have hardly a hope of his success. His situation is now that of a blind man walking strait to a precipice—one calls to warn him of his danger, when to one's horror one finds him deaf—one throws oneself in his path—one struggles to force him into another direction, but his is the greater power of action, and on he stalks to destruction. His vanity and self confidence which are unlimited, and based I am sorry to say upon no better foundation than ignorance and a lively imagination, prevent his learning the art of government, or understanding that it consists in any thing else than a succession of hits more or less lucky, with the practical execution or ultimate effects of which he, the inventor, has no concern. These same feelings make him not only greedy of glory, but of every scrap of *gloriole* which can be gleaned from off the surface of affairs, and in order to have the popularity of some two or three striking measures (or rather *decrees,* for in that abortive shape they usually wither and die) in each Department of the State, he monopolizes four Ministries and retains Noodle and Doodle for colleagues—ignorant that action is paralyzed and discontent is loud and just. I was with him nearly five hours last night, and much of the time was spent in endeavouring to fix his attention to his real position. I left him with his mind *grazed* by the truth, but it did not go deep enough to inspire me with any confidence that he would gird up his loins and proceed to battle either with a knowledge of his weapons or with that determination to conquer which is half way to victory.

One of the subjects—and a sad one it is—upon which I intended to write to you by the last courier, but was restrained by the fear of my letter being intercepted, is the English Legion. It has fallen into disorder and disrepute. The Government was originally in fault for not keeping its engagements, but this, though it may palliate, does not justify the total absence of discipline which prevailed almost immediately after their arrival at Vitoria. The clothing which they brought with them has nearly disappeared and the men are in rags—upward of 1,200 are in the hospital, many in consequence of hardship and the neglect of those charged by the Government to provide for them, but the greater part owing to their own excesses. Then the expence is tremendous,[1] whether from bad management or in accordance with original agreements I know not, but the contractors charge the Government with 10,000 rations daily while Evans hardly brings 5,000 men into the field. The pay, allowances, etc., are far greater than those of the Spanish army or the French corps, and this joined with their inefficiency has created much jealousy which the conduct of the Legion does not tend to diminish. Some time since a regiment either quartered in or marching through a friendly village maltreated the inhabitants (I fear killed a good many), desecrated the church, and robbed the plate, and the ornaments of the images. Evans subsequently sent for

373

the cura and made him give an account of damages which he paid.

Evans himself seems to be mild and indolent—an excellent honorable gentleman and in the field an intrepid officer, but no disciplinarian and wanting the energy—perhaps too the knowledge—necessary for making raw officers do their duty, and keeping in subjection many hundreds of men—not the very cream of society in Westminster. A very good officer, an Englishman, and a colonel in the Spanish service whom Evans has asked for is now going down to the Legion, and from him and some new Commissariat arrangements I hope for better things—but they are now in such a state that some severe examples among both officers and men appear to be necessary.

I have not mentioned this subject before because I hoped that the excitement of service might have improved the health and the morals of the Legion—but it was not so. I heard (though only from an inhabitant of Vitoria) that they have 800 baggage mules and 500 whores moving about with them, which must be pleasant but is not cheap.

Quintus Curtius Marquis of Miraflores has been *at* me again about saving the country, and I have again balked his patriotic ardor by asking him if his Government was to be based upon foreign intervention—he replied unquestionably, and that he would only devote himself to the infernal gods upon that condition. I then begged him to suspend awhile the sacrifice as I had lately heard from Lord Granville that *under no circumstances* would Louis Philippe allow a French soldier to cross the Pyrenees—this bit of authentic information I added that I had communicated to only one person and that person was the Queen. This was a blow in the wind that doubled up the little patriot, and he declared he should not come to the scratch again.

Much I fear that under *some* circumstances sooner or later Louis Philippe must depart from his resolution and that we shall all live to repent the non-adoption of a measure which eight months ago was insignificant, and of which the success was as certain as can be predicated of any event before it has taken place.

I hope you will send me a strong instruction with respect to the Captain General of Cuba's keeping the slave treaty in his pocket instead of publishing and executing it. . . .

Pray let me ask you again if any orders have been issued for the free admission of Spanish newspapers into England in return for the system now in operation here.

I enclose you an article from the leading journal of Catalonia as a specimen of the state of opinion which has been created in that province by premature discussion upon the Commercial Treaty.[2] Now that all chance of concluding one is over, for long before Mendizabal thinks the time for it is come he will himself be swept away and no more thought of, I must in all good humor express the great disappointment I have felt at the manner in which this important matter was treated in the Mother Country. Upon my original attempt I will say nothing, for I must have already bored you through and through about it though as you never answered any of my arguments I have seen no cause for changing my opinions, but it was the unnecessary publication of it in England, the announcement of it to the people here by Rothschild's Jewboy, the talking sine-tact Rennie and Grant that I regret en el alma, not on account of the past—let byegones be byegones—but because all this has incalculably augmented the difficulties of the future. I will however not be disheartened but do my best to repair the mischief.

PS. I send you the Gazette of today with the official article upon the King's Speech. Mendizabal was very grateful to you for the Spanish passage.

Enclosure: Gaceta de Madrid, *13 February 1836.*

Received 22 February.

GC/CL/241; Clar. Dep. C.452/2 (47-55)

[1] On 15 February Evans suggested to V that the best way to provide for the cost of the Legion would be to link it with the commercial negotiations then pending between England and Spain. (Evans to V, 15 Feb. 1836, Clar. Dep. C.460.)

[2] Enclosed in V to P, 13 Feb. 1836, no. 34, FO 72/457.

190   Villiers to Palmerston, 22 February 1836

Madrid. Private. I have received your letter of the 11th instant which was most welcome as it contained the news that you are strong and shall stand your ground against the formidable minority opposed to you. . . .

The general feeling of the House seems good upon foreign politics, but there are one or two passages in the King's and your speeches with reference to approbation of the Spanish Government, and to naval preparations which I look upon as argumentum ad Imperatorem, which stimulate me to offer you a few remarks upon the condition and prospects of this country.

You know my opinion of foreign intervention, and if I recur to arguments which I formerly used upon this question, it is only for the sake of drawing some deductions which may be useful for the future. If ten months ago England and France had jointly intervened *against Don Carlos,* tranquillity would at once have been restored here, and we should at once have reaped the moral fruit of our alliance with France, 1st by shewing that that must be done which we both chose to do, and 2dly that our interests were so identified that we could now meet for a common purpose upon the very field where we had for ages been giving each other battle. We should thus have gained a great moral victory of that kind which decides the fate of empires, for would Russia have dared to undertake any great enterprize seeing that England and France had buried their ancient rivalries in oblivion, and were sincerely making common cause to carry into effect the policy they had marked out for themselves? The obviousness of our common interests in settling the Spanish question or the ease and success with which it might some time since have been accomplished would not have been taken into consideration. The results and the moral effect would alone have been permanent—they might have given a different turn to the politics of Europe, and prevented those questions springing up which may hereafter put to a disastrous proof the sincerity of the Anglo-French alliance.

The reverse of all this must now have taken place, for Russia, long sighted and drawing accurate deductions from all that passes around her, must perceive that either from misunderstanding between ourselves, or embarrassments, whether political or financial, at home, we cannot effect that which we have publicly pledged ourselves to, or bring about the combination which should be a main feature in our new system of policy. She must accordingly look upon [us] as feeble for any operations in the East where every circumstance of difficulty which has prevented our taking a decided part in the Peninsula must be indefinitely multiplied—distance, expence, geographical position, are insignificant considerations with reference to Spain and to a task which we had sous la main, compared to what we should find them in the East.

The position of France as regards England should likewise be taken into serious account. Her alliance with us is founded upon no very solid or eternal basis—we are not *necessary* to the existence of each other—upon matters of commerce and national prosperity our interests are looked upon in both countries as rival—add to which the old national feuds are, on the part of France, rather slumbering than extinct, and may with facility be roused. The Alliance has hitherto been maintained upon the consideration that we were *politically* necessary to each other, and this is a consideration which may any day be changed, and we therefore any day left in the lurch either to wage a war single-handed against the most powerful nations of Europe, or dishonorably to retire from the contest, admitting our weakness or inability to continue[1] it. As the strength of England consists therefore in a great measure not only in what she may be able to effect conjointly with France, but in the conviction that other Powers may have, that wherever she is engaged France will neither be neutral or hostile, nothing should in my humble opinion be neglected for nailing France[2] to the system of the Western Confederation, and by committing her irretrievably and upon every occasion against the Northern Powers, secure her being actively interested in that which *must*, whether we will or no, be our policy.

This would have been effected had she been stimulated and *poked* into an intervention in which we had joined, and even if she had not honestly adopted our policy afterwards we should have avoided this exhibition of moral weakness, and have found in Spain a convenient, perhaps a powerful ally, whether in cooperation with France or as a check upon her—while if France were really with us it was most important to heal the sore which is now festering in her flank and which must paralyze her operations elsewhere.

But supposing, as has been said, that Louis Philippe regretting the ancient hold that France had over this country is desirous of marrying one of his daughters to Don Carlos's son, and that he therefore secretly wishes ill to the Queen's cause, we may arrive at an irreparable schism in our relations, for our efforts here will have been baffled and our national interests and feelings wounded. Who can pretend to say either that in consequence of the sinking state of the Queen's Government the cause of Don Carlos may not advance, that he may not take Vitoria or Burgos and then be recognized by the Northern Powers? Who will claim to exercise the same right in assisting him as we do in favor of the Queen? What will be our position then? Shall we retire from our ally because the danger which threatened her is more imminent, or shall we entamer une guerre sourde with the Holy Allies, or intervene then with every description of difficulty increased, and leaving to Don Carlos, even were he driven out of the country, the moral force of having been recognized, and of possessing powerful friends compromised in his cause whose support he will always be invoking, and through whose means he will be able to keep up a focus of rebellion in the Peninsula which will for years demand our anxious care and supervision?

These questions are grave not so much perhaps in themselves as with reference to our alliance with France, the general state of politics in Europe, and the threatening aspect of affairs in the East. It is for these reasons and because you may any day be called upon to take a definitive decision that I have inflicted upon you this treatise. Rely upon it that the contest here will never finish unless by the application of force *from without*. Spaniards against Spaniards are incapable of finishing any thing—much less a civil war. There is no use in waiting for circumstances or the vicissitudes of fate to befriend us—we have done so for $2\frac{1}{2}$ years, and things have got worse and will get worse still. Upon the score of humanity (as in the case of the Greeks) to which the British public is sensibly alive—and well it may be God knows—and *against Don Carlos*, it is yet time to take a decided part, but this time will be of short duration, for the Exaltados are rapidly getting possession of power, and no sooner will they have acquired it than they will infallibly plunge the country into revolution. To them intervention and the re-establishment of order would be destruction—they would appeal to national prejudices and the Jacobinical part of the community— the measure would then appear contrary to the national will—directed more against the *liberties* (!) of the country than the Pretender, and become impossible either for France or for ourselves.

Mendizabal during the short period that he may be expected to remain at the head of the Government cannot ask for intervention—he is too deeply pledged against it though in his heart he may admit its necessity—but it would not be indispensable to wait for the asking of the Spanish Government. Let but England and France announce their determination to support the Queen and the liberties of Spain and their readiness to *cooperate* in stopping the effusion of blood. Let British men of war protect San Sebastian's, Portugalete and the coast, openly, avowedly protect them.[3] Let Harispe *upon the demand of the Spanish general* lend 2 or 5 or 10 thousand troops to protect the Bastan and the other great vallies upon the frontier *which are ready to rise* in favor of the Queen the moment they feel secure of not being abandoned.[4] Let this be done and above all let the moral effect be produced upon the Carlists of knowing that England and France *intend the war should cease*—and *it will cease*. I would answer for it with my head. It is the only mode, except a large supply of money, by which we can save Mendizabal and avert that chaotic state of things which was about to come to pass in September last from whence difficulties may spring of which no man can calculate the magnitude or extent. It may not suit France—any more than it did 10 months ago—to take an active part in settling this question, but I beg of you to believe that danger of every description is more imminent than then, and that before a similar determination is again come to, the many bearings of the question require to be most maturely weighed.

Before I go any further I must beg of you to attribute to my zeal, and therefore to excuse, my thus venturing to offer suggestions to my Chef.

In answer to a question in your letter, Mendizabal can*not* get money without our guarantee, but he dares not make the treaty upon which alone we could help him. He and I had again resumed the subject and even had *drafted* another treaty—but his accounts of the state of opinion in Catalonia upon the subject have again obliged him multa gemens to abandon it. He gravely proposed that we should guarantee two millions in return for Spain's recognizing the South American independence (upon which he has behaved wretchedly as I shall narrate to you by the next courier)[5] but I told him we would not guarantee him two pence for that which it was the interest of Spain not to lose another day in doing.

He is mobbed on all sides poor man and I much fear he will not hold out till the meeting of the Cortes.

Received 3 March.

GC/CL/242; Clar. Dep. C.452/2 (55-62)

[1] 'which may any day' to 'continue' underlined, possibly by P.
[2] 'but in the conviction' to 'France' underlined, as n.1.
[3] 'Let' to 'them' underlined, as n.1.
[4] 'lend' to 'abandoned' underlined, as n.1.
[5] V to P, 27 Feb. 1836, no. 46, FO 72/457.

191 Palmerston to Villiers, [25 February 1836][1]

Your last accounts of the 13th instant are certainly not very encouraging, but I hope things will go on better than they then appeared likely to do.

Alava says at Paris that the Catalonian Carlists have been defeated with the loss of 600 men. That is something, if true. By the by did not Cordova play Evans a foul trick in leaving him after the advanced movement from Vittoria, without informing him that the Spanish troops were retreating? It seemed to us from the account we had of that operation that it was no thanks to Cordova that our people were not surrounded and cut off.

Mendizabal is certainly not exactly what a Prime Minister of a great country ought to be, but he is at present nearly the last chance Spain has left, and we ought therefore to do all in our power to support him. I have written to him to say that we wish he could point out to us anything we could do to help him, that as to money it would be very difficult to Parliament to guarantee a loan, unless it was accompanied by some considerable commercial relaxations; but perhaps a complete treaty might not be absolutely necessary.

I see you have not forgiven us for not adopting the treaty you sent, but we had as I told you at the time two insurmountable objections to it, the one that it was a measure to be taken in secret without previous communication with France, the other that the King could not take the engagement to guarantee the loan, but could only undertake to recommend to Parliament to empower him to do so. These two objections were not removed by the explanations and answers to them which you gave and therefore we could not ratify.

Your account of Miraflores amazes me; poor little man; nature did not destine him for an Atlas, however ready he is to offer his shoulders to support his country.

The Government here is getting stronger daily and we consider ourselves pretty sure of getting through the session.

I suspect that the change of Government in France will not make any essential difference in the foreign policy of Louis Philippe, it is a change of instruments and not of the directing will; at the same time we have lost the honestest man in France and in his room, we have got—Thiers! We must endeavour however to make the most of what we have.

Copy.

GC/CL/1257

[1] Docketed 'March 1836', but clearly the letter of 25 February to which V's letter of 7 March (no. 194 below) is a reply.

192   Villiers to Palmerston, 27 February 1836

Madrid. Private. There is of course but little change in things since I wrote to you five days ago, except perhaps that Mendizabal's downward progress has been arrested by the decree for the sale of national property which I sent you on the 22nd instant.[1] Among other things that it has been worth to him is the being elected Procurador for Madrid, which he assuredly would not have been at the beginning of last week, and I think I gave him good advice when I recommended him to put forth some bold and striking measures without waiting for the Cortes being assembled. He is trying to be elected for several provinces in which, vû the means at command of the Government for influencing so small a body of electors, he will probably succeed, but this will be a very fallacious proof either of popularity or strength, and unless some unforeseen event (that constant remedy for disasters in Spain) occurs, I have no idea that he can maintain himself. Too much has in fact been expected from him, or rather too much faith has been placed in the expectations which he himself raised. People forgot that his knowledge and experience were culled in the Stock Exchange; and that he was likely to apply the system which had been successful to him there to the government of his country. On the Stock Exchange lies and great promises fail or are successful, but they are forgotten in 4 and 20 hours. When a Prime Minister adopts such a system and makes time bargains with the nation, he must turn out, as poor Mendizabal will, a lame duck which is even less graceful in a statesman than a stock-jobber.

From what is hitherto known the new Cortes promise to be *muy calientes,* and greatly will Mendizabal regret having dissolved their predecessors among the majority of whom good sense, good will, and great fear were so nicely distributed that with tolerable management contending parties might have been kept down and the Government have scrambled on between them for a considerable time.

In order to render the state of things here complete, the dii superi seem to have united with the infernal ones (to whose special charge the management of Spanish affairs is usually left) and so severe a winter has never been remembered. Cordoba is as much snowed up as if he was in Siberia, and Evans reports that his men who were getting more healthy are again filling the hospitals. The British Legion is a melancholy subject upon which I hardly like to write, but from several persons who have lately returned from Vitoria I have had but too certain information of its want of discipline and its inefficiency. Evans too appears to have embarked in an undertaking which has turned out greater than he expected or is quite equal to, and at times he sinks into a state of desponding apathy. The Government was at first greatly in fault for having neglected the Legion as it did—they would more than once have absolutely perished if Cordoba had not made himself personally responsible for some money he raised for them. This hardly justifies however the disorders which were committed—the men selling their clothes, etc., etc., in short every evil which want of discipline can produce. Then Evans's high Spanish rank is an embarrassment—he ought to command every other general now in Navarre, but he is unacquainted with the language and above all with the country—this latter is matter of life and death to the troops in movement—and of course therefore he inspires no confidence. Then the higher pay of the Legion over the Spanish army and the French Legion (which by all accounts is one of the finest and best equipped corps of veterans ever seen)[2] creates jealousy particularly when this vast expence is coupled with their inefficiency. Upon the whole it is a miserable mess and the English name has sadly lost its prestigio. Was this horrible war like any other and was there a prospect of any fair fighting I have no doubt that the Legion would still distinguish itself above either Spaniards or French—but waiting in villages, expecting ambushes, long and harrassing marches after an enemy who flies or disperses at your approach, and at best a little brisk fighting are what regular troops have to undergo and all they must expect.

Evans complains bitterly of Cordoba, with how much or little reason I don't pretend to say. When the Legion first came to Vitoria Cordoba wrote to me in terms of high praise of its appearance, and he was *in raptures* with Evans himself. Since that time he has never mentioned either to me, but I know from the Minister of War that he was exceedingly annoyed at the want of discipline which he (the Minister of War) said was but too true and upon which he had in a friendly manner remonstrated with Evans. I hope however that some improvement will now take place. Evans has been reinforced with Spanish troops—his wants are better attended to—he has drafted some of his bad officers and men and incorporated some regiments which will diminish the expence. We have sent down to him La Saussaye, an Englishman and a colonel in the Spanish service who is an excellent officer and will help to reorganize the Legion, and when the severity of the winter is over I hope things will go better with them, but I still come back to my old refrain—without the exhibition of force *from without* the Spanish question will never be terminated.

The Queen Regent sent me a strange message the other day by Mendizabal—that she should be much obliged to me to get her brother and Miss Penelope to *marcharse* from Spain[3]. . . .

As public attention in England seems much directed to Spanish atrocities and that the subject may again be reverted to in Parliament I have thought it well to send you a dispatch in answer to your's upon the Barcelona massacres although it contains nothing that I have not already told you.[4]

Received 7 March.

GC/CL/244; Clar. Dep. C.452/2 (63-70)

[1] i.e. the property seized by suppressing the monastic orders and curtailing religious establishments. (Enclosed in V to P, 22 Feb. 1836, no. 35, FO 72/457.)
[2] See Evans to V, 14 Feb. 1836, Clar. Dep. C.460.
[3] Her brother, the Prince of Capua, had eloped to Spain with Miss Penelope Smyth.
[4] V to P, 27 Feb. 1836, no. 45, FO 72/457.

193 Villiers to Palmerston, 27 February 1836

Madrid. Private. Although I know not how you are disposed towards the commercial-cum-guarantee treaty question *in the only manner* (namely that of advance upon customs duties and therefore uniting together the two objects) which Mendizabal can make it, because you have never said one word to me upon the matter since I ventured to re-submit the matter to the consideration of His Majesty's Government, still I am unwilling to be disheartened or to let a subject so very important to England and to Spain drop so long as I see a prospect of success.

This is now the present state of things. Three times a week, but more commonly six, I bate Mendizabal upon a commercial treaty. The general one involving rights, privileges, interests, etc., as well as questions of law and practice we could not get under the most favorable circumstances in less than 3 or 4 months. The subject must go its round of juntas, informes, y expedientes—no hay remedio[1]—you might as well ask a Spaniard to forgive an injury as to dispatch business in any other mode. Mendizabal however wants money, and to get that he would make, as before, a partial treaty, but at the same time he wants courage, and has a mortal and well grounded fear of the Catalans—accès of valor come to him every now and then, and in one of these I shall some day catch him and make him sign if I have reason to expect your approval.

It is with this object and in order to save time when delay may be mischievous, that I now enclose to you the drafts of two conventions[2] to which Mendizabal may without damaging himself too much accede. I have made two conventions instead of one thinking it more likely to meet your wishes.

If you decide that the guarantee and the cottons shall not be mixed together there is an end of the matter for Mendizabal cannot make a loan—he says he *will stand loading* his pledge but not breaking it, and he will therefore accept an advance.

If you do *not* object, have the goodness to return me the drafts with the amendments and alterations that will make the conventions possible in England with reference to the House of Commons, and to France perhaps with reference to the latter you might chuse to omit the cottons 'being the genuine productions of Great Britain and Ireland'. Things may get so much worse here that Mendizabal may find it impossible to do any thing of the kind, but they may improve and then it would be important to me to know what His Majesty's Government opine in order to nail him.

Mendizabal would conclude a treaty tomorrow stipulating one thing which he has begged me to submit to your consideration—the keeping it secret for two months. He says he should only then communicate it to one house in London which upon the knowledge of the treaty being signed would furnish him all the money he requires—with this he should be able to carry on the war with an energy not hitherto attempted and at the same time give strength to his Government, while he should be buying a few of the principal manufacturers in Catalonia

384

and preparing public opinion in the province. Then at the expiration of the two months, he should be like a giant refreshed and proud to publish the treaty—for its political importance would be acknowledged by the whole of Spain and its commercial advantages by $\frac{3}{4}$ths of the country—the grumbling fraction he should then be strong enough to keep never minding.

Pray tell me what you think of the possibility of this scheme.

PS. I was going to have written to Poulett Thomson but as I would only say the same things I will beg of you to shew him this letter.

Received 7 March.

GC/CL/243; Clar. Dep. C.452/2 (71-74)

[1] 'juntas, reports and documents—there is no remedy'.
[2] The first dealt with the British guarantee for a loan, and the second with the lowering of import duties on British cotton goods. (Enclosed in V to P, 27 Feb. 1836, no. 48, FO 72/457.)

194 Villiers to Palmerston, 7 March 1836

Madrid. Private. I have received your letter of the 25th ultimo and I wish that in answer I could confirm your hopes that things would go better. They go very badly and will go worse—be assured of that. How far an out and out, rights-of-man Cortes, then the reign of unlicensed liberalism, then that of Don Carlos as the lesser despotism of the two, may suit England and more particularly France I cannot say—it is for them to judge—but this is the course we are now steering, and *within* the Peninsula I see no means of putting about—scarcely even of tacking. Diplomacy and good wishes and good advice may smooth difficulties in the way of ulterior measures, but they cannot guide political events, or do I believe that any other mode of doing so has been discovered than plenty of men and plenty of money. Both are wanting here—25 or 30,000 more troops are necessary to occupy the insurgent provinces. Recruits are raised it is true, but there is no money for equipping them and instead of at once being poured into Navarre and making a grand final operation, they will like former levies join their regiments by driblets, not doing much more than supply the average losses of the campaign, and serve to prolong but not to terminate the war. In the mean while the Exaltados will be to Don Carlos like Zumalacarregui redivivus and do more than that general to open the road to the throne and the Inquisition.

A few days since I wrote to Lord Granville that there were hopes of getting Isturiz into the Ministry and forming a strong Government which might make head against contending parties, but these hopes have vanished into thin air. Isturiz has been over-persuaded by his friends as well as alarmed by the probable ultra-ism of the newly elected Deputies, and he has now declined having any thing to do with the Government upon any terms whatever. Mendizabal intends therefore to meet the Cortes with his present inefficient colleagues and I expect that they will be all bowled down like ninepins within a short time. These Cortes are avowedly called for no other purpose than to pass an election law, but as no law could give them more radical returns than the late elections, where they have paid no attention to *any* law, they will probably have a fancy for making themselves a Constituent Assembly, or else the Government to avert such a step will give them the 'Estatuto Real' to *mouzle,* from which operation it will infallibly come forth the Constitution of 1812.

But I won't go on boring you with all the pleasing prospects I *have in my eye.* I have talked them over unreservedly with Mendizabal who does not agree with me, and begged I would tell you that he does not see things as blackly as I do—he thinks he shall manage the Cortes and keep within the pale of legality. I sincerely hope that these predictions of mine may turn out as mistaken as all those which I have hitherto made to him have proved true.

He is very grateful for your letter and says that *the* way of serving him in his principal embarrassment—want of money—would be to make the cotton and guarantee treaty and allow it to remain a secret for two months, till the money had given him sufficient strength to disregard the Catalonian uproar. I have not held out to him any expectation of your compliance, but unless he can find money he must be swept away and with him will go as you justly say nearly the last chance Spain has left.

Being once more upon this everlasting treaty topic you must allow me to make a remark upon a passage in your letter with respect to the two insurmountable objections to the treaty I sent. You say that it was a measure to be taken in secret without previous communication with France and without her being a party to it. Surely that was guarded against at the time. Did not Mendizabal give me a solemn promise that he would conclude a similar treaty with France, with similar advantages, and upon similar terms? There was nothing therefore to have prevented a free communication with France and, if she had been willing, the two treaties being signed on the same day. So far was it from being intended to keep the matter secret from France that, if you remember, I wrote a special dispatch upon the subject with the object of its being communicated to the Duc de Broglie *before* the English Government took any step in the matter, and how much less attention was shewn to France in the treaty which was returned to me, and which settled at once and in our favor many of those international questions which are of more importance to her than to us or even than commercial advantages.

The *concurrence* of France was not looked upon as indispensable as you told me that you would conclude the treaty whether France did so or no—neither was the fact of the treaty not being a general one an insuperable objection as the same reasons which then applied would be valid now when you say that it is not absolutely necessary.

With respect to the King's undertaking to recommend to Parliament to empower him to guarantee the loan, I took the liberty of offering one or two precedents upon a much larger scale where that recommendation had not been resorted to. And the King had guaranteed and *given* large sums of money without there being a question of Parliament. But granting that it was indispensable and that you had made that amendment in the treaty, Mendizabal would have had no difficulty in adopting it and he could have easily afforded to wait till the meeting of Parliament if he had then been certain[1] of getting the money. That however and every thing else of the kind was rendered impossible by Mr. Rothschild.

If there has been any thing in the tone of my letters upon this subject which makes you say I have not *forgiven* the unadoption of my treaty it was certainly unintentional and I pray you to excuse it—any feeling approaching to *resentment* would have merely been to make myself ridiculous. I take the affairs of Spain warmly to heart, and I regretted that a moment which will never return was not availed of for (perhaps) saving the country by making the Government strong and enabling it to carry on the war with necessary vigor.

As the English public seem to take an interest in Spanish affairs and that you are *therefore likely to be attacked* for Mina's ferocity I made a great row with Mendizabal and Almodovar about his shooting the mother of the Carlist chief, not that I had any idea that he would be punished or even reproved, but in order to shew in England that your opinion had been pronounced upon the act, and that you always endeavoured to confine the war within the bounds of *ordinary* barbarity.[2] It had not been the intention, *evidently*, of either of the above Ministers to take any step upon the subject if I had not remonstrated, and it was only by returning to the charge on three successive days that they did what they have done, which is a solemn farce but may perhaps not be understood so in England.

I have always been watchful over the security of the 27 Carlist prisoners and both at Coruña and Cadiz, through the Government, the local authorities, and the British consuls I have endeavoured to mitigate their sufferings. They were to sail on the 3d instant for Puerto Rico and the Governor of Cadiz has taken every precaution for their being treated as officers and gentlemen—their female relatives being allowed to accompany them. The prisoners themselves have expressed their satisfaction at being thus removed, as they felt their lives were always in danger from popular violence so long as they continued in Spain.

Colonel Wylde and General McDougall have arrived here in order to lay before the Government a detailed report of the miserable and inefficient state of the Legion in consequence of the neglect with which they have been treated and the violation of every engagement by which the Government, and the authorities upon whom they are dependent, were bound.

We had a conference of nearly four hours with Mendizabal but as yet nothing satisfactory is settled—the grand question being arrears of pay and Mendizabal having no money.[3] Some arrangement however must be come to or the Legion will be dissolved or mutiny and then pass over to Don Carlos who McDougall tells me offers, and *pays*, £30 to each English deserter. I am very glad these two gentlemen have come as the weight of their eye-witness testimony is of service to me in my remonstrances.

Mendizabal is a strange man—he really loves Evans and has a paternal affection for the Legion, but I have never been able fairly to fix his attention to the subject of their distresses or to make him believe that disgraceful inefficiency would be the consequence of his neglect. Even now I am by no means sure that he will do that which will satisfy Evans.

Evans sent me a copy of the letter he wrote to Mendizabal by

General McDougall and I herewith enclose a copy of it to you.[4]

You asked me whether Cordoba did not commit a foul treachery towards Evans by leaving him to find out that the Spanish troops had returned to Vitoria after the action of Arlaban, and as I did not consider myself a competent judge of the question I requested Wylde, who was upon the spot and whose testimony cannot be doubted, to give me his opinion in writing upon it. I enclose you a copy of his letter by which you will see that Cordoba was not to blame.[5] Evans is very furious upon the subject, Wylde says, and is quite certain he was thrown over, but that does not alter facts, and as he never saw or heard of an insurgent at the time he thought he should be cut to pieces, Cordoba's confidence that he would not do so appears to have been justified.

PS. I enclose you a copy of the private letter I wrote to Mendizabal upon forwarding to him the statement of McDougall and Wylde.[6]

Received 17 March.

GC/CL/245; Clar. Dep. C.452/2 (75-84)

[1] 'if' and 'certain' double-underlined, possibly by P.
[2] Mina ordered the execution by firing squad of Cabrera's mother who was over seventy. The Carlists retaliated by shooting the wife of a colonel in the Queen's service and the wives of three other officers. (V to P, 7 Mar. 1836, no. 51, FO 72/458.)
[3] For an account of this meeting, see V to P, 7 Mar. 1836, no. 53, FO 72/458.
[4] In this letter Evans threatened to resign. (Copy, Evans to Mendizábal, 29 Feb. 1836, enclosed in V to P, ibid.)
[5] Wylde to V, 6 Mar. 1836 (private), enclosed in V to P, ibid.
[6] V wrote 'not officially but as between friends'. He informed Mendizábal that the question of pay for the Legion 'is a very serious one, more so than I at first thought, and I do assure you it must be promptly and satisfactorily dealt with'. (Copy, V to Mendizábal, 7 Mar. 1836, enclosed in V to P, ibid.)

195 Palmerston to Villiers, 10 March 1836

Foreign Office. I brought yesterday before the Cabinet your last plan for a guarantee and a sort of commercial arrangement. Difficulties were felt about the guarantee and doubts whether it could be carried through Parliament. I fear we shall hardly find our courage up to the mark. My own belief is that we should carry it, at the same time the matter is not clear.

I must try now the other plan and see whether we cannot contrive to have the French cordon advanced as you suggest, a little way into Spain, so as to protect the frontier valleys, and to help to squeeze the Carlists into a still narrower space than that in which they are at present shut up. I think that at the same time we might give our ships on the coast orders to take an active part in defending sea ports, or in helping to recover them, and we might even authorize the landing of seamen and Marines to hold any post which the Spanish generals wished us to occupy, provided it was within reach of the shipping. I shall bring this arrangement more practically under the consideration of the Government, in the shape of instructions and dispatches, and I do not despair of carrying it. This would do something both with reference to the military operations, and also with reference to Mendizabal's finance.

I am convinced that in spite of all disclaimers Louis Philippe would be delighted to march even a corporal's guard into Spain.

I hope you will have succeeded in forming the new Spanish Cabinet, and that thus reinfused Mendizabal will be able to go on. I have written him a strong letter about the murder of Cabrera's mother. Mina ought to be dismissed. It's no use talking of his influence and power—a man who commits such atrocities cannot do good to any cause.

You see we grow stronger in the House of Commons as we go on. The Tories and their friends in high quarters are sorely disappointed and mortified at the last division.

Copy.

GC/CL/1255

196 Villiers to Palmerston, 12 March 1836

Madrid. Private. It is nauseous work sitting down once a week to tell you the number of steps we have made in the descensus Averni and I am inclined to send you no more extracts from my log till we have got to the bottom, where, as falling bodies descend with an increasing velocity, we shall speedily arrive—however here goes for another melancholy MS. To the curious in *black-letters* my correspondence would be valuable.

Mendizabal did quite right in summoning Rayneval and me to hear his difficulties and his resolves,[1] and you would do quite wrong if you believed that he has any means of meeting the one or of executing the other. Events will be too powerful for him even if he had double the skill and tact he is deficient in, and the day he dissolved the Cortes he let his last chance of governing the country slip through his fingers. *Now* I don't know what he will do for his friends, the press, and the funds are all against him and I see neither hope nor help for him, for such resources as he could command are either exhausted or have failed. It is melancholy to see him catching at such straws as Batanero's entering Castile with a few factious and the fall of a couple of little fortified places in the North, not for the purpose of saving himself but in order to account for his *going to be drowned.*

Isturiz and Co. will have nothing to do with him because they think they should have to share his unpopularity as well as his responsibility, and because they see that his cheval de bataille—finance—has completely broken down under him, and that as he has no means for carrying on the war, *civil* or *political,* he would be to them both a dangerous and useless colleague. He may *meet* the Cortes with his present colleagues but if he is able to maintain himself and carry on the Government, why, the age of miracles is not over. I fear too he has not availed himself of the recess to prepare any measures though I have worried him like a schoolboy to get forward with his holiday task.

In one thing which he said to Rayneval and me I am inclined to agree with him. Money might save things yet, for the want of it prevents the recruits joining their corps and proceeding to the occupation of the country—the *only* way of finishing the war. That done or in fair progress, public credit and confidence would quickly revive, money would bring money, and the Government would recover substance—it is now barely a shadow—but then where this money is to come from the Mighty only knows. France of course would not guarantee a centime and even if you were inclined to do so upon such commercial terms as Mendizabal can offer, perhaps France might take huff and either get up a wrangle with us or withdraw the army of observation from the frontier, in which case ten millions might not be sufficient to finish the war—it would merely be gambling with the Holy Alliance and seeing which party has the longest purse.

Mendizabal wanted me to sign another treaty with him of which je me suis joliment bien gardé as you may suppose—he shewed me a copy of the letter he wrote to you a few days since upon the subject, and I put down what I thought would be inadmissible in his proposals and such parts as with amendments you may find it possible to adopt. He agreed to what I suggested with the exception of the omission of Catalonian wines which I said would bring upon us the remonstrances of other wine growing countries. He contends we ought not to drive too hard a bargain but reserve that for the general treaty, as it is of great political importance to us to settle the Spanish question, and he asked me to beg of you *por el amor de Dios* to make some concessions in favor of Catalonian productions, and I accordingly *do* appeal to the religious feelings of you and Thomson, but without taking upon myself to offer an opinion upon the subject. Three months ago I would have gladly, had it been possible, stood the whole responsibility of the treaty—now however you know what I think of the prospects of this country and the risks which must consequently attend entering into any engagements with it upon a large scale. I send you a copy of my observations upon Mendizabal's letter to you.

Since my last letter I have learned a good deal more concerning the Legion and in justice to Mendizabal I must admit that he also has reason to complain or rather he has some kind of excuse for the non-fulfillment of his engagements. Since the Legion first set foot in Spain he has never been able to get a single account of what money has been received, of how it has been expended, of the supplies and stores which have been furnished from England on Spanish account and which should therefore be set off against arrears of pay—and it is therefore not correctly known by any body what in fact is due by the Government. A Mr. Grindley of the Commissariat is just arrived here, and after proper pumping a great many facts have been elicited from him. He tells me that it is perfectly true no accounts have been furnished because the captains of companies absolutely refuse to account to the paymasters for the money they have received. The Diputacion de Alava who contracted for the supply of the Legion he says has behaved shamefully, but that the disorganization of the Legion is not owing solely to them, but to the total inexperience of the officers and their ignorance of their duty. These things are told to Evans but he takes no notice of them. Baggage coming from Santander and accompanied by the recruits from England has been completely plundered in the road—arms and ammunition sold to the Carlists on its way to Vitoria —but Evans has not been moved to make enquiry, or has he once inspected the Legion since it left Santander. I have for some time past been receiving evidence which corroborates Mr. Grindley's statements,[2] and I think it right to communicate them to you though pray never let it be known[3] that you received them from me, as my constant endeavour is to uphold the character of the Legion—no easy matter under present circumstances when Mr. Grindley tells me that the day he left Vitoria a public subscription was talked of to get rid of the English.

As for Evans I believe him to be an honorable amiable man and a brave soldier, but I confess his conduct as a general does not surprise me. When Alava announced his appointment to me last year and said he thought I should be astonished that with his Tory opinions he should have selected such a radical as Evans to send to Spain, I said that I regretted the appointment not on account of Evans's political opinions which I was sure he would leave behind him on taking service in a foreign country, but because I was convinced (although I was unacquainted with him) that he would not be found a man of action, and my reason for this was that I can't recognize two distinct characters in the same man. In Parliament I saw that Evans was a man of mighty intentions and small performance—his notices of motions were fit to shake the universe and they always came off in the thinnest smoke, and I therefore feared that his fault of undertaking more than he can execute which had been displayed in the House of Commons would be equally manifest in Navarre—and so it has turned out.

I have done my best during the last week to goad Mendizabal into fulfilling his engagements with the Legion, and I am glad to say that General McDougall departs this evening quite satisfied. Wylde will remain about a week longer to watch over the execution of Mendizabal's promises which I hope you will approve.

The Prince and Princess of Capua have taken their departure for Paris. . . .

The sacred person of a newspaper correspondent having been meddled with by the Spanish Government, I have troubled you with a long dispatch upon the subject[4]. . . .

Enclosure: 'Bases of Commercial Convention proposed by M. Mendizabal' with 'Observations', and 'Bases suggested to M. Mendizabal', Madrid, 12 March 1836.

Received 21 March.

GC/CL/246; Clar. Dep. C.452/2 (85-94)

[1] See V to P, 12 Mar. 1836, no.59, FO 72/458. Rayneval reported to Thiers

on 5 March that the Spanish Government was prepared to resort to force if the new Cortes became too radical, but he was instructed to advise the Queen Regent against a preventive coup. (AMAE CP Espagne 771.)

[2] Evans freely admitted to V that the troops sold their arms and supplies, but he contended that he had stated at the outset that 'the sale of necessaries, indiscipline and inefficiency would be the inevitable consequence of want of pay and privation in point of quarters.' (Evans to V, 20 Feb. 1836, Clar. Dep. C.460.)

[3] 'never' to 'known' underlined, possibly by P.

[4] V to P, 12 Mar. 1836, no. 55, FO 72/458, about Mr. Honan, Madrid correspondent of the *Morning Herald*.

197 Palmerston to Villiers, 14 March 1836

Foreign Office. To save me the time necessary to write two letters, I send you the copy of one I write by this messenger to Granville.[1] I think the French Government notwithstanding the disclaimers of the King and Thiers are dying to[2] go into Spain, and have wished to do so all along; only they wanted to be a little pressed by us to do so. Mendizabal should write to Alava to urge the measure.[3]

You see we have adopted your military and naval plans though we have not your financial and commercial schemes.[4] I myself have some doubt whether we should be able to carry a guarantee through Parliament. The Tories would to a man vote against it, and the Economists would not support it; and if after all we were beat upon it in the House of Commons, we should cut a particularly foolish figure. When the Greek loan guarantee passed we were much stronger in the House of Commons than we are now; and that guarantee had been promised by a protocol signed in 1830 by Aberdeen. The Tories were as much pledged to it as we were. In the present case they would be free, and depend upon it they would fight it to the utmost.

To make the guarantee of any use it must immediately be submitted to Parliament in the shape of a Bill; and then the commercial arrangements about the cottons which would require to be kept secret for 2 or 3 months would be of no use to help the passing of the Bill; though it might gain us all great credit afterwards.

Rothschild was very pressing last week for the guarantee; I said, 'Well, but will not this sale of Crown lands give Mendizabal money?' 'Yes', said he, 'in time, but not in time for the May dividend. It is like telling me at 7 o'clock when I want my dinner, there is a calf feeding in a field a mile off.' If the French enter, it would perhaps be expedient that our flag should wave as well as theirs, and we might garrison with our Marines, if asked to do so, St. Sebastians or any place on the coast where a few hundred men would be safe, and could hold communication with their ships.

Now we have got our Navy vote we have a little more elbow room in these matters.

Copy.

GC/CL/1256

[1] In which P instructed Granville to inform Thiers 'that England and France would stand in a more commanding position with respect to the three other Powers on other questions if that of Spain were satisfactorily settled'. (P to Granville, 12 Mar. 1836, GC/GR/1602.)

[2] 'send' crossed out.

[3] Álava had already asked for increased Franco-Spanish co-operation on the border. On 3 March 1836 he had asked the French Government if they would agree to the following measures: (1) to allow Spanish troops to cross the French frontier where it was necessary and desirable to strengthen their military positions against the Carlists; (2) to provide the Spanish garrisons on the frontier with arms as it was difficult to supply these garrisons from Madrid; (3) to allow Spanish troops attacked by superior Carlist forces to take refuge in France; (4) to disarm and intern all Carlist troops who took refuge in France. (Álava to Broglie, 3 Mar. 1836, AMAE CP Espagne 771.)

[4] The British Government adopted the scheme proposed by V in no. 190 above. After a Cabinet meeting on 14 March P summoned Sébastiani, the French ambassador in London, and informed him that orders had been given to British ships to proceed to ports menaced by the Carlists and to defend them, if necessary, against Carlist attacks by putting Marines ashore. He invited the French Government to participate in these new measures of support, first by occupying several Biscayan ports, and secondly by sending troops into the valley of the Baztán. (Sébastiani to Thiers, 14 Mar. 1836, AMAE CP Angleterre 647.)

198 Villiers to Palmerston, 19 March 1836

Madrid. Private. I have received the apreciabilisima carta de Vuestra Excelencia of the 10th instant, and I feel as pleased as if some personal advantage had befallen myself that you are about to take some active measures in favor of Spanish civilization, for the longer the war lasts the nearer will this nation approach to barbarianism, and I am convinced it will be found that a little force of the right (or external) kind well directed will produce greater results than those who away from the scene of action can expect.

The question whatever it might have been a year and a half ago is not now a purely military one—this can never be too much insisted upon or kept in view—it is a political quite as much as a military question, and must be treated accordingly if any real good is intended to be done. The addition of any number of battalions to the English or French Legions will do but little for they will be in the Spanish service—it is the English and French flags and the associations of irresistible force which they carry with them which will alone strike panic into the rebel bands and extinguish the civil war. Much of course must depend upon the spirit in which it is done, and the energy which is displayed, but I believe the objects we have in view would be effected by the French cordon being advanced a little way into Spain, for much of the country to the east is disposed to rise in favor of the Queen and is only deterred by the fear of not being sufficiently protected afterwards. The Spanish and auxiliary troops then being at liberty to press upon the enemy, he would be driven up into the mountains—for out of their own country *the Navarrese will not go*—where it would be easy to cut off supplies by land, we taking care that none came by sea, and that the troops now constantly harrassed by marches to protect the sea ports, might be disposable to hem in the insurgents on the Biscayan side. The rebellion having thus an aneurism of its very heart, the Carlists who now circulate freely through the adjacent provinces would soon drop off, and the authority of Government and the law once more revive—a circumstance, which from the total impotence of both at this moment, is quite refreshing to think of.

I told Mendizabal just now in confidence that there was a hope of English Marines landing and taking possession of some of the sea port towns, and I thought he would have jumped out of his skin (he *did* out of one of his shoes) for joy. He said if he had his choice he should prefer that to the gift of a million by England, for the nigger knows in his heart that no number of Spaniards, even though el Gran Capitan were to rise from his grave to put himself at their head, can ever finish the war, but he dares not breathe the word intervention or cooperation after all his vaunts of not wanting it.

I only hope that if you cannot contrive the French part of the plan, that our assistance may still be given, and in the vigorous way we know how to do things when we set about them in earnest. When it is once seen that we are so, I would pay out of my own pocket for all the powder and shot the Carlists will give us occasion for expending, and I cannot believe that the measure would be otherwise than popular in England except with Mahon, Price and the prig genus omne, in retaliation for the butchering of Englishmen by Don Carlos.

In short I see a glimmering of hope through the black clouds in which we are now enveloped. The blindness with which the public of Madrid and the Procuradores seem determined upon casting out Mendizabal and his own determination not to understand or admit the dangerous position in which he stands are both equally lamentable. His opponents have not a thought or a care about how he is to be succeeded, and he contents himself with recounting his Portuguese exploits and hoping he shall get equally well out of his Spanish scrape.

I don't know in what terms Mendizabal intends replying to your letter respecting the murder of Cabrera's mother[1] but if he tells you the truth he will say that he no more dares dismiss Mina than he dares dismiss the Queen Regent. The Government has no power any where—in fact there *is* no Government—and Mina would laugh at any order he didn't chuse to obey just as the Intendentes of all the provinces do at the bills Mendizabal draws upon them and which they return protested.

I send you the copy of a note which I wrote to Mendizabal respecting the depredations committed upon the Duke of Wellington's estate . . . .[2]

Received 28 March.　　　　　GC/CL/247; Clar. Dep. C.452/2 (95-100)

[1] See P's strongly-worded despatch to V, 2 Mar. 1836, no. 54, FO 72/456.
[2] V to Mendizábal, 16 Mar. 1836, enclosed in V to P, 19 Mar. 1836, no. 61, FO 72/458.

199　Villiers to Palmerston, 22 March 1836

Madrid. Private. I have absolutely no time for writing today as Rayneval sends his courier early and the ceremony in the Cortes[1] has consumed every moment except those devoted to two long dispatches which I visit upon you.[2] My conversation with Isturiz will give you an idea of the opposition which Mendizabal is likely to meet with from the friends among whom he expected support.[3] There is a great deal of intrigue and double dealing on all sides as you may suppose— at the same time I must add that within the last three days a reaction has taken place here in Mendizabal's favor and a requisition to the Queen signed by 500 commercial men has been got up against his quitting the Government.

Victories, money, or some acts of assistance on our part as well as that of France may still save the Government *and the cause,* for when I tell you that only three days ago Arguelles admitted that he thought the success of Don Carlos inevitable, you may suppose that things here look *blackish.*

I sincerely hope you will publish my dispatch of today upon the 27 Carlist prisoners as an appendix to the papers already laid before Parliament. There is nothing in it which I am not prepared to stand to—*on horse or foot*—and it is high time that the humbug of My Lord Londonderry and Co. should be exposed. They induced these poor people by false promises and hopes to undertake the expedition and their pretended humanity is only an attempt to redeem their own unjustifiable pledges.[4] By 'certain persons' I mean Lord Londonderry and if you think it would be better to substitute *his name* I should be very glad.

Cordoba has permitted—if not caused—all the field officers of the army to sign a petition to the Queen not to accept his resignation—a most indecent and unmilitary act which, as he is a friend of mine, makes me highly indignant.

Mendizabal has been talking to Rayneval and me about another additional article to the Quadruple Treaty offering Spanish assistance to France and England (risum teneates) in the event of their wanting it, in return for French aid which should not come south of the Ebro and English which should not go far from the coast. He begged we would mention it to our respective Governments but it did not take a sufficiently official form to put in a dispatch neither would there be time to write one today.

Received 1 April.

GC/CL/248; Clar. Dep. C.452/2 (101-103)

[1] The new Cortes was opened by the Queen Regent.

[2] One concerned his efforts to persuade the Spanish Government to deport twenty-seven Carlist officers, prisoners at Cadiz, to Puerto Rico, on the grounds that deportation was the only way to prevent their being lynched by an angry mob. (V to P, 22 Mar. 1836, no. 64, FO 72/458.) The other concerned his meeting with Istúriz 'to induce that gentleman to change his

resolution of not forming part of the Ministry'. (V to P, 22 Mar. 1836, no. 67, FO 72/458.)

³ Istúriz's objections to Mendizábal were: (1) that he was despotic in his determination to run all Departments; (2) that he could not manage the Cortes; (3) that he had no coherent programme; (4) that he had failed to secure a loan, the hope of which was his main claim to power. (V to P, 22 Mar. 1836, no. 67, FO 72/458.)

⁴ V stated in his despatch that 'certain persons held out to the prisoners the hope that they would be exchanged for 27 Christino officers held prisoner by the Carlists'. (V to P, 22 Mar. 1836, no. 64, FO 72/458.)

200   Palmerston to Villiers, 24 March 1836

Copy. Foreign Office. Levees, drawing rooms, state dinners and petitions of constituents to be presented to the House of Commons, with the multa alia which the day brings with it, make it not an easy matter to have a letter ready when one is told 'This is the day for the messenger to such a place.' I must dine at St. James's today and have no more time to write, but I send you a copy of a letter I have written to Mendizabal, as it contains everything I could say to you.

I see from what Sebastiani hinted to Melbourne, though not to me, that Louis Philippe looks forward to taking the field in Spain to put down revolution with the consent and cooperation of the Holy Alliance.[1] This would be a mad attempt on his part, and one in which we could never concur.

Thiers has been much tickled, Granville tells me, with some yards of ribbon and a bit of enamelled silver which Mendizabal has sent him.

GC/CL/1258

[1] The French Government had declined to intervene in Spain in the way that P had proposed. (Thiers to Sébastiani, 18 Mar. 1836, AMAE CP Angleterre 647.) It also refused Álava's requests, with the exception of allowing Spanish troops to cross the border provided that they did not use their arms on French territory. (Thiers to Rayneval, 19 Mar., AMAE CP Espagne 771.)

201   Villiers to Palmerston, 26 March 1836

Madrid. Private. I yesterday received tidings that a messenger, who by *collateral evidence* I infer was dispatched by you on the 14th, has fallen ill at a place about 30 leagues off and I have sent a courier to fetch his dispatches—he wrote to me by Rayneval's courier to say he was poorly and to desire I would send a carriage upon springs for him. This highly characteristic request convinces me he is one of the real old English breed and I hope he may long be kept as a stallion messenger to prevent the race from becoming extinct.

By a letter of the 19th from Lord Granville I conclude that you have put into execution the intention you announced to me last week of trying to push the French a little way into Spain, and that as was to be feared the prejudices or aversion of Louis Philippe are not to be overcome—perhaps it would be more correct to say his sinister policy —for the system begun by Louis the 14th of keeping Spain poor and disorderly is so manifestly the easiest way for France to retain her influence over this country that I have not much hopes of his descendant voluntarily adopting any other. It may cost him dear however for though the ambitious policy of France may be unchanged, he should remember that neither Spain or Europe are what they were 150 years ago and that though the same means may be pursued now as then, the ends will no longer meet with the same toleration.

Things are if possible more entangled and bedevilled than when I last wrote to you. Mendizabal has unworthily and as I think imprudently prevented Isturiz from being elected President of the Chamber by means of a trick in the voting performed by a dozen and a half of his own immediate dependents. He swears to me that he had no hand in it but I know to the contrary and that he has sacrificed to his pique against Isturiz for not forming part of his Government, or as he declares for his intrigues against him, that which is at this moment a State necessity, for if ever it was important to have an inflexible sturdy President, it is now when the majority of the Deputies is undisciplined, hotheaded and bent upon all kinds of wild revolutionary and illegal projects. Mendizabal's enemies and the whole moderate party declaim loudly against the trick. The speculators and monied men are satisfied with it for the weakness of Mendizabal's character suits their purposes and they wish to retain him in the Government. Others again of the Exaltados who begin to fear Isturiz's energy and his determination to stick to the rules of the Chamber have become the most active against him—the result of it all is that I defy any human being, be he ever so much versed in Spanish absurdities, to tell what will be the course of events. The liberals are divided among themselves but the house will not fall because in Spain nothing happens regularly—not even a Scripture axiom.

I hope I have been the means of restoring better feelings between Cordoba and Evans—the latter writes me word that Cordoba was profoundly afflicted at the attacks made upon him by the English newspapers and in the House of Commons respecting, among many other things, his having sought to compromise the Legion after his retreat from Arlaban *which is certainly without the least foundation,* adds Evans. Now if as I believe Evans wrote in a very different sense to you and others of his friends upon this matter he certainly should undo the impression he has created now that he has seen reason to recognize his error.

The criticism in your dispatch No.13 is very just upon the discrepancy between the information sent by Wylde and myself. I am always very careful about sending any which I do not receive from Mendizabal, Almodovar or Cordoba. In the present instance it was from the Minister of War that I got the subject matter of the dispatch to which you reply and I will endeavour to trace the truth though it is not now of much importance.

I enclose you a long result of Miraflores's midnight oil—not because you will read it but because I could not help promising him you should have it[1]—he has been announcing it to me for weeks, and as I believe in charity, lest stumbling upon it by accident its excessive talent should be too much for me. If carefully examined I am inclined to think it relates to the Spanish question, and he tells me it is meant for the guidance of Europe in general but more particularly for that of France and England. He is really the most ridiculous creature of his inches I ever met with.

The courier is returned and I have received your dispatch and letter of the 14th. You will see by my dispatch the effect they have produced upon Her Catholic Majesty's advisers[2] and so they ought, for if I may be permitted to express an opinion they are a perfect specimen of adaptation of means to ends. Our assistance upon the coast will of course only produce local advantages—if it had been simultaneous with French aid it would I am convinced have put an end to the war. You could not however do more and we must turn to the utmost account what you have done. It will be very desireable not to *starve* so good a deed by not placing an efficient force upon the coast, and the more so as Lord John Hay, than whom a better or braver officer does not exist, is a little apt to underrate the Carlists and he may perhaps attempt too much with too little means. As he cannot let his forces go far from the ships I thought it very desireable that some inland support should prevent their being harassed in any places they may take possession of, and as Spaniards can never be reckoned upon for any thing except jealousy and disobedience, I have suggested to Cordoba to send the Legion to the coast, and I think you will agree with me upon the numerous reciprocal advantages which it and the King's forces may be of to each other.

I have asked Wylde what sort of addition he thought should be made to the force now under Lord John Hay's command, and he says Marines as many as you can spare, one large steam boat, and two small ones which should be able to go over the bars of the different rivers in order to supply places which will be entirely dependent upon what they can receive by sea.

If Cordoba agrees to my proposal and matters are carried on actively—if Fuentearabia is taken, the corner turned there, and a cordon stretched out eastwards—I think the French will hardly like to see us taking so vigorous a part while they are only spectators, and they may then perhaps lend a hand. It was for this reason, and to prevent the French Government being committed to a negative with that of Spain, that I shewed Mendizabal confidentially your dispatch to Lord Granville[3]—for otherwise he would have directed Alava to make an application, or rather he would have made it to Rayneval to whom for the last week he has had a note ready upon the subject, but which I recommended him not to send until we received some further intelligence from Paris.

I of course regret the failure of the millions cum cotton scheme, but you are the best judge of its practicability. Should the time arrive when you think that the two measures *together* might be carried in the House of Commons pray let me know for the chance of Mendizabal's being strong enough not to make the 3 months secresy a sine quâ non.

Received 4 April.

GC/CL/249; Clar. Dep. C.452/2 (105-111)

[1] Not found in the Palmerston Papers.

[2] Mendizábal expressed 'his admiration and gratitude for the frank and noble manner in which His Majesty's Government had come forward with assistance'. (V to P, 26 Mar. 1836, no.73, FO 72/458.)

[3] In which P had suggested that French troops should occupy certain key positions across the Franco-Spanish border.

202 Villiers to Earl Granville, 28 March 1836

Madrid. Private. I go to Toledo tomorrow morning and in case Rayne-val should send a courier during my absence I leave a line to say that the news of the English cooperation has produced a magical effect here, as well as at the head quarters of the army where Lord John Hay sent to Cordoba the offer of the force under his command. There is but one general sentiment of satisfaction among all parties (save Carlists) and this is the best answer to the doubts respecting the mode in which foreign intervention would be received. I am certain that if France had made the forward movement which was suggested we should have seen the insurrection crumble to pieces in a month or less, whatever may be the opinion of M. de Talleyrand.

However we must make the best of what we can get, and the willingness of France to give arms and provisions, but above all to take a more menacing attitude on the other side of the Pyrenees, may be turned to good account.

I find from Cordoba's aide-de-camp Colonel Alba, who is a *very* clever officer, that if Harispe would leave Bayonne and establish the cordon and his head quarters closer to the Pyrenees, that it would produce a great moral effect. The Carlists would look upon it as a *preparatory* measure of hostility of which they would not understand the extent, and it would introduce among them the distrust and alarm which it is so important to create. I have likewise suggested to Cordoba to *garnir* the French frontier with the French Legion, who will then be more or less in communication with their compatriots on the other *side of the hill,* and derive from that a kind of support and confidence which would stimulate their exertions—upon the same ground that I have recommended the British Legion's being sent to cooperate with the King's naval forces. Harispe should be ordered to advance to the utmost limit of the French territory or rather of the neutral ground —and I think that there will be the less objection to this as it will not be popular in France that the English should now singlehanded be taking so active a part.

I have used my best exertions that neither in the Gazette or in other papers there should be any laudation of England at the expence of France. Our interests properly understood are all the same and it is important that no petty jealousies should mar the good which our united exertions may effect. The turn which things are now taking may save Mendizabal and be the means of curbing the Exaltado party. Will you send this letter on to Palmerston?

GC/CL/250

203   Villiers to Earl Granville, 2 April 1836

Madrid. Private. I am just returned from Toledo in a state nearly approaching a jelly from a 12 hours journey to perform 12 leagues upon a road more like the sea in a storm than any thing else. It is almost impossible to believe that there should be no other communication between the ancient and modern capitals of Spain. However trouble was never better repaid, for Toledo with its innumerable associations and standing records of Goths, Arabs, and Spaniards down to the time of Philip II, is the most interesting place I ever visited in my life.

Upon arriving here I found your letter of the 26th. My remarks of which you justly complain were not made in forgetfulness of their conveyance, but in ignorance of any danger, as I had not then received your warning.[1] It is very easy to be more cautious in future though I am still at a loss to imagine how *such deeds* are ventured upon.

I did not mean to say that Mendizabal had confidence in his own stability—that I knew he had not—but that he was ignorant of his real position for nothing will bring him to believe that he has not the art of governing at his fingers' ends—and he is in consequence always attributing effects to causes which are not the real ones. His absence of tact and inconsiderate way of proceeding get him into trouble, and invite, I should almost say justify, the intrigues for ejecting him of which he complains and of which he magnifies the extent and influence.

I have just seen him and find that he is in better spirits than when I went. The reaction in his favor certainly continues, and it would be difficult to account for it in any other way than by the jealousy of Isturiz which has sprung up in consequence of his being supposed presumptuous in not choosing to have to do with a Government of which Mendizabal forms part, and the public though they were very angry with Mendizabal before won't allow him as yet to be maltreated beyond a certain extent. As far as he personally is concerned, I think he will have a majority, but that won't last if he cannot find better men than his present colleagues to join him in the Government.

I have not yet had any answer from Cordoba to my suggestion of sending the British Legion to the coast. Mendizabal is very desirous he should do it, and he implores of Palmerston to take energetic measures in order to render fully effective the assistance we are now lending—he wants one or two little British vessels in the Bidasoa among other things. I admit that they would be very useful but I think they would too openly give us the appearance of establishing a police against France—this should only be done by Spanish troops or troops in the pay of Spain. We might back them but we ought not to do any thing which is open to France, or rather her duty under existing engagements, to perform.

Mendizabal likewise wants a commissioner from each of the parties to the Quadruple Alliance to be stationed on the frontier in order to watch over the punctual fulfillment of the French part of the Treaty—with that ostensible motive such a proposition cannot be admitted I apprehend, although if it were thought desireable some other pretext might be found.

I shall be curious to hear what you think of Mendizabal's letter to Thiers which Alava is instructed to consult you upon before he delivers it.[2]

From one or two persons I have seen this evening and whose reports upon the state of public opinion are always correct I learn that the good effect at first produced by the news of English cooperation is wearing off owing to the conviction that France will take no part and that we shall be left singlehanded without being able to extend our aid further than the coast, and that that will leave the principal theatre of the war intact. The Carlists have accordingly regained courage and still look to the dissensions among the liberals as their security for ultimate triumph.

Will you send this letter on to Palmerston? I have not time to write more as Mendizabal's courier is waiting and I have too many bones unset to write a second letter.

I am very sorry to hear of this return of gout. . . .

GC/CL/252

[1] Granville had warned V that the bags he sent via the French courier were being opened. V was surprised 'as I thought bags were free from that danger. Pray tell me if the seal appeared broken either of the bag or of the dispatches.' (V to Granville, 22 Mar. 1836, PRO 30/29/421.)

² Mendizábal wrote to Thiers through Rayneval, requesting either tighter French control on the Spanish border or an Anglo-French loan guarantee. The French Government rejected both schemes. (Rayneval to Thiers, 7 Apr. 1836, and Thiers to Rayneval 30 Apr., AMAE CP Espagne 771.)

204 Villiers to Palmerston, 5 April 1836

Madrid. Private. As this letter will go by a French attaché to the mission at Lisbon, and that I do not suppose you will receive it much before my courier of next Saturday reaches London, I shall address you very shortly. The moral effect of our cooperation has considerably subsided. The Carlists were knocked down by the news at first, but they now consider that we must confine ourselves to the coast and that they shall still have the main theatre of the war as open to them as ever. In short, say they, nothing but France openly and effectually aiding the Queen will ever do them harm. I fear therefore we must look rather to local than to general advantages from our assistance, but this raises the spirits of the army and of Cordoba, for the sea ports have always been matter of great anxiety, the Carlists being able to attack them whenever they pleased and the nature of the country rendering it impossible to go to their relief without an immense force (a small one would be cut to pieces in the defiles) for which all the supplies and ammunition must be moved at the same time over the worst roads, and where artillery can hardly pass. All this trouble and expence having been incurred, the Carlists upon the approach of the Queen's troops are off like so many goats and hasten to attack the points which have been left weak. Cordoba therefore considers we have relieved him from a constant source of annoyance and he says the same feeling pervades the whole army which, so far from being jealous of foreign cooperation, 'la demande à hauts cris'—the same wish exists almost to a man among the partizans of the Queen's cause.

I have this day had a letter from Cordoba who gladly adopts my proposal of sending the British Legion to the coast—but of this more by my own courier.[1]

It is very desireable that one or two steam boats should be sent from England for the protection of the coast and that some Marines should come to garrison, though it were but for a short time, the two or three places which Lord John Hay will speedily retake.

As for Government there is none whatever in Spain at this moment,

for Mendizabal's *proceedings* cannot even in the most strained accepta-
tion of the term be called governing. He does and undoes just what
he pleases and as the fancy takes him, without reference either to the
law or the *prophets*—for I am sure it is not for want of warning that
he gets into his daily scrapes. How he will get out of their accumulated
mass I cannot foresee—he has not only made so many enemies and
retained so few friends, but he has involved every department of the
State in such confusion by ill conceived measures and unfulfillable
promises, that every body shrinks from sharing in the enormous
responsibility he has prepared for any new colleague he may happen
to catch. I pity him sincerely for he has the good of his country at heart
and he does his very best, but that best is awful bad to be sure. He
says he shall pay the dividend—and that he means to apply to the
Cortes for a loan of two millions.

Received 14 April.

GC/CL/253; Clar. Dep. C.452/2 (113-116)

[1] V to P, 9 Apr. 1836, no. 84, FO 72/458.

205   Palmerston to Villiers, 6 April 1836

Murrell Green. I write two lines on my way to my constituents at
Tiverton to say that your suggestion made to the Spanish Government
to send the Legion to the coast to cooperate with our ships is excellent.
I hope Mendizabal will adopt it.

The result would be a sweeping away of the Carlists from the whole
line of coast up to the French frontiers, and our ships would occupy
Passages which is now in the hands of the Carlists. Nothing would put
Louis Philippe to shame more than this because it would be doing by
English troops, that which we proposed to him to do by French
troops.[1]

PS. We shall send out some more Marines to Lord John Hay.

Copy.

GC/CL/1259

[1] P informed Granville on 5 April that his policy would be to shame Louis
Philippe 'into some effort in favour of the Queen. To say that he will do anything but give her pecuniary or military assistance is really to laugh at her
distress.' (P to Granville, 5 Apr. 1836, GC/GR/1608.)

206   Villiers to Palmerston, 9 April 1836

Madrid. Private. You will see by my dispatch that an unexpected but very decided manifestation of good sense on the part of the public makes me think a shade better of things here.[1] It is perhaps not wise in me committing myself to an opinion as to the duration of this good sense or of its effects, but it was tempting to report to you that there is at all events a *check* in our downward progress.

People here like people every where care more for what they can't get than for what they have, and there is perhaps more grief at what France refuses than joy over what England grants. I must do them the justice to say however that they are very grateful to us, and I have not heard a word in a different sense except from that fanciful old twaddler Arguelles who at the same time that he acknowledges the contest can never be finished by Spaniards, declares he should prefer Don Carlos at Madrid to a single foreign soldier in Navarre. His opinion however has no weight with any body, and the public only desire the largest possible amount of cooperation.

England and France may singly or conjointly with safety to themselves and successfully to Spain intervene as they please in favor of the Queen and against Don Carlos—but que la France se garde bien to attempt the plan to which you allude in your last letter of tranquillizing Spain by means of an army and an intervention sanctioned by assembled Kings in Congress. He who attempts to mettre le hola between two Spanish combattants is sure to unite them both against him and to receive their respective knives in his own side. If France were to make this attempt she would be involved in all those difficulties of which she has some experience. It would be the only way of bringing about again the year 1808, and now as then she would be exposed to the same dangers, expence and failure. That she would get the Holy Alliance consent to it I have no manner of doubt, for Nicholas would well understand (or if he did not there are those about him who would) that no measure so speedy or so effectual could be devised for crippling France or breaking up her alliance with England. It would be far more our interest to let Spain go to the Devil her own way if that contented France, mischievous and cruel as that policy would be, than to incur the disgrace of permitting such a measure or the risk of opposing it. I fear that Louis 14th's system of keeping Spain poor and dependent is still thought excellent in France, and it would only be by coaxing and good management that we shall prevent its being rigidly enforced.

I have at last convinced Mendizabal that he was not very likely to bully France, and that he had better shut his eyes to all he did not like and pretend to believe all he is told. His language, and I believe his dispatches to Alava, are now upon this subject what they ought to be.

I send you today copies of a correspondence of Cordoba's with Evans and myself.[2] He has been deeply mortified by the charges brought against him in the House of Commons and in the English press, but I believe what induced him to enter thus upon his defence was some sharp remarks of mine to him upon the language he was reported to be holding with reference to the Legion. The more I know of Evans the less fit I think him for the post he occupies—he is weak, touchy and eternally thinking of what will be said of him in Westminster which makes him mutinous against Cordoba's gradual occupation system as one not productive of military glory. His high rank in the Spanish service is an embarrassment to every body and I don't wonder therefore at Cordoba's sharing in the feelings of jealousy which the Legion excited, but I thought it very desireable that the expression of such feelings should be checked—and I wrote to him accordingly. His amende has been very honorable and among other things he has inserted in a Madrid newspaper an article upon the Legion which I enclose a copy of, and of which he has acknowledged himself to be the author at his head quarters.

Evans is highly pleased at being sent to the coast, and considers rightly that the Legion will at last have an opportunity of distinguishing itself. He writes me word that his troops are now very well clothed, and Mendizabal swears he has already taken measures for their being regularly paid by some bankers of Bayonne. Wylde leaves Madrid in two days and I have recommended (in which he entirely agrees as Cordoba is not likely, for want of means, to begin active operations at present) that he should go with the Legion to the coast and see them well launched in their new duties. I had another motive for this which is that he should explain both to Evans and Lord John Hay the expediency of avoiding all collision with the French ships at Pasages or with French authorities on the Bidasoa. I am sure you will think it important that what we are now doing in Spain should in no way give cause of complaint to France. On the contrary it should be made the means of shewing our friendly deference for her—then perhaps poco a poco if we can succeed in giving a favorable turn to the war she may be inclined to help us, and *until she does the war never will end*—but the better things become the less will be her fear of compromising herself.

As folks in England seem rather to occupy themselves about Spain and are constantly referring to the Eliot Treaty you may perhaps like to know the *exact state* of that treaty. In the 1st place it is impossible to speak of it in too high terms—without it the contest in the Northern Provinces (the theatre of the war at the time of making the Treaty and to which its operation was confined) never would have taken its comparatively civilized form—it has been punctually observed, and hundreds and hundreds of families have to bless its effects. In Catalonia every species of horror is committed, but to that province the treaty did not apply,[3] and this serves to set forth more prominently the humane effects of Eliot's mission.[4] Nobody can say that Cordoba has been guilty of a single act of cruelty, or of more oppression than the circumstances of such a disastrous contest rendered necessary.

Mendizabal's system of *not* doing business and of breaking his promises respecting the different matters I have to bring before the Government is enough to ruin the best of tempers—mine has been so these three months past, and it would be very useful if you would write me a strong dispatch upon the subject of delays and inattention. The Express Packet case may well serve as a text.[5] Nothing is gained with *any* Spaniard by soft words or fair usage—like their mules there is a good deal to be got out of them but it must be by dint of thrashing.

Were I in your place I should not hesitate an instant in ordering Sir George Cockburn to remove the troops which have taken possession of Cay Sal Bank and to begin building the lighthouse where it is wanted. Till some such measure is resorted to neither of the questions—the disputed bank or the lighthouse—will be satisfactorily settled.

Mina's letter to the Government respecting Cabrera's mother has not done much good here—the parts of it which are intelligible people don't believe.[6]

Enclosure: Newspaper extract comprising a letter from 'Un Official General del Ejercito' (Vitoria) to the editor of El Español, *30 March 1836.*

Received 18 April.

GC/CL/254; Clar. Dep. C.452/2 (117-121)

[1] V to P, 9 Apr. 1836, no. 90, FO 72/458.
[2] Evans had frequently complained of Córdoba, first that 'he troubles himself much about the state of parties at Madrid. If he would think more about

the war I think it would be better.' (Evans to V, no day or month, 1836, Clar. Dep. C.460.) He complained secondly that he 'is convinced that it is impossible to contend against the Carlists except by means of a French army of intervention. Having this opinion as Commander-in-Chief it is clear that he will avoid advancing on the enemy in any direction. The enemy are aware of it.' (Evans to V, 19 Mar. 1836, Clar. Dep. C.460.) He said thirdly that Córdoba's neglect of the Legion was so flagrant that Evans had no choice but to resign his command. (Evans to V, 5 Apr. 1836, Clar. Dep. C.460.) Córdoba defended himself against the charge that he had neglected the British Legion in his letter to Evans of 26 March 1836 and in a letter to V of the same date. Both letters are enclosed in V to P, 9 Apr. 1836, no. 85, FO 72/458.

³ See P to Backhouse, instructions for a despatch to V on the desirability of extending the Eliot Convention to Catalonia, 25 Apr. 1836, FO 72/456.

⁴ This paragraph has minor alterations, probably by P in preparation for its publication or use elsewhere. 'Folks' has been changed to 'people'; the phrase 'seem rather to occupy themselves about Spain and' has been circled, presumably to indicate omission; 'state' has been changed to 'effects'; 'In the 1st place' deleted; 'Lord' has been added before Eliot; and a paragraph end mark has been placed after 'the humane effects of Eliot's mission'.

⁵ The Spanish authorities seized goods from the *Express Packet* in August 1834 for, it was claimed, part-payment of customs duties. V had protested to the Spanish Government but had been waiting almost two years for an answer. (V to P, 9 Apr. 1836, no. 83, FO 72/458.)

⁶ Mina claimed that Cabrera's mother was not shot as an act of vengeance but because she was known to be involved in a Carlist conspiracy. This explanation was published in the *Madrid Gazette*. (V to P, 9 Apr. 1836, no. 87, FO 72/458.)

207 Villiers to Palmerston, 18 April 1836

Madrid. Private. I have received your Murrel Green letter of the 6th and am glad to see that you approve of the Legion going to the coast—Cordoba, Evans, Lord John Hay all like it too as you will see by the enclosed letter from Evans which is much more satisfactory than its innumerable predecessors.

The state of the war continues the same—that of politics is rather a strange one, though I hardly know if it is worth troubling you to read a history of them. The public has shewn itself far more reasonable than was ever remembered even by the *oldest inhabitant,* and the spectacle of Mendizabal strong has once again presented itself. About three weeks ago he thought he might have a majority of 30 in the Chamber—for which notion he drew upon his imagination, as he had no other data, and in his heart he did not think himself saveable. This state of things spurred on the opposition against him at the head of which rushed to place himself the brave Quintus Curtius Atlas Miraflores, in whom Nature evidently means to solve the problem of how closely a man can resemble an ass by the mere operation of vanity. Their intrigues with the Queen and the Camarilla, and between men of the most irreconcilable opinions were carried on in so open and so bungling a manner that the public began to murmur, and then upon the first shew of opposition in the Chamber loudly to express their indignation. This took effect and the orators began to outbid each other in orderly pledges. The violent demagogues complained that some recent disturbances had not been punished, and those who were most active members of the juntas in September last cried shame upon the Government for its weakness and not making itself respected. Not venturing therefore to oppose the Government they determined upon giving it thick and thin support, and the majorities last week were of 90 and 100 against 10 and 12.

Lazarus when raised from the dead could not have felt more surprized than Mendizabal at this unexpected accession of strength coming how or whence he had not a notion, every body at the same time feeling how unfit a Minister he is, and how entirely he has failed in fulfilling any of his wild promises—but the public did not choose he should be kicked out till they saw clearly he was not to be succeeded by other spirits more wicked than himself. The fear of this gives him negative strength, and I have been laboring to make him feel that now or never is the time for turning this accident to solid account by completing his Ministry, and asking for a loan—first however recognizing the South American independence in order to produce a favorable effect upon the foreign money markets. Proposing to Mendizabal to divest himself of any portion of power or to select colleagues who will not be subservient to him, is very like sailing against the wind and one makes about the same kind of way.

I consider that I saved him and his Ministry the other day by my interview with the Queen, for she hates him so cordially and is so pledged to Quintus Curtius and Co., that she was quite ready for a grand coup d'état. Now that may do in England but in Spain it would have played the Devil, and there would have been an uproar from one end of the country to the other—so I thought as it was asked I had better give my opinion though I abstained from directly advising.[1]

God help me if I did a bad deed—but I was impelled to it by a sense of duty, and repugnant enough it was to me, for our friend Mendizabal is as unprincipled a quack and liar as ever lived—a regular Stock Exchange bird with just a sufficient sense of right and wrong and meum and tuum to keep him out of any *very* great scrape. I may as well not write all Her Majesty said to me of him, but she can't endure him and was very frank in detailing her reasons.

I think you will approve my having sought an audience of Her Majesty upon the grounds stated in my dispatch. How much or how little the Camarilla were authorized in coupling her name with the shameful reports of which I complained I cannot pretend to say, but I heard of them from various quarters, and though they were probably only intended to injure Mendizabal and make people believe he was *selling his country to England,* yet as they were most offensive to our national good faith, and likely to injure the Queen's cause if known in England,[2] I thought it desireable to receive their contradiction from Her Majesty's own mouth, and to make her feel she must impose silence upon her entourage. It all came off very well, and I am sure she is profoundly grateful for the assistance we are affording her cause. She spoke of you con muchisimo cariño and desired me to say how much she should love you always.

The debate upon the address abounded in acrimonious personalities and if the Chamber had been Irish instead of Spanish about 18 duels would have taken place. One however was *verificado* the day before yesterday between Mendizabal and Isturiz, in consequence of some big words of the latter's who was in the wrong—there was no harm done, but Mendizabal took such particular pains to assure me that the pistols were loaded *with ball,* that I am inclined to believe the seconds had duly provided for the safety of the combatants.

The papers are full of a congress to be held upon the affairs of Spain which has produced a not agreable sensation here. I conclude there is no truth in it—but if either at London or Paris there is to be a junta formed with any such object let me suggest that Rayneval and I ought to be subpoenaed as witnesses.

I am sorry to say that the faction is daily increasing in the provinces of Galicia, Catalonia, Aragon and Valencia. The partizans of the Queen are tired and frightened to death and care not at whose hands or by what means they may once again enjoy tranquillity.

Enclosure: 'Extract of a letter from General Evans to Mr. Villiers dated Vitoria

April 11th 1836', reporting the restoration of good relations with Córdoba and the decision to move to Santander.

Received 27 April.   GC/CL/255; Clar. Dep. C.452/2 (122-127)

[1] V advised the Queen of the danger of intriguing against Mendizábal, whose fall might result in the population of Madrid turning against the new Government and demanding the Constitution of 1812. (V to P, 17 Apr. 1836, no. 93, FO 72/458.) P minuted on this despatch 'Entirely approve. 27 April 1836.'

[2] 'Reports had come to my knowledge that Her Majesty, so far from sharing in the general feelings of satisfaction which the active cooperation now afforded by England had produced in the Spanish public, was disposed to view it with jealousy and as covering an intention ultimately to take possession of those places on the sea coast which His Majesty's Government have now offered to recover or protect.' (ibid.)

208 Palmerston to Villiers, 21 April 1836

Copy. Foreign Office. I am glad things in Spain seem taking a better turn. Your suggestion for sending the Legion to the coast was excellent; when that corps and our squadron come into cooperation they will do something; and their successes will pique the French Government to take a more active part. Minto enters into our measures with zeal and energy. He has made John Hay a commodore, and is sending him a good supply of Marines, howitzers and steamers. We shall not starve the service.

Granville says that the French are going to reinforce the Legion from Algiers, and are really sincere in their cooperation. If Mendizabal will get the Cortes to give him a loan, and thus enable him to march up his new levies to the main army, the war may soon be put an end to. If Mendizabal can accomplish this, it will be a great triumph to him; and I hope he may. The thing to do is to raise a loan. 'Point d'argent, point de victoires.'

Our instructions to the cruizers on the eastern coast of Spain were given rather for the sake of uniformity than for any great practical good they can accomplish.[1] But they tend to shew we are in earnest, and that cooperation is our rule, and not our exception.

Alava writes me word that Talleyrand has never uttered to him a word about Spain—pretty well for the man who wanted for a long while to take credit for having invented the Quadruple Treaty.

GC/CL/1260

¹ The instructions were identical to those sent to the officers of the British Navy on the northern coast of Spain. (P to V, 21 Apr. 1836, no. 28, FO 72/456.)

209   Villiers to Palmerston, 23 April 1836

Madrid. Private. If this were not a regular courier day you would not have the advantage of an autograph from me as nothing good and nothing more than commonly bad have interrupted the monotony of our march to the Devil.

Notwithstanding all Mendizabal's promises to me that his Ministry should be formed a week ago, he had last night taken no effective step towards it. He cannot bear the idea of parting with the least scrap of power, or of taking into the Cabinet any man who will not be as subservient to his caprices and as blind to his want of judgement as his present colleagues against whom public opinion is so justly pronounced. We had a grand wrangle upon all this last night and the motives by which he was influenced, for if another week passes without his forming a Government after his repeated promises to do so, people will be furious and then no Government at all will be possible, for the individuals who might now be got to do so would not then venture. During the last six months he has been playing the same game, and by trifling with his friends and compromising them has disgusted and turned into bitter enemies all those who might have given him effective support.

I told him seriously that unless he mended his ways, it was my intention to make a formal representation to you upon the inexpediency of our committing ourselves any further in behalf of this country when there was no Government to afford us the slightest guarantee that our efforts would not all be thrown away. He growled horridly at this, and danced about the room while he invented the difficulties he labored under to find Ministers, till I thought we should have made a pretty study of a Savoyard and Bear. This morning however I got a letter from him saying he adelantado un gran paso—ahora se hace mas facil las combinacion y me prometo poderla concluir en terminos satisfactorios.¹

Mendizabal's bugbear is that every Frenchman, from the King and his ambassador here downwards, is intriguing against him. I have no reason for believing this, or has he any proof to give, but the notion influences his conduct. He shares however in the universal desire for French cooperation, 1st because he believes it necessary and 2dly because if he were thought to be opposed to it his Government would surely fall. You and Lord Granville must be better judges than me whether the French Government—or rather Louis Philippe, for it very little matters what his Ministers think if he is of a different opinion—is now acting with good faith. Never since the war began have the Carlists been so abundantly supplied with all they wanted from France as at this moment, and never were they up to the time of publishing the late decree reduced to such straits—they now have not magazines in which to store away all they have just imported, and my information is derived not from Mendizabal or Cordoba, but from private sources upon which I rely.

I have likewise good reason to believe that the principal people of Guipuzcoa have offered to place that province under the protection of France. How far the province would consider itself bound by such an offer—how much it would be resented by the whole Spanish nation —and what value the French Government may set upon it, are different questions but that such a negotiation has been set on foot I have no doubt.

I send you today a dispatch in answer to your's upon the murder of Cabrera's mother containing the justification such as it is of the conduct of the Government with respect to the transaction.[2] I don't believe that poor Mrs. C. was ever tried for a conspiracy, and that it has only been got up in consequence of the universal clamor upon the subject—whether she had been previously *condemned* to death or not, there is no doubt that she was *executed* by way of reprisal. Nogueras's order to that effect is extant.

In the event of its becoming necessary to publish the dispatches I would suggest that there is one passage in my No. 51 which had better be omitted stating that Mendizabal and Almodobar had not appeared to think any steps necessary before I remonstrated. It is most strictly true, but as it reflects little credit upon them, there is no use in proclaiming the fact, and it would put me on bad terms with them.

I hope too that if there is any more said about the 27 Carlist prisoners you will see no objection to publishing my No. 64, as it would be a sort of key to Tory interference in Spanish affairs, and an answer to Londonderry's unstoppable nonsense.

The idea of a congress upon Spanish affairs continues to excite great alarm here. I cannot believe that a measure which would shew such a total misapprehension of the Spanish character can be in contemplation. Let the results of such a congress be what they might, no measure that emanated from it would be executable here. Do you know what are the present feelings of the Northern Powers with respect to Don Carlos? I should much like to have the job of proving to them that upon their own anti revolutionary principles they ought to uphold the Queen's cause.

Lord John Hay is very anxious to have some more steam boats and Marines. Now that we have so manfully undertaken to clear the coast and protect the sea ports, it is very important that it should be well done and that our people for want of a little additional expence should not be exposed to unnecessary risk.

PS. Mendizabal sends me word he is *contentisimo* with the new Portuguese Government.

Received 1 May.

GC/CL/257; Clar. Dep. C.452/2 (128-131)

[1] 'advanced a great step. The combination becomes more easy' added in pencil, possibly by P.
[2] It reiterated the claim that she was executed 'not by way of reprisal' but 'for a conspiracy in which she had been clearly proved to be a principal agent'. (V to P, 23 Apr. 1836, no. 97, FO 72/458.)

210 Villiers to Palmerston, 23 April 1836

Madrid. Private. *Encloses a note from Evans, and praises Evans's address to the electors of Westminster.*

Enclosure: Evans (Vitoria) to Villiers, 15 April 1836, 5 a.m., announcing the departure of the third and last brigade of the Legion for Santander, and enclosing a packet for forwarding with this letter to Palmerston. The *do-nothing, risk-nothing* principle guides here—in fact it is a diplomatic not military war. . . .

Received 1 May.

GC/CL/256

211 Villiers to Palmerston, 2 May 1836

Madrid. Private. I have received your letter of the 21st ultimo and I do not wonder that you should think matters are taking a better turn here upon learning the majorities that the Government had obtained in the Cortes, because it is not easy with respect to other countries to lay aside views by which an opinion is formed respecting one's own —particularly when in such countries the same forms of government and therefore the same grounds for coming to an opinion exist as in one's own. But an application of English rules to Spanish things will generally turn out to be a fallacy. There is so little *consequence* in the ideas and actions of these people, moved as they are by passion, that nothing certain can be predicated of tomorrow from what they think or do today. In England and France large parliamentary majorities give life and strength to a Government—here they do not, for every one knows that for the merest trifle Ministers may in the next hour be left in a great minority. The instances of this have been repeated during the last two years, but then on the other hand minorities do not kill a Government here as in England and France. It gets up and shakes itself and nobody remembers its having been knocked down. Legality is the universal rule in England and whatever is done there is according to law—here it is the exception—the laws, such as they are, seem only made to be disregarded, and almost every act of Mendizabal's Administration has been in violation of legality and without any other sanction than his will. The same practice is observed throughout all ranks of[1] authorities—the newspapers and Gazette are full of official reports from the provinces of contributions levied without authority, and people shot without trial at the good pleasure of officers and alcaldes. Nobody thinks this irregular—and no complaint is made against Mendizabal's illegality—it is his want of success that irritates people. His majorities in the Chamber have not given him an atom more power or the public greater confidence in him, and he is as much at a loss now to find people to join him in the Government as he was two months ago.

Mendizabal increases the difficulties of his own position by his want of resolution, and at the same time his fear is so great of having abler men than himself in the Government that he addresses himself only to those who are his inferiors in acquirement, which of course *minimizes* the range of his choice of colleagues. Then whether from fear or old sympathy I know not but it is the canaille who lord it over him, and alarm the well intentioned part of the community. There is a revolutionary paper here advocating the abolition of the Upper Chamber and the calling a Constituent Assembly. It is edited by a Procurador of infamous character who Mendizabal knows is in the interests of Don Carlos (which are best served by creating disunion among the Queen's party) and yet nothing is done to check this paper although the censorship exists. I told Mendizabal the indignation which it excited against him, as he was supposed to be favorable to these subversive principles, for not checking their publication. He confessed that the Government were responsible but were *afraid* to do their duty—he added however that if I would write him a letter complaining of the articles that he might make that a ground with his colleagues for acting with energy. You may suppose what my answer was to this cool proposal of delivering me over to the tormenters of the press, and I merely state this to you in exemplification of the sorry plight to which Mendizabal is reduced.

He and Cordoba are now at daggers drawn—the latter swearing that he has been deceived and maltreated in every way by the Government, and the former swearing that he lies. I have done my best and with success for a long time to ward off this storm, car il ne manquoit plus que cela—but it has got beyond my reach I fear. The revolutionary party which though small is active and noisy, and that party of which the sage Miraflores is the digne chef, are equally interested in putting Cordoba and the Government ill together—the former want to get rid of him knowing his influence with the army which hates revolution and its agents in every shape, while Miraflores and Co. want his support for the same reason, and to gain it, loudly proclaim that Mendizabal's soul is as fairly sold to the anarchists as Peter Schlimmel's[2] was to the Devil.

Cordoba who like every military chief in a civil war is of necessity as much a politician as a soldier, is undecided between the parties. This tends to paralyze the exertions of the army, and the secret societies are in the mean while endeavouring to debauch the soldiers—so that every thing is in active operation except the means for conquering the common enemy who daily becomes more powerful from all this confusion and disunion.

The public hate all these manœuvres and manœvrers—they are in deadly fright—and I believe if prayers could be offered up for French intervention we should see all the churches crowded to suffocation. The idea gains ground every day that unless 30,000 foreign troops come to the Queen's aid, Don Carlos will be at Madrid before next spring—and you may suppose how such an expectation adds to the indecision and fear of compromising himself which seem inherent in every Spaniard.

Nothing will beat it out of Mendizabal's head that France is not playing false both with us and with Spain. I combat his notions because whether true or false he ought to talk and act as if he believed in the good faith of France, but I am far from feeling sure that he is wrong.

He assures me that his negociations for a loan have already made some progress in London, and as soon as he is sure of it he shall ask the consent of the Cortes who will give it gladly and instanter. Mendizabal says he has received great complaints of the *horrors* committed by the Legion on its way to Santander[3]—and Cordoba writes me word that the regiment of Lancers which Evans left with him and which he sent south of the Ebro to refresh the horses had been robbing and killing till the people were about to get up a new edition of the Vesperas Sicilianas. He sent an English officer to enquire into the facts who reported that the complaints of the inhabitants were most just and that the principal offenders were the officers. How far all this is true I know not, but I fear it is certain that the fame of England stood higher in this country before the arrival of the Legion than it does now.

You will of course hear what Evans is about on the coast sooner than I shall. We as yet only know of his arrival at San Sebastian.

Lord John Hay seems a fine fellow—his are the only letters from the insurgent country (or indeed from any other part of the kingdom) which are not desponding and womanish. He says he will clear the coast and take every place upon it now in the possession of the Carlists in the course of this month. I have suggested to him that in the places he takes or occupies for the purpose of protection, the Spanish flag alone should be hoisted. His tars would be very likely to hoist the British flag and quite certain thereby to alarm or offend the Spaniards.

Received 12 May.

GC/CL/258; Clar. Dep. C.452/2 (132-136)

[1] Possibly altered to ampersand. C.452 has 'and'.
[2] Peter Schlemihl, in the story by Chamisso.
[3] See also V to Granville, 27 Apr. 1836, PRO 30/29/421.

212   Villiers to Palmerston, 7 May 1836

Madrid. Private. Esto marcha—though not exactly in the right road.
We have had a very ugly revolutionary week, and the Cortes and the
press seem contending which shall do best service to Don Carlos
—which will win I know not—at present it has every appearance of
a dead heat. The majority of the first of these Powers which is composed of unadulterated canaille, is determined upon removing Cordoba from the army—and the present Captain General of Madrid
from his post, because he is a stern fellow who they know means to take
the opportunity of the first row in Madrid to render *quite* harmless for
the future some score of anarchy mongers—various other authorities
too upon whom the Government can reckon for the maintenance of
order it is proposed to kick out and replace by men *friends to progress.*
During two days the Procuradores debated with closed doors, and
amongst various useful suggestions taken from the French Revolution,
declaring the session permanent and appointing a committee to confer
with the Government upon the state of the nation, were brought
forward— the newspapers at the same time *proving* that it was the Constituent Assembly alone which enabled France to make all the necessary reforms so quickly and so wisely. Yesterday the debate was so
stormy that I am told the galleries called the Members to order, and
the President broke up the session to prevent their coming to blows
amidst a chorus of *Carajos* from the representatives of the people. An
agreable state of things and *like for more wet* as Noah said when he
looked out of the ark.

After the first day of the secret session Mendizabal did not exactly
see what it was leading to, but when he understood that it was a bad
joke instead of a good one as he thought it, he behaved very well and
was very active. During the night he sent to all the Deputies upon
[whom] he could count and succeeded the next day in preventing any
of the revolutionary measures from being taken into consideration.

The Queen's cause however is in more danger at Madrid than in
Navarre. The elements are likewise active against Her Majesty. Cordoba writes me word that after snowing the last week of April as it had
not done all the winter, such torrents of rain had fallen that the country
is like a great lake, and the army is *impossibilitated* from moving. I begin
to believe what was said to me some time ago that El mismo Dios es
faccioso. Lord John Hay too is prevented by the weather from being

as active as he otherwise would, which is much to be regretted as seven weeks have now passed since he announced his cooperation to Cordoba and nothing has yet been done. It is not his fault though, I am sure, for he appears the personification of zeal and activity. I trust that if larger vessels than his or senior officers are sent from Lisbon to the north coast of Spain that he will not be superseded in his command for he has the entire confidence of the natives. I know nothing of what Evans is about, though I have had two letters from him at San Sebastian. One was to ask me to buy a marriage present for a young lady and the other to recommend a captain of horse to command a ship.

As soon as it is brought to bear, the force you are sending out will I am sure be sufficient for all you propose to effect, and the war would have been knocked on the head before midsummer if the French had rendered themselves to your invitation—but of that we must clearly abandon all hope and do the best we can without it.

The journey of the French Princes in search of a Holy Alliance happens unluckily for the intervention question, as they probably go charged with sound despotic doctrines, and Louis Philippe would not at this moment do any thing displeasing to the hosts of his boys.[1]

You will perhaps be surprised to hear it from me, but I think that Cordoba cannot longer retain the command of the army with advantage. Notwithstanding my almost daily assurances upon the subject, he has been led into error by Harispe and other French correspondents, as well as by people here, that intervention would be granted if its necessity was demonstrated and if it was properly asked for—much being made likewise to depend upon a change of Government. All this turning out to be smoke and Cordoba having committed himself greatly with the public and the army that intervention was indispensable for finishing the war, the troops will necessarily lose their confidence in him, and a new general will be necessary to give them fresh courage. This is a very difficult matter to manage, for Cordoba is not a gentleman to be trifled with, and there is no general less unfit than another to succeed him. The Queen would have great objections to removing him and it is important not to let the revolutionists in the Chambers think they have gained a victory upon this matter—still I feel that it ought to be done, for Cordoba is in a false position and he may drag the army and the cause into one as well. You will admit I hope that my liking for him does not carry me to undue lengths in his favor.

With reference to your dispatch upon the extension of the Eliot Treaty[2] I have at various times mooted the subject with Mendizabal and the Minister of War but it offers innumerable difficulties. In Navarre there are two regular armies under their respective chiefs and the treaty is easy of execution. In Catalonia, Aragon, Valencia and Galicia—an enormous extent of territory—the Carlists are in irregular bands which pay a sort of obedience to the ragamuffin who has managed to put himself at the head of each, but who are quite independent of Don Carlos or his authority, and only espouse his cause for the sake of leading the guerilla life they all love. A treaty made with one of these chiefs would not be binding upon another, and it would be impossible for the Government to attempt making a score of distinct conventions which would raise these chiefs and their warfare into great *political* importance, as it would prove the extension and power of the faction. Should the Government however be disposed to the attempt, the public would not suffer it, or would any regard be paid to such arrangements. Neither perhaps would the object in view be attained by them, for the provinces I have mentioned are infested by robbers and malefactors of every kind, who would all when caught plead Carlism in their defence, and must either then go unpunished or be the cause of some horrid retaliations if treated as their crimes deserve.

All attempts to humanize the war where it is irregularly carried on will I fear be useless, because the sense of the nation is against it. The belligerents have no more wish to be separated than two bulldogs and will only fly upon those who try to pull them apart.

I am glad that Almodobar has come to the Foreign Affairs for he is a sensible right minded man—he has not the *felicitous inspirations* of our friend Mendizabal, but he is less shatter-brained, y tiene mas mundo[3] as they say here.

You will see by my dispatch what was the fate of the instructions to Captain Parker.[4] When the Admiralty wish to write to him I believe it would be better to send the letter to the consul at Marseilles to be forwarded by the steam boat to Barcelona. Writing viâ Biscay and Madrid is roundabout and very unsafe.

Almodobar admitted to me last night (what I was sure would turn out to be the case) his fears that Mina's story of Cabrera's mother having been already condemned to death for conspiracy was a lie, invented upon finding that his order for shooting her by way of reprisal had made him the object of general execration.

423

I wish Melbourne had read an extract from my private letter to the indefatigable Londonderry respecting the Eliot Treaty, as of course I am equally prepared to stand by what I write to you in a letter as in a dispatch. In consequence of the debate I have asked Almodobar what was his opinion respecting the execution of the treaty—he said he believed it had been scrupulously fulfilled. A Procurador asserted three days ago that Don Carlos shot all the National Guards whom he made prisoners. Almodobar says that never having heard of it or even seen it in the newspapers he does not believe it, but Cordoba has been written to for information.

Received 15 May.

GC/CL/259; Clar. Dep. C.452/2 (137-142)

[1] This refers to the visit of the Duc d'Orléans and the Duc de Nemours to Berlin and Vienna. See also Granville to P, 2 May 1836, GC/GR/762.
[2] See no. 206 above, n. 3.
[3] 'and has sharper wits'.
[4] 'A courier taking a dispatch from Lord John Hay to Captain Parker of HMS *Rodney* was robbed by a band of Carlists in Arragon and the dispatch taken from him.' (V to P, 7 May 1836, no. 114, FO 72/459.)

213   Palmerston to Villiers, 11 May 1836

Copy. Foreign Office. Well done Evans. The exploit of the 5th instant[1] is brilliant and must be important, but he wants more troops. I have written to Mendizabal to urge him to send reinforcements. Ten thousand men or more; as many more as possible—Spaniards, Portuguese and French. Evans may have his defects as well as his merits, but depend upon it, the men from these Islands are always for acting and getting on; while the Peninsular Gentlemen love to stay swaggering at fixed quarters.

Cordova is a clever fellow; but do you think he really wishes to put an end to the war? Does not its continuance suit him in various ways, political and pecuniary? Has he not an eye to Madrid as well as to Biscay; to high office, as well as to victory? And may he not think that a lingering war would serve all these purposes of his better than an early termination?

Whether he be sincere or not the best thing for Mendizabal to do is to strengthen Evans. If Cordova is in earnest, Evans will help him; if Cordova is playing booty, Evans will force him to run true. I will do all I can to get Evans reinforcements from hence by fresh officers and recruits; but that is a slow operation compared with the effect of marching 10,000 formed men on the spot, to place themselves under his orders.

GC/CL/1261

[1] The victory of the British Legion at San Sebastian.

214 Villiers to Palmerston, 15 May 1836

Madrid. Private. I am very much hurried today as Rayneval is desirous that no courier should get to Paris before his with the news of the downfall of Mendizabal's Ministry. The story and its denouement you will find in my two dispatches of this day's date,[1] and I will only add that Mendizabal has brought this, like every other disaster which has befallen him, upon his own head by his ungovernable obstinacy, and total want of tact in the management of men, *women*, and things. Seven months ago he held the grandest position which it is possible for a private individual to occupy—he had calmed a revolution without bloodshed, and the whole nation was obedient to his word—but he allowed a swarm of ragamuffins to cluster round him, to fill places of trust, and then dictate to him the conduct he was to pursue. Honest men (i.e. comparatively speaking for a *really* honest man I apprehend was never seen in this latitude) kept aloof—he treated the Queen with unvarnished despotism, and thus played into the hands of his enemies who surround her, and who have finally overthrown him. Do not however think that I have not always been just of the same way of thinking as yourself about him. I have felt that he was the Minister of Necessity, and though I have taken the liberty to warn him of his failings (and I have the satisfaction to think I have prevented *some* capital blunders) I have always upheld him in public and given it to be understood that the English Government thought him essential to Spain at this moment of crisis.

During the last week I have worked night and day to get the disagreement between the Queen and him patched up, though I stopped short of offering any advice unasked to Her Majesty for the reasons contained in my dispatch and which I hope you will approve.[2]

Much of the mischief which may now be expected lies at the door of the absurdest of God's creatures, Miraflores, who was so bent upon forming a Ministry which should satisfy the entire nation and be in itself a guarantee of perfect government—all which he saw personified in his own goodly self—that he kept urging the Queen to turn out Mendizabal, without its ever having occurred to him that other people could think differently of his perfection, or that he might not beckon to Isturiz or any one else like a hackney coach from the stand. And so it came to pass that, when he beckoned, all the hackney coachmen laughed but kept not coming, and the Marquis is left alone in his glory.[3]

The evils to which all this may give rise will I fear be very great. The different treasurers gave notice a week ago that on the 18th they must stop payment of every thing for want of funds, and beyond that day there are not the means of feeding even the garrison of Madrid. Where or how therefore Isturiz will *echar mano*[4] upon the needful I have no idea or I am sure has he. The anarquistas[5] some days ago sent emissaries to the provinces to prepare rows in the event of a change of Government and there is no bad prospect of tumult in the capital. When I went to the Foreign Office this afternoon I found all the ex-Ministers together—hypersulky of course—and rather chuckling over some information they had just received of an intended row tonight. I took the liberty of making them a formal speech upon how much it would redound to their honor to have it known that the last use they had made of power was to secure the public tranquillity and that it would be a satisfaction to them to think that no blood had been spilt owing to their want of precaution, etc., etc. This took very much and Mendizabal, who is really a good and rightminded man when left to himself, immediately sent notice to the different authorities of what was preparing, and did all that he would have done if he had been in the full exercise of his ministerial powers.

Evans's success has been most brilliant, and the renown of British arms is here greater than ever. I am convinced that if the Legion is properly reinforced and this victory followed up with activity, that the war may be ended before the autumn without French aid—barring of course internal commotion and national bankruptcy.

I send you an extract from a letter of Colonel La Saussaye's (an Irishman and a very distinguished officer in the Spanish service who I mentioned to you some time ago and that we had sent him down to help the Legion) written two days after the action. You will see from that what invaluable service would be rendered by a few more *British* troops. Do you think it possible to send any? I fear not—but it would be a right good deed—at all events I hope that British officers may be encouraged to come out, and I think that this victory will give such a turn to public feeling about the affairs of Spain, that many who before held back from the obloquy which was thrown upon the Legion would now be ready to come.

Isturiz's[6] feelings towards England, and all that is English, are quite what they should be. Although I have been working hard for Mendizabal I have taken care to keep well with him.

I must not write any more.

Enclosure: 'Extracts of a letter from Lieutenant-Colonel Lasaussaye to Mr. Villiers dated St. Sebastian May 7th 1836', on the action of 5 May and the need for reinforcements.

Received 23 May.

GC/CL/260; Clar. Dep. C.452/2 (143-148)

[1] V to P, 15 May 1836, nos. 121 and 123, FO 72/459. Mendizábal's Ministry collapsed when he gave in to the ultra-liberals in the Chamber and agreed that the Inspector of the Militia and the Commandant-General of Artillery should be dismissed and replaced by ultra-liberal nominees. The Queen Regent refused. Mendizábal then asked her to nominate successors of her own choice; failing that, he offered his own resignation, which the Queen accepted.
[2] V did not wish to arouse French resentment or weaken his position with a new Ministry. (V to P, 15 May 1836, no. 121, FO 72/459.)
[3] Miraflores was asked by the Queen Mother to form a Government, but failed to do so. (V to P, 15 May 1836, no. 123, FO 72/459.)
[4] 'lay hands'.
[5] 'The ultra-liberal party in the Chamber of Procuradores is not unaptly termed that of the anarquistas.' (V to P, 15 May 1836, no. 121, FO 72/459.)
[6] New President of the Council of Ministers.

215 Villiers to Palmerston, 17 May 1836

Madrid. Private. Although you will probably be desirous of hearing how we go on[1] I don't think I should have considered myself justified in sending a courier if it had not been for the urgent request of Mendizabal who wants some financial letters speedily sent which he says may save him from severe losses. He goes so tête baissée into whatever he undertakes that I fear he has ruined himself, for which his partner Mr. Carbonell is likely to care more than he seems to do.

He pleases himself with the thought that his position is like your's last year, and that the Queen will have to send for him again. Isturiz however won't make as good a fight as Peel did, for though he has more vigor and energy than I have ever met with in a Spaniard, he is without resources and above all without that host of thick and thin friends who backed Sir Robert. My conversation with him tonight disappointed me. I had no idea that his expectations of success would have made so poor a show, or that after laying his ground as he has been[2] for two months that he would be found without an inch to stand upon. I could not help expressing my surprise at his having engaged in such a hopeless enterprize, and he defended himself by saying that the Queen was *demented* by Mendizabal's conduct to her, and by his saying that he would abate nothing of his conditions though she were to go down on her knees to him for it. She had then appealed to him (Isturiz) to relieve her from such tyranny, and as a Caballero he thought himself bound to comply, though in the full expectation of breaking his (political) neck.

It is idle making predictions of what will happen here for the prospect is too black on every side to enable one yet to discover what evil will be the greatest or which will come first, for even supposing that the provinces remained tranquil, which they will not, the contributions to be expected from them have all been anticipated by Mendizabal for the next twelvemonth—there is not one farthing in the treasury, and Isturiz does not mean to apply for a loan until Aguirre Solarte[3] arrives (*if* he comes which is by no means certain) and then it will probably be refused.

The effect of this throughout every class of the community but particularly the army is enough to give occupation to any fertile imagination and I defy it to reach *all* the evils which are in store.

Galiano is a good speaker and is universally *dis*respected. The Duque de Ribas is an homme de lettres of small calibre—that is all the perceptible Ministry as yet, and they have about seven friends in the Estamento.[4] Don Carlos ought to be bell-ringing and Te Deum singing for verily his affairs are at a premium.

The cowardly authorities of the 'very heroic Bilbao' as it is called have done a bad deed in making Lord John Hay stop with 700 Marines to protect the 6,000 troops which form the garrison, instead of taking Pasages. In a war such as this where moral effect is so important successes should be followed up quickly. The Carlists are now recovering from 'late Panic'. Englishmen alone can put an end to the war—Spaniards can't, and the French won't.

Received 26 May.

GC/CL/261; Clar. Dep. C.452/2 (149-152)

¹ To Granville V admitted that since the fall of Mendizábal his own position had not been without difficulty: 'I have had great trouble in persuading people that I had not asked for my passport and had not directed the British Legion to withdraw on account of the change of Ministry, and last week I narrowly escaped a deputation from the Chamber of Procuradores to request I would use my influence with the Queen not to accept Mendizabal's resignation.' (V to Granville, 17 May 1836, PRO 30/29/421.)
² 'doing' added in pencil, possibly by P.
³ The new Minister of Finance.
⁴ One of the estates composing the Cortes.

216 Villiers to Palmerston, 21 May 1836

Madrid. Private. I have received your letter of the 11th and you will have already learned that every thing in my power to procure reinforcements for Evans was done immediately upon learning the news of his victory. Indeed, a fortnight before and in the anticipation of it, I had begged Cordoba to send him 5,000 more troops, but he told me that it was absolutely impossible for that the new recruits were as yet of no service to him, and he could spare none of the old regiments. The event proves that it *was* possible for he has sent four battalions, and if he had done so before, Evans's success might have been followed up immediately and not allowed to get cold as it has.

Your doubts with respect to Cordoba are perfectly legitimate though perhaps not *quite* correct. I have no prejudices for or against him or anybody else. I form my judgement upon people as I find them and from the best data I can get, but I don't believe that I am pigheaded or ever refuse to admit a proof of having been wrong. I came here prepossessed against Cordoba. I changed my opinion upon reading his dispatches from Lisbon, and the courageous and statesmanlike advice he gave Ferdinand upon his resolution to uphold Don Miguel, as well as upon learning the manner in which without waiting to know the effect produced in Spain by the King's death, he declared himself in favor of the Queen and saved her throne (as the Queen Regent has over and over again admitted to me) by his measures for preventing the return of Don Carlos to this country. On his arrival here I found him to be a man of larger views and more natural capacity than any I had met with, and full of that kind of ambition that leads a man to glory. As a personal favor to me he was sent to the army—his courage and talents gained the good opinion of every body—he afterwards commanded in chief when he remoralized and redisciplined the army, raised its enthusiasm to the highest pitch, gained a victory and fully justified the expectations of his friends.

Till last winter set in therefore I saw no ground for changing my opinion of him—since that time I have never been quite satisfied with his conduct—he has been constantly meddling in politics and blowing hot and cold about Mendizabal (whose eternal failure however to fulfill whatever he promised justified much of the disgust which Cordoba exhibited) instead of devoting himself to the duties of the campaign. His health is so bad and he suffers so much from nervous irritability that I have long since thought him at times insane (his brother died mad). The Queen has likewise done all in her power to irritate him against Mendizabal, and of late I strongly suspect that the French Government has got hold of him, and to that more than any thing else I attribute his inactivity.[1] What the bait may have been I know not, but his object in prolonging the war cannot be high office here, for if tranquillity were reestablished he knows that with the army devoted to him he might command and retain any post he liked, and if he had pecuniary objects in view he could make more as Minister of War with a large standing army than as Commander in Chief.

Be that as it may, and you see I don't put his morality very high, I believe him to have an understanding with the French Government which is determined upon this war dragging on.[2] The engagements which you say Louis Philippe has taken with the Northern Powers only adds one to the many proofs that have lately come to my knowledge of his desire that the attempt now making in this country to pass from an absolute to a constitutional form of government should not be successful.[3] I can well understand the Holy Alliance looking upon it with terror, for if in this strongest hold of despotism a representative system could be established, and that from it were manifestly to spring the improvement and prosperity of the people, the desire for imitating such an example might become uncontrollably strong among the subjects of the Northern Powers, and the interest of these latter is therefore pressing to have it shewn that all such attempts produce bloodshed and misery and end in failure. The solution is now as it has been all along in the hands of Louis Philippe, and what can he pledge that is more likely to get him received into the bosom of Nicholas than that despotism shall not expire in the West; or what marriage offering is better fitted to produce a Holy Alliance for his son than the nascent liberties of Spain?

Unfortunately Spaniards are playing his game and seem eager to prove that they are not yet fit to be free. Experience has taught them nothing—the same revolutionary vagaries are going on as in 1820 and now as then the (misnamed) liberals are forcing the nation to look to an Absolute King as a relief from their tyranny.

With respect to the present ministerial crisis, I have done all that lay in my humble power to avert its consequences. Not being able to see the Queen before she decided upon accepting Mendizabal's resignation, I procured that she should be fully warned of the danger of doing so—but to no purpose. She seemed blindly bent upon revenging herself upon Mendizabal. I afterwards managed to reconcile him and Isturiz which I thought a great point gained,[4] and Her Majesty once more put a spoke in her own wheel—so till something fresh turns up I am au bout de mon Latin.

I am enraged to think that Miraflores should have been able to produce all the mischief, and my only consolation is that this Sancho Panza who has been announcing himself for the last six months to the nation as a Messiah should, when he thought his hour was come, have knocked at every door for a colleague and have only got laughed at and told to get about his business. Not having been permitted to redeem his country the little Saviour now meekly solicits about 5 and 20 times a day (Isturiz tells me) to be sent ambassador to Paris, solemnly engaging that by return of courier he will dispatch to Spain 50,000 French troops which have not yet come because they have never been properly asked for, and because nobody but himself knows how to tackle Louis Philippe. Having met with an unaccountable (to him) hesitation about this appointment, he offered to put up with London and I found Isturiz really thinking of it, not so much to please the Marquis as to serve you, believing from Miraflores's account that you had never been well in health or quite right in your mind from pining at his departure from England. Upon my certificate that your Lordship's was a mens sana in corpore sano Alava, as you may suppose, will not be disturbed in his mission.

PS. May 22d. I have detained my courier till today in order to communicate to you the determination of the Government, but I don't believe I have any thing to add to my dispatch. The dissolution is a tremendous coup d'état for a powerless pennyless Government.[5] With this capricious people no one can ever feel sure of the turn things may take, but nothing can be blacker than the present prospects. The war was just beginning to take a favorable turn, for the Carlists are in extreme distress, and now comes all this devilment to send the Pretender up to a premium! Mendizabal's dismissal will probably alarm Evans and the Legion, and as I have received from Isturiz the most satisfactory assurances that every engagement of the Government with them shall be punctually fulfilled,[6] and that he looks to them as the mainstay of the Queen's cause, I have written to that effect to Evans and shall desire the courier to take my letter on to Bayonne as soon as he has delivered his dispatches to your messenger at Oleron.

Received 30 May.

GC/CL/262; Clar. Dep. C.452/2 (153-158)

[1] 'that the French' to 'inactivity' underlined, possibly by P.
[2] 'the French' to 'dragging on' underlined, as n.1.
[3] 'should not be successful' underlined, as n.1.
[4] V arranged a reconciliation between Mendizábal and Istúriz in the hope that it would result in the formation of a new Government of which both would be members. Mendizábal and Istúriz were prepared to work together but the Queen Regent refused to allow Mendizábal to return to office. (V to P, 21 May 1836, no. 131, FO 72/459.)
[5] The Chamber was dissolved on 21 May after it had debated a motion of no confidence. (V to P, 23 May 1836, no. 133, FO 72/459.)
[6] For Istúriz's assurances that money, arms and reinforcements would be sent to the Legion, see V to P, 22 May 1836, no. 132, FO 72/459.

217 Villiers to Palmerston, 23 May 1836

Madrid. Private. For form's sake I add a line of private letter to my pair of little dispatches.

Notwithstanding the swagger of yesterday about the great things that were to be done today in order to prevent the dissolution of the Cortes, the operation was successfully performed in about two minutes. In the galleries there was a chorus of Múeras but outside the Chamber a dead silence which may *partly* be attributed to the spectators counting among their number two detachments of cavalry.

The provinces seem *uneasy* as far as is known of them yet, but there has been no outbreak. Money is the great want, and where Mr. Isturiz means to look for it every body is asking his neighbours. *With* it I should not despair of his keeping the peace and carrying on the war.

The two *state papers*[1] I send you today are wretched performances considering that two literati, the Duque de Ribas and Galiano, are Cabinet Ministers.

Received 2 June.

GC/CL/263; Clar. Dep. C.452/2 (159-160)

[1] An Exposition of the Government to the Queen to dissolve the Cortes and a Manifesto of the Queen Regent to the Nation, both enclosed with V to P, 23 May 1836, no. 134, FO 72/459.

218 Villiers to Palmerston, 29 May 1836

Madrid. Private. Things are not looking quite so badly as might have been expected—that is the provinces have not set up their juntas, or done much more than manifest dissatisfaction. This however does not justify the step taken by the Queen, for there was every probability that it would throw the country into confusion, and Isturiz accepted office in the full expectation that such would be the case; he knew also that there was not a farthing in the treasury and that Mendizabal was about to contract a loan (I am by no means sure that the hope of coming in for larger slices of that than Mendizabal would have let them have did not influence the Queen and Her Majesty's Camarilla) and he was aware that during the time that must elapse before he could establish a [?loan] with foreign capitalists the army would run the risk of being starved. These considerations together with the state of the electoral law in the event of a dissolution, and the spirit of the Cortes which rendered such a measure probable upon a change of Government, should have made prudent and patriotic persons pause, but they are rare birds in Spain and we must take people as we find them.

The state of destitution and penury of the Government is beyond what I can describe, every paymaster's and contractor's office is closed like a broken bank, and though Spaniards are accustomed to every species of irregularity on the part of the Government they have seldom seen any thing to equal what is now taking place. Isturiz does nothing but shrug his shoulders—this does not however produce gold and he

433

intends to take his chance until the arrival of Aguirre Solarte who is a poor little tradesman not very likely to help the state coach out of the slough.

Rothschild and Ardouin are so deep in Spanish funds that they may possibly advance something in order to prevent complete ruin of the national credit, and they would do wisely for the war never looked so well as it does now. Evans's victory has given it an entirely new turn, and since the affair of the 5th the Carlists have been running about the country like rats in a barn of which they have long had undisturbed possession upon finding the ferrets and terriers turned in. They have been moving in every direction without a definite object and the country people who have hitherto been the stimulators of the troops are disheartened. Cordoba's army became furious at its inaction and at seeing the English success and declared itself anti French intervention. Cordoba was obliged to take the field, and although no official dispatches have been received from him since the 20th we know that he has been doing really great things. Destroying all their fortifications upon Arlaban and the lines behind which they intrenched themselves and shut out the Queen's troops from their country will produce a tremendous moral effect besides shortening the war in the material part *if there was but money*, for the country where the Queen's troops *ought to go* produces nothing for them, and every biscuit must be bought in Vitoria for the use of the army and its transport paid for or Cordoba must abandon his operations.

I learn by private letters from the scene of action during the last few days that the Navarrese (who are longo intervallo Don Carlos's best troops) are so disheartened that they could not be got to advance and Villareal was obliged to fetch the Alave[s] and Guipuzcoans from a distance in order to oppose any resistance to Cordoba—there appears to have been *some* hard fighting at first in which the Queen's troops were successful and they have since had it all their own way.

I have been glad to hear upon most impartial testimony that Cordoba is not to blame for his late inaction—the severest winter ever known in Spain had rendered the roads, the fords, the mountains, in short the whole country absolutely impassable.

Now would be the time, if you could possibly get them together, to send out 1,000 more Marines. They, together with those which Lord J. Hay has, might take care of San Sebastian, Pasages, Fuenterabia and Irun without hardly losing sight of their ships and Evans would then have his 10,000 men free and he would then go and meet Cordoba sweeping the country before him and placing the enemy between two fires. Think of this if possible and *we* shall have the glory of finishing the war. I am sure you have no reason to repent the assistance you have already afforded.

By your messenger of the 19th I had no private letter from you.

Received 6 June.

GC/CL/264; Clar. Dep. C.452/2 (161-164)

219   Villiers to Palmerston, 30 May 1836

Madrid. Private. *Introduces the Chevalier de Zayas, who is proceeding to London on his way to take charge of the Spanish mission at Copenhagen.*

Received 13 June.

GC/CL/265

220   Palmerston to Villiers, 2 June 1836

Copy. Stanhope Street. I am very sorry for the break up or break down of Mendizabal's Government, it is a most unfortunate thing for Spain. Where in the world is Isturiz to get that money without which the whole machine of government must come to a stand still? I hope one's anticipations of ill may be falsified, but the prospect is not bright. The French Government are so anxious to disclaim having had any participation in the intrigue that they convince one that Rayneval had much to do with it. Possibly he wished to have kept off the change for a little while till money matters were settled, as the Tories may be desirous of keeping us in, till the supplies are all voted—but it is evident that the French consider the present Government in Spain as *their* Government, and accordingly beg and intreat our concurrence with them in fostering the bantling. Be this however as it may, we support what *is* in Spain; and as long as Isturiz does his best to put down the Carlists, and govern Spain constitutionally, he ought to have all the assistance we can give him.

To be sure he has made a strange start as to governing constitutionally. His declaration about the way in which the elections are to be made[1] is much as if we in 1831, when we dissolved Parliament, had declared that the new elections should be made according to the Reform Bill which had been proposed to the House of Commons,

435

instead of according to the established law of the land. But this is the affair of the Spaniards and not ours; and if they like to be governed by ordinances instead of by laws, and think the acts of the Cortes so assembled will be valid, it is all well and good.

Pray plague Isturiz's heart out till he sends more Spanish troops; unless Evans has 10,000 disposable men, besides his garrisons, he cannot do what he ought to do, and what he would do with adequate means—why not send him the Portuguese contingent?

By the by Moncorvo came to me today to say Villa Real has written to him that the Portuguese Government had rather not have their second division of 3,000 men advance beyond Zamora, or wherever else it may be, near to their own frontier. That things were not altogether so quiet in Portugal as they might be, and they had little left within their own territory to keep order. I told him this opinion seemed to me very reasonable, and that I would write to you to beg you to ask the Spanish Government not to press these 3,000 Portuguese to go further away from their own frontier. Now that the Spanish Government has raised so large a portion of its 100,000 men, so small an addition as 3,000 men cannot be any great object to them; while the loss of that force by its removal to a distance from their frontiers would be a serious inconvenience to the Portuguese.

I am glad you assured Isturiz that I can live to the end of the year without my worthy little friend Miraflores. The poor little man seems to have lost all the small wits nature endowed him with. Alava does much better for us. If the Spanish Government could have raised a loan of two millions, they would probably have put an end to the war in 3 months, it is provoking to think that they should have changed their Government at such a moment.

The Tories are much elated with the hopes that these Irish Bills will bring them in. . . .

PS. The Rodney is ordered to join the fleet at Malta, but if a line of battle ship is wanted on the eastern coast, one can be sent from Lisbon.

GC/CL/1262

[1] The elections were to be in accordance with the Bill introduced during the session, not according to the existing law.

221   Villiers to Palmerston, 4 June 1836

Madrid. Private. You will have already learned by a letter of mine a few days ago to Lord Granville [of] Cordoba's arrival here, and his opinions en gros upon the state of the war. I look upon his visit as very important, and Mendizabal now bitterly repents not having allowed him to come to Madrid some months ago. All their quarrelling would have been avoided and Mendizabal would perhaps have been Minister at this moment. He was in the habit of not reading Cordoba's dispatches, but of sending him all manner of instructions with reference to the funds rather than the military operations, and making him brilliant promises of assistance which of course never were fulfilled. This used to drive Cordoba mad and was the occasion of his resigning continually and writing and speaking furiously against the Government. The correspondence which he has brought with him to shew me goes far, I must admit, to justify his resentment. Afterwards when I managed to make it up between them, and Mendizabal had consented to Cordoba's coming here, he (Cordoba) wrote the most urgent letter to the Queen (which he sent under flying seal to me) upon the inexpediency of changing her Minister. It arrived however the day after Mendizabal had given his resignation when he and the Queen had each embarked too large a share of amour propre in the question to yield.

I think it due to Cordoba to mention these circumstances as well as the language he has held every where since his arrival respecting the moderate party with whom he was supposed to be in league. He explains his vehemence for French intervention by the destitute condition in which the army was left and his having been led to believe that the objections of Louis Philippe to the measure were not insuperable, and he was the more desirous of it because the war is not merely one of strategy but of opinion, and moral effect is therefore of more importance than military achievements. He is now however convinced that nothing is to be hoped from France; his late operations have restored the enthusiasm of the troops, and he seems to be in better heart about ultimate success though quite positive that the system of wearing out and starving out the faction is the only means [of] restoring tranquillity, because when the country becomes entirely exhausted by the exactions which are every day becoming more intolerable, the population will of itself embrace, and afterwards stick to, the Queen's cause.

Cordoba is very clever and his arguments *appear* unanswerable, but I don't pretend to give an opinion upon whether he is right or not. I shall have some further conversation with him and then report to you fully his views. The confidence which the people of the country are beginning to manifest towards Evans is perhaps more important than his military success. If you write to him pray encourage every kind of protection being given to life and property in order that the English may be looked to as conciliators as well as conquerors, and that what is promised by them is scrupulously performed, for the Spaniards know each other far too well ever to take their own promises even into consideration.

The captain of the French ship of war at Pasages appears to have behaved very ill. He was asked in the civilest manner by Lord John Hay to move his vessel out of the way for a time lest she should receive any damage from the Carlist guns and he refused to do so. The place as it turned out was taken without damage to any one, but if resistance had been made, Lord John Hay in order to avoid collision between the English and French naval forces would have relinquished his co-operation and the Carlists would thus have received direct protection from the French man of war.

It is of course useless and might be mischievous to make much row about this, but a friendly observation upon their dog in the manger system would possibly prevent its repetition, without dangerously compromising the King of the French while swaining the Holy Allies.

The report of Evans having ceased hostilities till he knew the effect of the change of Government here was an infamous lie, like 100 others spread about by the revolutionary party for the purpose of creating confusion. Mendizabal pretended to have such entire confidence in the source from which he received it that I thought for a moment there might be some foundation for it. I have now called upon him to assist me in tracing the author of the calumny and he seems inclined to do no such thing.

The provinces are quiet and matters generally look better than *any body* expected, but the want of money is *espantoso*[1] and so is the prospect of getting any. I have as yet seen no reason to change my opinion of Isturiz—that he is not a man of resource, and although he has great vigor of character and can take a bold resolution he will fail in executing it.

I am trying as usual to push commercial matters and Isturiz promises fairer than any of his predecessors. I hope if Jabat comes to you for any assistance you will let him know that it is high time something should be done for us, especially as that something will be of signal benefit to Spain.

Mr. Renny is arrived. . . .

PS. By the same conveyance that this goes, my attaché Otway will return to the Mother Country. I know how little patronage you have and how many claimants there are for that little—it is therefore useless recommending Otway for a share, but it is only justice towards him to tell you that he is an industrious, docile, painstaking young man, always anxious to do his duty. He will never be a great ambassador but few secretaries will be better than him if ever he should chance to get made one.

Received 13 June.

GC/CL/266; Clar. Dep. C.452/2 (165-170)

¹ 'appalling'.

222 Palmerston to Villiers, 6 June 1836

Copy. Foreign Office. The state of things in the north of Spain induces me to send you off a messenger though he only carries to you this private letter. Are the Queen and her Camarilla stark staring mad, or have they acted upon secret promises of succour pecuniary and military from France? If the former, I hope the Turkish Providence will not desert them; if the latter, I wish the deities of Paris may not have lured them on with false hopes. But to dismiss a Ministry which was about to get money, and to replace it by one which has not a farthing and to all appearance cannot anywhere get a farthing, and to deprive that Ministry by a dissolution of all legal means of raising extraordinary supplies, and to do this in the midst of a civil war and at the opening of a campaign does look almost too much for madness, and can scarcely be accounted for, except by the supposition of treachery. But let Cordova and Mendizabal, the Spaniards and the French settle this matter among themselves as they may. It little signifies to us who is to blame. The result is what we care about.

But there is one matter in which we have a positive, a direct, a national, an urgent interest and that is the Legion and Evans's operations—and the Spanish Government, let who will be in office, is bound by every principle of honour not to desert the Legion, or mar the operations of Evans.

It was at the request of Spain that the Order in Council was issued; it was for the cause of the Queen that we encouraged Evans and his brave army to go; it was to save the Queen's throne that the military honour of England was embarked in her cause, in the persons of Evans and his Legion. We have done all we could to render that corps efficient and useful; that corps has done all it could to render itself worthy of the nation to which it belongs. The Spanish Government may if it pleases leave Cordova and his generals to kick their heels at Vittoria, or to rove about the country living on contributions; that is a national affair, and the disgrace begins and ends with Spaniards. But they have no right to abandon the Legion to distress, and by administrative misconduct reduce our people to a condition in which they might be broken down in spirit and body, and driven to acts that would disgrace themselves and their country.

Pray lose no time in putting this in the strongest possible light to Isturiz, and if necessary to the Queen. Say that if they mean to throw up their hand and relinquish the game, they are bound in honor to send the Legion home while it is in its present state of complete and honorable efficiency, while its laurels are fresh and untarnished by the consequences of suffering and privation. That if they think the throne of Spain still worth fighting for, and if they have the means of carrying on the war, they must take especial care that the Legion is kept well supplied, that the engagements made with Evans are fulfilled, and that ample reinforcements of Spanish troops are sent to Evans, to enable him to complete the important operations which he has begun.

Now the engagements made with Evans are:

1st. That arrears should be paid up.

2d. That officers and men should henceforward be paid monthly in advance.

3d. That proper magazines should be established in advance and in reserve for clothing necessaries, camp equipment, etc.

4th. That there should be depots of provisions always complete for two months.

All these things are evidently necessary, with these arrangements six thousand of the Legion will be worth twelve thousand men ill provided; so that it is a real economy to keep the corps efficient.

But besides this there are some expences incurring here, for clothing and necessaries and accoutrements due to the Legion in July.

Young Rothschild called on me two evenings ago to ask my opinion what he should do; he said he had bills drawn on him for the Legion amounting to £5 or £6,000 which he must either pay or refuse the next morning at 10 o'clock—he wanted to know whether the Government could help him. I said it was utterly impossible; we could not advance or guarantee a farthing, he must decide for himself—but it seemed to me that he could not hesitate to pay the bills because the evil of refusing them would be great and immediate, and there could be no doubt that if the Queen swims, she will pay. He said he would pay for the nonce, but more bills were in the wind, and pay them when they came he neither could nor would. I promised that if he honoured the £6,000 on Saturday last, I would write to you to let you know what had passed between him and me, and to beg you to urge the Spanish Government to repay him a sum which I had myself personally asked him to pay, and for the repayment of which I had pledged my *belief*, which was all I could give.

Some immediate communication about money matters to Jabat or Carbonell is absolutely necessary.

It is too provoking to think that the whole thing should go to the dogs, just at the moment when the sky was clearing up.

As to your friend,[1] I hope I do him great injustice; but I plainly confess his conduct is to me inexplicable upon any supposition which does not impeach either his honesty or his military ability. He might have been unable to move; but repeatedly he did move; and then only as it were to stop people's mouths, but not to do anything that could be of the slightest use. The Carlists have, it is said, 40,000 men; such an army, composed as you will, must have magazines and manufactories of powder and arms. Why does not Cordova, if he can do nothing more, make a dash at these establishments and destroy them? But if he and Evans and Bernelle were to cooperate upon a rational plan, and with equal good will, surely they would be able to squeeze Carlos and his army, *as an army*, out of the small district in which they at present are.

I have this morning received your letters and dispatches of the 29th ultimo.

I ought not to omit that Reid wrote to Hay of the Ordnance last September that the Legion was in great want of entrenching tools. Hay and I set to work immediately, and in a week after a supply was sent out specifically for the Legion. The supply reached Santander, was there clawed hold of by Cordova, and the Legion in its late operations lost actually *six days* from not being properly supplied with entrenching tools.

GC/CL/1263

[1] Córdoba.

223 Villiers to Palmerston, 12 June 1836

Madrid. Private. I have received your letter and dispatches of the 2d and am not surprised at your disapprobation of all that has been done here, but very happy you consider I did what laid in my power to avert the mischief. I read part of your letter to Isturiz and told him what was the public feeling in England with respect to the change of Government, intimating that if he was really sincere in his wish to prove that French influence had not been exercised of late, and that he was not unduly bound to France, he must immediately take measures for putting our commercial relations upon a better footing. He seemed then, as he has done before, fully to admit the importance of this and the advantage it would be to his Government, adding that it was an affair of amor propio with him to manifest how unFrench he was, *but,* and there is *always* a but in Spain, he was so overwhelmed with business that he could devote his time only to that which was of vital importance, and the state of Catalonia was such that the utmost caution must be observed with respect to measures which would be unpopular in that province. He understands the interests of Spain upon this question better than his predecessors *but* he is a Spaniard and will therefore do nothing.

The approaching elections give the Government great uneasiness for there is not time to get ready an apparatus for combating the activity of the anarchists and the apathy of the moderates—and the Queen is playing her va tout—if this opportunity is lost she will not have another. Mischief is brewing in Catalonia and Aragon, and the want of money paralyses every thing—so that Isturiz is not upon a bed of roses.

There is no necessity in my opinion to recur to French influence or intrigues in order to account for recent events here—their causes are evident. The anarchist party who formed the majority in the late Chamber declared their determination two months ago, as I reported to you, in a secret session to change the generals and all persons at the head of the military and civil force in order that no resistance should be made to the after projects they had in view. Mendizabal hating and fearing this party could not do without them, and in an evil hour proposed some of the changes they stipulated for to the Queen. She, aware of what they would lead to, refused—the Ministers offered to resign. She said, Don't resign but don't make me remove persons who are not incapable of carrying on the public service and in whom I have confidence. She left them 4 or 5 days for consideration and they still insisting, she accepted their resignations, believing it better to make her stand then than later. I quite agree with you that the whole was ill timed and ill done and will probably be productive of disasters, but I don't believe that any foreign influence was used upon the occasion, though plenty of French applause has been since bestowed upon the coup d'état. Thiers's speech on the 2d has been an immense lift to the Carlists.[1] What they most fear is the intervention of France, and the doubt in which the question was held had a considerable moral effect. That doubt is now removed, for Thiers says France will never intervene without the consent of the Chamber—the Chamber being known to be unfavorable to the measure and being about to be prorogued, the Carlists feel secure from harm for the next 6 months.

There is one part of Thiers's speech which if rightly reported requires some explanation and you may easily conceive the bad effect it has produced here. He says that we have engaged to give up to France whenever they are demanded of us the ports of Spain which we at present hold. I was not aware that we held any, or that the British Legion in the service of the Queen of Spain, having saved San Sebastian from the Carlists, could be looked upon as having given possession of that fortress to the King of England. As I said before I don't believe Thiers ever said this, but it is reported in five French newspapers and having been translated into the Spanish it has been mischievous in the extreme with an ignorant susceptible public like that of Madrid.

Cordoba has been here a great deal too long—he began by refusing to have any thing to do with the *interino* Minister of War who was not of rank for the post and being only an aide-de-camp of Quesada's was disliked in the army. Several generals gave and others were about to give in their resignations in consequence of having such a Minister of War, and Cordoba said he should have lost caste with the army if he had not insisted upon his removal. Several days were lost in the debates upon this subject, and several more in fetching General Mendez Vigo[2] from the army. I have this moment learned that he is arrived and I suppose that Cordoba will be off in a couple of days. He assures me he has reinforced Evans as much as he possibly can at this moment, but I still intend to get some more troops sent to the coast, though if Cordoba's account be correct, and I have myself checked it by the official returns, Evans has considerably more than 10,000 men under his command. As for any combination between Evans and Cordoba at the present moment it is out of the question, as there are absolutely no means of communicating together but by Santander or through France, and a combination 5 days old with all the contingencies of such a war in such a country might expose one or both of the combining parties to a serious scrape.

I cannot say I am in good heart about what Cordoba will do when he returns for he makes out a case of almost insurmountable difficulty if he is to be left without money or provisions—and the Government cannot furnish him *with a tithe* of what is *indispensably* necessary.

I have done my utmost to save the lives of the Carlist chiefs recently made prisoners in Aragon, but such is the state of rabid fury of the people in that province against the faction since the murder of 54 officers by Cabrera that I fear the lives of these men must be sacrificed to preserve the province from insurrection.[3]

I am sure that upon the score of humanity the state of Spain justifies foreign intervention quite as much as that of Greece ever did.

Received 20 June.

GC/CL/267; Clar. Dep. C.452/2 (171-175)

[1] For a report of the speech, see *The Times*, 5 June 1836.
[2] Appointed Minister of War on 8 July 1836.
[3] For a report of V's conversation with Istúriz on this subject see his despatch to P, 12 June 1836, no. 147, FO 72/459.

224 Palmerston to Villiers, 14 June 1836

Copy. Stanhope Street. I have received your letter of the 4th, but in spite of all that you say for Cordova, and Cordova says for himself, I must continue to think him a vapouring bragging coxcomb, with much say and little do. If he is honest and sincere in the cause of the Queen, and is doing his best, it is evident that he is deficient in military skill. None of his operations have been so devised that it was possible for them to produce any permanent result, and he studiously abstains from every movement which might be productive of such consequences.

Wyld foretold us exactly what would follow from Cordova's absurd attack of Arlaban and Oñate. Wyld said that Cordova could not maintain himself at either place and would be obliged to go back to Vittoria; that the Carlists, though beat in his advance, would pursue him in his retreat; and would boast and with apparent reason, that they had driven him before them. If instead of these useless marchings out and marchings in, Cordova would take possession of the Carlist magazines, occupy the valley of the Borunda[1] and open a communication between Vittoria and Pampeluna, order Bernelle to take possession of the Bastan, and to close in one way, while Evans adequately reinforced was to sweep the country downward from the coast and the French frontier, and effect a junction with Bernelle and Cordova, I am told by better judges than you or I or Cordova that the war would be over in something like one fortnight. But if Cordova with an army of upwards of ninety thousand men, and in the beginning of the summer, and with the Carlists disheartened, distressed, and cooped up, talks of pursuing a system of wearing out and starving out his enemy, depend upon it he is either playing false or totally incapable of playing at all. Pray press these considerations upon Isturiz, and urge him by his duty to his Sovereign, his love for his country, his hopes of fame, and his attachment to office, or if there be to a Spaniard a stronger motive, by that also, to stir up Cordova with a long pole, or if he will not move, to put somebody else at the head of the army who will.

I have had a long conversation with M. Zaya[s], the little man going to Denmark. He is intelligent, but overflowing with abuse of Mendizabal; I suppose he will talk in the same manner of Isturitz in a fortnight after the Cortes meet, when Mr. Somebody Else has been made Minister.

I suspect the Baron de los Valles had something else to say to me, if I had listened to his first overture about the Spaniards at Lisbon.[2] From some words that dropped from him but of which I took no notice, I think he was disposed, if encouraged, to have hinted an arrangement between the parties, marriage, etc., etc., and this I would lay a wager is Cordova's scheme.

GC/CL/1264

[1] Borunda was a hamlet which gave its name to a mountain pass in the Valle de Araquil in Navarre, formerly the scene of some of Zumalacárregui's most brilliant exploits.

[2] See P to V, 13 June 1836, no. 48, FO 72/456. Los Valles was an agent of Don Carlos.

225 Villiers to Palmerston, 18 June 1836

Madrid. Private. I have received your letter of the 6th and you will see by my dispatch that I have done my best to give effect to your instructions. In the first place I read nearly the whole of your letter to Isturiz and insisted upon a meeting with him and his Finance colleague where we came to an understanding as regards the present and future state of the Legion. Respecting that force there is not one word in your letter which would not have been equally applicable any time since Evans arrived at Vitoria as now—but as I rather think from the tone of your letter that you attribute the distress of the Legion to the neglect of the present Government, and as it is just each person (for there are several) should have the share of blame which rightly belongs to him, I propose to enter into the real history of the Legion though it will be long and tedious.

In the beginning of March General McDougall and Colonel Wylde came to Madrid to represent the state of the Legion which in their official letter to me they described as one of 'destitution, misery, disease and frightful mortality' in consequence of 'the callous neglect of the Government which had led to the inefficiency of a great portion of the corps'. You know the language I held to Mendizabal upon the subject and what I got him to agree to. Some time after McDougall returned to Vitoria he informed Wylde that none of the conditions stipulated for had been fulfilled, and that the deputation had never received the orders which Mendizabal asserted had been sent. Ever since that time it has been at least a weekly battle between Mendizabal and me to procure subsistence and pay to go on with (let alone the pay in advance and the stores in magazine), and the Legion when ordered to the coast was detained several days for want of money which was at last raised by selling some stores at a ruinous loss.

These circumstances shew how far the conditions were fulfilled during Mendizabal's time—but I must add in his justification that he objected to paying more money until the Government was furnished with the accounts of the Legion, and it certainly is a shameful fact that not a farthing has been accounted for, or does the Government know how the clothing or stores have been applied—and what is more they never will I am convinced, for the confusion has been so complete—I fear I might add something worse than confusion—that the accounts cannot be made up. Under these circumstances it was agreed upon with Mendizabal that the arrears claimed should stand over till their amount was correctly ascertained—instead of this however part of the money transmitted for the pay of the Legion has been taken for these very arrears and the troops of course suffered. Evans then complains loudly of distress and sends up a letter from a Spanish commissary saying that in a few days the Legion will be without provisions—on the very same day however arrives the commissary (Llanos) who was placed with the Legion three months ago by Mendizabal and declares that he has left supplies for two months. On the same day (of this week) too the Minister of Finance learns from the Intendente of Asturias that he has complied with Evans's order to send a large supply of cattle (Evans having no authority to give any such orders).

The Government accordingly, without accounts, without information, and receiving conflicting statements, is in a really embarrassing position for they have every desire to behave honestly and generously to the Legion whose great services they appreciate, but they contend it is hard they should bear all the blame of a state of things which they inherited, and be called upon to make large disbursements without being allowed to know their application. Within a fortnight after Isturiz came into office I pressed him to send money, and the Bayonne bankers advanced £12,000. This he believed, and so did I, covered the month of May—Evans *adverts* to it only as a trifle which has been sent, but he professes not to interfere with the Pay or Commissariat departments and is therefore I fear made the victim of persons whose conduct appears more than questionable.

Mr. Grindlay the Deputy Commissary General is here at this

moment and I have requested him to draw out a memorandum for your information of the manner in which the financial affairs of the Legion have been conducted. I enclose it and I think you will admit that the present Government should not be held responsible for a state of things which such long mismanagement could not fail to engender.

My courier this night is the bearer of a letter to Bayonne directing the bankers there to send £12,000 to San Sebastian which for aught the Government or I know to the contrary should cover the pay for the month of June. A courier has been sent to London directing the payment of the bills for which you *guaranteed your belief* to Rothschild and for £25,000 of bills for the Legion besides.

I now come to another and very painful part of my story—Evans. Since Mendizabal left the Ministry his language has entirely altered and it is evident I am sorry to say that he is bent upon going home and dissolving the Legion. A few days ago he wrote a letter to Isturiz couched in improper language after the assurances which I had sent him on the part of the Government (I have not missed a single opportunity of doing so since the change of Government but he has never acknowledged a letter of mine) and after desiring that remittances should be sent to Carbonnel and giving the reasons for his private friendship with Mendizabal, although accompanied with assurances of adhesion to the Government, he returns the diploma of the Order of San Fernando because it had been transmitted to him through the locum tenens of Cordoba. The effect this has produced upon the Queen and the Government has been terrible—they feel that the cause *depends* upon the Legion but that Evans will never act cordially with them. Isturiz is beside himself and has begged me to tell you the real state of the case. The diploma is signed by Rodil, the late Minister of War, and went through the course usual in the Spanish service without the remotest thought of offending Evans who is a *Spanish* general here or he is nothing. I enclose you a copy of the letter I wrote to Evans as he sent his to Isturiz under cover to me, and as indeed he does his dispatches to the Government since Mendizabal went out instead of direct to the Minister of War.

Yesterday I received from him another letter for Isturiz which I have taken upon myself not to deliver. I send you a copy of it as well as of my letter to him.[1] A more unprovoked insult cannot be offered and the Government if it has any self respect must quarrel with him. He complains that he has not been reinforced. He asked for 2,000 men at first—he has received 9 battalions amounting to 4,475 men—for I extracted the numbers from the official returns—besides recruits. It is not the fault of the Government that the greater part of the army is now composed of recruits, or that as many troops cannot be sent him as was at first intended in consequence of the numbers which must now be detached to Aragon and Valencia. If the reinforcements are not sufficient to advance he must remain awhile in his present position—it will be a misfortune and a great one to the cause, but it is not a reason for dissolving the Legion. He says that the clothing due in July will not be received in time—why, the Spanish army is in rags and he cannot expect that a pennyless Government at the end of 3 years of civil war should be able to provide for every thing punctually. He desires that Carbonnel should be paid but the Government may surely chuse its own agent and it does not see reason to be satisfied with Carbonnel. Evans knows that the artillery horses had all served their time in London cabs and he gave the whole of them to Cordoba who can make no use of them—and that so far from much of the clothing being cloth it is a courtesy to call it baize. He is furious at his recommendations for rewards not being acted upon but he must know that in every service in the world such recommendations should come through the General in Chief to whom, since he went to San Sebastian, he has given the go by completely.

All these things place me in a very painful position with the Government, for it is difficult to defend what is wrong and yet I can't allow my countrymen to be abused by any Spaniard.

Cordoba is however Evans's principal bête noir—in this he may to a certain degree be right but he is certainly unjust upon some matters. Cordoba may be jealous of Evans for aught I know—to myself and in outward acts he disguises it if he is, and he has begged of me to ask Evans if he has ever given him a single ground of offence. On Evans's arrival at Burgos Cordoba turned out of his house for him, afterwards raised money for the Legion upon his own credit and never objected to Evans acting contrary in every thing to his advice and instructions—he gave him up his secretary and best aides-de-camp upon his asking for them, and they parted apparently the best friends upon his going to the coast. Since that time he has only written once officially to Cordoba and never answered his private letters. Cordoba acknowledged in general orders that the affair on the 5th was the bravest and most important of the whole war and in short he knows not in what

449

he has failed towards him—he could not appoint him during his absence to the command of the army with which he could not even communicate and, so far from his having left instructions to Espartero to be inactive, he enjoined him to undertake any thing he was likely to effect. Espartero did *nothing* and yet he is the man Mendizabal wanted to put permanently in Cordoba's place. Cordoba was (or at least appeared to be so) indignant, and to regret the length of time that he had been induced to stay away—his original intention was to have been here 8 and 40 hours. As for his being a traitor to the Queen's cause *I will answer* that he is not—putting it upon no higher grounds his interests lie in quite other directions.

Pray do not for a moment think that any partiality for Cordoba makes me hold this language. I say to you with respect to him, to Mendizabal, to Isturiz exactly what I think—as it is my duty to do. I now believe, referring again to interests, that Cordoba is anxious to finish the war but I will add that after repeated and long conversations with him I incline to think that he is not equal to the difficulties he has to contend with, and that without some lucky turn (which is quite upon the cards in the present demoralized state of the faction) circumstances will get the better of him, particularly as the means at his command will now be more curtailed than ever.

I am ashamed of having allowed this tedious letter to run on to such a length and I will now conclude by asking you whether in Evans's present state of feelings you think it possible for the Government to go on with him? If so I hope you will write a letter of encouragement to him—if not, do you think it would be well to look out for another general? The latter I can see would be the most satisfactory to Isturiz since the receipt of Evans's letter but he only desires to be guided by your advice if you will have the goodness to give it to him.

In your letter of the 6th you ask me if the Queen and Camarilla are stark staring mad or if every body is committing treason. Things here seen from afar fully justify your enquiry, but as great events often spring from little causes and that you may wish to have a look behind a Spanish curtain, I send you a morsel of secret history which will amuse if it does not surprise you. As I hardly consider myself justified in making the communication (as you will easily see) I beg of you to have the enclosed decyphered by some one of your *entire confidence*.[2]

PS. I can easily conceive that you must feel dissatisfied with Cordoba and unable to explain his military movements. I can only say of him as you did of Mendizabal that he is the best general, indeed the only one, the country affords, and we must do as well as we can with him. I learn from an intelligent young English aide-de-camp who came to Madrid with him that the enthusiasm of the troops for him is now greater than ever. The officers don't like him much.

First enclosure: Memorandum by Deputy Commissary-General Grindlay on the financial affairs of the British Legion.

Second enclosure: Copy, Evans (Headquarters, San Sebastian) to Istúriz, 13 June 1836, returning a decoration.

Third enclosure: Copy (extract), Villiers (Madrid) to Evans, 16 June 1836, on the payment of the Legion, Córdoba's absence in Madrid, and Evans's behaviour over the decoration.

Fourth enclosure: Copy, Villiers (Madrid) to Evans, 18 June 1836, private, urging Evans to be on better terms with the present Government at Madrid.

Received 25 June.

GC/CL/268; Clar. Dep. C.452/2 (176-187)

[1] The copy of Evans's second letter is not now with the enclosures.
[2] See the following letter, no. 226.

226 Villiers to Palmerston, 18 June 1836

Decypher. Madrid. Private. During the two first months after he came into office, the Minister[1] made love to the Queen Dowager. She at length yielded, but he declined to avail himself of the victory. I do not know whether his reasons were physical zero, morality, or politicks: he declared to me the two latter. I said everything to induce him to *behave properly*, but in vain, and he wrote her a letter which no woman, being at the same time a Queen and an Italian, could forgive. Hence the animosity and desire for revenge, and the consequences to which they have led.

Received 27 June.[2]

GC/CL/269

[1] Mendizábal.
[2] So docketed; but the cipher had been enclosed in no. 225, which was received on 25 June.

227   Palmerston to Villiers, 20 June 1836

Copy. Foreign Office. I send you off another extra messenger because I begin to be in despair about Cordova and Evans and the war. The Spanish general seems likely to have too much of feasts in the capital, and the English general too much of frays on the frontier. I do hope and trust you will have been able to move Isturitz to send more troops to Evans; Evans is the only man who *has* done any good hitherto, and depend upon it he is the only man who *will* do any good. If he is furnished with troops enough he will put an end to the war in spite of Cordova and the French Government.

The arrival of Los Valles has let in not a new light but a broader light upon the secret manoeuvres that have been going on. It seems pretty clear to me that the scheme of Cordova and the French Government or rather of the French Government and Cordova was to spin out the war, and let the Carlists get a head, to reduce the matter to a condition in which French aid must have been invoked as a necessity, and for Louis Philippe then to have not only proposed but imposed the marriage of Carlos's son with the Queen. This would have reconciled Louis Philippe with Austria and the other members of the Holy Alliance; would have been a triumph of French influence in Spain; and would have freed the Tuileries from their apprehensions of the bad consequences which may arise to France from the firm establishment of constitutional government in Spain. If this plan was conceived it has been marred by our blundering policy which could not enter into such fine spun schemes and which simply imagined the expulsion of Don Carlos and the establishment of the Queen to have been the common objects of all the allies. But the existence of such a scheme is the only supposition which appears to me to account for the conduct of Cordova and of Louis Philippe.

Evans says Rodil is the man who is thought the most likely to succeed as commander of the Spanish army—of that we cannot judge. Sebastiani begged me the other day to write to you to ask you to exert your influence to get Cordova retained in his command and to prevent that command from being given to Mina. I said that in the first place we were not much in the habit of meddling with such matters, but to tell him the truth my opinion of Cordova was coming back to what it originally had been. That when first he took the command he seemed disposed to do more than his predecessors and had infused a new spirit into the army, but that for some months past this had changed; and that now one must impeach either his honesty or his military talent; that consequently so far from interfering to retain Cordova I should be delighted to hear of his being removed. But that Mina had shewn no capacity for general command and that his savage conduct in the case of Cabrera's mother and in many other instances prevented us from wishing to see him succeed Cordova.

It is curious that I received yesterday a letter from Evans saying that Rodil is the only man for the command, and that today I get a letter from William Russell at Berlin saying exactly the same thing, and expressing about Cordova much the same opinion that one hears from everybody who speaks of him.

Since I began this letter I have received yours of the 12th. I send you a dispatch to deny the pretension which Thiers ascribes to us of a right to order the Queen's troops to deliver up Spanish fortresses to the troops of Louis Philippe. Thiers spoke hastily and without exactly weighing the full import of his words.[1] The thing will have been forgot by the time my dispatch reaches you, but there it is nevertheless.

I hope Isturitz will peremptorily order Cordova to send more troops to Evans. What you say of the impossibility of quick communication between the separate divisions render[s] it still more necessary that Evans should be strong enough to act upon his own account. But armies and divisions have cooperated according to plans previously fixed with wider intervals of time and distance between them than those which separate Vittoria from St. Sebastians. Evans ought to have at least 10,000 men disposable besides the garrisons he has to leave in St. Sebastian's and Fuente Arabia (when he takes it). 5,000 Spaniards are a mere nothing—when double that number are with them it will be time enough [to ask] whether two or three thousand more will be enough. But Cordova's jealousy of Evans and spiteful wish to see him crushed show themselves in all his arrangements; as to foreign interference it is really now a joke to talk of it considering the relative condition of the two contending parties.

I am very glad you have done your best to save the two guerilla chiefs, though I fear from your account that your endeavours will have been unsuccessful.[2]

PS. Thomson tells me that Goldsmid of the City assures him that if Isturitz would give him and other capitalists the guarantee of a treaty

of commerce with this country, they would advance what money Isturitz wants, and without asking any guarantee from the English Government. I am to see Goldsmid tomorrow, but that is what Thomson
understands him to have said.

GC/CL/1265

[1] P to V, 20 June 1836, no. 53, FO 72/456. He points out that contrary to
Thiers's statement in the Chamber of Deputies, Evans and the Legion were
not under the direction of the British Government. They were British troops
in the service of the Queen of Spain. In fact, therefore, there were no British
troops occupying any part of Spain.
[2] P to V, 20 June 1836, no. 52, FO 72/456, approving of V's representations
to save the lives of officers belonging to the Carlist faction of Catalonia.

228 Villiers to Palmerston, 23 June 1836

Madrid. Private. The little I have to say this evening is rather favorable than otherwise as the accounts all agree in stating that the faction
never has been in the state of misery and discouragement that it is now,
and the desertion would be much greater than it is if the Carlist lines
were not as much used to keep their own people in as they are to keep
the Christinos out. The depriving Eguia of the command, too, is *or
ought to be* an important event, as he is the only officer of ability who
Don Carlos has in his service. It has been said, and I believe truly, that
until he took command the facciosos did not know what their energies
and activity were capable of—it is he who has organized all the espio-
nage, and who never failed to have his troops found in the place where
their presence was least desired by the Queen's army. Don Carlos knew
this perfectly and so did his Minister Erro (who is a very able man)
and the intrigues or rather the discontent of the population must have
been very powerful to have displaced him.

Villareal is by way of being a preux chevalier and a liberal unfortunately embarked in a cause which his honor forbids him to desert. He
has a mighty great mind however to throw over his honor if he could
do so decently, and I made a proposition to Cordoba founded upon
some information to that effect which he gave me—viz. that if he could
establish through his parlementaires a communication with Villareal
and make him feel the hopelessness of pursuing the contest he might
offer to him and the other Carlist chiefs the guarantee of England that

their lives should be spared, that they should quit the country in safety, etc., etc., and other terms which might be agreed upon hereafter, and that if they objected to treat with the Spanish general, that the British minister at Madrid might be induced to enter upon the negotiation, and that there would be no more shame for them in accepting the diplomatic intervention of Great Britain than submitting to the military intervention of France. If this event should ever *come off* it will of course be subject to 100 modifications. I hope you will not disapprove of my having armed Cordoba with this power; if you do, there is plenty of time for revoking or altering it as Cordoba said the suggestion would not come with force to the Carlists until they were a little more beaten and a good deal more distressed.

This change in the command is also likely to delay it awhile, as Villareal imagines himself a pretty considerable general and he will be desirous to livrer a battle or two which Cordoba declares is what his own soul pants for. Nous verrons.

Evans has sent me up a very heavy account of the Legion against the Spanish Government in which he does wrong, for although I am quite ready to make myself the agent of the Legion if any good were to come of it, yet the Spanish Government, whose servant Evans is, have a right to be offended at his never communicating direct with them—but this account is unaccompanied by vouchers or details of any kind, or even by an assurance from Evans that it is correct. Not liking to present an account to the Government upon the payment of which I did not feel myself quite warranted in insisting, I requested Mr. Grindlay's (Deputy Commissary General of the Legion) opinion upon the account—and he at once pointed out so many *errors* and of so large an amount that I was obliged to abandon all idea of presenting it to Isturiz until some explanations at least are received from San Sebastian. Grindlay informs me that the Spanish Commissary with the Legion is one of the greatest rascals unhung, but not greater than some of the paymasters of the regiments who he believes have robbed unmercifully, though until he was able to prove it he wished not to be quoted for the opinion, but he says he greatly fears as soon as the accounts which are come-at-able are audited that the Legion will be looked upon as a set of plunderers.

Evans is determined, as I told you, not to interfere either with the Commissariat or Pay departments[1] and he is imposed upon by people who have come out for the *purpose of being paymasters*. One of them, a

Mr. Burt, brother of two fellows who keep gambling houses near St. James's Street, said to a clerk of Grindlay's that it had not answered to him as he expected because he had never got hold of *swag enough to bolt with.* You may judge therefore of the state in which the *uncontrolled* accounts of such men must be.

Evans some time ago wrote me an indignant letter upon the treatment which the sick and convalescents left behind at Vitoria had met with from the Spanish Government and authorities, representing that several officers had died for want of a few dollars to buy themselves the necessaries of life—that money sent for their relief through the Spanish Commissariat had never been delivered, etc., etc. I was horrified at this report and immediately sent to Grindlay to say that as far as £3 or £400 of my own went I was ready to give it in order to remedy such a state of things, and I begged him to write to Vitoria to know the real truth and desire the Chief of the Medical Staff there to draw upon my banker if necessary. I enclose you a copy of the answer he received as it is probable the same reports may have been transmitted to England, and you will of course be glad to have an official statement as to their entire want of foundation. It is next to impossible in this country ever to get a word of truth.

Enclosure: Copy, Dr. A. Taylor, Principal Medical Officer to the British Legion (Vitoria) to R. Grindlay, praising the provisioning of the hospitals at Vitoria.

Received 1 July.

GC/CL/270; Clar. Dep. C.452/2 (188-193)

[1] 'He is quite right' added in pencil, probably by P.

229   Villiers to Palmerston, 28 June 1836

Madrid. *Recommends Mr. Brackenbury, son of the consul at Cadiz.*

Endorsed in Palmerston's hand: Register.[1] P.

GC/CL/271

[1] Altered to 'Registered', presumably by a clerk.

230   Villiers to Palmerston, 29 June 1836

Madrid. Private. I have received your dispatches and letters of the 14th and 20th instant. From the tone of the latter I almost fear that you look upon me as *personally* interested in upholding Cordoba which I should regret, first because it is not the case, and next because it might tend to weaken the confidence you have hitherto I believe placed in my reports generally from this place. Such reports are the results of my opinions impartially formed to the best of my ability, and written without reference to whether they may be agreed in by others or not.

When Cordoba first took the command I told you I thought him the cleverest man I had met with in Spain, and probably the best officer (though this latter is not saying much). He began by *re*moralizing the army and gaining a battle, after his predecessor had officially announced to the Government that the bravery of his troops could no more be depended upon than their loyalty. In September last Cordoba's presence of mind and firmness prevented a political mutiny in the army, and in October you wrote me word that you were quite ready and glad to do justice to him, that he had behaved nobly in his command, etc., etc. During the extraordinary severe winter, and crippled as he was for want of means, he could do little more than establish and maintain his blockade by which he all but starved the enemy until the French frontier was opened to them and their wants were abundantly supplied. When the spring came he had committed himself so much upon the subject of French intervention that I told you, *as it was not to be granted*, I thought he ought not to remain in the command. Mendizabal was of the same opinion and at his request I wrote to Cordoba proposing that he should go to Paris on an extraordinary mission. I afterwards considered the moment he had chosen for coming to Madrid a most unfit one, and that his stay was most unreasonably prolonged—although he had the excuse of its being necessary to change the Minister of War and to confer with the new one. I subsequently told you that I thought his military talents not equal to the difficulties with which he has to contend, and I think therefore I cannot justly be charged with undue predilection in his favor.

I am still of opinion with reference to the notorious incapacity of every Spanish general that he is the fittest man to command the army—the enthusiasm with which he has been received by the troops on his return to Vitoria would alone go far to justify my opinion, for it is what no other general has met with after a year's command. Certainly the appointment of Rodil would produce an effect the very reverse, as he is considered a man that always mars whatever he himself undertakes. For instance, he was only in the Government a few days and in his first *despacho* with the Queen he upset Mendizabal's Ministry. Of Mina there is no chance, as he is without talent for general command, is disliked by the army, and his appointment would be an insult to public opinion in England and France after his bloody deeds of the last few months. So much for the chiefs.

With respect to your plan of campaign it is exactly what Cordoba told me he wished to carry into effect—but of Carlist magazines there are hardly any, except a few small powder manufactories in the interior of their country—the troops all live by rations furnished by the villages and their arms are manufactured by artisans who move about and establish themselves for a time near the different iron forges of which the country. is full—the communication between Vitoria and Pamplona is open, and why Bernelle does not move towards the Bastan or at least give signe de vie I cannot tell unless he is waiting for the always promised never arriving reinforcements to his legion. There is no doubt that the Borunda is where Cordoba ought to establish himself, and I have written to him that such is the opinion of the highest military authorities in England.

Now as to the most important subject of all—reinforcements to Evans—and first let me beg of you not to believe that because I do not report to you all I am daily doing, or endeavouring to do, upon this and other matters, that I allow them to sleep—but I see no use in inflicting upon you the irritation and disappointment of which I get such a plentiful share. Every thing that Evans, the Legion and the Commissariat want or have to complain of come through me, and the difficulty of getting any thing done with this impracticable people, so blind to their own interests, so shifty, intriguing and confused, makes me sometimes feel as if I was in a madhouse. Such reinforcements as Evans has received have been sent in consequence of my importunities, and as he began by asking for 2,000 men I thought I did pretty well in getting him 5,000—not that that made me relax in my exertions however, and my parting request to Cordoba was that more might still be sent.

It is true he has an army of 90,000 men but you will have seen by my despatch on the 18th instant[1] how they are disposed, and that they are not as available as they may be thought. Upwards of 20,000 are in hospital—owing greatly to want of medicine and medical care. Upwards of 40,000 are in garrison—this appears enormous but there are 60 strong places, or places so called, where the inhabitants expect to be protected, and the neighbouring country is to be kept in order. The least neglect is sure to bring down the Carlists like hawks to pillage and burn and carry off the people capable of bearing arms, which immediately *dis*affects a district to the Queen's cause. Cordoba has therefore from one reason or another only about 24,000 men for his actual army of operations, and if you will look upon the map at the tract of country he has to guard and to be able to move in from Burgos to Miranda, Vitoria, Pamplona and up to the Bastan, you will see that this force is barely sufficient, judging by the impossibility in which Evans (who has far more dash and enterprize than Cordoba) finds himself of undertaking any active operation with a corps of less than 10,000 men.

I read your dispatch[2] and part of your private letter (of the 20th) upon this subject to Isturiz, and made him feel that they were proofs of the lively interest taken by the English Government in the Queen's cause, and that no sacrifice would be too great in order to meet your wishes. I proposed to him to write directly to Cordoba in his capacity of Minister for Foreign Affairs and insist upon reinforcements being sent to Evans as a measure of foreign policy which was of the utmost importance. This he readily undertook to do, adding that he not only felt himself bound to give effect to any suggestion emanating from you, but that he was convinced *every thing* depended upon the British Legion. I have managed to put him in good humor again with Evans who he thought had intended to quarrel with the present Government, and Cordoba at my request immediately that he returned to Vitoria wrote Evans a most friendly letter, and I trust that matters will now go on more *cooperatingly* between all parties.

I received from Evans a few days ago a letter with which I think I had good right to be dissatisfied. I send you a copy of it and of my answer to him—he is a man exceedingly difficile à vivre, always believing every idle report that is told him, and surrounded by a set of toad-eaters who make his life miserable by representing every thing as a premeditated insult to his dignity. His letters to me during the last month have been so full of his wish to withdraw from the country and

459

of the reasons why it might be as well to dissolve the Legion that I cannot but suppose he wants to appear in the House of Commons before Parliament is prorogued. I may do him injustice and am half inclined to regret having resented his letter for I got a very handsome one from him last night thanking me for not having returned the 3d Class Cross of San Fernando to Isturiz, and speaking of men and things in a much more satisfactory way.

I told Isturiz of Goldsmid's proposition to Thomson and he said he thought the best way of meeting it would be to desire Zulueta,[3] who is a man highly respected in London and thoroughly conversant in Spanish affairs, officially to communicate with the capitalists on the part of the Government, and to report the result to him, when he declared he would forthwith be ready to enter with me upon the whole commercial subject. I think it might do a great deal of good if you would see Zulueta and tell him what we want—his opinion is all powerful with Isturiz. Now that the Spanish mission in London is charged with the affairs of the Legion a word from you would probably make Jabat bestir himself and by Zulueta's assistance take care that no just ground of complaint occurs for the future.

In reporting to you last week the proposition for putting an end to the war diplomatically, I omitted to mention that I had told Cordoba we must not be expected to enter into any negotiations with Don Carlos under present circumstances—or at least that I would venture to hold out no hopes of the kind until I received instructions from my Government. We saved his life in Portugal and he escaped from England in order to decree the murder of Englishmen in violation of his own treaty and the usages of war among civilized nations—he was therefore entitled to no favor at our hands. I mention this in order to ask for your instructions as it is well to be prepared for every contingency, but I daresay the event will never *come off*.

First enclosure: Copy, Evans (San Sebastian) to Villiers, 19 June 1836 (recte 17 June), private, complaining of the lack of money and supplies, the attitude of the Spanish Government, etc.

Second enclosure: Copy, Villiers (Madrid) to Evans, [-] June 1836, in reply to Evans's letter of 17 June.

GC/CL/272; Clar. Dep. C.452/2 (194-201)

[1] V to P, 18 June 1836, no. 149, FO 72/459 : a long despatch on the military situation.

² P to V, 20 June 1836, no. 53, FO 72/456.
³ Presumably one of the family of bankers and merchants.

231   Palmerston to Villiers, 30 June 1836

Copy. Foreign Office. Thank you much for your piece of cyphering; it contains a truly curious and instructive matter of history; and explains what was before mysterious. The implacable resentment for sins of commission was unintelligible; that sins of omission should be unpardonable is quite natural under the circumstances of the case. I shall not betray you.

I have no time to write as I must go down in time for the first scene of the Tempest which is about to be enacted this afternoon in the House of Commons by the Irish Members upon receiving the Lords' rejection of our amendments in the Corporation Bill. But the Legion men here are in the depth of despair at the stoppage of the recruiting. They say they could have got 1,500 men in Ireland, and they are now only able to send out 150. To urge people that have no money to do things that require ready cash is of course uphill work; but it would be very important that the Spanish Government should authorize somebody or other to go on with the recruiting if it is only to fill up vacancies and not to let the Legion dwindle down to nothing.

Of course Cordova feels jealous of Evans and the British and his praises are only a thin coat of varnish to hide the bad wood underneath; and his talk must have had much effect on Isturitz and the rest of the Government; but do what you can to support the Legion and to get it reinforced by Spanish troops, and augmented by recruits. Since your account of Cordova's *plan of campaign*, I have no hopes for Spain but in Evans and his division. I verily believe that there is no other chance for the Queen.

As to the Legion not having rendered accounts, it seems to me that the memorandum you sent me explains that sufficiently, but I know by War Office experience how difficult it is to get accounts properly made out, and how next to impossible it is to make them out retrospectively, if the receipts and expenditure have not been properly recorded at the time.

GC/CL/1266

232 Palmerston to Villiers, 1 July 1836

Copy. I have received your letter of the 23rd and will reply another day to the first part of it. With respect to the accounts of the Legion, if the Spanish Government think those accounts are not properly rendered, why do they not send to the Legion a sufficient number of honest intelligent and trustworthy accountants to put matters to rights? Is not the Legion part of the Queen's army? And is not the Spanish Government as much to blame for irregularities in that corps as in any other in the Queen's service? But I have a curiosity to know whether the pecuniary matters of the Spanish regiments are conducted with more regularity, and whether the accounts of those corps have been rendered more punctually. Evans is perfectly right in declining to have anything to do with the Pay or Commissariat departments. They form no part of his proper business; and the military arrangements are quite enough to occupy the whole of his time; and moreover he is very wise not to give his enemies any handle to fix upon him pecuniary irregularities committed by others, and over which he could not by human possibility exercise any control. If, from the jealousy of Cordova and the want of due support from the Spanish Government, he should be compelled to abandon the Queen's service, unable to effect any great military result, he is quite right to have disconnected himself with the pecuniary affairs of the Legion, so as not to give any man a pretext for impeaching his personal integrity.

I confess to you that I do not like the step you say in the first part of your letter you have taken. I have the most rooted distrust in the man you mention,[1] and should be very unwilling indeed to give him any discretionary authority to act or speak for me.

GC/CL/1267

[1] Córdoba.

233 Villiers to Palmerston, 2 July 1836

Madrid. Private. I thought it prudent not to reply to certain parts of your letter of the 20th by a French courier. Every day appears to bring some fresh proof of the bad faith of the French Government towards this country—they have not only created hopes respecting reinforcements which it is evident they don't intend to realize, but there is some reason for *suspecting* that Bernelle has had orders not to make himself too active. A good deal of his recent conduct can hardly be explained upon other grounds, for he is a man of ambition and fight and he has of late been singularly dexterous in avoiding the gratification of his tastes—but *un indirecto*,[1] as they say here, from his own Government would of course have more weight with him than the salvation of the Peninsula and its Queens.

I mentioned to Isturiz in entire confidence that the French Government might perhaps with reference to pleasing the Northern Powers be desirous of bringing about a marriage between Don Carlos's son and the Queen, and he told me that the Queen Regent had been during the last 10 days in a state of great dejection from having, as she said, reason to believe that such was the project of Louis Philippe,[2] though Isturiz does not know from what source she derives her information.

During the last two years I have never varied in my opinion as to the policy of France or doubted that the longer the contest continued the more hostile she would be found to Spain, and indisposed to taking part with us for the establishment of tranquillity *from* constitutional government; but I have never had any grounds for believing that Louis Philippe was desirous of intervention, or that he had fixed in his own mind the period or the circumstances when such a course would suit his purpose. Every thing that I know would lead to a contrary opinion, but upon this you and Lord Granville must of course be better informed than me.[3] Louis Philippe's policy for a clever man, which nobody can deny he is, surprises me, for he must know that its tendency is to deliver up Spain to Carlism or democracy, neither of which can be indifferent to him unless he builds a wall of brass between the two countries, and if he thinks he can impose by force of arms either a King or a system upon this country he is wretchedly mistaken, for that would raise as national a feeling against France as in 1808, and what Napoleon failed to achieve is not left I guess for Louis Philippe to accomplish. Every class of society whose interests are opposed to revolution have ranged themselves on the side of the Sovereign de facto—most of them considering they have one de jure—and to promote such a state of things, and crush in the beginning the now small band of anarchists whom time and internal commotions may render powerful, and strengthen the Government whose conduct is much more likely to be adverse to than in favor of popular liberties, for every Government is as despotic as it dare, and for despotism there is an extraordinary toleration in

Spain—to do all this would only be acting up to his own principles on the part of Louis Philippe, and might be proved to be more in conformity with the substantial objects sought by the Holy Ones than any other course His French Majesty could adopt.

As for the marriage it is the most absurd and impossible of plans, proving only that he who desires it is profoundly ignorant of this country. I much doubt if Don Carlos, even were he ten times worse off than he is now, would hear of it. It would be opposed by a large majority of his party because if it came seriously on the tapis they would in the true Spanish fashion think the Cristinos were afraid of them and be for going the whole hog—then as for the liberals I am certain that they would rather make good terms for themselves and have Don Carlos himself than consent to the establishment of a perpetual civil war[4] of which they would by slow degrees all be the victims.

For these reasons, in which any one who had lived three months in Spain would concur, I feel certain that Cordoba, whom no one can accuse of being either a fool or remarkably blind to his own interests, has no arrière pensée whatever about the marriage—he never could gain any thing by it and he knows the Carlist party far too well ever to expect any thing but inextinguishable hatred at their hands. Neither do I think he has a desire to prolong the war—his incessant demands for French aid which would have finished it ingloriously for him, prove rather that he was in a hurry to put an end to the contest even at an immense loss of the popularity he is so desirous of. He knows too that if he leaves the command, the war unconcluded, he sinks into obscurity, but that if peace is restored by his means he may count upon the enthusiastic support of the army in any scheme for the satisfaction of his ambition. He has little doubt however that if no progress is made in the next three months against the faction, and that the winter again sets in upon the hostile camps neither the country nor the army will tolerate him longer and he will be crushed under the weight of public indignation.

I therefore think he *wants* to finish the war. Whether he has the military talents I don't know, but I much doubt it—more so since his visit to Madrid, and that I have had the opportunity of talking to him than before, for I believe that the talents required for contending with such varied and peculiar difficulties are of a higher order than any of us who have not been at the theatre of war are inclined to imagine. I hope I have contributed to reconciling him and Evans and that they will now go on more smoothly together but till I can get the latter properly reinforced I do not expect any important progress being made in the campaign.

I am now going to make a suggestion to you in which I can honestly use that hackneyed phrase 'for the good of the service' as I have no personal motive in proposing *that I should make you a visit for a few days.* I consider this to be a critical moment in the history of the Spanish revolution and one which ought perhaps to be a new starting point in the connexion of England with this country. In all probability the new elections will make it necessary to take some decisive course. The success of the Exaltados may, if they are left to themselves, produce the departure of the Queen Regent or an appeal to the army. England would be involved in the discredit of her ally. If however we were decided as to our course we could either withdraw in time or guide events by being clear as to the extent of the assistance we would give. The Exaltados will be quite as eager or more so than any others for the aid of England, but if they have it, whether in the shape of money, troops, or moral support, they ought to pay for it in commercial advantages and in submitting to the guidance of England.

I think that by personal communication better than by writing I could put you in possession of the real state of things, and that that might be useful considering how much you may have to reason and decide upon Spanish matters within the next year. To me personally it would be of great use not only to have the advantage of learning from yourself your own views, but on account of the importance which would be attached here to my visit to England, and my return would have all the effect of a special mission. Whatever objects it were desireable to carry would then come with great accumulated weight.

At Paris I might perhaps do some little good, at least that good that may be expected from the testimony of an eye witness. I am sure I could destroy the opinion that exists there of my anti-French proceedings in this country.

The moment is not a bad one for me to leave Madrid—the business of the next two months is more military than diplomatic—but I think I should return soon after the time that the Cortes meet and proceed to constitution making.

I must once more repeat that I have no other object in this proposal than what I have stated, and if you consider that I may do more good by staying here than passing a fortnight in London pray don't be deterred from saying so by any idea that I *am asking for leave* or have any desire for a *jaunt*—if I had, it should not be when the thermometer is at 800° in the shade.

By a letter from Mr. Shaw (who with Goldsmid had an interview with you upon Spanish commercial matters) to his correspondent here Mr. O'Shea, I see that you expressed surprise at my not having written to you upon the subject of their communication. The reason is a very simple one—because I knew it would all end in smoke . . . .

Received 11 July.

GC/CL/273; Clar. Dep. C.452/2 (202-211)

[1] 'a hint'.
[2] 'she' to 'Philippe' underlined, possibly by P.
[3] 'Palmerston's determination to think that Louis Philippe is longing to intervene here is the oddest quirk, you and I must have during the year sent him so much evidence to the contrary.' (V to Granville, 2 July 1836, PRO 30/29/421.) V asked Granville whether he thought it would be a good idea for him (V) to take leave of absence to visit London and 'put Palmerston straight on Spanish affairs'.
[4] 'perpetual civil war' underlined, possibly by P.

234   Palmerston to Villiers, 8 July 1836

Copy. Foreign Office. Lord John Hay complains much and loudly of the conduct of the Spanish admiral at Passages,[1] and of the admiral's secretary who have both of them since Mendizabal's retirement thrown every possible obstacle in the way of the naval service and who not only thwart Lord John but evidently want to get rid of the English officers and crews of the two Spanish steamers. Pray do what you can to counteract the folly of this old ass.

GC/CL/1268

[1] Ribera.

235   Villiers to Palmerston, 9 July 1836

Madrid. Private. I have just heard from Isturiz that a financial courier of the Government is about to start for Paris, and I avail myself of the opportunity to acknowledge your letter and dispatches of the 30th ultimo.

I don't wonder at your despairing of the Queen's cause for it does look desperate. Its best chance is that its enemies are Spaniards as well as its supporters, and that there is not more virtue, courage or ability on one side than the other. Its next best chance is, I quite agree with you, the Legion, and I need not tell you that every thing in my power has been and will be done to support it. I have just been speaking to Isturiz about sending out recruits from England and so far from wishing to check it he desires to have the greatest possible number sent out. He says that Zulueta has full powers to act for the Government and knows well that whatever he does will be approved. Isturiz said he knew it would be a great satisfaction to Zulueta to learn from you what you thought it best for him to do in behalf of the Legion and the cause and I said I had no doubt you would receive him if he presented himself. I believe him to be an honest intelligent man—possibly a little timid—and a stirring up from you would do him good. Isturiz told me again and again that any engagement made by him in the name of the Government should be sanctioned and carried into effect.

A general—a general—that is the desiderandum—a good Commander in Chief might save the Queen's cause—but I swear to you there is not such a man in Spain. I repeat what I have all along said that Cordoba is true to the Queen's cause, but every day confirms what I have for some time past thought, that he is not up to the difficulties with which he has to contend.

A large body of Carlists have succeeded in making their way to Galicia or at least to the Asturias. Espartero is still in pursuit but will no more catch them than I shall. Admiral Ribera has sent in his resignation which I have taken care should be accepted.

Received 21 July.

GC/CL/274; Clar. Dep. C.452/2 (212)

236 Villiers to Palmerston, 12 July 1836

Madrid. Private. I am glad I have not much to write today for I am so completely knocked up by the heat that I can hardly hold my pen.

The news of what the army is *not* doing becomes every day more alarming, as are likewise the increasing number and audacity of the factions every where. This expedition to the Asturias and Galicia[1] may be a death blow to the Queen's cause and a resurrection to that of Don

Miguel if it succeeds, which as far as Spanish generals are concerned it has every chance of doing, for it will meet with considerable support in both those provinces, and we know by Mr. Aubyn's reports from Rome that a combined insurrection in Galicia and the north of Portugal has long been meditated.

It seems almost incredible that a general with money and means at his command, and supported by the authorities and people of the country through which he is marching, should for many days not be able to reduce the distance *of 6 leagues* between his troops and the invading expedition, which has none of the advantages he can command, and is moreover encumbered with 500 prisoners and 4,000 spare muskets. But no day passes in Spain without one's being obliged to believe something that appears incredible.

Cordoba seems to me to have quite lost his head—he is without any plan of campaign evidently, for he has now let three weeks pass since his return without doing more than run about between Vitoria and Pamplona and suffocate 2 or 300 men from the heat in the march. Nobody I assure you would be more glad than I should to see him removed for I don't think he will ever do any good, but unfortunately there is no one to replace him—there are 600 Spanish generals and not one among them fit to command a brigade. It is one of the many unfortunate circumstances of this war that the very excellence of the soldiers should be neutralized by the incapacity of their commanders.

Notwithstanding the improved aspect of their affairs the Carlists avail themselves of every opportunity to desert, and in this I see some ground for hope as it proves that they are dissatisfied. What Cordoba's plans are, if he has any, I know no more than the Government does. We did not part very good friends when he went back to Vitoria, and I have since written him 2 or 3 letters which he has thought it more convenient not to answer.

Isturiz shewed me the copy of a handsome letter he had written to Evans giving explanations upon the different matters of which Evans had to complain and returning to him the Grand Cross of San Fernando. Reinforcements however is what I am laboring to get but cannot.

I send you the copy of a letter from Evans[2] principally on account of what it contains personal to myself, for I know both by published and unpublished letters from the Legion that the neglect and ill treatment they have experienced is attributed to my want of activity in their cause, and to my being *done* by Cordoba and his agents. I should have cared very little for this if I had not perceived something of the same tone in your letters, and I am therefore glad to avail myself of Evans's testimony in contradiction. I know that since the Legion set foot in Spain hardly a day has passed without my having been occupied in its concerns either in reconciling differences or attending to its wants. With Mendizabal I always enacted the part of a sturdy beggar first supplicating and then threatening before I could get him to fulfill his own engagements, as he used to say that Don Pedro's army in Oporto used to do with *nothing a day,* and that the British Legion must be broke in to the same system. In short I say it without fear of contradiction from any party that *not a single thing* has been done for the Legion but through my intervention and remonstrance with the Government.

Cordoba is indignant with the French Legion which is now worse than useless as Bernelle has evidently some reasons for remaining inactive even when attacked by the enemy, and Isturiz is rather desirous of getting rid of that corps than of reinforcing it.

The wish that is manifesting itself among the officers of the British Legion to retire at the expiration of the year's service is alarming, and I have agreed with Isturiz to write an official letter to Evans setting forth the mischievous consequences to the Queen's cause that a perseverance in such a determination would entail, appealing to their honor, etc., etc.[3] I hope you will likewise write to Evans in the same sense. I think that some progress has been made towards revoking the Decree of Durango[4] and Cordoba writes to the Government that he has much greater chance of success in his negotiation with Villareal than with Eguia.

Isturiz has applied to me to get Howard to arrange with the Portuguese Government that the Carlists now confined on board the pontoons at Lisbon should be given up on the application of Cordoba in order that they may be exchanged.[5] He does so upon the ground of thinking that the matter may be managed by the agents of the English and Spanish Governments without the Governments giving direct orders to the effect. I have told him that with reference to your conversation with the Baron de los Valles I must defer complying with his request till I had communicated with you. Will you have the goodness to give me your instructions upon the subject? The exchange of prisoners would be more beneficial to the Queen's army than to Don Carlos's.

Mr. Carbonell called upon me yesterday and delivered to me your letter. I hope I have already done him some service with Isturiz who has again assured me that any arrangement made by Zulueta with the house of Carbonell in London shall be approved without a question by the Government. He says that Zulueta in conjunction with the Spanish legation have carte blanche *for every thing* and that he had made that arrangement because he thought it would be the most satisfactory to the British Legion and the best mode of having their wants promptly attended to.

Received 21 July.

GC/CL/275; Clar. Dep. C.452/2 (213-216)

[1] 'The division of Carlist troops which on 27th ultimo defeated General Tello and the corps of reserves has passed on to the Asturias.' (V to P, 12 July 1836, no. 171, FO 72/460.)

[2] No enclosure found.

[3] For an account of what was discussed between Istúriz and V on this matter and the agreement they reached see V to P, 16 July 1836, no. 179, enclosing V to Evans, 14 July 1836, FO 72/460.

[4] By which foreigners were excluded from the provisions of the Eliot Convention.

[5] See V to P, 2 July 1836, no. 163, FO 72/460.

237 Palmerston to Villiers, 14 July 1836

Copy. Foreign Office. I will first reply to that part of your last letter which relates to your own arrangements. I have talked with Melbourne about your suggestion that it might be worth while for you to come over here for a short time; we both of us feel that upon many accounts great public advantage arises from periodical communications between foreign ministers and the home Government, by the return of the former on leave, and that every foreign minister ought to come home for such purposes every now and then. But we doubt whether it would be expedient for you to come to us just now. There is no particular question pending upon which you and we do not fully understand each other, or upon which personal instructions could be necessary for you—your coming, especially if it was only for a short time, obviously to communicate with us, and not for the ordinary purposes of leave, would create a general impression that there was some important matter pending, and all Europe would be set a guessing. This would excite suspicion on the part of the French Government. They would think there was something deeper in the matter than the explanation we should give them would account for. When nothing particular came out of your trip, people would say we had tried some secret scheme which had failed. Moreover you would be absent from Madrid at the meeting of the Cortes, a time when your presence there will be very important. On the whole therefore we think that the advantages of such a trip would not counterbalance its inconveniences.

Now as to Cordova and as to what I have written you about him—I certainly think you have a better opinion of him than he deserves, and at all events you have a better opinion of him than we have. My object in abusing him roundly in my letters to you has been to drive you to say what you could in his defence, in order that both you and I by comparing facts and opinions, might come as near as we can to a correct judgment.

We cannot bring ourselves to believe that he has been acting sincerely and single-mindedly for the interests of the Queen whom he serves. We think that the small use he has made of great means, and the very lame apologies he makes for not having done more are indications that his conduct is guided by unavowed motives, and when we look to his former history and to his general character we find nothing in either that forbids our entertaining any suspicion of his straightforwardness.

It is evident as you say that Louis Philippe fears the complete triumph of the Constitutional party. He has been led mistakenly to imagine that by dragging on the war that party may be weakened, and that at last both sides will agree from fatigue and exhaustion to a compromise which would render Spain a better neighbour for France than he thinks she would be, if purely constitutional. Hence Louis Philippe hankering after the marriage, and after a settlement by a European congress. This is all highly absurd, and shews a superficial knowledge of the particular facts and of general principles—but so it is.

Well, it is quite notorious that Cordova and the French Government understand each other, and are well pleased with each other in the main, notwithstanding some few decent complaints made by each, and my firm belief [is] that Cordova does not wish to put an end to the war just yet, and is resolved to do nothing which shall tend very decidedly to do so. What he is to gain by one course or by the other is more than we can any of us precisely know, but it is not impossible to conceive preponderating personal advantages that might be held out to him to do his duty or to neglect it. We cannot explain his military conduct even by the supposition of incapacity, because he is not a fool, but a very sharp clever fellow, though he may not have the talents of a general; and a clever man must see that to allow the Carlists to keep their magazines unmolested, to leave Evans with so small a force as to be unable to cut off the communication with France, to permit the Carlists to reap and carry the harvest without disturbance, are not the likeliest means of rendering the blockade system effectual. Fabius took very different measures to accomplish his success.

Pray push Isturiz again to reinforce Evans; 4,000 or 5,000 more Spaniards at least should be sent him, and the Portuguese corps if possible. The reasons given you by the Minister of War for not doing so are anything but satisfactory. Tell Isturitz plainly that our naval aid will not be continued, if a sufficient Spanish land force is not sent down to the coast, to render our cooperation effectual for some permanent advantage. We shall only render ourselves ridiculous by continuing to cooperate with persons who do not do their best to help themselves. They profess to mean to starve the Carlists out by blockade. They have been complaining for two years that the Carlists derive their chief supplies from France; instead of themselves occupying the frontier and cutting off those supplies they have been urging the French Government to do so by measures within France; at last comes one squadron into play and by its aid the Legion are on the point of doing this long desired thing, and then the Spanish Government cannot out of its 100,000 men find the additional 3 or 4,000 that would accomplish so important an object. It is difficult to imagine that 40,000 men can really be required for garrisons, but could they not try to do with 36,000, and send the odd 4,000 to Evans?

As to Cordova's incessant demands for French aid, that rather strengthens than allays our suspicions because why should a general go on declaring that foreign aid was necessary when he must know full well that such foreign aid cannot be had? Is not the tendency of such language to dispirit his own army, and to lay the ground for excusing himself for doing nothing?

The augmentation of Bernelle's Legion if it is to be carried into effect will be a capital thing. I wish he could increase Evans's in the same manner.

The Tories seem to think they shall throw us over before the end of the session . . . .

I am very glad you acted with so much promptness and energy about the stupid old Spanish admiral at Passages and that you saved the two steamers from the gripe of his Spanish candidates for command.

GC/CL/1269

238 Palmerston to Villiers, 14 July 1836

Copy. Foreign Office. Private and confidential. The King objected to my despatch 55, the draft of which was not sent to him till after the despatch had been sent off to you. I was obliged therefore to cancel the despatch as it was not worth while to argue the matter with the King.[1] I have no doubt that what he objected to, though he did not say so, but gave other reasons, was the passage praising Evans.

GC/CL/1270

[1] There is no copy of this despatch in FO 72/456, only instructions for its withdrawal.

239 Villiers to Palmerston, 16 July 1836

Madrid. Private. I only received your letter of the 1st yesterday. You ask me why the Spanish Government do not send down to the Legion a number of honest intelligent and trustworthy accountants. They do not for many reasons, the first of which will suffice, viz. that no such animal exists in all Spain, and a man with three heads might be as easily found as one who united honesty, intelligence and trustworthyness.

In the next place although the Legion undoubtedly forms part of the Queen's army it claims to be administered according to the regulations of the British service, and I understand that our system of accounts in the Commissariat is so different from the Spanish that a *native* accountant would produce only worse confusion. I quite agree with you that the Government was to blame for allowing these irregularities but that blame does not attach to Isturiz. He came into office and was immediately asked to pay up the arrears due to the Legion—he asked how any came to exist and was told that Mendizabal had refused to pay them until the accounts were rendered, not one of which he had been able to procure during ten months. Surely he was bound under these circumstances to pause before he paid them? He sent the money necessary for carrying on the service—he gave orders that the bills drawn on London should be paid—and he has now sent down Mr. Grindlay who appears to be an intelligent man of business (he is in the British service and therefore his character may be known) with full powers to call upon the pay masters for their accounts, and an assurance both to him and to me that upon correct accounts being furnished they shall be immediately liquidated.

I speak of people as I find them, and I have seen more reason to be satisfied with Isturiz as regards the Legion than with Mendizabal, and I have greater reliance upon his word.

You ask likewise if the pecuniary affairs of the Spanish army are conducted with more regularity. I don't believe they are—robbery and confusion prevail in the military as in every other Department of the State, but then the complaints of the Spanish army are never noticed—the soldiers are hardly clothed, not always fed and not often paid. The Government cares nothing about arrears due to their own troops for they pay them or don't pay them just as they please, and think that auditing is useless trouble till the day of settlement arrives.

Evans is quite right not to meddle with the accounts of the Legion. If he had he would have been sure to furnish his enemies with a handle against him. My remarks upon this subject applied only to his sending up accounts to me—the payment of which I was to insist upon—without having ascertained that they were correct—it was putting both himself and me in a false position with the Government. Before I took them to Isturiz I referred them to Grindlay who proved to me that at least one half of them should be knocked off. It was for this reason I said that Evans was imposed upon by some of the dishonest persons who have to do with the finances of the Legion.

I am sorry that you disapproved my project of diplomatic intervention as we were not likely to get any military. There never could have been a question of it until the Carlists were dead beat and wanted a pretext for laying down their arms as would have been the case last year if a French army had crossed the frontier. Under such circumstances the war *might* have been put an end to in a day, and we might have had the glory of it as well as the right afterwards to insist against persecutions. However there is no harm done—it is only one of the thousand projects which the state of things in this country is constantly engendering, and like most of them quedará en el aire.[1] I beg you will be assured though that I was not going to put my trust in Cordoba or to be *done* by him or any one else.

There is every appearance of the Government being beaten at the elections and Isturiz gave me to understand today he expected it.[2] If that is the case and he is either patriotic or wise he will resign before the Cortes meet and the majority compromises itself by violent acts or opinions. In any case we shall not have much of the *juicio*[3] necessary for a Constituent Assembly.

The next three months will be hyper critical.

As to the supposed dislike of the Spaniards towards the Legion of which the English newspapers are full, nothing can be more false. *The hopes of all the partisans of the Queen* are fixed upon Evans and the Legion. It is felt and *acknowledged* that they alone *have done* any thing and they alone are *likely* to do any thing.

PS. I send you a map of the theatre of war[4]—the country within the red line is the enemy's.

Received 24 July.

GC/CL/276; Clar. Dep. C.452/2 (218-221)

[1] 'will be left in the air'.
[2] In Madrid all seven Government candidates were defeated. (V to P, 16 July 1836, no. 181, FO 72/460.)
[3] 'judgement'.
[4] Not found.

240 Palmerston to Villiers, 18 July 1836

Copy. Foreign Office. *Sends an extract from a letter from Sir Edward Disbrowe, British minister to the Netherlands, about the Spanish chargé d'affaires at The Hague.*

No enclosure.

GC/CL/1271

241 Palmerston to Villiers, 18 July 1836

Copy. Foreign Office. *Sends a letter from Lord Ponsonby relating to Córdoba's conduct at the time of the Churchill affair,*[1] *and asking Villiers to communicate the substance of it to Istúriz.*
No enclosure.

GC/CL/1272

[1] See Sir C. K. Webster, *The Foreign Policy of Palmerston*, ii. 530-34.

242 Villiers to Palmerston, 24 July 1836

Madrid. Private. When I tell you that I am ill from the effects of the heat, that I have got the gout, and that I have just lost three if not four horses (from inflammation) each worth nearly 200 guineas here, you will suppose that my black report of today takes its color from these circumstances, but I assure you that paint as black as I may I should fail in giving you an accurate idea of the rapidity with which disasters of every kind have come upon us since I last wrote to you. The manner in which the Carlists from the North are overrunning the country is more like the coming in of the tide than any thing else. The army seems determined not to do like Mrs. Partington and try and mop out the ocean—it stands at present high and dry and *quite still* as if to wait the coming flood when it will probably by degrees melt away like sugar and be assimilated with the surrounding fluid. This is metaphorical if you please and appears a caricature but it is perfectly exact. The Carlist expedition to Galicia has already arrived at St. Iago—how much further we know not—always closely pursued but never near being caught. In Valencia and Aragon the Carlists carry desolation wherever they please, and from Navarre detachments are sent into Castille which alarm the country, rob the towns and villages and invariably elude the Queen's troops which are, or affect to be, pursuing them.

A large body of them arrived the day before yesterday within 8 leagues of San Ildefonso where the Queens and the Court are at present disporting themselves. I was on my road down there notwithstanding the gout as I was to have seen the Queen last night, when I met the relays of mules for the royal carriages and learnt that the Queen and the garrison of San Ildefonso were already upon the road flying from 5,000 factious who with their *corresponding artillery* were within 2 leagues. I accordingly returned to Madrid but this morning I have received so pressing a letter from Isturiz to go back again that I am about to start as soon as I have finished writing for a courier which Rayneval is about to send from San Ildefonso.

He writes me word that the confusion which prevailed there when it was known that the Queen was about to bolt was the most horrible and at the same time the most ludicrous exhibition that could be conceived—as no one individual there had the means of getting away. The grandees, among whom are many halt and lame and blind, crept off *on foot* with a foreknowledge that it would take them 6 days to reach Madrid after that fashion—the Court ladies were getting their affairs ready to be ravished and Rayneval himself, after storming about the necessity of not leaving Louis Philippe's representative at the mercy of the invaders, had allotted him *as the most special favor* une vielle rosse de cheval et un *âne* for the transport of his person, household and archives.

It seems after all that the number of the enemy was exaggerated and that they have taken another direction, so for the present I suppose we are quittés pour la peur as far as danger for the Queen's *person* goes. Her *cause* never was in such imminent peril. Cordoba's army is dismembered, discontented, without pay, without rations, and as it appears without hope, Carlists and anarchists both availing themselves of this state of things as best suits their respective purposes. I send you an extract from a letter of Cordoba's to me dated the 18th[1] which is as bad as any thing can be. I have another from him dated the 20th in which he begs I will support the urgent representation he has made to be relieved from the command which his retaining any longer in the present state of things and of opinion can only be prejudicial to the Queen's cause. I shall of course make a point both with the Queen and the Government that his resignation be accepted. I am too unwell and too much hurried to reply at this moment to your letters of the 14th respecting him but I will do so by my own courier on Saturday.

Then, as if to make the malediction of Heaven or its Antipodes complete, the movement against Fuentearabia[2] fails owing to the worst of all causes—the illness of Evans—and as if that was not enough two or three regiments of the Legion avail themselves of this happy moment to mutiny.

Nil desperandum in Spain is a favorite theory of mine as well as of every body's who knows this country, and I am obliged unceasingly to have recourse to the dram to keep up my spirits.

Nearly the whole of the garrison of Madrid is away and the brave National Guard, who during the last two days have been shaving off their mustachios and cramming their uniforms and muskets down the privies, may now be expected to resume their functions and create a political row. There is not *one* man in this country who has any head or any heart or who when he is tried is not *sure* to be found wanting.

I entirely agree in all you say respecting my coming home—circumstances however have changed so much since I made the proposition that I should not have left Madrid upon your simple permission to do so, or upon any thing short of an order.

You are aware, though possibly not to its full extent, how rabid the French Government has been against me for some time past (I should have thought their hands must have been full enough of more important business) accusing me of loving Mendizabal, and hating Isturiz, and not caring for Rayneval, etc., etc. As all they said was very false and very *little* I took pains through Alava and others to *rectify* their opinions, which might have had mischievous political consequences. Lord Granville also convinced them of their error—and the result has been that Thiers wrote a most flattering letter about me to Alava requesting that I would correspond with him, and he said the same to Lord Granville.

I have accordingly written him a letter of which I send you a copy—my object has been to shew the expediency of France still complying with your suggestion of last March that a forward movement should be made by the French army of observation now upon the frontier. I hope you will not disapprove for you *may be assured* that unless the Queen's army and public opinion become *reanimados* from without, we shall see all the best, or rather the least bad, classes of society running away and emigrating, the worst classes running into every sort of revolutionary excesses, and the civil war established in every corner of the country. Foreign aid will then be hopeless and the sooner both Lord John Hay and Evans then get away the better in order to leave the contending parties like the two Kilkenny cats to each other. Which bit of tail would ultimately be found the longest I cannot tell—possibly the Carlist end—but in the Queen's would still be found an almighty power of vibration.

I will end as I began by assuring you that it is neither the twinges of the gout or the Angel of Death having smitten my cavalry that have blackened my views today. A little time will I fear prove their correctness.

Many thanks for your arrangement in favor of Mr. Alonso.[3] You have made an honest man supremely happy.

First enclosure: Copy, Comte Harispe (Quartier Général de Bayonne) to Álava, 17 July 1836, on the affairs of the French Legion. (In French.)

Second enclosure: Extract from a letter dated 18 July 1836. (In Spanish.)

Third enclosure: Copy, Villiers (Madrid) to Thiers, 22 July 1836, regretting French reluctance to intervene in Spain, with a postscript dated 25 July.

Received 4 August.

GC/CL/277; Clar. Dep. C.452/2 (222-227)

[1] Enclosure not found.
[2] The attempt by the British Legion to take it from the Carlists.
[3] Alonso was Spanish secretary at the British legation, i.e. he copied and translated from and into Spanish. A memorandum signed by P, 12 July 1836, ordered that his salary should be increased from £150 to £200, and should be paid quarterly instead of half-yearly. (FO 72/460.)

243 Villiers to Palmerston, 24 July 1836

Madrid. *Asks Palmerston to tell Spring Rice that he has secured permission for Messrs. Strachan and Saunders to reside and trade in the Manillas.*

Copy.

Clar. Dep. C.452/2 (228)

244 Palmerston to Villiers, 25 July 1836

Foreign Office. I have received your letter of the 16th. Pray do not suppose that we do not fully appreciate all your indefatigable exertions in behalf of the Legion; I can assure you we are quite aware how assiduously you have toiled to assist them, and how irksome the labour must have been. You have however fully succeeded, and the Spanish Government seems to have now done everything that is right by that force, except send additional Spanish troops to cooperate with it. But if what Alava says is true, and Cordova has resigned, we shall probably do better, and the officer, whoever he may be, who may be appointed to succeed Cordova will find means either to send reinforcements to Evans, or to undertake some operations himself which may have the same effect as a reinforcement.

We by no means think that Cordova has *done* you, but looking at his conduct at a distance and judging by results, and by his own former life, we distrust him more than you seem to do; and impeach not merely his military capacity, but his honesty of purpose. I do not mean to say that he was in positive communication with Carlos, with a view to place Carlos himself on the throne, but he was certainly acting with a view to some other object than the simple and direct success of the Queen's cause. When first he took the command he seemed to be in earnest and to mean well; but his conduct for the last 6 months has led to a different belief, and the only chance of success for the Queen now lies in his removal from the command of the army.

I am very glad to find that Isturitz behaves so well. We meddle not with the making or unmaking of Administrations as the French Government does, our dealings are with Governments as permanent bodies corporate; and provided the mayor and aldermen for the time being act fairly and honestly by us, we are content, whichever ward they may belong to.

Copy.

GC/CL/1273

245 Villiers to Palmerston, 31 July 1836

San Ildefonso. Private. You are probably as sick of reading as I am of writing the hopeless accounts of this helpless people, and yet I don't bother you with more than a tithe of what happens. As I cannot help taking great interest in concerns where we are so much embarked, it is a most wearing process, I can assure you, never to get up of a morning or to pass the day without hearing some fresh disaster or crime of omission or commission. Then it is painful always to be complaining about something or other to a Government which has only the external attributes of one, and is totally powerless either for the dispatch of business or to control the conduct of its own agents. Chaos never was in greater confusion than every department here is, and to expect regularity from people desperate with the difficulties which surround them and caring only for the means of preserving existence is quite idle.

These are the reasons why I do not send you answers upon commercial and ordinary matters. It is for no want of remonstrance—that I give them till my notes and my face must be equally nauseous.[1]

I write no dispatches about the Legion supposing that you will of course have fuller information than I can give from Wylde, and as Our Gracious Lord the King is probably not in the best humor upon the subject there is no use in troubling him to read more than is necessary when nothing favorable is to be said. I fear Evans is very ill and not likely to be fit for work yet. I hope you will like my plan of sending Espartero to the coast.[2] I have no doubt that it will fail from the rivalries and difficulties which Spaniards cannot help creating, but I am sure if it were put in execution all the advantages which I allude to in my dispatch are upon the cards.

Isturiz means well and I really believe he comprehends all the advantages of English alliance to his country better than any of his predecessors, but he seems devoted to the infernal gods, and from the day of his entering the Ministry disasters have poured upon the land. I doubt any good happening so long as he remains at the head of affairs. I ventured a hint upon the subject in my interview with the Queen, and endeavoured to temper her royal ire against Mendizabal but it did not do.[3] Her Majesty seemed to think Isturiz might still have a turn of good luck, and that his predecessor was a very *impotent fellow* when put to the performance of his promises. I did not chuse to press the subject further and I was obliged to be doubly cautious for Mendizabal since he has been out of office has spared no pains to commit me, and try to have it supposed that I was hostile to the present Government and desirous of seeing him reinstated.

It is a matter of great personal satisfaction to me that Cordoba should have resigned and his resignation have been accepted,[4] for I was most errroneously supposed to be blind to his defects and to be his advocate with the Spanish Government as well as my own, till I got to be almost held responsible for his scrapes. I think he has done less ill than his predecessors and I don't believe that his successor whoever he may be will do better, but the trial is worth making. He was desirous of going to Paris and serving the cause there with or without a diplomatic character as he said he thought he might put the Spanish question to Louis Philippe in a way that must produce intervention. He requested me to speak to Isturiz about it. I did so and effectually prevented it. Isturiz was inclined to let him go, but there would have been no end to the intrigues real or supposed that would have taken place at Paris, and the British Legion and the British press would be attributing to them all the disasters which are going to occur here. If no intervention came it would be said that Cordoba had prevented it out of spite—if it was obtained Spain would be sold by him to France to the prejudice of English interests.

The only thing I like about Sarsfield's appointment[5] is the certainty I feel that he will refuse it. It may be an error or a prejudice on my part but I believe if he takes the command it will be the coup de grace to the Queen's cause. I did what I could to prevent the appointment and suggested one or two others who Isturiz could not deny were more likely men than Sarsfield—but then one was friendly to the Constitution, another belonged to some secret society and a third was a personal enemy of Isturiz's—and with these consequences of disunion one is met at every turn among a party whose best hopes of success are in being united.

Received 9 August.

GC/CL/278; Clar. Dep. C.452/2 (230-233)

[1] V had raised the question of a new commercial treaty between England and Spain with Istúriz 'several times since he came into office'. (V to P, 31 July 1836, no. 184, FO 72/460.)

[2] V had suggested to the Spanish Government that General Espartero and his troops should join up with the British Legion, take possession of Fuenterrabia, Irun and Hernani and occupy the frontier with France. (V to P, 31 July 1836, no. 190, FO 72/460.)

[3] In an interview on 27 July 1836. See V to P, 31 July 1836, no. 186, FO 72/460.

[4] V, in his interview with the Queen, strongly advised her to accept the resignation of Córdoba which she was at first disinclined to do. (ibid.)

[5] He had been offered the post of Commander-in-Chief. V pointed out that he was totally deaf and that in Madrid there were doubts 'as to his loyalty'. (V to P, 31 July 1836, no. 189, FO 72/460.)

246 Villiers to Palmerston, 6 August 1836

San Ildefonso. Private. I have received your private letter of the 25th. Your messenger of the 28th did not bring one. You must by this time have about the same kind of feelings with respect to my correspondence as I have towards that which comes from the British Legion—nausea attended with great doubt of whether to open it or not. If such is the case and you resolve not to read my dispatch of today I shall give you joy, for though it has all the couleur de rose which I have ventured to lay on, it remains a foul picture of a deplorable and I fear hopeless state of things. I say hopeless because Spaniards are sure to get into a scrape under the most favorable circumstances, and are quite incapable of righting themselves under adverse ones. There is but one possibility of saving the cause and the *Peninsula* but it is hardly worth adverting to for it is I presume an impossibility. If England and France thought it worth while to resort to great measures and lustily to intervene between the *three* belligerent parties, Cristinos, Carlists, and Jacobins, nominally in favor of the first, the two others might be crushed without difficulty—but such aid should not be given or if given not continued unless the conditions which Rayneval and I should be instructed to impose (more especially with respect to persons which are things in this country) were punctually complied with.

Rayneval and I should have no differences of opinion and these people thus gagged might be made to go strait. This is a strange mode of settling the affairs of a nation, but the people is a strange one and except by extraordinary means its affairs will never be settled.

If Louis Philippe understood the Spanish question in its real bearings upon France and his own policy he ought to wish well to the Queen, for an everlasting civil war between Carlists and anarchists at his gate (which will be the consequence of the Queen's being set aside) must sooner or later be a serious annoyance to him, and if his aversion to intervention is not insuperable he will never have a better moment for it than the present, for no liberal in or out of Spain could object to his opposing the Carlists, and as he would at the same time be putting down the Constitution ('el idolatrado codigo' as some of the addresses to the Queen call it) he would find favor in the eyes of the Holy Alliance.

This is however but a Spanish castle I fear, and is not worth further discussion—left to themselves it is impossible to say what will become of these people. Were the Queen to ask my advice I should recommend her to take Mendizabal again and I can give no greater proof of how desperate I think the state of affairs, for no man can have a more profound contempt for the character of another than I have for Mendizabal's—at first he fascinates and deceives but one soon finds him out to be an arrant cheat. I think however he would flounder and juggle out of the scrape which Her Majesty has got into and at all events gain time. She said however two nights ago that she would sooner cut off her hand than sign a decree appointing him Minister so I cannot *volunteer* the advice, and she is already rather upon her guard with me, by the advice of her Camarilla, as a radical.

The other day when all this bad news came pouring in Isturiz was taken very ill and remained so for 8 and 40 hours, upon which Quintus Curtius Miraflores, ever ready for his leap, came galloping down here *pour se faire nommer*, as he told me, President of the Council. He said he could not but consider the illness of Isturiz as a fortunate circumstance for affairs looked ill and required to be managed by a man of great calmness, commanding abilities and above all by one who united in his favor the esteem of all parties. I fancy therefore, said the little patriot, Her Majesty will not be sorry to see me here today. His fancy however was disappointed for I saw him after his interview and upon splicing together the bits of confession I extracted from him I made out that Her Majesty had told him he was a foolish little fellow and that he was to go back to Madrid, which he did with his tail between his legs.

I enclose you an extract from a letter which was shewn to me today respecting Cordoba. It is from a colonel in the Queen's Guards, a discreet and acute Scotchman who has a personal dislike to Cordoba with whom he has served during the last year and his letter is addressed to a relation here who bears the said General no good will. You cannot justly attack Cordoba on all sides. You quarrel with him for his eagerness to get French intervention which would put down the Carlists in a fortnight, and yet you say he does not wish to finish the war. Pray remember that every general who preceded him was *stumped* up in three months and fairly removed by public opinion and the execration of the army. Cordoba has never had a single disaster happen to him—he has never been surprised and has never lost any men who were under his own immediate command. You say none of his predecessors had so large an army and that he therefore ought to have done better than them, but it must be observed that if his army was doubled so was that of the enemy likewise and the country occupied by them when he took the command was extended four fold to what it was at any preceding period of the war. Here however comes the lack of generalship which I have always admitted—many a general may command ten thousand men with success yet fail completely with 100 thousand. With such a force distributed over 80 leagues of mountainous country he was of course dependent upon his subordinate generals and one may judge of the manner they must have failed him upon every occasion by their conduct now that they are acting independently in other parts. Look at Espartero who was the best of them now in Galicia—look at those in Biscay, Aragon and Valencia. Their conduct is such as would disgrace second rate old women. Yet with all the hardships endured by the soldiers and the little progress made in the war the enthusiasm of the troops for Cordoba up to the day that he returned from his foolish expedition to Madrid was beyond anything ever known in the Spanish army.

You say why does not he destroy the Carlist magazines and hospitals—they can hardly be said to exist or are they necessary in a country where every village contains an iron foundry ready for the itinerant armourers of Don Carlos and where every cabin contains a bed for a wounded soldier.

As for his objects in not finishing the war, I assure you I can understand none by which his interests could be served. If he had succeeded his military glories must have opened to him a great political career—he has failed and his avenir whether as a soldier or a statesman is destroyed.

However, be all this as it may, he is no longer Commander in Chief and few events here could have happened so personally satisfactory to me.

Santa Maria has begged me to call your attention to the scandalous conduct of the Government of the United States with respect to Texas. . . .

The Cortes having been dissolved, the South American recognition question remained in statu quo and having had nothing worth saying about it therefore I did not indict you a dispatch upon the subject.

You may easily conceive my anxiety to know the result of the debate in the House of Commons on the 2d.

Enclosure: 'Extract of a letter from Colonel Barrie of the Royal Guard, Vitoria, 1 August 1836.' The unjust treatment of Córdoba by the English press.

Received 15 August.

GC/CL/279; Clar. Dep. C.452/2 (234-240)

247 Palmerston to Villiers, 6 August 1836

Copy. Foreign Office. I send you a messenger to let you know that I learn from Vienna on the authority of Metternich that Louis Philippe and Thiers have proposed to the Austrian Government a settlement of the Spanish contest by a marriage between the Queen and Don Carlos's son, but that Metternich does not seem much inclined to enter into concert with France upon the subject of Spanish affairs.[1]

I also learn from Paris that Thiers is going actively to work to augment the French Legion in the Spanish service, and will carry it up to 10,000 effective men, and that he has a plan for sending a French marshal, probably Clauzel, to command the Spanish army if the Queen should consent to such an arrangement. The mission of Bois le Comte is said to be for the purpose of sounding the Spanish Government as to the appointment of a French marshal to the command of the Spanish army; but Bois le Comte is said not to know the name of the officer who would be sent if the proposal were to be accepted. I have no doubt however that Bois le Comte is also charged with some overture upon the subject of the marriage.[2]

I never saw Bois le Comte, but have heard much of him; and I know him to be a disciple of the intriguing school of French diplomacy. Busy, meddling, credulous of statements that make for his views, anti-English, and not much inclined to liberal institutions, building theories upon slight foundations and defending his castles as Palafox did Sarragossa.

Thiers is said to have been acting in these matters a little upon his own account, and without being fully authorized by the King from whom he is supposed to have withheld the knowledge of some parts of his proceedings. This I am inclined to doubt, Thiers would hardly venture, and this is more likely an invention on the part of those who have given my correspondents information, with a view to give more apparent value to their *confidential* communications.

You may if you think proper tell Isturiz and the Queen in confidence the statement which I have received of the proposition made by the French Government to that of Austria, supposing always that the Queen is not a party to the proposal. This information may be useful to the Queen in deciding upon the offer of a French marshal to command the army. A good general would to be sure be a godsend to the Queen, but it is a serious matter of doubt whether a French marshal would be of much real use to her, considering all the national prejudices on the side both of Christinos and Carlists which such an appointment would shock. It may also be questioned whether it would be quite prudent to give to the French Government that degree of influence over the management of the war which such an appointment followed up by the others that must necessarily attend it would create.

Why does not the Queen send Rodil to command? Everybody seems to say that he is the best Spaniard. If you are consulted about the offer of the French marshal state all the doubts and objections that may occur to you, and say that you will if the Queen likes write home about it to enable you to give a decided opinion; but that in the mean while they ought not to lose a day in appointing the best officer they have to carry on the operations while the season is favourable for action.

GC/CL/1274

[1] See Sir Frederick Lamb to P, 26 July 1836, GC/BE/163.
[2] P instructed Aston, chargé d'affaires in Paris, to inform Thiers that he was well aware of the marriage proposal, and that the British Government was completely opposed to it, regarding it as an attempt to 'restore absolutism in Spain'. (P to Aston, 4 Aug. 1836, FO 355/6.) But see below, no. 251, n.3. Aston kept V fully informed of Thiers's activities. (Aston to V, 26, 29, 30 July, 1 Aug., FO 355/6.)

248 Villiers to Palmerston, 9 August 1836

San Ildefonso. Private. Rayneval who went to Madrid yesterday has just sent me word that he dispatches a courier tomorrow morning and as Madrid is 50 miles off I must be brief in order that my letter may arrive in time.

Things are going their train but with a Montagne Russe[1] rapidity. We are of course waiting with the utmost anxiety for news from the army—not military but political. If as it is said one half the army is Carlist now and the other Constitutional the whole thing is over, for the garrison of Madrid will take good care not to be left alone in its glory of resisting the popular movement or of being backward in making conditions with the enemy. Upon the steadiness of this garrison or rather upon the hate it bears the National Guard much has depended during the last few days. If it had fraternized with the Constitutionalists we should without any doubt have had Isturiz and the Captain General *arrastrados,* which compliment to unpopular authorities means dragging their mangled remains through the streets, the capital without government and the Queen Regent and her daughters flying wherever the panic-stricken Camarilla drove them. However this *pleasant feature* in the present state of affairs has been avoided for the present but ce qui est differé, etc.

Evaristo San Miguel, the Captain General of Zaragoza who is now inviting the Queen's army to declare for the Constitution, was Foreign Secretary in 1820 and the author of the famous note to the Foreign Ministers.[2] About five months ago he volunteered writing a book to shew the mischiefs and dangers of the Constitution which was hated even to its name by the whole Spanish people, and that the chief obstacle which the Queen's cause had to contend against was the fear that existed among its partisans that sooner or later the Constitution might be reestablished. Not a month ago he wrote friendly letters to Isturiz approving all the acts of his Government, and now puts himself at the head of the party he has been condemning and tries to seduce from its allegiance the whole of the Queen's troops which are, or ought to be, operating against the enemy.

For all which he is thought a very fine fellow—he certainly is a very true Spaniard.

I feel every day more convinced that the original cause of all this movement was the discovery that the elections were turning out more favorably to the Government than had been expected. The Isturiz-haters could not bear this or did they chuse to wait as they at first intended to slay him in parliamentary fight, so they got up the Constitution cry in one or two places always ready for disturbance when there is no coercing force at hand, and then the example of revolt is too allur-ing not to be followed in other parts where the ill disposed are indus-trious and those who have good intentions have no zeal or activity.

I really don't know what to do about the Legion. The letters I get two or three times a week from Evans with accounts of distress and mutiny and all that is most unfortunate drive me to my wits ends. I never fail to remonstrate and go myself to all the different offices in order to follow up whatever I may be claiming. I am shewn by the Ministers the most express instructions or orders in compliance with my demand. I think I have succeeded and then a fortnight afterwards I get a letter from Evans shewing that these orders cannot have been received or at least have not been obeyed. Isturiz and his colleagues are beside themselves with all the difficulties which are daily closing

488

in upon them and as there is not one farthing in the treasury or a hope now that one will find its way there I cannot wonder that I am so constantly disappointed, but that is no satisfaction for the Legion and I know not what to do for them. Isturiz appears to me more distressed about this than any thing else that is occurring and I really believe if he had the money he would advance it out of his own pocket.

The day *may* come when I shall have something else than grievances to write to you but it does not seem very near at hand.

Isturiz shewed me the copies of dispatches he had written to Alava and Jabat requesting to know what would [be] the course of the French and English Governments in the event of the Queen Regent being forced to adopt the Constitution. I told him that we were not in the habit of giving opinions or binding ourselves upon hypothetical cases, and that he must therefore not consider it unfriendly on the part of the English Government if they declined to give a direct answer to this query, although I thought I might assure him that the imperfections and dangers of the Constitution of 1812 were well understood in England and that you would learn with extreme regret that it were adopted here because it would place the authority if not the office of the Queen Regent in abeyance.

I thought it well to say thus much to prepare him for the reply he may possibly receive. If you think it expedient to send him a more favorable one he will be better off than he expects.

Received 22 August.

GC/CL/280; Clar. Dep. C.452/2 (241-244)

¹ Switchback (railway).
² He was both Premier and Foreign Minister in 1823. (CG/CL/280 has 1820 in error; C.452 has 1823.) In his note to the Foreign Ministers of France, Russia, Austria and Prussia after the Congress of Verona he refused to make any changes in the Constitution which could be regarded as concessions to the King and the royalists in Spain, or to the four Powers. What he regarded as a gesture of defiance was seen by the four Powers as cause for intervention in Spain.

249 Villiers to Palmerston, 13 August 1836

San Ildefonso. Private. I have but a moment for writing by an opportunity which has just offered and Bois le Comte and I are desirous to lose no time in dispatching a courier lest when the events of this night become known at Madrid there should be a row and the exit of couriers stopped. We have passed as pleasant a night as 1,200 drunken mutinous soldiers could procure us, and the affair has only been over about 2 hours. I don't know that I have aught to add to my dispatch which is a narrative of what I saw myself with the exception of that which passed with the Queen Regent.[1] I did my best to get into the Palace in order to see if I could be of any service as I knew Her Majesty would be in a state of panic and that she was surrounded by arrant cowards, but it was impossible, and the soldiers looked upon people in plain clothes as Palace spies and to have said who I was would have done more harm than good and have only increased their exigeance with the Queen if they had known she was advised by foreigners.

It is impossible to say what will be the effect of this at Madrid but I do not reckon upon the fidelity of the garrison and the Queen will then be at the mercy of what the approaching Cortes may determine.

Valencia has declared the Constitution. We know nothing (here at least) from Catalonia or of the manner in which the army has received all the Constitutional movement—which is most extraordinary. Espartero appears to have obtained a considerable success over Gomez whose troops have nearly all fallen into his hands—at least according to his (Espartero's) dispatches—but until I see some practical confirmation of a victory I always doubt those said to be gained in the dispatches of a Spanish general.

Of Bois le Comte's mission I have no time to write this morning. Events travel too quickly here for such missions to have any importance or useful result.

Received 22 August.

GC/CL/281; Clar. Dep. C.452/2 (245-246)

[1] The mutineers demanded to see the Queen Regent, and informed her 'if she did not at once adopt the Constitution, that every person in the Palace should be massacred, and at 3 o'clock this morning Her Majesty signed a declaration to the effect that she adopted the Constitution for the time being and until the meeting of the Cortes'. (V to P, 13 Aug. 1836, no. 194, FO 72/460.)

250 Palmerston to Villiers, 15 August 1836

Copy. Foreign Office. I have received your letter and despatches of the 6th. Their contents are certainly not agreable; but nothing in Spain is desperate, as nothing there can inspire one with perfect confidence. It is a great thing that the movement at Madrid should have failed; and if the Queen can maintain her authority there, it will ultimately be established in all the rest of Spain. This seems to have been a last desperate effort of the ultra liberal party to anticipate the meeting of the Cortes; and fearing that the Government would have a majority in that body, they resolved to strike a blow before the meeting in order to upset the Ministry and get power into their own hands.

You say that a nearer acquaintance with Mendizabal has inspired you with profound contempt for him. I am sorry to hear you say so; because you have had opportunities of forming a judgment, which we who have known Mendizabal here have not had, and one regrets to find every Spaniard fail one after the other on being tried. I am bound to say that nothing which I saw of Mendizabal during my intercourse with him about Portuguese and Spanish affairs led me to the same conclusion. I found him honest and straightforward, and energetic, and full of resources; though as might have been expected from the habits and occupations of his former life deficient in the knowledge and extensive views which are requisite to form a statesman.

I hear that within a short period and not long ago large sums have been invested in the English funds in the name of Muños, amounting as is said to £300,000. Has this been done since Mendizabal went out?[1] And may his refusal to concur have contributed to his disgrace? As to Cordova, I cannot concur in the charitable view you take of his conduct. His preaching up the necessity of French interference was part of his system of intrigue and of connivance with Louis Philippe. It was safe doctrine to hold because he well knew that Louis Philippe would not grant the aid, and what could be better calculated to disorganize an army and to destroy its spirit than daily declarations from its own Commander in Chief that Spanish efforts must be unavailing, and that nothing would put down the civil war but foreign aid which was publicly known to be unattainable?

But, abiit, evasit, erupit, and I hope and trust there is an end of him. Depend upon it he is a man whom no one ought to trust. Sarsfield is obviously unfit, and by your account unwilling. Why not try Rodil again as a military man? His reputation stood high before his last command; and his fault was the reverse of Cordova's; he hazarded a little too much, and got beat, but that fault soon corrects itself. Cordova stood stock still while the enemy was gathering strength every day, and his avowed system was to *do nothing*. But wars are not brought to a successful issue by *doing nothing*.

I hear from Löwenhielm who is over here that it is well known to the bankers at Paris that Austria and Russia send Carlos about £50,000 a month. This all goes by Bayonne either in money or in stores, and the road by St. Jean de Luz is daily covered with carts conveying these things in open day to Irun and Ernani. If the Spanish Government would give Evans force enough to take possession of that road and to hold it, the difficulties of the Carlists would be very greatly increased; or I should rather say their facilities much diminished, for difficulties they seem to have none. Pray press this again and again upon Isturitz. If he really means to put down Carlism this is the first move he should make; there is no other single thing that would tell so much.

Docketed: By messenger. GC/CL/1275

[1] On 3 June 1836 V wrote to his brother Edward: 'I always forget to answer your information about the enormous amount of stock standing in Muñoz' name. I had known it for a long time past but whether it is his money or the Queen's I can't say. It is pretty barefaced, however, and shews great stupidity or great indifference to public feeling.' (V to Edward Villiers, 3 June 1836, Clar. Dep. C.467.)

251   Villiers to Palmerston, 17 August 1836

Madrid. Private. I send a courier just to let you know that His Majesty's minister at Madrid has neither deserted to Don Carlos or been shot by the Queen's troops. It is the one I ought to have sent on the 13th but nobody, nor even a letter, was suffered to leave San Ildefonso. In Madrid they knew nothing of us for three days, and none of the people even who I have yet seen have clear ideas of what has occurred there or how we got away.[1]

I can assure you it was a most diabolical position to be shut up in a little place with 1,000 mutinous soldiers whom wine and the fear of the consequences of what they had done made completely ungovernable—then the dreadful position of the Queen and the consequences of the act she was forced to commit, together with the illness and death of poor Rayneval, all tended to make the last week about the worst I ever passed, and I arrived at the conclusion that service in Spain ought to count double.

With respect to the future it is too dark and confused to hazard an opinion upon it. Of course the Constitution snatched from the Queen as it has been is illegal—that would not so much signify if it were practicable because legality is the last thing ever thought of in Spain, but I feel certain this country, or indeed any other, cannot be governed under it, although it may perhaps be at first turned to account and made a stimulating engine to the public mind against Don Carlos.

I have hardly had time to look about me or know the real state of things. Mendizabal who I have seen says that tienen compostura.[2] I doubt it—however in a day or two I will send back Waring who arrived this morning with your letter of the 6th having been detained 2 days at Zaragoza on account of the road being occupied by the Carlists. I believe your Vienna correspondent is wrong in the principal parts of the information he gave you.[3]

PS. Mina appears to have been the only one of the Queen's authorities who restrained the Constitutional movement, but he must of course now conform to what Her Majesty has done.

If you are curious in anecdotes of national character here goes for one. The assassins of Quesada[4] cut off his genitals while he was yet alive and his member decked with a green ribbon (the Constitutional color) was put upon a stick and exposed to the approving gaze of the public, and men, women and children are now singing all over the town some impromptu stanzas made upon the occasion and the *part!* I think *out* of Spain it would be difficult to match this story.

It was multa gemens that I urged the Queen to adopt the Constitution but a few hours more delay would *infallibly* have cost her and her daughters their lives and the Constitution would have been equally proclaimed.

GC/CL/282

[1] The Queen was allowed to return to Madrid only after she had consented to the publication of a decree promulgating the Constitution of 1812. (V to P, 17 Aug. 1836, no. 196, FO 72/460.) The rebellious regiments of San Ildefonso also came to Madrid, which according to V was under their dominion. (V to P, 21 Aug. 1836, no. 198, FO 72/460.)

[2] 'they have reached agreement'.

[3] According to V a marriage proposal formed no part of Bois-le-Comte's instructions. (V to P, 21 Aug. 1836, no. 202, FO 72/460. See also Bois-le-Comte to Thiers, 10 and 12 Aug. 1836, Bibliothèque Nationale, Paris, Thiers Papers, NAF 20603.)

[4] A general who had tried to resist the proclamation of the Constitution of 1812 at Madrid. (V to P, 15 Aug. 1836, no. 195, FO 72/460.)

252   Palmerston to Villiers, 20 August 1836

Foreign Office. *Forwards a letter from Sir Hussey Vivian, who wishes to obtain a mining concession from the Spanish Government.*
Copy.

GC/CL/1276

253   Villiers to Palmerston, 21 August 1836

Madrid. Private. The courier who arrived yesterday having given me reason to expect that the Carlists upon the Zaragoza road will intercept the dispatches which go today I shall reserve till a safer opportunity various details which would be interesting to you respecting the position of affairs here which is I really believe the most extraordinary and the most terrible that history has yet told of. The Sovereign—the Government—the lives and properties of individuals without any distinction, are at the mercy of common soldiers who are fully aware of their power but acknowledge no leader. I know of no other revolution where some chief was not apparent, or where responsibility though for however short a time did not after the first burst rest somewhere. Such however is not the case here—the spirit of disorder is daily increasing, and is fed by the impotent attempts of the Government to control it, and the panic and consequent inaction of the upper and middling classes.

The affair of San Ildefonso must donner à penser to every Crowned Head in Europe—what will be the result of these royal[1] reflections I don't pretend to guess, but it is certain that the body guards of Nicholas while rusticating at Czarskosoelo would be just as well able to screw a constitution out of His Imperial Majesty as Christina's were at San Ildefonso—a thousand armed men excited or bribed up to the point of making prisoners of the whole royal family may dictate their own terms to the country. It is an awful precedent and lets in a bran new light upon the mode of making revolutions which will occupy the attention of the *manufacturing interests* in that line quite as much as that of the Sovereigns.

And yet what is to be done? The Holy Alliance won't come crusading in favor of Isabel I suppose and they can't decently interfere in favor of Don Carlos to avenge his rival's wrongs. Then England and France can hardly continue their support to a prisoner Sovereign and to a cause managed by common soldiers—and yet after mature reflection I believe it is the only course to be pursued. I believe that putting down Don Carlos is the only chance for the Queen's Government, or *any* Government, to recover existence and then to combat revolution i.e. constitution in its present shape. Then some energy might be hoped for from the thinking and possessing classes—to them the word constitution is loathsome—they look upon it as equivalent to proscription, robbery and unbridled licence, and those who believe that the present movement represents the national opinion or the national will are grievously in error. All the small towns take their *cue* from the large ones where a few demagogues raise a cry of constitution and under the name of liberty possess themselves of the means of vengeance and taxation. The National Guards who in the provinces are nearly all proletaires share in the booty, and the army is in favor of the Constitution because it considers itself relieved from discipline under its aegis, and the soldiers think they have a right, as they are now doing here, to command their officers and satisfy every wanton caprice. There, with the exception of some dozen visionaries like Calatrava and Arguelles who have never missed an opportunity for proving their unfitness for the practical business of government, are the only real likers of what they call a constitution and only understand in their own sense.

And yet these people have the nation as much their prisoner as the Guards had the Queen last week.

If Don Carlos were not the man he is—the devoted instrument of a sanguinary party which has far more revenge to satisfy than upon its return to power in 1823—he would be invited to the throne by 9/10ths of the nation—but there is no trust to be placed in him or his. The position therefore of the moderate well affected partizans of the Queen is very much that of corn between two grindstones, and I suppose when their pulverized remains disappear the two grindstones may have at each other and see which lasts longest. An attempt by the united efforts of the British and French Legions to drive out Don Carlos might I think be successful and, besides offering the only chance now left for the Queen, would enable us if we pleased to retire afterwards from the contest with something like credit, having *done* what we pledged ourselves to *assist* in doing. Then, if Spaniards love blood and war better than tranquillity, we may leave them to their tastes —though I do not think it could be for long—Spain forms too important a part of Europe to be left for any considerable time in the condition that the South American States were reduced to.

Even Mendizabal sees but little hope.

There is of course not a farthing of money in the treasury or in expectation and unless some means can be found in England for advancing 3 months pay to the British Legion in the same way that the French Legion's is secured it had better not act with the latter but go home. That however with this logical people will be looked upon as an act of overt hostility on the part of England.

As yet houses here have been respected—this may only last a few hours longer and I have no reason for thinking that diplomatic hotels will fare better than their neighbours. In such an event, and the Government not being able to give protection or redress will you tell me what you should wish me to do?

Received 29 August.

GC/CL/283; Clar. Dep. C.452/2 (247-252)

¹ 'royal' deleted in pencil, possibly by P.

254   Palmerston to Villiers, 22 August 1836

Foreign Office. No. 76. His Majesty's Government deeply regret the disturbances which have lately taken place in Spain and the illegal and violent interference of military bodies with the civil administration of the country. His Majesty's Government are not called upon to pass judgement on the measures of the Queen Regent, but no impartial spectator of events could well have avoided foreseeing that the decision taken by Her Majesty in May last to dismiss her Ministers and to dissolve the Cortes must produce consequences most injurious to the cause of the Queen Isabella . . . . His Majesty's Government however are sensible that these are matters which concern the Spanish nation alone and with which foreign Powers are not entitled to interfere and upon these points I have no instructions to give you.

It is necessary however that you should be instructed as to the course which you ought to pursue in certain possible contingencies. In the first place then I have to state that as Great Britain does not pretend to interfere with the decisions of the Spanish nation as to its form of internal constitution, the complete and general adoption of the Constitution of 1812 by the Queen Regent and the nation would make no change in the relations between Great Britain and Spain, and you would in such case continue to perform your functions without interruption; in the same manner as His Majesty's diplomatic agents in Spain did from the year 1820 to 1823, when that Constitution was in nominal existence.[1]

In the next place I have to point out to you, that you are accredited to the Queen who is Sovereign of Spain and not to the Queen Regent, and that therefore a change in the regency, how much soever to be lamented such an event might be, would not of itself put an end to your diplomatic functions. If such a case should occur, you would report it, together with the circumstances under which it had happened, to His Majesty's Government, and you would wait at Madrid such instructions thereupon as might be deemed advisable to send you.

If indeed a more serious change were to take place in the state of affairs in Spain, and if the Queen Isabella were to be deposed and a republic were to be established or Don Carlos were to be set up in her room, in either of these cases your functions would necessarily cease with the authority of the Sovereign to whom you have been accredited, and it would then become your duty, without waiting for further orders, to leave Madrid and return home.

Extract.

Minuted by Under-Secretary (William Fox-Strangways): If Mr. Villiers under these instructions should quit Madrid, will he be authorised to leave Lord William Hervey or any other person there, in a private capacity for correspondence and observation?

Minuted by Palmerston: Yes. Palmerston. 23/8/36.

FO 72/456

[1] P informed Bourqueney that he hoped that the French Government would give similar instructions to their diplomats at Madrid. He said that as the Queen's authority was under such attack it was the duty of the representatives of friendly Powers to remain at Madrid and to be seen to support her cause. (Bourqueney to Thiers, 18 Aug. 1836, AMAE CP Angleterre 648.)

255 Palmerston to Villiers, 23 August 1836

Copy. Stanhope Street. I am just starting for Tiverton to attend the races and have not time to write more than two lines. We do not think so ill of affairs in Spain. This Constitution cry only means new men, more vigorous measures, and a revision of the Royal Statute. The first two are necessary, the last may be very proper for anything we know to the contrary.

The moment there was a notion here of a change, Zulueta stopped payment for the Legion, like a true Spaniard. I fear the Legion will suffer during the interval that must still elapse before the Cortes can grant any money. But I hope it will make shift to keep together. Reid, whom I have seen, begs me to press upon you and through you on the Spanish Government in the strongest manner, the absolute necessity of getting the Legion out of the corner in which it is at present embayed. The only way of doing this is to make the French Legion advance and join it, letting the two together operate along the Bastan and upon Fuentarabia and Irun. They will then come down upon Ernani which has been made very strong, and may be able to take it. Reid says the Carlists have fortified convents at Ernani, as the French had at Salamanca, works which took the Duke of Wellington many days of regular attack to carry. Things not to be walked into at the point of the bayonet.

I begin to have hopes of Spain, and think it not impossible she may save herself without French assistance.[1] I return to Windsor on Friday and to town on Monday and then mount guard here for five or six weeks.

GC/CL/1277

[1] To Aston P wrote blaming the 'mistaken policy of the French Government' for the recent events in Spain. 'The French Government ought now to make haste to give the aid they intend to afford . . . .' (P to Aston, 19 Aug. 1836, FO 355/6.)

256 Villiers to Palmerston, 27 August 1836

Madrid. Private. As far as the capital is concerned our position is greatly improved since I last wrote to you when it was really very formidable as 2,000 soldiers were already in a state of tumultuous riot,

2,000 more were upon the eve of becoming so, the National Guards and inhabitants being frightened out of their wits, and the 'barrios bajos'[1] which for ferocity and desire for plunder need not fear competition with any canaille on earth, were only waiting till confusion became a little worse confounded to sack the town. However thanks to the courage and tact of the Captain General this addition to our other pleasures has been averted.[2]

Of other matters I will say as of a lady just brought to bed that they are as well as can be expected—the action of the Government is imperceptibly small, that of the secret societies visibly great and important. There is hardly a decent person throughout the country who does not deplore what is passing, and the accounts given in the newspapers of universal joy and happiness are of course most false—nobody rejoices except those dregs of society whom such a state of things as the present throws up to the surface, and a few doctrinaires who think that the reestablishment of the Constitution wipes away the stain of the French invasion. They have now got it however and they must make what they can of it. In Spain nothing need ever be despaired of, and as both good and evil here spring from causes the least expected, it is possible that in the general shaking which this revolutionary movement will give the country that the Carlists may get crushed, and as that is the declared object of every liberal of every gradation of opinion I see no reason why England and France should not now continue to assist this object.

The presence of the representative body will give great force to the Government[3] but the difficulty is how to get over the intervening time before the Cortes meet and to prevent the Government being debordé by its partizans. If it could be passed in military successes and Don Carlos be driven from Spain before the middle of October the great cause of excitement and alarm would be removed, and people *might* then think of political tranquillity and consolidating themselves. At all events *there* we might take leave of them with some credit to ourselves if we had prevented that which we have declared we would not permit—the occupation of the throne by Don Carlos.

Aston says[4] and Bois le Comte admits[5] that the active assistance which a month ago was promised would not have been withheld for the mere fact of the Queen's having been obliged to swallow the Constitution—so that if Louis Philippe now turns his back upon his niece it will not be on account of what she has swallowed but of the manner in which it has been forced down her throat. I admit that this is extremely difficult to get over, but if it could be treated as cosa Española and taken no notice of and the military aid be still given all parties would I believe find their account in it—Spain in having the civil war put down—France in having 10 or 12,000 troops in the Spanish service who the Exaltados would feel might any day put on the tricolor cockade and the next be on their march from Pamplona to Madrid—an *enormous* check upon their proceedings—and England would find her account in both the above grounds for satisfaction to France and Spain, *plus* that assistance afforded at this moment by Louis Philippe to the Queen would cause an irreparable breach between him and the Holy Allies. I think then that he should be urged to continue his military aid against Don Carlos. He will get into a very serious scrape if he intervenes against the Constitution. Every thing will be reenacted here as in 1823 but the Queens may possibly not leave Cadiz as triumphantly as Ferdinand did—the approach of the French army may cost them their lives.

Calatrava[6] in compliance with my suggestion is quite willing to leave Alava either at Paris or London but I suppose Alava won't continue serving a revolutionary Government.

In my dispatch of today I give verbatim what Calatrava said in answer to my queries respecting the regency[7]. How he reconciles his opinion with the spirit of the Constitution I know not—he cannot pretend to do so with the letter.

I have been very ill since my last courier and am not yet in working trim or I should treat of various other subjects.

Received 5 September.

GC/CL/284; Clar. Dep. C.452/2 (253-256)

[1] 'poor quarters'.

[2] Five battalions were sent by the Captain General of Madrid from the capital to the war in the North, including two which had taken part in the mutiny of San Ildefonso. They agreed to go after they had received arrears of pay. (V to P, 27 Aug. 1836, no. 204, FO 72/460.)

[3] The Cortes was convoked, according to the Constitution of 1812, for 24 October. (V to P, 27 Aug. 1836, no. 206, FO 72/460.)

[4] 'I conceive therefore that any hopes of cooperation are entirely at an end. Not a man or a musket will be allowed to be sent to the Legion.' (Aston to V, 23 Aug. 1836, Aston Papers, FO 355/6.)

[5] For V's conversation with Bois-le-Comte, see V to P, 27 Aug. 1836, no. 205, FO 72/460. For Bois-le-Comte's memorandum on the crisis in Spain, sent

to Thiers on 22 August 1836, see AMAE Mémoires et Documents 352.

[6] Appointed principal Secretary of State and described by V as 'a passionate admirer and advocate of the Constitution'. (V to P, 21 Aug. 1836, no. 199, FO 72/460.)

[7] V questioned him on this matter after he heard rumours to the effect that the partisans of the Constitution of 1812 intended to deprive the Queen Mother of the Regency. Calatrava said that neither the Government of which he was the head nor the party of which he was a member intended to deprive her of her position or drive her out of Spain. (V to P, 27 Aug. 1836, no. 204, FO 72/460.)

257 Villiers to Palmerston, 31 August 1836

Madrid. Private. I send you back the messenger Waring who I hope will arrive safely. He sets out half dead with fear at all he is likely to meet with upon the road.

A calm has succeeded the *borrasco*.[1] The Government is getting some hold of public opinion—they have adopted some clever measures (in which Mendizabal has been of great use) and things upon the whole look as well as can be expected on the revolutionary side. The Carlist is not altogether so fair, at least today, for Mr. Gomez is but 10 leagues off at Guadalajara, the authorities and inhabitants of which place came flocking in here this morning with their goods and chattels. The garrison and Rodil[2] marched out last night. All day there has been panic and Carlist commotion and now Calatrava has this moment sent to beg my courier may not go till tomorrow in the hope that some better news may arrive to render null all the evil reports that would be written tonight.

You will see by my dispatch that the Ministers, Constitutional and hyperNational as they are, have very decided opinions upon the necessity of foreign aid[3]—I added the opinion of Seoane the Captain General of Castille, because the Ministers look upon him as one of the Cabinet and because I think him the most sensible and practical man I have met with in Spain. They all likewise understand the awe which a foreign force, although employed against the Carlists, would inspire and that the Exaltados would take care to keep themselves within bounds lest the wrath of their allies should be turned against them. I must do the Duque de Ribas, one of the ex Ministers, the justice to say that he holds the same language, and considers that the only means of saving the country is to strengthen the present Government.

I was very desirous that Mendizabal should join these Ministers, because in a crisis like the present one and before the business of regular government begins he has not his equal for throwing dust in people's eyes—and I offered to speak to Calatrava upon the subject, and to try and remove any royal objections, but he would not consent, 1st because his friend Ferrer is appointed Minister of Finance and until his answer is received (he is in France) he would not take his place, 2d he wants to prove by not taking office that he had no concern in all this revolutionary movement which he is accused of, and 3dly because he is bent upon going to Paris and London for a few days upon a diplomatico-financial mission in order to shew the French and English publics that Spain is in the high road to tranquillity and prosperity and then to get his hands as far down in their pockets as they will let him, returning with the spoils for the opening of the Cortes. I don't think this a bad project, and if he succeeds in defending his own Ministry at Paris, and proving that he was not a revolutionist, and that he can pick up some money in England he might then join the Ministry here and he would bring great weight.

I think you will approve of my having got a reprieve for Alava and prevented the commission of two or three acts which would certainly have been considered offensive at Paris.[4] In the present circumstances of this country meddling with the embassy at Paris is a matter of political importance or I should not have thought it worth while to treat of it in a dispatch.

Your character of Bois le Comte is a very correct one as I have daily means of observing. I knew him twelve years ago at St. Petersburg and he has turned out all he then promised to be. I don't know what weight he has with his Government—he talks as if he was King of the French, and expects to have his credentials of minister by the next courier.

I am more than ever embarrassed about the Legion—it is at this moment useless to Spain and discreditable to England. The accounts brought up by Colonel De Lancey, which are no accounts at all, will never pass with the Government even if it was solvent, but as it is pennyless advantage will be taken of the confusion which prevails in every pecuniary transaction of the Legion not to pay (or rather *acknowledge*, for paying is quite out of the question) what is justly due.[5]

There is no doubt that a most disgraceful system of plunder has been permitted, and the Legion must either be got rid of or be put upon an entirely new footing. I should be for dissolving and then reorganizing it, sending home the malcontents as well as the 4 brigadiers and all the useless costly paraphernalia sufficient for an army of 20,000 men—4,000 (*at the very utmost*) useful men might in this way be procured, and they would do good service *if* they are kept in activity and *if* they are punctually paid—two important conditions which as they depend upon the Spanish Government and generals are not very likely to be fulfilled.

I omitted to mention that Calatrava proposes in the event of Alava's resigning altogether or electing Paris for his mission to appoint a certain Mr. Campuzano to London—he was a colleague of Frederick Lamb's at Lisbon and Vienna and he (Lamb) has a very good opinion of him—he is a well meaning sensible man and a considerable bore. Calatrava asked me if I thought he would be agreable to you—I said you would probably not object but that I hoped nothing would be settled till we knew more of Alava's intentions—to which he agreed.

PS. September 1st. I have nothing to add to my dispatch of this day—the town was in a great state of alarm last night at the approach of Gomez. What do you think of the Captain General of Old Castille's dispatch on the 29th to the Government saying he had chased Basilio across the Ebro, the said Basilio having at the time he wrote joined himself with Gomez and on the following day beat the Queen's troops within 10 leagues of Madrid? The pitch to which cowardice and lying have arrived with Spanish generals is beyond any thing recorded in ancient or modern history.

Rodil has done very ill to come back to Madrid as the skrummage is by no means over and Gomez is a much better man than any of those he has against him.[6]

Received 12 September.

GC/CL/285; Clar. Dep. C.452/2 (257-261)

[1] 'storm'.

[2] The new Commander-in-Chief of the Queen's army.

[3] In V's conversations with Calatrava, Cuadra, Rodil and Seoane all argued 'that the Governments of England and France should not at this moment relax in the efforts which they have hitherto generously made to uphold the Queen's cause' and that they should 'overlook' the events of San Ildefonso. (V to P, 31 Aug. 1836, no. 213, FO 72/461.)

[4] Álava, Spanish ambassador at Paris, wrote a letter of protest to Calatrava against the events of San Ildefonso. Calatrava wanted to dismiss Álava on the grounds that he did not support the Government and the Constitution, but

V persuaded him to leave Álava at his post as his dismissal would cause great offence to the French Government. (V to P, 31 Aug. 1836, no. 210, FO 72/461.)

[5] See V to P, 31 Aug. 1836, no. 209, FO 72/461.

[6] Postscript omitted from C.452/2.

258 Villiers to Palmerston, 4 September 1836

Madrid. Private. We have had panic the second since I last wrote, and I must say it was not an unfounded one, as it is pretty generally felt that whatever depends upon the valor or skill of Spanish generals fails.[1] Luckily the enemy is Spanish as well, or Don Carlos would at this moment have been proclaimed at Madrid. If Cabrera had not been jealous of Gomez and refused to join his forces (9,000 men) with those of Gomez at Guadalajara, the Queen's tenure of the capital would not have been worth 6d., for the garrison which does not amount to 5,000 men is without discipline, and the National Guards, even if they had not been employed in shaving off their mustachios and hiding their uniforms—the first object of a National Guardsman on the approach of the enemy—would have had quite enough to do in defending themselves against the Carlist populace. If the panic had lasted a few hours longer we should have had a change of Government and all the other vagaries in which the frightened and the mischievous are wont to indulge at such moments.

There are now in Castille upwards of 16,000 troops who are or ought to be occupied in destroying Gomez and his 4,000 men, and yet I feel confident he will return to Navarre or beat the Queen's troops in detail just as he pleases. He really is a fine fellow, and one cannot help feeling a respect for a man who marches from Navarre through a by no means friendly country to Coruña, and back again in defiance of pursuers in treble force, and then advances within ten leagues of the capital without knowing that the reinforcements he reckoned upon for attacking it would be at the place he expected them or not.

I did my best to animate Calatrava and Co. to take some measures for the protection of the town, arming the citizens, etc., etc., and I was assured every thing had been thought of, but I saw nothing was done. Some of these recreant generals should be punished as a warning to others against treachery or cowardice, or one of these mornings the

Queens, duly escorted by facciosos, will be on their road to Oñate to visit their amiable and illustrious relative.

I have received your letters of the 15th and 23d which came together per tot discrimina rerum or in other words by the courier who had to play at hide and seek with the Carlists in the mountains, and to walk those stages where there were no mules or *asses* to be hired.

I have the misfortune not quite to agree with you about persons in this country, but I don't know that it is worth while to discuss our differences of opinion, for I at least have long since arrived at the conviction that no Spaniard is worth even a discussion. Of Cordoba as a general during the last six months I think as you do. As a traitor I have no reason for agreeing with you—but of him I will say nothing, 1st because there is an end of him, and 2d because I am sure his very name irritates you—but I think it just to say one word respecting his journey to Madrid. He had long wished to come and I had recommended Mendizabal to give him leave *as the best means of removing him altogether from the army,* which you may remember I wrote to you in the month of April last I thought indispensable. Mendizabal was about to comply when the brouillerie with the Queen happened. The day before he went out of office Cordoba sent to me under flying seal a letter to the Queen declaring in the strongest terms that quarrelling with Mendizabal would be madness and bring great evils upon the country. Mendizabal was delighted with this letter and when the Queen accepted his resignation he begged me to send a courier to Cordoba to desire he would come to Madrid in order to advise the Queen, and he wanted to antedate a leave of absence for Cordoba. I declined the one and prevented the other, but foreseeing that the Chamber would oppose Isturiz and knowing that Cordoba had immense influence with the Queen, I recommended him to come here if he could leave the army safely for a few days in order to prevail upon Her Majesty to take back Mendizabal. When he arrived the Cortes were dissolved, and the Queen thinking she had gained a victory would hear of no ministerial changes or modifications.

That Cordoba should have remained here upwards of a fortnight instead of 8 and 40 hours was, under the circumstances, a *crime* admitting of no palliation. With respect to Mendizabal, if you gave credit to the opinions I expressed concerning him in my letters during the whole time of his Administration I think you cannot be surprised at my feeling contempt for his character. Your intercourse with him *en gros* was of a very different kind from the daily relations I had with him for 8 months, when I found that he hardly ever spoke the truth, and hardly ever kept a promise, and that his selfishness and vanity were beyond what I had ever met with in the same man. These are qualities which I think you will admit are calculated to inspire contempt. Still however I thought him necessary in the Government and I exerted myself to have him retained until I became an object of suspicion to the Queen and the whole moderate party. If things were now going on smoothly I should not think his return to the Government particularly desireable—in their present state I wish very much to see him there because his energy and resources are longo intervallo superior to those of any other man in Spain, and in a moment of crisis they far outbalance his bad qualities.

Then Rodil—I am glad he is appointed Commander in Chief because you have several times expressed a wish upon the subject, and because the Legion have a fancy for him, but I fear you will be disappointed—his failure in the last command arose not from attempting too much but from executing what he attempted badly. His orders were to catch Don Carlos à tout prix and he set about it with a tail of 10,000 men always dragging after him up and down the mountains, and he of course did not catch his man but lost many joints of his tail. He has now been appointed to the army upwards of a fortnight but is not yet thinking of going there, and by his conduct last week he has now lost all his prestige. He went from Madrid in order to go to Guadalajara when Lopez was defeated. He went half way there and was back here in little more than 24 hours, leaving $\frac{1}{2}$ a dozen divisions which are coming up in different directions, each commanded by its colonel or brigadier, to act or not act against the enemy just as they please for want of some one to command them all, and to force them into what each hates like poison, cooperation. The public are angry and Rodil will go to the army *disvirtuado* for he has given a miniature specimen here of what he will do there. Au reste he is a very good sort of man—well disposed to the English—and I shall endeavour to make him *uncorner* the Legion.

Calatrava is delighted with your answer to Jabat's note.[2] He takes the resolution of Louis Philippe[3] with calmness and says very properly that it should be an additional stimulus to Spaniards to try and get out of their scrape by themselves.

Received 15 September.

GC/CL/286; Clar. Dep. C.452/2 (263-268)

[1] Gómez, the Carlist general, defeated an army commanded by Rodil in pitched battle some thirty miles from Madrid. Gómez was, however, forced to retreat as Espartero brought troops to the relief of Rodil. (V to P, 1 Sept. 1836, no. 218, FO 72/461.)

[2] Jabat resigned his post in the Spanish legation in London as a protest against the adoption of the Constitution of 1812. He informed P of his decision and the reason for it. In reply P said that the British Government saw no reason to change its Spanish policy merely because the Spanish Government had changed.

[3] Louis Philippe, who had only reluctantly consented to the measures of assistance that Thiers proposed, withdrew his consent after the collapse of the Istúriz Government and the formation of the new radical Ministry in Spain.

259   Villiers to Palmerston, 7 September 1836

Madrid. Private. I have had so little notice of the departure of this courier (who is dispatched for the safe conveyance of a young gentleman who wants to give himself importance by declaring he is in danger here)[1] that I have only time to write you a few lines of dispatch respecting military operations for upon them the little hope which still exists for the Queen's cause depends.

Rodil as well as his colleagues are true Spaniards and never provide against an evil or believe in its advent till it is actually upon them. They accordingly take no concern about Gomez and his faction and think that because troops *ought* to be pursuing him they will therefore catch him. I differ with them entirely and look upon this Gomez as a fellow capable any day of giving the coup de grace to things here. One of two movements he seems to be meditating, either to join with Cabrera or Quilez and then return upon Madrid by Guadalajara, avoiding or beating the Queen's troops (the one being as easy for him as the other). His information from this place is frequent and accurate and he knows that he would find here no opposition whatever. The troops in garrison are much inferior in numbers to those he would bring with him—the National Guards if they took any part at all would be fully occupied with the Carlist pillaging populace, and the whole town would be in such complete confusion that running away would be the only *real* business of the Court, the Government, and the Military. The other project which Gomez may attempt is to march through Valencia and take possession of Andalusia which would be to him as easy as to sack it afterwards—and then with all his money and forced recruits to march up upon Madrid by a combined movement with Villareal who should cross the Ebro and meet him here from the North. Then I think you will allow we should be rather *en apuros*,[2] for as the enemy approached, the liberals would of course be changing Governments and executing traitors as the best means of defence against facciosos. I have suggested all this to Rodil and Co. who are far from denying the possibility of such events *coming off*, but when they add that the attempt would be too *arriesgado*[3] for Gomez their conscience and their exertions seem equally stilled.

Rodil won't go to the army without money because he says that the arrears of pay due are a fair pretence for the mutinous spirit which already exists there, and if he takes the command without anything but promises to give the soldiers he shall have no chance of being obeyed. He is certainly right in this and in fearing that some of these mornings we shall hear of the army having disbanded itself and the men having gone a sus casas which is the great ambition of a Spanish soldier always. He is thinking of taking the command of the troops in Aragon and of urging Sarsfield to take that of the army of the North—but in the mean while nothing is done and the Government is sinking in public opinion.

I might, and perhaps ought, to add to this nauseous catalogue of ills present and to come in order to lay before you fully the state of the country but you have probably enough for this time and there is a very handsome reserve for future couriers.

One more only I must however touch upon and as far as we are concerned it is the worst—the Legion. Mendizabal has promised first one thing, then another—in short all except money which the Government has not got, and he is I fear almost reduced to the conviction that it will be necessary to ship them off to England. I shall be able to write you something decisive upon this subject by my own courier on Saturday. Every exertion should be made by the Government to retain the Legion in preference to any other troops in the Queen's service, but if provision cannot be made against their falling into a state which would ensure their being useless to this country and a disgrace to their own—which by Colonel De Lancey's account I am sorry to say is the case at present—then I think that it would be better at once to send them home *upon the ground* that the Spanish Government is unable to fulfil its engagements with them.

Your instructions to me in the events of Don Carlos or a republic being acknowledged are perfectly clear and satisfactory—there is however one more that I should beg to be furnished with. If either of those events should occur *partially*—at Madrid for example—and the Queens think it necessary to go to Galicia or any other part of the kingdom where their authority is recognized I conclude it will be my duty to accompany them and remain with them so long as a chance exists of reestablishing the not-altogether-upset throne of Isabel.

PS. Calatrava tells me he has information that the frontiers are more open than ever, and that all the Carlist chiefs whom Mina forced to take refuge in France where they have been detained are coming back again. The Carlists look upon the Quadruple Treaty, as far as France is concerned, as at an end.

Received 17 September.

GC/CL/287; Clar. Dep. C.452/2 (269-270, 280-283)

1 'The Austrian chargé d'affaires' added in P's hand.
2 'in distress'.
3 'risky'.

260 Palmerston to Villiers, 9 September 1836

Copy. Foreign Office. The last accounts we have received from you are more encouraging. The proclamation announcing the intention to alter the Constitution looks well; the getting the mutineers out of Madrid was a grand measure and if Louis Philippe's finger can be kept out of the pie things may go on well. But the great matter is to get money to pay the troops; and you should urge Calatrava to set to work immediately to raise a loan: not a forced loan but a good spanking one of sufficient amount to finish the war. Though the transaction may not be capable of being concluded till the Cortes can sanction it, yet if it were known in the money market that such a measure were resolved upon, people would probably be found willing to make advances on account. Of course Calatrava will take care to pay the Legion who are greatly in arrear; but it is of infinite importance to get them united with some good troops and extricated from the corner in which they now are.

Reid told me that from their great want of officers the discipline of the regiments was at an end and that he should be very sorry to see them put to do anything difficult by themselves. He saw an instance of the bad order in which they were a few days before he left them. Some little demonstration was ordered in front of St. Sebastian's. The regiment which was ordered to make it, instead of doing what it was told, ran on hurra-ing and shouting much further than it was meant to go. It then got into difficulties and retreated faster than it had advanced: other battalions were obliged to go to support it, and more was brought on than Evans had any intention of doing. It is therefore of urgent importance to reinforce Evans or to place him in connexion with some larger force.

I hope we shall soon see Mendizabal in office again. The Queen's objections to him ought to be overcome; they are founded in French intrigue and in no good reasons; and his accession to the Ministry would give great financial facilities to the Government.

Alava and Jabat decline swearing to the Constitution and retire. To be sure it is disagreeable to *swear* to a thing which is announced only as temporary, and an affirmatory declaration might have been sufficient. But if I mistake not Alava was a Constitutionalist in 1820, or between that and 1823.

If the Spaniards would do their duty I should be rather glad of the shabby conduct of Louis Philippe, because it would be better that Spain should save herself than that she should be saved by the French[1]—and one is not without hope that the Spaniards may now succeed by their own exertions.

Howard tells me that Isturitz, in order to leave no doubt as to whose protégé he considered himself, rushed to St. Priest immediately upon arriving at Lisbon.

I have ascertained beyond a doubt that in March 1835 £300,000 stock was placed in the books of the Bank of England to the name of Muñoz; no wonder the army remained unpaid.

GC/CL/1278

[1] To Granville P suggested that the best course for Louis Philippe 'would have been to have gone boldly to work in conjunction with us to expel Don Carlos, establish the Queen, tranquillize Spain and secure his rear, and then to have made proposals of marriage which, though refused when made by timidity and vacillation, would have been accepted when proceeding from confidence and strength'. (P to Granville, 2 Sept. 1836, GC/GR/1627.)

261 Villiers to Palmerston, 10 September 1836

Madrid. Private. In addition to the numerous causes of embarrassment which exist here the anxiety produced by the tardy ministerial parturition at Paris comes very mal à propos.[1] The Carlists are full of hope that the Quadruple Treaty is virtually at an end and I don't suppose they are far wrong. If Louis Philippe does not[2] mean at once and openly to favor Don Carlos he will not withdraw the troops from the frontier depôts at this moment. That would be a coup de grace, for every body would feel that as these troops do not cost the country more at one place than another their dispersion could only mean no assistance in future, and every possible damage at present.[3]

As far as Navarre is concerned the moment would be particularly propitious for active military operations as the intrigues and disunion at the Court of Oñate are far greater than at that of Madrid, and of more importance as their sphere of action is smaller. I believe that the Northern Provinces would look upon a foreign force which was sufficient to protect them against Carlist reaction as the greatest blessing which Heaven or the *Virgen Generalisima*[4] could send them. I have upon the authority of General Seoane that the *original* insurgents have nearly all gone home to their villages, that there are not 8,000 Navarrese or men of the Basque Provinces now in the army of Don Carlos, and that his force consists of deserters from the Queen's army and peasants taken by force from Castille and the adjacent provinces.

The success or failure of the Constitution as a system of government depends upon the war. If an end can be put to that it matters very little whether the Constitution modified or the Estatuto liberalized is the machinery adopted for carrying on the affairs of the country—but if no military successes are obtained then *all government*, be the form what it may, *is impossible.*

A new bother has sprung up within the last few days. The Infante Don Francisco, moved by his Devil of a wife,[5] is intriguing with the lowest of the Exaltados in order to get himself proclaimed Regent and Generalisimo of the Army. Some measures will have to be taken about him shortly if he does not mend his ways.

Calatrava is as I told you upon his coming into office not à la hauteur des circonstances in which he is placed and he is constantly committing important errors. He and I however have become such friends that his colleagues request me to speak to him or send him to consult me whenever they want to carry anything of importance[6]—for even in Spain he is proverbially obstinate. The last few days I have been endeavouring to impress upon him the necessity of reinforcing his Ministry for as it is now composed it cannot last a month. I want him to take in Mendizabal (of whom he is somewhat jealous) and one or two young active men who should satisfy the Exaltado party and give the public to understand that the Government is not the patrimony of the Emigrants who are now considered and with reason *gastados* (stumped up). We are still in negociations and I am not without hopes of getting together a Ministry of courage and action notwithstanding the royal and official opposition.[7]

Alava having *childishly* in my opinion, for it deserves no other name, refused to swear to the Constitution it was impossible for the Government to retain him in his post, and they have named Campuzano, who was to have gone to London, but he will do much better at Paris as he is well thought of by Metternich, and Louis Philippe cannot look upon him as an emissary of revolution. Under the circumstances I do not think they could have made a better appointment. He goes with the rank of minister because the Constitutional Cortes do not permit embassies and Calatrava thought it would be less of an affront to send him with his present character than have to haul him down from his rank of ambassador by order of the Cortes, to whose resolution Louis Philippe would have had to conform with respect to his own representative here. Bois le Comte has made known that he is every day expecting his credentials as minister which justifies the nomination of one from here and will prevent Louis Philippe's sending an ambassador unless he chuses.

Aguilar, the man who was to have gone to Paris, will probably be sent to London—he is a bon diable who will thankfully receive and execute any orders with which you may favor him.

I saved Isturiz's life by sending him with a courier to Lisbon. I don't know whether I did a good deed—but I believe if it had not been for me he would have shared the fate of poor Quesada.

Miraflores has likewise thought it necessary to flee on account of a book which he wrote two years ago and which nobody ever heard of, much less read, but which—*I have it under his own signature*—he considers to be the cause of the present revolution. His book had nothing to do with it but he himself had and upon no man's shoulders do the disasters of Spain weigh so heavily as upon his. Every thing which is now happening I predicted to him in April last and warned him against the stupid use he was making of the influence he had unaccountably got with the Queen—he swore the country wanted to get rid of Mendiza-bal's Government and that he knew perfectly what he was about. The Queen took his advice because it fell in with her own private feelings but laughed Miraflores to scorn when he suggested himself as rempla-çant. I really wish the people of Santander had caught him as they were near doing, mistaking him for Toreno—one short fat man for another—and he escaped on board the Castor from which he writes me word no human power shall remove him until Lord John Hay gives him a passage to Bayonne. He begs me to let you know that he has been received with every mark of distinction par *l'honorable* Capitaine Robertson.

Received 20 September.   GC/CL/288; Clar. Dep. C.452/2 (284-287)

¹ The fall of the Thiers Ministry as a result of a disagreement between the King and Thiers over the question of aid to Spain. See no. 258 above, n.3.
² 'If' and 'not' double underlined in pencil, and 'but he *does* evidently mean to do so' added in P's hand.
³ 'no assistance' to 'present' underlined, possibly by P.
⁴ The Virgin Mary was appointed by the Carlists to be Commander-in-Chief of their army after the death of Zumalacárregui.
⁵ Donna Luisa.
⁶ V's willingness to co-operate with the new Ministry was regarded with great suspicion by the French. (Drouyn de L'Huys to Thiers, 21 Aug. 1836, NAF 20604; V to Granville, 4 Oct. 1836, PRO 30/29/421.)
⁷ On 12 September V claimed that he had suggested to Calatrava that the following changes would strengthen the Government, and that Calatrava was contemplating making them: Mendizábal to be Minister of Finance, López Minister of the Interior and de la Cuadra Minister of Marine. (V to P, 12 Sept. 1836, no. 226, FO 72/461.)

262 Palmerston to Villiers, 13 September 1836

Copy. Foreign Office. My last Thursday's messenger has been detained at Paris because I have been in discussion with High Quarters¹ from that time to this about the wording of my dispatch. It has now been settled to the satisfaction of both parties and so I send it you.² As I expected from day to day to be able to send him on I thought it not worth while to let him go without it and to delay my dispatch for another ten days.

I had a long conversation today with a person to whom you lately rendered a very important service;[3] and who spoke of that service and of yourself with a warmth of gratitude that did honor to him as well as to you. I am very glad that you were able to do for him what you did. He is going to Paris tomorrow but thinks of returning again to England.

The decrees you have sent us betoken some activity and vigour in the present Government of Spain and if they are executed they may do much towards a successful issue. The French Government of course abide by the decision on which Thiers returned; and for the present at least refuse to send a man into Spain. They assure us that they will at last execute their engagement as to stopping supplies. I doubt both their will and their power to do so.

Spain has nothing at present to hope from France and must rely on its own resources. It is impossible for the French Cabinet to turn *against* the Queen, so that the Spanish Government know the worst that can come to them from France.

You have given very sound and wise advice on all occasions, and it is fortunate that it has on many important occasions been followed. The Queen would have acted most imprudently in longer resisting the Constitution of 1812, or in not keeping faith about it although she had acted under duress. It is to be hoped that those who have the remodelling of the Constitution will see that in a country like Spain great existing interests must be incorporated with the national institutions and that it would be unfortunate, as such, not to give the nobles a share in the Upper Chamber. It would of course be impossible to carry a second Chamber purely and entirely hereditary; but in some way or other the nobility ought to be represented in it independently of popular election or of nomination by the Crown.

The readers of history will hardly believe that Espartero could have followed Gomez with such respectful deference and preserving his interval with such military accuracy during so long and harrassing a march. It has been like the fore and hind wheels of a carriage; and the thing would be truly laughable if it was not seriously lamentable—and yet one hears that Espartero is one of the most promising of the Queen's generals! To be sure they seem all to be men of promise, rather than of performance.

Jabat has given up and has presented one of his attachés in his stead. Jabat has behaved very well throughout and is an honorable man. He told me a creditable trait of Calatrava. He said that when Calatrava was here as a refugee in the time of Ferdinand some friends of his desired him to draw on Lubbock for what he wanted, in addition to his own scanty means and the wretched allowance which the Government was able to give the Spaniards who were here; that Lubbock never announced any drafts; that at last Calatrava fell ill and it appeared on enquiry that his illness had been brought on by his denying himself throughout a severe winter the indulgence, if it may be so called, of a fire, in order that he might not have occasion to draw upon the purses of his friends. There is something fine in such sturdiness.

I hope Mendizabal will take the Finance Department, his name will be of use here; as a city man said to me yesterday, he understands the wisdom of keeping engagements made by Governments.

GC/CL/1279

[1] For P's correspondence with the King and related papers 9-12 September 1836 see Palmerston Papers RC/A/488-496.

[2] P to V, 12 Sept. 1836, no. 78, FO 72/456, regretting the recent violence and urging the vigorous prosecution of the war.

[3] Probably Álava.

263 Villiers to Palmerston, 14 September 1836

Madrid. Private. I am getting very anxious to learn what you think of all that is passing here. I as yet only know of your having received my dispatch of the 13th ultimo from San Ildefonso.

The Government cannot help hoping that we shall do *something* for them though they know not what, and they will hardly take my assurances that with all the good will in the world it is absolutely impossible for us to do anything en grand for them and the day for minor succours is past. At least this is the language that I think it prudent to hold, but I wish to God you had 10 or 15,000 men with a little money at your disposal. Things would soon right themselves then and England never could make a sacrifice which was better worth while—not for the advantages which Spain will offer to us, but for the evils which will be averted elsewhere by the restoration of tranquillity here—the foremost of them rupture, or *as* good *as*, between England and France, and when that is said all the rest is implied. It is like unlocking the gates of Hell and letting out all the devils upon the earth.

That question is doubtless more important than any other and every thing we desire *here* would be dearly bought at the price of our alliance with France—and time presses and the utmost skill is necessary if it is to be avoided. Don't think me impertinent for communicating to you an idea that has just occurred to me.

Could you not without compromising yourself run over to Paris during the vacation and have some talk with Louis Philippe and the new Ministers and at least save matters with France if they cannot be helped in Spain? If such a scheme were feasible at all the advantages might be very great, for *be assured* that as far as this country is concerned the face of affairs will be entirely changed before the meeting of Parliament. I will not enter upon my reasons for saying this for they are composed only of details with which you are already acquainted and must be heartily sick, but believe me if the Spaniards are left to themselves there is neither Constitution, or any other form of government or set of men that can avert the catastrophe which has always been predicted, that from one end of the country to the other a civil war will rage disgraceful even to barbarous nations and to which Europe must mettre le holà, but in a manner and with objects which we shall not chuse to cooperate in, and we must then either oppose or be shut out of the arrangement. There are 100 things upon the cards for which you must be prepared any day now. The advance of the Carlists upon Castille, the proclamation of Don Carlos at Madrid and of the republic in twenty other places—the Queens wandering about and Ministries changed by dozens. I don't wish unnecessarily to make myself a bird of ill omen, but it is absurd not to be prepared for the worst, and what I now mention is *more likely to happen than not*. As to my pretensions to being believed I will appeal to my dispatches of June 1835 and my letters to you at that time and subsequently whether I rightly judged the course which events would take here.

I hope you will approve of the steps I took to have Mendizabal admitted into the Ministry. I don't believe it would have succeeded if I had not taken Calatrava by storm. Mendizabal might have come in later but it would have been at the head of a revolutionary party and he would have done nothing but mischief. Now he joins some decent old Constitutional Gentlemen who will not let him play any of his most outlandish pranks, and he in his turn has given their Government a new lease in public opinion.

Mendizabal implores of you to grant the muskets that will be asked for and to find the means of sending them in order that the arming of the National Guard may be proceeded with rapidly.[1] *He says* that 56,000 Nationals, all good men and true, are ready each for his musket in Estremadura and that in that province the Queen's party might be collected and the last stand made if we are driven by Don Carlos from Madrid.

As for any measures being taken to put Madrid in a state of defence or rather for defending the approaches to it, it is useless to hope for it. Rodil has satisfied himself, the Mighty only knows how, that the Carlists won't come here, y basta.[2] You will be disappointed in Rodil I fear and so will Evans who has been looking for his nomination as a summum bonum. He has already lost his head in consequence of the difficulties which surround him—he at one time inclines to take the command in the North, at another of the army in Castille and Aragon, and in the mean while does not budge or does he intend to do so that I can gather from my conversations with him, and yet it is always till his arrival at his head quarters that he must wait to see what means are possible for taking the Legion out of that corner and making it effective. Not a step further can I get, but I must at the same time acknowledge that Evans sick and the Legion mutinous make it very difficult for a Minister to order from hence what would be most expedient for the service.

I hope we have scraped together some money for the Legion and that Colonel De Lancey may return with satisfactory news to San Sebastian. I am glad he came here, for he has had a taste for three weeks of what I have had to endure for a twelvemonth with small thanks from the Legion. He admits that if he had not himself had proofs of it he could not have believed the extent to which shuffling and bad faith are carried in every department of Her Catholic Majesty's Government.

I am sorry that Alava should have got himself into such a foolish scrape and forced his old friends who are now in power to take a severe measure against him,[3] but they learn from all quarters of the mischief which has been done by Alava's resignation and the language he has held to the Government and the diplomats and the salons of Paris, and as in moments like these Ministers are the slaves of public opinion, if they had favored Alava and with him all those who have imitated his example they would merely have weakened themselves without ultimately saving their friend.

Toreno has suddenly left Madrid for France and I have some reason to believe that that worthy intends to compound with Don Carlos. He, Isturiz and Miraflores will be three dangerous men to the Queen's cause at Paris—far more so than the representatives of the Northern Powers for they will work with all the zeal that a Spanish desire for vengeance can give and with better connoissance de cause than MM. Pahlen or Werther can have.

Mendizabal has begged me to ask you whether you would direct an article to be put in the Chronicle respecting the dangers to which all French holders of Spanish stock are exposed if Louis Philippe plays foul with Spain and the Quadruple Treaty. Nothing of course can be hoped from Don Carlos, and the more Louis Philippe keeps not helping the Queen the more chance there is of confusion and poverty here, consequently of non-payment of dividends, and of ruin to small French shopkeepers. As they form a class that is very criard, this subject well handled might stir them up to protest against the Carlist leanings of the King, and it might not be without its effect in England.

This evening we have the news that in Lisbon the soldiers have enacted their edition of our La Granja melodrama and forced the Queen to adopt the Constitution of 1820.

Que gusto[4] to have to do with Peninsular men and affairs! What would you give to have them all lowered a few fathoms in the sea for an hour or so? Mendizabal says that he has received positive proofs from Lisbon that the whole has been the work of the French minister at Lisbon. It may be so—but I know that half Madrid consider at this moment that they have positive proofs of the affair at La Granja being all *my* doing.

Received 24 September.   GC/CL/289; Clar. Dep. C.452/2 (288-295)

[1] See Calatrava to V, 14 Sept. 1836, asking for a hundred thousand muskets, enclosed with V to P, 14 Sept. 1836, no. 232, FO 72/461.
[2] 'and that is enough'.
[3] Álava, as a result of his protest against the Constitution, had been deprived of 'all honours and emoluments'. (V to P, 14 Sept. 1836, no. 227, FO 72/461.)
[4] 'What pleasure'.

264 Palmerston to Villiers, 16 September 1836

Foreign Office. I hear that it is reported from Madrid that attempts are likely to be made by the Spanish propaganda to excite disturbances in Portugal with a view to cause the Constitution of 1820 to be adopted at Lisbon. Of course the Spanish Government will do all it can (and that perhaps is little) to prevent this; but pray speak to Calatrava about it, and say that such an event would very possibly lead to our withdrawing altogether from the Partie Quarrée.

Copy.

GC/CL/1280

265 Villiers to Palmerston, 17 September 1836

Madrid. Private. My courier from Oleron due yesterday morning has not yet made his appearance and I only write you a line by the French courier this evening for form's sake as I have nothing to say—a circumstance in Spain which is nearly equivalent to good news.

The order for sequestrating the property of factious emigrants from their country and the Constitution[1] will I daresay be cried out against and represented as a revolutionary measure, but in my opinion it was one of absolute necessity, and I think it is done with all the moderation and tact that could be expected. Miraflores and id genus omne may not like the Constitution—nobody does—but they have no right to embarrass the Government and increase the difficulties which they themselves have had so much hand in creating. The effect has been very mischievous here for some days past, and I am glad the Government have taken the step they have—indeed since the accession of Mendizabal and Lopez to the Ministry there has been much more vigor in its march and the public is much better satisfied.

Calatrava is a worthy and well meaning man but being an old lawyer it is difficult to make him lay aside forms which are nothing but impediments in critical moments of revolution. For instance there are 200 French ragamuffins here who have lately imported themselves and are doing a power of mischief[2] but Calatrava won't eject them or meddle with the Spaniards they are acting with because the Constitution does not point out the means of doing so. Our suspension of the Habeas Corpus Act and our Alien Bill have made some impression upon him but he still allows all this canaille to be beating the Government in different parts of the country and preventing the mobilization of the militia and the contribution to the National Loan.[3]

A propos to the loan, I have as you will see written to Calatrava to have British subjects exempted from it,[4] but there is much to be said on the other side and I doubt my succeeding. If you think it adviseable to take the opinion of the Law Officers of the Crown upon the construction of the Treaty it might be of use to me in the wrangle I shall probably have with Mendizabal who I know reckons upon bleeding the Britishers freely.

Alava, from whom I had a letter yesterday, makes a poor defence of his conduct which was very irréfléchi to say the least of it—he falls back upon his years and his desire to make his peace with God before *he is fetched,* but if he had put it off for a few weeks I daresay in the long run it would have made no difference to him, and it did a great deal of harm to Spain. He says that even without the affair of San Ildefonso the French Government would have been broken up when the King discovered that Bugeaud had been sent for without his knowledge to command the Legion, which was to have been increased to 10 or 12,000 men. This I don't believe. It is possible that Louis Philippe may not have known about Bugeaud or the instructions given to Lebeau but he made use of these circumstances in order to quarrel with Thiers and get out of his compromise—for Bois le Comte told the Queen Regent that the French Government would increase the Legion to at least 10,000 men and that it was by no means intended to limit the aid to that number of men should circumstances render their further increase necessary—and he told me afterwards that the nature, the object, and the amount of this assistance had been discussed and agreed upon between the King and Thiers in his presence. The only thing he was not to mention to Rayneval (and Aston wrote me word the same) was the appointment of Bugeaud because it was not *definitely settled* with the King.

The Holy Alliance representatives[5] availing themselves of the affair of San Ildefonso have done all the mischief I should think—I trust they will live to repent it and more improbable events than that have happened in the world.

I send you a copy of a letter I have received from Thiers—it is a pity he was not sooner of his present way of thinking—if he had done what you asked at the time that orders for active cooperation were sent to Lord John Hay nothing of what is now happening would or could have taken place. One must be fair however and admit that the moment was not a lucky one. The King and indeed the French public were so much engrossed with the visit of the Princes to Germany and the hopes of their picking up a wife that an act so unpopular at the Holy Courts as active aid to the Queen of Spain would have been looked upon by every body as suicidal.

Enclosure: Copy, Thiers (Paris) to Villiers, 7 September 1836, in reply to Villiers's letter of 22 July, attributing his resignation to his views on Spain, which are the same as those of Villiers, and regretting the failure of the French Government to strike a fatal blow against Carlism. (In French.)

Received 26 September.

GC/CL/290; Clar. Dep. C.452/2 (296-300)

[1] See V to P, 17 Sept. 1836, no. 235, enclosure, FO 72/461.
[2] See V to P, 14 Sept. 1836, no. 231, FO 72/461.
[3] A forced loan to be made by 'individuals of substance' to the Government. In the case of employees of the Government, it was to be a percentage of their salaries.
[4] V to Calatrava, 15 Sept. 1836, enclosed with V to P, 17 Sept. 1836, no. 235, FO 72/461.
[5] At Paris.

266 Villiers to Palmerston, 21 September 1836

Madrid. Private. I am totally unable to account for the non arrival of the courier from London who should have been here upwards of five days ago. Nothing can have happened to him on this side of the Pyrenees as the road has not been so clear of facciosos this month past as it is at the present moment. Whatever may be the cause it alarms this Government very much as they had been in hopes to tell their friends that England was unchanged by the late events, and to draw a contrast between our policy and that of France[1] which should revive the drooping spirits of the liberals, but as Jabat writes them nothing they have no tidings about you since the news of the melodrame at La Granja reached England. The public of Madrid which is always well informed about the incomings and outgoings of couriers have magnified the consequences of the non-arrival of mine most absurdly, but lo cierto es that never was a courier more important here than the one which seems to have no intention of arriving.

I have told you all along what kind of man Rodil is who Evans has been sighing after so much. After delaying here a month upon one ground or the other and being at last forced by the growling public out of his inactivity he could not bring himself to the scratch and has appointed Espartero who is ill at Burgos to command the army.[2] He has himself gone in the direction of Valencia, but the Government even don't seem exactly to know whether he intends to command the troops there or only to inspect and direct and then return *here* or to *Navarre*. He is a poor devil and Mendizabal told me last night he was afraid some disaster would befall him.

I must however do him the justice to say that he has been very obliging in granting every request of Evans's without even looking at their justice or propriety—even to the Star of the Order of Charles III to Evans's brother Captain Arbuthnot R.N. (who has nothing in fact to do with the Legion) for his activity in embarking stores a year ago from Santander! Rodil's only condition has been that in future Evans should in his capacity of Spanish general enquire what are the fixed rules of the Spanish service before he makes recommendations which violate them and then complains of the Government because his requests are not immediately complied with.

I have screwed the money for the Legion out of the Government le couteau sur la gorge, and under the influence of fear it was scraped together God knows how,[3] but I gave notice that if the engagements were not fulfilled I should require of Evans to take the Legion home to prevent the national name being disgraced by acts which must be expected from disappointed starving men, and that the public then would consider that England was taking the same course as France and we had retired from the contest.

Calatrava's Government has a new lease since Mendizabal and Lopez joined it, there exists now here all the confidence in the Government which can be hoped for independent of military successes, and there is nothing I have done since I came here which affords me more gratification than having been instrumental towards these ministerial modifications.

GC/CL/291; Clar. Dep. C.452/2 (301-304)

[1] On 20 September 1836 Calatrava made an official protest to the French chargé d'affaires at Madrid that, as the French Government now refused to give the aid which Bois-le-Comte had promised, the Spanish Government considered that the French no longer attached any importance to the Quadruple Treaty. (V to P, 21 Sept. 1836, no. 239, FO 72/461.)

[2] Espartero was appointed Commander-in-Chief by a royal decree of 19 September 1836.

[3] In his despatch V wrote: 'Mr. O'Shea the English banker of this capital

has accordingly commenced remitting the sum of twenty five thousand pounds to St. Sebastian for the use of the Legion.' (V to P, 21 Sept. 1836, no. 238, FO 72/461.)

267 Villiers to Palmerston, 22 September 1836

Madrid. Private. I had some despatches and letters ready to send to you yesterday by a courier of Mendizabal's, but when they were about to be *embagged* the said Minister changed his mind and determined not to send the courier till tonight. Mine the day after tomorrow will probably arrive as soon but for fear of accidents I write you a line to say that a most important victory has been gained by Alaix over Gomez—1,200 prisoners have been taken without loss on the Queen's side. The thing was done by surprise and by the cavalry just as Iribarren did in Navarre a month ago. Never did a lucky event happen more opportunely, for if Gomez who had with him on the day of the action 7,000 infantry and 1,000 cavalry, all good troops, had beaten Alaix, which judging from the experience of the last 6 months was more likely than not, he would have marched to Madrid in a day and $\frac{1}{2}$ and then all I predicted to you in my letter last week would have happened. Everybody would have fled from here, Don Carlos would have been proclaimed in the capital and then a long list of etcs. Now all fear of that is over for the present. Gomez is still formidable and he will probably retreat to the mountains and continue to worry and baffle the Queen's troops, but the moral effect of this action must be great on both sides. The Carlists will be dispirited and the Cristinos take heart. Who knows therefore whether the generals might not for once make a combined movement and operate as if they intended to defeat the enemy instead of each other? One or two more successes like this and the Constitution might be modified to any extent with ease. Your letters and dispatches of the 13th arrived last night.

Received 3 October.

GC/CL/292; Clar. Dep. C.452/2 (305-306)

268 Palmerston to Villiers, 22 September 1836

Copy. Foreign Office. I have received your letter of the 10th which reached me the day before yesterday, and we received last Saturday the account of the revolution at Lisbon. It was to be expected that what happened in Spain would be imitated in Portugal.

This is all very unfortunate, but it is the natural consequence of the Louis Philippe and Cordova intrigue by which Mendizabal was removed when he was about to raise money, and the Cortes dissolved at a moment when its aid and authority were absolutely necessary.

You say that the Carlists are full of hope that the Quadruple Treaty is at an end. That Treaty *is indeed* and has long been at an end as to the spirit in which it was framed;[1] but it is still a restraint upon the French Government and prevents them from taking openly part with Don Carlos. What the King of the French is about it is impossible to say. One thing is certain, he has thrown us over, which indeed some of my Tory assailants in the House of Commons always told me he would do. His motives may be various. Desire to curry favor with the Holy Alliance; fear of over popular notions prevailing in Spain; a wish that Spain may remain weak and distracted, on the same principle that Russia wishes to keep Turkey barbarous and powerless; a hope that the monarchy may be split up, a federal republic formed, and that the provinces adjoining the Pyrenees may place themselves under the protection of France; all or any of these and many other motives may sway the King of the French but we have only to deal with the effects—we shall continue to work at him, but unless the Molé and Guizot Government falls, and another succeeds it, France will of course not depart much from the system for not yielding to which Thiers was turned out.[2] The only thing for you now to do therefore is to endeavour to get the Spaniards to rely upon their own resources, and to bring those resources into play, and to try to finish the war themselves.

I am glad Mendizabal is likely to join the Government; whatever his faults may be, depend upon it, he is one of the best men they have; and have not pains been taken by Cordova and his family and friends to exaggerate to you those faults, and to set you against the man? So it is said here by persons who hear from Spain, but this may rest upon slender foundation.

In my conversation however with Isturiz, Cordova was mentioned. I said that he (Isturiz) had undertaken what appeared to be an almost desperate task when he took the Government in hand, without a shilling in the treasury and no means of getting any till the Cortes should assemble. He said, Yes, it was, and indeed nothing but military successes could have carried us through. True enough, said I, but you did not exactly go the best way to work to obtain such successes, when you left Cordova at the head of the army. He then defended him and I stated my opinions. He said, Well, but Mr. Villiers thinks very differently of him; I know he does, said I, but I think he is too indulgent. Well, said Isturiz, perhaps truth lies in the middle, and Cordova deserves neither your bad opinion nor entirely the good opinion which Mr. Villiers has of him.

I asked him what he thought of the future; he said, After all, Carlos has as good a chance as any body. Well, but you have our[3] army of a hundred thousand men and more—what are they about? Why, they are thinking of nothing but of turning silk into metal—that is sergeants and corporals into commissioned officers. Bad enough occupation, but what do you say of the National Guard? Oh! Vous pouvez compter sur la Garde Nationale. I am delighted. Stop a bit—pour faire des révolutions, but not to fight the enemy. He said nothing ever struck him more than the contrast of the prosperity of Portugal with the misery of Spain; perhaps he carried in his eye the image of a Madrid mob, the absence of which in Lisbon gave a soothing repose to the scene. His gratitude to you was really affecting and did him great honor.

I suppose Calatrava is a stubborn gentleman to deal with . . . .

The King objected to my dispatch about the Legion; and it was not worth while to press him about it.[4] You will therefore only remember to report in a private letter any steps you may have taken thereupon. I hear a good account of the present state and efficiency of the Legion —if they can be supplied with money and if they and the French can be united, something may yet be done on the frontier.

I hope we shall hear no more of the intrigue you mention for a change in the regency. I believe Latour Maubourg who is going from Brussels to Madrid is a good sort of man, and will be an improvement on Bois le Comte—as to the influence which you say our little friend Miraflores had over the Queen, I presume he was only a conductor and that the shock came from Paris.

GC/CL/1281

[1] In his instructions to Granville P stated: 'I think the tone for you to take with Molé is that we look upon France as backing out of the alliance as fast as she can. That we are sorry for it but wash our hands of the consequences, and upon those who have advised or who may execute the plan must rest the responsibility for any inconveniences which may follow. That we shall pursue

our own course without in the least being put out of our own way by the desertion of France.' (P to Granville, 20 Sept. 1836, GC/GR/1628.)

[2] In conversation with Aston Louis Philippe claimed that he had remained
faithful to the Quadruple Alliance, and blamed 'the deception practised upon
him by Thiers' for the apparent inconsistency of French policy. (Aston to P,
19 Sept. 1836, FO 355/6.)

[3] *Recte* your.

[4] For the draft of this despatch, dated 13 September 1836, and suggesting
that the Spanish Government should begin by paying the twenty thousand
pounds admitted to be due to the Legion, see FO 72/456. The King would
not approve the draft because he did not acknowledge the Legion, and it was
therefore sent as a private letter.

269   Villiers to Palmerston, 24 September 1836

Madrid. Private. I am very unwell with a kind of ague. I can shiver
famously but can't write at all so you must excuse me today. I have
little to add to my letter of the 21st enclosed and to that of the 22d
which I sent by Mendizabal's courier. If it were not that Spaniards
were pursuing Gomez I should say it was impossible for him to escape
from the net of troops which is weaving all round him.

Received 4 October.

GC/CL/293; Clar. Dep. C.452/2 (307)

270   Villiers to Palmerston, 1 October 1836

Madrid. Private. Since I last wrote to you a week ago I have not stirred
from my bed which together with fever and regimen have reduced me
to the lowest state of weakness, but this time I have avoided Rayneval's
example and the Carlists can't say that a murrain has come upon the
Quadruple Alliance representatives.

You will not lose much by my incompetency today for there is little
worth communicating. The victory of Alaix has in the true Spanish
fashion not been turned to account and Gomez, who appears to be a
very undauntable dog, has advanced towards Andalusia. On the other
hand Villareal's second in command with several battalions seems to
have crossed the Ebro and is now near Santander. Whether his object
be to sack that province, to take the port or to carry the war into the
Asturias we know not, but now would be the time for marching to
Oñate and common offensive operations, but—whatever requires fore-

sight, wisdom or courage we must put out of all calculation. Chance may every now and then do a good turn as in two instances during the last six weeks—but nothing else—and the odds, as I have often had to observe before, are greatly in favor of a succession of disasters throughout the winter.

Rodil frightened by public opinion stole away some time ago like a hare and has now made his form a few leagues from here where there is every reason to expect he will remain—until an enemy approaches.

I have no reason to believe that this Government had any thing to do with the recent commotion in Portugal—on the contrary they sincerely regretted it, but every one here expected that Portugal would on this as all other occasions run the same rig as Spain.

I did not make any use to this Government of your dispatch respecting the Legion because as far as the Legion was concerned matters were settled before I received it, but Colonel De Lancey's back was no sooner turned and O'Shea had been got well into his advances to San Sebastian than Mendizabal violated every promise—verbal and written—with a degree of impudence and fraud that I believe would hardly find its equal in Stock Exchange Alley. O'Shea then came here and said he would make no more remittances and the Legion might fare as it could, and I then gave him a kind of guarantee that he should be repaid as I had that day received official instructions to press upon the Government the payment of the very sum he was advancing. This quite satisfied him and he went on and things are now smoother between him and Mendizabal.

It has occurred to me that in the despatch in which I gave you an account of my conversation with Calatrava respecting the appointment of Aguilar to Paris[1] I rather denigréd that diplomat, and our sovereign lord the King may think that what was not good enough for Louis Philippe ought not to do for him, and that I should have opposed the appointment. My objections to Aguilar however were exclusively founded upon reasons which would have ensured his failure at Paris and would consequently have made matters worse. His having been the lover of the Queen of Naples—the acquaintance of Louis Philippe in Sicily who afterwards dropped him entirely—his having lived here during the last 2 years with all the Exaltado rabble which is just what Louis Philippe would have had exaggerated to him and have disliked —all these together with an intellect rather below par would have made him a very unfit man for such a post as Paris. In London where all is good faith and good will it little matters whether the requests for muskets are signed by a consul or a minister and you will find Aguilar a very decent sort of fellow.

A propos to muskets they *certainly* are wanted very much and might be made use of tomorrow if they were here. Pray back me up about taxing British subjects here—this is a good opportunity and you might say that you only allow the muskets to be furnished upon the understanding that the principle of not exposing British subjects to the *ir*regular and *extra*ordinary taxation of the country is admitted.[2]

I am unequal to any more.

Received 10 October.

GC/CL/294; Clar. Dep. C.452/2 (309-312)

[1] V to P, 7 Sept. 1836, no. 222, FO 72/461.
[2] 'How stands our treaty right on this point?' (Minute by P, 10 Oct. 1836.)

271 Palmerston to Villiers, 6 October 1836

Copy. Stanhope Street. I was sorry to hear by your last note that you were unwell, and indeed the handwriting shewed that it was so. I am anxious for the next accounts and hope to hear that you are better. We are much obliged to you for Gomez['s] defeat. Pray send us some more events of the same kind. They will be most thankfully received and are much wanted.

You have done a right good thing in getting Mendizabal in again. In the kingdom of the blind the one-eyed reign, and though he might not make a very good successor for Spring Rice he will do good service in Spain.

Your predictions about Rodil seem likely to be confirmed, but however if he takes the Legion under his protecting care that will be something.

I have had a long talk today with Sebastiani who came back yesterday. He says we must keep our eloquence to ourselves, for it will certainly not induce Louis Philippe to send a man into Spain; *anything else* he will do with pleasure to shew his zealous interest in the Queen's favor. The French squadron is to look into the Spanish ports and to assist the Queen's cause, and then to go on to Lisbon to do the same by that of Donna Maria. However the Spanish Government must not deceive themselves, and must lay their account with having no help from France. If they had activity and energy which of course they have not, they would not require French aid.

I hope by the by they have not done anything ungenteel with poor Miraflores' estate. It would indeed be hard that the man who signed the Quadruple Treaty, which has certainly been of some considerable service to the Queen's cause, should first be obliged to fly to save his life, and then be told because he has saved his life, he must lose his estate. This would indeed be propter vitam, vivendi perdere causas. Pray intercede in your persuasive manner in favor of our little friend, who may have made a goose of himself, and may have taken needless alarm and have fled without cause, but who still cannot deserve to be proscribed and ruined. Perhaps after all his fears for his estate are as groundless as were those for his person but he writes me a most doleful epistle from Paris, in the spirit of a beggared martyr whose only remaining resource lies in the sale of a collection of bad pictures.

I have had a communication indirectly from Burshenthal[1] wanting to come to England to give me some information which he pretends to have got hold of . . . .

Easthope is very anxious that Mendizabal should place his man on the footing of the most favored nations and not give facilities to the Times agent which are not equally granted to the Chronicle man. Pray ask Mendizabal to do this. As to the Times he will never get any good out of that paper, do what he may for its correspondent at Madrid. Old Barnes and Walter and the rest will take their own line, he may depend upon it.

St. Priest seems to have been playing the devil at Lisbon, to have been deep in the plot which brought about the late revolution, and to have said to members of the Diplomatic Body that if any of the former Ministers were to be brought back again by a reaction which he deprecated, he should quit, and France would not send a chargé d'affaires even in his stead for that he had been ordered to turn out the last Government and had done so. I must say our good friends and allies the French have a most marvellous turn for intrigue and underhand proceedings; but we must take them as we find them and make the most of them as they are.

PS. If as we hear the Portuguese Corps in Spain is in favor of Pedro's Charter and if it will march back to Lisbon and reestablish that order of things, it will be a capital measure and may not be without its use in Spain.

I understand that Ludolf, a most singularly wise man, has taken upon himself to address a note to the chargés d'affaires of Austria, Russia and Prussia at this Court to propose to them an armed interference of the three Powers in the affairs of Spain.

It is a burlesque upon diplomacy. The three chargés d'affaires have it is said taken the communication ad referendum.

There is no reason to believe that the accident which has happened to Nicholas was anything but an overturn.

GC/CL/1282

[1] Büschenthal was a German Jew, involved in Spanish and Portuguese financial deals.

272 Villiers to Palmerston, 8 October 1836

Madrid. Private. I am glad that there is little to relate today first because I am still too unwell for work and next because little to say means here not much bad news to tell.

Owing to the usual want of foresight and proper precautions we have passed this entire week in ignorance of Gomez's movements—by private accounts it is known that he entered and taxed[1] the town of Andujar, but the Government knows nothing officially of all that is so important and passing some 40 or 50 leagues off! There is not the least doubt that if Alaix had followed up his victory of Villarobledo he would have utterly annihilated Gomez, but he lost *six* days in wondering what he should do with his prisoners, and it was not *the business* (just like English servants) of any other division of the Queen's troops to come to his assistance. The routed rebels in the mean while gathered themselves together again and were able to enter Andalusia.

There has been what is called a *magnifico pronunciamiento*[2] in that province. National Guards bustling about in every direction and swearing to spill the last drop of their blood, the authorities publishing kill'em and eat'em proclamations and making forced loans—the two invariable companions of every pronouncement—but as yet nothing has been *done*, and although Gomez appears to be surrounded on every side by *exterminators* I shall not be surprised to hear of his winding his way back along some of the sierras to Aragon or Navarre.

There is a passage or two in your letter of the 22nd in which you speak of my too indulgent opinion of Cordoba [which] annoys me much because added to others of a like nature they make me think that you believe I was the cause of Cordoba's having latterly been retained in his command and *consequently* of all the disasters that have come upon the country. That I did not and do not join in the cry that has been raised against him or believe the reports half of which contradict the rest about him is perfectly true, but that is no proof that I wished him to remain in the command of the army. And ever since January last I have thought meanly of his abilities as a general, although I knew of no one better to put in his place, and certainly none who at that time would have found the same favor with the soldiers—but you may remember that in the spring I recommended Mendizabal to send him on a mission to Paris or any thing to get rid of him from the army, and so far from my having said anything in his behalf to Isturiz, further than that I was convinced he was no traitor, I urged him to appoint Rodil or Seoane to the command, and he peremptorily refused because they were enemies of his own or friends of Mina, and he it was who resolved upon maintaining Cordoba coûte qui coûte because he thought, and in this he was right, that he would vigorously oppose the anarchists. The Queen even asked my advice about removing Cordoba and agreed with me he could no longer be retained with advantage— *even then* Isturiz resisted. I have therefore nothing whatever to blame myself for except thinking that Cordoba was just as good or rather as bad a general as any that could be put in his place. It is now two months since he was removed. Oraa, Rodil, and Espartero have succeeded him and I see no reason to change my opinion.

When you say that Cordoba was instrumental in turning out Mendizabal, I think you must have forgotten the letter I told you he wrote to the Queen warning her of the dangers she incurred by changing her Ministry at such a moment, and Mendizabal's earnest desire that Cordoba should come to Madrid in order to advise the Queen upon the step she had been urged to take by Miraflores and others.

Then as to what is said in London by persons who hear from Spain about Cordoba's family and friends having exaggerated to me Mendizabal's faults, I will not allow myself to believe that such a story can have made any impression upon you. Of friends here Cordoba has none, or has any man in Spain who has risen rapidly in his career. His family consists of two sisters and an old orangewoman of a mother who went about abusing me like a pickpocket because as a general and a politician I had found fault with Cordoba—but surely I did not want

531

such aid to find out Mendizabal's faults after 8 months' daily intercourse with him and learning by experience that he never keeps a
promise or ever speaks a word of truth? However I think of him as I
did of Cordoba at one time, that with all his faults he is the best man
one can find—a necessary evil in short—and I therefore took upon
myself to overcome the objections both of the Queen and her Prime
Minister to him. If I had *not* done so I assure you that Mendizabal
would not at this moment have formed part of the Government.

I will not again trouble you with these matters but I am naturally
anxious to remove the erroneous opinions I believe you to entertain
with reference to me as regards both Cordoba and Mendizabal—and
I have been also moved to say what I have from believing that these
reports originate with that fretful fellow Evans whose conduct to me
has been shabby and ungrateful.

Mendizabal cannot pay the dividend, and on the 15th instant the
English, French and Spanish publics are to be simultaneously informed
so. It is unlucky but unavoidable I really believe, and it is better at
once fairly to say so and offer the best terms that circumstances admit
than to shuffle with the creditors or to make tremendous sacrifices at
a moment when Spanish credit is at its lowest point, and which would
probably incapacitate the Government from keeping faith in future.

Mendizabal has been here today and has begged me to bring under
your consideration a project which he does not despair of your adopting. He wants England to guarantee a loan for Spain of two millions
repayable by instalments of £200,000 a year for which the revenue of
Cuba would be mortgaged to England, who would therefore at any
time or under any form of government that may exist in Spain during
the 10 years in which the loan is to be paid off be able by means of
the British ships in the West India station to repay herself should the
Spanish Government of the day fail in booking up the instalment. Part
of this loan would go to the immediate discharge of the debt now due
to England for arms supplied under the Quadruple Treaty. I of course
proposed to him the treaty of commerce at the same time. He said his
only difficulty, exclusive of the standing one of Catalonia, was the
jealousy of France and the additional hostility on the part of that
country that it would produce, but that as soon as ever the *mobilized
Nationals* can occupy the fortresses and the troops close the frontier that
then the Government may snap its fingers at France and be too happy
to draw closer to England.

Will you let me know with the least possible delay whether you think this project *entertainable* for in that case something might be done about it before the Cortes meet? Afterwards it would be necessary to consult them.

I am convinced that the muskets are *really* wanted—had they been here now they might have produced very important results. I hope therefore you will grant them but pray at the same time back me up about not exacting extraordinary contributions from British sojourners in Spain.

Received 16 October.

GC/CL/295; Clar. Dep. C.452/2 (313-318)

¹ Gómez was said to have collected an immense amount of booty, as well as arms and ammunition, including the plate of the cathedral.
² 'grand uprising'.

273 Villiers to Palmerston, 15 October 1836

Madrid. Private. I have this morning received your letter of the 6th instant and I wish I could obey your injunction to send you more Carlist defeats but we don't prosper here—that you will say is nothing new—untoward events however thicken and the horizon gets more and more black.

Upon Gomez marching to the South the Andalusians who are good for nothing on earth except smuggling, singing and murdering were all overflowing with patriotic ardor—all resolved to conquer or die—all marching against the enemy and surprising every body here who expected from them nothing of the kind. I can't say that I for a moment swallowed their blatherumskyte, because I saw no reason for their now belying all their former history as they have never failed to swagger and fly—and consistently at all events have they now behaved, for every column which advanced against the enemy found upon approaching them that it was necessary to fall back upon some town or village the defence of which was most important to *the cause of liberty* to defend and Gomez quietly advanced sacking every town through which he passed till he arrived at the city of Cordoba where 1,500 National Guards shut themselves up in a convent, and after Gomez had pillaged the town they all surrendered and allowed themselves to be disarmed and stripped of their clothes with which Gomez equipped as many of the old realistas who had opened to him the gates of the town and helped him in its sacking. Don Carlos was then proclaimed in the town and (as it is understood) in the principal places of the province of Cordoba, and Gomez after having remained there 7 days unmolested retired with all his prisoners and booty which is estimated at £200,000 value—leaving the territory in charge and under the dominion of the Carlists. This has encouraged various other towns to imitate the example, and the patriotic Andalusia where the juntas were first established in 1835, and the Constitution proclaimed in 1836, is the only province of Spain through which a Carlist expedition has passed which has given the example of rebellion and reared the standard of despotism.

This is a new and terrible as well as quite unexpected feature in the wars, for the Queen's troops, slow and timid under the best circumstances, all at once find themselves in a hostile country where they expected to meet nothing but friends—their difficulties and dangers are therefore increased, and it is always in proportion with them that a Spaniard's courage sinks. 14 or 15,000 of the best troops which are desperately wanted in the North are now kept in the South—probably to do nothing—and if the Carlists in Navarre have but the pluck for it now is their time for a coup de main upon Madrid where things would not turn out very differently from those at Cordova.

In the mean while the patriots of Malaga, Grenada and other Exaltado towns are frightened out of their senses, and instead of acting in concert against the enemy, the greater part of whom are mere rabble, they are murdering and plundering each other! The Government has little or no information of what is going on, and we know not whether Rodil has yet given over manoeuvring strategically against nobody on this side of the Sierra in order to descend into Andalusia to the assistance of Alaix who must be in great need of it.

Then just the same game is playing in the North. The troops which Evans sent to intercept the Carlist expedition to Galicia and whose absence nearly cost him very dear were not allowed by the authorities of Santander to proceed to their destination Gijon, from whence they *must* have pounced upon and annihilated Sanz, but were sent to lose themselves in the army of reserve, and General Peon, who with double force is following the Carlists, ought upon his own shewing in his own dispatch to be shot, for he admits that the enemy was close to him and he stops 3 days in Oviedo because the weather was bad and the troops wanted to rest and CLEAN THEIR ARMS. In short on every side there is cowardice and incapacity, if not treachery, as I am obliged every day to tell Calatrava and Mendizabal when they cry out for foreign aid, and I ask them how we can venture to do anything for people who have either not the will or the courage to avail themselves of the abundant means at their disposal.

The face of things *may* change, some lucky (though improbable) accident *may* happen, for after all the enemies of the Queen's cause are Spaniards as well as its partizans, and therefore do not avail themselves of a tithe of the opportunities for triumphing which the Queenites are constantly offering them. The Carlists however have this advantage —that they are comparatively united. They have at present but one object—the overturning the Queen's throne and Government. Should they succeed, then all the same jealousies and quarrelling between themselves would begin as now exist among the liberals. They have another advantage too—that they live upon the country through which they pass, and kill and exact just as they please, not professing to be any thing else than freebooters and invaders of a hostile country. The Queen's troops are compelled to affect legality and order, and are consequently always in want of money, clothing and food, while the Carlists are always living in plenty. Among the liberals too there is every division and subdivision of political differences, and as the animosity of sectarians against each other is always greater than against those of a different creed, so the liberals hate each other much more intensely than they do the Carlists, and are far more ready to compound with the latter than to attempt coming to an understanding among themselves.

The Cortes that have just been elected are moderate to a degree that disgusts the Exaltados, but it shews that the country when left to itself, which it has been at the late elections, is adverse to all this political jangling and splitting of hairs about forms of government when a deadly foe is at the gate, and the people have therefore sent up Deputies who they consider men of discrimination, committed to the cause, and who have something to lose by the destruction of that cause. The Constitution may be practicable as would have been the Estatuto Real or any other system if the war had been put an end to—if it lasts, no form of government, though it were octroyé by the Almighty himself, will be *possible*.

I sent you a couple of dispatches two days ago by a Spanish courier because I did not venture to send them by this opportunity. One of them is a pretty sufficient answer to Sebastiani's communication to you.[1] The other is worthy of attention because Seoane is a man much respected and of considerable influence, and his position as regards the Government causes him to be looked upon almost as a Cabinet Minister.[2]

Miraflores is an unadulterated blockhead and really deserves the scrape he has got into. He is the origin of most of the disasters that have occurred[3]—he chose by way of giving himself consequence to run away though his life was in no more danger than mine and I will underwrite his safety and nobody's taking any notice of him at $\frac{1}{2}$dy. per cent if he likes to return—but the Government have adopted a general measure and they cannot make an exception in favor of a man who, although he did sign the Quadruple Treaty, is now at Paris intriguing as hard as his faculties will permit against the present Government and order of things, and furnishing arguments accompanied by entreaties for a Holy Alliance intervention in the affairs of Spain. I regret this and every other measure of proscription and confiscation. I did all in my power to prevent it, or at all events to get exceptions made in favor of Miraflores and one or two others, but I could not succeed, except in the case of Alava who stands upon different grounds. How then can the Government make any exception in favor of one who is acting as that goose is at Paris? All I can do, and that I will try my utmost for, is to prevent the decree being put in execution against any body though it may hang in terrorem against all.

You are quite right about Büschenthal—his metier is a spy . . . .

I have spoken to Mendizabal about Easthope's man to whom he will give every facility but the said correspondent never goes near him. He helps the Times man and he in consequence never writes a word, or the Times either, against Mendizabal personally, which is an *immense point* for him—the nigger knows how much there is to say against him.

The Portuguese Corps in Spain is much more inclined to Don Pedro's Charter than to the present Constitution but they cannot well be spared from here, and if they were the Portuguese Government would not let them come to Lisbon for they are sending away all the troops they can in order to leave the town under the dominion of the National Guards. Nobody here thinks or cares a straw about what passes in Portugal, and the affairs of that country exercise no influence over those of Spain. The Spanish Government however are ardently desirous of a reaction there.

Ludolf's note is probably a clumsy execution of instructions, but the matter is worthy of attention. We have here some information which may be relied on of a good deal of similar work going on elsewhere but I don't venture to write upon it now.

Calatrava hugged me and almost cried for joy when I told him you consented to give the 100,000 muskets.

Received 24 October.

GC/CL/296; Clar. Dep. C.452/2 (319-326)

[1] The commander of the depot at Pau, on the French side of the Pyrenees, had dissolved the depot of troops because 'a state of things existed in Spain which the French Government neither approved nor recognized'. (V to P, 13 Oct. 1836, no. 253, FO 72/462.)
[2] He called upon V and informed him that 'the Cortes about to assemble would probably be found the most moderate and reasonable that have yet met since the publication of the Estatuto Real with the exception of a few hothead individuals'. (V to P, 13 Oct. 1836, no. 254, FO 72/462.)
[3] He left without a passport, and was therefore in danger of having his property confiscated.

274 Villiers to Palmerston, 19 October 1836

Madrid. *Advises Sir Hussey Vivian to abandon his mining project until the country is calmer.*

Copy.

Clar. Dep. C.452/2 (327-328)

275 Villiers to Palmerston, 20 October 1836

Madrid. Private. I have thought it worth while to send a courier to you with the proposal of the Spanish Government for an English guarantee.[1] I have done nothing more than amend the proposal in favor of England and pledge myself to its transmission. I hope you will think I could not have done less. A loan guaranteed by England could give new life to the Queen's cause, restore the discipline of the army which is starving, and revive the drooping spirits of the liberals—in short to all except the hyper-Exaltados and the Carlists who each for their own purposes desire confusion it would be like manna from heaven—for things can scramble on for a very little while longer in their present state. The Constitution and its offspring—the forced loan and the new levy—have completed the disgust of the masses, and when the money arising from those two measures is spent, which it is even before it dribbles in, the disgust of the army will be complete—and then—sauve qui peut. Every body foresees this and is preparing for the day of wrath, so that there never was a moment when two millions of English money would so completely fulfil every condition of a blessing.

Now for the English side of the question. In the first place we shall get immediate payment of £500,000 which is about as bad a debt as ever tradesman had upon his books, and likely therefore to become a plausible ground of attack for Carlist Maclean[2] and Co. when Parliament meets. This would be so much saved out of the fire, but then it might be said that we were throwing good money after bad, but I think it would not be difficult to repel that charge considering the mortgage we should have upon the richest and most flourishing colonies in the world—and the political value of the transaction to us should not be lost sight of . . . .

With respect to the financial details of the proposal I have left them pretty much as Mendizabal suggested not knowing whether you will think it worth while to entertain the matter at all, and being quite certain that any alterations or suggestions you may like to make will be readily agreed to here. I do not venture to recommend the measure to you as I did the commercial treaty last year, but upon the whole I do not think it a bad speculation.

I have of course borne in mind (indeed it is never out of my mind) a commercial treaty, but I must confess that the moment is a singularly unpropitious one for it—the Government is powerless, and by the Constitution cannot make a treaty without consulting the Cortes where they would be beaten if they were to try the question. Catalonia would be *all*, instead of *half* of it, in arms against them, the smugglers of the South whose occupation would be gone would turn Carlists and be a formidable nucleus of faction. The Government are not prepared for a treaty with France, and if they made one with us only, the indirect hostility of France might become direct.

These are too great odds against a Government at such a critical moment, and would furnish their opponents with formidable political weapons.

If you reject, as you probably will do, the loan proposal I hope you will give some plausible and friendly reasons, for the helpless condition of these people merits compassion, and in any case it is important to them that the most profound secrecy should be observed upon the subject.

M. de la Tour Maubourg is a calm cold man of gentlemanlike manners and moderate abilities—whether it is his aspect or the instructions of which he is supposed to be the bearer[3] I know not, but the impression he has produced here is not favorable. I have no doubt that I shall get on well with him, and he is a great improvement upon Bois le Comte who returns to Paris next week.

As soon as the ambassador arrived he was informed of the uproar which the advent of his compagnon de voyage M. Cazes had made here, and he immediately sent a passport for him to be viséd at the Foreign Office by the secretary of embassy who went to announce to Calatrava the arrival of his chef.[4]

I never mentioned before the conversation I had with Bois le Comte upon his arrival here respecting the conformity of views between Louis Philippe and Thiers because I did not consider it of importance until M. Molé advised himself to tell Campuzano that the promised reinforcements, the depôt at Pau, etc., etc., were all got up à l'insçu du Roi. Campuzano quoted these words of Molé or I should have been inclined to think he had made a mistake, for the King must have known that Bois le Comte was sent to Spain, and that his mission had probably some object.[5]

Of military matters I can tell you nothing more than the meagre account in my dispatch. The Government are absolutely without any information at all either of the movements of the Queen's or the Carlist troops. Rodil has not written for four days, and the public is getting frantic with the disgraceful conduct of the generals.

I hear that the chargés d'affaires of the Factious Powers (as they were called here) have received orders from their Courts to remain upon the frontiers—I suppose to be in readiness to assist at the coronation of Charles V.

PS. Upon reading over and signing my dispatches I find that an important omission has been made in the loan bases—there is no security for the payment of the interest. It is now too late for communicating with Mendizabal upon the subject, but I enclose the project of an additional article which will meet the difficulty.[6]

Any other mode however which you might suggest would be adopted here—as it is of course only an omission.

I shall keep my ordinary courier of the day after tomorrow till Monday in order to send the Queen's Speech.[7]

Received 29 October.

GC/CL/297; Clar. Dep. C.452/2 (329-334)

[1] A loan of two million pounds, secured on the customs duties of Cuba, Puerto Rico and the Philippines. In the event of default the British Government could send a commissioner to Cuba 'in order to preside over the punctual fulfilment of the contract'. (V to P, 20 Oct. 1836, no. 263, FO 72/462, enclosing Calatrava to V, 20 Oct. 1836. P minuted: 'This proposal must be considered as perfectly secret', 29 Oct. 1836.)

[2] Donald Maclean, M.P. for Oxford.

[3] For Latour-Maubourg's instructions, see Molé to Latour-Maubourg, 26 Oct. 1836, AMAE CP Espagne 772. He was instructed to adopt an attitude of reserve and 'la circonspection la plus extrême' towards the Spanish Government. He was informed that he must give no opinions on Spanish politics and offer no advice on the conduct of the war. In the event of the deposition of the Queen Regent, he was to have no contact with a revolutionary Government and should await the instructions of his own Government.

[4] The Spanish Government suspected Cazes of Carlist sympathies and indicated that he would not be a welcome addition to the French embassy at Madrid. (V to P, 20 Oct. 1836, no. 261, FO 72/462.)

[5] V wrote a despatch on his conversation with Bois-le-Comte in which he put on record Bois-le-Comte's assertion that he received his final instructions from Thiers in the presence of the King. (V to P, 20 Oct. 1836, no. 262, FO 72/462.)

[6] Enclosed with his despatch no. 263, FO 72/462.

[7] 'I' to 'Speech' omitted from C.452/2.

276 Villiers to Palmerston, 24 October 1836

Madrid. Private. Barring its truly Spanish length I think you will approve of the Queen's Speech. Calatrava promised me it should contain no invidious comparisons between France and England, and nothing that should give offence to Louis Philippe upon his change of policy, and I think he has kept his word without neglecting his duty. He said he could not deprive the Government of the benefit of acknowledging English favors, or entirely pass over in silence the non cooperation of France, but both have been done with tact.[1] The Speech besides stops up several holes, and varnishes over some bad passages in the history of the last two months and is altogether I think as good as could be expected.

Seoane has frightened the Frenchmen out of their wits—they neither know what to make of him or of the prospect of affairs here, and La Tour Maubourg will doubtless represent this place as the head quarters of all the devils upon earth (in which I fear he is not far wrong but I hate it being thought so in France). Seoane has had a long conversation with him in which he held the same language as to me and which I reported to you respecting the system of terror which it may become necessary to adopt upon the failure of measures of moderation in putting down Carlism and earning the good will of other countries.[2] La Tour Maubourg was greatly shocked, for he at once saw that Seoane was no bragger, but a mild intelligent *gentleman*, who was resolved to throw himself headlong into all that he abhorred as a last though doubtful resource rather than deliver up his country to what he believes would be its perdition or let himself quietly be hung like a dog. La Tour Maubourg appears to have said, not with much tact, that his Government never would tolerate such a state of things and that there would immediately be an intervention. Oh, said Seoane, you would be able to find armies *then*, should you? It's a pleasant diversion for you now to see us cutting each other's throats and losing battles against the arms and ammunition and cavalry with which you supply our enemies, but when we find our prayers to you are useless and that we give over entreating and do what we can for ourselves in our own way, then all at once you find that you have got armies at your disposal, that you no longer fear the unknown lengths to which an intervention may lead you, or the contagion of revolutionary Spain for your soldiers; but, M. l'Ambassadeur, we are not so ignorant as to have to learn that in these times armies are not so easily moved, and that the consequences of moving them are very grave. France could not make war upon Spain with a less force than 100,000 men. Would she venture thus to expose herself to the animosity of Powers who any more than the Carlists of Spain will never forgive the King for the means by which he ascended the throne?

All this I understand was said in a mild unblustering tone which made all the more effect upon the ambassador. I trust however that we shall never see Seoane's views attempted to be carried into effect, for setting aside the horrible nature of them, I believe they would be unavailing for the objects he contemplates, and as the masses would be against them they would shortly have to be abandoned. Such measures would be much more likely to produce a general rising in favour of Don Carlos than any thing else.

Bois le Comte has received instructions to supersede St. Priest and sets out for Lisbon the day after tomorrow—he has been here for *three hours* this evening and I have done all in my power to secure his drawing well with Howard. He swears he knows nothing of the cause of St. Priest's recall or of the disagreement which appears to exist between him and Howard, but I think he seems to pique himself upon reestablishing harmony—his opinion is that France has no important interests to uphold in Portugal and ought always to play a secondary rôle to England. I should think it would be desireable in the event of our ships having any thing active to do at Lisbon to invite Admiral Hugon to take part with us also, if he should be there at the time—*that*, Bois le Comte says, is the only possible ground for disagreement which he can foresee because if the French ships were to be excluded from any coup d'état we might perform the officers might be piqued, and the newspapers be saucy and the envoy ad interim embarrassed. He says Hugon is most desirous to be on good terms with our naval officers.

I have spoken to Mr. Büschenthal . . . .

Rodil, Gomez and Alaix are playing at hide and seek upon the Sierra somewhere. Very little however is known here of the movements or intentions of any of the parties.

Received 2 November.

GC/CL/298; Clar. Dep. C.452/2 (335-340)

[1] The Speech mentioned British naval and military assistance and the recent supply of a further hundred thousand muskets. It also commended the activity of the French Foreign Legion but regretted that the French Government 'has seen fit since not to carry out the preparations made for extending the co-operation on the part of France'. A copy of the Queen's Speech is enclosed with V to P, 24 Oct. 1836, no. 271, FO 72/462.

[2] See V to P, 13 Oct. 1836, no. 254, FO 72/462.

277 Villiers to Palmerston, 27 October 1836

Madrid. Private. I write a line by Mendizabal's courier for the chance of Lord Granville's having an opportunity of forwarding my letter.

Mendizabal made a much lamer defence of the instructions he had given his financial agent than I have put in my dispatch,[1] and he told as usual about four dozen lies upon the matter. I don't know how he will get any body to believe that his own envoy and two such men as

Ardouin and Ricardo would publish and act upon such a measure without positive instructions from the Government—he intends to try however.

You will probably be in no want of loopholes to get out of the not overtempting loan proposal—otherwise the priority of mortgage being now disposed of affords an excellent one. Mendizabal even cannot deny that it would much increase your difficulties were you ever so well disposed. The want of money is appalling and if ever a little is scraped together and sent to the army the generals rob it.

The proposition made yesterday in the Cortes for confirming to the Queen Regent her present title and authority which is signed by nearly 80 Deputies is important, and will I hope settle that question, but I have no great confidence in these Cortes. Calatrava, who is always sanguine about every thing, continues to think, or to say he thinks, them patriotic amenable gentlemen, but I believe the majority of those who are yet arrived to be ignorant and hot-headed. Some such presentiment must have likewise seized the Government to have induced them to abandon the initiative upon the reform of the Constitution which they had reserved to themselves until within the last few days. They had their project ready as I communicated to you[2] but now they think it adviseable to leave this important measure to be introduced by some chance Deputy and decided upon according to the *generosity* of the Cortes.

La Tour Maubourg told me yesterday that he had received a letter from Count Molé stating that the Northern Powers had made up their minds to the triumph of Don Carlos not being *prochain,* and that M. Ancillon had been the first to volunteer an explanation respecting the recall of their chargés d'affaires from Madrid which was, that the Spanish Government persisted in looking upon them as diplomatic representatives which they were not and that the time was therefore come for withdrawing them. This (in order to avoid circumlocutions and the chance of finding a less correct term) is a lie. Calatrava treated them exactly as all his predecessors did—with indifference—tolerating their presence rather than thinking it desireable as it was always known that they were not faithful reporters of passing events. They were at first greatly alarmed that Calatrava was going to do less than his predecessors, for when we returned from San Ildefonso and the town was in the power of the mutinous garrison La Grua (the Neapolitan chargé d'affaires) came to me in the name of them all to ask for refuge in my house because M. Calatrava had sent them no official notice of his appointment, and they supposed therefore their persons were not considered to be under the protection of the Government. I immediately represented this to Calatrava, when it was found that a trick had been played him in his office and that the notes in question which he had signed some days previously had never been delivered. They were immediately sent and no other communication that I am aware of took place between the Government and the diplomaticos facciosos as they were called.

I told all this to La Tour Maubourg who said he should write it to Count Molé, but he can think of nothing but Seoane's conversation with him, and I am inclined to believe he does not look upon his own head as very safe on his shoulders. I am sure he will represent me at Paris as a revolutionist and as not disapproving of much of what goes on here because I claim to know something more of this country than he does and will not admit his preconceived opinions with which he is determined to make every thing fit.

From the different theatres of war we have hardly any information, but the constantly-exterminated rebels go where they please and do what they like. Nothing since the war began has been so disgraceful to the Queen's arms as the expedition of Gomez to Andalusia.

Mr. Büschenthal has just been here . . . .

Received 5 November.

GC/CL/299; Clar. Dep. C.452/2 (341-344)

[1] Mendizábal had instructed the financial agent of the Spanish Government in London to issue bonds 'chargeable on the revenue of the island of Cuba', whereas in the recent loan discussions with V he had stated 'that there were no charges on the revenue of Cuba'. (V to P, 27 Oct. 1836, no. 273, FO 72/462.)

[2] See V to P, 15 Oct. 1836, no. 255, FO 72/462.

278 Villiers to Palmerston, 29 October 1836

Madrid. Private. I have but little to add to my letter of the day before yesterday except that which is not pleasant—the successful retreat of Gomez from Andalusia with the whole of his enormous booty and all the prisoners he has thought worth keeping after having attacked and burned the town of Almaden and destroyed the quicksilver works!

Flinter and Puente, two of as good officers as are to be found in the Queen's army, made a gallant defence for 8 and 40 hours with 1,200 men almost destitute of ammunition and provisions against the whole force of Gomez which amounts to 13,000 *individuals,* but of which there are not above 5,000 fighting infantry and 800 good cavalry. This attack was contemplated by Rodil and announced by him in his dispatch to the Government, but though he was only eleven leagues distant with a large force he appears to have done nothing either to prevent the attack or to succour the garrison. You see how unfortunately true my prophecies about that man have turned out. Pray let William Russell know it as he wrote to you from Berlin that Rodil was a general. Rodil's safe and short promenade in Portugal hardly afforded sufficient grounds for forming such an opinion.[1] Public indignation against him is raised to the highest pitch, and if he were to return this evening to Madrid he would perhaps share the fate of poor Quesada.

All this of course tends to render the Cortes more unmanageable and the position of the Government more precarious. I cannot perhaps give you a better version of what I conceive to be the position of the Government at this moment than by enclosing to you a copy of a letter I wrote two days ago to Mendizabal. It was before this last disaster was known and in consequence of Calatrava's telling me that the Government had done all in its power and that nothing more remained to be done. There is a great deal that they might do but I feel sure they won't—there is no energy or courage or savoir faire. A fatality seems to attend what little they attempt, and I begin to believe that el mismo Dios es faccioso—at least he seems to inspire the Carlists with all that our side is deficient in—*they* never miss their opportunities, and when they undertake a thing they are generally successful with far inferior means.

I am afraid they are meditating some great coup at this moment. They have been actively employed in fortifying all the accessible points in Navarre, and as they will know the Queen's troops have no intention of acting on the offensive this looks as if they were about to leave their strong holds and to descend en masse upon the plains. We have accounts likewise that a large force with a good deal of artillery is moving upon Bilbao which it would of course be an immense object to them to take, and if they attack it as they did Evans's lines in the beginning of this month they will probably succeed, for the season of the year will make it difficult for Lord John Hay to assist as he would like, and Evans having been weakened by detaching the two regiments against Sanz (which by some villainous trick on the part of the Santander authorities were never allowed to proceed to their destination) will be able to do little towards the defence of the place, having besides to take care he is not himself simultaneously attacked. I believe too that the Governor of Bilbao is a cowardly thief who will do nothing but augment the panic of the inhabitants. However I may as well cut my doleful story short though I have not half emptied my budget. I try only to tell you what is strictly necessary in order that you should be gradually preparing yourself for the worst. A month ago I thought we were sure of passing the whole of the winter in Madrid. I am now beginning to doubt it.

Mendizabal has begged me to send you the enclosed extract from the report upon his Department which he read to the Cortes in justification of himself with you as respects his agent's proceedings upon the non-payment of the dividends.

The courier of the 20th from London brought me no letter from you.

First enclosure: Copy, Villiers (Madrid) to Mendizábal, 28 October 1836, private, recommending vigorous action by the Government and changes in the military commands.

Second enclosure: Copy, report by Mendizábal on the Ministry of Finance, 25 October 1836.

Received 10 November.

GC/CL/300; Clar. Dep. C.452/2 (344-346)

[1] He was commander of the Spanish force sent to Portugal in 1834 to help in the action to expel Don Carlos and Dom Miguel.

279 Palmerston to Villiers, 29 October 1836

Copy. Foreign Office. I send you a note which I have received from Minto upon the subject of the inactivity of the Spanish steamers on the northern coast of Spain; pray communicate it to the Spanish Government.

Enclosure: Copy, the Earl of Minto (Admiralty) to Palmerston, 29 October 1836. The Spanish Government by leaving Commodore Henry's squadron without pay or provisions throws the whole duty of the coast upon our ships and sailors—their own remaining inactive . . . . If the Spanish Government will do nothing for itself, there can be no use in our keeping our ships on that bad coast in winter, and we had better order Lord John Hay home immediately . . . .

GC/CL/1283

280   Villiers to Palmerston, 30 October 1836

Madrid. *Introduces M. Büschenthal.*   GC/CL/301

281   Villiers to Palmerston, 1 November 1836

Madrid. Private. I avail myself of a courier which Mendizabal is about to send to write you a dispatch upon military matters. There is no use talking of any others for they are all subservient to the war, and the Devil in person seems to be commanding the Queen's troops at this moment. The Devil is of course Carlist and right well he is serving his protegé.

A few days ago I was all for depriving Rodil of his command, but I confess I think differently now upon the matter. The apprehensions stated in my dispatch seem to me well founded,[1] and I have moreover reason to believe that Rodil is connected with some of the secret societies who would support him in resistance to the Government, and rejoice to see his army march upon the capital in full mutiny that they might turn the confusion to account. There is another fear also, that Rodil might possibly give what Calatrava calls *un escandalo a la Europa* or in other words march over to Don Carlos with his men—thinking the *ingratitude* of the Government no bad excuse for passing to what they must be beginning to consider the stronger side. It is only fortunate that he did not take the command of the army in the North where he might have done worse than Espartero who only does nothing. But what a dreadful position the Government is in—blamed on all sides for not taking vigorous measures—not able to do so—or to state the grounds upon which they act, and fully aware of all the consequences political and military which may ensue. I really feel for Calatrava who is an honest man, and is fit to hang himself for despair.

Mendizabal tells me that La Tour Maubourg had a long interview with him yesterday at his (La Tour Maubourg's) own request. He remonstrated in *lively* terms about the non payment of the dividends and complained of the distress which it occasioned to French small shopkeepers. Mendizabal said that no one could regret more than he did not having money but as he had it not it was plain he could not pay, but that France was solely the cause of this disaster as well as of most others that had befallen Spain within the last two years. This franchise startled the ambassador's calmness mightily, and he said he could not permit such an assertion. Mendizabal replied that Mr. La Tour Maubourg might entertain a contrary opinion but that he had his, and they were that the French Government had turned him out last May not because he was considered revolutionary or for any of the other causes that were alleged, but because he was thought in France to be an Anglomane and desirous of destroying French influence in Spain—that the French Government had set up Isturiz who had been the means of bringing about a state of things which would not otherwise have existed here—that having done so the French Government withdrew the assistance they had offered and in the manner most hurtful to the Queen's cause and useful to that of Don Carlos—and lastly had by their official organs of the press so misrepresented all political events here as well as military, that they had knocked down the Spanish funds at the most critical moment and rendered all financial operations impossible.

La Tour Maubourg replied that there could be no doubt of the preference which it was wished to shew towards England as Mendizabal had made a commercial treaty—but Mendizabal denied *it like a man* and swore it was utterly fabulous. The ambassador then said he had heard that there was some new negotiation on foot with Mr. Villiers[2]—utterly false again, replied Mendizabal, but he added that even if there was he would propose nothing to England that he should not be prepared to do with France. Mais cela ne nous arrangeroit nullement, was the answer, we don't want any thing with you—which of course Mendizabal qualified as very unfriendly and very unjust. This conversation he assured me passed in a friendly tone without any asperity on either side, but after shaking hands with him as he went away La Tour Maubourg said, Monsieur Mendizabal, si vous voulez conserver l'amitié de la France, prenez bien garde à vous et à ce que vous faites—this was with reference to England as Mendizabal understood. He begged me so much not to say any thing of this conversation that I only report it to you in a private letter.

Received 11 November.   GC/CL/302; Clar. Dep. C.452/2 (347-350)

¹ That the dismissal of Rodil would be followed by a mutiny of his troops. (V to P, 31 Oct. 1836, no. 283, FO 72/462.)

² Latour-Maubourg, in his account of the interview with Mendizábal, said that Mendizábal's denial that the British and Spanish Governments were involved in commercial negotiations did not convince him. He informed Mendizábal that France would not be duped in this matter. (Latour-Maubourg to Molé, 31 Oct. 1836, AMAE CP Espagne 772.)

282   Palmerston to Villiers, 3 November 1836

Copy. Foreign Office. I am glad you have quite recovered from your illness, I wish Spain had recovered from hers. But the Cortes has at last met and that is something. A representative Government with no assembly is the weakest of all; it has not the vigour of despotism, nor the power which representation affords.

Your plan for a loan shall be well considered; unluckily Minto and I are the only Cabinet Ministers in London, but we shall all meet in ten days, and I will then let you have our decision. I think the plan rather tempting myself and the security unobjectionable; but we must know what Melbourne and Rice say on the subject.

I have seen Aguilar who seems a good humoured, plain minded man and with whom we shall get on very well. He seems to have justly enough appreciated Louis Philippe's feelings and policy about Spain.

I am very glad you succeeded in getting the Queen's Speech free from any passage which France might have thought offensive; it was very wise to abstain, especially as it was tempting not to do so.

The list of sulphur, flints, pounds of lead, single horses and mules stopped on the frontier and enumerated in the Moniteur are ridiculous, but they shew at least some consciousness that there is ground for blame.

Has the Spanish Government no cavalry and horse artillery or light artillery moveable by horses? Why do they not pursue Gomez and the rest by such forces? Surely if the pursuers were always hanging on the rear cutting up stragglers, and cannonading columns, these scampering marches might not be thought such good fun by the Carlist peasantry? But probably so natural an idea has struck everybody; and there are insuperable difficulties to prevent its being carried into execution.

It will be too bad if Louis Philippe allows the Holy Alliance Conference to establish itself at Bayonne. The French Government is very sore about the attacks made upon it by newspapers here; il n'y a que la verité qui blesse. Latour Maubourg is I believe a very honest honorable good sort of man; cold and repulsive in his manners, and without much scope of mind, but a gentleman. He was not popular in Belgium; but you will probably get on pretty well with him.

We are doing well and I have no apprehension that the Tories will be able to disturb us.

The Emperor of Russia is ill . . . .

GC/CL/1284

283   Villiers to Palmerston, 5 November 1836

Madrid. Private. Although I think it probable that you have already received it from Lord Granville yet I send you a curious document which Calatrava put into my hands a few days ago. He was discreet as to the means by which he became possessed of it, and only told me it came from the head quarters of Don Carlos, but I know he had it from Cordoba or at least I believe so, and in that case Lord Granville would have it directly, as Cordoba for reasons which I suppose he would tell Lord Granville was desirous that you should have the information.

I hardly know what to make of the paper, and whether to believe or not the part which is attributed to the Duke of Wellington. The matter is *meditated* after his manner—parts of the memorandum are sufficiently in his style, and there are one or two traits that look original. Still however I hesitate to think that the Duke of Wellington would commit himself to un misérable like Aznarez, that he would enter into such details respecting the agent it is proposed to send to Cuba or speak so warmly in favor of *any* Spaniard, that he would authorize a project altogether unEnglish, or that he would run the risk of being discovered in a plot which might almost be called treasonable against the Government and the solemn engagements of his Sovereign. These are the considerations which induce me to send you the papers privately, and not to leave officially on record in the Foreign Office so grave an accusation against the Duke of Wellington under the doubt which must exist of the authenticity of the charge; but if upon further enquiry you have reason to believe the story is well founded I can write you a

550

separate dispatch with this date covering Calatrava's letter and communication. Southern has made an excellent translation of the paper but I think it sufficiently important to send likewise a copy of the original—or rather of the copy which was sent to me.

My conversation with the Duque de Bailen[1] took place on the very day I received Lord Granville's dispatch containing Molé's denial of French instrumentality in dismissing Mendizabal and it appears to me worth reporting, but at the same time I should observe that too much consequence ought not to be attached to it as the Queen is quite capable of having *improvised* the story in order to stop the mouths of her Councillors and satisfy her hate against Mendizabal.

Whether La Tour Maubourg acts upon his own view of the crumbling state of things here or in accordance to instructions I know not, but he is at no great pains to disguise that his stay at Madrid will be short and he told the Danish chargé d'affaires the other day that for the present he should neither furnish his house or even take a cook. I believe, though God only knows why, that he thinks me a tremendous revolutionist and always big with some plot for advancing the interests of England in Spain at the expense of those of France. I see that he attaches more weight to Seoane's opinions than to Calatrava's and the revolutionary measures contemplated by the former are never out of his head. Since the arrival of the courier he asked for another interview with him and I have suggested to Seoane to throw out as his own idea and that of the party in the Cortes whom he influences that there is one other way of avoiding the revolutionary measures which the civil war fomented by France will render necessary—which is, frankly to throw themselves into the arms of England and to make it worth while for the English public to support their Government in some great measure of assistance which of course could only be done by a considerable territorial sacrifice, but that that would not be paying too dear for peace and prosperity in what would then be left—adding however that all these measures which at best must be a disturbance to Europe would be avoided by the loan of 30,000 troops for a month, whose besogne would be over and they returned to France before the much feared remonstrances from Berlin and St. Petersburg could be received and taken into consideration at Paris.

I had a curious proof yesterday of how much the personal feelings of Louis Philippe are embarked in the policy he has adopted towards this country . . . .[2]

The military news upon which every thing else here depends, is of rather an improved quality today. The taking of CantaVieja, the defence of Bilbao with the loss the Carlists have sustained there, and the miserable remains of Sanz's faction being up to their chins in snow and without a bit of *wittles* are all good in their way, and highly disgusting to the Carlist and the *Moderate* party, which latter would greatly prefer the success of the Pretender to that of the present Government.

Still however the cause of Rodil v. Gomez makes no progress and is still as it has been for the last 6 weeks in a disgraceful state. If ever two men deserved being shot as incapable cowards it is Rodil and Alaix, each with a force sufficient to beat Gomez, both afraid to go near him, and yet never able to combine an operation. The division of Narvaez which went through Madrid yesterday and which is as fine a body of troops *as ever was seen* in *any* country, will probably be the finishers of Gomez if they can come up with him. If he goes into Portugal I have recommended the Government not to wait and be negotiating whether Spanish troops are to pass the frontier in pursuit or not, but to be after him at once. The cause is the same in both countries and if Gomez was allowed to go quietly to the Algarves there would be a Miguelite rising directly. Orders to this effect have been sent to Rodil.

Espartero's army is of course too weak to allow of any reinforcements being sent at this moment to Evans, but I am so perpetually harping upon the necessity of it, that if Gomez can but be destroyed and all the troops which he now keeps employed set at liberty, I believe I can reckon upon 10,000 men to send to San Sebastian, and we would then have the French frontier closed before the end of the year—that would soon change the face of affairs—though the starving state of beggary in which the Government is paralyzes every thing.

I have never held out the least hope that you would accept the proposition I sent to you 10 days ago, but do you think there is *any* mode in which it might suit England to guarantee a loan? There is no reason why we should not turn an honest penny if we can, and Spain would accept any conditions with gratitude. Some of the East India Company and several great commercial houses of London were desirous a twelve-month ago of *hiring* Manilla for a term of years provided the transaction was under the protection of the British Government. Do you think this could be renewed? I believe Goldsmid, and Wilson and Co. were the people who came forward on the occasion. If it be *possible* an effort should be made to give things here a decisive turn before Parliament meets.

Mendizabal called upon me this evening and told me in strict confidence that the Ministers had been *watching* and *praying* all night as they had reason to believe the Queen Regent intended to escape, instigated and assisted by the French ambassador. I have since seen Seoane, the Captain General, who does not believe in the story, which however seems to have originated with one of the Queen's coachmen. Several people have written lately from Paris that Louis Philippe wished the Queen Regent was out of Spain as then his treaty obligations would be at an end—but the Queen would hardly expose herself to such great dangers as she would have to incur.

Mendizabal likewise told me that Alsager, one of the editors of the Times, had privately written to him to say that the Duke of Wellington and Baring had become proprietors in the Times concern and that they were going to take up the cause of Don Carlos.

Calatrava wants you to kick out Mr. Aznares from England but I have told him that that no puede ser.[3] The more I think of Mr. Aznares's paper the more I incline to believe the Duke of Wellington's name has been taken in vain—if not, you will have a powerful weapon against him in Parliament—if it has, you may possibly think it well some time or other to communicate with him upon the subject and let all these Carlist conspirators be shewn up. Mr. Büschenthal's information related to Cuba—perhaps he may throw some light upon this matter.

PS. Mendizabal has just sent me his report upon the finances of the country which he read in the Cortes. It is not likely to amuse you much but as it is possible you may like to see the kind of paint that is put upon the empty boxes I send it.[4] Do you ever see Ardoin?[5] I believe he knows more about Spain and above all about Spanish finance than any foreigner and he is now in London.

First enclosure: Copy, Calatrava to Villiers, 2 November 1836, 'confidencial y reservada', enclosing documents from Don Carlos's headquarters, and asking whether the British Government would expel Aznares, the Pretender's chargé d'affaires in London.

Second enclosure: Translated copy of a despatch from Aznares to Erro, Don Carlos's Minister, 20 September 1836, reporting a conversation with 'Prudencio' (alleged to be the Duke of Wellington) in which the latter advocated a declaration for Don Carlos by Cuba; together with a memorandum by 'P' elaborating the scheme, 18 September 1836.

Third enclosure: Note by Melbourne (South Street), 16 November 1836, expressing disbelief that Wellington had anything to do with the Cuba proposition.

Received 15 November.

GC/CL/303; Clar. Dep. C.452/2 (351-356)

[1] A member of the Council of Regency. Bailén told V that Rayneval had urged him to advise the Queen to dismiss Mendizábal. (V to P, 5 Nov. 1836, no. 186, FO 72/462.)

[2] The story concerned Baron Taylor, in Spain on business for the Louvre, who greatly annoyed Louis Philippe by reporting on the need for French intervention.

[3] 'it is not possible'.

[4] Possibly the second enclosure with no. 278 above.

[5] Ardouin, the French banker.

284   Palmerston to Villiers, 11 November 1836

Foreign Office. I send you a letter for Mendizabal about the Legion; read it, seal it, and send it him; tell him I have sent [it] you open that you might read it, in order that you might be better able to converse with him on the subject to which it relates. If I could believe that it was written in the Book that Carlos could succeed, certainly I should imagine the fulness of time was approaching. When every plank is rotten, how can the ship not founder?

You have been but too right about Rodil, and Alaix and all of them. The defence of Bilbao is a set off—but that was the result of the defence of St. Sebastian's.

I much fear the Cabinet will not agree to the guarantee of the loan. It would require of course the consent of Parliament, and with what face could we propose to Parliament to saddle England with the possible charge of the interest of a loan, for a set of people so utterly incapable of doing anything for themselves? Men would say that if money was the chief want of the Queenites a loan might set them on their legs, but that the Rothschilds will not contract to supply military skill and willingness to fight and honesty of purpose, and common sense, and without all these things the loan would only enrich a few more generals, without advancing the Queen's cause a step. The two millions would be gone in a crack and two millions more would be wanted. The pounds sterling would disappear like the muskets and with as little good result. Carlos would get to Madrid, Cuba would declare for him, and we might go whistle for our security, unless we sent an expedition to conquer an island in the Tropics; however the question shall be duly considered.

PS. Lord Holland asks why the young Princes, sons of Francisco, and such other young grandees as profess attachment to the Queen should not raise regiments for rank and admit foreigners to hold commissions in such corps?

Copy.   GC/CL/1285

285 Villiers to Palmerston, 12 November 1836

Madrid. Private. I have received your letters and dispatches of the 3d this morning—they came later than usual owing to the snow on the mountains and, the French courier going early, I have but little time for answering.

I shall be glad if the loan guarantee is considered practicable by My Lords of the Treasury for without money it is hopeless work here. You see an example of it in the condition to which the naval force on the North Coast is reduced—the Legion is just the same—the army is if possible worse off, and neither discipline or obedience can be expected when the Government on its side fails in all its engagements. Representations and complaints are of no use for there is not a farthing in the public chest and blowing up never yet produced anything out of nothing.

To return however to the guarantee .... If you thought it adviseable to invite the French Government to join in the transaction it would not be otherwise than well viewed here as compromising them and offering some security for their interest in the cause—at all events it would prevent French complaints against England and Spain, and France could not play dog in the manger. If she did not chuse to go halves with us she would have no right to growl at our helping an ally and taking care not to lose by it.

The surplus revenue[1] is worth consideration, and at all events if you do not shut the door entirely to money aid let me beg of you to state what it is you think practicable, and it will be accepted here, for of course all you will want is to cover your responsibility with the public and with Parliament. If such a measure were accompanied by payment for the arms we have supplied, and followed by a commercial treaty, public opinion would I think be in its favor.

As to the commercial treaty I have little to add to my dispatch[2] except earnestly to beg you to let me have an answer without delay, for a Spanish Minister's tenure of office is not worth three days purchase, and I shall have to wait three weeks before I hear from you. In the draft of the treaty you sent to me the article relating to the 20 per cent duty on British manufactures was framed with reference to the proposal of guaranteeing a loan of 2 millions—that is not now in question, and we cannot expect that in return for such a vast concession to us that the Spaniards will be satisfied with a pledge on our part to revise the Spanish part of our tariff. For that there should exist here enlightenment and despotism—the former in order to understand the advantages that Spain would derive from liberalizing her commercial system though we did not make a pennyworth of return, and despotism to stifle the yell of indignation that it would create throughout the country. Now as there is neither force or intelligence here at this moment we must take things as they are and not expect too much, for prejudices are deep-rooted and easily converted into political weapons, and there is as you know the greatest apathy among this people with respect to whatever concerns their own interest, be the road to it ever so clearly pointed out. But Calatrava is, to my mind, better disposed than any of his predecessors—be assured however that we shall have a formidable enemy in Mendizabal who will not like that another should overcome difficulties that he was afraid to encounter. It is likely that in consequence of the fears with which he may inspire Calatrava that I shall not manage the most important part of the treaty—the tariff—but there are many others which it would be most desireable for British subjects resident in this country to have regulated, and which it would be well worth while to come to a decision upon even though they were unaccompanied by what is most wished for in England. But if they do not get something out of us in order to make a push with the war, or we do not get something out of them to make a shew when Parliament meets, I sadly fear that folks in England will run sulky and that the state of opinion will be a source of embarrassment to you in any thing you may wish to do in Spain, whereas if we had really established a commercial or financial *raw* the Commons would help you to *keep* it.

Soublette[3] will be in England shortly after you receive this letter. . . .

Poor Santa Maria is seriously ill.

Mendizabal has just been here and has told me so much of Rodil's dispatches, acts and operations that I cannot refuse to join in the opinion which is now becoming general—that he is a traitor. It is only lucky that he did not assume the command of the army of the North. I always knew him to be incapable as I have often told you, but I never had any reason to suspect his principles. I now fear that he will not quickly resign his command. The debates in the Cortes and the virulence of the press have greatly disgusted the army and added to the apathy with which military operations are proceeded with.

I have no time for more.

Received 24 November.   GC/CL/304; Clar. Dep. C.452/2 (358-360)

[1] Of Cuba.
[2] V to P, 12 Nov. 1836, no. 291, enclosing V to Calatrava, 10 Nov. 1836, FO 72/462.
[3] He had failed to secure Spanish recognition of Venezuela. (V to P, 12 Nov. 1836, no. 293, FO 72/462.)

286   Palmerston to Villiers, 17 November 1836

Copy. Foreign Office. I am sorry to say Rice will not hear of the guarantee for the loan even upon any of the conditions suggested by you. In truth it would be a desperate attempt to ask Parliament to sanction such a measure in the present state of military affairs in Spain, and of the money market in England; Spain must therefore make some effort herself, and after all she will only have to pay a little dearer for the money she may want to raise.

We are sending out Colquhoun with brevet rank of major to Lord John Hay, and he takes with him a detachment of Royal Artillery, 3 officers and 30 men. This is something and may be of some little use.

I do not believe Prudentio to be the person asserted; I think that person not capable of entering into such schemes. But the papers are curious and it is clear that somebody or other has been fishing in troubled waters.

PS. What an exhibition of folly and cowardice the Portuguese have made in this bungling attempt at counter-revolution at Lisbon. If the Queen had only waited till things were ripe she would have found little difficulty in carrying her point. But to attempt a revolution without being sufficiently provided either with physical force or moral courage was truly Portuguese.[1]

GC/CL/1286

[1] The Queen of Portugal regarded the September revolution which replaced the Charter by the 1822 Constitution as a threat to the Crown. She left the palace at Belém, proposing to go aboard a British warship. She was warned that to seek foreign aid would be to endanger the throne, and urged to return to Lisbon. This incident, the Belémzada, left the Septemberists in the ascendant.

287 Villiers to Palmerston, 19 November 1836

Madrid. Private. I have received your letter and dispatches of the 11th by my courier who is certainly a good goer. I immediately sent your letter to Mendizabal and asked him to dine with me today in order that we might talk over its contents, and I shall be able before my courier goes tonight to tell you what he *says*—that he will be able to *do* any thing, I conceive to be impossible, for every day during the last 2 months I have been urging the payment of the Legion but without effect, indeed I may say that my chief occupation with the Government for a twelvemonth past has been advocating their claims, and screwing out by good words and bad partial instalments. On the other hand I am bound to say that if proper economy and *common honesty* had been observed by those connected with the financial affairs of the Legion money enough has been *actually paid by the Government* to have prevented its falling into its present unfortunate condition. As for exertions of mine I can do no more than I have done to make dollars out of empty chests, for the Government is now reduced to the insignificant revenue of *Madrid* for meeting all its clamorous creditors.

The villainy of Rodil by means of which Gomez has overrun and exhausted the most productive provinces of Spain has caused all the resources upon which the Government had a right to count to fail. A little money would now be of more importance than at any moment since Ferdinand's death, and I think its application is too plainly pointed out to allow much of it to go astray, for if Narvaez beats

Gomez, which is more probable than not, because he is a brave and ambitious *young* man (which is all that is wanted here) every effort would be made to blockade the French frontier. The Government recognize the necessity of it—the public would insist upon it—and I believe now as I always have that that offers the only chance of concluding the war singlehanded. However it is written in the Book that nothing shall turn out well here, and so to the Devil it will all go—unluckily it will drag a good deal of the surrounding materials with it.

I translated Lord Minto's letter to you and gave it to Calatrava insisting that it should be read at the Council of Ministers.[1] £2,000 were immediately sent off to Commodore Henry and Mendizabal says he will try to scrape together a few pounds more.

I have assisted at the debate upon the regency today and nothing could be more satisfactory.[2] I don't know what M. La Tour Maubourg reports to his Government about the Cortes, but nobody who really looks for the truth and is not afraid to speak it can justly complain of the course *hitherto* taken by the Cortes—there is not among them a great deal of talent, but there is much good sense and still more fear which together make a malleable compound for a Government.

The Lisbon affair produced a sensation but no effect here. Calatrava and indeed all the people in authority bitterly lament the failure of the counter-revolution, as they think it would have helped the march of reaction here—in which I believe they are mistaken, for nothing will produce a solid effect but military successes and if they are obtained reaction may be left to itself. If the passage in your letter to Mendizabal respecting the assistance given from this country to the late revolution in Portugal alludes to the Government either individually or collectively, I must assure you of my conviction that you are wrong. What the secret societies may have done I know not, but the present Government had far too great an interest in checking revolution here to think of promoting it in a country so situated, politically and geographically, as Portugal is with respect to Spain.

You see what a pretty boy your *re[c]omendado* Rodil has turned out, and yet all the evils of Spain were supposed to be augmented by his not being put in the place of Cordoba. I know all these worthies well and can gauge the good-for-nothingness of each accurately. I was sure he would never do any thing—why, the blundering way in which he executed the orders of the secret society he is connected with, to propose revolutionary authorities to the Queen, was the prime cause of breaking up Mendizabal's Administration. She would never have ventured to turn him out if so just a cause of complaint had not been furnished to her.

During the last 3 or 4 months I have had various conversations with Santa Maria upon the necessity of keeping faith with the English creditors of Mexico . . . .

The Spain of Lord Holland's time must have been very different from that of the present day if he thinks it possible that young grandees would raise regiments at their own expence—there is not one of them that has the soul of a mouse or a shilling in his pocket. They have done nothing—absolutely nothing—for the cause which from the servile degradation of a palace raised them to a political existence, and they now, for the most part, would prefer the triumph of Don Carlos, provided he left them their estates, than that the Queen's cause should succeed with the present order of things. Francisco's sons are two half-witted little boys of 15 and 16 years old.[3]

I have talked longly with Mendizabal about your letter—he is much flattered at your having given yourself the trouble of writing directly to him such a letter. He had not time tonight to answer either you or Lord Holland as he could desire but he is preparing a statement which he will send to you in the middle of the week to prove that the Legion has not been by any means so neglected as it is represented. He solemnly swears that since he came into office in September £30,000 has been given to the Legion and that he has not been able to furnish more than that to the whole Spanish army. £30,000 he contends is sufficient to have kept the Legion, which does not consist of 6,000 men, out of distress for 3 months—however he says he will try what he can do by bills and other means to raise some more money for them—but he is almost mad with the emptiness of the treasury and the Juntas de Armamento y Defensa, as they are called, laying hands upon the sums which the recent measures of the Government have extracted from the pockets of the people.

Mendizabal is in my worst books, for he has already been working at Calatrava against a commercial treaty. If he continues to do so by the Lord he shall suffer for it both here and in England, let what will be the consequences.

We have repeatedly offered to do something to prevent smuggling from Gibraltar in exchange for a more liberal commercial system. How could we carry these offers into effect? I believe it would be found extremely difficult if not impossible, but Poulett Thomson may have some plan which might at all events be a bait.

Received 30 November.

GC/CL/305; Clar. Dep. C.452/2 (361-367)

[1] See no. 279 above.
[2] The confirmation of the Queen Mother as Regent. The question was put to a vote and the result was 124 for, 6 against. (V to P, 19 Nov. 1836, no. 299, FO 72/463.)
[3] In fact the Duque de Cadiz was fourteen years old and the Duque de Sevilla thirteen.

288   Villiers to Palmerston, 26 November 1836

Madrid. Private. There is a great dearth of news this week as you will see by my *war* dispatch[1] which is the only one from here that ever signifies, for all the rest is but leather and prunella compared to the war. I daresay there is a great deal of news from different parts which wants telling if it could get here, but unfortunately the only avenue open to Madrid now is the road from France and that I suppose is blocked up with snow for the courier from London due yesterday morning is not yet arrived. All the remaining roads are very unpleasant for travelling, for where the ever-chased and never-caught Gomez has been he has caused the Carlist sympathies of the people to spring up like mushrooms, and as every patriot has run away there issue forth unmolested bands of Carlists of from 25 to 200 who rove about the country seeking whom they may devour. They intercept the couriers (these they always murder) and diligences, rob the villages, and eat up the land, spreading terror far and wide. It is not then much to be wondered at if revenue is not collected, and that the forced loan of two millions remains still in the pockets of the right owners.

This is the real reason why the Legion is reduced to such straits, for although Mendizabal gets up a wrangle about the accounts (many of which I am sorry to say tell ill for the morality [of] the paymasters and commissaries) he would pay now and settle afterwards if he had the money, but what little is scraped together in the provinces the Juntas de Armamento y Defensa immediately grab. Remonstrances are quite vain and only serve to shew more clearly the weakness of the Government, or rather that out of Madrid there is no Government at all. I have not been able to see Mendizabal today but he had not prepared his answer to your letter yesterday—he just sends me word however that he shall answer you *muy satisfactoriamente*—perhaps he may as regards the sums total that have been transmitted to the Legion, but he cannot as to those which are due still. I have of course done all that is in my power to assist General Godfrey who, although much disgusted with Mendizabal personally, is not without hopes of obtaining several things which are much desired by the Legion—one of which is pensions for officers and men wounded, and for the widows of those who are killed. I likewise hope that in the beginning of next week we shall send to San Sebastian £10,000—some bank or Mont de Piété being probably robbed for it—otherwise I have not an idea where the money can be got from. I have unusually good assurances—i.e. from others than Mendizabal—that the money shall be sent but I cannot promise that it will. Godfrey will write fully upon his proceedings to Le Marchant.

I shall write to you upon the subject of my commercial dispatch of today[2] by my own courier next week. I hope you will approve of the step I have taken. I had more than one reason for it.

I have been constantly pressing Calatrava to get forward with his reform Bill and to commit the Cortes to certain bases rather than wait for a remodelling of the whole Constitution. I have likewise been in communication upon the subject with one of the leading members of the commission, and I hope that these bases will be presented very shortly. They are much the same as Calatrava promised me they should be two months ago—the Crown to have the veto and the power of dissolving and proroguing the Cortes—two Chambers—election direct—Deputies may be Ministers, and a few other minor but not unimportant improvements. Calatrava assures me he has no fear of these not being carried—if they are, nobody will have a right to say that the Cortes are not behaving well and doing what is in their power to check the progress of revolution.

Two months ago Bois le Comte told Calatrava that the promises of military aid had been withdrawn for a time because France desired to place herself in observation and see what was coming to pass here. I don't know how long this process was meant to last, but I think if she has observed impartially, she must see in what has passed as much guarantee for the future as people under such critical circumstances could be expected to give.

PS. The courier is just arrived having been detained by the snow. I am not surprised and can hardly regret the refusal of the guarantee for charity begins at home, and things being worse than when the proposal was made a month ago we might have got into a serious scrape. It will be bitterly felt here and the more so as I see no chance of their getting on without money or any of their being lent money, make what sacrifice they may.

Received 7 December.

GC/CL/306; Clar. Dep. C.452/2 (368-373)

[1] V to P, 26 Nov. 1836, no. 309, FO 72/463.
[2] V to P, 26 Nov. 1836, no. 306, FO 72/463, reporting Latour-Maubourg's hostility to the Anglo-Spanish commercial negotiations. See also Latour-Maubourg to Molé, 26 Nov., AMAE CP Espagne 772.

289   Palmerston to Villiers, 26 November 1836

Copy. Foreign Office. I send you a special messenger with my answer to your questions about the commercial treaty,[1] because even a few days may be of importance in the present state of affairs in Spain. Indeed by Quin's account of the state of the road as he returned, it seems doubtful how long quadrupeds will be found to convey messengers backwards and forwards.

You may say to Calatrava that not only are Spanish bonds very low at present in England; but that the Queen's cause is very low also. That the failures of all their military commanders, and the want of energy and success which has appeared in all parts of the country, has entirely damped all enthusiasm, and has rendered the public here extremely indifferent as to the result of the civil war.

The only things which could revive the interest which was heretofore felt in favour of the Queen's cause would be military successes and a commercial treaty. The first it seems the Government cannot command; the second they can have whenever they chuse. A treaty of commerce and navigation is really almost the last card they can play with reference to this country. With all the clubs and societies we hear of in Spain the one called 'aide toi, le ciel t'aidera' seems to have no affiliations in the Peninsula unless indeed Carlos may be supposed to belong to it.

We are in hourly wish, I can scarcely say hope, of hearing that

Espartero has relieved Bilboa. As to Gomez we have ceased to think about him, knowing he can go where he will and do what he likes. You were quite right about Rodil, and we were all of us entirely wrong. He seems to be worse than Cordova.

Parliament will meet the 31st of January; I fear we shall have no great things to announce by that time. However one comfort is that even if we should fail and all should go to the dogs, England will have fulfilled its engagements, and have stuck by its principles; and we shall be able to say that we have done everything short of actually going to war, in order to uphold the cause we have espoused.

GC/CL/1287

[1] 'I regret to have to say that the British Government does not think it could, with any prospect of success, propose to Parliament the guarantee in question; and such a guarantee could not, as M. Mendizabal is aware, be given by the Crown, without the authority of an Act of Parliament for that purpose.' (P to V, 26 Nov. 1836, no. 112, FO 72/456.)

290   Palmerston to Villiers, 30 November 1836

Copy. Stanhope Street. I send you Lord Carnarvon's book on Spain.[1] Read Chapter 13 about the Basque Provinces and send me as soon as you can any materials for an answer to his assertions.

Enclosure: Instruction by Palmerston: Get the book and send it him by the messenger tomorrow.

GC/CL/1288

[1] *Portugal and Galicia with a review of the social and political state of the Basque Provinces,* 1836.

291   Villiers to Palmerston, 3 December 1836

Madrid. Private. I am at last able to announce something like a turn in the tide of adverse things which has so long been rolling in upon the Queen's cause. How long it will continue or what use will be made of it I will not predict, and indeed I refrain from thinking upon the matter, for where Spaniards are concerned the lasciate ogni—not *esperanza*—but *confianza* must be the prevailing feeling in anybody that knows them. However the manner in which the mutiny of the Guards here[1] (which was far more serious than it appeared and which might have upset *every*thing) terminated, is a new element of strength for the Government who may get on pretty well now if the restrictive measures they have asked of the Cortes[2] are granted—but they are absolutely indispensable. No Government can exist with such a liberty of the press and such a liberty of conspiring with impunity as now obtain here in the midst of abject penury, excited passions, and contending principles. Calatrava says the Government will have a hard battle upon the subject with the Cortes but he has confidence in the good sense of the majority. The reforms of the Constitution are as ample as could have been expected under the circumstances—their announcement has been well received by the Cortes and the public likewise views them with favor. The discussion upon the recognition of the South American States proves that these Cortes have more sense and less prejudice upon this always-trying subject to a Spaniard than their predecessors in the last Constitutional epoch, and that we may therefore hope to escape from the many follies which distinguished the parliamentary heroes of that period.

Then if the news that has been scraped together, for nothing official is known, of the raising the siege of Bilbao is confirmed it will be by far the greatest moral blow that the Carlists have received during the war, because far and near, at home and abroad, they have announced to their partizans that their success was certain and the advantage to their cause incalculable. And lastly Gomez having been fallen in with and beaten is, as I need not say, of immense importance both in the South and the North. He is however not yet finally destroyed and we must not sell the skin before the bear is killed—but I think he cannot escape because the country is sure to be against the beaten man and wherever he or his scattered remains present themselves they must expect to meet avengers of the atrocities he committed when, thanks to Rodil, he was in prosperity. Andalusia will then be free and there will be a hope of some revenue from it if those cursed juntas, which in an evil hour the Government legalized with their consent, do not continue to lay hands upon everything they extract from people's pockets and which should of course find its way to the general treasury.

Ribero's division of 8 or 9,000 men will then proceed by forced marches to Espartero's army, and I hope to secure Narvaez with about the same number of men to send to San Sebastian—he is the general upon whom I fix my hopes, and I must do Cordoba the justice to say that from Paris he sent Calatrava word that Narvaez was the only officer capable of dispatching Gomez, and of fulfilling whatever duties the Government intrusted him with.

Narvaez's marches since he left Madrid would be incredible in any other country than Spain where the soldiers march better than in any other, and when he fell upon Gomez with his whole force he had not more than 4,000 infantry and no cavalry. Money however is the rock we must split upon even though every thing else were to go well—a million at this moment when fortune seems turning would be worth five in ordinary times when throwing good money after bad would seem only to be augmenting future difficulties without relieving the existing ones. Do you think any help could be given in return for the cession of sovereignty over Honduras and the adjacent islands[3] respecting which I anticipate some demur in the Cortes?

Bacon is very desirous of raising and commanding 2,000 cavalry and feels sure, as I do for him, that he would sweep the country south of the Ebro clean of factious, but the Government having no money I intend to discourage Bacon's offers in order not to have 2,000 more complaining Englishmen in Spain. Should you venture to make a present to Spain of the horses and equipments[4] for this number of men, which Bacon would raise, and the pay for which might I think then be raised upon the provinces they protected, in return for the Honduras matter being *satisfactorily* settled?

Some time ago Goldsmith and the house of Wilson and Co. were desirous of paying largely in order to obtain a commercial footing and exclusive rights in the Manila Islands—but they all at once ceased to moot the matter here. Mendizabal would have no objection to treat with them now if they are still desirous of it—perhaps you would let somebody sound them, for they may now think that matters are looking more stable here. I mention these things not with much hope of their success but because I want to leave nothing untried in order that Spanish affairs may present the least bad appearance possible at the opening of Parliament. You say that Spain must look to her own resources and will only have to pay a little dearer for the money she raises, but every door is shut against her in the present state of her credit, and with the insecurity which a civil war presents and the excited passions which increase the difficulties the Government finds in taking any decided measures, I do not see what Spain can at this moment promise, pawn, or sell which would induce foreign capitalists to come to the rescue.

I cannot report any final measures with respect to the Legion, but Godfrey is satisfied with the disposition he finds here to strain every nerve in order to meet their wants. The importance of doing so was never more felt than at the present moment when the Government is at last convinced that San Sebastian and Irun must be the points de départ and the line of the Pyrenees the only base of operations—but what is to be done? They can't coin for want of the proper metals, and begging produces them nothing. I am certain, and so is Godfrey, that if the money existed or could be got at any price it would be given at once and without wrangling about old debts. If Andalusia is set free there may be a prospect of raising funds in a short time, but I doubt Evans *allowing the Legion to wait* and I do not *say this unadvisedly.* He has now, as he has all along had, Westminster and nothing but Westminster in his eye—he is determined to go home coûte qui coûte, and would sooner take the Legion with him upon financial grounds than leave it behind. Evans is as brave as a lion in the field, but he is deficient in most of the important qualities which a general ought to possess. I have innumerable proofs of this which have probably not reached you.

PS. I send you the report of the commission upon the reforms of the Constitution.[5] It is a creditable document and worthy of being made public in England.

Received 13 December.

GC/CL/307; Clar. Dep. C.452/2 (374-379)

[1] A mutiny on 1 December of a battalion of the fourth regiment of the Guards. The mutineers attempted to kidnap the Queen, but failed, and the mutiny was quelled. (V to P, 3 Dec. 1836, no. 312, FO 72/463.)

[2] The Government had asked the Cortes for special powers to tighten up press censorship and the right to forbid public meetings directed against the Government. (V to P, 3 Dec. 1836, no. 315, FO 72/463.)

[3] 'in return' to 'islands' underlined, possibly by P.

[4] 'a present' to 'equipments' underlined, as n.3 above.

[5] Enclosed with V's despatch no. 315.

292 Palmerston to Villiers, 8 December 1836

Copy. Foreign Office. I send you a copy of the translation of a letter from Espartero to Evans, sent by John Hay to Minto.[1] It is not fair by Espartero to pronounce judgments upon him till we know the result of his operations for the relief of Bilbao, but the impression produced upon me by the perusal of this letter was that Espartero like Rodil has been bought by Don Carlos; and that he wanted to entice Evans and the Legion away from St. Sebastians in order that that fortress might fall into the hands of the Carlists; while on the other hand it was his intention to leave Bilbao to its fate.

I think you should show the letter to Calatrava, it reads like a mauvaise plaisanterie.

GC/CL/1289

[1] No enclosure survives.

293 Villiers to Palmerston, 10 December 1836

Madrid. Private. The courier from London is not yet arrived which is hardly to be wondered at for snow upon the mountains, Carlists in the plains, and no horses upon the road *are* impediments to travelling. Webster however arrived in the beginning of the week, but I have not as yet been able to *trade* much with what he brought me from you, for events crowd upon each other so rapidly in this land of confusion, and every body leads such a from hand to mouth life that it is impossible to get any business attended to which does not concern the immediate interest of the day. People accustomed to the self-working machinery of office in England can have but little idea of the labor it is here to get through *any thing*, or of the annoyance of having perpetually to dun a bankrupt Government. It is about as easy to see the Kham of Tartary as Calatrava, for he passes his whole day in the Cortes, his evenings in Cabinet Council, and half the night he travaille's with the Queen. He and I are the best of friends. He knows I want to see him upon various matters, yet though I wrote to him yesterday morning for an appointment he is not able to receive me before 12 o'clock tomorrow night. I mention this in order that you may know the kind of difficulties which attend the *discussion* of a treaty but you may be sure that nobody is more anxiously desirous to get on with it than I am.

Mendizabal will be our chief obstacle as I have always foreseen, and long before the treaty is signed or broken off I shall have to thrash him, for such a low-lived pedlar I never had to do with before. He would *sell* the treaty as he would his father's skin or any thing else, but look at the question like a statesman he can't or won't. Whether some fifty years ago he chanced to be baptized or circumcised I can't say, but that he has the *soul* of a Jew I have no manner of doubt. I won't deny, though I didn't admit, that he is justified in some of his objections—he begged me to remember what was to have been the price of articles 1 and 13 last year.[1] Nothing of the kind is offered now—only vague promises by way of commercial reciprocity—and the Cortes and the Constitution have to be consulted upon the matter. Nil desperandum however in Spain, and if all does not go to the dogs within a few days—of which there is a possibility—I shall still hope to do something.

I beg of you to take into your consideration the additional articles to the treaty which I send today,[2] and I hope you will then not forbid me to continue the negotiation even though articles 3 and 13[3] should be rejected or modified, for I believe if British merchants in Spain had to chuse between these two articles and the rest of the treaty as it now stands, they would take the latter, because it more immediately affects them in their business and personal security and comforts. The old treaties are not denied but they are not fulfilled, and never will be, because they are out of date and very *doubtful*. Privileges were granted to British subjects some 150 years ago[4] it is true, but subject to the condition of paying an annual sum to the King—at least the treaties are so worded as to authorize a doubt—therefore a wrangle—therefore never doing anything but what suits a slovenly Government and corrupt employés. The old treaties revised, compressed, translated, and circulated as law, would be as valuable to our countrymen in Spain as sweeping away the customs duties, and should the French Government make such a treaty and bestow these benefits upon French subjects we should all be handsomely abused for rejecting the opportunity because we could not get all we wanted.

It is certainly written in the Book that if ever any improvement does take place here it shall be of the shortest possible duration. Last week I had good hopes—they are all now in mourning for the treason and mutiny perpetrated by the villain Alaix. He alone is responsible that Gomez and all the remains of his faction are not at this moment prisoners in Madrid. Narvaez had them all in a net, panic stricken and exhausted, demanding to capitulate, when Alaix—true Spaniard!—sacrificing every thing to his jealousy makes his division mutiny—a day is lost, and the rebels escape, Narvaez having narrowly escaped being shot by one of Alaix's officers before his eyes. He has of course complained to the Government and desired to resign if this mutiny is not punished. The Government is afraid and rather more inclined to sacrifice Narvaez than to chastise Alaix, the latter being a cowardly incapable common soldier, and the former, if I am not greatly mistaken, the only man in Spain capable of finishing the war. I have written a series of letters upon the subject to Mendizabal and told him amongst other things that if he and his colleagues did not act vigorously that I should consider it equivalent to breaking off the relations of Spain with England as the British Government was accustomed to treat with *men* and not *eunuchs*.

Bilbao is a subject of extreme alarm. Espartero who is no more fit than I am to command 20,000 men has placed the army of the North —which is the only plank between the Queen and destruction—in a position to be completely cut to pieces if he fails in his attempt to save Bilbao, and his hesitation to move forwards is a fearful omen.

For the Legion I am almost in equal alarm—my dispatch will tell you what we have been able to effect in the midst of beggary and confusion. Godfrey has returned so far satisfied that he feels nothing has been left undone which there was a possibility of doing.

Received 19 December.

GC/CL/308; Clar. Dep. C.452/2 (380-383)

[1] A loan from the British Government to Spain.
[2] Enclosed with V to P, 10 Dec. 1836, no. 322, FO 72/463.
[3] Article 3 stipulated that goods passing from either country to the other could be carried in British or Spanish vessels, and Article 13 admitted British manufactured cotton goods into Spain.
[4] The Anglo-Spanish commercial treaty of 1708.

294 Palmerston to Villiers, 15 December 1836

Copy. Foreign Office. Peninsular affairs begin to look somewhat better. If Gomez has been well beat and shorn of his tail as is said, and if Bilbao has been finally set free as I hope, the Queen's cause will assume a more favorable aspect. But I still doubt Espartero's honesty, and believe that if Wylde had not gone to him, he would not have come near Bilbao. Wylde says he is a poor creature; I suspect he wishes to make himself less poor by means of Don Carlos's money. If this is so he ought not to be left in command.

Mendizabal's letter to me is not very satisfactory; tell him I am looking with impatience for accounts of the arrival at St. Sebastians of the money which he promised to send thither; and tell him moreover that it is most important that the Legion should not be left without food. An Englishman is nothing without his rations.

The French are getting very jealous of our cooperation in the north of Spain, and do not like the arrival of our guns and artillery men and the works which John Hay has thrown up at Passages. You will see by a dispatch of Granville's that the French claim Passages as belonging to them and not to the Queen of Spain—do not fail to let Calatrava into that secret. It is right he should know it.

I mean to send out a couple of officers to assist Wylde as the Queen's armies are getting back to the North. This may be of use. I shall try to get two scientific officers who speak Spanish, Engineers or Artillerymen. I doubt much whether any of your plans for money or money's worth would be practicable.

We have no cavalry equipments in store, they are found by colonels of regiments and not by the public; we have therefore no stock of them; and we have no money available for buying the number that Bacon would require for his cavalry corps.

The only thing that has occurred to us [as] feasible, and perhaps the Spanish Government would not think it so, would be that the Spanish Government should make a loan here, pledging some revenues to the contractors as security, or giving any other security which might be deemed sufficient, and that the transaction should take place with the cognizance of the English Government in such manner that the contractors should have a right to claim the assistance and interference of the Government if Spain should not keep faith with them.

That the money so raised should be applied exclusively to the service of the Legion, which corps should be augmented, and that for this purpose the money should be paid into the hands of commissioners appointed here by the Spanish Government. I know not whether all my colleagues would agree to such a plan, but at least it would avoid the necessity of any vote of Parliament.

It seems to me to be of the first importance in the present state of things that the Legion should be kept up and if possible increased. That corps has kept Villa Real in the North and has prevented him from making a dash on Madrid; it has preserved to the Queen important points on the Northern Coast, and has identified England with the Queen's cause. It would be a great calamity for the Queen if the Legion were to be broken up. It may be that Evans may be chiefly guided by views to his own personal interest, most men are so where their own country is not concerned. But I think him incapable of acting otherwise than honourably; and when one places oneself in his position with all the various difficulties he has to encounter: wants of the Legion; just complaints of the officers and men, for which he can obtain no redress; promises of the Spanish Government repeatedly broken; himself and his force left by the fault of others in a condition so wasted as to be unable to achieve any decisive results; his Spanish troops taken from him; his arrangements thwarted by the jealousy of some and the incompetence of others; no paramount authority to appeal to, to back and support his own; when one considers all these things, it cannot excite one's surprise if he should wish himself well out of his position. He may want many of the qualities which make a general, but good generals are rare productions of nature; much more so than eminent men in other lines.

I have seen Burschenthal; he had only a cock and bull story to tell me about designs of the United States on Cuba . . . .

PS. This failure of the French at Constantina[1] which we have only today learnt, ought to be a lesson to them to fulfil their promises, instead of going buccaneering. If they had employed in supporting the Queen the 7,000 men who have been repulsed in an unjust attack on Constantina they would have had to boast of success and honour, instead of having gathered shame and discomfiture from the mud plains of Africa.

GC/CL/1290

[1] Marshal Clausel, who had gained the consent of the French Government to direct an expedition against Achmet Bey, encountered extremely cold and wintry weather, and was forced to retreat from Constantine with heavy losses on 24 November.

295 Villiers to Palmerston, 17 December 1836

Madrid. Private. Before you receive my dispatches of this day you will probably know how much value is to be attached to Campuzano's communications respecting French intervention and guarantee. As regards the first we know nothing except that Louis Philippe is a good deal squeezed by public opinion and is supposed to be desirous of doing *something* to neutralize the opposition to be expected in the Chamber upon Spanish affairs—of course if he could make that something disagreeable to Spain he would be killing two birds with one stone, and he would like to try intervention in order to establish French influence here and the institutions which might suit his taste. This would be a gross miscalculation on his part, but his whole policy with respect to this country has been a tissue of errors, and there is no reason for supposing that he will now turn away from the wickedness he has committed—he may therefore wish to intervene and I think the line which Calatrava takes upon the subject a very proper one.

With respect to the guarantee[1] I have known for some time past that they have been nibbling at the loan and the surplus revenue of Cuba through some of the blind agents which the French Government are so fond of employing, but Aguado having taken the initiative upon it is to my mind a proof that the King is in its favor, and that it is a speculation in which none of the *parties to be concerned* will lose. Aguado has the whole press and most of the Government offices at Paris in his pay, and he must be a clever fellow to have made himself, from a retail dealer in sherry and cigars which he was, one of the richest men in Europe out of the mangled remains of this country. Aguilar will submit to you the terms of the proposal which from what Calatrava tells me does not differ much from the one I sent to you some time since.

I know not whether you will think better of it now but if you reject it again the Spanish Government will of course conclude the agreement with Louis Philippe if he is really willing, for money they must have, or the army will disband itself in order to levy its own pay and food and clothing upon the country.

Your disgust and indignation will be equal to mine—it cannot be greater—at the miserable jealousy displayed by the French Government upon the subject of our concluding a commercial treaty here, and the insolence both towards England and Spain with which they have manifested their paltryness.

I have not seen La Tour Maubourg (who is not over cordial with me) since he received his instructions upon this and Calatrava has not told me of any communication from him, but of one thing I am certain and that is they will find all the support they can desire in Mendizabal *who will never allow us to improve our commercial relations with Spain if he can help it.* He succeeded in alarming Calatrava and *he* it was who was the cause of my being compelled to communicate with the French ambassador upon the subject—which I omitted to tell you by my last courier. The first day that I took the draft of the treaty to Calatrava

I found him quite changed and his zeal very much cooled. He said that France would be indignant if a commercial treaty were made with England without her participating in it, that they could not afford to increase French hostility, etc., etc., and asked me whether he had not better desire Campuzano to communicate with Molé upon the matter. I said I thought I had much better do so with the ambassador which Calatrava preferred as well. I did so, and if La Tour Maubourg wrote as he said he should it would be in favor of my procédé with him and of the desireableness of revising the treaties which was the ground upon which I said I intended to apply to the Spanish Government, leaving a revision of the tariff for such arrangements as we might respectively be able to make. I did not shew him Article 13.

The conduct of the French Government upon this will not so much signify because we ourselves by offering nothing in return pretty well smother the nascent hopes of a treaty.

The Queen Regent has been frightened by her amiable relative on the other side of the Pyrenees respecting the guns we have lately sent to Pasages,[2] and Calatrava tells me she had spoken seriously about it to her Ministers who of course treated the matter and the suggester of the Queen's notion with contempt.

The Cortes are still displaying much good sense and there is every reason to believe that the reforms of the Constitution will be carried without delay or serious opposition.

I have received the copy of Lord Carnarvon's book which you sent me. I had already got one a few days before and had determined upon answering his assertions for my own satisfaction. I shall have a double one in doing so now that you have expressed a desire for it. All I ask is a little more time in order to do the thing well, and get together the necessary information, but I can promise you that my *pamphlet* shall be out before the meeting of Parliament, and I will keep your messenger here till the MS. is finished, for I understand that Lord Carnarvon's book has produced considerable sensation and it is of importance therefore that his hollowness should be shewn up without delay.[3]

PS. I hope you will instruct Sir Augustus Foster to assure the Count of Turin that there are no hostile intentions here against Sardinia. M. Quadado the late Spanish chargé d'affaires there is just returned and has called upon me. He says that Solar[4] is believing or affecting to

574

believe that Spain is animated with a bellicose spirit against them. Nobody thinks about Sardinia.[5]

Received 29 December.

GC/CL/309; Clar. Dep. C.452/2 (384-387)

[1] A loan for Spain to be secured on the revenues of Cuba and 'guaranteed by the French Government in conjunction with that of England in order to avoid the jealousy which might be expected in that country if France alone were to contract such an engagement'. (V to P, 17 December 1836, no. 328, FO 72/463.)
[2] It was said that Louis Philippe had informed the Queen Regent that the British might establish a permanent naval base on the north coast of Spain, and that the guns set up at Pasajes were part of this plan. (ibid.)
[3] 'I have no doubt that Carnarvon's book must have done harm and damaged Palmerston with all those who don't want much reasoning à son égard, which are not few I believe. Events have certainly not come off lucky for him.' (V to Edward Villiers, 17 December 1836, Clar. Dep. C.467.)
[4] Count Solaro della Margarita.
[5] Postscript omitted from C.452.

296   Villiers to Palmerston, 24 December 1836

Madrid. Private. Having nothing to say I say nothing, and write you no political dispatch by this opportunity for the past week has been particularly uneventful. We have no news from Bilbao—the troops that were in the South are all moving up to Biscay—the Cortes are wisely and steadily proceeding in the reforms of the Constitution,[1] and the state of public opinion is improving. If Bilbao is saved and some money could be had I should consider the Queen's prospects to be better than they have been for many months past. The Carlists are less confident, the war is more concentrated and the necessity of a juste milieu system of government is more generally acknowledged.

The Carlists have learned how little active sympathy their cause meets with when it is carried out of its strong holds in the North. The provinces are clearer of formidable bands of facciosos than of late and might easily be brought to order, and the liberals having got the ne plus ultra of their hopes which is a vast deal more than their expectations—the Constitution—find that it neither protects them from the enemy or increases the resources of the State. Thus things have been brought by a natural course to just that state most fitted for establishing a system that would have a chance of taking root and becoming permanent. The knowledge that the Government had some money would give it the strength necessary for consolidating all these good embryo materials provided there are no new military disasters, and except at Bilbao I do not anticipate any, for these harrassing expeditions into the Queen's country may now be looked upon as at an end.

Five days ago I received a courier from Evans informing me of the increased distress of the Legion, the mutiny of two regiments, his own intention of going home, etc., etc.—as disagreable a batch of letters as ever courier was charged with. I set to work immediately with the *circumcised Head* of the Finance, and I believe few sheriff's officers have worked harder to catch a slippery debtor than I have to recover the money due to the Legion. I kicked up such a row and threatened the Jew so roundly to shew him up both in Downing Street and Change Alley that I got £10,000 out of him, and in order to avoid the usual protestation of Spanish treasury bills wherever they are presented, Rothschild's agent here was induced to give us bills upon his correspondent at Bayonne with which I sent off the courier the day before yesterday, and I can assure you that is not bad work considering the people I had to do with. Mendizabal moreover swore to me that the money promised to Godfrey, and which was not sent from Santander according to agreement, must have been received a week ago by Evans at San Sebastian, as the bank here had given directions for its payment. I don't believe it—but he is very positive. He has likewise given me his *word of honor* (there's a pledge!) that in the first week of January another £10,000 shall be sent to the Legion. It is not his fault I will admit that the provisions have failed at San Sebastian for he has a letter from the Intendente of Coruña saying that 600,000 rations destined for the Legion had for some days past been on board a vessel which was unable to put to sea on account of the weather and that they would go at the first possible moment. The weather has indeed been diabolically Carlist of late. He further assured me last night that he had letters from Santander saying that provisions in abundance had left that place for San Sebastian.

I have received your letter of the 8th with Espartero's to Evans which I had already seen. I agree with you that it looks like a mauvaise plaisanterie but it is merely the work of a frightened man shrinking from responsibility and knowing he was about to undertake that which it was probable he should fail in performing, but it is nothing else. Espartero is not a traitor—he is a common soldier, that's what he is, and no more a general than I am, but he is not Carlist. I know pretty well by this time what each of these gentlemen are worth and I did my best to prevent his being appointed Commander in Chief knowing that he has no head and no moral courage and it is only by accident that he commands. When Rodil went to the South[2] in order *not* to catch Gomez Espartero was named *ad interim* to the Chief Command. When Rodil got found out Espartero was necessarily confirmed in his appointment—first because there was nobody else to send and 2dly because he is very popular with the army. You may depend upon it he is doing the best he can and very bad that best is.

PS. The courier is just arrived and has brought me your letter and dispatches of the 15th. I have no time for replying as La Tour Maubourg's is just going.

I have nearly finished my anti-Carnarvon brochure and as soon as it is copied fair I will send it off.

GC/CL/310; Clar. Dep. C.452/2 (388-391)

[1] It was decided to have a second Chamber which would not be hereditary. (V to P, 24 Dec. 1836, no. 334, FO 72/463.)
[2] C.452 has 'North', which is correct.

297 Villiers to Palmerston, 30 December 1836

Madrid. Private. I send the messenger Webster today instead of my ordinary courier tomorrow. He is the bearer of my lucubrations upon the Basque Provinces in answer to that most poetical historian Lord Carnarvon. I send them to my brother Edward with directions not to lose a moment in having them printed and published as a pamphlet. Should you have time or inclination to look at what I have said pray send to Edward at the Council Office who will bring you the MS.[1]

Should any thing fresh occur in Spain or any measures be adopted or contemplated by the Government you might like to add a postscript, and there might be an advantage in so doing as the whole would then smell less of Madrid, but if the *facts* I have stated are to have any influence in rectifying public opinion upon the Spanish question the brochure should come out before Parliament meets and people have finally made up their minds.

I believe there never was a grander opportunity for striking a coup than at this moment, and with far better chance than at any previous

577

one of its being successful, because the nation not having been put through its entire course of revolution would have been uneasy and prone to listen to those restless spirits who would have promised better things by the very means which have now been proved to be worthless, but at this moment the cry of revolution has ceased to have any echo, there is quite a desperate wish for repose, and you may depend upon it that we might *Portugalize* Spain with little difficulty and expence. I cannot believe that if the whole question were broadly stated in Parliament and the political and commercial advantages that we should secure by terminating the civil war in Spain were generally understood, I cannot believe that the Macleans and Stormonts and Carnarvons would be permitted to annoy you or that the good sense of the country would not be in favor of a national support to the Queen's cause. That which has hitherto been given has been of the Government. Parliament and the public have not disapproved but they have not been invited to take their share in the undertaking. If we were masters in the Peninsula how effectually we might *jam* France at both ends and *make* her go *strait* in spite of her crooked tendencies. The policy of France towards this country has been anti-English throughout, we owe Louis Philippe no consideration, and the best mode of asserting our own dignity and putting him in the position he deserves to occupy in public opinion is to do that which of all things he would feel the most—obtain a preponderating influence in Spain. It would be a rap of the knuckles to him that would make him think twice before he practised his double-dealing upon us again.

I am afraid your proposals for raising money are as little practicable here as mine appear to be in England. No capitalist would lend money to Spain at this moment upon the guarantee of the *cognizance* of the English Government, or could this Government raise a loan exclusively for the service of the Legion. The unpaid army and employés would never permit it and the Government is not sufficiently strong to disregard public opinion.

For my own part and having an almost daily cognizance of what passes at San Sebastian I regret to say that I cannot concur with you in opinion either about Evans or the Legion. In the first place you may be assured that the Legion has had nothing or very little at least, to do with keeping Villareal in the North. If Gomez had remained in Galicia as he was ordered and had Maroto's expedition to Catalonia succeeded we should have had Villareal upon Madrid in despite of the

Legion and Evans, but Gomez chose to go larking to Andalusia (for which to judge of the language held about him at Oñate he is not unlikely to get shot when he returns) and Sanz, who was directed to do what Gomez left undone, having failed as well as Maroto, the Carlist Camarilla were able to prevent Villareal's leaving the mountains which he wanted to do despite of all these adverse circumstances.

The Legion and Evans are in very bad odour at this moment for neither doing any thing to assist Bilbao or to create a diversion by an onward movement. The Government have intelligence that the greater part of the force which was before San Sebastian has been quietly withdrawn and is now at Bilbao—2 battalions and 1,000 armed peasants being all that is left, the Carlists counting upon the mutiny and inactivity of the Legion, and yet the Government is charged with 15,000 rations daily consumed by the Legion. There may be exaggeration in both these accounts but they are official and not contradicted by private communcations. I agree with you in thinking Evans incapable of acting otherwise than honorably, but he may be very honorable and yet totally unfit for command. He should, knowing the distressed state of the Government he was serving, have had some regard to economy although he might have said, like the servants, that it was not his *dooty*—but he has done all in his power to augment expence, and then to irritate the Legion when those expences were not paid. He says he has not 5,000 men and yet he has a staff more than enough for 20,000—he has made God knows how many brigadiers and the field allowances are at this moment £4,000 a month! But he fancies himself Napoleon, and when reductions have been proposed to him he replies that *he* cannot carry them into effect as he commands a corps d'armée.

This last mutiny has been solely caused by Evans—he assembled all his field officers, declared to them his own sentiments upon the bad faith of the Government and the necessity of strong measures in order to force a fulfillment of engagements and he then desired them each to give his opinion in writing which of course they did in the sense he desired, and this volume of round robins was sent up to the Government. The subalterns not having been called upon to give their opinions to the Commander in Chief gave them to the soldiers and mutiny was the natural consequence, and what means had the officers, supposing them to have the inclination, of punishing that which was in accordance with what they themselves had been publicly preaching? When Godfrey was here I saw a private letter from Evans to him saying 'Under Espartero I will *not* serve'—he would not serve under Cordoba either—but he has repeatedly written to me that *Rodil* was the only man who inspired him with confidence and who he wished to see at the head of the army. He is as brave as a lion in the field and no man in Spain, perhaps not in England, is better fitted to inspire his troops with courage and enthusiasm when in action, but he has no knowledge of men and his zeal for the cause he serves is perpetually checked by his notions of his own self importance. He came out here for English and not Spanish political purposes, and his position with the Government, his operations in the field, and the discipline of his corps have all suffered from the phantom that has eternally pursued him of—What will they say of me in Westminster?

If you could hear the *candid* opinions of Lord John Hay, Wylde and others you would find they confirmed mine, and if, as is not improbable, Evans when he gets home attempts to set himself right with his constituents or the House of Commons at the expence of the Government I shall be ready to prove what I have now advanced.

Many thanks for your conversation with Büschenthal....

PS. Calatrava begs me to thank you much for your information respecting the French claim to Pasages of which he had never heard before. He wanted to know under what treaty or what possible construction of treaty the claim would be put forward. I of course could not tell him and I suspect our neighbours would be equally puzzled to do so. Calatrava remarked that it proved the wisdom of only asking for the cooperation of France conjointly with that of the other parties to the Quadruple Treaty.

I shall delay sending my ordinary courier till next week.

Received 9 January 1837.

GC/CL/311; Clar. Dep. C.452/2 (392-397)

[1] See also V to Edward Villiers, 30 Dec. 1836, Clar. Dep. C.467.

298   Palmerston to Villiers, 3 January 1837

Copy. Broadlands. I send you an extract of a letter which Poulett Thomson has received from Mr. Cobden of Manchester, the author of the pamphlet in defence of Russia, but whose statistics seem better than his politics....

Aguilar has read to me today some dispatches from Campuzano and

Calatrava about the propositions to be made to us and to the French. I told him that there is obviously no use in again pressing the French about cooperation. We have long known that Louis Philippe will not as at present advised grant it, and with his speech still ringing in our ears[1] to repeat the application would only be to court a refusal and to degrade ourselves.

I said therefore that unless the Spanish Government want a document to lay before the Cortes, Campuzano had better not present any note; and that even if he does do so, we cannot instruct Granville to take any step upon the subject. With regard to the loan which they want England and France to guarantee jointly, I told him that I much doubt our Cabinet agreeing to the proposal, but if he will make me a written communication, it shall receive all possible consideration.[2] But the best guarantee would be a liberal system of commercial intercourse.

I congratulate you upon Espartero's success at Bilbao,[3] and on the share which our people have had in it. This little exploit contrasts well with the Constantina disaster;[4] and our conduct as allies of the Queen stands a good comparison with that of Louis Philippe. The only inconvenience of the victory would be a demur about placing some other general to command the army of the North. But that ought to be done forthwith; Espartero is brave and he seems after all to be faithful, but he is totally incompetent; and ought to have some better man put over him without a moment's delay. If the advantage gained at Bilbao has been followed up the Queen's forces ought by this time to be at Durango. At all events the moral and military consequences of the success which has been achieved must be very considerable. The Spaniards may still be able to extinguish the war without French aid; and if they can do so it would be incomparably more advantageous for them to do it.

First enclosure: Extract, Richard Cobden to Poulett Thomson, November 1836, on the folly of Spain's restrictive commercial policy.

Second enclosure: Instruction by Palmerston, 5 January: Send under flying seal to Lord Granville begging him to seal and forward. *Endorsed by clerk :* Sent.

GC/CL/1291

[1] The Speech from the Throne, in which Louis Philippe stated that France would adhere loyally to the Quadruple Treaty but would not intervene in Spain. (Aston to P, 21 Dec. 1836, FO 355/6.)

[2] 'His Majesty's Government have every reason to think that there is not the smallest probability that the French Government would become parties to such a guarantee, even if Great Britain was willing to enter into the arrangement.' (P to V, 3 Jan. 1837, no. 3, FO 72/475.)

[3] The Queen's troops under Espartero and with the assistance of the British Legion relieved Bilbao on 25 December 1836. For an account of the action, see V to P, 4 Jan. 1837, no. 1, FO 72/477.

[4] See no. 294 above.

299 Villiers to Palmerston, 4 January 1837

Madrid. Private. I am glad I had not to write to you the day that the news from Bilbao arrived here as you would probably have thought me *intosticated,* and so I was, for I hardly remember an event which gave me equal pleasure. Both parties were playing their va-tout and one side has won. If Bilbao had fallen Don Carlos was to have received a large sum of money and I have no doubt would have been recognized by the Northern Powers or their dependents, which would have made a very agreable complication of the question, and not facilitated your redaction of the King's Speech. It would have cast dismay with all its (in Spain) numerous consequences through the Queen's ranks, and the good conduct of the Cortes and the sound political feelings which are growing up in the country would no longer have been to be depended upon—in short we should have tumbled down hill and perhaps lower than we have ever fallen before. All this mischief is averted from us, and has fallen upon the enemy, and as moral effect is of the first importance in a war like this I cannot but hope that the Carlists have received a mortal blow. Still however I work late and early to make Calatrava and Mendizabal act with energy, and not to let this success get cool and be wasted as Spaniards love to do—but I must say that both Government and public seem desirous to push on and the conviction of ultimate triumph by which all are now animated is an excellent element to work upon.

The main difficulty is the weather for never was such a winter known in Spain, and it is as favorable to the Carlists as it is disadvantageous to the Queen's army. The former occupy the centre of their own country, they have no provisions to seek or to carry, and have no long and dangerous marches to make. The latter in order to get at the enemy will be exposed to the *utmost danger of perishing* from the cold and storms on passing the tremendous puertos[1] of the mountains, and in addition to the usual dangers of being cut to pieces in the defiles they will have to dig their road through the snow. The transport of troops by sea even from Santander to San Sebastian is almost impossible and the transport of ammunition and the sufficient quantity of provisions under all these adverse circumstances will be a Herculean labor—diminished however by the nonexistence of such provisions, for Mendizabal is equally aux abois for dollars or lies wherewith to induce the contractors to make further advances, and here will be a grand difficulty.

Vû all these circumstances then, you must not be disappointed if great progress is not made immediately. I do not venture to expect it. I hope more from the demoralization of the Carlists than the activity of the Cristinos.

I have succeeded in getting 8,000 men and Narvaez, who is the best officer in the Spanish service, sent to Evans or at all events ordered to go to him, although I really do not know how they will get there. Mendizabal has sworn to me today that Evans by this time will have received £24,000 and that on Saturday next he will send him £6,000 more. I shall therefore hope to see the Legion make an onward movement before long.

I told you rightly when I said that Espartero was no Carlist. I still continue to think he is no general, but we must be just towards a man suffering agonies from the stone and who leaves his bed on such a dreadful night as that of the 24th ultimo in order to put himself at the head of his battalions to storm a fortress which was considered impregnable. It does him honor too that in the first moment of victory his first thought was to thank the British officers, and to declare before the people of Bilbao that without them the assault would not have been undertaken—nor would it have succeeded.

I have not the least doubt of the truth of the declaration and that Wylde, Colquhoun and Lapidge[2] are the men to whom the victory is really due—but in a country like Spain it is as pleasant as it is unusual to see an act of justice done, and I must say that the public of Madrid are not at all behind Espartero in gratitude for the assistance we afford them. Would that 10,000 red coats were at this moment disembarking upon the coast and I think I could promise you Don Carlos *in hand* before the meeting of Parliament.

Under the altered circumstances could you have any London capita-

lists sounded as to whether they would advance *a trifle* upon the cognizance of the English Government as you suggested in your last letter,
which with Bilbao saved and the improving spirit of the country might
almost stand for a guarantee?

PS. A comparison between Bilbao and Constantina I think ought to
take down French vanity a peg or two.

Received 14 January.   GC/CL/312; Clar. Dep. C.453 (1-4)

[1] 'passes'.
[2] Both officers with the British Legion.

300   Villiers to Palmerston, 4 January [1837][1]

Madrid. *Private. Complains of the dilatoriness of the messenger Draffen, and
cites another example of Draffen's misconduct.*

First enclosure: Note by Palmerston, 16 January 1837, asking for information.

*Second enclosure: Memorandum by John Backhouse, 17 January 1837, exonerat-
ing Draffen.*

GC/CL/233

[1] V has written '1836' in error.

301   Villiers to Palmerston, 8 January 1837

Madrid. *Private.* I have nothing to tell you today for no news has
arrived here since I last wrote. We are generally in a state of blockade
here from one cause or another, for whenever the Carlists are not doing
duty they are relieved by the elements. We have now a wall of snow
which appears to be impenetrable, for nothing has been received from
the North or from Bilbao since the day the Queen's troops entered
it—now nearly a fortnight—and the sea appears nothing behind the
land in hostility. The news of Bilbao was six days getting to Bayonne
—the military and therefore the political consequences of this are disastrous—the troops have got blocked up in places where there are no
provisions, provisions going to places where troops are starving can't
proceed—operations to be begun cannot be undertaken, and those
begun cannot be continued. In short Heaven seems to be imitating the
example of certain sublunary Powers and determined to assist the Carlists whenever the Queen's cause looks prosperous.

The paralyzation of the activity produced by the success at Bilbao is a most fortunate circumstance for the enemy who will have time to recover themselves, and to shake off the moral effect of having played for and lost their grand stake. In another week they will probably be making comme si de rien n'etoit, and if they do recover their courage they will be like rats in a corner when the new plan of operations commences and prepared for some desperate act of biting or bolting which nuestros valientes may be unable to withstand. Then as usual the money difficulty meets one—if the Government had about £300,000 to be applied solely to the uses of war Sarsfield's project[1] might succeed, but if it is undertaken with insufficient means a very disastrous failure may be the consequence, for everything necessary for the campaign *must* be carried with the army when it commences offensive operations.

I have mentioned to Mendizabal the possibility of assistance being given by capitalists if they did so with the *cognizance* of the English Government and he this day writes to Aguilar and Goldsmith upon the subject—the latter is I believe about to be (if he is not already) appointed financial agent of Spain in London *vice* Ricardos resigned, and a little official encouragement might make him open his purse strings. The opportunity *for distinction* in this way is really excellent and he might at once make himself *a name in Spain*. The Spanish Government has securities in bonds, etc., which they might give (they are already in London) and which would rapidly rise in value as military operations advance.

Closing the French frontier is I am certain the most important thing to do, and I never let a day pass without drumming it into the ears of the Ministers, and whenever the snow melts I have as much certainty as one can have of anything in Spain that it will be vigorously set about.

I send by this courier a PS. to my review of Lord Carnarvon's work which my brother will shew you if you have time or inclination to look at it.

Received 17 January.

GC/CL/313; Clar. Dep. C.453 (5-7)

[1] 'The plan of operations proposed by General Sarsfield was last night definitely adopted by the Council of Ministers—to act upon the offensive, to blockade the frontier of France, to abandon several fortified places and to carry the war into the heart of the enemy's county. It is hoped that this plan may

be put into execution in the beginning of next month.' (V to P, 8 Jan. 1837, no. 8, FO 72/477.)

302   Palmerston to Villiers, 11 January 1837

Copy. Broadlands. I shall be in town again tomorrow but I write to you today to make sure of the messenger. I congratulate you on the victory of Bilbao. In any other country than Spain, it would be a most important and almost a decisive event, perhaps it may prove so, even though it has happened in Spain—at all events now is the time for pressing the Spaniards to make an exertion. If Narvaez, Ribero and the rest all get up to the North, surely they will be able to effect something decisive against an enemy beaten, discouraged and cannonless. The weather and season are to be sure adverse, and must make campaigning amid the mountains a severe amusement, but these difficulties must press nearly though perhaps not quite so much on the Carlists as on the Queenites.

All you say in your letter of the 30th ultimo about Evans may be true, but there he is in command and whatever his faults may be, they do not afford ground for dismissing him, nor would it be expedient to do so if there was even a pretext for it. Therefore the best policy for the Spanish Government is to make all they can out of him. But to do this they ought to reinforce his corps, or put it into direct cooperation with some stronger one. I do not wonder that Evans should refuse to serve under Espartero; no man who ever had any character to lose would risk it by making his movements, his success or defeat depend upon the orders of a man so utterly incompetent as Espartero to act as a Chief in Command.

The experience of the last six weeks or two months ought to convince the Spanish Government of the danger of leaving Espartero a single day in command of any separate corps. He is undoubtedly brave and may be faithful, but he can only be trusted to obey, and not to give orders.

What you say of Sarsfield's wish to make a dash during the siege of Bilbao encourages one to hope that now that the Carlists have been defeated something bold and well-concerted will be attempted. It would be an immense thing for the Spaniards if they could finish the war by their own means without assistance from France; and it really seems possible now for them to do so. As to guarantee and the like of that I fear that they must not look for it from us; and I admit the force of the objections to the other plan which I suggested—a little more military success will however raise their funds, and then it may be possible for them to make an arrangement upon their own account.

It is not unlikely as you say that Burschenthal's proposal to me was a trap. . . .

The Spanish Government should recollect what facilities our naval people have in cooperating with the Legion; and this should be reason for reinforcing the corps under Evans, so as to enable it to accomplish something effectual.

I shall get your pamphlet tomorrow and read it as I go to town.

GC/CL/1292

303 Villiers to Palmerston, 14 January 1837

Madrid. Private. The Carlists are very low in the world but the weather and absence of money or credit prevent our taking all the advantage of their position which we might, and when one has to depend upon Spanish generals I dread some disaster befalling the troops in those old scenes of their misfortunes, the defiles and mountain passes of Biscay, which may serve to give the enemy courage. Mendizabal too, who thinks that when the army moves on the funds will move up, is desirous of persuading his colleagues that Espartero and the generals of divisions will find rations and clothing on their march, but I hope that nothing will be undertaken until all the materials without which success is impossible are got together.

The thing practicable and indispensable is reinforcing Evans, and that I have no doubt will be done although the slowness with which it is set about drives me mad. The orders given by the Government are precise and satisfactory. They have desired Espartero to keep a sufficient force upon the Ebro to guard all that line, which is not difficult at this time of year when the river is unfordable—to send to Evans 7 or 8,000 men which is all he wants in order to take possession of Irun, Hernani and other places which will close the frontier, himself (Espartero) to enter Guipuzcoa from Bilbao and cooperate with Sarsfield who is to advance from Pampluna—but he is to endeavour to combine all this beforehand in order that the movement of these different corps shall be simultaneous and that the net shall be drawn round the game on the same day if possible. Now it must be confessed that this plan although very desireable is very difficult to execute at a moment when an English steam boat is five days going from Bilbao to Bayonne, when it takes six to go to Vitoria from Bilbao, and when Pamplona where Sarsfield is is nearly inaccessible. There is the difficulty of the first communication, and then of moving the troops to given points at given times which Spaniards are sure to fail in—then there will be the average amount of starvation, nakedness, mutiny and jealousy of generals to be taken into the account, so that upon the whole I do not reckon much upon military operations, but I do upon closing the French frontier which will reduce the Carlists to the greatest straits, and upon the weakness which disunion will create among them.

I am very near screwing up my courage to the sticking place and to expend a little secret service money in order to send a man of my own to the Carlist[s] to buy disgust and defection. It would be much cheaper and more effectual than another remittance of muskets. Should you disapprove?

I am much pleased at seeing the universal readiness which exists both in the army and the public to attribute at least $\frac{7}{10}$ths of the success at Bilbao to Wylde.[1] I hope you will be able to do something for him, and if the King is not much averse to it pray permit all the British officers (including those of Gibraltar) to accept the crosses which the Queen is desirous of bestowing upon them[2]—they attach an immense value to them and it stimulates their zeal, so that they make up in energy what they are deficient in numbers.

I have not much hopes about the commercial treaty though the manner in which I mixed up political with commercial considerations in my last note to Calatrava[3] have had an effect upon him, but I doubt our ever doing any thing so long as that scoundrel Mendizabal is in office. I say scoundrel in the fullest extent of the word, and public execration of him increases every day.

You will see by my dispatch that he has failed as usual in his word to me,[4] and I do hope that you will support me in neither speaking to Rothschild or Goldsmith until we have some pledge that the Government will bonâ fide endeavour to meet our wishes upon the subject of the treaty. Pray also speak to Aguilar upon it and in the sense of my last note—that we shall be compelled to retaliate. We can only ask that the Government shall do its best. I know all the difficulties which the treaty will meet with in the Cortes to which according to the Constitution it must be submitted, and where of course the utmost ignorance and narrowmindedness prevail. Our having liberalized our system is nothing to them, they will say—we did so to benefit ourselves and not Spain, and upon the same ground they will resist all innovations, but we have a right to expect the Government to take it up in a different manner to what they have hitherto done and now or never is the time to force them when they are most in need of our assistance.

Carbonell's agent M. Alvarez is returned to England, and I have no doubt that Mr. Carbonell if he chooses might pay the English creditors—as I have private information of large sums of money which Mendizabal abstracts from the treasury to send to him, ostensibly of course for the public service. Thus 2 or 3 months ago some thousand pounds were sent to Carbonell for the *purchase of muskets*—at the very time that the English Government gave 100,000—and today I know that £10,000 is to be remitted to Carbonell *for the conveyance to Spain* of the muskets we let them have—the greater part of them having I believe been brought in ships of war or Government steam boats—but if they had not, their carriage never could have cost any thing like that sum. You must not admit that you had this information from me, but if Mr. Carbonell or the creditors bother you again it will be well to bear it in mind.

I have written a dispatch to you founded upon Lord John Hay's letter to me[5] thinking that Lord Granville may shew it to Molé in its way through Paris, as after what has occurred about Pasages we may be liable to less suspicion by that course than if the representation were to come direct from London or that I had made it to that thick headed gentleman the French ambassador.

Received 26 January.

GC/CL/314; Clar. Dep. C.453 (8-13)

[1] His efforts were praised in a decree published by the Queen Regent. (Copy and translation enclosed with V to P, 14 Jan. 1837, no. 10, FO 72/477.)

[2] For their part in the victory at Bilbao.

[3] In this letter V stated that if new commercial arrangements were not made 'public opinion will compel the British Government to adopt a measure of retaliation by which our political alliance must be weakened in the eyes of Europe'. (V to Calatrava, 3 Jan. 1837, copy enclosed with V to P, 4 Jan. 1837, no. 3, FO 72/477.)

[4] See V to P, 14 Jan. 1837, no. 19, FO 72/477.

[5] Pointing out Hay's difficulties 'in consequence of the increased number of French vessels of war now stationed at Pasages'. (V to P, 14 Jan. 1837, no. 18, FO 72/477.) Granville did raise the matter with Molé and the French agreed to remove two of their frigates from the harbour at Pasajes. (Granville to V, 16 Feb. 1837, PRO 30/29/422.)

304 Villiers to Palmerston, 21 January 1837

Madrid. Private. I have received this day your letters of the 3d and 11th instant. There is nothing you can say of Espartero that I have not multiplied by ten and said to the Spanish Government,[1] but you must not argue upon the matter as if the Government were a free agent, or had the power to do in every instance that which they may think best for the country. The success at Bilbao has given Espartero great weight in public opinion. Neither the Cortes or the people are aware of his errors and misconduct during the six weeks previous to raising the siege—they only judge of the end and care little for the means by which it was brought about, and after the debates in the Cortes, and the rewards that have been granted, and the eulogies of the press, no Government here however convinced it might be of the necessity of removing Espartero could venture to do it—a mere announcement of the intention would be sufficient to turn out even Calatrava, and upon his remaining in office the political tranquillity of the country depends. There are other considerations likewise which must not be left out of account—the fact of Espartero's being no general and a mere soldier makes him beloved by the army, and in its present state of indiscipline it is probable, I would almost say it is certain, that the soldiers would not allow themselves to be commanded by any other general. Then again where is that other general? And I assure you that although I know what each commander in the Spanish army is worth better than the Government, for they only judge by the lying dispatches of their officers, I should be greatly embarrassed who to appoint if the nomination were left to me. This is an unfortunate state of things but we must take both men and things as they are here and above all not argue upon them with reference to what would be done in other countries where no civil war exists, and where Governments are strong and rich.

All that is possible here at the present moment is to prevent Espartero from doing much mischief—not to allow every thing to depend upon his incapacity and to cut out for him by others work that it will be impossible for him not to undertake and which he will be capable of performing. With this view I induced the Government to write the most pressing orders to Espartero to send 7,000 men to San Sebastian. I wrote to Evans to induce him to stay—I requested him to send a trusty agent to Sarsfield in order to combine their movements—I asked Lord John Hay to have all his steamers ready to transport the troops—and I begged Wylde to go to Espartero at Bilbao with an ostensible letter from myself which I thought was likely to facilitate all this operation. My plan was that Evans properly reinforced should take Irun and Hernani, and by closing the French frontier cut off the supplies upon which the Carlists depend for existence. That Sarsfield then advancing towards Tolosa should be able in conjunction with Evans to afford protection to the Bastan and other vallies which only wait for that to declare for the Queen. That they should then advance into the heart of the enemy's country, and *thus* enable Espartero to leave Bilbao and fall upon the enemy from the west and south while Evans and Sarsfield pressed them from the north and west—in short to draw a net round the game.

All that I suggested was punctually performed, but to my inexpressible mortification I received late last night from Wylde a letter dated Bilbao the 13th instant stating that nothing was to be hoped from Espartero, and that unless the Government could send troops to San Sebastian Espartero would not abandon his own plan of campaign, which is one he will not venture, in the first place, to undertake and if he did he would be sure to fail. I went in a towering passion to Calatrava, to Mendizabal and to the Minister of War where I was till 3 o'clock this morning (nothing shall be lost that can be gained by any exertion of mine); they all ended by agreeing with me, but I begged to see the whole of the instructions sent to Espartero and I am bound to say that nothing could be better or in more entire conformity to what we had agreed upon three weeks before. I must also add that it appears these instructions had not yet been received by Espartero and I will not therefore entirely abandon the idea of their being obeyed, but I have requested that they shall be repeated and given to me to send—which was agreed to.

I told you just what was the case respecting Evans but I expressed myself ill if I gave you the idea that I thought the Government ought to remove him from his command—so far from it, I have done all in my power to persuade him not to go home, and he is the only man I would at this moment give the command of the army to if I didn't know that every officer in it would be night and day employed in undermining him and securing the failure of whatever he undertook.

Provisions, clothing and money are getting together as fast as possible, but the poverty of the Government and the totally impassable state of the roads have naturally retarded this all important measure, and to undertake any military operations at this season and in a country destitute of resources *for the Queen's army* is not only to risk destruction but to render it inevitable.

Pray do not relax in your friendly exertions for the cause. Your very dry dispatches nos. 2 and 3, as well as the tone of your letters, make me think that some change is *effectuating* in you with respect to Spain, and now or never is the moment to reap the reward of the sacrifices you have made and the worry you have had for the last 3 years.

If the King's Speech contains any complimentary allusion to the good sense of the Spanish people and the prudent conduct of their representatives it will produce an admirable effect here, and tend more than any thing else (I do not say this unadvisedly) to confirm the Cortes in the course they have hitherto pursued.

Will you oblige me by telling Thomson that I only received his letter this morning and I do not answer it till next Saturday as I prefer not writing upon the subject of which it treats by a French courier?[2]

Wylde tells me he sent you a copy of Lord Ranelagh's[3] letter. I think the conduct of that youth in taking part against the King's troops and in favor of ferocious Carlists whose intention it notoriously was to murder and pillage and ravish every thing English in Bilbao deserves to be held up to public indignation.

If I had ventured I would have employed some secret service money upon the business I alluded to in my last, and I would have employed the individual who told you some time ago that he and I did not understand each other,[4] for he did the same kind of thing admirably in Portugal and Mendizabal was very anxious that he should be again employed in a similar way. After conquering his fears I could not overcome his avarice, and as he insisted upon £4,000 which *I* had not the power or the *Spanish Government* the means of giving, the scheme has been abandoned which I am sorry for, as I have abundant information to shew how much something of the kind is *wanted*. There are innumerable waverers waiting for some one to take the initiative with them or to help them to do it for themselves.

There is here a certain Mr. Mackenrot, the correspondent of the Morning Herald. . . .

Notwithstanding what I said to you last time and at the risk of appearing somewhat inconsistent I hope if it is not too late that you will give the moral guarantee of which I wrote a week ago. I am more than ever convinced that until the war is finished we shall not get what we want here. I shall write fully upon this subject next Saturday.

PS. What do you think of Ranelagh's correspondent? It would appear that there is a real or assumed sympathy in their political views.

Received 30 January.

GC/CL/315; Clar. Dep. C.453 (14-21)

[1] 'I expressed to His Excellency my great apprehension of the evils that threatened the Queen's cause, not from General Espartero's want of loyalty, for of that there is no reason to doubt, but from his incapacity as a general, and his total want of moral courage to face the difficulties of the responsible position in which, by a succession of errors, he had placed himself.' (V to P, 21 Jan. 1837, no. 25, FO 72/477.)

[2] The letter from Thomson was on commercial affairs. V was convinced that the French Government was determined to prevent the satisfactory completion of Anglo-Spanish commercial negotiations, hence his unwillingness to entrust a commercial despatch to a French courier.

[3] Ranelagh was a British officer who joined the Carlists in October 1835, but left for Italy in January 1837.

[4] Büschenthal.

305   Palmerston to Villiers, 25 January 1837

Stanhope Street. *Encloses a letter from Easthope.*

Enclosure: Copy, John Easthope (Morning Chronicle Office) to Palmerston, 21 January 1837, in favour of W. Edward Murta, who is replacing S. Derbishire as Chronicle correspondent in Madrid.

Copy.

GC/CL/1293

306   Palmerston to Villiers, 26 January 1837

Copy. Foreign Office. I should like well enough to do what you recommend, and to give the Spanish Government no assistance as to their money affairs until they agree to do what they ought to do about commerce; but on the whole it seems so important to put an end to the war, at least into a better train, that I still do what I can to persuade Goldsmit to advance 3 or 400,000 £s. I saw him indeed on this subject two days ago, and was to have seen him again today, but that he was one of those who come to the office, and finding me engaged with another man did not chuse to wait. He is to come to me again tomorrow. I do not however expect much success, as he seemed disinclined to stir without a positive guarantee from England or France; and I told him that any guarantee from us is quite out of the question.

In the meanwhile this order of the French Government against the importation of provisions into Spain[1] will have a good moral effect, and it shews that the French are convinced that Evans and his coadjutors will very soon succeed in doing practically that which Molé decrees upon paper. I understand this order to mean, 'You will do the thing in spite of us, in less than a month; we will make a virtue of necessity and endeavour to forestall you in the merit of doing it.'

I will let the Gibraltar people accept their orders if I can possibly make out that their cases come within the regulation.

Wylde has been very inadequately rewarded and injustice has been done him, but some other day I shall be able to make compensation to him. I wanted him to be immediately made brevet colonel, but the jealousies of military authorities were too strong for me, and I could only get him for the present the local rank. I am very glad you wrote the dispatch in his praise; it will be of use to him.[2]

We are delighted with the moderation of the Cortes and with their good sense Spain will yet become a Power, and much we need an additional Power like her, as a fresh element in the balance of Europe. It is manifest that no firm reliance can be placed on France.

Our opening will probably be stormy, but the relief of Bilbao will render the attacks on foreign affairs easy to be dealt with.

The pamphlet[3] is really excellent and will produce a great effect.

GC/CL/1294

[1] The French Government prohibited the export of foodstuffs, clothing and other goods from the departments bordering Spain. This was after both the British and the Spanish Governments had made representations on the matter. (Granville to V, 10 Feb. 1837, PRO 30/29/422.)

[2] V to P, 8 Jan. 1837, no. 7, FO 72/477.
[3] Published as *The Policy of England towards Spain*.

307 Palmerston to Villiers, 27 January 1837

Copy. Foreign Office. I have seen Goldsmit today and I think that if the Cabinet agree to the moral guarantee he will advance the £400,000. By the moral guarantee I mean an agreement by which if the Spanish Government failed to pay the interest, the English Government should have an acknowledged right to compel them to do so, and should undertake to him that they would exercise that right.

I have no time to say more.

GC/CL/1295

308 Villiers to Palmerston, 28 January 1837

Madrid. Private. I am afraid you will be sick of my schemes for helping this country, but I really believe that the one I send you today contains more than average elements of success.[1] As its projector[2] is about to go to London and to present himself to you I have not thought it necessary to develop it more in my dispatch. . . .

In the mean while the termination of the war must not be forgotten and until that is effected no speculation is secure. The Government are greatly embarrassed about Espartero for the reasons I have stated in former letters, but if he fails now in reinforcing Evans I think they will be willing, because more able, to remove him. Very little is wanted to put an end to the contest in the present demoralized state of the faction. If the temper of the House of Commons is good do you think that 1,500 or 2,000 troops could be sent, or such a batch of Marines spared from Lisbon as might occupy San Sebastian and Pasages so as to leave Evans with 10,000 men to finish[3] the war off his own bat? He would do it easily, and it would be a very glorious termination for us here. The principle of direct intervention we got over at Bilbao, and I hope that its application will not be found an insurmountable difficulty. If you are able to render any service to this country pray give me timely notice in order that I may turn it to account upon commercial matters, with respect to which I am more anxious than ever in consequence of the conduct and speeches of the French Government. The bank and the treaty would be ample and most sweet revenge.

The Government are very desirous that Büschenthal should go to the Carlist camp in order to promise pensions and the recognition of their rank to the different chiefs who there is every reason to believe only wait for such a guarantee in order to be found wanting when Don Carlos calls, but the Government have no funds, and Büschenthal, thinking he may possibly get hung for his pains, is desirous of leaving £4,000 or at least £3,500 to his widow, and he would insist upon receiving it before he crossed the frontier. Mendizabal says he did marvellous good service in the same way to Don Pedro, and he has no fear of trusting him upon such a job. Would you be disposed to advance such a sum for secret service? If so, will you let me know it by the earliest opportunity because if Evans advances the panic among the Carlists will be general, and then would be the time when Büschenthal's proposals would meet with a favorable acceuil?

I have written to Thomson upon commercial matters—he must really bear in mind that the Government has as difficult a set of fellows to deal with in the Cortes as an English Minister would have had 50 years ago in the House of Commons upon commercial matters, and they will have little or no support from public opinion and the press. I know there will be difficulties in pledging ourselves by treaty to a reduction of duties, but if we really intend it, some form equally binding upon both parties might be devised in order to keep up an appearance of reciprocity.

The speeches of Molé and Guizot[4] have produced a bad effect here and have dispirited the Queen's party rather—they are the only favorable events that have happened to the Carlists for some time past.

Received 6 February.

GC/CL/316; Clar. Dep. C.453 (22-27)

[1] The proposal was for a Joint State Banking and Commercial Company to advance money to the Government and thus ensure the termination of the war. (V to P, 28 Jan. 1837, no. 35, FO 72/477.)

[2] Count Jelski, a Pole living in exile at Madrid.

[3] 'occupy' to 'finish' underlined in pencil, possibly by P.

[4] In speeches on 14 January 1837 in the Chamber both Molé and Guizot criticized the Spanish Government's conduct of the war and the new Constitution in Spain.

309 Palmerston to Villiers, 30 January 1837

Copy. Stanhope Street. I have just received yours of [the] 21st. If my letters and despatches have seemed dry it is because my hour glass has run dry; and when one has no time for half the things one has to do, each thing is likely to be done by halves. What you say of Espartero is unanswerable, and I was quite aware that after the night of Bilbao it would be impossible to remove him. The only thing to be done is to swamp him by some such arrangements as you suggest. As to the employment of Secret Service funds which you advert to, I think it a dangerous course, and our means are too scanty. You never can be sure that you have got Punch even when you have bought him, and uno avulso non deficit alter; and if once a bridge of gold is thrown over the gulph, no man will pass it by any other road.

I shall be glad to have from Mr. Mackereth[1] any proofs he makes against our consul and vice-consul at Lisbon. . . .

I think I shall be able to manage the matter with Goldsmit, but there are many difficulties in the way.

PS. I suppose it would be quite impossible to persuade the Spanish Government to let us send them a Commander in Chief.

GC/CL/1296

[1] *Recte* Mackenrot.

310 Villiers to Palmerston, 4 February 1837

Madrid. Private. I am very glad you have spoken to Goldsmith and that he appears inclined to let himself be persuaded. If he consents it may be the salvation of things here, for great as the exertions of the Government are they will not be sufficient to put an end to the war without some additional help. Provisions, clothing and a little pay are got together with immense difficulty but not in amount sufficient to enable active operations to be commenced although very burdensome to those who have to contribute. Nothing is done—people are disgusted—and the Government can't screw out any more from the country. In the mean while much valuable time is lost and the Carlists are recovering from the blow they received at Bilbao.

Nothing can excuse the apathy or, I suppose, the motives of jealousy which have impelled Espartero and his tutor Oraa to delay sending reinforcements to Evans. I hope however that they have at last been brought to a sense of duty for Espartero has written officially to the Government to say that all the troops Evans stands in need of shall be immediately sent, and Wylde in a letter dated the 25th ultimo tells me that Espartero had given him his honor that so soon as Ribero's division (which had been sent for three days before) arrived that reinforcements to any amount he asked for should be sent to San Sebastian. After giving me some further particulars of a long and confidential conversation with Espartero, Wylde concludes by saying, 'Under these circumstances I am sure you will agree with me that it is infinitely better for the Queen's cause that the command of the army should remain in the hands of a loyal soldier and honest patriot, although his abilities may not be first rate, than in those of perhaps a cleverer officer but who does not possess those qualities in so imminent[1] a degree, and the operations necessary to be carried on to bring this war to a successful termination appear to me to be so simple that it does not require a Napoleon to put them in execution. The only things needful are supplies of all sorts and MONEY—without this last, Espartero cannot enter into the heart of the enemies country or strike a serious blow. Pray therefore move the Government upon this point and support Espartero as with him I can deal but with a new one I should have all my work to do over again.'[2]

I have copied this because it is the testimony of an intelligent witness upon the spot and that it confirms what I have already said respecting the difficulties the Government would experience in removing and replacing Espartero, not that I have any confidence in him unless his work can be cut out for him by others. And this would be done if there was money, for Evans being reinforced (of which a little sooner or later there is no doubt) Sarsfield would take the field and as he cordially cooperates with Evans and that they would have at least 20,000 men between them, Espartero would be compelled to do something, and if he did not it would be comparatively unimportant. My great fear at this moment is that the Carlists should attempt some expeditions into Castille and Aragon—at least it is so clearly the only game for them to play that I cannot but expect they will try it. If they do, Espartero alone will be to blame for it. The Carlist chiefs might at this moment give an expedition of the kind a character which it would not have if Evans was in a condition to be advancing upon them—it would then be a flight and the Pretender would not have ventured to leave himself so bare of troops and the country would have risen to oppose it, but now Espartero and Evans being both from different causes quiescent, it would assume the appearance of a useful military operation. It would not eventually help the Carlist cause, but it would produce a great deal of confusion, and of embarrassment to the Government.

It is quite astonishing how little is now wanted to put every thing right here, and the conduct of the Cortes and the spirit which now animates the nation are solid guarantees that Spain will become a Power as you say. *I* have never had any other opinion, and I am certain if the war were at an end that this country would spring into a Power with the rapidity of magic, and under circumstances which of all others would be the most *useful* and *agreable* to us—*but* if the little that is wanting for the base of all this be not given, it is not yet too late for every thing to go to the dogs. If the House of Commons really understood its own and the country's interest it would *peremptorily invite* you to send here the British standard and 5,000 red coats. I should not care if there was a condition attached that they all were to be back in London before the autumn—the spring would see their work ended.

Should you have any difficulty in letting this Government be furnished with provisions and stores such as salt meat, flour, biscuit and rum instead of the muskets which you have consented to give under the Quadruple Treaty and of which 50,000 are I believe still undelivered? Pray give this your serious consideration. Mendizabal is most anxious for it. I know you could render few greater services to this country and as all these stores are properly naval and might be taken from the Government dépôts it does not seem to me that you would have any great difficulty in allowing them to be furnished *instead* of the arms which we are bound to give and which are already promised. If they were sent for the most part to San Sebastian it would be a means of attracting troops there and securing that Evans should have an ample force under his command. Depend upon it, it would be a great thing to do.

I am glad you approve of the pamphlet[3] but I regret that its publication should have been delayed so long—ten days just before the meeting of Parliament of circulation lost are calculated to mar any good effect it might produce. I hope you will have given it all the shove into the world you could.

PS. Mr. Easthope of course takes the measures he thinks most advantageous for his paper, but he never did a more foolish thing than recalling his correspondent here, Mr. Derbyshire, who is a gentlemanlike man and the only one of the numerous reporters for newspapers that have been at Madrid since I arrived here that I consider worthy of confidence. He knows the country now, speaks the language and is generally liked, and this is the moment when affairs are most critical here and that it is important during the session of Parliament to keep the British public well informed that Mr. Easthope chuses for recalling Derbyshire and replacing him by a man who will have all to learn and who I may very likely not think as trustworthy as the present incumbent. All too as I understand for a paltry wrangle about £40 of expences incurred by Derbyshire in accompanying Narvaez to Andalusia which procured for the Morning Chronicle some of the most interesting letters it has published from Spain.

Received 13 February.

GC/CL/317; Clar. Dep. C.453 (28-35)

[1] C.453 has 'eminent'.
[2] Wylde to V, 25 Jan. 1837, enclosed with V to P, 4 Feb. 1837, no. 39, FO 72/478.
[3] See also V to Edward Villiers, 4 Feb. 1837, Clar. Dep. C.467.

311   Palmerston to Villiers, 10 February 1837

Copy. Foreign Office. I have such a cold in my head I can hardly see to write, but I have seen Goldsmith several times, and he has at last suggested a plan which one should think would do. He was to see Aguilar about it, and send a messenger to Madrid. I do not know whether either of them write by this messenger of mine. The plan is that in return for the £400,000 the Spanish Government should give Goldsmit a certain number of licences for the importation into Spain of cottons and other English goods now prohibited, a moderate duty to be fixed, such as would underbid the smuggler; half the duty to be paid to Goldsmit here in reimbursement of his advance, the other half to be paid in Spain, and to be an additional gain to the Spanish Government. This is very much like a scheme of yours last year. The Spanish Government could not do better than to adopt it.

The pamphlet has had a wonderful success. It is praised by all sides.

GC/CL/1297

312   Villiers to Palmerston, 11 February 1837

Madrid. Private. The King's Speech arrived yesterday. We look upon it here as just *the least taste in life* cold with respect to Spain—un peu pâle as La Tour Maubourg called it although he said so before he was aware that at Paris it is considered of a couleur tres prononcée. The no mention of France was sufficient to arm against you the vanity of Frenchmen for I believe they would prefer being abused to not being taken notice of, and such being the case, it would have been easy and desireable to have warmed up the Spaniards and encouraged them in the prudent course they are now pursuing by $\frac{1}{2}$ a dozen words of praise bestowed upon the Cortes. However I have no doubt that opportunities for saying something of the kind will be given you before long, and I am sure it will not be thrown away here.

The sending these two military Deputies to the army is a good plan[1] —they are very intelligent men—well acquainted with the position of the Government and the feelings of the country as regards the operations of the army—and in their double capacity of Royal Commissioners and Deputies they will speak with weight, as well as enable the Government to judge of the real condition and spirit of the army more correctly than they have yet been able to do from the dispatches of the generals.

I asked officially to have an interview with them before their departure which was readily acceded to. I explained how much my Government had done and how much might still be expected from England if Spaniards were but true to themselves. I represented that our cooperation and every circumstance connected with the British Legion afforded constant grounds for attack against the Government by the Tories, and that it was therefore the duty of every loyal Spaniard to lighten the burden of the Government in Parliament by contributing to render our cooperation effective, as success would fully justify our measures in support of the Queen's cause—that this could only be secured by reinforcing Evans in a manner that should enable the Legion to distinguish itself and our naval forces to take an active part as they had done at the siege of Bilbao. I added that in thus serving the English Government they would best advance their own cause for it was from San Sebastian alone that the war could be carried on with a chance of final success by closing the French frontier—by enabling the Bastan to rise in favor of the Queen—thus opening the road for the cooperation of Evans with Sarsfield when both advancing upon the heart of the enemy's country they would not only give protection to the inhabitants who are exhausted by the war and desirous at any price of its termination, but they would render it possible for Espartero to come out of Bilbao with the large force now under his command, which he will never be able to do so long as the numerous defiles and passes through which he would have to move are occupied as they now are and that the attention of the enemy is not drawn off to other points. The Deputies agreed with me entirely and as I took care to mix up a great deal of general and European politics in all I said, I saw that I raised the importance of their mission greatly in their own eyes. I have given you an account of this in a private letter rather than in a dispatch lest my language about Evans and the Legion might be displeasing in High Quarters.[2]

Although I never believe in any thing here but that which is actually accomplished I can hardly permit myself to doubt that Evans will at last be reinforced, and if he is I shall take some credit to myself for it, as I have never left the Ministers quiet day or night for a month past upon the subject. I only hope that the said Evans when he does get the troops he said would be sufficient for his purpose will not disappoint us.

As you said that the moral guarantee affair was to be settled with Goldsmid on the 30th in one way or the other and that I have heard nothing from you or the Government from Aguilar upon the matter since, I am afraid that Isaac is not to be hooked with such a bait. I hear too that the Ricardos are likely to make a difficulty about giving up the securities they hold which may account for Goldsmid's unwillingness. If so, Mendizabal will have himself alone to thank for it, as he has alienated the Ricardos and Ardouin in the same manner that he has every one else of the same class who was inclined to serve the cause by his want of good faith and the precipitate and passionate manner in which he acts when he encounters the smallest opposition to his will. He ought never to have quarrelled with these men, because it is much easier to make those who are already up to the chin in Spanish affairs advance a few steps further than to induce new men to enter into them. Mendizabal during his first Ministry made a joint stock purse of the Spanish treasury, his own private property and the House of Carbonnel—he managed them in his own scrambling way and they all went to the dogs together—when he left office in May last

Carbonnel was on the eve of bankruptcy and Mendizabal asked Ardouin to lend him £20,000 which the latter declined and the former has never forgiven. The consequence is that Spain has lost some very zealous and friendly financial agents at a moment when it is of most importance to have money—without some supply from abroad we cannot hope to see the war ended for the extraordinary exertions that have been made during the last month cannot be sustained, and all the money that has been scraped together is forestalled revenue for the next six months.

PS. Since writing the above Captain Maitland, Lord John Hay's 2d in command, has arrived here on leave of absence. He informs me that 6,000 troops were to arrive on the 6th instant at San Sebastian. He saw them about to embark on the 4th at Portugalete. He says also that Evans is so short of provisions that he is afraid he will be unable to move notwithstanding the arrival of the long-wished for reinforcements. If you can consent to the proposition of furnishing victuals instead of muskets they would now be of inestimable value.

Received 21 February.

GC/CL/318; Clar. Dep. C.453 (36-41)

[1] Luján and Del Valle left Madrid on 6 February, the former to go to the headquarters of General Espartero, the latter to General Sarsfield.
[2] i.e. to the King.

313 Villiers to Palmerston, 18 February 1837

Madrid. Private. The courier from England is not arrived and I have therefore nothing to answer and little that is worth communicating.

We are all on the tenterhooks of expectation to see whether the army, or rather the generals, will be pleased to do any thing, and I always tremble for events which are dependent on them. Evans has now got the reinforcements he desired and even more than he stated to be indispensably necessary.[1] In his letter to me he said that 3 or 4,000 men would be sufficient to execute the work he had to do—he has now at least 6,000 in addition to the Legion and the Marines and Artillerymen. I have been working hard, and I hope with success, to secure his being well supplied with provisions, and if all the letters that Mendizabal has received from the consul at Bayonne and the Corporation of San Sebastian are not lies the troops will be amply provided for. Unluckily the north-west wind appears to have set in and at this time of year it is capable of lasting six weeks during which no vessel can leave Bayonne or Socoa—this is an additional reason for taking possession of Irun and securing the land communication with France. Captain Maitland who has arrived here with Lord John Hay's answer to the President of the Cortes[2] says there ought to be no difficulty whatever in taking Fuentearabia, Irun and Hernani—veremos.

Sarsfield, having got the money[3] and provisions he stipulated for as the condition of his taking the field, now appears to consider that his force is insufficient although he had agreed to march to Oyarsun and meet Evans there. The idea of the defiles and mountain passes through which they will have to march appears to cow them all.

We continue of course much dissatisfied with Espartero but the same difficulties exist about removing him. Calatrava told me yesterday that if the Government were strong enough to carry such a measure he would immediately set about looking for a foreign general to command the army, but he is quite right in thinking that unless such a general was accompanied by a foreign force, as in the case of the Duke of Wellington, which would serve as a pretext for taking a step so derogatory to the national conceit, it would be unwise to attempt it, for whatever might be the prestige of such a general's name, if he came single-handed it would be insufficient to get him well received by the army, and whatever his talents might be he would find himself thwarted and betrayed. We must therefore, until you send us out 10,000 red coats, make the best of the very bad materials we have. Seoane's determination of going to the army for the purpose of acting as Espartero's adviser is one of the best things that could have happened. He is an excellent officer—very discreet but very determined, and Espartero has a personal regard for him, and will never be jealous, for Seoane refuses all commands and promotions or even pay. The only drawback to his undertaking is that his good sense and high-mindedness will be wanting in the Cortes, and that as he has an open wound and a paralyzed leg the journey may cost him his life.

Captain Maitland has been very well received here—he is to be presented to the Queen this evening. She has given him the Order of Charles III and on Monday 40 or 50 Deputies of all shades of opinions give him a dinner in order to shew that whatever differences they may have among themselves they are all united in gratitude to England. They say that this is the first living specimen of cooperation they have caught at the capital and they will not let him go without taking back to his countrymen the assurance of the feelings which animate all parties in Spain towards them. Pretty demonstrative this is of the Tory assertion that English influence in Spain has totally declined. Apropos to that I am sorry that among my proofs to the contrary[4] you cut out the probability of Englishmen being allowed the free exercise of their religion and the favorable disposition towards some commercial arrangements which exists. I am sorry too that you introduced Lyndhurst's name because I particularly avoided alluding to individuals, and it is therefore personal to go out of my way to speak of Lyndhurst with whom I have for many years lived upon terms of intimacy and with whose politics I, here in Spain, have nothing to do.

I say this because I conclude the authorship will not long remain a secret, as I have heard that the Poodle[5] has somehow nosed it out.

The project for reforming the Constitution is ready and will be presented forthwith to the Cortes—it has one great advantage over the Constitution of 1812 that it consists of only 84 articles whereas the latter had nearly 400. I don't foresee the probability of much opposition, and I think the new Constitution will be such as can give no cause for alarm to foreign countries and will be likely, under the blessing of Divine Providence, as Mr. Plumtre would say, to take root and flourish in Spain.

Received 27 February.   GC/CL/319; Clar. Dep. C.453 (42–47)

[1] Six thousand men arrived at San Sebastian on 7 February. (V to P, 18 Feb. 1837, no. 56, FO 72/478.)
[2] Captain Maitland was sent by Lord John Hay to thank the Queen for the decorations given to officers and men of the British squadron, and to reply to the letter of congratulation from the Cortes. (V to P, 11 Feb. 1837, no. 52, FO 72/478.)
[3] Twenty thousand pounds. (V to P, 18 Feb. 1837, no. 56, FO 72/478.)
[4] In the pamphlet *The Policy of England towards Spain*.
[5] Frederick Gerald Byng.

314 Palmerston to Villiers, 23 February 1837

Copy. Foreign Office. Our majority this morning exceeded our expectations. . . .

I had a letter today from Evans, saying that he meant to begin last Saturday, or if the weather was unfavourable a day or two later. He does not seem to reckon much upon the cooperation of the Spanish generals, and therefore his calculations may turn out right. He is very grateful to you for the assistance you have given him in getting reinforcements. If he is able to do anything brilliant or useful the Spanish Government will be better able to get money.

I really begin to hope that the course of this summer will bring this war to a close. If once things take a decidedly favourable turn, facilities will spring up on all sides. Those who do not want aid can always get assistance in abundance. It is only the needy man that cannot find a friend. One friend however Spain has found in her hour of need and that is England; and I trust that she will long continue to remember the good services we have done her.

By long I mean at least 12 months which is an eternity for national gratitude; but which would give us time to settle our various relations with Spain in a satisfactory manner.

GC/CL/1298

315 Villiers to Palmerston, 25 February 1837

Madrid. Private. I received together on Monday last your letters of the 30th ultimo and the 11th instant. I don't know why your first was so long delayed.

Mendizabal won't hear of Goldsmid's proposal for the licences and in this instance I think him right—he could not do it or any thing else which affects the revenue without the consent of the Cortes, and he asks whether it would be worth while to create all the uproar which the admission of a small quantity of British manufactures would produce, just as much as if he had signed our treaty, and perhaps to get beaten, and put Catalonia in a rage, and render our future negotiations more difficult—all for £400,000—to be negotiated and repaid in a manner not very respectable for a Government which pretends to have some remains or some hopes of credit. It must therefore be abandoned. Mr. Goldsmid seems to have very little pluck, and not to be fit therefore for the financial agency of a country in a state of civil war—he ought to risk something for he knows that if things turn out well his gains would be enormous. He should remember what a few bold men did for Don Pedro when the chances were 500:1 against him, and remember what they did for themselves as well. He has no right to look for security as if he was dealing with a settled country, and for all the advantages which the varying events of a civil war give to the capitalists who are concerned in them. I fear that this connexion with Goldsmid which Mendizabal established in a passion will have little other result than disgusting such powerful and enthusiastic friends to Spain as the Ricardos and Ardouin and obtaining the abortive good wishes of Mr. Isaac Goldsmid.

Calatrava shewed me Aguilar's dispatch reporting various conversations he had had with you upon commercial matters and urging upon his Government the necessity of doing something to satisfy public opinion in England. Calatrava feels it, but believe me as long as Mendizabal is in office no wish of ours will ever be attended to, and in this case he acts *upon principle.* He says there is no advantage in obliging one's friends because friends ought not to require *that sort of thing,* and that as for England she has sufficient political motives for upholding the Queen's cause without requiring commercial sacrifices from Spain. These *principles* he emits in a torrent of professions that he is going to do all we want, but I *know* he is playing us false and assuring the Catalans that *he* will never sacrifice them to England.

I forced him the other day into an appointment in order to discuss the treaty, and he then told me he had four *bases* to propose—the 1st to postpone indefinitely any act of navigation (a good idea of a *basis*), the 2d was to admit English manufactures into Spain at 20 and 25 per cent, the 3d to admit Spanish produce into England at the same duties, and the 4th a guarantee by England for 4 millions sterling. It is useless reporting to you what my answer was, but he was very indignant at my refusing to send off a courier with these brilliant propositions as he called them, and he said he should do so himself notwithstanding my remarks that the English Government had already refused to entertain a similar but much more favorable project in which there was no mention of his 1st and 3d bases, and the guarantee for a loan was 2 instead of 4 millions.

Of course he has sent no courier as the whole was only one of his impudent schemes for gaining time. Calatrava can't bear him and feels that his tricks discredit the Government and expose them every day to defeat in the Cortes, but in the present circumstances of the country he is like many other evils unavoidable. Calatrava is placed with respect to Mendizabal as the partners in Marsh's Banking House were to Fauntleroy—they knew they ought to be bankrupts and that they were kept going by some means they were not well acquainted with but which they felt they had better not ask Fauntleroy about. So it is with Mendizabal. Spain has long been unable to keep her engagements, but she must pay her army and Mendizabal cheats every body, leaves all the employés to starve or steal, robs the hospitals and Mont de Pieté, and forestalls the next year's revenue—but his colleagues *make as if* they didn't see all these crimes (and, as an atrocious abuse of power, they can really be called by no other name) until some lucky turn comes, and the Government can depart from the wickedness it has committed and do that which is lawful and just.

Calatrava is I am sorry to say seriously ill, and if any thing happens to him I should look upon it, next to a total defeat of the Queen's army, as the greatest misfortune that could now befall this country. He is a discreet and honorable man and his conduct in the difficult circumstances of the last 6 months has rendered him a guarantee to foreign countries of order in Spain, as well as of better government in his own.

My letter of the 19th[1] will have replied to the query I have since received from you as to the possibility of Spain admitting a foreign Commander in Chief. I think you will admit the propriety of Calatrava's reasoning upon the subject, though nothing would please him more than to do it, as he says the country is now, just as during the war of independence, in a state of subjection to the intrigues and incapacity of the military chiefs who eat up the land and are dreaded by everybody except the enemy. Calatrava was the Deputy of Cortes who first proposed giving the Command in Chief to Lord Wellington, and he would now pursue a similar course if he dared, i.e. if public enthusiasm was as great and public opinion as unanimous now as that time. Had you any body in your eye to send out when you made the suggestion? It might be well to know in the event of circumstances making such a measure practicable. I have never said a word upon the subject to anybody, but supposing that this Government wished to give Wylde the command of a division with the corresponding rank in the Spanish service would the Horse Guards object?

I believe I told you in my last letter that a certain number of Deputies of all shades of opinion intended to give a public dinner to Captain Maitland in order to mark their gratitude to England. I tried to fight off dining there lest my French colleague should as usual represent my conduct here as revolutionary—but I found my refusal would be an offence so I accepted the invitation. Upon my health being drunk the spirit moved me to make a speech, and as I am probably the first foreign minister who ever addressed a meeting of Deputies in Spanish, and that what I said took the fancy of the audience it had a marvellously good effect. It has likewise taken with the public, and I had the satisfaction last night of hearing myself hawked about the streets though at *rather a low price*—a dos quartos[2]—El Embajador de Inglaterra—a dos quartos—resounded through Madrid, but it was the whole put for the part, the *Embajador* for the *discurso*. I send you a report which appeared in the newspapers, not because it is worth your reading but because I may be attacked for having spoken at all, and that you may see I said nothing that any body has a right to be offended at.[3]

I have spoken to Mr. Macenrot and invited him to give me his information respecting the consular department at Lisbon. . . .

The reformed Constitution is deserving of all praise, and I think it will be well received by the Cortes and the country.[4] What a pity it is that when everything bids fair for the regeneration of Spain all should be held in doubt and danger by the continuance of a war which ought to be so easily finished. Can't you get some friendly M.P. to bully the Government into sending out a few troops with a good general? We would aggregate to him any number of Spanish troops you might chuse, and in that way and by degrees he might get the Chief Command and ensure the tranquillity of the country for a while after he had put an end to the war.

I think you will approve of Calatrava's project of amicably but completely breaking with the Pope.[5] It will be a grand thing for the civil and religious liberties as well as for the revenue of Spain, and if the war is at an end and the measure cannot be turned into a political weapon not a voice will be raised in favor of His Holiness. The only service he has done to this country is to render a rupture with him easy for the Government.

PS. Would there be any objection to establishing a system of office boxes for the safer transmission of dispatches between London and Madrid? They are generally rubbed in the journey between this and Oleron which is always performed on horseback.

If you know where Jelski *puts up* will you have the goodness to send him the enclosed?[6]

Enclosure: A. Mackenrot (Madrid) to Villiers, 25 February 1837, private. The political bias of members of the British consulate at Lisbon.

Received 6 March.

GC/CL/320; Clar. Dep. C.453 (48-57)

[1] In fact, the letter (no. 313 above) was dated 18 February.

[2] C.453 has 'cuartos' (copper coins), which is correct.

[3] GC/CL/388 is a newspaper report of V's speech, with a minute by Stratford Canning dated 28 March 1838. V sent Granville a long defence of his conduct over the dinner since he felt that it would be misinterpreted at Paris. (25 Feb. 1837, PRO 30/29/423.)

[4] A copy of the new Constitution was enclosed with V to P, 25 Feb. 1837, no. 59, FO 72/478.

[5] See V to P, ibid. Diplomatic relations were broken off later in 1837.

[6] Not found. The final sentence is omitted from C.453.

316 Villiers to Palmerston, 4 March 1837

Madrid. Private. The courier from London is not arrived. I have therefore nothing from you to answer, and Calatrava's illness puts a stop to all business. He is out of danger but it will be a long while before he can resume the duties of his office, or attend the Cortes which is very unfortunate just as the discussions upon the Constitution are about to commence and as his word is law with the Deputies. He *ought* to be waited for, but still it is very important to get the question settled— these Cortes dissolved—and the two Chambers elected, for if no great disasters occur we shall then see all the best men that the country can produce elected, and public opinion will be settled and conform itself more than it has yet done to the constitutional system, because it will then more than at any former period have a character of permanence and solidity.

This however like every thing else in the futurity of Spain depends upon the conclusion of the civil war—or rather of that part of it which is still waged in Guipuzcoa, for that being over all the rest dies a natural death—and the nation and the cause have yet to be saved from two great dangers: the insurgents in the North and the Queen's generals. It is only the latter which render the former powerful. During the last month a little decision and dash rather than generalship would have sufficed for their extermination, but just as in the war of independence intrigues, rivalries, and avoiding the enemy are the sole occupations of Spanish generals, and now as then the work will not be finished but by a foreign hand. It is the unvarying nature of the beast—there is no use in preaching or advising, but as we find them we must take them. A very grave question however arises out of the results of this nature of theirs. The consolidation of constitutional government in the Peninsula and the regeneration of Spain depend upon the speedy termination of the war—the war will be everlastingly protracted if its management is left to Spanish generals. A few weeks ago I thought otherwise, not because I changed my opinion of them but because the work they had to do was so simple and easy that I thought they could not help performing it—they have however—it has now become more difficult and my expectations have in proportion diminished.

The question then is whether with reference to the manner in which we have embarked in Spanish affairs, the past sacrifices we have made, the hopes we have of Spain for the future, and the moral engagement that we have almost taken with Europe that the cause we espouse here shall triumph, whether with reference to all these considerations we ought not to do something more—whether we shall not be greater losers politically and commercially speaking by leaving these people to themselves than by at once making the sacrifice necessary to establish that which is on every account so much our interest here. Would not our policy immediately gain moral force in Europe? Should we not be positively stronger when we had Spain as an ally bound to us not by gratitude, for of all ties that is the slenderest, but by necessity and the desire of self-preservation? I think there can be no doubt of it, and the arguments in its favor assume a stronger color if we reflect upon what will be the position of England and above all of the Whig Government if during the next summer the Carlists again descend from their mountain holds to carry the war through the country, and again place in doubt and danger all that is upon the verge of being beyond their reach. When I talk of the sacrifice we should make I mean such an expedition as Mr. Canning sent to Portugal—6,000 men under a good general to which might be added here any number of troops you might chuse to require, and of as good troops as any in the world. They want but to be well commanded and if 25,000 men were thus placed under the orders of an English general the whole would be essentially English and the military and political results don't require to be expatiated upon, but I should look upon them as certain.

If you grant the expediency of such a measure you will perhaps deny its practicability, and upon that I must of course be silent, but I repeat what I say in the pamphlet that I wish some friendly M.P. would give you an opportunity of feeling the pulse of the House of Commons upon this very important question—there is so much analogy between the state of things here now and during the war of independence that I think old associations might not be appealed to in vain. Should all this be impossible, would it in your opinion and Lord Granville's be hopeless once more to tâter le terrain with our neighbours? Circumstances have changed in France within the last two months and many things wear a very different aspect there now to what they did in December, while events here must, if any thing can, have undeceived Louis Philippe as to the state of opinion in Spain and the little fear he need have of being obliged to send his troops beyond the Ebro if once he decided upon allowing them to crush the war in Biscay.

The victory at Bilbao paralyzed all the petty factions in the remotest parts of the country—what would not 10,000 French troops and the tricolor flag do? Where are the Carlists who would make a fight when their Pretender was gone, their chiefs *amnestied* and their army dispersed?

If the expedition to Constantina should not take place—if the spirit of indiscipline which seems spreading in the French army ought to be met by occupation—if Louis Philippe despairing of Northern Alliances should wish again cordially to unite with us—Harispe with a good division might be suffered to cross the Pyrenees, and I believe that Louis Philippe would kill two birds with one stone. He would secure moderate government in Spain, and he would do more to set himself right with public opinion at home and to restore the prestige of the Royauté de Juillet than any thing else he has done within the last four years. In his place I should rejoice at so cheap and so easy an opportunity to *fausser* all the attacks and charges that are made now and not without apparent reason. A few French troops could cow the Carlists completely, and give all these recreant generals of the Queen courage, while the assistance being afforded by France conjointly with us and under the Quadruple Treaty would shew to the French nation and to Europe that our alliance is itself again, and that their hopes of our disunion and weakness must be abandoned.

Two months ago I should have felt the inutility of making these remarks about France but as a change in her policy is possible and that possibilities should not be excluded from political considerations I could not refrain from once again *réchauffé-ing* the arguments I have so often before submitted to you.

It is not fair to judge Evans without knowing the motives of his present strange conduct but with the unreasoning public he is damaging the English name and fame. He was so loud in his demands for assistance, and so confident in his promises of striking an important blow, declaring himself independent of other generals, etc., etc., that his present inactivity makes him appear very small. The fact is that he cannot help looking upon himself as the Great Captain of the Age, and fancying that he is the Duke of Wellington, that that squinting little boy Don Sebastian[1] is Napoleon and that if he moves from San Sebastian it is to fight the Battle of Waterloo. All of them very great errors.

Received 13 March.

GC/CL/321; Clar. Dep. C.453 (58-65)

[1] Commander-in-Chief of the Carlist army.

317 Palmerston to Villiers, 10 March 1837

Stanhope Street. I have no time to write today, as I must go down to the House to defend you and myself against Mahon.[1] I wish my English speech may be as good as your Spanish one.

I had nobody in my eyes as a general to command the Spanish army, but we could easily find one if the Spaniards would accept. I should be delighted if they would give a command to Wylde. They would do a very wise thing.

Copy.

GC/CL/1299

[1] P's defence of his policy in Spain on 10 March 1837 contained no reference to V, an omission which V described to his brother as 'both shabby and unfriendly'. (*Parl. Deb.*, 3rd Series, XXXVII, 256-71, 10 Mar. 1837; V to Edward Villiers, 25 Mar. 1837, Clar. Dep. C.467.)

318 Villiers to Palmerston, 11 March 1837

Madrid. Private. A few hours after the departure of the last courier I received your letter of the 23rd ultimo. The majority of 80 is a great triumph. . . .

I fear that my correspondence from hence is again falling back into the black-letter epoch. Military and therefore as usual political prospects are sombre, and we know by experience how rapidly bad becomes worse in this land of passion and intrigue. I can't undertake to explain what nobody understands—the inactivity of the generals. I can only report that which takes place, and it is the same that I have had to report a dozen times before—disappointment succeeds hope and then come fear and rage. Every body—Government and public —made exertions to have the success at Bilbao turned to account. Evans got all he wanted—Sarsfield all he asked for—and if Espartero didn't likewise it was because he appeared to be wilfully unreasonable in his demands, and to make that which he knew to be impossible the sine qua non conditions of his moving, but if some screw had not been loose in his politics (not his loyalty, of that there is no reason to doubt) or his courage, he would in the course of nine weeks have left Bilbao and gone somewhere else to eat his 40,000 rations a day—but not one of them have stirred. First they hadn't provisions enough—when *they* arrived they hadn't troops enough, and when the troops came the rations were short again. Then the three were to cooperate with each other, but each wanted the other to begin, which made each think that the other wanted to compromise him and leave him en las astas del toro as they say here. In short it has been enough to drive one mad with rage and disappointment, for all three generals have over and over again failed in their engagements and their own offers both to the Government and themselves. Sarsfield is the one I distrust most—I believe he is mad, and in his lucid intervals I doubt his loyalty. Espartero is a moral coward and does not dare risk operations which he knows he has not the abilities to direct. Evans is the best of the three and the only one of whom I have hopes, but doubting is more his forte than acting. I have a letter however from him of the 4th written in great spirits and promising great things as soon as he gets 2 or 3 fine days. May the sun shine upon his vows! For some military feat is urgently wanted to stop the progress of discontent, and restore the calm which the Cortes impelled by the public are beginning to lose, and which it is so essential they should bring to the discussion of the Constitution.

This state of things is being exploited by different parties with devilish activity—the Moderados fancy their time is come for again *saving the country* as they did under Isturiz, which salvation would probably end in a republic or a federal division of the country—and the anarchists are appealing to the fears of the public and representing the inaction of the army as the natural result of the incompetency of the Government. Calatrava's absence unfortunately gives them beau jeu—he was the only man of the Government who gave it stability or to whose guidance the Cortes were willing to submit.

The execration that Mendizabal is held in by all parties cannot much longer be restrained within bounds, and I do not wonder at it for destruction of whatever exists seems his only occupation or pleasure. This tithe abolition measure of which I give you an account in my dispatch today[1] is pregnant with mischief both to the country and the liberal cause and is one of the most wanton acts of mischief that even Mendizabal has yet committed. It would require all the vigor of a well established Government in order to abolish tithes with safety, and all the local data and administrative knowledge that this Government has not in order to have a chance of supplying the deficiency the measure will create.

From all I can learn Goldsmid appears to be acting very shabbily, promising just enough to prevent this Government from establishing relations with any other capitalist—doing absolutely nothing to help them, but laying by snugly without committing himself during the storm in the hopes of reaping what he has not sown if ever fine weather should return, but I suppose there is attraction in circumcision and Mendizabal therefore clings to Mr. Isaac G.

As you are now todo poderoso with this brilliant majority in the House of Commons can't you do any thing for us in the way of men, money, or victuals? We want a coup de main sadly, and if it is given now it may be an economy in the end.

I have just received the Quarterly Review which I consider very satisfactory in re my pamphlet as shewing how little they find to say against it—however I don't intend to let that little pass unnoticed.[2]

PS. My bit of a speech at the dinner has had success in the provinces and, absurd though it may appear that important consequences should spring from such a trifling cause, I hear that even the Exaltados say that they ought not to falsify such flattering predictions or impair the opinion which they suppose is entertained in England of the importance of Spain.

Received 20 March.

GC/CL/322; Clar. Dep. C.453 (66-71)

[1] V to P, 11 Mar. 1837, no. 65, FO 72/478.

[2] The *Quarterly Review* (cxv, Feb.—Apr. 1837) reviewed *The Policy of England towards Spain* on pp. 281-96. The reviewer used the pamphlet to launch a general attack on the foreign policy of the Whigs.

319   Palmerston to Villiers, 16 March 1837

Copy. Stanhope Street. It is very natural that you should urge us to send 10,000 men to Spain, and I have no doubt that such a force gathering the Spaniards like a snowball around it would decide the war; but go through in your mind all the various proceedings necessary for the execution of such a measure, and you will see that it is impossible. We have not the men disposable; at most could we spare 5 or 6,000, money would be required, votes of Parliament, etc., all of which in the present situation of domestic affairs, and in the relative position of parties at home would present insurmountable difficulties. I hope however from what we hear today that the operations commenced by Evans on the 10th have been supported by Sarsfield and Espartero and have been attendant with important results. Would there be any use in sending another officer like Wylde, and to act in the same capacity with any other Spanish corps? Would the Spanish Government like it, and would it be acceptable to the army? This we could easily do, and a good practical officer might be of use to Sarsfield or to Espartero.

Our debate on Spanish affairs went off very much in the way described in the pamphlet. Carlos was thrown over by Peel; the treaty was admitted to be binding; a mere doubt was thrown out whether we have not gone beyond its binding engagements, but the point was not insisted upon; and Mahon candidly said that his reason for not making his speech till after the House had actually gone into the Committee of Supply was in order to prevent a resolution of approval from being carried by a large majority. Grove Price and Mahon bore testimony to the merits of the pamphlet by the bitterness with which they attacked it.

Our majority last night was small. . . .

PS. Count Jelski could do nothing here, and is gone back to Paris. In fact the Spanish Government seem to employ too many financial agents at the same time. It is like one man sending two agents to bid against each other for him at an auction.

GC/CL/1300

320 Villiers to Palmerston, 18 March 1837

Madrid. Private. God is great! And the army has moved,[1] which is a prodigious, and as I have for some time past thought, an unattainable object. There is not much done yet to be sure, and the weather which never misses an opportunity of shewing its Carlist predilections will probably now prevent any more being effected—for Evans will not be able to move his artillery if the rain cuts up the roads—Sarsfield won't pass the mountains if it snows[2]—and if it blows provisions can't get by sea to Espartero. However all three generals are fairly unkennelled, and as neither of them liked to be the first in going out, so I hope there will be an equal disinclination to be the first in turning back.

This onward movement in the North has stopped a similar operation in the public spirit at Madrid. Los Señores revolucionistas are calmer, and good news will prevent much nonsense. The absence of Calatrava however is irreparable—he is the only man who exercises just that kind of influence which the ignorant but docile Cortes stand in need of, and in this most important question of reforming the Constitution upon which the future welfare of the country and the prospects of liberal government depend, the Deputies are all like hounds at fault before the huntsman arrives, tossing up their noses, and tearing wildly about without a chance of hitting off the scent. I don't like the turn that things are taking in the Cortes, but it is impossible to wait for Calatrava who is no better, and it is very difficult to replace him as President because it would break up the Ministry, and that would open a door to all sorts of ambitions and intrigues. Men are not disinclined to pull well with or to tolerate the Ministers who have borne the brunt of office since the revolution of La Granja, but if others are to be selected then all think themselves equally fit, and we shall have to endure the usual course of turbulent opposition with its consequences.

Almodovar is ill too, and the Under Secretary likewise, so that all business with the Foreign Office is at a standstill (which does not produce any great change to be sure) and Mendizabal and an insane Minister of the Interior[3] are the only ones that are up, but they are *alarmingly well* and take the opportunity of playing the devil in other Departments as well as their own. After all this can any body say that Spain is a difficult country to govern?

I had very little idea that my bit of a speech would have produced such a hubbub in the political or rather in the newspaper world, but it does not seem to me that I said any thing new or any thing that the whole world was not aware of when the Quadruple Treaty was signed. Spain *is* necessary to the West against the East of Europe—the necessity of such a confederation is no work of ours—Russia denounces vengeance against whatever is revolutionary, and she is pleased to consider France and England and Belgium in that light, and she either enlists or forces Austria and Germany and Italy into her views. Are we not to look out for support where we can get it—geographical if not political? And are we to neglect availing ourselves of occasions to promote our own interests? The Holy Alliance know perfectly well that if the tranquillity of the Peninsula can be established, the thrones of the two Queens consolidated, and moderate government secured here, that not a shade of difference would then exist between England and France and that the union they so much dread would then recover all its original vigor. They know all this—they do all they can to prevent it—and our silence upon it would neither deceive nor propitiate them.

Wylde laments very much an order sent from the Admiralty to Captains Lapidge and Le Hardy[4] to return to England. . . .

I am very sorry you were not able to do what you wished for Wylde—he is deserving of any reward that could be bestowed upon him. . . .

Received 27 March.

GC/CL/323; Clar. Dep. C.453 (72-75)

[1] See V to P, 18 Mar. 1837, no. 69, FO 72/478.
[2] 'Sarsfield' to 'snows' underlined in pencil, possibly by P.
[3] Pita Pizarro.
[4] W. F. Lapidge, captain of HMS *Ringdove*, and T. P. Le Hardy, captain of HMS *Saracen*.

321 Palmerston to Villiers, 23 March 1837

Foreign Office. We have this morning received Colonel Wylde's account of the unfortunate event of the 16th.[1] It is a sad disappointment after the expectations which the success of the preceding day had inspired. At least however this calamity vindicates Evans from the charge of timidity for not having sooner made a forward movement, because if notwithstanding the reinforcements which he had received before this affair, he still found himself so inferior in numbers to the force which the enemy was able to bring against him, it is evident that it would have been madness on his part to make the attempt before he received those reinforcements. This misfortune seems to be mainly owing to the return of Sarsfield to Pamplona on the 12th, the day after that (namely the 11th) on which he left it. What reason Sarsfield may be able to give for his retreat remains to be seen. He may succeed in accounting for it, but it has been the cause of a great misfortune.

The defeat of Evans does not in a military point of view signify a great deal. The loss on both sides was probably equal; he saved his guns and retains the advanced position on the Ametzagana.[2] But in a moral point of view, it is very unlucky, and will give confidence and spirits to the Carlist party all over Europe.

The great mistake the Spanish Government has made has been not keeping up the Legion in officers and men. A corps that is not recruited; which feels itself gradually dwindling down to a regiment; whose officers see no future prospect before them; and who are suffering daily under privations of all kinds; such a corps *cannot* be animated by that spirit of hope which cheers men on to great exertions. You will say that want of money has been the cause of this, and to that I have no reply.

What is to be done is the question now to be solved; and that can be answered only at Madrid—in London we have done all we are able to do. We have gone to the utmost length of our tether as to Marines, ships, artillerymen, stores, ammunition, etc.

I can understand easily the difficulties felt by the Spanish Government as to its generals. But it has been proved that three generals acting independently and with separate corps at the several angles of a triangle cannot do much against an enemy occupying the centre. Buonaparte shewed this in the campaign of 1814 before the allies entered Paris. With a very inferior force acting from the centre, and even in an open and flat country, he kept in check superior numbers, and beat them one after the other. The Carlists will continue doing the same thing. The proposition may be demonstrated mathematically, that such a central force may always bring a majority to bear on either angle; unless the three were equally active, zealous and of one mind. I am just going down to the House to be crowed over I suppose by Maclean and Mahon and the like.

The best chance of retrieving the bad effect of this defeat would be that the Carlists should make an attack on Evans's lines. He would probably repulse them with as much rout as that which attended his discomfiture.

Copy.

GC/CL/1301

[1] The defeat and partial flight of the Anglo-Spanish army at Hernani. (See copies, Wylde to P, nos. 105 and 106, enclosed with P to V, 23 Mar. 1837, no. 33, FO 72/475.)
[2] A fortified hill taken by Evans and the Legion on 10 March.

322   Villiers to Palmerston, 25 March 1837

Madrid. Private. You must have already known for some time the disaster which befell us at Hernani on the 16th. Bad news always travels fast and I daresay it arrived time enough before the Prorogation for the Tories to congratulate each other in Parliament upon Englishmen having disgraced themselves. That the Legion did so is a melancholy fact. Whether Sarsfield acted with good or bad faith I know not though if he had been active and done his duty it is clear that the enemy he was holding in check would not have dared to leave the road open to him and march off to Guipuzcoa—but even the arrival of these reinforcements is no excuse for the battalion of the Legion which ran away before it was hurt, and threw an irrecoverable disorder into the whole line, Spanish as well as English. The officers did what they could to check it, but the men were without pluck and it was impossible to recover the day. If it had not been for the Marines every thing, artillery, provisions, ammunition, all would have been left behind in the panic.

Evans cannot be blamed for the cowardice of his men. From what I can learn all that can be laid with justice to his charge is having delayed his attack on the 15th for 3 or 4 hours, by which he was unable to finish the whole or nearly the whole of the work at once—not having commenced operations on the 16th till 10 in the morning instead of at daybreak, knowing as he must the importance of time and that reinforcements were likely to arrive (the distances for the Carlists who occupy the centre of the country being all so short) at any moment, when it became clear that he was attacking in earnest a place which the enemy had so much interest in preserving as Hernani—and lastly having allowed money to be distributed to the troops on the 15th when before the enemy—the consequence of which was that the Irish regiment was drunk and would obey no orders, and I fear a good many of them were made prisoners.

I have always thought that much caution was necessary in talking of the Legion—they should be looked upon as Spanish troops recruited by the Spanish Government to which we wish well as countrymen in the service of an ally, but it will not do to stake the national honor upon them, for the original formation of the force, the character of its commander, and the Government they serve all unite to render impossible that discipline without which troops, and English troops in particular, are worthless if not dangerous. We know how the men were collected together and what class of people they are. They came out here to earn a livelihood, and they consider they have not much honor to gain and little disgrace to fear. Evans is a brave man, but deficient in the qualities requisite for a general—he is besides M.P. for Westminster before every thing else, and the thoughts of what will be said of him in England make him nervous and cramp such energy as he possesses, in Spain. This is the reason why he has often compounded with mutiny, and why discipline has never been maintained in the Legion, besides which the Law in England might on his return fall heavily upon him for the hanging or flogging of his countrymen here.

The Government then has of course had its share in the periodical demoralization of the corps by not fulfilling its engagements, and the officers, thinking that the mutiny of the men was a good way of getting their own arrears paid, have never been inclined to check it, and I am afraid they have too often given it encouragement. Still however with all these drawbacks courage is so innate in Englishmen that I never expected them to fail on the day of battle, or that English prestige should have been knocked down as it has been by them. It is a bad job altogether, and as yet I don't know of any thing having been done to put matters right—as I have nothing from Wylde later than the morning of the 17th when he said that he was *trying* to animate Evans and the field officers to get their men into something like order. I have written to Evans with the same object, for Lujan reported he was *inconsolable* and Wylde wrote to me that he was going to resign. I have told him that if he were to do so it would be the greatest blow the Queen's cause had received for it would be the greatest victory the Carlists had gained—that 3,000 facciosos arriving at an unlucky moment should be able to drive him and the Legion (for no one else could keep it together then) to England was an idea not to be tolerated. I wrote to Wylde and Lord John Hay in the same strain. Mendizabal assures me that he has complied with my request of doing so likewise, and that 1,000 troops shall be got together in Galicia and sent to Evans forthwith. In short we have done what we could here to raise their spirits.

A reward should be offered for any one who will bring news of Espartero and the army—the date of his last dispatch was just a fortnight ago and since then nothing has been heard of him except by report. It appears certain however that the Queen's troops have been well received in the enemy's country—that the people have not fled from the towns—that provisions have been furnished by the authorities—and that pretty strict discipline has been maintained. So far so good—it now remains to be seen whether these apparently friendly dispositions arose from the people thinking that the Queen's forces must be irresistible, and that the war must be put an end to, and whether now that Evans has been beaten they may not return to their old ways again. If so Espartero who has been allured on into the enemy's country may find himself in a tremendous scrape either from want of provisions, or from being waylaid in defiles and having his retreat cut off. In short the sky which was pretty clear a fortnight ago looks very lowering just now. The storm *may* blow off but the wind has not yet set in to the right quarter for it.

I don't think that prig Mahon took much by his motion upon Spanish affairs, though from what I can gather of the tone of the debate[1] it appears to me there is no great inclination to help this country more than we have done or are doing. It is a great pity, and I am sure that those who would deny the trifling sacrifice necessary to settle matters here take a very narrow view of the interests of England, not as regards Spain only but Europe—there is no way by which we could so cheaply raise our political power to a greater eminence than we have already attained and that would be an event not only necessary for ourselves but universally useful.

I see that you are going to have a field day upon the commercial relations of England with Spain and I have accordingly sent you today some more letters which I received (at the same time as the one from Cadiz) from British merchants at different places here.[2] I do so for two reasons, first because I know that the Tories are doing every thing to get up a case. I learned yesterday from a private source that one of the principal merchants at Alicante had received a letter from a friend in England (written at the request of BINGHAM BARING who was about to bring the subject before Parliament) begging to know what complaints they had to make upon commercial matters, and particularly against me for any want of official protection or attention to their interests.[3] Now this is so ungentlemanlike and dishonest that it deserves to be shown up though it must of course be done with care so as not to commit my informant. My other reason for sending these letters is that they are the best defence of my conduct. No other minister has received such before in this country, and if you consider that I have done my duty I hope you will make them known—it will be the most satisfactory reply I have at present the means of making to the abuse of the Tory papers which I suspect is attributable to my being considered the author of the pamphlet.

Your speech on the 10th has produced a very good effect here. The part which relates to commercial matters has however been laid hold of by the opposition press with a view to exciting the public feeling against England and this Government which at a moment like the present will increase the difficulty of coming to any arrangement of the question. I send you the article in case you should have time to read it. It is very difficult to treat this subject satisfactorily in the House of Commons for you have two audiences with opposite interests and both should be conciliated. As far as the Spaniards are concerned it would be expedient to disconnect as much as possible our cooperation from commercial considerations, and to point out how much the morality and the revenue of Spain would gain by checking the contraband trade which must always exist under the present prohibitive system, and with such unguardable frontiers and coasts—that the Spanish people must when they turn their attention to the subject see what is most for their own interest and that we ask nothing of which the advantage is not reciprocal, or the injury of any native industry which requires that rational protection we afford to our own. In short if you could give a lecture in Political Economy to Spain in the House of Commons it might help matters here more than official notes will ever do.

In defence of this Government it may with truth be said that a moment of such excitement as a civil war is not a favorable one for any radical change of a system defended by prejudices and fierce passions —it should be remembered how long and arduously Huskisson labored and all the obloquy he was exposed to in *enlightened England* for endeavouring to introduce trifling changes in a system not much better than that which now obtains in this country.

If the Tories quote the treaties of 1810 and 1814 and ask why they have not been fulfilled, they may be asked in their turn why during 16 years of tranquillity in this country when they had to deal with both despotic and constitutional forms of government they never were able to obtain any thing—not even to remedy an act of oppression or injustice to British subjects—whereas the present Government has shewn good will in its feebleness. We have obtained from it the slave treaty—an almost cessation of the piratical acts of the Guarda Costas, and the exemption of British subjects from extraordinary taxation. These are not trifles when the state of the country is considered and the slowness and unwillingness with which the Spanish Government ever does *any thing*.

By this opportunity I send to my brother Edward my answer to the article in the Quarterly Review upon my pamphlet.[4] If you have any time for reading it will you send for it to him? If as I hear Lord Carnarvon is coming out with a pamphlet in reply to mine I shall answer that likewise and the one I send today will not be published until I can kill the two birds with one stone.

Enclosure: Newspaper cutting of a leading article from El Español, *25 March 1837, describing the attitudes of the British Government and Opposition towards Spain.*

Received 3 April.   GC/CL/324; Clar. Dep. C.453 (76-85)

[1] On British policy towards Spain in the House of Commons, 10 March 1837.

[2] V to P, 25 Mar. 1837, no. 74, and enclosures, FO 72/478.

[3] 'at Alicante' to 'interests' underlined in pencil, possibly by P.

[4] The 'Reply' was sent to his brother by the same messenger. (V to Edward Villiers, 25 Mar. 1837, Clar. Dep. C.467.)

323 Villiers to Palmerston, 1 April 1837

Madrid. Private. I yesterday received together your letters of the 16th and 23rd ultimo. My report today is somewhat less gloomy for the public mind is more tranquil upon finding that the disaster at Hernani in a military point of view is not what it was at first represented, and that the great loss sustained by the Carlists[1] prevents their reaping much moral benefit from the event. In short it would signify very little if Evans were in a situation to begin offensive operations again, but I doubt his being able to do so alone with troops he can have no confidence in, and who to a certain degree have lost theirs in him, and I have no expectation that he will be cooperated with to any effectual purpose.

Iribarren who has succeeded Sarsfield[2] is a brave man and much liked by his troops but they do not amount to 10,000 and if he goes by the Bastan and skirts the French frontier in order to effect a junction with Evans (by which something certainly may be done) he will leave Pamplona and all the eastern part of Navarre exposed. I can't say that *I* should hesitate about doing it but I suppose he will. From Espartero I expect nothing except a collecting together of all the troops he can lay hold of in the place where they are least likely to be useful—his love of pottering in a corner and his inability to act upon any plan that he adopts will continue to inutilize an army sufficient in itself if well commanded to put an end to the war. The plan which Wylde has proposed to him is the only one likely to be effective.[3] I have preached and proposed it ever since Cordoba first took the command of the army, feeling as I have always done the truth of what you say concerning the inefficacy of separate corps at the several angles of a triangle against an enemy occupying the centre.

I do not think there would be any advantage in sending another officer like Wylde to act in the same capacity with the other Spanish corps because it would be long before he could acquire that knowledge of the country and the war which have given Wylde so much weight with the Queen's generals, and have induced them to lay aside the jealousy they always feel towards foreigners. A second Commissioner coming out would very likely be regarded as a private tutor by Espartero who might out of obstinacy do just the contrary to what he was advised by El Ingles—however I will consult Calatrava about it, and I hope in a day or two he will be well enough to see me. The Minister of War[4] is still in bed, and talking about *any thing* to Mendizabal is mere waste of time.

I quite agree with you upon the impossibility of sending troops here but the conduct and achievements of 500 Marines on the 16th are sufficient proof of what 5,000 *real* red coats would do here. The war would have been finished on *that day* by us. Public opinion however does not take a right direction upon the subject and there is no use bothering any more about it, but if it were likely to be useful I could shew from all that has happened here within the last 3 months how perfectly borne out I am in all that is advanced in the pamphlet respecting public opinion in Spain, and the state of the war and the little that is necessary to bring it to an end. If I had ordered and arranged the facts myself they could not have turned out more favorably to my assertions.

If there is no political commotion here and the Tories are kept out of office we may perhaps win yet, although the odds in our favor are lowered and notwithstanding the immense difficulty of ever making Spaniards succumb to Spaniards. If Spring Rice was as Spanish as you and I are I still think that a moral guarantee would be possible.

I don't envy you the debate you were going to when you dispatched your messenger on the 23d—being crowed over by Maclean and Mahon is not a pleasant pastime. Evans may thank himself for much that will be said in England—he wrote a dispatch to Espartero on the 16th under his first gloomy impressions and sent a copy of it to the Government which very wisely did not publish it, but in accordance with his cursed practice of putting every thing into the newspapers he gave another copy of it to the correspondents at San Sebastian and they have published to the whole world a dispatch that he would now give his ears not to have written.

Received 11 April.　　　　　　　GC/CL/325; Clar. Dep. C.453 (86-89)

[1] The Carlists were said to have been more numerous and better armed, and also to have suffered heavy losses. (V to P, 1 Apr. 1837, no. 80, FO 72/479.)

[2] As commander of the army of Navarre.

[3] 'Wylde urged Espartero either to come himself to San Sebastian with the greater part of his army, or to send 10,000 men there in order that General Evans, making the Bidassoa the base of his operations and uniting his army with that of Navarre, should be able to move upon the centre of the enemy's country and drive him towards the Ebro.' (V to P, 1 Apr. 1837, no. 80, FO 72/479.)

[4] Facundo Infante.

324　Palmerston to Villiers, 3 April 1837

Copy. Stanhope Street. *Encloses a letter from Lieutenant-Colonel Reid.*

Enclosure: Copy, Lieutenant-Colonel William Reid (Portsmouth) to Colonel Fox, 29 March 1837, private, advocating the concentration of the French and English Legions in order to establish and keep open the direct communication between Bilbao and Vitoria.

GC/CL/1302

325 Palmerston to Villiers, 6 April 1837

Copy. Foreign Office. I send you a memorandum which has been given me by McDougal of the Legion[1]—valeat quantum. He is a good officer and a clever man. The Spanish Government should come without delay to some decision about the Legion and the first thing they should do is to apply to us for a prolongation of the Order in Council permitting British subjects to enlist in the Spanish service. It ought to be continued for two years longer; but it should be done upon a note from the Spanish Government. It is probable that most of the officers and men would re-engage, especially if they were assured of a permanent footing in the Queen's service. Why should she not have an Irish brigade; unless there is anything in the Constitution to prevent it? The Tories will of course try to prevent the renewal of the Order in Council, and the sooner the thing is done therefore, the better.

If there is to be a change here, which I begin to think not likely, it may be as well for the Queen to get this from those who will give it; from Peel and the Duke she would not have it most certainly.

It was to be expected that the disaster of the 16th should produce an unfortunate effect at Madrid; I wish and hope that better things may soon happen, in some degree to repair the evil. All you say about sending 10,000 men is quite true and if it depended upon my single will to do so, and we had the men to send, they should go next week, and they would beyond the slightest doubt decide the war, but these things are impossible, and there is no use in talking about them.

I will attend to what you say on commercial matters, when that subject comes under discussion in the House of Commons.

Tomorrow Mr. Hay takes the Legion and the Marines under his protection.

Macdougal who ought to be a judge of military merit is inexhaustible in praises of Quarter Master General Jochmus of the Legion. . . .

GC/CL/1303

[1] Enclosed with P to V, 6 Apr. 1837, no. 34, FO 72/475.

326 Palmerston to Villiers, 7 April 1837

Copy. Foreign Office. We hear from those who have lately returned from Bilbao that Espartero has done nothing to fortify the place, and has not even destroyed the aggressive works erected by the Carlists.

Would it not be well for him to keep his 20,000 men in health by the wholesome exercise of the spade and pickaxe so as to strengthen the defences of the place?

Docketed: Sent open to Lord Granville to forward.

GC/CL/1304

327   Villiers to Palmerston, 8 April 1837

Madrid. Private. I daresay you would like to put the Durango Decree in execution against me for again mentioning the subject of guarantee to you but as I am not disheartened by my repeated failures so I hope you will not be disgusted at my again returning to the charge, for the proposal I send today is greatly superior to any of its predecessors, and if it can be carried into effect it would be the greatest service that under existing circumstances could be rendered to the Queen's cause. In that cause we are too far embarked and too much compromised to hold back if there is a possibility of advancing, or to refuse to strain a point if it is likely to lead to definitive results.

Aguado is the greatest capitalist in Europe—at least he has a greater command of ready money than Rothschild. He is a Spaniard and thoroughly well acquainted with his own country—his voluntarily coming forward therefore at this moment to offer so large an amount of pecuniary assistance to the Queen's Government is a sign that will not be mistaken by the Carlists of his opinion that their cause is desperate, and for its moral effect I would sooner have nine millions advanced by Aguado than twelve by Rothschild. The latter would be viewed as an ordinary loan transaction, but the latter[1] will be felt from one end of the country to the other as a guarantee of the futurity of Spain. Aguado takes upon himself to obtain the guarantee of France. He is upon intimate terms with Louis Philippe and I see no reason to think that he would without sufficient grounds have made the offer he has, and declared he was sure of the King's consent, and induced Marliani to make the journey here to lay the whole before the Spanish Government, and have written to him during the few days he has been here to repeat his conviction that if no difficulties are made here to the plan it will experience none at Paris.[2] The terms of the loan are honorable[3]—its amount sufficient to relieve the difficulties of the country—it is to be appropriated exclusively to the payment and support of the army till the war is over—and if I had to chuse between it and the armed intervention of France I should not hesitate to give my vote in favor of the loan.

Supposing that Aguado has made no mistake about the guarantee of France,[4] he will advance the money immediately whether the guarantee of England is granted or refused, but he is most desirous to obtain it not only as a greater security to himself, but because he knows the advantage it will be to his country to have the name and power of England associated with its concerns, and that it is important so great a service should not be exclusively rendered by France. The Government is of course far more eager for it than Aguado, for they know all that they owe to England during the last 3 years and Calatrava would bitterly regret that we should have borne all the heat and toil of the combat that France should make an exception to her general rule of hostility and at the eleventh hour render a vitally important service to Spain in which England refused to join. The risk is really trifling—the revenue of Cuba is more than sufficient to bear us harmless, and it would not be without its political importance to us to have such a lien upon Cuba for it would make the inhabitants of that colony feel they must not think of declaring themselves independent—which in other words a little sooner or a little later would mean falling into the clutches of the United States which are lying in wait for Cuba as a tyger does for its prey.

I have no doubt that you will be disposed to view the question with favor but I am afraid that your Colleagues of Treasury and Trade are not benevolently disposed to Spanish things, and all I beg of you is to suspend any adverse decision until Marliani's arrival in London. Hear what Louis Philippe has done and what Aguado will be prepared to do,[5] and then judge whether France should be allowed single handed to render this service to Spain with a chance of ultimate intervention in Cuba, and whether our taking part in the guarantee might not be the best mode of setting to rights our coolness with France upon the subject of Spain—and further that as the termination of the war depends upon money, and the payment of the foreign creditors of Spain depends upon the termination of the war, it would seem that the British Government is justified in taking some steps for the preservation of so large an amount of British property.

I mentioned to you in my last that I had sent to my brother an answer to the Quarterly Review and as he has delayed the publication of it I send today an addition in the form of another appeal to the English public for assistance to Spain with reference to the events which have occurred here during the last three months, and to Peel's speech of the 10th ultimo.[6] It will be no compromise to you as you had an opportunity of declaring that you were not the author of the pamphlet, and if you are able to bring forward the question of the guarantee I think I have stated some facts which will not fail to strike that small minority of reasoners who do not make up their minds before they enter upon an argument.

I am afraid the Legion is past remoralizing—the men all declare that it is not worth while to get themselves hurt for the short time they have yet to serve and if they go into action again I dread a repetition of the disgrace of the 16th. I have written at the request of the Government to beg Evans will use his utmost endeavours to make the whole stay 6 months longer and the best men one year or two, offering a bounty or any arrangement respecting pay that are likely to be most *taking,* but I suppose we shall not succeed, and the moral effect of the Legion's departure will be very bad. I send you the copy of a letter I received from General Seoane this morning upon the subject—he is one of the most sensible rightminded men I have met with in Spain and a good officer. He seems to approve of the plan of campaign which is going to be undertaken, and it may be a very good one, but to me in my civilian ignorance, it looks very like a wildgoose chase.

Enclosure: Copy, General Antonio Seoane (San Sebastian) to Villiers, 1 April 1837, urging a plan for reinforcing Evans, and for a joint offensive by Evans and Espartero against the Carlists. (In Spanish.)

Received 18 April.

GC/CL/327; Clar. Dep. C.453 (90-93)

[1] *Recte* former.
[2] 'it will' to 'Paris' underlined in pencil, with superior 'Q?', possibly by P.
[3] See V to P, 8 Apr. 1837, no. 85, FO 72/479.
[4] That it would involve no difficulty, because Marliani had already secured the unofficial approval of the French Government for a guarantee.
[5] 'Hear' to 'do' underlined in pencil, possibly by P.
[6] Not enclosed with this letter.

328 Villiers to Palmerston, 8 April 1837

Madrid. *Introduces M. Marliani.*   GC/CL/326

329 Villiers to Palmerston, 15 April 1837

Madrid. Private. I have received your letter of the 6th and in the midst of all the disasters here it is a crumb of comfort to learn that you don't think the Tories likely to come in. It always gives poor Calatrava a relapse when he thinks of the possibility of such an event. The Duke of Wellington and Peel would of course not renew the suspension of the Enlistment Act but I fear the Spanish Government is not at this moment in a condition to make the request or at least not to avail themselves of it if it were granted in consequence of their inability to pay the Legion its arrears which is the sine qua non condition of a single officer or man remaining in this country.

The affairs of the Legion almost drive me mad—the despondency of Evans—the shameful robberies of the contractors and pay-masters—the impossibility of getting any accounts—the clamors of the public at the enormous expence of the force—the trickery of Mendiza-bal—the conduct of the Legion on the 16th and the manner in which both officers and men declare their satisfaction at having taken the only effectual means for living to fight another day, are enough to disturb greater equanimity than I possess.

Yesterday I received a courier from Evans in answer to my enquiries on the part of the Government as to the best means of getting the whole Legion to re-inlist[1]—he says that the utmost number which could be induced to remain is 1,500, and that only upon receiving the uttermost farthing of what is due to them together with a fresh bounty. As for the rest he declares that if they are not equally paid and means provided for transporting them to England that they will become an ungovernable rabble, and that they will be most dangerous to the lives of their officers and the property of the inhabitants of San Sebastian which place will probably then fall into the hands of the Carlists, and the partizans of the Queen at Madrid had better be thinking of putting their houses in order if such a catastrophe should occur! I tell all this to Mendizabal and receive the answer which I knew beforehand I should get—that he has not a farthing. I passed the night in consultations and redispatching the courier to Evans but I have sent him little beyond solemn promises and offers to *do bills* at 6 and 9 months. I am afraid however that neither will bear a premium at San Sebastian or even be accepted there *without a consideration*.

Mendizabal has made a fine appeal to the brave men who have been devoting themselves to the cause of liberty—but as these braves have just run away and never thought of devoting themselves to any other cause than that of $7\frac{1}{2}$d. a day which they see no chance of getting, the appeal is not more likely to be successful with the soldiers than Mendizabal's promise to their commander a few days ago to make him either Count of Oriomendi or Hernani according as he took the one or the other place. Evans has been mightily offended at this mode of getting at his generalship through his vanity and he resents it as a soldier and a radical.

I am sorry to say that Wylde confirms all Evans's apprehensions as to what will happen on the 10th of June if means for paying and conveying away the men are not provided, and as their sacking San Sebastian would be a most unsatisfactory wind up of their services and our quasi intervention I hope there will be no objection to Lord John Hay's lending a steam boat or two to take them home. Perhaps some arrangement may be made by the Spanish Government for paying in England those who insist upon returning there, and settling at San Sebastian with the men who can be induced to remain.

The Durango Decree however makes them very shy of the Carlists and it must be allowed that the knowledge that they are to be shot like dogs if they are taken prisoners and that our Marines and the Queen's troops are to be spared is not calculated to inspire the Legion with a surplus amount of courage. Still a battalion might be induced to remain if money could be found, but without military successes nobody will lend a halfpenny (for I do not venture to hope anything from the loan proposal I sent you last week) and how can they be hoped for with such a general as Espartero at the head of the army? Yet the Government have hardly the power to remove him and if they had they have no one to put in his place.

Lord John Hay says he is expecting some more Marines. I hope you may be able to send them but I should almost doubt it in the state of public opinion now in England. I believe he could take Fuentearabia if he were allowed by the Admiralty. Would there be any objection to his doing so? I don't look upon it as of much importance unless as a part of offensive operations to be undertaken at the same time by the

Queen's army. If they do not begin shortly and do not succeed we shall be having juntas all over the country and a repetition of all the summer diversions of last year. Zaragoza which is generally foremost in these sports is already laying the ground for them.

The question of making the Senators tenants for life of their dignity was yesterday lost by 8 votes in the Cortes which I attribute entirely to Calatrava's having been again taken ill, for the Deputies had all agreed to the expediency of the measure, i.e. the ministerial majority, only two days before when Calatrava harangued them, but yesterday he was away and the Deputies who are not bad boys if the schoolmaster has his eye upon them are the most mischievous dogs in the world whenever his back is turned.

I am not sorry that the question is lost because popular election and a life charge seem quite incompatible and I am sure would have produced here very mischievous results. The Senate would now be elected under circumstances of popular excitement, the number of persons likely to be thought eligible would therefore be small, and men might therefore be placed in the Upper Chamber for life who in a couple of years' time, if tranquillity is restored, would probably be ill viewed by the very electors who sent them there, and who would elect Deputies to the Lower Chamber more in harmony with their opinions; which would be to render a rift inevitable between the two bodies and the unchangeable Senators would either usurp all the functions of Government or be an eternal pretext for revolution, and the nation's not adapting itself to its new constitutional forms. Calatrava with whom I have often discussed the subject has some plausible arguments on the other side which are not worth troubling you with as the question has been thrown out, but as it is one of importance to the futurity of Spain I shall recur to it another day when the Government has decided in what way the lapsus linguarum of the Ayes and Noes yesterday may be best repaired.[2]

My brother writes me word that opinion is so little favorable to our intervention with armed force in the affairs of Spain that he is averse to publishing my supplement. You will perhaps think with him—if not, and that you have $\frac{1}{2}$ an hour to dispose of upon such matters, will you send to him for the MS. and give your opinion as to the publication of the whole or a part of it?

I will bear in mind Captain Jochmus. . . .

Received 27 April.   GC/CL/328; Clar. Dep. C.453 (94-99)

[1] Instead of one or two years, Evans suggested 'till the end of the war. For we apprehend deplorable consequences to have resulted both in discipline and in action latterly from the definite period having been originally adopted.' (Evans to V, 10 Apr. 1837, Clar. Dep. C.461.)

[2] Revised proposals were put forward on 20 April, whereby 'each time the Chamber of Deputies is dissolved a third of the Senate shall be removed in the order of antiquity and the members so excluded may be again re-elected.' (V to P, 22 Apr. 1837, no. 99, FO 72/479.)

330 Palmerston to Villiers, 20 April 1837

Copy. Foreign Office. We have had a most triumphant debate of 3 nights on Spanish affairs[1]—all the good speaking was on our side, and some capital speeches we have had. Sheil, Lushington, Lytton Bulwer, your brother, were the best; many others very good; on the other side all poor, but Follet and Peel. The division was better than we expected. But that is not material. The arithmetical proportion of the two sides of the House is well enough understood by the public. The Spanish question was very little understood, but will be better understood in consequence of this discussion. I was very glad it lasted 3 nights, and that so many persons unconnected with the Government had the opportunity of speaking upon it.

From what Granville writes to me of his conversations with Louis Philippe[2] I fear there is no chance of the French Government guaranteeing the loan; and much as I should wish that we could do so, there is no use in deceiving oneself on such matters, and it is perfectly evident that there would be no possible chance of persuading the two Houses, nay either House of Parliament to pass a Bill of Guarantee. I am sorry for this *petit ministère* in France,[3] because until it has run through its little span of life we can hope for no more active assistance to Spain from France.

GC/CL/1305

[1] From 17 to 19 April. In a closing speech on 19 April P said: 'I am bound to say that the respect which Spain has for this country is very much owing to the able and judicious conduct of the representative of the British Government at Madrid. The high character which that minister has personally established and the good faith which the British Government has observed in its dealings have indeed rendered the character of an Englishman a passport throughout Spain.' (*Parl. Deb.*, 3rd Series, XXXVIII, 484-85.)

² Granville to P, 17 Apr. 1837, no. 139, FO 27/540. See also Granville to V, 19 Apr. 1837, PRO 30/29/422.
³ On 15 April Guizot, Persil, Duchâtel and Gasparin left the Ministry and were replaced by Salvandy, Barthe, Lacane Laplagne and Montalivet. Molé remained President of the Council and Foreign Minister.

331 Villiers to Palmerston, 22 April 1837

Madrid. Private. I have very little to communicate today for except with a few articles of the Constitution no progress has been made any where since I last wrote to you.

I have a letter from Wylde dated the 13th by which I find that he takes the same view that I have already expressed in my dispatches respecting the inexpediency of this roundabout operation of Espartero's by Pamplona, and the extreme danger of not taking the field immediately. He was accordingly going to Bilbao to see if he could persuade Espartero to go by sea with 20 or 25 battalions to San Sebastian and at once to recommence the campaign. Wylde says that he will pledge his life that in a fortnight after his arrival the frontier will be closed and Irun, Fuentearabia, Hernani and Vera in the possession of the Queen's troops. This has always appeared to me the proper plan of campaign, and if there was no other reason for adopting it it should be resorted to out of mere *curiosity* and as an experiment—every other has been tried. Attempts to penetrate into the enemy's country have been made from the south and east and west but never from the north, and yet it is in that quarter that the greatest amount of immediate advantage might be expected—all the really fortified places which the Carlists hold would fall—the Bastan and all the country well disposed to the Queen's cause would be enabled to emancipate themselves. The French frontier which is the very life of the war would be closed, and if the line of the Ebro is properly guarded the enemy when driven southwards would be between two fires, and if they were to pass the Ebro pursued by a victorious army they ought to be annihilated in the plains of Castille within a fortnight after they leave their mountain holds.

But I have no confidence in Espartero—he is ignorant, weak, idle and diseased—in short the very man fit for ruining the cause which now depends upon his incapacity. Yet the position of the Government with respect to him is unchanged—for although the public would see

635

his removal with unconcern if not with satisfaction, the army would not—the chiefs like his inactivity, and the soldiers his disregard for discipline, and as long as the war lasts *they* are our worthy and approved good masters. If they chose, and they would choose, to retain Espartero and to be commanded by no other general the Government would be worse off than it is at the present moment—its weakness more discovered—and its relations with the General in Chief and the army would be those of open hostility.

Besides if they stood the shot of all this, they have literally no one to put in Espartero's place. According to the information given by Campuzano to his Government Marshal Clausel is nibbling at the appointment of Commander in Chief of the Queen's army,[1] but Calatrava throws cold water upon it, as the measure would bring neither military nor political advantages. Marshal Clausel is not acquainted with the country where the war is carried on and without that all the military knowledge and strategy in the world would be of no avail, and the Spanish officers would be sure either to refuse to serve under him or to play him some trick in the course of his operations. Clausel likewise being in bad odour with Louis Philippe the French Government might have recourse to the innumerable means which unfortunately are at their command to ensure his failure. Calatrava is therefore right I think in wishing to avoid this *compromiso*.

I have been fighting another hard battle for the Legion as you will see by my dispatch[2]—the matter however was one of pressing necessity for if Espartero does not send troops to San Sebastian before the 10th of June when the Legion ceases to be Spanish soldiers and re-enters the category of British subjects, our braves are very likely not to defend the lines, and still more so to pillage the town in order to pay off to themselves the arrears owed to them by the Government. Incidents which however pleasant they might be to His Majesty's Opposition are very much to be deprecated by His Majesty's Government, and I accordingly left no stone unturned to procure the arrangement which I yesterday sent off to Evans—ready money does not exist and cannot therefore be sent. I *hope* the arrangement may give satisfaction though I know that Mendizabal's bills enjoy very little more credit than his promises.

As the Legion seems to be converted into a virulent party question by the Tories and that I do not know what feelings may exist upon the subject in High Quarters I have been very cautious in the wording of my dispatch and marked it separate for *greater convenience*.

Mendizabal made to me yesterday two very characteristic propositions which shew his accurate knowledge of England and his nice perception of what is honorable or decent. The 1st was that the English Government should recognize the Legion as British troops and give the officers their present Legion ranks in the British service. The other that the English Government should furnish 50 or 100,000 muskets more to some Spanish agent in London who instead of exporting them to Spain should raise as much money as he could get upon them. I wonder what Maclean and Mahon would have given to overhear him.

PS. Calatrava will make an official application to you for a renewal of the Enlistment Bill suspension directly that he is certain the Legion will consent to re-enlist. We think it would not be fair to expose you to a hard fight in Parliament without being sure that its results could be availed of here. In another week I suppose we shall know.

Received 1 May.

GC/CL/329; Clar. Dep. C.453 (100–105)

[1] Clausel informed the Spanish Government that 'he left it to the Government to propose to him the "splendid" reward to which his services would be entitled'. (V to P, 20 May 1837, no. 125, FO 72/479.)

[2] See V to P, 22 Apr. 1837, separate, FO 72/479. On 18 April Evans wrote to V complaining about a letter he had received from Mendizábal, and warning V of the trouble that would break out if the Legion's arrears were not settled by 10 June. (Clar. Dep. C.461.)

332 Villiers to Palmerston, 29 April 1837

Madrid. Private. I give you de Corazón, la enhorabuena[1] for the result of the debate upon Hardinge's motion.[2] It has indeed been a great triumph. I have been reading the speeches with an intense interest and have seen with pleasure that your own was, as it ought to be, *the* speech of the whole debate[3]—a more effective and masterly and statesmanlike exposition of your policy and the whole bearings of the Spanish question cannot be, and infinite good it will do here, in England also I hope, for besides setting public opinion right upon the part which we are taking in the affairs of this country, I trust that the blow aimed by the Tories against the Government will recoil upon themselves and that the unworthy manner in which they sought to take advantage of the disaster at Hernani will be duly appreciated. I am very grateful to you for what you said about myself—to have merited the public expression of such an opinion is all the reward I ambition, and it is an ample compensation for my uphill and somewhat thankless task here.[4]

The disappointment which the failure of the loan scheme has produced is bitter. I cannot say that it has surprised me for I always felt and told Marliani himself, that there must be a mistake *somewhere*, for it seemed little less than impossible that Louis Philippe should so far depart from his policy towards this country as to sanction so great an act of succour. Yet Aguado who is not a mere stock jobber but a man whose *hobby* is now his name and reputation, spoke so confidently that it is not to be wondered at if the Spanish Government believed it to be practicable and reckoned upon it as done. Poor fellows their mouths have been watering sadly for the past three weeks, for the offer was not only of the crumbs which fall from the rich man's table but all Dives's best entrées. It was a kicking out of the strange bedfellows that poverty has made them acquainted with—it was the prospect of salvation to men who distress is about to drive into any rash act of folly or crime —and the mortification has been in proportion to the hopes excited. What they are to do now the Mighty only knows, for every possible source of revenue is dried up—forestalled for the next twelvemonth at least—not a farthing is to be had and the pressing wants of the army *must* be attended to or the cause perishes. It is a desperate situation—a hopeless one in any other country than Spain which is always hobbling out of one disaster into another, and has now become as used to misery as the eels to being skinned.

Of a guarantee on the part of England I have of course always recognized the impossibility, i.e. of such a one as would require the sanction of Parliament, but would it be practicable to revert to our old idea of a moral guarantee in the event of its being satisfactory or sufficient for the capitalists concerned? . . .

I hope that the vote in the House of Commons will enable you to renew the Order in Council suspending the Foreign Enlistment Bill[5] and still more do I hope that you may be able to strain a point in order to send out another battalion of Marines. The opposition of the Tories will be just the same whether we have 800 or 1,500 of that corps here.

Wylde writes me word that the loan of two steam boats in addition to those already upon the North Coast is of the utmost importance for the prompt conveyance of troops to different points in the event of the

Carlists making incursions to Castille or Galicia—they likewise want 1,000 or 1,200 tents. We have already done so much and we are so completely compromised that going a little further cannot much signify, and if this new plan of campaign is carried into effect (which will be known in London sooner than at Madrid) it is a last card upon which every thing may depend and we should really exert ourselves to make it turn up a trump—marking it or any of the most approved means used at Grahams being I think justifiable to resort to for the object. Such a cause and such a contest as this may be won in a day and at a blow provided that Spaniards are not left entirely to themselves.

I have been working like a banker's clerk during the whole week to obtain money for the Legion, for upon attempting to negotiate all those fine securities offered by Mendizabal I found they were worth absolutely nothing, and that he was making me the instrument for deceiving Evans and the Legion, totally regardless of all the tremendous consequences which a failure of his promises would entail. Neither in public nor in private have I yet had to do with such a man as he is. I have addressed myself to all the monied men here for an advance of £40,000 and having arranged the terms upon which they would do it I have *canvassed* each Minister for his vote in the Cabinet *(always unofficially of course)* and have so far succeeded that £20,000 goes to Bayonne tonight and the other half will I hope follow in a day or two.

PS. The discussion upon the reformed Constitution is over and I think that upon the whole the Constitution is excellent and will work well if tranquillity were once restored. The fact of its having been begun and ended on the two fête days of the Queen, although apparently insignificant, is here an evidence of loyalty and a mark of respect to the throne which would not have been hoped for a few months ago when one remembers the circumstances of popular excitement under which these Cortes were elected.

Since writing the above I have seen Calatrava who has begged me to convey the respectful thanks of himself and his colleagues to you for your admirable speech on the 19th instant and to tell you that the Queen is as pleased and as grateful as her Ministers.

Received 9 May.

GC/CL/330; Clar. Dep. C.453 (106-111)

[1] 'heartfelt congratulations'.

[2] See no. 330 above for P's comments on the debate.

[3] To his brother Edward, V wrote somewhat differently: 'The Tories and their atrocious lies now seem to have gotten the upper hand on Spanish affairs. What an opportunity for a Foreign Secretary to distinguish himself, but it is not in Palmerston and he must take the consequence.' (V to Edward Villiers, 22 Apr. 1837, Clar. Dep. C.467.)

[4] V was not really satisfied with the praise from P. He wrote later to Granville: 'It is true that Palmerston paid me a compliment some time since in the House of Commons but it was not till fifty opportunities for doing the same thing had passed. . . .I didn't know either till afterwards that Lord Clarendon had gone to Palmerston to speak to him upon the subject of his never saying a word on my behalf so that I have no good reason for thinking a friendly feeling exists towards me.' (V to Granville, 8 July 1837, PRO 30/29/423.)

[5] See V to P, 29 Apr. 1837, no. 102, FO 72/479, enclosing a translation of a despatch from Calatrava to the Spanish minister in London.

333 Palmerston to Villiers, 1 May 1837

Copy. Foreign Office. Pray dissuade Calatrava earnestly from employing Clausel. His recent exploit in Africa shews that he is a most dangerous commander; and unless he is greatly belied he has also proved during his employment in Africa that he is an unscrupulous and insatiable peculator.

GC/CL/1306

334 Palmerston to Villiers, 4 May 1837

Copy. Foreign Office. My last accounts from Wylde of the 24th, and those from John Hay of the 26th encourage us to hope that we shall in the next fortnight hear of the occupation of the frontier next to France by the Queen's troops—such an operation will have a powerful effect on public opinion here, and will help the Spanish Government to money.

I have seen Marliani and Aguilar about the plan for a loan, and so has Thomson. I told them that a pecuniary guarantee is out of the question—that it would be altogether a new and not a convenient thing for England to sign a treaty with a foreign Power, by which that Power should engage to England to execute pecuniary engagements to a set of private individuals. Treaties are concluded between Sovereigns for matters in which both sides have something to do; but this would be a one-sided engagement—and then the meaning would of course be that England should by force and by war if necessary compel Spain to pay the dividends regularly; but what an inconvenient duty for England to perform! And suppose all the stock so created were to pass into the hands of foreigners, how awkward it would be for England to be interposing for the benefit of Frenchmen, Germans and Hollanders.

I told them therefore that the only way in which the English could be brought as a party into the transaction would be by the conclusion of a commercial treaty between England and Spain, by which for a limited number of years English goods should be admitted at certain rates of duty. That such an arrangement would immediately create a revenue for Spain out of which she might pay her dividends, and that the knowledge that such an arrangement would continue during the time specified in the treaty would give confidence to those who might be disposed to advance money to the Spanish Government.

Thomson held exactly the same language when he saw them afterwards. The result has been that Marliani has written to Aguado at Paris; and when he gets Aguado's answer, if it is satisfactory, he is to give me some proposition in writing. You will have heard that the French Government will not give Spain the slightest help direct or indirect in these matters.

Admiral Napier has offered himself to go and succeed Evans if Evans comes away—at first his being a naval and not a military man startled one as a difficulty. But extreme cases require extreme remedies. In the Spanish service such transfers from sea to land and from land to sea are not wholly unknown. Napier says he was some months with the Duke of Wellington's army and was wounded at Busaco; that he has always had a greater fancy for land than for sea operations; that he commanded 3,000 men in Portugal and took fortified towns; that he would be assisted by his cousin Colonel Napier brother to the historian, by Colonel Shaw, and by many others. On the other hand we know his daring and enterprize; and we have seen that he knows how to acquire influence over the people of the Peninsula. He says he should require to be invited by the Spanish Government, to have £100,000 in his military chest to start with; to have the command of Spanish troops like Evans, and also to have the Spanish flotilla placed under his orders. I can only say that if I was Spanish Minister I should accept the proposal. What the Spaniards most want is energy, decision and enterprize. Those qualities Napier possesses. He has also been invariably *fortunate*. There is no time to be lost if they mean to have him. Speak about this to Calatrava.

I have written to Evans to tell him what has passed between Napier and me. I told Napier, the first thing to be done was to communicate with Evans, and to ascertain whether he was positively determined to come home, that there might be no appearance of an intrigue to supplant him.

Napier wrote to Evans himself.

GC/CL/1307

335 Villiers to Palmerston, 6 May 1837

Madrid. Private. The weather as usual continues to be hyper Carlist and by not allowing the troops to be transported from Bilbao to San Sebastian much of the advantage to be expected from the new plan of campaign has been already neutralized. The secret was exceedingly well kept—on the 24th ultimo the Carlists had no idea of what was intended and they were concentrating all their forces in the direction of Estella preparatory to an expedition into Castille or Aragon. Had the weather permitted of the main body of the Queen's army being moved to San Sebastian at that time, a great blow might have been struck at once, but the gods not only would not permit that but they did just what was the most mischievous for us. They allowed the gales to moderate sufficiently for transporting a number of troops, not enough to begin operations, but quite so in order to make manifest to the enemy what it is they are threatened with, and of course now the Carlists are agglomerating their hosts towards the spot where their presence is least to be desired. Espartero is to have upwards of 30,000 men at San Sebastian, but there must be at least 10 or 12,000 yet to be moved from Bilbao, so that when these operations will commence we know not.

A new difficulty seems to have arisen likewise as General Seoane in a letter from Bayonne of the 29th ultimo informs me. Fuentearabia and Irun cannot be attacked without a violation by cannon balls of the French territory. I think it would have been much better to have said nothing about this—to have attacked and taken the places *without having an idea* that French lives or property would be endangered but if any casualties occurred the Spanish Government should have indemnified the parties concerned. However a Council of War seems to have determined otherwise, and Seoane was dispatched to negociate upon the subject with General Harispe (who is I believe an ardent well-wisher to the Queen's cause and always inclined to stretch a point or exceed his instructions against the Carlists). He first proposed that Spanish troops should be allowed to cross the French frontier in order to attack the places in question. Against this Harispe replied that he had already positive orders from his Government. It was then suggested that Fuentearabia and Irun should be taken and afterwards immediately occupied by French troops which would do away with all future question of attacking or defending them. To this Harispe inclined, and agreed to receive and to consult his Government upon a letter addressed to him by Seoane upon the subject. Calatrava however objects to it,[1] 1st because the admission of foreign troops into Spanish territory without the previous consent of the Cortes is an infraction of the Constitution—but principally because he is certain that Louis Philippe would never consent to such a measure. He has refused armed intervention in every shape—he won't allow a Spanish soldier to pass the French territory—how can it be expected that he should send garrisons to Spanish towns? Calatrava therefore objects to ask the permission of the Cortes for that which Louis Philippe is likely to refuse, and he objects to negociations and references to Paris as tending only to create delay and disappointment. You will I think be inclined to consider him right.

I have written to Evans, Lord John Hay, Wylde and Seoane deprecating all this diplomacy and recommending, at the same time, that nothing is done to offend the King of the French, yet that nothing should be expected of him—that the Spaniards should rely upon their own resources and the moment they have everything ready move forward without a thought of what might be got by asking from France or England. If Espartero unites 30,000 men he ought to carry all before him—the army is in excellent spirits and Espartero himself writes in a tone of unusual confidence.

After infinite trouble I have managed to arrange the financial affairs of the Legion between the Government and some monied men here. The commissary returns today quite satisfied and considers with reference to the miserable state of the treasury that a miracle has been performed.

I have likewise obtained a promise from Calatrava that the officers and men of the Legion who may be induced to reinlist on the 10th of June shall be retained in the Spanish service for 3 years which is what Evans desired. I hope too that it is settled that Seoane acting by and with the advice of Wylde, Lord John and one or two more shall be the man to make the arrangements necessary for reorganizing the Legion. Evans is so weak and is so devoid of any opinions of his own that he cannot be depended upon for any thing—he is never of the same way of thinking two days together. I have suggested that the present commercial crisis and distress of the lower orders in England may be turned to account in inducing the men to stay in this country, for nothing but starvation will await them if they persist in going home.

La Tour Maubourg leaves Madrid for Paris on Monday next—he says his journey has no political object and that his objects are purely connubial, as he is going to be married, and that Molé has given him six weeks leave of absence for the purpose. I have great difficulty in believing it and I see many reasons for thinking that Louis Philippe intends to withdraw his ambassador, and that this leave of absence, which might well have been postponed to a period less critical in Spanish affairs, has been given in order to make the retreat decent. As far as the ambassador himself is concerned the relations between the two countries will probably be improved by his absence, for a more cantancorous quarrelsome gentleman never bothered affairs, but if there is to be no representative of France here it will be a new source of triumph and satisfaction to Don Carlos.

Will you permit me to renew a suggestion that I made to you some time ago—viz. to bear in mind when you speak upon Spanish affairs that you have two audiences, and that every word of yours is caught at here with avidity and scrupulously weighed and discussed? In your speech on the 19th you made some remarks upon the bloody national character of the Spaniards and the ferocious manner in which they have always waged war. Il n'y a que la verité qui blesse and accordingly the effect that those remarks have produced here is beyond anything I can describe. The press has been furious, and many persons without being able to deny the correctness of what you stated have expressed their regret to me upon the subject, because they said that such opinions, in the mouth of one who was so proved a friend to Spain as you have shewn yourself, stamped an indelible stain upon the national character of Spaniards.

I have received a letter from Captain Hackett of the Jaseur begging me again to move you to recommend him for the King's permission to accept the Order of Charles III. Sir Alexander Woodford would likewise be made very happy if he could accept the Order that has been offered to him. . . .

I send you today the copy of a letter to Mr. Renny (who by the bye pretends to be acting in accordance with Poulett Thomson) from the British merchants at Alicante. They have informed me privately that they could not refuse to answer Mr. Renny's queries, but considering his proceedings very unhandsome and to have solely party objects in view, they officially communicated to me their letter as they knew they were under greater obligations to me than to any of my predecessors. There can I should conceive be no objection to make use of this letter and my dispatch in the House of Commons against our worthy friend Bingham Baring who will deserve to be turned into ridicule for his meddling with matters he has no business with and does not understand.[2]

Marliani is I know gone to London. I have not (neither did I give him or Calatrava any) the slightest hope that you will be able to do anything for him in the way of guarantee but if by any unexpected chance you saw a possibility of facilitating the measure, its being made conditional upon commercial arrangements might check the clamor it would otherwise raise—for the manufacturing districts at this moment of suffering would attach far greater value to a treaty with Spain than at any other, and at no time would it do the Government at home so much good as now. As for Spain it would be salvation and I have little doubt that the French would be so jealous and piqued with our treaty that Louis Philippe would be compelled to assist the Queen in order to get commercial advantages for France.

The courier from Paris is not yet arrived.

Received 14 May.

GC/CL/331; Clar. Dep. C.453 (112-119)

[1] 'and very wisely' added by P in pencil.
[2] See V to P, 6 May 1837, no. 107 and enclosure, FO 72/479.

336 Villiers to Palmerston, 13 May 1837

Madrid. Private. I have received your letter of the 4th and in reply to your arguments respecting the guarantee I have nothing to say—they are conclusive, and Calatrava to whom I read that part of your letter considers them so likewise. As regards your *counter-project* I must reserve what I have to say until I can write by a safe opportunity which will occur in a day or two, but I may in the mean while mention that during the last ten days I have made more real progress in this important question than any time since I have been here.

The circumstances of the country and the unruly state of Catalonia have been of service to me, and as I have succeeded in making a Cabinet question of it I think that our great obstacle which I have always told you was Mendizabal will be overcome.

I have spoken to Calatrava and Mendizabal about Napier and both are much pleased with the offer and inclined to accept it. His being a naval man is no objection, for his military talents are well known here and his feats in Portugal have made his name a glorious one in Spain. Only two objections have presented themselves—the money he requires to have at starting in the Legionary Chest—and the command of the Spanish flotilla. With respect to the latter he need not in my opinion insist—in the first place it is an insignificant force and 2dly there is little or no sea work to be done, and there will be none if Fuentearabia is taken. The Carlists only possess one or two havens on the coast where they have a few boats which hardly ever dare shew themselves as the British steamers are always cruizing backwards and forwards, and if the Queen's troops have any success inland a battalion or two would soon eject the Carlists from their forts on the coast if they did not previously retire of their own accord. Moreover if any thing were necessary on the coast Lord John Hay would do it better than Napier could with the whole Spanish navy which he would find but a lumbering machine.

With respect to the £100,000, that's a different question and Napier with reference to all that has passed since the Legion came to this country is quite right to insist upon it, but if I could give you any idea of the trouble I have had and the *personal responsibility* I have taken upon myself in order to raise £40,000 and prevent a scandal and a catastrophe, you would understand how near akin to impossible it is that any such sum should be placed in deposit. Entirely agreeing however with Napier as to the necessity of *some* previous provision being made, I must add that the sum he requires is far beyond what is absolutely necessary. If he has money always in advance for 3 months pay and allowances of every description he ought to feel himself secure, provided that all arrears are settled up to the time of his taking the command, and that clothing is furnished by the Spanish Government from England and that Spanish contractors keep him regularly supplied with provisions. When the Legion was at its greatest numerical strength and the Government had to provide for all its absurd paraphernalia of staff, medical department, etc., etc. (sufficient for an army of 30,000 men) the monthly expence was from 12 to £15,000. Its numbers will now be reduced to 3,000 *at the utmost*.[1] All unnecessary expence will be curtailed, and I do not apprehend that the calls upon the military chest would then exceed £2,500 to £3,000 per month.

Under these circumstances to require so large a deposit would be unnecessarily to distress the Government and to have a great sum of money lying idle. I should say that if he could always have £10,000 in hand he would be secure from all the difficulties which Evans has had to encounter, for he would of course have nothing to do with the payment or provisioning of the Spanish troops he might command.

There has been a good deal of fighting during the last ten days in Valencia and Catalonia, and we have every reason to believe that the advantage has been on the Queen's side, but we are sadly in want of official details. The Government have received indirect accounts that Oraa has twice beaten Cabrera's faction in Valencia and that the Baron de Meer has done the same with Tristany's in Catalonia, but these beatings which are always doubtful matters even when reported by the generals themselves are still more so when they arrive through bye channels.

The row at Barcelona, although for the present force est restée à la loi, was a very *unnecessary* occurrence.[2] I believe it to have been mainly caused, as well as similar movements at 3 or 4 other places in Catalonia, by foreign agency working through the secret societies. The Government have some curious evidence upon this subject both here and in the provinces.

There is no doubt that the policy of those Powers who wish ill to this country is to endeavour by every means to produce confusion, to disgust and weary out all parties—to make them believe that constitutional government is the source of all their sufferings, and that liberal institutions are impossible in Spain. *Then* to settle affairs as may be thought most convenient to the rest of Europe which for that very reason never could be a national or a final termination of the struggle. The Catalans who are the curse and the scourge of this country easily lend themselves to such intrigues—a nothing excites them for they are never contented, and when their blood is once up they are ferocious, vindictive and persevering. So general however is the feeling of exhaustion and desire for repose throughout the country that I should fear neither Catalan impatience or foreign intrigues if a really effective blow could be given to the Carlists in the insurgent provinces.

Of this, if it were not for the many disappointments we have already had, I should now conceive hopes. The Queen's army is for *the first time* going to commence operations upon a fixed plan, and in a manner likely to produce great results, *sure* to produce them if others than Spanish generals commanded. 30,000 men are now collected at San Sebastian—they ought to take Fuentearabia, Irun and Hernani beyond all doubt—the enemy at most can only bring 25,000 men to oppose them, and that will be by withdrawing all their troops from the most distant parts of the country they hold and which at a recent council of war they have agreed to abandon if necessary in order to defend at all risks the communications with France. They doubtless occupy tremendous positions which are fortified and entrenched in every direction and they have a great deal of artillery—still they ought to be beaten, and if they are the demoralization of their forces will be instantaneous and the desertion general. The troops which are now guarding the line of the Ebro should then close in upon them and catch them between two fires—the whole question *might* be settled in a week —*but* a defeat in the present state of public opinion and of the disunion among parties which the duration of the war creates might be fatal. It is an anxious moment.

The feelings of satisfaction produced here by the nomination of Major Owens (Marines) as aide de camp to the King are universal. . . .

Received 25 May.

GC/CL/332; Clar. Dep. C.453 (126-131)

[1] In a letter of 13 May to Edward Villiers, V recounted how he had prevailed on all the superior officers and 2,500 to 3,000 of the best men of the Legion to remain in Spain after 10 June. (Clar. Dep. C.467.)

[2] A revolt of the Militia suppressed by regular troops on 5 and 6 May. Over one hundred people were killed. (V to P, 13 May 1837, no. 114, FO 72/479.)

337 Villiers to Palmerston, 15 May 1837

Madrid. Private. When I received your letter of the 4th instant I had been laboring for some days to prove to Calatrava that now if ever was the time for making a commercial treaty, that it would be the best punishment for the turbulent Catalans, and a coup d'état as regards France whose hostility becomes every day less disguised. He agreed with me and made it a Cabinet question as I told you in my last, and he considers that he has to a certain degree conquered the *repugnancia* of Mendizabal (the supposed friend of English interests!). Then arrived Marliani's proposition founded upon his conversations with you and with Thomson for uniting the treaty and the guarantee and the ground was well prepared for receiving it, but I have told Calatrava that I think Marliani's wish is father to the thought of your having under any circumstances held out hopes of the only kind of guarantee which could be satisfactory to capitalists.

Mendizabal promises and Calatrava who is a man of his word is really anxious, so that we now have a hope—a victory on the frontier and a commercial treaty would put Parliament and the country in good humor with our foreign policy for a twelvemonth and over both the Tories and the doctrinaires it would be a triumph which does one's heart good to think of.[1] We must not conceal from ourselves however that the treaty will be extremely difficult to carry here under any circumstances and will only be possible if on our side we offer reciprocal commercial advantages or that we guarantee a loan—pray therefore take these into consideration and at all events let me have the answer I ask for to my dispatch respecting the reduction of duties upon Spanish commodities.[2]

I wrote to Mendizabal today to know what answer he should send to Marliani and whether it would be in the spirit of his recent promise to me. I enclose you his letter in reply.[3]

Marliani wished that powers for signing any treaty should be sent to him but this would be quite impossible for of all the questions which this Government can moot either with the Cortes or the country that of a commercial treaty with England is the most delicate and difficult. There is so much ignorance, prejudice and national vanity to temporize with that a despotic Government would find it a hard task. For *this* one, feeble in public opinion and in the midst of a civil war, dreading to increase the number of its enemies, additional precautions are indis pensable. Circumstances vary every 4 and 20 hours and the Government must adapt to them its language with the Deputies. If it were known that a commercial treaty was being negociated in London a cry would be raised instantly that the country was sold to England and the whole would be *quashed* at once. We must take people as we find them and only endeavour to adapt our means as well as we can to our end which is really worth some trouble and sacrifice.

I have written you a long dispatch about the French ambassador and Calatrava[4] but as the former threatened an explosion and that he appears to me for the last 3 months to have been laying the train I thought it right to put you au fait of his operations.

Received 26 May.

GC/CL/333; Clar. Dep. C.453 (132-135)

[1] 'foreign' to 'think of' underlined or circled roughly in pencil, possibly by P.

[2] 'I am convinced that no treaty of commerce will have a chance of being sanctioned by the Cortes unless it is either based upon entire reciprocity of commercial interests, or it is concluded simultaneously with the guarantee of a loan by England.' (V to P, 15 May 1837, no. 118, FO 72/479.)

[3] No enclosure found.

[4] V to P, 15 May 1837, no. 117, FO 72/479.

338 Palmerston to Villiers, 18 May 1837

Copy. Foreign Office. We are in hourly expectation of hearing some good results from the concentration of Espartero's army at St. Sebastians.

The French telegraph announces the occupation of Hernani, and if that is so, the whole country up to the French frontier must fall into the hands of the Queen's troops. This will be an important event. Don Sebastian is supposed to have broken cover, and to have made for Madrid. If so, and if his pursuers go the requisite pace, he must be run in upon in the open.

I hear from Granville that Aguado has signed his loan contract; he has done wisely if he has done so. But he has had no promise of guarantee from us, of any kind. We told Marliani that we could guarantee neither interest nor islands—and that the best and only security which could be offered the loan contractors would be a treaty of commerce with England, securing for a certain number of years the admission of

British commodities into Spain on payment of reasonable duties. We said that such an arrangement would secure to Spain a revenue, out of which interest could be paid. Granville however tells me that Aguado gave out in Paris that we had promised some guarantee or other. If he has said so he has told an untruth.

The improved posture of the Queen's army in the North seems I think to supersede Napier's proposal. It might have been well to employ him for a long shore operation; but it would hardly answer to metamorphose him into a regular general, to act in the interior of the country. We are meeting with great difficulties about the renewal of the Order in Council in a quarter where objections to it might have been expected.[1] I hope and trust however that these difficulties will be overcome. But they have arisen very much from personal dislike to Evans, for before he was named to command the Legion, there was all possible zeal to assist its recruiting and formation; and from the moment he was selected coldness began, and has matured into aversion to everything belonging to the Legion.

I rather think all things considered that the wisest course the Spanish Government could pursue would be to instruct d'Aguilar to apply to the English Government to select some experienced military officer to command what will remain of the Legion after the 10th of June. We should then take the Horse Guards with us by asking Lord Hill to recommend; some little field to patronage would be opened to head quarters, and we might get the military authorities over to our side, without having a bad choice of officers. This is worth considering if the Spanish Government mean to retain, and especially if they mean to recruit the Legion.

We made a mistake in the outset by not following this course, but here is an opportunity of falling into it, and it would be unwise not to take advantage of it.

GC/CL/1308

[1] From the King.

339 Villiers to Palmerston, 20 May 1837

Madrid. Private. I have been very *puirly* for two or three days past and as I have made myself worse by going out this afternoon and having long palavers with Calatrava and Mendizabal I shall not address you privately at any great length. You will be better and more quickly informed about military events in the North than we are here for nobody seems in a hurry to write to the Government when there is not bad news to communicate.

I am very sorry that the Carlists adopted the prudent part of valor and would not wait for the thrashing which *even* Espartero could not have helped giving them,[1] because a great victory would at once have produced those moral effects which are absolutely necessary for putting an end to a struggle such as this and which we must now obtain by slower steps and subject to all the chances of Spanish direction. However the abandonment of all the positions which it was known the Carlists had so great an interest in retaining and their occupation by the Queen's troops[2] will not be without their moral effect, and disunion among themselves together with a scarcity of victuals will not render the already exhausted followers of Don Carlos more zealous in his cause.

I don't doubt now that their plan is to generalize the war by sending expeditions to other provinces—it is a desperate plan and ought to be their total ruin—still however I hope it may not be put into practice for whenever great results have depended upon timely measures or upon zeal and activity, our friends here and particularly those who command armies are sure to fail. The only general in whom I am inclined to feel any confidence is Iribarren and I think if any man here can, he is the one to prevent the enemy from crossing the Ebro i.e. until the time when it becomes fordable every where, or not to run away from them if they do—but the Carlists will have various matters to take into consideration before they execute their plan. In the first place they have not *altogether* above 24,000 men. Of these at least a third will hardly be persuaded to leave their mountains, or their homes and families to the mercy of the Queen's troops. If they are left behind Espartero will have no great difficulty in hunting them down, and the country will no longer be so much in their favor for the great—the only—desiderandum there now is peace, and if the people after the enormous sacrifices they have made to support Don Carlos find themselves deserted by him because he considers it convenient to carry the war elsewhere they will have an additional motive for seeking the protection of the Queen's generals, and the more so if, as I hope, the measures adopted by Espartero are all of a mild and conciliatory nature.

Another question for the Carlists will be *where* to send their expeditions. It is believed the first one will be viâ Aragon to Catalonia. Take what direction they may they will have great difficulty in subsisting for the country is everywhere exhausted—break through the line of the troops (nearly 20,000 men) now guarding the Ebro where they may, they will be pursued by an equal or greater number of troops with cavalry far superior to anything they possess. All the towns are held by the Queen and there alone will provisions be to be found and the pursuing army will be in far less want of subsistence therefore than the Carlists who will be in distress and consequently will find no active sympathy in the country they traverse. Then again what is to be done with the royal person of Don Carlos? He will be very little inclined to go *Gomezizing* over the land and still less so to be left behind with a force insufficient for his protection. If he does sally forth however in the direction that is now supposed he will not have so clear a field before him as Gomez had, because he will be marching towards the Baron de Meer in Catalonia or Oraa in Valencia, both of whom have a respectable force and are tolerable generals, and the more he *dis*occupies the Biscayan Provinces the more troops can be detached after him. My principal fear is the inactivity of Espartero—he is sure to go to ground in any little town he may take and it always requires a week to dig him out.

Calatrava received a courier from Marliani this morning bringing the news that he had arranged a loan, etc., etc., with Aguado but I cannot bring myself to believe that Marliani's patriotic enthusiasm has not led him into error. I cannot believe, much as I should wish to do so, that you have offered him any guarantee such as would induce the capitalists to lend a large sum to Spain—he talks with confidence of this guarantee but in none of his communications can I find its terms specifically stated, and I have therefore put both Calatrava and Mendizabal upon their guard against expecting that which there is every reason to fear may not be realized.

I have made further progress with the treaty of commerce and I have this evening agreed with the two above mentioned Ministers that we shall proceed directly to the discussion (and if possible to the conclusion) of the draft of treaty I presented to them long ago and as soon as this is done we shall according to circumstances either send it off to you or wait to know how far you can go in re guarantee, for without some pecuniary advantages we shall never, notwithstanding all the zeal and tact with which the affair may be managed here, obtain the sanction of the Cortes—but be assured that such a glorious opportunity of making *Spain ours* may never occur again. Everything helps us at this moment—there is more gratitude towards England—less fear of France and a greater desire to shake off the Catalan yoke than ever existed before. It is possible also that the successes upon the frontier may dispose people in England more favorably towards the cause, and the manufacturing stagnation may make people more desirous of a commercial treaty with Spain. I know that it will not be for want of exertion on your part if this brilliant wind up of our policy towards Spain does not take place.

If you are able to give such a guarantee as will satisfy Aguado it would perhaps upon the whole and as a saving of time be expedient to send a courier here with the terms and your ultimatum.

Received 29 May.

GC/CL/334; Clar. Dep. C.453 (136-141)

[1] The Carlists made no attempt to defend Hernani and retreated with thirteen battalions on 11 May. (V to P, 20 May 1837, no. 124, FO 72/479.)

[2] Hernani and Irun, the two most important, were occupied.

340 Villiers to Palmerston, 28 May 1837

Madrid. Private. The Saragoza road must still be unsafe and as my last courier was within an hour of being nabbed by the Carlists I shall say nothing by this one that I should object to see in the Gazettes de Oñate or de France.

This affair of Iribarren is a sad calamity,[1] not so much for what we have lost as for what we have missed the opportunity of gaining. Iribarren has with him the heroes of La Granja and the troops (or rather banditti) which composed the division of Alaix last year when in pursuit of Gomez, and their discipline has never been properly restored. They insisted upon attacking the enemy who was much superior in numbers and within a walled town—they probably went at them with about as much order as a parcel of Cossacks and were, as might be expected, repulsed. The death of Leon, who was as distinguished a cavalry officer as any in Europe, and Iribarren, the only general in the Queen's service who really seems to *be* one, having on account of his wound to leave the command to an incapable successor[2] may have serious consequences.

At all events we must abandon the idea of finishing the war at a blow as I was almost rash enough to expect three days ago, and now its theatre will be carried to Catalonia and several acts may have to be performed there before the curtain drops. There never was a country where things are so wont to occur between cup and lip as in Spain. Don Carlos had brought out of his strongholds and concentrated together in a hostile country the élite of his army, his Government, his Court, his hopeful nephew[3] and himself. Troops nearly equal in number to his own, in better spirits, better supplied, and unencumbered with all the civilian apparatus which Don Carlos has to drag with him, were waiting for the proper opportunity to fall upon this emigration of the Carlist question, and if the enemy had been attacked under the favorable circumstances which a little patience must have afforded they would soon have fallen into confusion and every man that escaped the Queen's cavalry would have been the prey of the Arragonese peasants who armed and in number about 6,000 were lying in wait for them among the mountains. It is a great coup lost —but *paciencia y Cataluña*, for I still think that in that province Carlism ought to find its grave as there the chiefs will not be found obedient, or the troops disciplined, or the people patient.

Don Carlos has succeeded in extracting a far greater number[4] of native troops from Navarre and the Basque Provinces than was expected. How he managed it or by what promises or bribes he induced them to do that which they are so notoriously averse to is not known, but we hear that they are in a state of extreme discontent and if that is the case great desertion may be expected—moreover the Navarrese and the Catalans detest and despise each other—they speak entirely different languages, and never yet have been made to draw together. We shall see what they do now.

There can be no doubt that this movement of Don Carlos is not a voluntary one—he had intended to defend the lines of Hernani and the communications with France à toute outrance, but he ran away in the 1st place from Espartero's overwhelming army, and then the necessity of carrying on the war in a mountainous country as well as of maintaining communications with France[5] made him turn Catalonia ways, and the advantage of approaching nearer to Italy as regards either escape or supplies was probably an additional inducement. Our cruizers upon the east coast should now be vigilant, for arms and provisions are known to be coming both from Sardinia and Naples and there is likewise some plot hatching by those two sagacious little Powers to get up a Carlist insurrection in the south of Spain.

The additional expence which this change of provinces must entail upon the Spanish Government will be enormous—all the supplies and contracts have been made for the *far west* of the frontier—they must now be carried or provided fresh at the extreme east. The state of things financial is that which most alarms me, and your letter of the 18th is not written in *golden characters*. It was of course no surprise to me or (in consequence of the language I have held since the question was mooted) to the Government.

Calatrava and I had come to the same opinion as yourself respecting Napier previously to the receipt of your letter. He adopts with many thanks the proposition of asking that an experienced officer should be selected for the command of the Legionary fragment. What should you say to the Considine who is recently returned from Constantinople? It was Wylde who suggested him to me—he says he is an excellent officer and all the officers of the Legion would be well pleased to serve under him.

Espartero—his sowl to the Divil—is at his usual pranks and he will have to be dug or smoked out of Hernani probably to run to ground again at Tolosa for another fortnight. We must however do him the justice of admitting that he has behaved nobly towards Evans and left him the undivided glory of these recent successes.[6] His proclamations also to the people of the provinces and the soldiers of Don Carlos do him infinite credit,[7] as well as to Seoane who I believe had great part in them.

These documents as well as the memorial of the Carlist prisoners at Irun should be made much of both in Parliament and by the press. Surely Spanish affairs should not always wait for an attack (i.e. when they look ill) in order to be brought before the public. Ought not some friendly Member to move for any papers which might give you an opportunity of pitching into the Tories for their conduct after the disaster at Hernani which was really disgraceful to Englishmen and gentlemen?

Received 5 June.

GC/CL/335; Clar. Dep. C.453 (142-147)

[1] On 24 May Iribarren attacked the Carlists at Huesca in Aragon. The Carlists made good their entry into the town and the Cristinos retired to Almudé-

bar. Iribarren was mortally wounded and General Léon was killed.
  ² General Buerens.
  ³ Don Sebastian, Commander-in-Chief of the Carlist forces.
  ⁴ 'number' supplied in pencil by P.
  ⁵ 'maintaining communications with France' underlined, possibly by P.
  ⁶ The surrender of Fuenterrabia and the previous engagements at Hernani.
  ⁷ 'Both are remarkable for the spirit of conciliation in which the benevolent dispositions of the Government are made known to the insurgents.' (V to P, 28 May 1837, no. 130, FO 72/480.)

341   Palmerston to Villiers, 1 June 1837

Copy. Foreign Office. I have not time to write more than two lines; I send you a dispatch telling you what I have done with Marliani.¹ I take the fact to be that Marliani has signed with Aguado some engagement to get a guarantee of some sort from us; hoping to be able to make good his engagement. As that cannot be done, he must now try to persuade Aguado to stand by his loan without any other guarantee than the treaty which is the only real one possible.

I will send you in a few days Thomson's answer to your 31.

Things seem going better in the seat of war, but depend upon it the Carlists will make an attempt upon Madrid or on Barcelona. Cut off from the French frontier they must either get a new line of communication for money and supplies; or they must take the chance of a dash on the capital. With decent management they are beat, and a glorious event it will be when the free Government of Spain can call itself safely and securely established.

Napier acknowledges that the war is now got beyond his scope. Why should not Wylde have the command of the Legion after Evans leaves it? Wylde has sufficient talent and military skill, and knows all the people he would have to deal with. Perhaps he might be more useful as he is—but I should think the command of the Legion especially if it is to be recruited would be a gratifying finish for him.

GC/CL/1309

  ¹ P to V, 1 June 1837, no. 68, FO 72/475. P informed Marliani that it was impossible for Great Britain to guarantee the loan.

342   Villiers to Palmerston, 3 June 1837

Madrid. Private. This has been an eventful and critical week and the events and the crises are far from being over. The loss of the two best officers in the Queen's army[1] is an irreparable one at this moment, but Don Carlos has no great cause to cantar victoria for the action at Huesca, as nearly 1,000 of his best troops were put hors de combat and he was unable to leave Huesca during four days. This must have disconcerted him greatly as there is now no doubt that the Ebro, Castille, and Madrid were his intentions, but he was fairly outmanoeuvred and pushed northwards by Iribarren. Once there he probably was forced to look to Catalonia for a place of refuge or else to come into Lower Aragon or Valencia where he would have been joined by the factions of Cabrera and others—but he remained at Huesca because he didn't dare move from it, being there exactly as the Queen's army in Navarre, without information and with all his communications cut off. He had also a difficulty about carrying off his wounded as the Navarrese troops he has with him would not suffer them to be left behind, the whole of Upper Aragon being eminently anti-Carlist and 6,000 armed peasants were prowling round Huesca like wolves attracted by the enormous quantity of baggage which goes with the expedition and waiting to suck the blood of the Navarrese which is the favorite food of the peasants of Aragon. Buerens however, who is an idiot and the slowest of all the Spanish generals (you may judge what kind of a coach he must be), allowed the enemy to slip down to Barbastro unhurt and unattacked though he ought to have annihilated them in the level country through which they passed—he did however prevent their passing the Cinca, and they were obliged to hark back again to Barbastro.

In the mean while Oraa has arrived from Valencia and has taken the command of Buerens's army—he is a better general, and more active and intelligent so that something may now be expected, particularly as the Baron de Meer is at Monzon and the left bank of the Cinca is pretty well guarded. How the expedition is able to live is to me incomprehensible, for the supplies they can have found in Huesca and Barbastro must have been trifling, and the peasantry are very vigilant in preventing the arrival of any. It would appear therefore that there is only left for the Carlists to attempt to force their passage over the Cinca or to retreat to Navarre, in either of which cases they ought to be destroyed, or else to sally forth and give battle to Oraa who should then have all the advantages of position and be able to turn to the best account his superior numbers, cavalry, and artillery. Still however we have been so often disappointed and have so often met with failure when success appeared certain that I am far from feeling sanguine upon the present occasion. If the Carlists *were* routed hardly a man would escape for the peasantry and the National Guards would make main basse upon all those who got away from the Queen's cavalry. The matter is perhaps decided at this moment.

Espartero is a pleasant kind of man to have a great cause depending upon at a critical moment! With his usual irresolution, arising from incapacity, he has allowed the successes of Evans to grow cold and the enemy to recover from their panic. He entered Hernani on the 14th—went to bed as usual directly—and on the 28th in bed and at Hernani he was still!! He must have known that Irun and Fuentearabia would fall and his preparations should have been made for marching on the following day to Tolosa, and occupying all the adjacent country in order to narrow as much as possible the theatre of the war, particularly as the expedition of Don Carlos had diminished by one half the forces which have hitherto occupied the Basque Provinces. If he had done so Lerin would not have been betrayed to the enemy,[2] Lodosa would not have been attacked or the Ribera endangered, and he might have detached 10,000 men to render certain the destruction of the Carlist expedition to Aragon.

The public indignation is great and the position of the Government with respect to this man is lamentable—they of course desire to remove him but they dare not risk the danger and the scandal of his refusing to give up the command or turning to his own account the popularity which his lax discipline gives him with the troops. I understand however that on the 29th he did march to Pamplona alarmed by a report which had reached Hernani that Don Carlos was descending upon Castille—when he finds that such is not the case he will probably go to ground for another fortnight at Pamplona.

I am again in great trouble about the Legion for Wylde writes me word on the 27th ultimo that the money which I scraped together with so much toil (and with some official if not personal responsibility) amounting to £40,000 and which the Commissary of the Legion assured me would be sufficient, will not do at all, and that unless I send £20,000 more the Legion will not only refuse to reinlist but there will be the devil to pay on the 10th of June. Now I might as well ask Mendizabal for 20 millions as for £20,000—there is not *one farthing* in the treasury and every general is asking on every side for 10 or £20,000 saying that he neither answers for his troops nor his operations if he is not instantly assisted in preference to every body else. So at this moment I am au bout de mon latin. If Oraa had the good luck to destroy the Carlist expedition at Barbastro the question and the prospects of the war would then so materially change that a good excuse would present itself for the Legion going home and it really then would not be wanted. As long as it remains in this country it will always be more or less a thorn in your side and God knows its departure would to me be an indescribable relief. I am somewhat at a loss too how to proceed not knowing whether the Order in Council will be renewed or whether you will lend the means for conveying home the men who are unwilling to stay.

We hang fire rather about the commercial treaty—without a single advantage commercial or pecuniary on the part of England the Government is *not* strong enough to carry the affair with a high hand in the Cortes unless a decisive victory was gained, for there is no more certainty that capitalists would lend money upon the customs duties to be levied upon English commodities than they would upon any other part of the Spanish revenue. What they want is security against loss in the event of affairs turning out ill here or Don Carlos coming, in which event the customs duties would be no more available for the payment of the dividends than the revenue of Cuba which is now offered as a security. We must be just and in order to judge of what is possible we should put ourselves in the place of the Spanish Government and ask with what face they could present themselves to the Cortes in the present state of the war and of public opinion and ask them to sanction the destruction of the Catalonian manufactures and the little shipping interests of Spain for no other advantage than that of increasing the public revenue by a process which the Cortes are too ignorant and too prejudiced to appreciate.

If Don Carlos is driven out I shall have hopes, *even* though Mendizabal continues Minister of Finance, but not till then.

Since writing the former part of this letter I have seen Calatrava who informs me that you have told Aguilar the Order in Council will be renewed for a year.[3] I shall now set to work and see if I can raise some money—if I do I shall consider myself quite fit to take Spring Rice's place if he likes to resign.

Pray help us in re vessels for conveying home the non-staying Legionists.

I think you will be pleased with the conciliatory measures upon the proclamation of the Constitution.[4] If the war was once put an end to I should really have great hopes of this country.

PS. The division on the Church rates has produced great alarm here in which I cannot deny that I share cruelly.

Received 12 June.

GC/CL/336; Clar. Dep. C.453 (148-153)

[1] Generals León and Iribarren.
[2] Lerin was betrayed by its garrison to the Carlists.
[3] See P to V, 1 June 1837, no. 67, FO 72/475.
[4] These were: 'A general amnesty for all political offences for those who are *not* in arms against the Queen's Government. A removal of the sequestration upon the property of emigrants. The restoration to their rank, pay and honours of all those who, in the month of August last, refused to swear to the Constitution of 1812, upon their now swearing to that of 1837'. (V to P, 3 June 1837, no. 145, FO 72/480.)

343 Villiers to Palmerston, 10 June 1837

Madrid. Private. I have received your letter and dispatches of the 1st. I was always aware, and took care to make the Spanish Government so, that Marliani's patriotic enthusiasm had made him overrun the scent a little, and that he would soon find himself at fault. I have not much hope of any thing being done because a commercial treaty is not and cannot be a guarantee for capitalists even though it were to be productive of any amount of additional revenue to Spain, for what security could the lenders have that such revenue would be applied to the payment of their dividends unless they were in some manner or other placed under the protection of a foreign Power? . . .

Oraa's repulse owing to the cowardice and indiscipline of his troops is a sad business, and more than anything else that has occurred lately destroys my confidence in the future.[1] There is not the least doubt that this system of expeditions *ought* to be the ruin of the Carlist cause,[2] but if the Queen's army from one reason or another cannot take advantage of the goods the gods send them, why there is an end of things. A month however has not passed since a Carlist council of war determined upon defending coûte qui coûte the lines of Hernani and the communications with France, but they were obliged to abandon their plan and to leave the country where their cause had grown and prospered and where alone the prestige of Carlism existed. They lost Hernani, Irun, Fuentearabia and all the lines that they had been fortifying at such vast cost and labor—they lost 28 pieces of artillery, their ammunition and provisions, and their force is diminished by nearly 5,000 men, yet with all this it is possible that the Queen's cause has not gained owing to that invariable Spanish custom of things turning out just the reverse of what might reasonably be expected. I still adhere to my opinion that Don Carlos will be annihilated in Catalonia if he only depends upon the assistance of the Catalans—but in the event of his being able to establish communications with France or to receive money and supplies from Italy, the Catalans may find it worth their while to share his gettings with him, but they will not be moved by any real devotion to his cause like the Navarrese, or by any other than selfish considerations.

The French papers have been making a great row about the secret session of the Cortes on the 18th ultimo. I did not mention the subject to you because I considered it of no consequence, and I could not possibly foresee that such a violent clamor would have been made about reports which were entirely false. The opposition press had for a long time been trying to run down the Government by declaring that every European Power was hostile to the Ministry of La Granja, and that its existence was the only bar to French intervention and all manner of benefits that might be expected from abroad. The Cortes, who are well intentioned but very ignorant, hardly knew what to think of these repeated assertions because they had no arguments or facts with which to reply to them, and Calatrava therefore in a secret session communicated to them some information upon which he said he could rely with respect to the policy of the Northern Powers, the intrigues they were employing at Paris, and the course which the French Government had thought it expedient to pursue, but he never said that this information was derived from Campuzano, whose name was not even mentioned, there was not a disrespectful word uttered with respect to France or the King, and I believe that no observations were made at the time by any Deputy, although upon breaking up the sitting many of them expressed to Calatrava their obligation for having enlightened their darkness and prevented their falling into the trap set for them by the Carlists and the Moderados who are even worse enemies of the Queen's cause than the Carlists. This is the whole story and if any mischief has been done it has been entirely owing to the *gobbemoucherie* of the French papers who all vie with each other in cramming down the throats of their readers with all the apparatus of Gospel the most malignant and unfounded calumnies respecting the cause and Government of the Queen, as well as the general state of this country. If they were all, and the Journal des Débats at the head of them, in the Pretender's pay they could not more diligently serve his interests than they are now doing.

I have entitled myself, *according to my own opinion* and as I told you in my last, to succeed Spring Rice for I managed to have £20,000 more raised, or rather perhaps I should say I laid violent hands upon what was destined for the Spanish army and sent it off to San Sebastian in time for it to arrive on the morning of this important day to the Legion, and it may possibly prevent some disaster.

The idea of Wylde taking the command of the Legion is very much liked by Calatrava, who I have seen since writing the above, but I should be afraid that he (Wylde) would not accept it, for 2 or 3 months ago I asked him whether he would take a command and he said nothing should induce him to do so. I am going to write to him directly upon the subject for I am certain that no man in Spain at this moment is so well fitted to command the Legion, or the whole army of Spain, as Wylde.

It would be very desireable if possible to reinforce the naval station at Barcelona. A steam boat or two there now would be worth their weight in gold.

Received 19 June.   GC/CL/337; Clar. Dep. C.453 (154-159)

¹ On 2 June General Oráa attempted to drive the Carlists out of Barbastro. The Carlists attacked his force and he retreated. (V to P, 10 June 1837, no. 149, FO 72/480.)

² 'Don Carlos will pass into Catalonia ... but I persist in thinking that the change of theatre ought to be the death blow and final ruin of Carlism.' (V to Edward Villiers, 27 May 1837, Clar. Dep. C.467.)

344   Palmerston to Villiers, 15 June 1837

Copy. Foreign Office. The King has been a little more easy since yesterday morning, but there is no alteration in the prospect as to his recovery. It is impossible that he can struggle long against his disorder, and all one can hope is that he may suffer as little as possible during the short period which he has yet to go through.

What the Princess will do when she becomes Queen no one of course can pretend at present to say; but it is probable that she will make no essential change in her Government. . . .

The communications which Thomson and I have had with Aguilar and Marliani, the results of which I send you,[1] really lead me to entertain a hope that a commercial convention will be concluded by you.

Marliani tried hard to get a guarantee out of us in some shape or other direct or indirect; but finding that impossible he betook himself like a wise man to what was practicable, and contented himself with the arrangement for receiving the duties in England instead of in a Spanish port. This in fact ought to be a security to Aguado, and will be so considered by him; though he may give something per cent less to the Spanish Government upon that arrangement than he could have afforded to do if we had consented to a guarantee. Sign away then if you find them in the mood, without further reference to us.

We have said nothing on the subject to the French Government, and do not mean to do so. Of course we can have no objection to a similar convention being signed the next day between Spain and France; but if we were to give France a hint beforehand she would try to thwart us, for the double purpose of depriving both England and Spain of the expected benefit.

You will make what you can of the Gibraltar arrangement. . . .[2]

I have told Aguilar in reply to his request that we would recommend an officer to command the Legion which he has addressed to me in accordance with what I wrote to you, that for the present O'Connell will probably do well enough, and we may as well wait to see what the Legion is likely to consist of in point of numbers before we take any further steps.[3] Perhaps if the corps is only to be one of 1,500 or 2,000 men, Wylde can be more extensively useful in his capacity of Commissioner, advising the general who commands the whole Spanish army, than he could be in the subordinate character of commanding officer of a brigade. Indeed it would be throwing Wylde away so to appoint him unless he were to have an extensive Spanish command as Evans had.

Considine set off some time ago to return to Constantinople; he might be brought back, but it would take some time to fetch him. The

Spanish Government therefore should determine what sort of officer they want if they want any. If they require only a man to command the 1,500 of the Legion, and such additional numbers as may be recruited and sent out to it from here, perhaps O'Connell is as good a man as they could get anywhere. If on the other hand they think of placing a division of the army under the man we should send, and a wise thing it would be for them to do, then we will look out for a good man for them.

Evans is not yet arrived, but I have seen Arbuthnot who stormed Irun. The attack seems to have been a sharp affair, and might have failed with less determined people.

GC/CL/1310

[1] See P to V, 15 June 1837, no. 71, FO 72/475, proposing as an addition to Article 13 of the draft treaty that British merchants exporting goods to Spain should have the option of paying the duty on them to Spanish agents in England.
[2] More effective measures for the prevention of smuggling of tobacco from Gibraltar into Spain. (ibid.)
[3] P to V, 15 June 1837, no. 73, with enclosure, FO 72/475.

345 Villiers to Palmerston, 18 June 1837

Madrid. Private. I have detained my courier till today in order that he may carry an account of the important event which is about to take place this morning: the swearing to the Constitution by the Queen —which will put an end to the hopes and intrigues of the Jacobins, the Isturiztas, the Estatutistas and the French that a reaction might be brought about and the new fundamental law set aside. I think very well of the reformed Constitution and see every reason to hope that it may take root and flourish in the country, and when it is remembered under what auspices it was begun and under what trying circumstances it has been continued and ended, I consider that the Regent, the Government, and the Cortes are entitled to high praise, as well as to the gratitude of all those who desire to see the spread of liberal institutions and this country assuming the place among nations to which it is entitled and from which it has so long and so perversely been debarred.

The arrival yesterday of the news of the Baron de Meer's victory[1] was very opportune, and the people of Madrid are in the highest state of enthusiasm. We have as yet no accurate details of the affair but I hope it is as complete as it is represented to be. My fear as usual is after any success that it will not be followed up—if it is I don't know how the faction is to escape for by going south towards Cerbera and Verdù they place themselves in a cul-de-sac—however they have often been in similar *culs* before and have got out unharmed, so till *we* are out of the wood I shall not begin to whistle. The predictions contained in my dispatch a fortnight ago with respect to Catalonia have not been falsified. Don Carlos was not able to proceed along the skirts of the Pyrenees but has been obliged to move southwards. The Catalan factions have viewed his advent with displeasure and have done nothing to assist him—and as for the people we have as yet not heard of any symptom of movement in his favor. If he has now really been defeated all this will increase for in Spain and more particularly in Catalonia there is no sympathy for a beaten man—like a hunted deer the herd drives him off.

I have been almost mad this week with the Legion affairs—another courier has arrived from San Sebastian with a demand for £100,000 more, notwithstanding all the money that in the midst of this abject penury has been scraped together for them, and letters from Wylde saying that upon my influence and my exertions it depends to prevent a horrible catastrophe, the sacking of San Sebastian and I don't know what besides. Where or how to get any more money I know not—I have devoted all my time to it these last three days and perhaps I shall succeed but what between gratifications, bounties, widows' pensions and arrears, etc., etc., it seems impossible to satisfy these people who insist upon every claim being paid that is brought forward without any of the accounts being audited or even presented in a regular way.

I have looked here into the accounts of money issued to the Legion and I see that in hard dollars upwards of £600,000 has been paid to them since they arrived in Spain, exclusive of clothing and rations—yet when the Legion was at Vitoria at its greatest numerical strength the monthly expence was calculated at from 12 to £14,000.

I am not at all satisfied at having a man of such little experience as O'Connell to command the new Legion, and I shall be anxious to hear whether you have been able to give any effect to your suggestion of inviting the Horse Guards to appoint a good officer. I proposed it to Wylde but I have not yet got his answer.

I believe Evans went off very sulky and did nothing to help the reinlistment on account of his services at Irun not having been acknowledged with sufficient warmth and rapidity, but he has been long enough here to know that things are not done in Spain as in other countries. He was aware too that the Minister of War was ill, and he had no right to disbelieve the assurances I gave him of the gratitude and goodwill of the Spanish Government and their earnest desire that he should remain in the Queen's service upon any conditions he liked to impose. Upon my suggestion that something marquant should be done for him they gave him the Grand Cross of Charles III. Calatrava has written to him himself—and the royal decree of which I send you a translation today cannot be couched in handsomer terms.[2] He has therefore no reason to complain of his *bene decessit*.

I don't advance with the commercial treaty—the reasons that I have stated to you before still hold good—or bad—and without some cotemporaneous money advantages the Government cannot at this moment risk the unpopularity of such a measure. Four months too I must add have now elapsed since I requested on the part of this Government to be made acquainted with the relief which the Board of Trade could grant to importations from Spain to England, and I am always obliged to tell Mendizabal that as yet I have received no answer, which does not look like much empressement on our part. I hope by the next courier to send a satisfactory answer respecting the additional duties levied upon British vessels that have touched at Gibraltar. Calatrava has been so overwhelmed with business this last fortnight that he has not been able to attend to it but I have got the matter through the Ministry of Finance.

I know that a courier was sent to you from Zaragoza with the account of Meer's victory. The person who dispatched him is at this moment employed by me. I do not like however in the present unsafe state of the road to say how or for what purposes but they are such as I thought well worthy of £2 or 300 secret service money which I hope you will not disapprove—he certainly had no authority whatever to send a courier to London and as he did so, I doubt not, for stock jobbing purposes I hope you will not pay the expences of the said courier.

I have just returned from the ceremony at the Cortes which has gone off extremely well. The Queen was accompanied by her daughter which has pleased people greatly and I think that advantage has been well taken of it in the speech. The National Guards of Madrid (nearly

667

10,000 men) are in the best possible spirit—as a proof of their gallantry they strewed the street from the Palace to the Cortes—$\frac{3}{4}$ of a mile— with flowers.

A little naval assistance is sadly wanted upon the coast of Catalonia. Could you let us have a steamboat or two?

Received 27 June.   GC/CL/338; Clar. Dep. C.453 (160-165)

[1] An action on 12 June between the Carlists and Baron de Meer on the plains of Gra. A despatch from Baron de Meer stated 'that the enemy suffered great loss, and abandoned their positions in the utmost confusion after an action which lasted from 9 o'clock in the morning till seven at night'. (V to P, 18 June 1837, no. 158, FO 72/480.)
[2] Enclosed with V to P, 18 June 1837, no. 153, FO 72/480.

346   Villiers to Palmerston, 24 June 1837

Madrid. Private. I yesterday received your letter of the 15th and am much pleased to find you take so favorable a view of the ministerial prospects in the event of the King's death. . . .

I have not yet been able to discuss with Calatrava and Mendizabal the two very important dispatches I have received from you by this courier but I really have hopes that they will be productive of good results. I abstain from saying any thing more upon the subject at present as I am writing by a French courier and will only advert to that which is left to *the option of exporters.* This appears to me to be an error for if you consider it you will see that it *might,* and there are abundant reasons for considering that it *would,* vitiate the whole arrangement.

Calatrava entirely agrees with you that it would not be worth while to send out a really good English officer to command so small a force as the Legion is likely to become, and we both think that Wylde would be far more usefully employed at the elbow of the Commander in Chief than at the head of his unruly compatriots—but Calatrava would be most grateful if you would endeavour to find an officer of experience whose name would be a prestige, and whose rank would enable him to command a division of the Spanish army. Such a man would be received with open arms by the Spanish Government—he might nominally come to command the Legion but 5 or 6,000 national troops would be immediately placed under his orders. This would make the Government independent of the General[1] in Chief, and they are far from being so under present circumstances which compel them to retain a man at the head of the army who they have every motive for wishing to remove. Should you be able to find such a man it might be well to let us know here of it first, before he becomes in any way publicly committed, lest as in the case of Napier, any events may have occurred to render such an appointment less desireable or feasible. I feel very anxious for it as the best mode of getting out of the military embarrassments upon which all others depend, and that it should be settled quickly in order not to lose the season for campaigning. Such an individual should if possible be a general, have served in the Peninsular War and if in the Basque Provinces all the better, he should have great activity and decision, not care for hardships and be a strict disciplinarian—he ought likewise to take some interest in the cause and in the spread of liberal institutions. A rare bird this would be, but not of a genus unknown in England.

The formation of the new Legion goes on slowly and unsatisfactorily for want of money, but there is no contenting those worthies and the exigéances of the officers and men down to the last drummer, together with the scandalous irregularity of the accounts, en masse drive me almost as mad as they do poor Wylde in detail. He declines the command of the Legion upon very sufficient reasons.

It is vexatious that when such gros jeu is playing in Catalonia that we should be ignorant of the results, but since the 14th nothing has been known here. The total dispersion of the Carlists however on the 12th and the enthusiasm and political union which that event produced in Catalonia are undoubted facts, but Spaniards being concerned it is wiser to doubt than to expect that any success will be complete.

The good spirit of the people and National Guard here upon the promulgation of the Constitution has been displayed in a remarkable manner. The Government are very strong in the Cortes as regards a compact majority and the dissensions which increase every day among the party systematically opposed to them, so that a victory or two (or in other words a good general) and a little money would now produce more important results than at any period since the King's death, for the country is exhausted and would take good care to keep the peace if it could once be made, and a new Constitution having been formed to the satisfaction of the vast majority of liberals there would no longer remain any political bones to pick.

Lord Carnarvon has I see published a reply to my pamphlet[2] and I suppose I must have another touch at him, but the weather is very hot and does not incline one to *extraparochial* work.

PS. Don't adopt any measures of retaliation yet against the Spanish Government. I hope in a few days to settle all pending matters of dispute.[3]

Received 3 July.

GC/CL/339; Clar. Dep. C.453 (166-171)

[1] 'Commander' in C.453, which also has '600' instead of '6,000'.

[2] Second edition of *Portugal and Galicia, with a review of the social and political state of the Basque Provinces* (London, 1837).

[3] In connection with the seizure of the *Express Packet* for carrying arms and seditious literature. The owners denied this charge and appealed to the British Government for the release of the ship. Voluminous correspondence on this matter is in FO 72/477-480.

347 Palmerston to Villiers, 29 June 1837

Copy. Foreign Office. We have had so much to do here, and the Queen has had so many things to attend to, that I have not yet been able to get the new credentials of our ministers abroad ready to be dispatched. I shall however in a few days send them off and yours shall be among the first sent away.

Nothing can be more prosperous and promising than the new reign has hitherto been. . . .

I hope you will have found the Spanish Government willing to conclude the commercial treaty. Marliani was very anxious about it and Aguado seems to have been brought to consider such a treaty as a real guarantee—either sign it or send it here to be signed as may be most likely to nail and clench the matter. Your former full powers will do, notwithstanding the demise of the Crown.

Sebastiani asked me the other day by desire of his Government whether we were going to guarantee a loan, or rather without asking any question he read me a private letter from Molé saying that it was reported we were about to do so in consideration of a commercial treaty. I said that he knew as well as we did that both the French and English Governments have repeatedly been asked to guarantee a loan for Spain; that our answer invariably has been that we could do no such thing. That we could give no guarantee direct or indirect, pecuniary or territorial, of dividends or of islands. That we long ago sent you a draft of a commercial treaty with instructions to take every opportunity to press it and that those instructions are still in force. That we have twenty times over told the Spanish Government that commercial treaties with us and with France and with any and every body else, upon the principle of freedom and reciprocity and universal and undiscriminating equality would be the true and only and best guarantee they could give for a loan and that this opinion I repeat to Aguilar every time I see him and he talks to me on the subject.

It is evident the French Government are much alarmed and annoyed at the idea of our making a treaty with Spain; and they will probably do all they can to prevent it. But we must trust that the emptiness of the Spanish treasury and the pressing demands of the war, will compel the Spanish Government to disregard French intrigue and Catalonian cabal.

The men, about 500, who have come home from St. Sebastian are detained at Portsmouth for want of bills on the Spanish treasury at six or eight months for the gratuities due to them. This is inconvenient as the contractors will not supply them any longer with rations for which as yet no payment has been made. The men cannot live on air; and it is not easy for the Admiralty to feed them.

We must however prevent them from starving till the bills arrive and the men can be sent to Ireland.

It has been reported here that the Spanish Government is disposed to convert some of their pictures into money, and especially the Rafaels of the Escurial. If that is so (and pray enquire about it) Spring Rice wishes to have a bid for them for the National Gallery, and he would no doubt make a liberal offer.

We hear that Emperor Nicholas has sent somebody to Madrid to negotiate about this; but if Spain means to sell, England ought to have the first offer. Pray let us hear about this.

It is difficult to understand what is the true state of things in Catalonia but Carlos's army seems wasting away and if the Catalans do not join him we may hope for a good result. What a triumph it will be for you and for us when we are able to boast that the civil war is over.

GC/CL/1311

348 Villiers to Palmerston, 1 July 1837

Madrid. Private. It is most satisfactory to see that your predictions respecting the commencement of the new reign have hitherto turned out so correctly. I trust that they will continue so and that La Reyna nuestra augusta ama will not cease to deserve the popularity which she has already gained for herself. . . .

I wish I had any satisfactory news with which to greet the accession from this part of the world, but the past week has been one of disappointment. I had almost been fool enough to expect some important results from the action at Grà, but the Baron de Meer for want of bread, or shoes, or money or from the simple fact of being a Spanish general, let the good effects of his victory slip through his fingers, and staid a whole week inactive at Cerbera. The Carlists appear, as we have seen twenty times before, to have recovered first from their panic at being beaten, then from their surprize at not being pursued—then they reorganized themselves just as if nothing had happened, and now there is reason to believe they are taking the offensive again and for aught I see to the contrary will cross the Ebro and come into Lower Aragon, which will be by no means a pleasant feature in the war.

Espartero of course does nothing and if it is a system there certainly never was one followed with greater pertinacity or worse results. He will continue however as he has begun unless Wylde can join him, and that cannot be until the affairs of the Legion are finally settled—£3 or £4,000 is all that is wanted, but here we are à sec and although I have applied all my instruments of pressure which at other times have been successful not a piastre have I been able to squeeze out now. The war is now in its financial stage and I really consider the whole question as one more of money than fighting.

My second disappointment has been the suspension of the negotiations of the commercial treaty. Upon this subject I have little to add to what I have told you in my dispatch.[1] The treaty and the loan *must* be united and go hand in hand to the Cortes—it would be quite as hopeless to expect the Cortes to consent to the one without the other as it would be for you to hope for the guarantee of the loan in Parliament. . . .

If I can hit upon any thing before the courier goes I will either suggest it to you or enclose it to Thomson who appears as anxious as either you or I can be for the conclusion of this good work. If the treaty was concluded either one way or the other I meditate asking you for a leave of absence before the autumn when I shall have completed four years of uninterrupted residence in hot water.

PS. No ideas have occurred to me upon the subject of the guarantee, but Southern has given birth to two which I think well worth sending[2]—the one an apparent guarantee which you would probably have no difficulty in granting as it consists only of appointing a commission which would protect the interests of the lenders—the other might necessitate an appeal to Parliament, as the Government might possibly be called upon to make some advance, but in order to place the whole trade of Spain in our hands and to secure the exportation of at least 2 millions worth of British goods surely there can be no doubt of obtaining the consent of the House of Commons—at least I know that I should ask no better than to have for an opponent upon the hustings in a manufacturing district the man who had voted against such a measure.

My courier account is rather high this quarter which is occasioned by having constantly to communicate with the Legion—the additional couriers have saved much additional mutiny among our worthy compatriots at San Sebastian.

If you think either of the projects admissible it will be well to let Marliani know. I have not communicated them to him.

First enclosure: 'A Convention *between Great Britain and Spain for providing a satisfactory mode of paying the interest of a loan contracted for by Spain, out of the proceeds of Spanish duties levied in England on goods exported to Spain under Treaty of Commerce.'*

Second enclosure: 'Convention for the levying 20 per cent duty on the admission of British cotton goods into certain ports of Spain and into the Spanish colonies.'

Third enclosure: 'Convention for the guarantee of the half-yearly dividends upon two millions sterling.'

GC/CL/340; Clar. Dep. C.453 (172-177)

[1] V to P, 1 July 1837, no. 172, FO 72/481.
[2] All three enclosures are in Southern's hand.

349 Palmerston to Villiers, 7 July 1837

Stanhope Street. *Asks Villiers to use his influence with the Spanish Government in favour of Colonel De La Saussaye ('Anglice Colonel Sauce'), and encloses a letter of recommendation from General Evans.*
No enclosure.
Copy.

GC/CL/1312

350 Villiers to Palmerston, 8 July 1837

Madrid. Private. I have received your letter of the 29th ultimo which is even more satisfactory than its predecessor respecting the prospects of the new reign. . . .

I do not wonder at the state of things in Catalonia (and passim) appearing incomprehensible to you, for I myself upon the spot can hardly make out whether the execrable conduct of the Queen's generals is owing to treason or idiotism. No advantage was taken of the victory at Grà. The Baron de Meer remained first a week at Cerbera because he had no money nor provisions—and then when he got them he remained ten days longer—in order to consume them I suppose, but absolutely ignorant according to his own dispatches of where the enemy was all that time. He moved then towards Barcelona, the Lord only knows why, I am sure the Baron does not, and the Carlists who were well acquainted with *his* movements slipped down behind him to the Ebro which they appear to have crossed on the 29th without opposition—Meer informing the Government of the agreable fact and adding that he had no doubt Oraa had *hostilized* them in their passage across the river. Oraa however was of a different way of thinking for, though he must have known that the Carlists could not maintain themselves in Catalonia and though he *did* know that they were approaching the Ebro, he took his army to an opposite part of the province, writing to the Government that he had ordered Brigadier This and Colonel T'other to defend the Ebro. The brigadier and the colonel were at a considerable distance from each other with not 2,000 men apiece and of course they could oppose no resistance to Don Carlos who came to the banks of the river with 7,000 men and whose passage was protected by Cabrera on this side with about 7,000 more.

This being the *fifth* opportunity that has presented itself within a month for annihilating the Carlist expedition, and opportunities they have been such as the gods rarely send their most favored generals —quite equal to some of those bits of intervention prearranged in Olympus of which Homer tells—I say therefore that it is most difficult to decide whether treasonable incapacity or treason pure is the cause of Don Carlos now being in Aragon and thereby frightening the cowardly inhabitants of the 'muy heroica Madrid' out of their senses instead of being on his road to join Don Miguel where it would have been easy to send him if men with heads of asses and hearts of mice had not had the direction of military affairs.

We are now just in the same position that we have always been only in a more alarming degree—everything depends upon a good general and a little money—the former more than the latter for if military successes were obtained money in abundance would soon follow.

With respect to the subject of a long dispatch I wrote you last week[1] and upon which I can say nothing now as this goes by a French courier, we are of course *in statu quo* and must remain so till the answer is received to the question which it was absolutely necessary to ask.

You can hardly suppose that I have not long had my eyes upon the magnificent pictures both here and at the Escurial with a view of transferring them to our National Gallery. Four or five months ago I took the opportunity when Calatrava was in the depth of despair at the emptiness of the treasury to insinuate that he might become a second Aladdin and convert old canvas into solid gold—but he was so horrified at the idea and swore so often that he would sooner sell the shirt off his back than part with a single one of the pictures which the nation valued as the apple of its eye that I have not ventured to renew the subject with him.

I am in the way of knowing all that passes in the picture dealing world, and I have heard nothing of an agent from Nicholas being here for the purpose of buying pictures of which the Government has the disposal, and I am certain that none is in treaty with the Government. The Russian consul at Cadiz was here two years ago buying pictures from private collections for the Emperor, but the greater part of what he sent to Petersburg was looked upon as rubbish. Spring Rice ought to have sent out some really good judge here to pick up the splendid pictures that were to be found in the convents. Louis Philippe did so and his agent has carried off some prizes.

I wish my patriotism moved me to cede to the National Gallery three pictures by Herrera (the master of Velasquez) which I *got privily* from Seville and which have been diligently searched for by the authorities of that place and by the Government ever since, but although my treasury is in a most Spanish condition I should, like Calatrava, prefer a state of shirtlessness to parting with them. I merely mention the subject to shew that valuable pictures may be got here *in spite* of both Government and authorities—indeed it is the best or rather the *only* way of going to work in Spain. A thundering royal decree was published a short time ago against foreigners who were robbing the national pictures, and the Queen's authorities were enjoined not to suffer one to leave the country. The week afterwards I exported a case 14 feet square full of pictures without let or hindrance either here or at Santander.

I wrote some time ago to Alava urging him to swear to the new Constitution and not to stand aloof when the union of contending parties was so desireable for the success of a cause which all classes of liberals have such an interest in securing. I have a long twaddling reply from him saying that it is utterly impossible—that he considers the new Constitution worse than the old—and that he can never forgive the restoration of the latter though it has only been for a few months—how very Spanish and how very foolish.

I think the Queen's letter to the Queen Regent[2] should have been *a trifle* more cordial under existing circumstances and have contained some allusion to the Quadruple Alliance.

GC/CL/341; Clar. Dep. C.453 (178-183)

[1] A despatch on commercial affairs (V to P, 1 July 1837, no. 172, FO 72/481.)

[2] A letter in Queen Victoria's hand, delivered by V to the Queen Regent on 10 July 1837. (V to P, 15 July 1837, no. 187, FO 72/481.)

351   Villiers to Palmerston, 15 July 1837

Madrid. Private. I shall be brief and *not important* today for the road between this and Zaragoza is not in a state to write what it would be objectionable for the facciosos to see. The French courier of last Saturday was detained by about 1,000 of these gentlemen at Fresun[1] (between Calatayud and Zaragoza) and the one who is just arrived was also detained by them 14 hours. They have hitherto contented themselves with cutting open the bags to look for money and have not molested the dispatches, but a continuance of this moderation cannot be depended upon as the troop is commanded by one who I daresay well deserves the nickname he assumes of La Fiera. I leave you to judge of what the man must be who in despite of the claims of Cabrera and others to the honor has been able to win and keep for himself the title of *The* Wild Beast.

His principal object seems to be the intercepting of couriers—he has already stopped several from Oraa, and what is worse he has prevented the arrival of one which Campuzano dispatched on the 7th from Paris and who must be the bearer of answers which it is so important to us to receive.[2] We do not know whether he has been detained only, or shot, which is probable if he has fallen into the hands of these rascals.

You will see by my dispatch of today[3] how very little is known of the movements or rather of the intentions of Don Carlos. He has hitherto failed in all his attempts to take any place that had the least pretensions to be fortified and it is evident that he dares not stop any where or run the risk of an engagement. It is also clear that the course he is now pursuing *ought* to be fatal to the prestige of his cause. If he had left Navarre in order to march upon the capital or to *establish* the theatre of war in another province it might have been viewed as a coup d'état or a military manoeuvre, but when it is seen that first he was pushed out of his original direction by Iribarren—that he was compelled by absolute want to advance where he ought to have been annihilated—that in Catalonia he met with no assistance from his self-styled partizans, could get into no place of consequence and after wandering about with his army exposed to every kind of hardship that can occur in an unfriendly country he was obliged to leave that province —that although Valencia is more favorable to him he appears unable to fix the objects of his march—in short that he has entered the category of Gomez or Don Basilio, running about à la bonne aventure and supporting himself by exactions and plunder, his kingly dignity ought to sink very low in the estimation of his lieges, and the prospects of his cause should be less favorable both at home and abroad. I daresay however that such will not be the case for besides the endurance and unwillingness to yield which characterize Spaniards, illiberals all over the world be they Carlists, or Tories, or Solar de la Marguerita[4] are so convinced that God Almighty made them to have the upper hand, they have such an insatiable desire for command, and above all they are so united, that they come into the field with prodigious advantages against those whose infinite variety of opinions prevents that union which is the first element of success.

I daresay therefore that we shall see the Carlists every where extolling the Pretender's military prowess and skill, and the Holy Alliance more active than ever in remitting money.

I incline to think that Don Carlos points towards Andalusia where he will certainly find more support and be able to do more mischief than in any other part of Spain.

Calatrava yesterday called my attention to a curious article in the Phare de Bayonne of the 8th instant of which I send you a copy. The only thing which makes it worthy of attention is that the Sous Prefet of Bayonne informed the Spanish consul (who is his intimate friend) that he had received the article lithographed from the Minister of the Interior with orders to publish it.

You and Lord Granville must of course know best whether it would be worth while to make any new attempt with Louis Philippe at co-operation in order to put an end to this deplorable state of things here. Any real demonstration of force would be sufficient for the purpose, because the country is groaning for peace, but if left entirely to themselves neither party will yield to the other. The longer the war continues the more will the peace of Europe be endangered and the sooner it is put an end to the more chance will Spain have of establishing moderate government and of not becoming troublesome to her neighbours.

By the next courier I hope to send you satisfactory answers to all our most important grievances—differential duties at Gibraltar—duties on coals—passengers by steam boats, etc.

PS. Should any measure of intervention ever become possible you know as well as I do how much tact will be necessary in order to make it completely successful. These people, however tremendous their distress, can only be assisted in their own way, and any thing that savored of 1823 would be sure to fail, but with a due regard to *forms*, the *substance* is always attainable in Spain.

There is no Russian agent here in treaty with the Government for pictures and Calatrava when I mentioned Spring Rice in connexion with the Escurial nearly cried with despair at being thought capable of selling the only jewels which are left to the Spanish Crown.

Enclosure: MS copy of an article (presumably from the Phare de Bayonne), *advocating the intervention of a large English and French auxiliary force to end the war in Spain and ensure the continuance of constitutional government.*

GC/CL/342; Clar. Dep. C.453 (184-187)

[1] C. 453 has 'Fresno'; El Frasno, between Calatayud and Saragossa, is probably the place meant.

[2] From Aguado about the commercial treaty.

[3] V to P, 15 July 1837, no. 192, FO 72/481.

[4] Sardinian Minister of Foreign Affairs; Sardinia was important because it was the channel through which the Carlists received funds from Austria and Russia.

352   Villiers to Palmerston, 22 July 1837

Madrid. Private. I have not time to write much today for I have been working like a horse in order to get my reply to Lord Carnarvon finished. It goes today, and I am horrified at its length, but I make up my mind at being read by fewer people than before in consideration of the *necessity* which I feel of replying to the lies and the charges which have been brought against the first pamphlet, and I can only say that it has not been for want of good intention if I have not discredited Lord Carnarvon, by shewing that he is grossly ignorant of his subject, and has displayed a levity in his mode of dealing with facts and a *onesidedness* in his views, very derogatory to a historian and destructive of the claim which he puts forth in every page to impartiality.

Upon the Basque Provinces much more might have been said but the subject is dry and has lost its principal interest now that the theatre of the war has been carried elsewhere. It is with respect to the commercial part of the attack that I have endeavoured to render the answer most complete, because if what Lord Carnarvon advanced had been true it would have damaged you and the policy that has been pursued towards Spain, in England—but *facts* have come marvellously to my support.

I don't know whether you will have time or means to give the pamphlet a helping hand when it comes into the world, but a moment of electioneering excitement is so unfavorable for the appearance of any thing upon foreign politics that unless a leading article or two in some newspapers loudly call the public attention to the matter, it will not be diverted from questions of domestic interest. My brother

Edward too who was my factotum with the first pamphlet is abroad, so that I must rely a little upon your good offices as the matter is as important to you as it is to myself.

Affairs here are less black than upon the two last occasions when I have written to you. If the Queen had a general my prophesy that this expedition *should* be the death blow to the Carlist cause would turn out as correct as what I foretold would be the consequence of the Pretender's going to Catalonia. The Queen's generals have to be sure neglected every opportunity which the gods have sent them, notwithstanding which Don Carlos has failed completely—he has met with favor nowhere—he has been unable to gain admission into any place which had as much wall about it as would serve for a kitchen garden in England, and he has shewn himself, although adopting the same course as Gomez did last year, to be greatly inferior to that chief in his mode of putting it in execution. The latter came with a certain sort of prestige as the emissary and lieutenant of the King—the former was the Royal Presence itself, robbing, plundering, sacking, and running whenever the Queen's troops advanced, in short every thing that could destroy kingly prestige has been done. In Aragon and Catalonia Don Carlos is only called Rey de los ladrones[1] and the Valencians in their patois all say of him *Quin Rey tan pobret.*[2] All this has produced its effect even among his own partizans, and the valiant resistance made by several fortified places, and the public spirit which has been displayed upon the occasion in towns where the loyalty of the inhabitants was doubtful and their cowardice more than suspected has been a most unexpected surprise, and a very important event for the Queen's cause.

Oraa had a brush with the enemy on the 15th and put several hundred of them hors de combat. Since then the desertion has been very great and would be more so did not the troops of Cabrera form a cordon round the Navarrese who Don Carlos brought with him, and who are disgusted beyond measure at the scrape in which they find themselves. In order to induce them to leave their country they were told that all the strong places in Catalonia were held by the King's forces, and that he would find no obstacle in marching into Madrid. I suppose he has tried to keep up the lies in the manner that Napoleon did from Moscow (though except in lying Don Carlos has not *much* in common with Napoleon) for we hear that there have been three days rejoicing at Estella on account of the King's having entered Madrid at the head of 30,000 men. His Majesty is now wandering among the barren mountains of Valencia, subsisting nobody can conceive how, and although he ought to be destroyed, I have no doubt that he will escape and if he pleases recross the Ebro (which at present *seems* the only course left to him) and get back to the Northern Provinces where he will arrive with a plentiful harvest of glory, and a fine tale his troops will have to tell their countrymen. Of the 12,000 that left Navarre with him it is calculated that at least 6,000 have disappeared in one way or the other.

As I am writing by a French courier I cannot do more than allude to the answers that we have for some time past been expecting here.[3] They are of a nature so unsatisfactory in every way—so *hyper-Hebrew* in the terms and so infinitely small in the result, that even *I*, anxious *ab imo corde* as I am upon the subject could not advise their being accepted and the two important *aids* that were hoped for must I fear for the present be looked upon as postponed.

Your dispatch No. 87[4] gave me great concern. Of course my views may be all wrong but if you saw matters here as I do both with reference to England, France, Spain and Europe, we should make some exertion in order to do *the* thing needful, and I verily believe that it might be done without your being in any way committed with Parliament more than the corresponding advantages would justify.

Received 31 July.

GC/CL/343; Clar. Dep. C.453 (188-191)

[1] 'King of the Robbers' added in pencil, possibly by P.
[2] Possibly 'What king so poor'.
[3] 'About Aguado's Loan' added in pencil, possibly by P.
[4] 'saying that England could give no guarantee for a loan' added in pencil, possibly by P. See P to V, 13 July 1837, no. 87, FO 72/476.

353   Villiers to Palmerston, 25 July 1837

Madrid. *Introduces Don Pascual Gazangos, an expert in Spanish MSS. whose knowledge would be helpful to the British Museum.*

Received 13 September.

GC/CL/344

354   Villiers to Palmerston, 29 July 1837

Madrid. Private. After the ponderous amount of dispatches which I have inflicted upon you today you will neither expect nor desire a long private letter.

My dispatch No. 202 is almost another pamphlet,[1] but I was moved to write it because it was an opportunity for saying something upon the present state of Spain, and because I thought it just towards Calatrava, who is an honorable, well-intentioned man, that there should exist in the Foreign Office a counter-statement to the unfounded charges brought against him by the French Government. Louis Philippe and his Ministers doubtless believe what they told Lord Granville[2] and I can only then say that their sources of information are most incorrect, and relying upon them as I suppose they do it accounts for the strange and mistaken policy which France has pursued towards this country. Either the French embassy writes the information it receives from the opposition and French party at Madrid which is anything but the truth, or else conforms itself to the taste of those who read the dispatches. Or, Count Molé adopts the views of Isturiz and Toreno who having no stake or interest in Spain think only of satisfying their desire of vengeance, and of proving that others cannot succeed where they so signally failed. If any of these hypotheses be true, and they are probably all so more or less, it accounts for the divergent policy of England and France which on general grounds as well as those which regard Spain are so much to be regretted.

Since the civil war began there has not been any moment when a small demonstration of active goodwill on the part of France would produce such great results as at the present one. The expedition of Don Carlos undertaken as if to prove that he had no moral force in the country, has turned the scale in the Queen's favor to a degree that few persons out of Spain will imagine. The prestige of the Pretender is destroyed in Spain, and in the insurgent provinces it is greatly diminished but there the pride of the people is more engaged not so much in behalf of Don Carlos as in their determination not to be beaten by the Queen's troops, and it is in that country that the exhibition of a foreign force which should mediate as well as occupy for a short time would instantly produce its effect.

There has not been a moment either like the present when so small a force would be sufficient for the purpose—there are no Carlist troops now in the Basque Provinces that could offer any resistance to 8 or 10,000 foreigners, and the moral effect would conclude the whole business. It may be said, Why don't the Spaniards do this for themselves? And I answer, Simply because they *are* Spaniards—they are inactive and incapable—there is not a single man capable of commanding an army among the generals, and the Government with its old inherent Spanish vice of adhering to forms will not or dares not set aside good for nothing men who are generals in order to bring forward many valuable ones who are colonels. The *nation* is full of defects and vice but we should be to them a little blind, and *malgré* all we dislike and despise endeavour to put an end to a state of things which may ultimately be so embarrassing to us.

The manner in which the price of national property has risen lately is an evidence of increasing confidence and the enormous number of buyers is a pledge that property will be interested in tranquillity as a means of constitutional government—while all the accounts from the provinces shew that the people are alive to their own interests in the coming elections and the indications are that the Senate will be aristocratical and the Deputies men of property—a result which of all others will be the most satisfactory to the country at large, and if [in] the mean while some demonstration in decided favor of the Queen were made by France and England either by money or men, confidence would take a prodigious spring and the revolutionary spirit which a civil war always foments would be *completely* extinguished.

I daresay you think me a bore for repeating these opinions so often, but if I take a right view of the duty of a diplomatic agent towards his Government, he should not disguise the opinions which he has peculiar opportunities for forming, and I am very certain that the tranquillizing Spain would repay some trouble and risk and sacrifice on the parts of England and France.

Aguado's answers are a great disappointment—my dispatch will give you an idea of their nature,[3] but the details which it is not worth while to enumerate are still more onerous and offensive than the principal provisions. I would not have hesitated to advise the Government to accept any conditions though they entailed a loss of 50 or 60 per cent, so as they got money, but Aguado's proposition does *not* ensure that vital point. . . .

Anxious as I am that these people should get money, and desiring with my heart and soul to conclude a commercial treaty, I declare that

683

if Calatrava were to put the whole matter in my hands and desire me to give a decision I could not *as a gentleman* recommend him to accept so preposterous a bargain, though as I have not been called upon to give an opinion I have merely suggested that a counter project should be drawn up but I have no hope of its being successful.

You considered a guarantee impossible with reference to the House of Commons, but if the elections turn out well *would* such a measure be impracticable? . . .

If Mr. Goldsmid or any other capitalist wished to turn some honest guineas rapidly, they ought to come out here now, for there is a great deal to be done and the Spanish Government in its present difficulties would submit to conditions that would not be heard of afterwards if things took a more favorable aspect. You may be very sure that a commercial treaty unaccompanied by money is *impossible* in Spain, but if what the British Government could do were satisfactory to Goldsmid and his friends he might make a great deal of money himself and help us to the treaty, but he should come here himself.

Don Carlos has for the last fortnight been in a most critical position—he has been pursued (for the rôle of King and Conqueror or even of attacker has been quite laid aside by His Rural Majesty) with somewhat more activity than usual by Oraa, and Espartero was marching upon him, but there is *of course* a rivalry between these two, the result of which will be inaction, and there is besides a great difficulty in subsisting the army and I suppose another brilliant opportunity for finishing the war will be lost. The Navarrese also who have just sallied forth to the rescue—about 7,000 in number—may produce a great deal of mischief. However the expedition has done much service upon the whole to the Queen's cause both by proving the absence of moral force in the country in behalf of Don Carlos and by the loss of about 6,000 of his best troops.

Notwithstanding all the misery which exists here I have managed by soft words and foul to send off nearly £7,000 this week to the Legion. In a few days I shall be able finally to arrange the question of bonds for the exportation of barrels destined to contain palm oil. I have already a satisfactory note from Calatrava upon the subject and there is only a matter of form to settle arising out of a misunderstanding of the obligations contained in our form of bond.

GC/CL/345; Clar. Dep. C.453 (192-199)

¹ V to P, 29 July 1837, no. 202, FO 72/482.
² See ibid.
³ V to P, 29 July 1837, no. 203, FO 72/482. This despatch details the same conditions as V spells out in his private letter.

355   Palmerston to Villiers, 4 August 1837

Copy. Stanhope Street. *He advised the Queen not to invite Osuna to dinner, and the report in the* Chronicle *is untrue.*

GC/CL/1313

356   Villiers to Palmerston, 5 August 1837

Madrid. Private. I have had no letter from you by either of the last two English messengers. I suppose you have been electioneering. . . .

I have very little to say from hence—Espartero and Oraa who at first seemed inclined to quarrel now appear to be cooperating cordially, but it is rather after the fashion of two individuals mentioned by Mr. Joseph Miller. What's Jack about? Nothing. What's Tom about? He's helping Jack. The same may be said of the two generals —they have now been for many days within a very short distance of Don Carlos whose situation is represented to be miserable, yet they don't run in upon him, or do they seem to know or at least to care for various other expeditions that are creeping over Castille and will present themselves one of these nights at the gates of Madrid. Ever since the taking of Irun nothing has been done by the Queen's troops in the Northern Provinces, and the weaker the enemy the more he has been respected. It is necessary to be in Spain and au courant of their proceedings to believe that there exists in nature such a genus as that of Spanish general—he is quite unlike any other animal, and it is really grievous to see a great country and a great cause disposed of by such wretches.

There is not a farthing of money and I see no chance of getting any. Mendizabal is too ignorant and likes the atmosphere of bankruptcy too much to think of turning to account the real resources of the nation. I wrote you word in a dispatch some months ago all the mischief he would do by persisting in his abolition of the tithes, and so it has come to pass. He has indisposed all that portion of the clergy who were well inclined to the Queen's cause, and he is now obliged to keep on the tithes a year longer, but his measure is put in the most unpopular form, viz. an extraordinary war contribution, after having proclaimed that tithes are a *noxious contribution*, and the measure only passes the Cortes after the greater part of the harvest is got in and will of course be duly gaspillé.

It becomes every day more lamentable that the English and French Cabinets do not understand each other upon the Spanish as they did upon the Belgian question, for the one is quite of as easy solution as the other. If it were once known here that England and France were determined to put an end to the civil war it would cease almost without the exhibition of force—the greater part of the Carlists being as exhausted and as tired of the war as the Cristinos. Nothing can be worse, except the triumph of Don Carlos, than the present state of things. Our hands are supposed to be tied and our naval cooperation is laughed at by the expeditions invading Castille and Aragon, and France is believed by the Carlists to be more inclined to their cause than to that of the Queen, while the Northern Powers must be chuckling at the tendency which all this has to produce coolness between us and France, and I am convinced it is much more on that account than caring for what happens in Spain that there is such an opposition on the part of the Holy Allies and the Tories to prevent a termination of the civil war. If that were once brought about there would be nothing to check the intimacy of our Alliance, for Spaniards might then be fairly left to themselves—England and France might then retire from all intervention in the affairs of Spain, and if these people were unable to settle what would then be only their own party squabbles they would find no sympathy among the liberals of France and England whose Governments would not be worried by public opinion—but the two Governments although professing to have the same ends in view—of tranquillity in Spain and the Queen's throne based upon liberal institutions—adopt means widely different for bringing them about and the inevitable result is distrust and jealousy.

You and Lord Granville, as I have often said before, must know better than me whether this vicious state of things has any remedy—if so it is worth an effort to bring it about—if not we must bide our time and the very disastrous results that time will bring forth.

What am I to do about Hanoverian subjects? A case has already arisen where one has disappeared and I am afraid poor man he has been murdered. I have ordered the seals of this mission to be put upon his property to prevent its being robbed by the authorities here, the same as I should have done during the life of the late King, but my right to do so may be disputed and I have nothing to shew in support of it.

PS. The French ambassador arrived here the day before yesterday—he is reposing after the fatigues of his 3 weeks journey and I have not yet seen him.

Received 14 August.

GC/CL/346; Clar. Dep. C.453 (200-203)

357   Villiers to Palmerston, 12 August 1837

Madrid. Private. All that I wrote to you last Saturday has already come to pass. Segovia has not only been attacked but taken, and the Carlists have been so close to Madrid that the citizens might, if they had had the smallest inclination that way, have walked out yesterday evening to see a bit of an action which took place between 4,500 of the enemy and 3,000 of the Queen's troops—the former were fortunately repulsed and we have not had occasion to try the mettle of the National Guard. I think however they would behave well, for when the Minister of War announced the night before last that the enemy had got between Mendez Vigo and the capital and that they were about to occupy the Pardo which is at the gates of Madrid, hardly a man among 11,000 was found absent from his post, and this too in spite of their not having the slightest confidence in either the civil or military authorities of the town—a feeling in which they are perfectly justified, for these authorities occupy their places not because they are fit for them, but because they are *patriots* of 1812 or 1820 and I leave you to judge what a parcel of old files good for nothing 20 years ago must be now[1]—so that the good spirit which has prevailed here is doubly credi-table to the people. Nevertheless I have no doubt whatever that if the Carlist force which took Segovia had marched on the same night upon Madrid they would have had no difficulty in getting in, and though they might ultimately have been kicked out or killed yet as all the lower orders here are little better than Carlist banditti a great deal of confusion and pillage would have taken place, and the moral effect both in Spain and abroad would have been very bad. As it is, I fear that Segovia having been taken, San Ildefonso occupied in the name of the King, and Madrid being quasi-besieged for a week will be very prejudicial to the Queen's cause, and Espartero having been obliged to draw off his forces from Aragon where he was really squeezing Don Carlos very tight will give the latter a great élan, and I shall not be surprised to hear that he has taken Valencia or at least some of the strong places in that province.

The Barham appears to have done some right good service the other day by firing upwards of 100 shots at about 6,000 Carlists who were creeping down towards Valencia, and by driving them from the sea coast. Wylde's presence here has likewise been of use. The affair of this week however will do more harm out of Spain than in it. The French Government and French newspapers will magnify it all and great will be the joy of the Carlist Courts.

When I wrote to you last week upon the subject of coming to an understanding with France about the Spanish question I had not yet seen the ambassador whose repulsive manner and querulous language render him a most emblematical representative of his Master's policy. It is clear he has returned with instructions which his own disposition will prompt him to comply with to the fullest extent of their letter and spirit[2]—he is very reserved with me and with Calatrava he hardly disguises his intention of picking a quarrel.

Howard on his side has but a bad report to make of M. Bois le Comte and it would seem that the policy of France in the Peninsula is more anti-English than anything else. I wish I thought we were strong or bold enough to beat her.

Wylde tells me that the new Legion consists of about 1,000 good infantry and an excellent regiment of cavalry if the Spanish Government will give a few horses. He recommends its being brought into the interior and actively employed.

The consul at Bayonne will have told you the trick I have for the *second time* been played by Mendizabal respecting payment of the Legion—twice with infinite labor and as a personal favor to myself I have induced people who had sworn to have no further transactions with Mendizabal, to advance the money. I had the written assurances of Mendizabal that it was destined for the Legion—I sent the courier with it and the first time it was taken by the Spanish consul at Bayonne (acting upon orders *which my courier took*) to pay some contractors, and the second it was all applied by the Commissary to similar purposes

—not one farthing having been given either to the old or new Legion! And Mendizabal like a thief at the Old Bailey impudently swore to me that he had never given the orders upon which these men acted. But there was no thief that ever was brought to a bar who I would not sooner trust than Mendizabal. O'Connell who now commands the Legion is come here to represent about this felony, and Captain Lyot of the Reyna Gobernadora has arrived to claim his dues, so that I am really almost driven mad with these just demands and the impossibility of satisfying them.

I daresay that the French Government will be fire and fury about a speech which Arguelles made this week about Camarillas and foreign influence, and to a certain degree they will be right for I believe the speech will have disarranged their plans grievously. The fact is that the return of the ambassador and his known hostility to the Government set all the 'Moderados' and their intrigues to work—they were tampering with the National Guard and using the Queen's name to the right and left. Arguelles accordingly delivered a thundering denunciation of the plot but in the *calor de la improvisación* his allusions to the Queen were in bad taste and he did not separate her sufficiently from the intriguers by whom she is surrounded. Calatrava ought certainly to have answered Arguelles at the moment, and then all would have been right—but he did not, and the Queen was justly offended. She will probably have complained to the ambassador of her Minister—however on the next day but one Calatrava made an admirable defence of the constitutional good conduct of the Queen for which she warmly thanked him, and Arguelles also explained satisfactorily. I believe the result has been a useful one for it has put the Cortes upon their guard as well as the Nationals, and it may perhaps have saved the country from another French coup d'état—an *Isturizada* like last year.

In the midst of all the bother of the last ten days the Portuguese Government thought proper peremptorily to order home their Legion just at the only moment since it came to the country when it could do any service. I believe however that I have succeeded in persuading the Portuguese chargé d'affaires to take upon himself the responsibility of delaying their departure until the matter could be again referred to Lisbon and I have written to Howard to insist upon the Legion being left here for the present.

PS. I have drawn for a little more Secret Service money[3] which in moments such as these I am obliged to employ rather more liberally than before. I have likewise been printing a pamphlet upon commercial subjects. I don't know whether I go beyond the mark in this expenditure but I have been so well convinced of the necessity of what I have paid that I would rather have *deposited* myself than have gone without *what I have bought*.[4]

Received 19 August.

GC/CL/347; Clar. Dep. C.453 (204-209)

[1] C. 453 has 'be worth now'.

[2] 'In reply to a question from me whether there was any change in the views or the policy of France with respect to Spain, Count La Tour Maubourg said, with a look of some surprise, most undoubtedly not, and all that had of late occurred here only confirmed the views, and justified the policy, of his Government.' (V to P, 12 Aug. 1837, no. 224, FO 72/482.)

[3] The sum drawn on 12 August was three hundred pounds. (V to P, 12 Aug. 1837, separate, FO 72/482.)

[4] Postscript omitted from C.453.

358 Palmerston to Villiers, 12 August 1837

Copy. Foreign Office. I have been obliged to detain this messenger a few days because I have been too busy to write. There are so many matters of form to be gone through on a new reign, so many people to see about nothing and so many complimentary missioners to present to the Queen that half of every day is lost for real business.

Aguilar showed me the other day Marliani's letter to O'Shea answering the objections made to Aguado's conditions for the loan: I do not feel myself very competent [to judge] which of the two is most in the right, but this I know that no Government can go on without money even in time of peace and much less in time of war. That the Spanish Government and the Queen's cause are suffering every day great and irremediable injury from the want of money; and that especially in this country the most extreme discredit is daily attaching more and more to the Spanish Government from its total cessation of all payments whatever; and when the stream of the current service has been dammed up for a certain time it will sweep away everything before it by the accumulated indignation which it has created—widows, orphans, wounded and maimed officers, discharged men, contractors, every kind and description of claimant appeal to us against the non-payment of Spain. I tell them all that Spain will pay when she can, but has now no means, but even this excuse will only for a time keep these matters quiet to say nothing of the public creditors of various kinds. But what is the conclusion to be drawn from this? Why, that Spain must have money and that to get it she must pay its price, and that almost any sacrifice is worth making for a sum which would enable the Spanish Government to get out of its difficulties and conclude the war.

Colonel Lacy of the Artillery is about to start to act with the Southern armies in the same capacity as Wylde with the Northern[1]—Lacy is a man of whose professional talents Vivian speaks highly; and he is said not to be merely a technical man but to have higher capacities. I hope he may be of use. You will post him where he can be of most service, he will take two subalterns with him.

Our elections do not turn out as well as we expected. . . .

I have read through the manuscript which was sent me; it is very good, and I kept it only two days. I hope soon to see it in print.

The Queen continues to be as favorable to us as ever; she takes great interest in the Spanish question, and is most anxious for the success of the Queen of Spain. She naturally is eager for the well being of Leopold and for the stability of Doña Maria's throne. Here are several leading points in which the Queen agrees with her present Ministers, and differs with the Tories.

GC/CL/1314

[1] See P to V, 16 Aug. 1837, no. 105, enclosing a copy of Lacy's instructions, FO 72/476.

359 Palmerston to Villiers, 14 August 1837

Foreign Office. I have received yours of the 5th which gives not a very encouraging account of the state of affairs in Spain—and matters will not improve till the Spanish Government gets money. As to doing anything to alter the divergence of opinion which you allude to, that I fear is beyond our power. So we must trust to il tiempo e la pazienza.

You may perhaps as a matter of courtesy continue to take charge of Hanoverian subjects, and by the diplomatic usages of Europe when a Government has no representative in a country, the representative of the Court most nearly allied by blood is allowed to stand proxy; I conceive therefore that the English minister at Madrid ought to be permitted to look after Hanoverian interests till a Hanoverian minister arrives.

I send you a report of our Tiverton proceedings; we had things very much our own way there.

Copy.

GC/CL/1315

360   Villiers to Palmerston, 19 August 1837

Madrid. Private. I am so much pressed for time today owing to the early hour at which the ambassador is pleased to dispatch his courier that I can do little more than refer you to my official account of what has passed here during the last few days.

We are in a second edition of La Granja,[1] only Luchana is a very inferior man to Serjeant Garcia—the latter at least did the whole thing in person and stood the consequences of his act, whereas the General in Chief sets fire to the building and when the flames burst out he sneaks off to avoid the responsibility and to perform his duty as a general when the enemy has got far away and his army is too demoralized to pursue them. Circumstances have made that man the curse of his country—vain, presumptuous and incapable, sluggish from habit and bad health, beloved by the soldiers for his own crimes as a general, viz. a reckless indifference to discipline, upheld by his officers because from his love of ease and desire for popularity he acceded to all their monstrous demands for promotion without regard to their merits or the exhausted state of the treasury. In short during the last critical year of the civil war when the Government, the cause, and the country depended upon the army it appeared equally dangerous to leave Espartero at its head or to remove him. To my mind the latter has always been the lesser evil and I have worked in that sense, but the Government has been weak and as men poverty stricken cannot make themselves respected they have been timid and nothing has been done.

A fortnight ago I thought the Queen's cause was more than ever in the ascendant, I now think that that of Don Carlos is, from the disunion of the liberals and not from his own success, in a state of unusual prosperity. I fear you will think my letters and dispatches contain opinions often at variance with each other upon the affairs of this country, but the truth is that *facts* are constantly at variance with each other, and Spaniards the most sagacious and the best versed in things here are as often at fault as the most ignorant stranger. There *is* no foretelling what the vagaries of ignorance, incapacity, and insubordination may be, and thus whenever things look most favorably they may be on the brink of an abyss which at the moment is concealed from view, and the direction even in which it lies is unknown.

On the other hand however it must be said that affairs when they appear utterly boulversés do scramble up again and right themselves in a manner that it would be impossible to hope for in any other country than Spain. Even today when confusion never appeared more confounded I do not absolutely despair, for if Espartero accepts the Ministry[2] and a more capable man is put at the head of the army and *any* success is gained over the enemy the new Government may maintain itself until the elections, when men more likely to possess the confidence of the country may be found in the Cortes. The indiscipline of the army however and the exhausted state of the treasury are obstacles of gigantic magnitude to the existence of this or any other Government.

The intrigues of the Moderados, who are now the real Jacobins of Spain, have increased prodigiously *within the last fortnight* and the Queen has unfortunately lent her ear to advice which she may have bitter cause for repenting—however more of that another day; as the next 8 and 40 hours will probably be fertile in events and the avenir will be rather more discernible than at present I shall probably send a courier by whom I may write ad libitum.

The courier from England who should have arrived yesterday has not yet made his appearance and as the Zaragoza road is free I conclude the delay must have been occasioned in London.

I grieve to see how unfortunately correct my prognostics have proved respecting our own elections and I am, as you may suppose, most anxious to learn what are your opinions respecting the prospects of the Government in the ensuing Parliament.

Wylde has been most active and useful in the recent events.[3] I believe if it had not been for him and for his reading to Espartero a very strong letter which I wrote to him upon the misconduct of the officers and the disgrace which would fall upon him (Espartero) as their general, that there would have been an outbreak and violent means would have been resorted to for putting down the Government.

Wylde having been obliged to march with Espartero I promised to make his excuses to you for not writing by this courier.

Received 28 August.

GC/CL/348; Clar. Dep. C.453 (210-213)

[1] On 17 August Espartero, who had been in Madrid with his army for several days, left the capital and marched to Arabaco, a league from Madrid. He then sent back word to Madrid that he would not continue the war until the Queen Regent changed her Government as he no longer had any confidence in the Government. The Government stated that they had no confidence in Espartero, but he was so popular in the army, especially with the ranks, that they could not dismiss him, so the Government resigned. V says that the Queen Mother and the Moderados had for the past fortnight been openly intriguing against the Government, and that Espartero was their chosen instrument. A new Ministry was appointed, with Espartero (i.e. Luchana) as President of the Council. (V to P, 19 Aug. 1837, no. 229, FO 72/482.)

[2] Espartero had been offered the Ministry of War but had not yet accepted it.

[3] Wylde was with Espartero at Arabaco where the latter and his officers made their demands for a change of Government.

361   Villiers to Palmerston, 26 August 1837

Madrid. Private. I have received your letter of the 12th and have communicated to that worthy old gentlewoman Bardaji[1] all you say upon the absolute necessity of getting money at any price. She quite agreed with you but has no idea where to get it or how to look for it. Esto no marcha—or rather it does marchar towards complete dissolution, and society (if this set of wild beasts can pretend to be called social) is all but resolved into its original elements. With a thermometer at $100°^2$ (I believe) I cannot write much, neither would there be any use in detailing to you the intrigues of parties—the treachery of generals—the mutiny of soldiers—the disorder, the beggary, the fear, the chaos in short which exists here at this moment.

I cannot say I see my way out of it at present, for though I believe the heat has much to do with all that is passing now, and that Spaniards being mad in August convert Spain into one great Bedlam, still they seem to be carrying their freaks far beyond what their lucid intervals can repair.

If Don Carlos eventually succeeds one half of his kingdom would hardly be a sufficient reward for Espartero who is the only man who has ever done him real service—yet he is not an intentional traitor. I wish he was, for knowing the objects or interests of a rogue one can deal with him—but upon a fool and a weak man no dependence can ever be placed—he is sure to throw one over at the moment of need. What is to be done with him I know not—this Government is not strong enough to take active measures with a mouse; much less with a blockhead to whom they owe their places and who is at the head of 8,000 men whose only desire is to come to Madrid—whether as friends or foes it is quite indifferent to them. He must be left to fret his hour I suppose, and it will probably not be a long one for the same fate as Escalera's[3] awaits him or any other general who winks at mutiny.

As for military operations they appear to be quite forgotten and the civil war with Don Carlos is lost sight of in presence of that between the liberals themselves. As usual my hopes rest upon the Carlists being Spaniards likewise; and as they must therefore be exposed to the same canicular influences, I trust they will not take advantage of our disasters and their own most favorable position. They are reported to be quarrelling among themselves both at Canta Vieja[4] and in Navarre but they are not cursed by a free press wherewith to excite their passions and publish their shame, so if they right themselves sooner than the Cristinos do and proceed steadily to work the whole game may be up before the end of the autumn, which is what the French Government and its most faithful representative here reckon upon.

Their plan is (and I have other reasons for saying this than mere conjecture) to give *direct intervention* in favor of confusion—to frighten and disgust the Queen with her position—to induce her to run away to the coast where she would be received on board a French ship. She then would be invited to Paris with her daughters and her position there rendered as royal and comfortable as may be, and with these hostages for Don Carlos's good behaviour towards France in his hands Louis Philippe would look with indifference at the Pretender's success —not only with indifference but with pleasure, for upon the ruins of Spain and the establishment of the Inquisition he would take his stand, and claim to have qualified himself for admission into the precincts of the Holy Alliance. Can you devise any counter-project?

I fear that the manner in which the elections have turned out will tie your hands upon questions of foreign policy, and that you will be unable to carry any large measures. . . .

I am happy to hear that the Queen takes so warm an interest in Spanish affairs. Do you think it would be worth while to give her my pamphlet as I have endeavoured to expose the Tories and their policy with respect to Spain in it and against them it would be desireable to indispose the Queen as much as possible? If you agree in this and think that Her Majesty has either time or inclination to devote to such matters perhaps you would desire Ridgeway for me to have a copy properly bound.

Almost a month ago I mentioned to you that a short leave of absence, to be used according to circumstances, would suit my case this year, for my life here is rather a weary one, but you did not give me an answer.

Received 4 September.

GC/CL/349; Clar. Dep. C.453 (214-217)

[1] The new President of the Council.
[2] GC/CL/349 probably has '100°'; C. 453 has '200°'.
[3] Generals Escalera and Sarsfield were murdered in August 1837, at the instigation it was rumoured of civilian radicals.
[4] Cantavieja in Lower Aragon was Cabrera's stronghold.

362 Villiers to Palmerston, 1 September 1837

Madrid. Private. This letter will be taken by a courier who I send to the frontier for two purposes—one I shall mention upon a future occasion, and the other is to try and keep the remnants of the Legion in order, for on the 10th of September by the terms of their new contract they are entitled to a year's gratuity and their discharge in the event of their not having been paid by that time. I am in hopes to conclude an arrangement today or tomorrow by which they shall be settled with and all the poor devils in London enabled to receive some money and have their claims put in a course of regular settlement.

I am so far pleased with the new Minister of Finance[1] that he does not attempt to juggle and deceive as his predecessor did or to give bills which he means to protest or ask me to send money to the Legion which upon its arrival he has ordered to be disposed of differently. Pio Pita the present Minister makes no disguise of the stupendous difficulties with which he has to contend, but he is determined to settle the affairs of the Legion as quickly and satisfactorily as circumstances will permit of. He did not however find one single dollar in the treasury when he came into office—the whole of the revenue of the State is pledged over and over again—the contributions in one way or another are paid in advance for the next two years and consequently not a farthing is received by the Government and the army is everywhere in a state of mutiny for want of pay. The situation is appalling and the difficulties I fear quite insuperable, for military successes alone can restore confidence or credit and what successes or even military *operations* are to be expected from an army which has been able completely to throw off all the restraints of discipline?

Fear is now the predominant feeling here, and at Madrid as in other places it is likely to lead to acts of folly and desperation. The Cortes are capable of doing something rash with respect to the regency of the Queen, and the clubs are already marking out for assassination some individuals who they politically or personally dislike. I have mentioned Seoane's duel in a public dispatch because it may possibly have public consequences.[2] If he were to die now or be killed in a continuance of these duels I have no doubt that the National Guard will assassinate all the officers concerned, and then we shall have a parcel of ferocious soldiers, headed by their officers too, rushing back to Madrid to chastise the National Guard. In short this is a chaos in which blind wild beasts are tearing about quite mad, and the Mighty only knows how soon they will all devour each other or how it will all end. Not that anything which is occurring now is new or inconsistent with the Spanish character. During the war of independence, which was a purely national one and not like the present where adverse principles are struggling for mastery and shades of the same opinions still more hotly opposed to each other, the same misery and mutiny were always to be observed, the Government was always out at elbows and the generals assassinated then as now, but in the midst of all that disorder there was a nucleus of discipline and good spirit in the British generals and their forces which prevented the national cause from ever sinking too low and enabled the Spaniards when the moment of fury was over to collect again their scattered elements of resistance against the enemy.

It was always foreseeing and dreading this state of things that I advocated intervention, for now the Queen's cause has nothing to rely upon but people who are incapable of any great or vigorous exertion, of measuring the consequences of their own acts, or of bringing *anything* to a successful conclusion. Thus the most brilliant prospects that ever opened to a nation have been gradually frittered away and the triumph of Don Carlos, if he succeeds, will be exclusively due to his opponents.

The French newspapers are I see all applauding the military insurrection which overthrew the Ministry of Calatrava and joying over the defeat which they suppose England to have sustained in the revolutionary Government.[3] I think it would be very expedient to have some articles put in the Chronicle denying that England has ever taken part in making or unmaking of Governments in Spain or done anything but faithfully fulfill the stipulations to which she was bound by treaty.

Received 11 September.

GC/CL/350; Clar. Dep. C.453 (218-221)

[1] Pío Pita Pizarro.

[2] Seoane was challenged by one of the officers whose conduct at La Granja he had criticized in the Cortes. (V to P, 1 Sept. 1837, no. 246, FO 72/483.)

[3] See *Journal des Débats*, 26 Aug. 1837. C.453 has 'movement' instead of 'Government'.

363 Villiers to Palmerston, 2 September 1837

Madrid. Private. Your dispatches of the 24th ultimo arrived here last night, but I had no private letter from you, and I have not much to add to my letter of yesterday except that the progress of dissolution has been about as great as it could be in 24 hours—nobody seems to think of anything but their own dissensions and those who have no quarrels upon their hands or do not mix in those of others are dispirited, and resigning themselves to a more than Turkish fatalism.

The Government is null and the Cortes very little disposed to support it. In short all looks like a break up and unless a favorable turn takes place the Queen's cause will shortly have to receive extreme unction, which is what has long been desired by certain people whose interests would seem to lay in a directly contrary direction.

With respect to your dispatch No. 111 and *one* of its enclosures, there appears to exist a wish to réchauffer relations which have cooled and the interest of the *wisher* is very plain in doing so, but if you *render yourself to the amiable invitation* I hope it will be upon condition that something is done to forward elsewhere what you have for some years now had at heart,[1] and it seems to me you might turn the crisis which is considered so alarming to account in more ways than one.

I don't know whether I make myself clear but I don't venture to write more plainly.

Poor Seoane is in great danger and will I fear die.

I will use my utmost exertions to get money sent to London next week for the Legion.

PS.[2] I hope you will have the pamphlet helped a little in the Chronicle—it will want it at this inauspicious moment for its publication. Pray tell me if you have thought it worth while to give a copy to the Queen.

Received 11 September.

GC/CL/351; Clar. Dep. C.453 (222-223)

[1] Commercial relations and a possible commercial treaty.
[2] In C.453 only.

364 Palmerston to Villiers, 7 September 1837

Windsor. The last accounts we have had from Spain are certainly not encouraging; but nevertheless I do not despair. It is very provoking that our good friend and ally Louis Philippe should do us as much harm as our opponents the arbitrary Courts; but the object we are striving to attain is great, and the condition attached to the attainment of great objects is a long and painful struggle against disappointments and difficulties.

I will give the Queen a copy of your pamphlet. She will I am sure read it with interest.

Leopold and his Queen are here; I fear that he is not altogether free from participation in the French Estatuto attempt; he probably thought that it would assist the Charter Party in Portugal.

General Romorino came to me two days ago, and asked me to give him a note of introduction to you which I did. He said that he and six other French officers were going to Spain to offer their services to the Queen—that all he wanted was the command of a division and that he would engage to do something with it. I never saw him before, and know nothing of the people who are going with him. He tells me he is a Genoese by birth, has served in the French army under Buonaparte; volunteered to assist the Poles, and being now a general in the French service has obtained leave to go to Spain through England instead of going straight by Oleron, is[1] that he thinks he can get to

699

Madrid more easily by Vigo than through the country which is the seat of war, and that he hopes to get some pecuniary assistance in England. He has asked me for £200 which I shall probably give him from Secret Service. I should advise the Spanish Government however to be on their guard about him. He may be a good officer, and he *may* be an honest man; but his famous march away from Warsaw when the Russians were going to attack it, lost the cause of Poland. If he could raise a Polish corps he might be put on his trial, and something at least might be got out of him while he was behaving well to inspire confidence; but it would not be prudent to give him at once an important command. I cannot but feel some sort of instinctive suspicion about him.

We can do nothing to assist the Queen more than we have already done; I am sorry for it, but so it is.

I preach to Leopold that his father in law has other objects in view than the welfare of Spain and the end of the war. He does not and of course cannot acknowledge it, but it is impossible he should not feel it.

Copy.

GC/CL/1316

[1] *Recte* in?

365　Villiers to Palmerston, 9 September 1837

Madrid. Private. I hardly know how or where to begin extracting from the great chapter of confusion here in order to give you any clear ideas upon all that is so dark and damnable. After all I believe I must leave to your imagination to conjecture what are the probable results of political intrigues, angry uncompromising passions, Carlist hopes and liberal fears, a weak and disunited Government, a mutinous army and universal beggary, all acting and reacting upon each other. If these are not the elements of chaos I don't know what are, but that *chaos reigns in Spain* there can be no doubt—where the light will break from or when, is beyond my powers of prophesy to say, and I shall therefore confine myself to things as they are at the present moment.

The 'Moderados' or would-be French doctrinaires but who are in reality no better than French Jacobins have had their coup d'état in changing the Ministry recoil upon themselves—they made their 18

Brumaire but the part of Napoleon like that of Hamlet was left out by particular desire. Espartero was totally incapable of understanding what he was induced to do,[1] and the Moderados were totally deficient in the courage necessary for availing themselves of what he had done. The change of Government accordingly became only a change of men's names and neither French nor Spanish intrigues have advanced in their objects, further than by adding to the confusion which already existed. The present Ministers are as anxious to be upon good terms with the Cortes as their predecessors—they as cordially hate and despise Espartero—they are as distrustful of France and as eager to deserve the support of England as ever Calatrava shewed himself to be. Unfortunately they have very little talent or energy and without military successes, of which I see not the most distant prospect, they like every other Government which has gone before them cannot exist. As for the two Ministers—of Foreign Affairs and of Finance—with whom I have to do I am well satisfied. Bardaxí is ultra English in his opinions and from Pita I have met a far greater desire to behave fairly towards the Legion than in Mendizabal from whom I never extracted sixpence except with le couteau sur la gorge.

That worthy has been playing some of his accustomed tricks. The consul at Cadiz writes word that in order to make himself popular there and to secure his election he wrote to some of his friends saying, that he had been compelled to consent to the suspension of the exceptional duties at Gibraltar but that they would soon be reimposed. This he did while Minister—and I know that he gave assurances to the Catalan Deputies that he never would consent to a treaty of commerce with England. He is much disappointed at Pita's making exertions to pay the Legion and even Captain Lyot, a simple-minded mariner, said he had found out that Mendizabal was putting difficulties in the way of his claims being settled. I don't know whether you are still laboring under any delusion about him, but you may be assured that there is not a greater rogue between this and London than el tal Mendizabal.

In all the intrigues and plots he is now engaged in he pretends to be supported by England and whenever he has 20 or 30 people gathered together in his room he sits down as he tells them to write a letter to me which letter I need not tell you never arrives, but this may in some measure account for the reports carried to the French embassy by the canaille from whom the ambassador gets his information that I am helping the ultra revolutionary party, and it is from the French embassy that has probably emanated a most false and injurious attack upon Southern in the Journal des Débats of the 1st September. I have thought it absolutely incumbent upon me to reply to it and Southern has done so likewise. I shall send my letter under flying seal to Lord Granville as I have the most profound respect for his judgment but I trust he will see no difficulty about sending my letter to the editor.[2]

I have written a longer dispatch than perhaps was worth while respecting the difference between Calatrava and La Tour Maubourg about the offer of mediation in Sardinian affairs,[3] but I was desirous of placing upon record that the mistake, if any existed, was not mine. I have no doubt either that it was not Calatrava's but that the ambassador, moved by his Sardinian sympathies, gave at the time an official character to communications which he is now pleased to call confidential.

I doubt the truth of the reports which have been received here within the last 24 hours[4] and I do not think that Don Carlos, at least, can be as near Madrid as it is said, but it is certain that the factions are approaching on all sides and this place may be the theatre of some very ugly events before I write to you again.

Is it true that Bowring is gone upon a mission to Egypt? If so I think it would do no harm if he were to return home viâ Barcelona and see if he can make the manufacturing smugglers of that province take a different view of their interests.

I am very little pleased with the notice taken of the pamphlet in the Morning Chronicle. At this season of the year and in the present state of politics at home any publication upon foreign affairs requires a great deal of puffing and pushing by the newspapers in order to attract attention to it. If you approve of the pamphlet and think it likely to do any good it should have a helping hand from you.

PS. I omitted to mention that my principal object in sending a courier last week was in order to enable the Duke of Ahumada to escape—we knew he was destined by the secret societies here to be murdered as Sarsfield was—he could not have got away without my assistance. He is now safe at Oleron, and I have the satisfaction of having saved the life of one of the best—I should say the best—and most honorable men in Spain.

Received 18 September.

GC/CL/352; Clar. Dep. C.453 (224-227)

[1] Espartero did not accept the Presidency of the Ministry.

[2] The *Journal des Débats* for 1 September 1837 alleged that V and Southern had had contacts with the disaffected battalions in the army before the events of La Granja, and that Southern actually took part in the military insurrection which made the Queen a prisoner. Granville did not send V's letter to the editor as he 'did not think there is much point in engaging in controversy with newspapers'. (V to Granville, 9 Sept. and 7 Oct. 1837, PRO 30/29/423; Granville to V, 10 Sept., PRO 30/29/422.)

[3] V to P, 9 Sept. 1837, no. 252, FO 72/483. The conflict between Spain and Sardinia was about commercial relations. The Sardinian Government did not recognize the Government of the Queen Regent, and refused to allow Spanish consuls to function in Sardinia-Piedmont. Spanish merchants complained that they were harassed by the Sardinian Government and had no consuls to protect them. Both the British and French Governments were anxious to mediate; the conflict thus became as much an Anglo-French as a Spanish-Sardinian one.

[4] 'Yesterday reports from different towns in the provinces of Cuenca and Madrid were received that the main body of the Carlist army was rapidly advancing upon the capital, and this morning it is said that the Pretender himself is at Tarancon about twelve leagues from hence.' (V to P, 9 Sept. 1837, no. 259, FO 72/483.)

366 Villiers to Palmerston, 16 September 1837

Madrid. Private. The ugly things which I said in my last might possibly happen here this week have not come to pass as yet, but you will see by my dispatch[1] that as far as the intentions of the Pretender and the incapacity of the Queen's authorities are concerned I was not without grounds for my prediction.

It is always gros jeu in Spain to depend upon the good management or cooperation of any body, but I could almost wish that Madrid had been seriously attacked for the results might have been decisive. Don Carlos was evidently deceived by false information as to the state, or rather means of defence here as well as the popular feeling towards him.

The moral effect ought to be good abroad of his having approached the capital (which of course there were no means of preventing) and hovered about it for a week without daring to make an attack and without there being here a single seditious cry or any one punished for attempting to disturb the public tranquillity. He has now been four months out of the Northern Provinces and though the Queen's generals on the one hand and political intrigues with financial distress on the other have done their best to assist him, not a town of consideration has he been able to enter, not a district even has he been able to raise in his favor, nor has any assistance been afforded to him but that which terror has compelled.[2]

I was glad to see by your letter of the 7th that you do not despair of the cause—there are moments when I do, but it is not on account of the Pretender's strength but the villainy and incapacity of the Queen's partizans, for I know that there exist abundant elements of success still—so sure am I of it, that (although it sounds very presumptuous) I would gladly accept the post of Minister of War tomorrow, and answer with my head for changing the aspect of affairs within a month.

These people however will not believe or at least will not act as if they were in revolution—in Government they make blundering attempts at legality, and in war they have no other guide than the army list—their appointments are regulated not by fitness but by seniority, and the older a man is the more likely he is to get named to a post where youth and energy are indispensable.

I have been upon my knees almost to Calatrava ever since Evans went to have O'Donnell appointed to the command in Guipuzcoa but could never obtain any other answer than that he had not the age or rank for it—it was at last done and within a week you see that he achieved more than that old fool Jauregui (who Evans allowed himself to be dry nursed by) did in 3 months. So there are $\frac{1}{2}$ a dozen more young officers quite able to look for the enemy with a determination of finding and beating him, which is all that is wanted here because the waiting policy is the only game that the Carlists can play with any chance of success. Living costs them nothing for they subsist by pillage, while delay and uncertainty exhausts and disunites the liberal party.

The present Minister of War San Miguel is mad and I have no hopes of any thing good from him, but this Government from the circumstances of its origin is so weak that any change is dangerous.

Those who think that a doctrinaire or 'Moderado' Government here would have helped the cause of the Chartists in Portugal display a miserable ignorance of this country. In the first place no one could have deplored the stupid struggle which is now going on in Portugal more than Calatrava did. He heartily wished that the Chartists might succeed, and although threatened with the withdrawal of the Auxiliary

Legion he refused to give any aid to the Constitutionalists upon the frontier, or to allow the Government to adopt the measures they proposed for their own preservation.

If a Moderado Government had succeeded that of Calatrava, their first act *must* have been to dissolve the Cortes, and the first result of that *must* have been independent juntas—nothing but 100,000 foreign bayonets could have prevented them, or have stopped the assistance which they as revolutionists would have given to the revolutionary party in Portugal. The Government there would have wished for nothing better than a doctrinaire Government here. Within a month the whole weight of Spain would have been turned in their favor—the Government would have had no power to prevent it, if indeed the Ministers could have had a month's existence, for I believe that the Government which it was intended to place here would not have been supported by the National Guards and if they (the National Guards) had not replaced it by one of their own choice they would upon the approach of Don Carlos have been more inclined to immigrate than to fight.

All this is so palpable and so clearly to be demonstrated that nothing shall make me believe it was not known to all those who were principals in the late ministerial change intrigue, or doubt that their manoeuvres were founded upon a knowledge of the consequences.

It is more than doubtful whether this courier will be able to get through the different factions which are à cheval upon the Zaragoza road, and I am therefore shorter and more careful in what I now write than I should otherwise be.

As for the assassination or deposition of the Queen Regent by the secret societies, I firmly believe that there is not and has never existed the slightest danger. It was sufficient to see her driving through the streets on the 11th in an open carriage without escort and the *enthusiasm* with which she was received by 12,000 National Guards to be certain that any body who chooses to be informed upon the subject may profess but cannot believe in the reality of the danger.

Some danger to the Queen's person would certainly exist if by a coup de main or other means Don Carlos got possession of the capital though only for 4 and 20 hours.

I am not prone to ask for instructions because they are difficult to give for all the varying circumstances of such a contest as this, and might be difficult to follow if they did not exactly fit the case which happened to arise. Still however I should much like to know your wishes as to the course I should pursue in the event of Don Carlos getting into Madrid—taking the Queens prisoners—or the Regent being forced to capitulate.

September 18th. At the moment the courier was about to start on the 16th the French ambassador decided upon not sending him, and as he still seems animated by the same decision I have determined upon dispatching one, for I am by no means sure that some political or Holy Alliance objects are not to be served by keeping people abroad in the dark as to what has been passing at Madrid. Accounts were sent on the 14th and 15th that Don Carlos was at the gates here with 30 or 40 thousand men and *some folks* may choose to look upon the climax of the war as having arrived and to act accordingly. It is to counteract such intentions by making known the truth that I send a courier, though I am aware that his journey will be attended with considerable risk.

If the Queen's generals were worth the value of the ribbands with which they are so profusely decorated the situation of Don Carlos at this moment would be very precarious, for Madrid which is his object is tolerably well defended from a coup de main, and the more he continues to *rôder* about it the more exposed he becomes to falling in with the Queen's troops, who *I think* would beat him, and so does he probably, to judge from his desire to keep out of their way. If he *is* beat the face of affairs may change completely in 4 and 20 hours—however we must not reckon upon these Spanish heroes.

Do you think it would be possible to send out a few more Marines to San Sebastian in order to assist in garrisoning the lines there, as well as Pasages, Fuentearabia and Irun which I fear will remain very weak now in consequence of the number of troops which must be withdrawn from that part of the country to form another corps d'armée in Castille, and it would be a great pity to lose any of those hard-earned conquests. If 4 or 500 English could be added to those already at San Sebastian it would set free at least 1,000 Spaniards, and the getting together a large force to be exclusively devoted to pursuing the Pretender must now be the grand object as it is the only chance. I am pressing this point with all my might now, for we must if possible have a better state of things here than the present for you to meet Parliament with.

I hope you will be able to make Leopold understand that Portugal is to Spain as a skiff to the steamer which is towing it, and that the only chance for the former is getting out of the troubled waters in which both are tossing about now. If tranquillity is once established in Spain, Portugal will subside down into the same state within a month.

I send you the memorandum of a conversation which Southern had today with an intelligent man who was caught by the Carlists in the town where he went to fetch his wife—he was well acquainted with Don Carlos in former times and was summoned to his presence in order to be interrogated. Their information upon the state of things at Madrid is very erroneous—the greater part of the Carlist army seems little better than wild beasts.

PS. I thank you for giving the Queen a copy of the pamphlet. It might be well to send one to Leopold also.

I send you under a separate cover a letter to Aguilar which pray have delivered immediately— it contains, *as I am most positively assured,* good bills upon London for £15,000 to be applied to the payment of the Legion.[3]

Enclosure: Memorandum by Southern of a conversation with a Spaniard who had been captured and interviewed by Don Carlos.

Received 28 September.

GC/CL/353,354; Clar. Dep. C.453 (228-235)

[1] V to P, 16 Sept. 1837, no. 262, FO 72/483.
[2] 'town' to 'compelled' underlined in pencil, possibly by P.
[3] Final paragraph omitted from C.453.

367 Villiers to Palmerston, 20 September 1837

Madrid. Private. I have little to add to what you will find in my dispatch[1] which contains an account of a very successful skirmish of Espartero's with the Carlists. He was yesterday in all his glory and doing just what he is fit for—commanding a brigade—the moral result however will be good, for it will animate the Queen's troops and increase the respect with which the enemy are already inclined to view them. I think you will admire the *true Spanish* [?character] of the manoeuvres on both sides—20,000 Carlists march to Alcala thinking that Espartero was at Guadalaxara and Espartero fast asleep at Alcala knows nothing of their having been upon him till he sees their footsteps next morning.

It is a proof however of what I said in my last about the Queen's army being upon much more equal terms with the Carlists here than in Navarre, for the latter are quite as deficient as the former in that first necessity of a war like this—good information.

If they had come on to Madrid yesterday night I hardly know what would have been the result, for as usual here when the immediate danger ceases there are no more recollections of it or measures taken to guard against its return than if it had never existed. As long as the Carlists hover about here as they are now doing I consider that the moment never was more favorable for striking a great and perhaps a final blow, because the whole of the factions are united, and Don Carlos is with them—they have no base of operations—they have no considerable town to fall back upon in case of reverse, and if they get to the mountains such large numbers as they have with them will be strangely puzzled to exist—they have neither hospitals nor magazines and though Espartero's army may not be so numerous as that of the Pretender it is in far better condition and discipline and spirit.

Upon the whole then things have mended within the last week, for the Carlists have received a great check here—their hopes of taking Madrid have been frustrated—the National Guard has shewn itself admirably—not the slightest popular movement in favor of the enemy has been observed, and Don Carlos in his precipitate retreat from the Queen's army has had his posteriors lanced. So that all that now appears necessary is to keep *at them*, and here I am afraid of Espartero's inactivity though I really believe in his good desires. Oraa is a man of more talent as a general than Espartero, and they might cooperate together with good result but then, as usual between Spaniards, they hate each other like poison and I therefore don't depend upon any of those good effects which a bonâ fide wish to do their duty might produce.

The taking of Valladolid[2] is a very bad affair indeed and will produce a just outcry against this Government which like every one that has preceded it will insist upon appointing no one to important commands except from among worn-out lieutenant generals or those cursed old emigrants. Till those two fléaux disappear from off the face of the land or at least of affairs there will be no saving the country.

Received 29 September.

GC/CL/355; Clar. Dep. C.453 (236-239)

¹ V to P, 20 Sept. 1837, no. 267, FO 72/483.
² The Queen's army left Valladolid in order to reinforce the army in Castile and the Carlists entered it without opposition. (ibid.)

368 Villiers to Palmerston, 23 September 1837

Madrid. Private. We are not going on badly but I don't begin to whistle yet for we are a long way from being out of the wood. Come what will however the result of the last fortnight ought to be very great in Europe, and to convince both Russia and France that Don Carlos cannot reign in this country. He has now in person made a campaign of four months in the provinces he considered most favorable to his cause—he has never been able to get into a town that had a wall round it, and has not procured as much popular demonstration in his favor as Gomez did for him last year when this system of expeditions first commenced and which the people soon found out meant nothing but rapine.

The display of loyal feeling and resolute determination that were made in the capital on his approach and the mauling he has since received put the *comble* to the proofs which already exist of his having no moral support, and no real physical force if he is attacked with determination. Those who uphold him therefore uphold nothing but a *principle* of civil war, and the disasters, disorder and *revolution* which necessarily flow from such a state of things.

Now, if ever, appears to me the time to make the Northern Powers understand if possible what is the truth respecting Spanish affairs, and to induce them to withdraw the support they are giving to Don Carlos, which, without advancing his cause an inch, serves, by prolonging the contest, to promote here a state of things which they must be anxious to avoid and that we, as much as they can do, deplore.

Now too, if ever, appears to me the time for asking France *what it is she wants in Spain,* for Louis Philippe has objected to and opposed and confused every thing which has existed since Ferdinand's death. It can hardly be believed that he has not some settled opinions or views respecting this country, and if they are not such as he is ashamed of, in God's name let him say what they are, and if possible let us cooperate with him; for the apparent coolness between the two Governments does more to feed party spirit here than any thing else, and to prevent that union between the liberals which is not only necessary for the termination of the war, but the future tranquillization of all those elements of discord which have been called into activity. Louis Philippe would not help Martinez de la Rosa and the Estatuto—he was openly hostile to Mendizabal's Ministry—he kept none of the promises by which the Queen was encouraged to adopt Isturiz and his coup d'état, and he has worried the Calatrava Cabinet to death. All these have been successivly swept away, and he now appears to be no better satisfied with the present Government,[1] although the most active member of it is M. Pita whose ejection from the last Ministry the French ambassador bemoaned himself over as revolutionary, disrespectful to the Queen and I don't know what besides. When this is coupled with his fast and loose system upon the frontier—his own assurances from the throne that he wished success to the Queen, and his Minister's in the Chamber that France could manage very well with Don Carlos, it really makes up altogether a policy such as no King and no gentleman ever I should think adopted before.

But there is no use to revenir sur le passé, and there may be some in trying to make arrangements for the future. The elections, as I said they would, promise to be in favor of the moderate party which does not mean that the Deputies chosen will be anti-Constitution of 1837, but men anti-revolutionary, and from having something to lose, inclined to respect property more than has been the case since Mendizabal began pulling down every thing. I should think that the whole of the present Cortes together do not represent £10,000 a year, and these gentlemen have therefore had little scruple about being generous with what did not belong to them.

In the moderate sense then a Government could be formed such as would be palateable to the country and likely to perform both its war and peace duties well. I would engage that such a Cabinet might be formed immediately—that it should not lean too much either to France or England though it would seek to cultivate the best relations with both, and in short that it should be essentially Spanish, and striving to bring about the state of things that England really and France professedly desire to see established here. I know the elements for it exist, but people will not come forward or commit themselves unless they have some kind of assurance that they are not to be galled by the perpetual bush fighting kind of warfare that France has hitherto adopted. Nothing would be asked of France beyond a bonâ fide fulfillment of the Quadruple Treaty;[2] and the knowledge that France and

England were cordially agreed upon their Spanish policy would be considered a sufficient guarantee. This is not much to ask though it may be impossible to obtain—it is however worth trying for, and if Louis Philippe still persists in his present course I should then consider that his policy was more anti-English than anti-Spanish, and I would see if something was not to be got out of the Holy Allies by retiring a little from France. The holy sanctuary which is for ever shut against Louis Philippe would soon open its doors to receive us, and if they once could be made to see that the reign of Don Carlos was impossible, they might recognize the Queen as a civility to us for being more cordial with them and less so towards France. This may appear to be a Chateau en Espagne, but whether it be so or not I know I would try it if the means of doing so rested with me.

Things here too are in a state for being turned to account, though the war is *not exactly* over, and the large force that has succeeded in crossing the Tagus does not help matters. I am not *partial* to the Queen's generals, but I don't know that they are to blame for this event as when 18 or 20,000 men divide into different bands in an open country where all is road, and any direction good for those that are flying and have an understanding with each other what point to make for and where to reunite, pursuit is excessively difficult for a general who must not weaken himself too much by dividing his forces for fear of being beaten in detail, and who must be at a loss to decide upon which detachment of the enemy it is most important for him to pursue.

The system of Don Carlos is always to keep ahead with the best of his troops from the main body of the army which latter nine times in ten does not know where he is, but receives orders to wait till the Queen's troops approach, or to move towards a particular point while he (Don Carlos) a few hours before takes an opposite direction. He is thus constantly moving with a screen behind him, and he does not care how many of the banditti portion of his army are sacrificed in protecting him.

I have had a letter from Cordoba complaining and regretting most bitterly that you should have said (*in public*, he tells me) that he and Alava had been intriguing at Vichy to overthrow the Calatrava Ministry.[3] It is very unlikely that you should have said any such thing but if you did I can most positively assure you that whoever gave you such information led you into error. Cordoba's *avenir* is for the present ruined by Calatrava's going out of office. They have for many months past been in correspondence together and Calatrava being highly pleased with Cordoba had not only requested of him to return here, but was about to comply with his wish to help him return as Deputy to Cortes, which he (Calatrava) considered Cordoba's best mode of reestablishing himself in public opinion. Cordoba was accordingly on the point of setting out to return to Spain when the news arrived at Bordeaux that a Government of Moderados was about to be formed. They are now his most bitter enemies and have persecuted him in every way since he swore to the Constitution of 1812 upon entering France last year. He at once therefore gave up coming here and though the Moderado Government failed he does not think of returning because *Calatrava was his friend and protector* and the only man of that party upon whom he could rely. It is therefore impossible he should have intrigued against his Government for it was entirely destroying his own prospects of being a Deputy which is his great ambition. When Don Carlos crossed the Ebro from Catalonia and that there prevailed here the greatest alarm, Calatrava shewed me the official request he had received from Cordoba to be employed by the Government under any general and without reference to his own rank—offering to serve as a volunteer or a common soldier if it was thought by the Government that he could be useful.

As for Alava I am as certain that he no more intrigued against Calatrava's Government than I did myself[4]—besides an intrigue at the Baths of Vichy against the Government at Madrid would have been one of the longest shots that ever was fired by plotters, and I don't see how two men quite alone, without any means of influence, political, moral or pecuniary, could by merely laying their heads together injure a Government 500 leagues off, which Louis Philippe has been unable to disturb during a twelvemonth and which was at length upset by a general who is the most avowed foe of Cordoba and who would have delighted in upholding Calatrava if he had thought Cordoba had been opposed to his Ministry.

PS. Is the Morning Chronicle in the pay of Don Carlos? It seems to have taken the Journal des Debats for a model and under the mask of good wishes never to lose an opportunity of injuring the Queen's cause.

Received 2 October.

GC/CL/356; Clar. Dep. C.453 (240-247)

[1] Relations between the new Government and the French embassy at Madrid were better than V realized. On 23 September Latour-Maubourg forwarded to Molé a memorandum from Bardaxí, asking yet again for French intervention. He stated that only the Queen Regent, Bardaxí and the Foreign Minister knew of it, and that V had deliberately been kept ignorant of it. The request, however, was refused. (Latour-Maubourg to Molé, 23 Sept. 1837, and Molé to Latour-Maubourg, 6 Oct., AMAE CP Espagne 779.)

[2] By the same courier V wrote to Aston to ask him whether there was any possibility of renewed French vigilance on the frontier. (V to Aston, 23 Sept. 1837, FO 355/6.)

[3] P has added in pencil: 'I have long left off thinking or speaking about Cordova.'

[4] P has added at the top of the page: 'I did not know that either was at Vichy'.

369   Palmerston to Villiers, 23 September 1837

Copy. Windsor. The turn which affairs have taken in Spain is certainly discouraging, but we must bear in remembrance our school boy lore 'aequam memento rebus in arduis servare mentem haud secus ac bonis',[1] and trust that when things look worst they are about to grow better; as indisputably we find that when they appear best, they may be expected to become worse.

Nothing has yet happened which ought to lead us to think that the cause of Carlos will triumph. The war will however linger, and one does not see exactly what is to bring it to an end.

I can assure you I have long since got over all my predilections for Mendizabal. He has shewn himself unequal to the difficulties of his position and not to be depended upon in any way or for any thing. But he was of use for his time; and it is well that he should be now succeeded by somebody else.

As to interference by France, I own to you I do not wish it. I doubt whether in the present state of the war such a measure is applicable: because the contest is no longer on the frontier but in the heart of the country; and the French army could not well march into Andalusia after Don Carlos. It is hard therefore to say what one wishes; or rather what means one could devise, if one had unlimited power, in order to obtain the wished for result.

I gave a note of introduction to you to General Romorino, because he called upon me, and I could not well refuse to do so, but I have declined giving him any money to pay the expences of his journey, or to mix myself up in any way with his expedition. From all I hear about him, I take him to be a slippery fellow who cannot in any way be trusted. He and his officers might perhaps lead well a forlorn hope in order to gain confidence; but they would abuse confidence if once gained.

[1] Horace, *Odes*, II, iii, l.1.   GC/CL/1317

370   Villiers to Palmerston, 26 September 1837

Madrid. Private. I am writing by a commercial courier and have expended all the little time that has been given me in the dispatches I send herewith. I can therefore only add one line respecting this most untoward event of poor Lacy and his companions.[1] What a bit of bad fortune to have waited two days in order to proceed safely, and then to drive right into the jaws of the faction of whose approach probably nothing was known in Alcolea, as Don Carlos was 40 leagues off four days before and the people on the road would never have expected his returning so rapidly.

Such a very short time has elapsed since I have become certain of the fact that I have hardly made up my mind as to the course I shall pursue. I shall do my best but that best will be little, for I shall not venture to hold a language to Don Carlos which would soon make him drop his prey if I did—but as I don't know that Her Majesty's Government would be able to support me in it, I must, multa gemens however, refrain, for it is bad policy growling when one has no teeth to bite with.

I have no information about Lacy since he was marched off from Alcolea on the night of the 22d. I cannot therefore feel certain that he has not been shot but as he was not at the first moment I think it un-likely—it is probable that he has been taken to the head quarters of Don Carlos and there his life will be perfectly safe. I hope you will give me immediate instructions as to how far I may go in menacing. You may be very sure that nothing else will be of use but an appeal to Don Carlos's fears to obtain the release of Her Majesty's officers.

In military matters a most extraordinary improvement has taken place.[2] If it were to continue next week as it has done the last the Queen's cause would be landed high and dry.

Received 5 October.   GC/CL/357; Clar. Dep. C.453 (248-249)

[1] 'It is with sincere regret that I have to inform Your Lordship that Colonel Lacy, together with Captain Williams and Lieutenant Crofton, have been made prisoners by the Carlists. He was on his way to join the headquarters of General Oraa in the same capacity which Colonel Wylde was attached to the army of Count Luchana.'(V to P, 26 Sept. 1837, no. 274, FO 72/483.)

[2] Don Carlos and his army were in retreat and had been for several days. The advance of the Queen's army had suffered no major setbacks. (V to P, 26 Sept. 1837, no. 275, FO 72/483.)

371 Villiers to Palmerston, 30 September 1837

Madrid. Private. The courier due yesterday from England has not arrived, so I suppose the road to Zaragoza is again embarrassed—however *I* am much less embarrassed upon the subject connected with the insecurity of the roads than when I last wrote to you as Lacy and Co. have arrived. You will see by my dispatch[1] that I was about to send William Hervey to the head quarters of Don Carlos. His readiness and indeed desire to undertake this mission which would have been dangerous and disagreable, reflect much credit upon him and deserve I think some expression of your approval.

Colonel Lacy appears to have no doubt that they should have been shot if they had been Legion officers which is perfectly consistent with the bloody and vindictive character of Don Carlos and his advisers. As to the declaration not to take arms in favor of the Queen which the three officers were made to sign in the understanding that if they refused the two who had no diplomatic character would be retained as prisoners of war, I think to say the least of it it is *impertinent,* but I suppose we must *put up with it,* as well as with the massacre of the English taken at Andoain on the 13th.[2] We have no official intelligence of this last event but I fear there is too much reason to consider it true. O'Donnell sent word to the Carlist chiefs that if the English were killed he would send for the garrison of Irun from Coruña and shoot them all before the Carlist lines. This would be a horrible act of reprisal but for my own part I hope he may put his threat in execution, for nothing else will have a chance of making these monsters desist from such unheard of deeds of ferocity.

It is now quite clear that the moral force of Don Carlos in the country is null, and that his physical force is little else whenever he is pursued with a determination of finding him and attacked with a determination of beating him. It is equally clear too that he has no other plan or system than to exhaust the country and to destroy every thing that he despairs of making his own. As far as this goes he is, and will I fear continue to be, completely successful and I assure you that the accounts which daily arrive here from all parts of the murders and outrages that are committed by detached bands of Carlists make one's blood run cold. They are disgraceful not only to Spain but to the age in which we live, to the Powers which uphold such barbarians, and to those which might interfere to check such horrors. If Don Carlos were put down all these marauding rascals would soon die the natural death of fear, for a few troops detached from the North would give the people confidence enough to arm themselves in their own defence, and they would in the course of three months make an end of their present persecutors. I suppose that some of these days the same motives which induced foreign Powers to put a stop to the effusion of blood in Greece will compel them to adopt a similar course in Spain.

Just because military affairs have been improving this last week political things have gone badly. The Cortes have been running Pita breast high ever since he came into the Finance, and yesterday they killed him by a great majority, censuring his conduct[3] which though not very wise or very able is a great improvement upon the Mendizabal chaos. He was scraping money together by degrees, and above all introducing something like order into the administration so that for the first time money was beginning to be applied to its legitimate objects of public service instead of being gaspillé by intendants and contractors. The army being better attended to, there has been something like a return to discipline during the last month, and the soldiers accordingly killed more Carlists and fewer generals.

The Cortes however have a personal dislike to Pita and as of course they only thought of satisfying that we are in a ministerial crisis again which will end the Lord knows how.

The existence of the Cortes at this moment is a ridiculous anomaly that could be seen only in Spain—they are sitting and acting under a defunct Constitution of which however they adopt all the forms. They are not in sufficient number to make a law, but enough to pass resolutions and turn out Ministries, and this too at a moment when their successors in a new Cortes are actually elected, and that it is known not a third of the present Deputies will be returned.

They ought to have been prorogued a fortnight ago, and would have been if old Bardaxi had taken my advice and the present mess would have been avoided. *Now* it would be somewhat dangerous and savoring of a coup d'état to do it in the face of such a vote of censure as was passed yesterday upon the Minister of Finance.

Received 9 October.

GC/CL/358; Clar. Dep. C.453 (250-253)

[1] 30 Sept. 1837, no. 276, FO 72/483. V reported that 'It was stated on Colonel Lacy's passport that he was attached to the British legation at Madrid.' P minuted on this despatch: 'Attach all the inferior officers to the mission, as well as Colonels Wylde and Lacy', 9 Oct. 1837.

[2] On 14 September the Carlists attacked Andoain, which General O'Donnell had taken on 8 September. The Spanish troops fled without telling the British (the remnants of the Legion) what was happening. The British were forced to surrender and the greater number were said to have been killed.

[3] Pita was censured on the grounds that his financial measures were unconstitutional. 84 voted for the censure motion, 27 against. (V to P, 30 Sept. 1837, no. 281, FO 72/483.)

372 Palmerston to Villiers, 5 October 1837

Copy. Foreign Office. I submitted to the Queen before she left Windsor, the propriety of sending you the Bath, and she most graciously agreed thereto; the next messenger will therefore bring it out to you; I give you this notice confidentially, and for your own personal satisfaction.[1]

Your last accounts are more encouraging; the tide seems to have turned with Carlos. Thus far shalt thou go and no further, appears to have been more successfully said to him than to the Channel sea; and one may trust that he may find a retreat a more difficult thing than an advance. At all events Madrid has escaped. The National Guard has displayed courage and the Queen Regent has shewn confidence in the people; and when a great attempt has failed, those who make it are not left as they were before they made the trial. I hope that now the Government will have in the North the troops necessary to defend our positions there. It would have a bad effect if our Marines and ships were obliged to evacuate in consequence of being abandoned by the Spaniards. Coming back is a different thing from staying, and we might not be disposed to begin over again—pray press this upon the Spanish Government.

Molé has talked some nonsense to us about our offer of aid at Ceuta,[2] and has proposed a combined demonstration; we say we decline any combined demonstration on the coast of Africa, because it would connect us with the French proceedings in that quarter; but if the French want a combined operation, they have only to give to their ships on the coast of Spain orders to act in conjunction with ours. If the French should offer to help the Spaniards to defend Ceuta, it might not be amiss for the Spanish Government civilly to decline the offer, saying it does not at present need their assistance.

The story you have heard about my having said that Cordova and Alava were intriguing at Vichy to upset Calatrava is pure invention. I have neither spoke nor thought of Cordova for a long while past, considering him as a piece off the board; and as to Alava I never should suspect him of intrigue. I was not aware that they were at Vichy.

The Charter men in Portugal have shewn themselves unfit for the character of conspirators and rebels. They may be worthy men but in future they should keep within the pale of the law.

The French Government is profuse in professions of its desire that we should again act together.[3] We shall see whether this will produce any change in their conduct, I doubt it. I fear however that we should make but little of the Holy Allies; they would at the utmost only listen to an arrangement founded upon a marriage.

I am very glad that Lacy and his men have got away from the Carlists; it would have been awkward if any thing had happened to them. They must of course be allowed a fresh outfit, if as is said they have been wholly plundered of all they had with them.

GC/CL/1318

[1] Granville hoped that V would see in the conferment of the G.C.B. 'proof that Palmerston appreciates your services'. (Granville to V, 21 Oct. 1837, PRO 30/29/422.) Earlier V had regarded the giving of the Bath to another diplomat as 'a personal slight'. (V to Granville, 8 July 1837, PRO 30/29/423.)

[2] On 5 August 1837 V reported that the Moors were attacking the Spanish garrison at Ceuta, which was in no position to repel them. (V to P, 5 Aug. 1837, no. 219, FO 72/482.) On 24 August P instructed V 'to ask M. Calatrava whether the Spanish Government is desirous that one of Her Majesty's ships of war should visit that place'. (P to V, 24 Aug. 1837, no. 113, FO 72/476.) The Spanish Government accepted the British offer and P gave instructions for the British Mediterranean fleet to assist the Spanish authorities at Ceuta in case of need. (P to V, 23 Sept. 1837, no. 123, FO 72/476.)

[3] Molé agreed with Granville that the British and French Governments

'should instruct their missions to be on better terms with each other', and wrote to Latour-Maubourg and Bois-le-Comte in that sense. (Granville to V, 7 Oct. 1837, PRO 30/29/422; Molé to Latour-Maubourg and Bois-le-Comte, 5 Oct. 1837, AMAE CP Espagne 779.)

373 Villiers to Palmerston, 7 October 1837

Madrid. Private. I have received your letter of the 23rd ultimo and am glad you have not been disappointed in expecting that when things looked worst they were on the eve of becoming better. They have mended greatly, and although not a tithe of the advantage has been taken of the improvement which might have been, still I think the impossibility of Don Carlos reigning or even obtaining any substantial triumph has been so clearly demonstrated that the Queen's cause must at least have gained morally, and the Northern Powers whose vision when money is concerned may be reckoned upon as pretty acute, must see that subsidizing such a man as Carlos is one of the most expensive and unprofitable caprices they can indulge in. I do therefore think that the moment is a good one both with reference to the late military events and Don Carlos's useless five months campaign as well as to the anti-revolutionary feeling which is everywhere displayed in Spain and the moderate and substantial men likely to compose the new Cortes, I do think the moment a good one for trying to move the Holy Alliance, not to recognize the Queen, but to desist from upholding the Pretender, in order that the country should have a chance of subsiding into a state of tranquillity, when its liberal institutions would do the Powers of the North no more harm and exercise no more influence in their countries than those of France and Belgium have done.

It is the civil war and the struggle to establish liberal institutions which call the attention of Europe towards Spain, and it is the state of revolution which the civil war keeps up which is dangerous and infectious. If the contest were over, Spain would sink down into the repose of exhaustion, and one country never can have anything to fear from the tranquillity of another, let what will be the cause of it.[1]

If this is true for the Northern Powers how much more is it so for France, who in addition to other motives has that of wishing to be well with us or at all events of wishing to appear[2] to be so. I quite agree with you that the moment for intervention is gone by—certain as the success of it would have been as long as Don Carlos confined the theatre of the war to the Northern Provinces, doubtful and inexpedient did the measure become when he went *a-campaigning*—so that there being no longer this bone of contention to pick, some arrangement between England and France by which moral support might be given to the Queen's cause appears to be more easy, but that it is absolutely necessary in order to render the consolidation of affairs here *possible* I have had ample proof during the last ten days, both in the difficulties which have existed in forming a new Government and the manoeuvres which have been resorted to in the elections.

With respect to the latter the 'Moderados' have obtained their success by assuring the people that if they came into power a French army would be sent here to put down Don Carlos, and as the desire for repose prevails over every other feeling in Spain the people gladly gave their votes to those who offer it to them upon any terms. As a Moderado Government however, or one likely to tamper with the new Constitution, would not obtain French intervention more than any other, and that its measures being anti-national would be likely to produce discontent and rebellious juntas, it would be most desireable that Louis Philippe and his Ministers both in their language to those Spaniards they are in the habit of consulting as well as by their official organs of the press should declare that the events of the last month clearly prove that if the energies and resources of the country are but well directed they are evidently sufficient for putting down the Carlists, who have neither moral nor physical force in Spain which ought to give concern to the partizans of the Queen if they really chose to unite against the common enemy. That France accordingly would not grant to *any* Government or any set of men, be their principles what they may, an armed intervention which would only embarrass herself and was likely to answer no good purpose—that a new era is commencing in Spain—that the Constitution of 1837 is a practicable form of government and a standard round which liberals of every class may rally—and that in proportion as they are seen united among themselves will France and England agree upon every measure possible to encourage and protect their efforts and to thwart those of their enemies both at home and abroad. Such language used with frequency and sincerity would go far to produce union among Spaniards because it would do away with the doubts and the hopes that keep them asunder, and it would soon settle the intervention question which as well as the wavering policy of France make the great difficulty of composing a

Government equal to grappling with the arduous crisis in which the country is placed.

No man who feels he has anything in him or who really is capable of rendering service will take office unless he has some security that the formation of a reasonable Government will be marked by such a change of affairs either within or without as shall make moderation and independence of party broils palateable, and save them from the first onset of their adversaries—or some security at least that such a Government will not, as every preceding one has been, become the puppet and the victim of French caprice or want of good faith. During the last ten days I have been a witness to the repugnance exhibited by every able man (and there are many quite equal to the management of affairs) upon these grounds to taking office. Olozaga is the one who in my opinion is the fittest to be Prime Minister of Spain and I have pressed him to form a Ministry with those who are of the same caste as himself and who would be ready to join him and offer themselves to the country (tired as it is and disappointed with the two parties which have successively governed it and led it to perdition) with no other colours than that of the Constitution of 1837—war to the death with Don Carlos—respect for property and the better administration of justice.

This experiment has never yet been tried but I am sure it would be successful, and Spain for the first time would have a Government which suited herself and would draw well with England and France. I enclose you the translation of a letter I have received from Olozaga in reply to my recommendation to him to form a Government and I think it might be useful to shew it to Count Molé without however stating that it was addressed to me although it should be known it came from Olozaga.[3] The Isturiz and Miraflores click [?clique] of impotents at Paris will of course not like such a man, for he was in fact the sole author of the reformed Constitution, but Louis Philippe must in his heart know that the *Estatuto emigrants* are people who have been tried and found wanting, and that as their only objects are to satisfy their ambition or their vengeance at the least personal risk to themselves, their opinion upon the affairs of their country can only be calculated to mislead.

En resumé then if England and France will come to an understanding with respect to the affairs of Spain and will cordially and openly countenance a Government that does not ask for material aid or any thing more than a bonâ fide fulfillment of the spirit of the Quadruple Treaty—which will eschew wild reforms and endeavour to adapt liberal institutions to the wants and taste of the *Spanish people*—which will make war against anarchy as much as against Don Carlos—which will respect property, improve the laws and endeavour to develop the resources of the country, I believe that such a Government could be formed and that the ensuing Cortes would give to it an efficient support. A manifestation of approval such as I have already indicated (and which if the will exists there [are] a hundred ways of doing) on the part of England and France, and such measures as might be taken on the frontier together with the cooperation of the English and French fleets, is all that would be asked from the two Powers. The certainty that they took the same view of Spanish affairs and had united for the same objects in this country would be the greatest blow that could under existing circumstances be dealt to Carlism and Jacobinism and would as I have said before be the best means of uniting together Spaniards of different political shades. It would also give confidence to monied men and the pecuniary necessities of Spain would have a fairer chance of being satisfied. But if it is done there is not a moment to be lost—a hot iron soon gets cool in Spain, and if we wait too long for events or expect too much from these people, opportunities for doing great and good things and relieving ourselves from the embarrassment which the Spanish question creates, may be lost and may never again present themselves.

I must now say two words upon a matter personal to myself. Not long after the King's death I wrote to you to say that I should much wish to have a leave of absence this autumn, but you gave me no answer, or to a second letter upon the same subject which I confess has mortified me considerably, for I think you must know me well enough to feel sure that I would not have pressed any wishes for leave if you had thought it better I should remain on here, or that even if I had obtained leave that I should have made use of it if by doing so the cause I have so much at heart was likely to be prejudiced by a suspension of such services as I can render—but your giving me no answer looks as if I had asked for that which I am not entitled to and as I am now in my fifth year of boiling hot water here without ever having stirred from Madrid I can hardly believe that you thought my request an unreasonable one.

Bidwell tells me there are some thoughts of sending the correspondence to and from Madrid viâ Vigo—if such an arrangement is seriously in contemplation I hope you will have the goodness to call for some remarks which I send him today upon the inexpediency of it and upon a plan for reducing the present expences nearly £2,000 a year.

Received 17 October.   GC/CL/359; Clar. Dep. C.453 (256-261)

¹ 'one country' to 'it' underlined in pencil, possibly by P.
² 'to appear' underlined, as n.1.
³ No copy of the letter survives in the Palmerston, Clarendon or Granville Papers. On 21 October 1837 Granville reported to V: 'I read to Molé the letter of which you sent me a copy as well as to Palmerston. He acknowledged it to be, as in fact it is, very ably written, which seemed to me rather extraordinary, but he doubted the possibility of forming a Ministry which could stand, if all those without exception who had been inefficient and were found wanting were excluded, for the exclusion would unite even those of the most opposite opinions against a Government founded upon the principles propounded by the writer of this letter.' (Granville to V, 21 Oct. 1837, PRO 30/29/422.)

374   Villiers to Palmerston, 14 October 1837

Madrid. Private. I have been very ill and am still in bed with one of those violent seizures peculiar to Madrid—a kind of ague which attacks the brain and the bowels and doubles one up in as masterly a manner as the cholera itself could do. I shall soon be quite well but today I can only acknowledge your letter of the 5th and tell you how sincerely obliged to you I feel for having recommended to the Queen to bestow upon me so great a mark of favor as the Bath. It will give me much moral weight here but I assure you my chief gratification consists in the public both in England and abroad seeing such an undeniable proof of *your* approbation.

Your letter and dispatches which came separately in a little bag were all that the courier was able to save from the hands of the Philistines—he was seized upon the road from Zaragoza by about 40 Navarrese lancers who so far from listening to his claims for diplomatic privileges told him they had orders to send his dispatches to *the King*.

Things are looking better here and though I have no doubt we shall have some reverses still, yet the Queen's cause has gained prodigiously within the last month.

Received 23 October.   GC/CL/360; Clar. Dep. C.453 (254-255)

375   Palmerston to Villiers, 20 October 1837

Copy. Foreign Office. I am glad to say that this messenger carries out to you the Bath in due form with all the dispensations necessary to wear it. It is well conferred, and the Queen did it most graciously.

Sebastiani assures me that the French diplomatists have been or will be instructed to become very cordial and intimate with the English ones, and I assured him that the Englanders will meet the French half way. I fear however that this will only end in words, because Molé does not appear to think with us on any European question, and those who do not think together cannot well act in unison. It is a lucky thing that we tied up the hands of France by the Quadruple Treaty; if she had been free she would have done still more mischief (if that be possible) in the Peninsula.

Howard says there are at Vigo Saldanha and a large number of Portuguese officers lately belonging to the Chartist troops; and that these persons would willingly engage in the service of the Queen of Spain, and raise a Portuguese Legion. It seems to me that this would be a very advantageous arrangement for all parties; and that such a corps might be of great use to the Spanish Government at this moment, and might take the place of that under Antas which they have lost.[1] These men are some of the best officers in the Portuguese army and among them are some good artillery officers. If the Spanish Government are inclined to do anything in this matter they should lose no time. If Saldanha was empowered to raise a corps at Salamanca or elsewhere he would be joined by Schwalbach and Torres, and a great number of good soldiers would flock to their standards. The Spanish Government might perhaps say that the formation of such a Chartist force in Spain might give umbrage to the party now dominant in Portugal; but in reply it might be urged that the employment of these people in fighting the Carlists in Spain would be actually a relief to the present Government of Portugal, by taking out of Portugal a number of dissatisfied and penniless men who if they remain in their own country are likely to breed disturbance.

We are constantly told by the Carlists at Paris that they have an understanding with Espartero, and that they know he will never do anything to hurt Carlos much; I do not believe this; but if one were inclined to credit it, his conduct of late would certainly not destroy the suspicion; he never throws the gloves off, and seems to have no other object in view than just to have the best of the sparring match, without ever flooring his adversary.

I am very glad you spoke to Bardaji about the island in Port Mahon;[2] this must not be lost sight of and I shall instruct Granville to ask Molé about it.

GC/CL/1319

[1] The Visconde das Antas, who had been in command of a Portuguese auxiliary division in Spain, returned to Portugal against orders and defeated Saldanha and Terceira and the Chartists in September 1837.

[2] P wrote that he had heard that the French Government wanted to rent harbour facilities in Port Mahon 'as a place of dépôt for coal'. He instructed V 'to state to the Spanish Government that the British Government could not view with indifference any arrangement which might lead to giving the French a permanent footing in Port Mahon or in any other part of the Spanish islands in the Mediterranean'. (P to V, 16 Nov. 1837, no. 157, FO 72/476.)

376   Villiers to Palmerston, 21 October 1837

Madrid. Private. I am a much better man than when I scrambled you a few lines last Saturday but another reason will prevent my writing you much of a letter today, which is the almost certainty of its falling into the hands of the Carlists for to any but them the road to Zaragoza is nearly impassable except by a chance, and the odds are five to one against a Cristino. Detached bands of forty or fifty have been crossing the road to Aragon for the last week and as they are not deserters and all say their orders are to go to Canta Vieja I suppose it is a measure that Don Carlos has been compelled to resort to by the impatience of his troops at being kept any longer from their respective provinces, and as the Aragonese and Valencians would not go to Navarre or remain in Castille he has ordered them to that part of the country where they would otherwise have deserted to. There is no doubt that the demoralization of the faction is very great, and that the position of Don Carlos is therefore very critical—it would be desperate if the Queen had a general capable of taking advantage of it, but from Espartero nothing must be expected except an occasional charge of cavalry if ever he comes upon the enemy by surprise.

What Don Carlos most dreads and will I believe only resort to in the last extremity is returning to Navarre—not on account of the ill effect it would produce there, for the people of the provinces are so brutally ignorant and stupid that they can be made to believe anything, and if the priests told them that the Emperor of Russia had promised his ally 60,000 Cossacks in the spring if he would only pass the winter among his faithful Navarrese they would be perfectly satisfied—but it is the effect it would produce in Europe and the stopping his pocket money from the Holy Alliance that Don Carlos fears, for as long as he remains out of Navarre it can always be asserted that he is pursuing a system and that his disasters are all according to his plan of campaign, but if he once returns to his old haunts the fact cannot be concealed and the cause will hardly be denied even by those who are most determined not to admit that the events of the last five months have proved that Don Carlos can only exhaust and destroy the country but never reign over it. Those Holy Allies might be well shewn up for their support of a Pretender whose standard of revolt out of the bigotted precincts of Biscay has been voluntarily joined only by the outcasts of society—who is fighting against all the respectable classes—who in the name of religion generalizes crime and whose unfounded claims have occasioned the deaths of more than 150,000 Spaniards and been the cause of misery which is beyond all calculation to his fellow countrymen.

If all this was well set forth in opposition to the principles professed by the Holy Ones it would not make an uninstructive picture of what their practice is.

The Moderados here, who I will compare to the Duke of Newcastle and Lords Winchelsea and Roden in England though they have not even the small amount of wisdom and foresight with which nature has endowed those noble lords, are doing the only thing they understand a little—which is intriguing. They think that the anti-revolutionary spirit shewn by the country means fondness for them and indifference to liberal institutions, but an evil hour it will be for them if availing themselves of the Queen's tendencies they attempt once more to govern. I would not insure the skins of any of them for they would be swept away like chaff before the wind but I should then consider the Queen's throne in greater danger than it has ever been from Don Carlos. I *hope* she may understand this danger and not give ear to evil counsellors but I have my doubts and fears upon this subject.

I hope that the Ceuta business will be arranged without the use or exhibition of force. I have agreed with Bardaxi that if the[1] offer alluded to in your private letter of the 5th is made that it shall be civilly declined.

I have no faith whatever in the fair words and cordial professions of France. This is the month of October—Parliament meets in November and I daresay there is a desire to be mentioned in the Queen's Speech and some good might perhaps therefore be got out of our trusty ally, but in the mean while La Tour Maubourg is as evil disposed towards the Government as usual, and never since the war began have the French authorities upon the frontier given such open and official protection to the Carlists as at present. 'Bayonne est une petite Navarre' was the expression of a native of that town whose letter to a friend here I saw this morning—and he is a man whose testimony can be relied upon.

Remorino has not made his appearance though I believe he left Vigo more than three weeks ago for Madrid. In selecting the route he did for getting to Castille from Paris he either shewed very little alacrity in favor of the cause he means to support, or the most complete ignorance of the geography or the state (probably both) of the country where he wants to figure. Under any circumstances he is coming upon a wild goose chase for he is no more likely to get the command of a regiment even than I am.

Howard wants the Spanish Government to take into their service the expatriated Chartist officers, but there would be all sorts of difficulties in this which would not I think be balanced by any military advantages judging from the recent prowess of these heroes.[2]

Received 31 October.

GC/CL/361; Clar. Dep. C.453 (262-265)

[1] 'French' added in P's hand in GC/CL/361.
[2] C.453 has 'persons' instead of 'heroes'.

377   Villiers to Palmerston, 28 October 1837

Madrid. Private. The courier from London has not yet arrived and I am afraid that some mishap has befallen him for the road to Zaragoza is lined with facciosos who hop over it backwards and forwards like rabbits across a ride. Nothing would be more easy, and it is certainly very important, than to protect this only communication with *Europe* which now remains open, and I have even presented a plan to the

Government for doing it without any expence and merely by employing the troops which are inactive in adjacent garrisons, but though it was mightily applauded it will never be put in execution, for since I have been in Spain I have not seen such a mockery of Government as the men who have recently been collected and have the presumption to call themselves one. I saw them all together the other day and they reminded me of old London watchmen—the united ages of the six cannot be less than 500—they are all deaf, nearly blind, and quite dumb, particularly in the Cortes—they shrink from giving any orders or taking any measures except appointing their cotemporaries to active employments—they are frightened out of every thing (except their places) by the Cortes, the press, and public opinion, and they are merely indebted for not having been long ago sent to the hospital or the workhouse to the general wish that exists not to make any fresh change till the Cortes meet and it is seen whether any men capable of forming a Government will be found among the new Deputies.

In the mean while the old Cortes which still continue sitting because men always cling to power as long as they can and the Government dares not by proroguing deprive them of it, but having no longer the fear of Calatrava who was their schoolmaster before their eyes, they have become extremely vicious in their old age and seem determined to moot every question that it would be wise to leave alone.

During the whole of this month I have by my own exertions (Bardaxi having fairly told me he could give me no assistance) staved off a discussion in the Cortes upon the exceptional duties at Gibraltar[1] but I fear I shall not be able to do so much longer if the Deputies are not sent about their business, and through the malice of some of them and the ignorance of others, with a Government incapable of taking any part, the question would assuredly be lost, which I should regret very much, not on account of the loss it would be to English interests, for in Spain more than in any other country the smuggler corrects the blunders of the legislator, but because it would be such a triumph to the Tories who would apparently be justified in throwing in our teeth the ingratitude and narrow-mindedness of our protégés. In the event of this taking place I should like to have your instructions as to the course as [sic] I should pursue, as well as with respect to the Extraordinary Contributions[2] which in every part of Spain are now being levied in the most arbitrary manner upon British subjects.

Day after day I have attacked Bardaxi upon this matter until I have exhausted my store of threats and expostulations, which however is more than my compatriots have done for I am overwhelmed every post by their complaints. Bardaxi admits our rights to the fullest extent, and says he would gladly issue orders to the local authorities not to molest British subjects, but he knows if he did so the Cortes would hold him responsible for exempting *any body* from the payment of a contribution which is so much wanted, and as he considers the wrath of England and France (for both claim under the same treaties) more distant than that of the Deputies he adopts the course which will afford him the longest chance of tranquillity.

Under these circumstances I should like to be authorized by you to say that if Spain does not observe the treaties by which she is bound to England we shall consider ourselves absolved from the Quadruple Treaty upon which the fate of this country in a great measure depends.

Our Peninsular wards are mischievous monkies and give their guardians a great deal of trouble, but I still think que le jeu vaut la chandelle[3] and that a little sooner or a little later we shall see liberal institutions taking root here and by degrees producing the benefits we expect.

I conclude that by this time Don Carlos will have reentered the Northern Provinces unmolested of course by Espartero, who will thus have lost another (which is about the 20th) brilliant opportunity for destroying the Carlist army which from all accounts appears to be in such a state of panic, discontent, and complete demoralization that the mere sight of the Queen's troops would be sufficient to produce its final dispersion. This state of things however will soon cease when the Carlists get home, and for the reasons stated in my dispatch of today I disagree with the general opinion entertained here of the evil consequences to his cause which will attend the Pretender's return, and I only hope that some successful attack upon Hernani and Irun may not prove that I am right. It would doubtless be difficult to make the troops undertake another expedition just now, not on account of the Queen's army but from the fear and hate that the Navarrese have of the Carlist factions in other parts of Spain, by whom they have been looked upon as invaders of their territory and sharers in their spoils and treated accordingly.

As an instance of the feelings which animate the Navarrese upon this subject I heard the other day that a colonel with a small escort was bringing the prisoners (chiefly men of the North) taken by Oraa from

Cuenca to Madrid, when a faction which was recognized to be part of Cabrera's appeared on a neighbouring hill. The colonel formed the few troops he had with the prisoners in the middle upon the high road expecting to be attacked, when the prisoners to his great surprise asked for arms and to be led against the faction which for the last 3 months they had looked upon as greater enemies than the Queen's troops, offering at the same time that half their number should be left behind as hostages with the understanding that they were to be shot if their comrades did not return. The whole of them unanimously proposed these conditions and I have no doubt from the character of the people that they would have faithfully fulfilled their offer but the Valencians sheared off and there was no necessity for putting the Navarrese to the proof. The battalions left by Don Carlos in Catalonia have been obliged to leave that province as they are run down and shot like mad dogs by the Catalans so that for some time to come at least I consider that we are free from Northern incursions.

I send you a letter from Wylde who has requested me to support his petition for three months leave of absence this winter in the event of active operations ceasing and upon the understanding that he is not to use it if he or I consider it would be useful for him to remain at Espartero's elbow. Besides some private affairs which make him wish to go to England he has lately owing to the bad food they have had in the *Pinares*, contracted a diarrhoea which he cannot cure and he is afraid of its becoming chronic as happened to him once before in the West Indies.

I know you have the same high opinion as myself of Wylde and I doubt not that if the opportunity offered you would like to do him a good turn . . . .

I have also received a request from another quarter where I perceive there is a little discontent lurking—Evans . . . .

I have omitted to mention Mr. Semple Browne[4] who you were desirous should obtain a commission in the Spanish army . . . .

PS. I have only time to add before the departure of the ambassador's courier that mine has just arrived safe and sound.

Received 6 November.

GC/CL/362; Clar. Dep. C.453 (266-271)

[1] Whereby Spanish ships that had called in the course of a voyage at Gibraltar paid duty on all cargoes; those ships which had only put in at Spanish ports did not. The matter was in fact raised in the Cortes the preceding week

although discussion was postponed. (V to P, 21 Oct. 1837, no. 301, FO 72/484.)

² To be paid by all households as a special contribution to the cost of the war. British and French residents claimed exemption by treaty right.

³ C. 453 has 'le jeu ne vaut pas la chandelle'; GC/CL/362 makes better sense and is probably right.

⁴ *Recte* Temple Browne?

378 Palmerston to Villiers, 3 November 1837

Copy. Foreign Office. This messenger takes out to you what the last could not, a star which can be worn.

I have received your letter of the 21st ultimo. There can be no doubt that if Carlos is compelled to go back to the north of the Ebro, such a move on his part will be a confession of failure which must make some considerable effect in Europe, and which it will be impossible to explain away. I agree with you that when this has happened some kind of appeal might usefully be made by England and France to the three arbitrary Powers; and that we might put it to them, ad verecundiam, whether they are now any longer justified in continuing to foment the civil war, since setting aside the question of which party has the best right, it must now be evident to all mankind that Carlos has no chance of success. It is objected to this by some, that the reply of the three Powers would be a proposal for a congress or a marriage; but that would not signify; we should decline the congress and object to the marriage and I think we could easily place on record that the three Powers are wholly without excuse in continuing to inflict upon Spain the calamities of the civil war. This however will require further consideration.

In the meantime I wish you would send me all the well authenticated details you can collect of the atrocities committed by the Carlists in the summer excursions through the country; such I mean as can be decorously stated remembering all the eyes by whom your despatches are to be read.

The French Government assure us that they are most anxious that all apparent differences between their foreign missions and ours should everywhere disappear, and that the union between the two countries should everywhere be understood to be as close as it really is. Instructions will have been sent to Latour Maubourg to place himself upon a footing of greater cordiality and intimacy with you, and we wish that you should on your part meet him more than half way.

We no longer ask France to send troops into Spain; first because we know the French Government will not do it, and there is no use in pressing for that which cannot be obtained; secondly because in truth the present state of the war does not admit of any partial and limited move of French troops into Spain with the chance of any material advantage to the Queen's cause; and as to any military interference upon a great scale, with a large force, and in the interior of the country, we have always admitted that the French objections to such a measure are conclusive and unanswerable, nor have we indeed ever recommended such a scheme. In fact the more the deliverance of Spain from Carlos and the Inquisition can be the result of Spanish exertions, the more likely the liberties of the nation are to be securely and permanently established.

Our accounts from Ceuta are satisfactory as far as the Moors are concerned, but there are too many prisoners in the fortress, and too few cruzados to pay the garrison. Custodes ipsos, quis custodiet? The Spanish Government should have an eye to this; but General Takeon should some day be forced to Take off.[1]

I have no time to say more but pray leave Maubourg no excuse for the absence of at least outward and apparent cordiality between the two missions. I know he is a dry piece of goods.

Granville sent you a letter from our friend the Doctor,[2] of which he also sent me a copy . . . .

GC/CL/1320

[1] The Moors took advantage of the disturbed state of Spain to invest Ceuta in North Africa. General Tacon, as Captain-General of Andalusia, was the Spanish general nearest to the trouble.
[2] Dr. John Bowring.

379   Villiers to Palmerston, 4 November 1837

Madrid. Private. I must begin by repeating to you my cordial thanks for the Bath which together with the gracious manner in which it was bestowed by the Queen I of course feel that I owe entirely to you, and, believe me, this distinction is of far less value in my eyes than that my services, such as they have been, should have deserved such a testimony of approbation. To yourself I shall always feel indebted as long as I live for having taken me from the Custom House and placed me without the sphere of mere drudgery, and I am therefore doubly glad that you should have thought yourself justified in thus publicly making known that I have not disappointed you. Politically speaking the Bath is of great value to me in this country, and it would appear absurd if I were to tell you the sensation it has produced here—it is looked upon however as a proof of the friendly disposition of your Government towards this country and cause, for every body is aware that [it] is only by my zeal in helping things in Spain that I can have won my spurs. The congratulations have been universal and apparently sincere except with my French colleague whose face has been additionally acid ever since and whose only consolation is that this decoration must be a polite precursor to a recall.

You may be very sure that I shall meet him more than half way towards a good understanding, but our visiting each other a little more and Molé's pseudo-instructions to him to be cordial are all *blatherum-skyte* and tend to nothing either here or anywhere else. La Tour Maubourg is a man incapable of a large or generous view of a question—he hates this country and the liberal cause—he has no connexions or acquaintances here and has therefore no means of informing his Government correctly. What good can be expected from such a man or from the Government which relies upon his reports? Take him all in all however he is a most worthy and faithful representative of Molé and the present policy of France.

He told me two days ago that he had heard from Paris that the French Government were much pleased at your having renounced all idea of armed intervention on the part of France, and having proposed that the two Governments should cooperate *moralement* to support the Queen's cause. For this the ambassador said that Molé was quite ready, and I don't doubt it for as his interpretation of *moralement* will be arbitrary he will be able to pursue the same hostile course as usual. If Sebastiani really wishes to know what his Government might do without compromise or expence let them order French ships to do what ours are doing on the coasts of Spain, and let them do it together. Let the Journal des Débats which is paid by the Government hold language favorable to the Queen's cause instead of, under the pretext of doing so, as at present, disfiguring every fact and never missing an opportunity to prove the weakness of the Queen and the power of her

733

enemy. Let the Government publish some bonâ fide orders to the authorities of the frontier to prevent the enormous traffic with the Carlists that is still carried on—let them watch over the fulfillment of such orders and let them eject from Bayonne the swarms of foreign conspirators which infest that town and make it another Navarre. Let the French Government permit the passage of unarmed Spanish troops across their territory, and let them hold language favorable to the cause they profess to support, instead of courting the advice and quoting the opinions of renegade Spaniards whose objects are personal vengeance or by misrepresentation to justify their own baseness.

In all this there is neither compromise nor expence, but there would be sincerity which is what we must not look for. But this would be real moral cooperation and its effects would be prodigious—confidence would revive directly and with confidence would come money which is the stumbling block at this moment, and for the want of it I look upon affairs here as in greater danger than ever, for *every* resource is exhausted and the expedients of the last two years cannot be repeated. A million of money would be sufficient to give breathing time and allow the country to recover a little from its present state of syncope, yet I see no chance of getting it, strange as it certainly appears that Spain with all her real and yet unexplored wealth should be on the brink of destruction and that the cause in which so many both here and abroad are interested should be so endangered for want of a sum so trifling—but such is the case, and at present I see no possible means of getting through the winter unless France will shew herself more hearty in the cause.

If you ever see Goldsmid now would you ask him if he thinks there would [be] a possibility of finding a million sterling which should bear an interest of 10 per cent—repayable in 5 years and guaranteed upon the customs of Spain—the whole prohibition system being done away with, and foreign production being admitted at a duty averaging about 25 per cent? I believe that this latter might be effected here if the former part could be done in London, and if the commercial system of Spain were liberalized it would be a revolution well worth all the suffering of the last four years, and the plan I have now mentioned would save Spain for the present and render her futurity safe. I should think that the people of Manchester alone, if those Cotton Lords have half the enterprize and wealth that is attributed to them, might do such a job. It is well worth thinking of and Master Molé would then be left alone in his glory, but we have no other mode of effectually combatting his policy.

Espartero and Lorenzo have certainly done their work and lost their opportunities like true Spanish generals, but I am inclined to say with Wylde that this has been the most successful campaign since the war began. The little power of Don Carlos has been proved—he has been foiled in his intention of wintering in Castille and has been compelled to return to the provinces where he publicly announced he should not come back—so we must make the best of it and I hope there will be an opportunity of setting forth these advantages in Parliament before any new reverses occur.

I suppose the Tory newspapers will be making a row about Messrs. Groneisen and Henningsen and I have accordingly sent you in detail what has passed with respect to them . . . .[1]

I believe I have rendered the Infanta a service by making her abandon her travelling project[2] which I believe was never political but merely had reference to family differences . . . .

Many thanks for my leave of absence. I shall keep my word not to use it if I think I ought to stay on here, and at the present moment when the new Cortes are about to meet and the formation of another Government may give rise to many domestic and foreign intrigues my going away might perhaps produce a bad effect.

Hervey is greatly pleased with having received the thanks of Her Majesty's Government for his projected expedition—he really deserved them.[3]

Remorino has never made his appearance.

PS. Temple must be cautious not to commit the Infanta in any communication of my dispatch that he may make to Prince Cassaro.

Covering letter: Earl Granville (Paris) to Palmerston, 11 January 1838, private, regretting the delay in forwarding Villiers's letter of 4 November 1837, which he had 'thrown into a drawer in the hurry of my departure from Paris in November last'.

Received 15 January 1838.

GC/CL/363; Clar. Dep. C.453 (272-279)

[1] See V to P, 4 Nov. 1837, no. 306, FO 72/484.
[2] See V to P, 4 Nov. 1837, no. 311, FO 72/484.
[3] The British Government thanked him for his willingness to go to the Carlist headquarters to negotiate the release of Colonel Lacy. (See no. 371 above.)

380   Palmerston to Villiers, 10 November 1837

Foreign Office. Moncorvo tells me that the Portuguese Chartist officers who were at Vigo have by order of the Spanish Government been marched up into the interior of the country, and he requests me to ask you to endeavour to obtain good treatment for them, and liberty to go where they like. The object of most of them in stopping at Vigo was, if they should not be able to get employment in the Spanish service, to return quietly one by one to their own houses, and a good many had done so before the rest were marched away from the sea coast. It can hardly be politic in the Spanish Government to take so decided a step in favour of a small faction in Portugal. The party of Franca and Mantas[1] cannot permanently govern the country; the Chartists must in the end gain the ascendant, and how can it answer to Spain to excite just and well founded resentment against the Spanish Government in the minds of the Chartist party?

Copy.

GC/CL/1321

[1] Leaders of extremists centred about the Lisbon Arsenal. França was an Inspector of the Arsenal and commanded the Arsenal battalion, and Mantas was commander of the Fifteenth Battalion.

381   Villiers to Palmerston, 11 November 1837

Madrid. Private. The courier from London has not arrived and I have very little to communicate. The last week has been one of complete paralyzation both military and civil—the former because the Carlists are occupied in reorganizing themselves and Espartero is of course unwilling to disturb them in so important an operation—and we have been politically tranquil because every one is waiting for the new Cortes from which so much is expected that general disappointment will probably be the result, for let them be ever so wise and enlightened I fear they cannot make money which is what the nation wants, and the knowing that it had got it would be more acceptable than any other kind of knowledge.

The two parties, Exaltado and Moderado, are now eying each other with no particular good will, and each is endeavouring to measure the strength of the other, but this is difficult, for the number of Deputies who are really moderate and desire to form a useful Government and to support it by a strong majority, is daily increasing, and they will not declare in favor of either party. The Queen is in an embarrassing position. She knows that war, finance, everything in short is going to the dogs, in the hands of the ancient ignorami who now compose her Government and who in their best days can never have been fit for anything above a porter's place, but are fit now for nothing but the workhouse. Yet if she charges a known Exaltado or Moderado with the formation of a Ministry it would produce general discontent, and if she selected an unknown and untried man he would find no one worth having to join him. The Queen must therefore wait to see which way the majority inclines in the Cortes, and as some time must elapse before that question is decided and a new Ministry gets into its harness, I am afraid that the army will die of hunger or go over to Don Carlos in search of food.

Of one thing there is no doubt which is, that if we wanted any concession from Spain whether commercial or any other, and were inclined to pay a little for it in the shape of a guarantee for a loan however small (say a million or a million and a half)[1] we should have no difficulty in obtaining what we want, for the conviction has become so general that this is a war of resources and that Spain unassisted cannot furnish them, that the moment was never so favorable for any foreign Government or capitalist to impose their own conditions. If a new Government were formed and could reckon upon a million sterling I think that military matters might go on pretty well, and there would not be much danger from anything else for the anti-revolutionary spirit that has every where been displayed of late is most remarkable. With the exception of Cadiz and Barcelona during the elections where the disturbances were promptly quelled there has existed a firm determination to preserve tranquillity, and the National Guard of Paris is not more peaceably disposed than that of Madrid. This is of good omen for the future if this horrible war could but be put an end to.

I conclude you are aware of the reports which are industriously circulated at Paris that England is tired of the Spanish question and is desirous of backing out of the assistance we give under the Quadruple Treaty. I know that Thiers has been made to believe this and I daresay he was nothing loth to do so.

I asked Bardaxi the other day what he was going to put into the Queen's Speech from the Throne—he said hardly anything because it was the *principle* of the Government to make it very short—only a few words—for the best of all reasons too because as there is not the $\frac{1}{4}$ of an idea in the whole Cabinet they don't know what to say and so call their compulsory brevity a principle. I remarked that although long speeches were to be avoided yet that it seemed to me this was a brilliant opportunity for the Queen to say something to Europe, and that as Don Carlos had been so obliging as to solve in person the problem which was before doubtful respecting his moral force in the country, that he had nowhere found any sympathy and had been joined only by the refuse of society, it might be well indirectly to make the Powers of the North feel that they were supporting a hopeless cause and that by feeding the civil [war] they did nothing but foment revolution for which in reality there exist neither elements nor desire in Spain, etc., etc. Bardaxi seemed to think this *principle* of a speech better than his own and promised to adopt it, but I am sure that $\frac{1}{2}$ an hour afterwards he will have forgotten it all.

I have had some conversation with an intelligent man who has arrived here deputed by all the authorities of Navarre to represent the disastrous state of that province. He speaks in the highest terms of Cordoba (whose political enemy he says he was formerly) and declares that nothing has gone well since he left the Command. The establishment of the line of Zubiri had been the means of keeping the faction in check, of protecting the Bastan, and of opening communications with the frontier and that the loss of this line now will shortly prove the extent of its value. He assures me that if the system of lines, which never had any other object than to prevent the introduction of provisions, had been maintained that the faction must have starved or have abandoned the provinces.

I cannot say I am sorry that Espartero does not put those two rogues Groneison and Henningsen at liberty . . . .

PS. I reopen my letter to say the courier has just arrived unscathed.

Enclosure: Copy, José Arias Tejeiro (Quartier Royal de Quintanar de la Sierra) to 'Milorde', 16 October 1837, thanking him on behalf of the 'King' for the copy of his work on Spain. (In French.)[2]

Received 20 November.

GC/CL/364; Clar. Dep. C.453 (280-285)

[1] 'that if we wanted' to 'half' underlined in pencil, possibly by P.

[2] The original of this letter was found among Captain Henningsen's papers, with evidence that 'Milorde' was Lord Carnarvon.

382 Palmerston to Villiers, 11 November 1837

Copy. Foreign Office. I hear from what is likely to be pretty good authority that the Carlists have at Tolosa a large store of money, shoes, clothing, ammunition, etc., and that it was partly to replenish from these stores that the Carlists retired across the Ebro. This may be a wrong conclusion; but it would be worth while for Espartero to see what these stores contain.

GC/CL/1322

383 Palmerston to Villiers, 16 November 1837

Stanhope Street. The most pressing thing at present is to reinforce O'Donnell at St Sebastians. If Bilbao, Irun, Hernani or Fuentearabia are taken we shall all cut a very foolish figure—Lord John Hay thinks that Espartero should push on to Durango, and that by being there he could protect Bilbao. Of this I cannot judge; but it is to be hoped that Espartero will not consider the campaign as finished, and give us a second edition of a winter's blockade of three provinces. This is a plan the absurdity of which has been demonstrated by experiment. If the communications of the Carlists with France can be kept closed, and the Queen's troops can press the Carlists vigorously, we may hope to see some important advantage reaped from the defeat of the Carlist attempt on the South.

The Spanish Carlists at Paris are always saying to people who send me private accounts that Espartero is bought by them and that they are quite sure that he never will do them any mischief if he can help it. This may be true or it may only be said for the purpose of exciting in our minds distrust of a man whom they have *not* got; but certainly if it were true, he could not well have acted any differently from what he has done.

I am very glad you were so active and successful in favour of Gruneison and Heningsen, but I should not have liked to receive the letter which you wrote the former 'et non potuisse refellere'.

They say in Paris that Aguilar is to be recalled as well as Campuzano, pray try to prevent this. We like Aguilar very much, he is honest and gentlemanlike and a man of business. I can deal with him, and know what I am about. He is heart and soul in the cause of his country;

and has gone through much that has been most painful to his feelings as a gentleman in consequence of the Government not supplying him with funds to pay claimants of various kinds. It would be an act of personal injustice to him to recall him, and the Spanish Government would find it difficult to get another man who would serve them so well.

I do not much like this coal store of the French in Minorca, but it would be much better to have it as you propose in the town and on the mainland than in the little island. But the Spaniards should remember that steamers are now ships of war, and that an unlimited permission for French ships of war to make Port Mahon a permanent storehouse for articles of indispensable necessity is a first step which may lead hereafter to embarrassing questions.

You will see that the Speaker has been reelected without opposition. . . .

Copy.

GC/CL/1323

384   Villiers to Palmerston, 19 November 1837

Madrid. Private. I was only able last Saturday before the departure of the French courier to announce the arrival of your letter and dispatches of the 3d, but in times and roads like those of Spain such information is not matter of indifference to those who don't wish to figure in the Oñate *Portfolio*.

According to your desire I send a select list of the Carlist atrocities which though not exactly a *dish to set before a Queen* will not offend.[1] If I had ventured to insert in the catalogue all that has come to my knowledge respecting the conduct of the Carlists and the manner in which they carry on their brutal exterminating warfare the picture would I am sure have still more excited the commiseration of the Queen. As you wanted these details in order to make an appeal ad verecundiam of the Holy Allies I have thought it expedient to write a covering dispatch for them which may serve you as a text from which to preach your sermon to those benevolent Sovereigns. It is too long I am afraid, but it is not half of what I might have said respecting the horrible state of this country.

Nothing but the termination of the war in the Northern Provinces will put an end to the hordes of banditti which infest every other part of the country, for it is only then that the Government could detach a sufficient number of troops for the purpose. The factions are able to evade and laugh at the forces now destined to pursue them, for no correct information of their movements can be got by the Queen's officers as they intercept all dispatches and then shoot the alcalde and the principal persons of the village which sends the intelligence. In short nothing can be more lamentable than the state of the country and Spain will before long be reduced to the condition in which the South American provinces were ten years ago. Yet the disposition of the people is good—all classes are wearied of war and revolution and all have so far profited by experience that if tranquillity were once again restored, the nation would be more easily governed and make more rapid strides in prosperity than at any former period of its history. During the absence of that scoundrel Cabrera for a month when he came with Don Carlos towards Madrid, Aragon and Valencia seemed to have a new life imparted to them—not a discontented voice was heard—agriculture was carried on briskly, and the contributions were again punctually paid to the Queen's authorities, and this would take place in every part of Spain were these marauders but got rid of. Since Cabrera's return every thing is panic and devastation again.

The great object would be to make the Northern Powers understand that the Queen's cause is not and cannot be that of revolution, and that that of Don Carlos is and must continue to be so. I would make a considerable sacrifice to be able to have an hour's conversation with Nicholas upon this subject, for my convictions of the truth are so complete that I could convey them to the mind of another more effectually than they ever can be by writing. It was one of my objects in asking for leave to go to Europe awhile, to palaver with the ambassadors of the Barbarous Powers (as Bowring always calls those of the North) and with our Cordial Ally Louis Philippe. It probably[2] would have done no good but it would have been an experiment like another, and every thing is worth trying in order to get this unfortunate country, and with it ourselves, out of the present mess.

You may rely upon it that La Tour Maubourg shall be met three parts of the way by me in any advances he may persuade himself to make towards a good understanding between us.[3] Since I received your letter I have dined him and his wife and invited 30 people to witness our cordiality, but I have no doubt that you are of the same opinion as myself that all Molé's professions are false, and that while he desires to make an outward show of union between the missions of the two countries in different parts, he will continue under cover of that union to thwart us politically and commercially wherever he can. What for instance does this country gain or how are the objects served which we profess to have in common by the ambassador and I visiting each other, if French ships do not cooperate with ours—if the French ministerial press is every day more rabid against the Queen's cause—if Bayonne was never more the head quarters of Carlism and the French frontiers never more open to the Carlists than at the present moment? It is a mockery which is not very far distant from an insult.

I hardly know what to think of the new Cortes—they would do well enough if there was no civil war, but I fear they will be too moderate for the strong measures and that kind of bold bad energy which are indispensable in times of revolution. The Moderados are decidedly in the ascendant, and as I am sure they will not use their victory with moderation I shall be afraid of some reaction although the country is heartily sick of the independent junta farces. As yet I cannot tell what elements there are for composing a decent Government, but whatever men are selected they will have the advantage of succeeding to the Charley[4] Cabinet, and however badly they may do they can't do so badly as the present men.

I told the Queen last night I hoped she would be able to find some Ministers whose united ages made rather less than five centuries, and she admitted they were shocking old gentlemen but said Bardaxi had de très bonnes intentions, to which I observed Her Majesty must be aware that an old man of 70 had often *the best* intentions of doing that which he did at 30 but that he generally made a miserable failure of it. She admitted this and I don't think it will lengthen Bardaxi's tenure of office.

The Speech today[5] is just what I expected—a failure and like true Spaniards the Ministers have thrown away a brilliant opportunity for doing service to the country. The avenir which the new Constitution and Cortes offer to Spain and the result of the Carlist expedition might have been turned to good account both at home and abroad.

I have written several times to Wylde respecting reinforcements to San Sebastian, but although he quite agrees with me as to the urgent necessity of the measure I doubt if he will be able to induce Espartero to break through his rule of never detaching a man from his head quarters—a rule which is really fatal, for 5,000 men are the very utmost he knows how to command and the consequence is that the more force he gathers about him, the more his ignorance of what to do with it compels him to remain inactive, and he cares not a straw for the troops being wanted elsewhere.

No sheriff's officer ever looked after a debtor more sharply than I do after these people in order to get some money for the Legion but there is not a maravedí in the treasury, and as for sending the bad bills with which people are paid here and which are sold at 75 per cent discount it would be of no use, for in London they could not be got rid of at any price.

If the gods would send a bold foreign capitalist to the rescue all might go well, but without some such miracle being worked I have not much hope of the war and none for the unfortunate Legion.

PS. I really believe that Gruneisen and Henningsen were upon a spying expedition.

Received 29 November.

GC/CL/365; Clar. Dep. C.453 (286-291)

[1] V to P, 19 Nov. 1837, no. 325, FO 72/484, enclosing 'A list of 25 atrocities committed by the Carlists between May 9th and November 3rd 1837'.
[2] 'probably' underlined in pencil and 'certainly' added above by P.
[3] See also V to Aston, 19 Nov. 1837, FO 355/6.
[4] A nightwatchman.
[5] A copy of the Queen's Speech was enclosed with V to P, 19 Nov. 1837, no. 336, FO 72/484.

385   Villiers to Palmerston, 25 November 1837

Madrid. Private. I have received your dispatches and three private letters of the 10th, 11th and 16th instant. I quite agree with you as to the immense importance of reinforcing O'Donnell, and as you will have seen by my dispatches[1] I urged it upon the Government from the first moment that Zariategui turned his horses' heads towards the Ebro, but what with the idiotism of these Ministers and the pigheadedness of the General in Chief nothing is done or attempted but that which it might be well to leave alone—although I do not mean to say that Espartero does wrong in punishing the excesses which have arisen from want of discipline (nobody is more to blame than himself however for the state into which the army has fallen)—on the contrary he is doing a most important service to his country—but he might have performed all his Provost Marshal's work in one week instead of six, and not have allowed the Carlists to refit and reorganise as they are doing now thanks to the money of the Holy Allies and the zealous assistance of French authorities. A few days ago I all but took Bardaxi by the collar when I asked him if he was aware that Irun was in danger of being taken by the Carlists—he shrugged up his shoulders and said *bien puede ser!*[2]

With respect to all political or military measures the Government is a completely dead body and I don't believe that the application of a galvanic battery to the President of the Council would produce any sign of life in the Cabinet. With respect to financial affairs and my daily and hourly occupation of dunning, the Government reminds me of a knocked up mule—it is dead beat and cares for nothing—you may break any number of sticks upon its back but it will make no attempt at moving or dragging the cart out of the mud.

I could easily turn out the Government by telling the Queen that I would no longer hold any communications with such a set of men, but just at the present moment she would have great difficulty in replacing them till it is seen how the majority of the Cortes is composed and to what party a new Government would have to look for support. Much time cannot now pass before this becomes evident, and then, but not till then, some of the duties of Government may be performed at home, and some of the obligations of the country towards ourselves fulfilled.

Nothing can have been more absurd than Bardaxi's conduct about the Portuguese refugees[3]—he would not see that he might at the same time relieve Portugal from an embarrassment and the provinces of Estremadura and La Mancha from factious by disseminating these troops among the Spanish regiments, which they were quite ready to have consented to, and he has now received a remonstrance from the Portuguese Government for allowing them all to be embodied in one or two depôts where they will be ready to return en masse to Portugal upon the first new Chartist rising. A great number of these men have returned home, and the rest will I hope shortly be received into the Spanish service, as I wrote a letter to the Portuguese minister upon the military and political advantages to both countries of such a measure, and he sent a copy of the letter to Lisbon as he said he was sure his

Government would entertain similar views. I am likewise stirring up the Deputies of Estremadura to insist upon the measure being adopted by the Government and I hope therefore that Moncorvo's wishes upon this subject will soon be accomplished.

Remorino is at Valladolid and the Government won't let him come on to Madrid. I have spoken to Bardaxi about this too, but I could get nothing out of the old idiot[4] except that for his own part he wished that Remorino should come, but *then what would the Northern Powers say?* It was in vain to point out that *they* could not claim much deference on the part of the Queen's Government, and that their hostility was not likely to be increased or diminished by such a man being at Madrid or Valladolid—but it was of no use, and there Remorino remains writing furiously to every body here. I can't say I care very much about it nor I believe will you, for it would be impossible to give an unknown foreigner any command of importance, and if he were here idle he might probably be made the instrument of the intriguers both foreign and national who swarm at Madrid.

You will see by my dispatch that I have put en train more friendly relations with the French ambassador.[5] I attacked and carried him by storm a few days ago, but I don't know whether I shall be able to maintain my ground. I will do my best.

I only heard from Paris last week that Aguilar was to be, or had been, recalled. Bardaxi did not say a word to me about it or to the ambassador respecting that of Campuzano. I asked him upon what grounds he was dissatisfied with his minister in London, and he had no reason to assign except that everybody here thought him unfit for his post. I begged that no successor might be appointed without my being previously informed, as I doubted his being able to find a man you would like better than Aguilar. This he promised and as he told me two days ago that he had not been able to fix upon anyone to send to London I may perhaps be able to have Aguilar retained—though there is no certainty of anything with such a man as Bardaxi. He is the seventh Minister for Foreign Affairs with whom I have had to do since I came to Spain, and the only one with whom I have had the slightest cause to be personally dissatisfied. Lord Wellesley was I believe compelled to turn him out of office at Cadiz on account of his stupid and intractable character, and everybody makes the same complaint of him as myself. I trust therefore he will soon be ejected.

My fears about the intemperance of the Moderados are beginning to be realized and if they are not quickly controlled by a strong Government having the confidence and support of the Queen they will be playing all manner of mischievous tricks for they are a hundredfold more intolerant than the Exaltados. I think, though of course I never answer for any Spaniard, that Martinez de la Rosa is going to behave like a gentleman and a patriot, and if he does he is in a better position than anyone else to check the retrograde movement. He drew up the Address to the Crown in answer to the Speech, and it is a very masterly performance. I am the more inclined to think so perhaps as it contains all that I recommended to Bardaxi to put in the Speech. You are not likely to have time to read such documents but I enclose it in case you should,[6] as it may be considered the programme of the party which Martinez is likely to influence and which might become what appears almost an impossibility in Spain at such a moment—a tiers parti. The discussion upon the Address begins on Monday. May it go off as well as I flatter myself yours has already done.

The no opposition to the reelection of the Speaker is good as far as it goes, but I fear the rabid unscrupulousness of the Tories upon the election petitions.

Enclosure: 'Proyecto de Contestacion al Discurso de la Corona, leido en la sesion del Congreso de Disputados el dia 23 de Noviembre de 1837.' (Printed, Madrid, 1837.)

Received 6 December.   GC/CL/366; Clar. Dep. C.453 (292-297)

[1] V to P, 25 Nov. 1837, no. 340, FO 72/484.

[2] 'It may well be.'

[3] 'Some weeks ago and immediately after the arrival in Spain of a number of Portuguese troops upon the defeat of the Chartists, I urged M. Bardaxi in the strongest terms to take these forces into the service of the Queen in order to operate in Estremadura. He objected to the measure saying it would offend the Portuguese Government and would be attacked by the Exaltado party here, who looked upon the Chartists in the same light as the Estatutists of Spain.' (V to P, 25 Nov. 1837, no. 347, FO 72/484.)

[4] 'the old idiot' crossed out and 'him' substituted by P, presumably for publication.

[5] V called on him and suggested more active and friendly co-operation between the two legations. (V to P, 25 Nov. 1837, no. 345, FO 72/484.) By the same courier V wrote to Granville that Latour-Maubourg's suggestion that he (V) had made no attempt to meet the latter half way was false, and that it was part of an attempt by the French Government to discredit him. (V to Granville, 25 Nov. 1837, PRO 30/29/423.)

[6] V to P, 25 Nov. 1837, no. 346, with enclosures, FO 72/484.

386 Palmerston to Villiers, 30 November 1837

Copy. Foreign Office. I have been gradually increasing the strength of our representations to the Spanish Government on behalf of British claimants,[1] and indeed I live in fear of some break out in Parliament which will greatly embarrass us. I have lent Aguilar £2,000 out of Secret Service to pay off the invalids still remaining at Portsmouth; he has given me accepted bills for the amount, payable some time next month; I hope they will be paid. But you may as well say nothing about this to the Spanish Government, who might be encouraged still more to withhold payments if they thought there was any fund here from which money could be advanced for them.

I was very glad to get your letter giving an account of your having dined Latour Maubourg, as it enabled me to send an opportune reply to some renewed complaints of Molé that you were not as cordial with Latour as Latour was disposed to be with you.[2] All this is miserable childishness if it is sincere; or it may as you suppose arise from a wish that an outward appearance of union should serve as a cloak for the real divergence of views and action between the two Governments. But in either case I am glad you have taken the line you have, and I very much wish you to continue it. Be as civil as you can to Latour, it cuts all ground of complaint from under the feet of Molé, and on the whole, and on a balance of good and evil, it is best that an outward good understanding between the French [and] English missions everywhere should at least wear the appearance of union even though there be a divergence of action. It may perhaps tell best for Spain alone that we should not seem to be taken in by the French; but with reference to Europe at large it is better that the Holy Allies should see that France and England can even differ without quarrelling.

I will see whether I cannot out of the materials you have sent me indite a pathetic appeal to the good feelings of the Holy Allies; but it will only be by way of putting the attempt on record, and not with the slightest expectation that it will have any effect upon the conduct of the Despotic Courts. I hear from Paris that Cordova is gone back to Madrid; I wish he may not be charged by Louis Philippe with some intrigue.

It is clear that Heningsen and Gruneison were spies, but nevertheless it would be useful here if they could be released; the lesson they have had will probably keep them out of the like for some time.

Cannot the Spanish Government be brought to face some commercial relaxations, if not a treaty? That seems the only way by which they could get some money.

GC/CL/1324

[1] The claims from the officers and men of the Legion for back pay, pensions and compensation for wounds. He instructed V to ask the Spanish Government 'to consider how it will any longer be possible for the Spanish Government to claim from England the continued performance of the engagements contracted by Great Britain towards Spain if the Spanish Government on the other hand allows engagements which it has contracted with a great number of British subjects to remain unfulfilled'. (P to V, 16 Nov. 1837, no. 165, FO 72/476.)

[2] Molé's complaints are in Granville to P, 13 Nov. 1837, no. 350, enclosed with P to V, 16 Nov. 1837, no. 164, FO 72/476.

387 Villiers to Palmerston, 3 December 1837

Madrid. Private. The French ambassador's courier who left Madrid last Saturday was robbed, half killed, and had his dispatches taken from him on the road to Zaragoza. We understand that part of the dispatches were afterwards found by some National Guards who went *to look at the place* where the man had been robbed, and that these 'membra discerpta' of our correspondence were sent on to the Captain General of Zaragoza (the courier being too ill to continue his journey) with a request that he would forward them to France. I know not therefore what has been saved or what will reach your hands, but I have suspended the fabrication of duplicates until I learn, with the exception of two dispatches which I send as those which may be of the most interest to you.

The French ambassador and I have made a joint verbal representation to old Bardaxi upon the necessity of protecting the only road now open and the only communication with Europe which remains to the capital of Spain. We mean also to fire a note at him, for the thing is easily done and if the Government had chosen to adopt the plan I got drawn up for them travellers might now pass in tolerable safety. I believe it will be necessary to give up sending the couriers on fixed days as the hours at which they pass is known on the road and thieves lie in wait for them. This is the reason why I have delayed till today the departure of the courier who should have gone yesterday.

I don't believe that I have much to add to my dispatches with respect to the state of things here. The Government is very anile and Espartero is very inactive—both ought to be got rid of but the difficulty is in finding successors in a country where revolution has turned up so few able men and where among those few political dissensions have narrowed the power of chusing. As yet I do not see any elements for forming a vigorous Government—there is no lack of general talent or of good speakers and good principles in the Cortes, but the generality of the Deputies are untried in public life, and as there is no one of them better entitled than another to command the votes of his companions all are waiting with their mouths equally wide open for the goods the gods may drop into them. In the mean while the country is giving proof of how easy it would be to govern it, by going on without any Government at all, and as different generals have now made it a fashion to restore military discipline more progress towards order has been made during the last three months than at any time for the last three years.

Really when one considers the civilization and prosperity of England and sees the violent party spirit which rages there and the foul licentiousness of the press, it is impossible not to look with respect upon these half savage and unhappy Spaniards. We as if in the mere wantonness of prosperity make mountains of such molehills as a clause for appropriating what does not exist, or repairing old churches by one kind of rate instead of another, and we defend our molehills inch by inch and use prohibited arms, and carry the war into the innermost precincts of private life, but here a struggle is going on not only for freedom from the most atrocious despotism, but pro aris et focis and for life and for all that can give value or charm to life—the struggle too is carried on amidst blood and privations, with exhausted vigor but untiring resolution. Fierce passions are necessarily excited in so long a contest and deeds to be deplored are committed in moments of phrensy, but social forms and decorum are upon the whole wonderfully preserved—a spirit of order reigns in the parliamentary debates, and the press, which is without legal check, has hardly in any instance attacked private character. Above all it must be observed that a feeling of religious respect towards the Crown pervades every rank and class, and that no sentiment but of devotion for the Sovereign has ever been uttered in public or appeared in print—let it be remembered what are the frailties of the Queen Regent and that for the maintenance of her and her daughter £400,000 a year is punctually paid by this beggared nation, and that neither a jeer nor a murmur are ever heard respecting the royal family. I think that when all these things are considered and the circumstances to which Spaniards have for three centuries been exposed, it cannot be denied that there must exist here an instinctive tendency towards what is good, and that such a people is worthy to be saved. We should perhaps find it hard to prove that mutatis mutandis we might not have been worse and more degraded than they are.

I am anxious to know whether you will have thought it expedient to make any démarche with the Northern Powers—not that I should expect any good results from it but it is worth trying, and I should think that even Nicholas who is not over particular about his way of dealing with either men, women, or children would hardly approve the slaughter of travellers by Palillos or the imprisonment of 600 women in order to make their relatives enlist—at least it will hardly be thought a proof of Don Carlos's wisdom to reward such acts as the first, or that the second is any demonstration of his moral force with the people— those people too being of Biscay, the head quarters of rebellion against the Queen and the focus of love and sympathy for the Pretender. If there were but a few thousand pounds available now I would engage to buy all the Carlist chiefs and put an end to the war, England becoming a party to any arrangement that might be made by the Spanish Government for securing to these men a decent existence out of their own country.

The want of money however paralyses everything and for that I see no remedy, but if the war could once be staunched in the North its circulation in the provinces would soon dry up.

I do not believe we have any thing to apprehend from the occupation by the French of the island at Port Mahon.[1] A territorial cession however insignificant will never be granted by the Cortes (unless it were in return for some such services as France is never likely to perform) and without their consent it would not be valid. Still however I think it will be well that the French should rent the buildings they may stand in need of at Minorca rather than upon the island in question and I shall keep Bardaxi up to that mark.

The Marquis de Espeja[2] is not a fit man for the post he is about to occupy—he is a proud, hot-tempered, unconciliatory man and though he will not sin in the same manner as Campuzano he is not likely to be more popular than his predecessor with Louis Philippe and his

Government. There is a circumstance too about Espeja which will not make him the more agreable to his French Majesty who when Duke of Orleans came to Spain and offered to command the Spanish army against Napoleon's—an offer which was peremptorily and not over courteously rejected by the Cortes at Cadiz, and the invitation to quit the country forthwith was communicated to him by Espeja who happened to be Chief of the Staff at the time.

I sent a message to the Queen (not relying entirely upon my friend Bardaxi) respecting your opinion of Aguilar and the injustice it would be to remove him. I got a very civil answer directly, saying that as far as Her Majesty was concerned there was no wish to remove him and that she should oppose any intention to that effect on the part of her Government.

Remorino is still detained at Valladolid and writing furiously to Madrid. He is very anxious that I should insist upon his being permitted to come here, and probably very angry at my not doing so, but I believe he is a troublesome restless fellow and I have no mind to godfather all the nonsense he would be likely to perpetrate if he got into this hotbed of intrigue.

PS. I told you that I would take care to bring about a good understanding between La Tour Maubourg and myself. We are now like two turtle doves together.

Received 12 December.

GC/CL/367; Clar. Dep. C.453 (298-303)

[1] See V to P, 3 Dec. 1837, no. 351, FO 72/485.
[2] Appointed Spanish ambassador at Paris.

388   Villiers to Palmerston, 3 December 1837

Madrid. I have taken upon myself the responsibility of delaying to carry into effect the instructions contained in your slave trade dispatch No.14 for the following reasons.

The mixed Court of Justice released the 'General Laborde' in spite of its appearing in evidence that that vessel was equipped in every respect for the slave trade, and you say it is not the wish of the British Government to disturb the sentence, but if that sentence is to remain as a precedent, the Equipment Article will become a dead letter and the advantages expected from the treaty of 1835 destroyed, for in the

state of public opinion in the Spanish colonies no vessel will find difficulty in procuring regular papers for a European port and of thus proving that it is engaged in a legal voyage . . . .

As the slave trade correspondence is published I have thought it
better to make these remarks in a private letter in order that if you
concur in them you may make any alterations you see fit in your dispatch No.14. If not I can still act upon the instructions it contains, and
no harm will have been done by the delay as at this time of year few
vessels go to the Havana and none will sail before I receive your
answer.

Copy.   Clar. Dep. C.453 (304-305)

389   Palmerston to Villiers, 8 December 1837

Copy. Foreign Office. I have good reason to believe that the recall of
Campuzano and of Aguilar was pressed upon the Queen Regent by
Louis Philippe; and I wish you would state, if necessary, to the Queen
Regent herself, that this report has reached me in a manner which
prevents me from entirely disregarding it; that we have nothing to do
with the appointment or recall of a Spanish minister to Paris, but that
we cannot allow the French Government to have anything to do with
the appointment or recall of a Spanish minister to London, and that
as this opinion has prevailed, and is so much in accordance with the
general conduct of the French Cabinet that it is likely to be believed,
we should consider the recall of Aguilar under these circumstances and
at this moment as a slight put upon us, at the bidding of the King of
the French, and as a declaration to all Europe that the Spanish
Government was entirely insensible to the difference between the relative claims which England and France have respectively established to
the good will and gratitude of Spain. It may be as well to make this
communication in the first place to Bardaxi or his successor; and only
in case of need to convey it to the Queen; but this I leave to your judgment.

GC/CL/1325

390 Villiers to Palmerston, 10 December 1837

Madrid. Private. The courier from London is not arrived and I have very little to communicate today, for this week incessant rain and idle discussions in the Cortes are the only things that have occurred—the first will probably save the country from a famine (the only disaster that is wanting)—the second is of benefit to nobody.

During the fortnight's debate which has taken place in the Cortes the Ministers have sat mute upon their Bench looking like so many corpses brought there for decent interment, but the Cortes have hitherto refused them these last honors because parties are so equally balanced that each is afraid of opening a door to the other if they create a vacuum too soon. In the mean while old Bardaxi sticks to his post although two of his octogenarian colleagues have dropped off their ministerial perches,[1] and all his attempts to induce men worth having to unite themselves with him have of course failed. The Queen is equally embarrassed to know who to address herself to for the formation of a Ministry and this unfortunate state of things may go on for some time longer, affording, as it does, an additional proof of how easy it would be to govern this country when one sees it existing even with an appearance of order in the midst of every conceivable disaster which a civil war can bring, without any Government at all for the space of four months. Everybody is preaching union and oblivion of the past but I believe they are doing so only the more effectually to bring into play their different passions and to satisfy their rivalities and vengeance. I have little hope of union being brought about and none of any good being done without it. There are no eminent men it is true, and it is a great blot upon the nation that in the course of four years' revolution not one individual superior to his fellows should have come forward either in the field or the Cabinet. Still however there are men of sufficient capacity to save the country if there were any means of bringing them together and of making them lay aside their hates and jealousies and work cordially for the general good, but in this lies the, I fear, insuperable difficulty. The greater part of the emigrants are returning from France which I regret, for none of them have sufficient talent to do any good and they will come back as emigrants always do, be they of what class or country they may, without having learned or forgotten anything, but confirmed in the opinions they held previously to their emigration, and desiring only to revenge the causes which led to it. These people will therefore set to plotting immediately and they won't even know how to do that for they belong to the Moderado party among which I have seen hundreds of intriguers but not one conspirator.[2]

I see therefore little chance of parties uniting for any common purpose although that purpose should be their common salvation from ruin. There is to be sure a ground for hope, that things rarely turn out in Spain according to one's expectations, and that there will not be any quarrelling about political institutions for it is admitted on all sides, with one or two foolish exceptions, that the Constitution of 1837 will do very well and that it is the only rallying point which the liberals have left.

There arrived here a few days ago a certain Herr von Nordenfels who brought me a letter dated the 2nd July from you, and who seems desirous of getting kicked about and then killed in the Queen's service. . . .

The death of Alonso is a grievous loss to this mission—he was as good a public servant as ever I met with, and unless another man of the same kind can be found the business with the Spanish Government will suffer considerably for it is the custom always to send a translation in Spanish of the notes which are addressed in English to the Minister for Foreign Affairs—otherwise if the translation of them was left to the Foreign Office the business which now God knows is done slowly enough would never be dispatched at all. As the place of consular agent here is of small emolument, leads to nothing, and requires special qualifications (otherwise it is totally useless) you will perhaps allow me to look out for some person really fit for it and recommend him to you for the appointment.

Since writing the above the courier has arrived and brought me your letter and dispatches of the 30th. I have been dreading as you seem to do some outbreak in Parliament with respect to the unsatisfied British claimants, and you may be sure that I have left no stone unturned in order to find money, but nothing I can say would give you a true idea of the dreadful state of beggary in which these people are. The old Legion itself is not worse off. If ever I hear of the Minister of Finance getting a dollar I am at him for it like a bailiff, but the wants of the army are so urgent that I am seldom able to succeed—however poco a poco I hope to get remittances made.

I shall work at commercial relaxations which I think more practicable and better than a treaty, as soon as there is a Government but from these men nothing can be expected.

I am glad you will make an appeal to the sympathies of the Northern Powers because I think that it is worth putting the attempt on record. If they wish to promote order and prevent revolution (upon general principles) in Spain, it is only to be effected by the consolidation of the Queen's throne. Is not Austria more inclined to listen to reason just now than the others? I shall have something to say upon this subject when I write by my own courier—and I will then also give you my reasons for feeling sure that Cordoba is not coming here with the object you suppose.

PS. You may rely upon nothing being omitted on my part to keep well with my French colleague.

Received 19 December.

GC/CL/368; Clar. Dep. C.453 (306-311)

[1] The Minister of War was dismissed and Baron Solar de Espinosa appointed in his place; and Perez, the Minister of the Interior, resigned.

[2] The Moderados, unlike the Exaltados, hoped for French intervention to end the war. (V to Aston, 10 Dec. 1837, FO 355/6.)

391   Palmerston to Villiers, 16 December 1837[1]

Foreign Office. I am very glad you have been able to put a stop to the Paris intrigue to procure the recall of Aguilar. It really would be a little too bad that the Tuileries should prescribe who should or should not be minister at London. We cannot stand that.

I hear that Cordova has been stopped from entering Spain, by order of Bardaxi at the desire of the French Government, and that the supposed motive for this interference on the part of France was that Cordova indiscreetly showed about in Paris a letter from you in which you intimated to him the wish of Calatrava and Mendizabal that he should come to Madrid to help them to form a Government in substitution of the present one. This might be a very good thing to do, but Cordova need not have shown your letters.

Your account of Palillos' barbarous treachery makes one's blood boil; is the fact so certain and well authenticated that I could venture to state it in the House of Commons in any future discussion on Spanish affairs?

The Carlists here in London such as the Bishop of Cuba and Agnares tell their Tory friends who come and tell me that two expeditions are immediately about to take place across the Ebro; the one to Castile and to menace Madrid, the other probably for Gallicia. If Madrid is safe from a coup de main, such a movement would lead to the defeat of the Carlists provided there be any sufficient authority and energy on the part of the Queen's troops.

Louis Philippe seems for the moment to have bought the Camarilla and Government; it will remain to be seen how long this acquired authority will [last] and what good it will do to him. Now that Spain has got a Constitution and a representative Government, foreign influence cannot extend much beyond the wishes of the Executive. Their acts will be controuled by the Cortes, and that Cortes cannot fail to be Spanish. At least so it will be in the long run, and therefore I mind very little these temporary ascendancies, even if they do exist.

I am very glad that you and Latour Maubourg are so well together again, and I hope that you may be able so to continue. I know that he is a dry stiff and repulsive man, but upon an average you make a very conciliatory pair of diplomatists.

I have not addressed any communication to the Powers who back Don Carlos, because if he gets on his legs again and sends forth an expedition to Castile, they would answer me by saying that so far from being in a hopeless condition and therefore a fit person to be abandoned by them, he was on the contrary on the high road to his throne.

Ricardo has been here to propose another scheme about the Quicksilver[2] . . . .

Draft.

GC/CL/1326

[1] An incomplete draft in P's hand, not docketed and presumably not sent.
[2] By which the quicksilver contracts would be fixed to the payment of the arrears on the Bonds. (P to V, 14 Dec. 1837, no. 185, FO 72/476.)

392 Villiers to Palmerston, 17 December 1837

Madrid. Private. I have delayed my courier till today partly to puzzle the footpads and partly because I expected the ministerial crisis would conclude last night. With respect to the latter I was not wrong, but I could almost wish it had been indefinitely prolonged rather than end as it has done. Ofalia[1] is an able man and knows his country well enough, but he was the humble servant of Calomarde and the colleague of Zea which must ensure his being ill received by the Exaltado party, and he is a man so timid and irresolute that far from taking any of the vigorous measures which the state of the country requires it will be his utmost ambition to maintain the statu quo. The fatal hand of France is as manifest in the appointment of this Ministry as it was in that of Isturiz, for if you will refer to my dispatch in which I report the Queen's language to me respecting the Moderate party[2] (language which was not only used to me but to several others who have told it to me) and bear in mind that Ofalia is so cowardly that his only object hitherto has been to be forgotten—not a fortnight ago he declared that nothing would induce him to accept the embassy to Paris—you will I think agree with me that some hopes must have been held out of aid by France in order to have worked so complete a change in the sentiments of the Queen Regent and of her present Prime Minister. Hopes which of course will never be realized and which will hereafter as upon a former occasion be declared to have had no foundation.

If the Queen had only held to me the language she did respecting the Moderados I should say that she had been conforming herself to what she might have thought to be my opinions, and that she had not been sincere in approving as warmly as she did the course I suggested to her to adopt with regard to the formation of a new Ministry, but to all the persons in her most intimate confidence she has expressed herself in the same way. Since I saw her however Toreno arrived and I know that he has told her Louis Philippe made the most ardent vows for the success of the Moderate party, and this has been sufficient to create in her mind hopes of intervention and to induce her to appoint men who will have no means of sustaining themselves without the aid of foreign bayonets which they will not get, and Louis Philippe well knows that such a Government as has just been appointed is of all others the most calculated to prolong the war and to promote revolution. He is able without the least compromising himself to give the advice he has done because it comes under the cloak of moderation and anti revolutionary principles, but Her Majesty is too well acquainted with the state of this country not to know that it must be by other than milk and water means that order can be made to issue out of the present chaos.

Since I have been upon more intimate terms with La Tour Maubourg who is the feeble echo of his master's views, I have seen more into the policy of Louis Philippe and I find that he is now even opposed to the union of different parties. He cannot openly proclaim the diabolical doctrine, but he says that union is so impossible to achieve that it would be most dangerous to attempt it. In short I don't believe that in the annals of history there is to be found an instance of more selfish and inhuman policy than that pursued by Louis Philippe towards this country.

I can devise no other way of neutralizing it than the Austrian project[3] I send you today, which I have put in a separate letter and a semi-official form in case you may like to make any use of it with your colleagues. The Queen Isabel is of course too young to be married now—she is seven *off*[?]—but if she were betrothed to the youth in question and that he were to come here in order to make himself Spanish, and were accompanied by the Arch Duke who although upon a temporary visit might easily advise and direct, all the objects sought in the marriage would soon be attained. It would be a prodigious feat to disarm the hostility of the Northern Powers for it would at once disarm the Carlists here, and if the Arch Duke were to take the affairs of Spain in hand he would be far too wise to attempt an abolition of the constitutional system though he might seek to temper the impetuosity of the liberals—a course which would consist perfectly with the real interests of that party and with the general feelings of the nation.

The grand difficulty which I should apprehend would be to persuade the Arch Duke of the desireableness and practicability of the scheme and then to overcome the opposition of Metternich and Tatistscheff, but for that I should look to the annoyance which the marriage would cause to Louis Philippe as the most persuasive argument. Another difficulty would be as to the person to negotiate the affair because he ought to be well acquainted with the state of Spain in order to reply to the numerous misstatements and the profound ignorance which exist at Vienna respecting this country. I would offer myself if you had no one better whenever I make use of my leave of absence, if I did not think that my journey to Vienna might perhaps excite too much suspicion.

However these are minor considerations but I shall be really happy if you think the scheme practicable, and the present policy of France makes some counteracting course more than ever necessary, not only for the sake of Spain but our own, because through Louis Philippe's means we shall cut a sorry figure here next spring.

The animosity which Maubourg has been ordered to display against Cordoba is the best reply I can give to your suspicion that he was charged with an intrigue by Louis Philippe, and the Queen Regent in order to meet the wishes of her august uncle lent herself most kindly to the measures for preventing Cordoba's arrival. He (Cordoba) denounces Louis Philippe and his policy too loudly and imprudently, but in other respects his conduct since his return has been all that it ought to be.

I have been assured upon good authority that Espartero is in correspondence with Louis Philippe's aide-de-camp General Athalin and that the only instructions he obeys are those which proceed from the Tuileries. If this is the case it is an additional reason for supporting him in the way that Maubourg does, although the certainty that he will prolong the war and consume all the resources of the country must be sufficient to secure him the favor of the King of the French.

I hope you will approve the course I pursued with respect to the disarmed Legion at San Sebastian.[4] I think we should have been justly blamed if we had for the sake of a satisfaction (to which in my opinion we have no claim) deprived the Queen of one of her most promising officers[5] and been the cause of Irun and the lines of Hernani falling into the enemy's hands—for the purpose of rearming 3 or 400 fellows who according to Lord John Hay's accounts to me are absolutely worthless and quite incapable of becoming soldiers. The cavalry and artillery are of a different class and they you will observe took no part and were not disarmed.

I have been dissatisfied with O'Connell ever since he took the command of the Legion for which he never was fit—he is a raw Irish dandy, brave in the field they say, but full of potatoes as to the head—he has not been well used as to money but then he has not used well the money that was given to him and he has been eternally quarrelling with every Spanish authority he has had to do with. I hope the affair may be made up—it will be the best way and with Lord John's aid I shall not despair of it.

Your Lordship must have been in a very bad humor when you wrote me the slave dispatch No. 16. I hardly think the present note required a rebuke so tart.

Received 26 December.

GC/CL/369; Clar. Dep. C.453 (320-325)

[1] The new President of the Council of Ministers.

[2] V to P, 17 Dec. 1837, no. 371, FO 72/485. The Queen described the Moderados as 'a weak, intriguing, cowardly party'.

[3] Suggesting a marriage between the Queen of Spain and a son of the Archduke Charles of Austria. (See no. 393 below.)

[4] General O'Donnell, commander of Guipúzcoa, disarmed the British Legion. The Minister of War informed V that the Government intended to deprive O'Donnell of his command and to restore arms to the Legion, in order to assure the British Government that the Spanish Government had not been a party to the decision to disarm the Legion. V argued that O'Donnell had had no choice; because the Legion had not been paid, the men would not accept O'Donnell's command. He persuaded the Spanish Government that O'Donnell was a successful and efficient commander who should stay at his post. (V to P, 17 Dec. 1837, no. 372, FO 72/485.)

[5] O'Donnell.

393   Villiers to Palmerston, 17 December 1837

Madrid. Private. I am about to develop to you an idea which may be but an idle dream—if so it will be but one of the many which occupy me day and night respecting the means of relieving England and Europe from the hourly increasing embarrassment which the Spanish question creates.

It is impossible to believe that the state of things which now obtains in Spain can be permanently permitted—that Spain should be perpetually deluged in blood, and that Spaniards should be the pariahs of Europe. This country contributed too largely to the present peace and prosperity of Europe to leave it alone in its distress, and to proclaim that nothing is owed to it. It would be easy to show that all the misery which Spain is now enduring dates from the sacrifices she made and the dreadful ordeal she went through to secure her independence in 1808, and in asking of Europe to heal her wounds, Spain applies rather for the payment of a debt than for aid, and humanity no less than the political and material interests of Europe demand that the appeal should not be made in vain.

Intervention is impossible. The Quadruple Treaty is a dead letter —and the Spanish nation is exposed to destruction under the accumulated evils of a long minority—a disputed succession—a civil war—and a national bankruptcy—the exactions of the Queen's Government and the rapine of the Pretender's partizans.

These dangers and more than any of them the long minority strike the mind of every Spaniard, and give to all a feeling of insecurity—the liberal party which this very feeling divides, rallies feebly round the institutions upon which the Queen's throne is insecurely based, for it has no confidence in the future and the uneasiness and disunion which doubt produces aggravate all the horrors of civil war. If a change could be wrought in this and Spaniards be made to think that they were toiling and suffering for something real, and that they were building up their futurity upon a solid foundation, a phalanx of the partizans of order would spring up, and a *positive fact* would quickly swell their ranks. In the present state of things when no aid is to be expected from without and all is confusion within this *positive fact* is only to be sought for in the marriage of Queen Isabel. That alone at the present day seems capable of being a substitute for the Quadruple Alliance—of healing the wounds of Spain and of placing her prospects upon a permanent basis.

Every Government which has existed in France has had an instinctive yearning to possess itself of supreme power in Spain—this desire was never more strongly exhibited than at the present moment although circumstances may now forbid the use of means which on other occasions have been resorted to. But the balance of Powers in Europe now more than ever demands that Spain should be independent, and in order to secure this and to save her from the grasp of France the marriage of the Queen is an occasion such as may never again present itself.

The three Northern Powers which support Don Carlos are moved less by sympathy for that weak and fanatical Prince than by hatred for the spirit of innovation which is manifesting itself in the West of Europe, but if they were invited to act in a sense contrary to the policy of Louis Philippe and with an object of monarchical consolidation they might hesitate before they rejected the proposal.

Louis Philippe before every thing else is *Bourbon*, and in receding as far as he is able from the principle which placed him upon the throne he almost has created a necessity to favor Don Carlos whose triumph would afford him an alternative of advantages. If Don Carlos were a ferocious and sanguinary despot Louis Philippe would hold him up to the people of France as the image of the restoration of Henry V. If he were a humane and docile despot he must inevitably be dependent upon France. On the other hand if the Queen triumphs the dynastic monument of Louis XIV falls to the ground and the Constitution of 1837 which is more liberal than the Charter would be an object of envy and emulation to the French. Louis Philippe then both as Bourbon and with the views he now entertains as King must desire the success of Don Carlos, or in other words the destruction of Spain under the double yoke of that Prince and of France.

The policy of England is to promote by every possible means the prosperity of Spain, and any measure which tended to render Spain commercially rich and politically strong would at the same time promote some of the most important interests of Great Britain.

Russia is far from being reconciled with *France of July* and she might be expected to look with pleasure upon any influence contrary to that of Louis Philippe raised up in Spain, provided it was not that of England, and England on her part would not object to the creation of a new force in the south of Europe which should act at the same time against the ambitious views of Russia and the influence of France.

The wise and moderate Government of Prussia would hardly oppose any measure likely to contribute to the repose of Europe which it well knows how to take advantage of.

There only remains then Austria to be taken into consideration, and it is an alliance by marriage between Austria and Spain which would seem to offer what this country now most stands in need of, a futurity which will unite scattered opinions, and conciliate in favor of Spain the general interests of Europe, save those of Louis Philippe, which are not strictly identical with those of France.

The military glory, the statesmanlike talents and the private virtues of the ArchDuke Charles are well known in Spain and his children are known to have received an education worthy of their birth and of their father. One of these children, Frederick William (I believe), was born in 1821—the approximation of age would appear to indicate him as the husband of Queen Isabel.

Whatever may be said to the contrary by absolute Governments and legitimists of every class, the rights of Don Carlos have been for them all but a pretext—an occasion to maintain a question of principles. History is there to prove that the Salic Law never had any real existence in Spain, and if the Northern Powers had been better informed with respect to the state of this country they would perhaps have found no flaw in the legitimacy of the Queen and have hesitated to adopt a course from which retreat was difficult.

Many of their illusions must have been dissipated during the last four years and the last campaign of Don Carlos must have shaken their convictions of his success, but they cannot look calmly upon the future state of Spain. The existence of a permanent revolution is a fact of enormous gravity. The monarchical principle can nowhere receive a shock without its essence being every where altered, and can it be believed that if the convulsions of Spain are prolonged that the fever of revolution will not at the same time increase? In 1835 the people rose against a Government—the Government fell. In 1836 a revolution took place against an institution—it perished. If a third commotion takes place it may only stop at the foot of the throne. Every King has an interest in averting such a catastrophe if they will remember July of 1830 when the peace of Europe was placed in such eminent peril.

The triumph of Don Carlos is a social impossibility. He can never reign but over sepulchres and ruins. His triumph would be more fatal to monarchy than to liberty—he would have but a Sovereign's title while its power was exercised by the dregs of the people. The Powers of the North cannot desire so abominable an alliance.

The triumph of Queen Isabel is on the other hand a guarantee for monarchy, for she is supported by all those classes which society every where is wont to respect, and whose opinions as well as interests are the most opposed to revolution, though they are now kept in agitation by the want of a solid object on which to fix their hopes. Such an object would be at once presented by the marriage of the Queen with an Austrian Prince. Spaniards would see in it a reconciliation with the Powers of the North and an abandonment of the cause of Don Carlos. The Pretender's partizans who are as wearied as their adversaries of this f[r]atricidal contest would find a guarantee in the word of the Prince and an honorable motive for laying down their arms, while arrangements honorable for all might be made, without even excluding the Prince who has caused such misery and bloodshed, and all would see that certain futurity which they are now vainly seeking.

Spain would then acquire a new life and soon resume that place among nations from which she has so long been excluded. Prosperity would revive under a strong and paternal Government which established order in every branch of public administration, and the well-being of the people would soon make them love the Government from which it emanated.

Peace—peace at any price, is upon the lips of every Spaniard, and no means for procuring it would seem more effectual than the alliance of constitutional Spain represented by Isabel II with a Great Power which should bring to her the force she stands in need of for establishing her monarchy upon the bases of a prudent liberty, of public prosperity, and of reconciliation with Europe.

Received 26 December.

GC/CL/370; Clar. Dep. C.453 (312-319)

394 Villiers to Palmerston, 24 December 1837

Madrid. Private. The courier due the day before yesterday has not arrived. Whether the delay originates in London or has been occasioned by Cabrera Ist, King of Aragon, I know not, but I hope the former.

This week has been uneventful which is pleasant as it implies absence of catastrophe—the next may not pass so well for I fear some outbreak in the provinces against the new Ministry. If any does take place it will be both mischievous and unjustifiable for the electors have no right to complain of a Government being taken from the majority of the Cortes, and it is their fault if they made that majority too Moderado.

For my part I am very glad that such a Ministry as the present one has been formed, for it will set at rest the intervention question which is the cheval de bataille of the Moderados. This party admit that intervention cannot be solicited through an organ more likely to obtain it than Ofalia who is known and respected in Europe and intimately acquainted with Louis Philippe—and that if it is refused to him it is useless for anyone else to try. Nothing but experience and forcing France to give a more decided negative than she has already done will convince these idiots that all does not depend upon the form of the petition and the character of the petitioners. They will get their *no*, for every reason which two years ago induced Louis Philippe not to intervene in Spain is now in ten times greater force than then.

The country will accordingly see that it has been imposed upon by the Moderados, and they will be done for as a party, for they have no vigor, no talents for governing in troublous times, and no leg to stand upon except their foreign one which will turn out to be a stump.

Ofalia is a very agreable man to deal with, and I was pleased with my conference with him. He is an experienced diplomatist and knows his own country perfectly, but he will want the vigor for carrying into execution his own ideas. His language about England was very satisfactory and the same as I have always heard from him since I came here. As I write by a French courier I have put a few lines in cypher upon the reasons I have for thinking that we may possibly find this Government more worth supporting than any which has preceded it.[1] Its origin is bad but its originators are, if Ofalia continues in his present mind, likely to be disappointed for I am confirmed in the opinion I gave you last week as to the influence under which this Ministry was formed.[2]

Ofalia had no idea till I told it him frankly how the Spanish question stinks in the nostrils of the public both in England and France, and that nothing was to be expected in the shape of pecuniary relief from those countries until the Queen had a general able and willing to do his duty—but Espartero is the stumbling block of every Ministry. I am the last man to defend Espartero's inactivity, but I am not sure that it has done harm during the last two months, for the dissensions among the Carlists are of a different character to any previous ones, and they have increased and ripened rather than otherwise by being left alone, whereas if Espartero had entered the enemy's country a common danger might have reunited the Carlists, and I am convinced that internal division among them is the only means of finishing the war. As for conquering Navarre, i.e. storming and taking about 500 Gibraltars and afterwards occupying the whole country over which they are scattered, *it is impossible* if the people are united and choose to resist.

I give Espartero no credit for his inactivity which is not the result of any plan but merely in pursuance of the only *system* he knows, which is to lye in bed, do nothing and prevent others from doing any thing. In the present instance however I believe it has been useful, and you will see by my dispatch today that Don Carlos is in a very awkward predicament,[3] and it is one which will become worse if, which I fear, Cabrera does not come to the rescue. The Spanish Government with its usual apathy never tries to foment discord among the enemy or to turn it to account when it exists. Now when all the Carlist chiefs are in disgrace or under arrest would be the time for making some terms with them, but they will not I am sure put faith in the Government or believe in the reality of any offers which are not guaranteed in some shape or other by England or France. Will you take into consideration whether it would be possible for us to be parties to any arrangement of this kind which would be a work both of peace and humanity? I shall perhaps be able to submit to you a plan upon the subject by the next courier.

I hope that sufficient reinforcements are about to be sent to San Sebastian and there is no doubt that those lines ought to be made quite secure, but Lord John Hay who always screams if he thinks there is a chance of his Marines being meddled with has perhaps augmented the danger which threatened Irun, Fuentearabia and Hernani. If those places were to fall tomorrow I hardly think it would be a reason for withdrawing our naval force as the loss of those places *ought* not in any way to endanger Pasages. The 2d line was taken by Evans before Irun was thought of and Lord John never considered his people in danger for the want of those places. Both he and O'Donnell have been somewhat inconsistent in taking and garrisoning Guetaria which from being utterly useless as a defensive position only serves as a drain to the force which they represent to be insufficient, and the lines ought consequently to have been concentrated rather than extended.

Wylde tells me that on looking over the returns from San Sebastian he finds that O'Donnell has now without reckoning the Legion 12,038 rank and file, of which 9,208 are effective under arms, and reckoning the garrisons at 6,000 which is a very large proportion, he will have a reserve of 3,000. This Wylde says ought to be enough for defence only, but with the force about to be sent he ought to be shot if he loses a single post.

No answers have yet been received from San Sebastian respecting the disarmed Legion, but the more I hear of O'Connell the more discreditable I think his conduct upon the occasion—he was bored, and considered any means good for setting himself at liberty and he has shewn very little regard for the men he commanded or the cause he was serving. Much of the distress of the Legion which led to the final catastrophe would have been avoided if O'Connell had not chosen to appropriate to other purposes part of the money which was sent to his men.

GC/CL/371; Clar. Dep. C.453 (326-331)

[1] 'I have more hopes on the commercial question with Ofalia than with any of his predecessors. He is the only Minister I have yet communicated with who views it like a statesman. He admits the expediency under any circumstances of better commercial relations with England and the absolute necessity if, as

he expects, France refuses to give more efficient aid to this country.'(V to P, 24 Dec. 1837, private (enclosure in cipher), with V to P, 24 Dec. 1837, no. 388, FO 72/485. Copy in Clar. Dep. C.453 (338).)

[2] 'Louis Philippe and Molé both deny that French influence has been exerted to effect the nomination of the present Ministers . . . , but I can see no disposition to support the men who are known to be liberal or who have had any hand in the establishment of the constitution reformée and I observe that any requests from the Spanish Government coming from Ofalia through Latour-Maubourg are more favourably listened to than during the time of Calatrava or even that of Bardaxi.' (Granville to V, 31 Dec. 1837, PRO 30/29/422.)

[3] The Carlists had divided into two hostile factions. The Castellanos were the 'uncompromising and sanguinary' party, and Don Carlos was entirely in their hands. The Provinciales were ready for a settlement that granted independence to the Basque Provinces and Navarre under Don Sebastian. (V to P, 24 Dec. 1837, no. 388, FO 72/485.)

395   Palmerston to Villiers, 27 December 1837

Copy. Stanhope Street. I have received your letters of the 17 and answer them before I start to spend five days in Hampshire.

I never was more surprized than when I heard of Ofalia's appointment. It is as if Decazes or Villère[1] were appointed at Paris. This Government cannot last; but the question is who set it up, and for what purpose. Aguilar tells me that he hears privately from his friends at Madrid that there is a notion there that this Government is put up by Louis Philippe in order to get the Cortes to propose a marriage between the young Queen and a French Prince. I have always been convinced that such a marriage is the real object of Louis Philippe, and is the key to all his strange policy about Spain, and that he thinks the best way of bringing such a scheme to bear is to bring Spain to an extreme of misery, and then to say to her that on such conditions he will come to the rescue.

To such a plan of course we never could consent, and we should resist it with all our might and main. Pray let me know if there seems to be any foundation for the report and lose no time in taking whatever steps may be the best calculated to defeat such a plan.[2] If there is reason to think such a scheme is in agitation we must of course take measures at Paris to prevent it.

I do not think however that your Austrian marriage would do. There is an inherent incompatibility between Austrian influence and constitutional liberty, and though Archduke Charles may pass for a liberal at Vienna, his son would probably be thought a despot at Madrid. That the young Queen should marry is desirable, but she should take for a husband some prince of a small family; not belonging to any Great Power; some man of personal talent and character which would enable him to govern, and who having no deep roots in any other country would soon and easily become a good Spaniard.

It is highly probable that Espartero is, as you have heard, in correspondence indirectly with Louis Philippe, and that his inertness is the consequence of French orders. This is an additional reason for wishing him at the Antipodes.

I am very glad you took the high and generous line about O'Donnell; and it was no less wise than courteous.

I have seen O'Connell who arrived yesterday; he seems a very gentlemanlike man, and the account he gives of the state of privation to which both officers and men of the Legion have been reduced makes one wish them all home, whatever the consequences to the Spanish cause may be. I begin to lose all patience with these Spaniards, and to wish them again under the heaviest rod that despotism can lay upon them; at least as far as they themselves are concerned; but we must rescue them for our own sakes.

I do not feel much uneasiness about Canada . . . .

GC/CL/1327

[1] *Recte* Villèle?
[2] See also P to V, 27 Dec. 1837, secret, FO 72/476.

396 Villiers to Palmerston, 30 December 1837

Madrid. Private. I have received your letter of the 16th instant. I am glad to see that you have so correct a view upon the impotence of foreign influence here so long as there is a Constitution and a representative system—*they* cannot be done away with, and although the Executive may be foolish and base and for a moment find support in such a course when the country is distressed and alarmed, yet a Spaniard is Spanish before everything else and the Cortes will always be the representation of the national feelings. If *we* had bought or 'ticed the Government and Camarilla for a moment as Louis Philippe has done, he would not have borne it with the same philosophy as you do or with the same knowledge of the worthlessness of the purchase.

I am flattered that you should think La Tour Maubourg and I make upon an average a conciliatory pair of diplomatists because that is giving me conciliation *for two*—he not only has not a particle of it in his dry stiff composition, but he seems determined to misrepresent all my efforts to be upon good terms with him. His charge against me upon the Contribution question[1] was scandalous, and if I were not a double-barrelled conciliation diplomat I should have broken his head instead of civilly calling him to account, and then turning off the conversation when he could not find the lies he was looking for in answer. Be assured however that nothing, short of a downright bassesse, shall be wanting on my part to keep up an outward show of harmony—that we should really pull well together is impossible. Louis Philippe is a Carlist—heart and soul Carlist—Molé is the feeble expression of his will as Maubourg is of Molé's. You are Cristino—heart and soul—and you may be certain your opinions are shared and acted up to by me. Louis Philippe desires the prolongation of the war—we wish for its termination—witness the succour we give the Queen, and the supplies he allows to reach the Carlists, as well as his *direct intervention* in favor of Espartero who all know has not the sufficient capacity even if he has the desire to finish the war. We care little for a few revolutionary antics provided they are accompanied by measures of vigor and produce men capable of giving peace to the country. Louis Philippe cares nothing about the restoration of tranquillity and declaims only against revolution, *never against Don Carlos or his partizans* has he said a word.

With policies so opposite then what chance have Maubourg and I of ever meeting—except occasionally at dinner?

The ambassador's animosity and therefore that of the Government against Cordoba is amusing for it is founded upon his being *sold to England,* being an instrument of mine, and I don't know what absurdities besides. To be sure Cordoba who knows how to hate à l'Espagnole repays them with interest, and has done more to expose the policy of France towards this country since his return than any one has since the war commenced. The text he preaches from is free trade and intimate alliance with England and he has already made a good many converts.

When I wrote to you a week ago I had hopes that we were immediately about to enter upon the treaty of commerce question for Ofalia was then determined upon it. I had left all the preliminaries to Marliani, whose zeal and activity are prodigious, in order that it should appear a matter of exclusively Spanish interest and he had made much progress in the question when the French got wind of it and have frightened both the Queen and little Ofalia out of their intentions to amend the tariff, and their hopes of raising money upon such a guarantee. In short they meet one at every turn and as they are determined that nothing good or useful shall be accomplished here I have no doubt they will succeed.

A few days ago Ofalia begged me to call upon him—I found him in a great flutter with a dispatch from Espartero in his hand which he said had thrown consternation into the Cabinet. It was a remonstrance of the said Espartero against the copy of your dispatch which Wylde had put into his hands respecting reinforcements to San Sebastian. He said that he was much hurt by a foreign Government having sent him orders in such a peremptory tone, and that you had done him injustice in supposing that he had disobeyed the orders of his own Government as he had never received any whatever to send troops to O'Donnell.[2] Having reason to believe that this latter statement is true and that Bardaxi who is imbecile and never spoke a word of truth had deceived me[3]—seeing moreover that Espartero's dispatch was conceived in terms most respectful towards England and to yourself personally and that it was a little Castillian pride ruffled which however the Government did not know to smooth down, I offered to write Espartero cuatro palabras[4] of dulcification. This was a great relief to the Government who were equally afraid of offending you and Espartero, and I had the less hesitation in doing it because I think it important that Espartero should remain on good terms with Wylde who is the only man capable of stirring him up occasionally to do his duty. I enclose you copies of the letter which Ofalia (at my desire) wrote to me asking that I should pacify Espartero and of mine to Espartero as well as to Ofalia in reply. In case Ofalia should not communicate to him what passed between Bardaxi and myself about reinforcements to San Sebastian I have written it to Wylde to use if necessary. I have not made translation of the letters because I believe it is immaterial to you whether you read Spanish or English.

With respect to the treacherous atrocity of Palillos I related the event as it was current in Madrid and upon what I had reason to believe was good authority. I now find that there was an exaggeration as to the number of the passengers in the diligence but all the rest is true. I have obtained from a brother of one of the murdered individuals—Señor Alvarez—an exact account of all that passed and I herewith send you a translation of it—and the money for the ransom was sent through the house of O'Shea so that there can be no doubt about the matter and you may safely make any use you please of it in the House of Commons. I think that the facts you will find in the statement—the treatment the victims received before they were massacred, and then their being butchered after their ransom was paid and the aide-de-camp and the mistress of Palillos having received the money they required in order to save the lives of the poor wretches, are likely to produce a powerful impression and hardly be considered defensible by Lord Carnarvon (whose direct correspondence with Don Carlos by the bye should not be forgotten whenever a discussion upon Spanish affairs comes on). Señor Alvarez was a quiet inoffensive man, never meddling with politics and occupied solely with the cloth trade and going to mass three times a day.

I was in hopes to have sent you a project about our guaranteeing to all the Carlist generals and principal people in the Northern Provinces pensions abroad if they would abandon the Pretender's cause but the treasury here is not in a state to bear this most productive outlay and it of course did not enter into my calculation to propose to you that we should be put to any expence upon the matter.

William Hervey's brother is at Pau on the point of death from consumption. Lady Bristol and some other members of the family have come there to him and I have given William Hervey leave of absence for 3 weeks to join them to which I hope you will have no objection as the case is too urgent to admit of asking previously for your permission.

First enclosure: Copy, the Conde de Ofalia (Madrid) to Villiers, 26 December 1837, 'confidencial y reservada', asking Villiers to write a pacifying letter to Espartero. (In Spanish.)

Second enclosure: Copy, Villiers (Madrid) to the Conde de Luchana (Espartero), 26 December 1837, 'reservada', explaining that Palmerston's suggestions were not meant to reflect on Espartero's military competence. (In Spanish.)

Third enclosure: Villiers (Madrid) to Ofalia, 27 December 1837, 'confidencial', reporting a satisfactory exchange of explanations with Espartero. (In Spanish.)

Fourth enclosure: Translation of a description of the capture and murder of some hostages by the Carlist General Palillos.

Received 9 January 1838.

GC/CL/372; Clar. Dep. C.453 (332-337)

[1] The extraordinary war tax levied on property.

[2] 'as he had never' to 'O'Donnell' underlined in pencil, possibly by P.

[3] 'Bardaxi', 'and never' and 'a word of truth had deceived me' underlined, as n. 2.

[4] 'four words'.

INDEX

Places are in Spain unless otherwise indicated

Evans, Lieutenant-Colonel (Sir) George de Lacy, in command of the British Legion in Spain (1835–37), 24, 257 and n., 264, 275, 292, 309, 319, 320, 322, 325, 326, 328, 332, 373–4, 375n., 382–3, 388–9, 392, 393, 394n., 401, 409, 410n., 411, 413–14, 417, 420, 422, 424, 432, 438, 447–50, 451, 452, 455, 456, 459–60, 462, 464, 468, 473, 474, 475, 477, 481, 510, 517, 521, 522, 532, 534, 567, 571–2, 578–80, 586, 591–2, 605–6, 613, 618–19, 620, 621, 626, 631, 632, 641, 642, 644, 651, 704, 730

see also British Volunteer Legion

Évora (Portugal), surrender of Don Carlos at, 142, 148, 158

exaltados, 177, 243, 268, 277, 278, 287, 293, 300, 309, 325, 335, 345, 349n., 367, 378, 385, 400, 404, 465, 500, 501, 511, 512, 534, 535, 537, 615, 736, 746n., 757

Exclusion Bill, *see* succession, proposal to change the order of

Express Packet, case of, 410, 411n., 670n.

Extremadura, *see* Estremadura

Faxardo, Antonio, deputy commissary of the British Legion, 262–3

Fay, Armand Charles Septime de, Comte de Latour-Maubourg, French ambassador to Spain (1836–37), 17, 525, 539, 540n., 541, 543, 544, 547–8, 549n., 550, 551, 553, 563n., 589, 601, 644, 650, 687, 688, 690n., 702, 710, 727, 748, 757, 759, 769
his personal relations with V, 573, 731–2, 733, 741, 745, 746n., 747, 751, 755, 756, 769

Ferdinand VII, King of Spain, 11, 51, 66n., 72, 95, 123n., 187n., 230, 245n., 252, 269
death of (1833), 39, 40, 44, 47, 52, 155, 250, 261

Ferdinand Philippe Louis Charles Henri, Duc d'Orléans, eldest son of King Louis Philippe, 112, 424n.

Ferrer, Joaquín, politician, 502

Figueras, 309

Finance, Minister of, *see* Aguirre Solarte, José Ventura de; Ímaz, José de;

Mendizábal, Juan Álvarez y; Pita Pizarro, Pío; Toreno, Conde de

finances, Spanish Government, 14, 23, 102, 224, 231, 290, 317, 365, 372, 391, 426, 428, 433, 435, 438, 439, 489, 532, 543, 546, 558, 561, 566, 638, 656, 685, 690, 694, 696, 716, 750
Toreno's scheme to meet foreign debts, 178, 186, 190, 195, 198–9, 202, 203–4, 206, 209–15 *passim*, 219 and n., 221
see also Cortes bonds; loans and loan guarantees; taxation, extraordinary

Finisterre, Cape, 191n.

Flahault, Auguste Charles Joseph de, Comte de Flahault de la Billarderie, French diplomat, 49

Flinter, George Dawson, with the Queen's army, 545

Floridablanca, Conde de, *see* Pando

Follett, Sir William Webb, M.P., 634

Foreign Affairs, Minister for, 296, 299, 754
see also Bardaxí, Eusebio; Istúriz, Francisco Javier de; Mendizábal, Juan Álvarez y; Ribera, Ildefonso Diez de

Foreign Enlistment Act, British, suspension of, 15, 254, 257, 260, 627, 631, 637, 638, 651, 660
see also British Volunteer Legion

Foreign Legion, French, *see* French Foreign Legion

Foreign Legion, Portuguese, *see* Portugal, military assistance to Spain by

Foster, Sir Augustus John, 1st Bt., British minister to Sardinia, 574

Fox, Colonel Charles Richard, secretary to the Master-General of the Ordnance (1835–41), 626

Fox, Henry Richard Vassall, 3rd Baron Holland, 7, 65, 113, 257, 351, 352n., 358, 555, 560

Fox, Henry Stephen, British minister to the United States, 285

França, —, Portuguese Chartist officer, 736 and n.

France, policy of towards Spain, 15–17, 26, 48–50, 58, 59n., 61, 130n., 131, 133n., 177, 185, 190, 198–9, 202, 276–7, 305, 332, 338 and n., 341, 342n., 359, 376–7, 380, 391, 394, 395n., 399 and n., 400, 406n., 408,

INDEX

Shaw, —, financier, 466
Sheil, Richard Lalor, M.P., 634
Silva Pereira, Francisco Xavier da,
    Visconde das Antas, Portuguese
    general, 724
slave trade treaty, 45n., 61 and n., 91,
    92, 141, 146, 156, 159, 161, 163,
    165, 195, 201–2, 204, 206, 211, 218,
    221–2, 223, 225, 227, 228, 234, 240,
    243, 247, 249, 253, 255, 257, 259,
    263, 264, 274, 275, 278, 281, 285–6,
    296, 314, 362, 374, 751–2
Socoa (France), 604
Solar de Espinosa, see Espinosa
Solaro della Margarita, Conte Clemente,
    Sardinian Foreign Minister, 574,
    677
    minister to Spain (1834), 118
Solarte, see Aguirre Solarte
Soublette, General Carlos, Venezuelan
    plenipotentiary in Europe, 258, 287,
    557 and n.
Soult, Nicolas Jean de Dieu, Duc de
    Dalmatie, French marshal and
    statesman, 26
Sousa Botelho Mourão e Vasconcello,
    José Luiz de, Conde de Villa Real,
    Portuguese statesman, 436
Sousa Manoel e Manezes Severim de
    Noronha, Antonio José de, Duque
    de Terceira, Portuguese general and
    politician, 135, 136, 725n.
Sousa-Holstein, Pedro de, Duque de
    Palmella, Portuguese politician and
    diplomat, 60, 61n., 72, 76, 77n.,
    211, 323
    and Dom Miguel (1833), 64, 66, 71,
    73, 80, 81, 82
South American States, recognition of,
    45n., 65, 66n., 94, 99, 107, 138,
    142–3, 218, 274, 275n., 299, 329,
    336, 341–2, 346, 347, 364, 379, 412,
    485, 565
    see also Montilla, Mariano; Soublette,
    General Carlos
Southern, Henry, private secretary to V,
    attaché, British legation in Spain, 9,
    118, 119n., 221, 275, 281, 333, 551,
    673, 702, 703n., 707
    mission to the Cadiz junta (1835),
    304–5, 306 and n., 307–8, 315, 317,
    322, 324, 326
Stanhope, Philip Henry, Viscount
    Mahon, later 5th Earl Stanhope,

Under-Secretary for Foreign
    Affairs (1834–35), 269, 270n.,
    271, 397, 613, 616, 619, 622, 626,
    637
Statella, Antonio, Principe de Cassaro,
    Neapolitan Foreign Minister, 735
Strachan, —, merchant, desire of to live
    and trade in the Philippines, 479
succession to the Spanish throne,
    proposal to change the order of
    (1834), 174, 175n., 176, 178, 184,
    187 and n.
Sweden, 105

Tacon, Miguel, Captain-General of
    Andalusia, 732 and n.
Tagus, river (Portugal), 37, 109, 112
Talleyrand-Périgord, Charles Maurice
    de, Prince de Benevento, French
    ambassador to Great Britain
    (1830–34), 15, 150, 175, 183, 403,
    414
Tarancón, 703n.
tariffs, see commercial relations,
    Anglo-Spanish
Tatishchev, Dmitri Pavlovich, Russian
    ambassador to Austria, 758
taxation, extraordinary, exemption of
    British subjects from, 519-20, 521n.,
    528, 533, 624, 729, 731n., 769
Taylor, Dr. (later Sir) Alexander,
    surgeon with the British Legion, 456
Taylor, Baron Isidore Justin Séverin, in
    Spain on behalf of the Louvre, 554n.
Tejeiro, José Arias, Foreign Minister of
    Don Carlos, 738
Téllez-Girón y Beaufort, Pedro, Duque
    de Osuna, 685
Tello, Juan, Cristino general, 470n.
Temple, Sir William, British minister to
    Sicily, 735
Terceira (Azores), 104
Terceira, Duque de, see Sousa
Texas, 485
Theresa, Princess of Beira, daughter of
    John VI of Portugal and 2nd wife of
    Don Carlos, 328, 330n., 345
The Times, 363n., 529, 553
    correspondents of, 208, 529, 536
Thiers, Adolphe, French statesman, 312,
    737
    Prime Minister (1836), 372n., 380,
    394, 399, 443, 453, 478, 486, 507n.,

Printed in the UK for HMSO
Dd736190 12/84 10170 (2750)